T0207156

Lecture Notes in Computer Science 13118

More information about this subseries at https://link.springer.com/bookseries/7410

Joseph K. Liu · Sokratis Katsikas ·
Weizhi Meng · Willy Susilo · Rolly Intan (Eds.)

Information Security

24th International Conference, ISC 2021
Virtual Event, November 10–12, 2021
Proceedings

 Springer

Editors
Joseph K. Liu (iD)
Monash University
Clayton, VIC, Australia

Weizhi Meng (iD)
Technical University of Denmark
Kongens Lyngby, Denmark

Rolly Intan
Petra Christian University
Surabaya, Indonesia

Sokratis Katsikas (iD)
Norwegian University of Science
and Technology
Gjøvik, Norway

Willy Susilo (iD)
University of Wollongong
Wollongong, NSW, Australia

ISSN 0302-9743   ISSN 1611-3349 (electronic)
Lecture Notes in Computer Science
ISBN 978-3-030-91355-7   ISBN 978-3-030-91356-4 (eBook)
https://doi.org/10.1007/978-3-030-91356-4

LNCS Sublibrary: SL4 – Security and Cryptology

This Springer imprint is published by the registered company Springer Nature Switzerland AG
The registered company address is: Gewerbestrasse 11, 6330 Cham, Switzerland

Preface

On behalf of the Program Committee, it is our pleasure to present the proceedings of the 24th Information Security Conference (ISC 2021). ISC is an annual international conference covering research in theory and applications of information security. Both academic research with high relevance to real-world problems and developments in industrial and technical frontiers fall within the scope of the conference.

The 24th edition of ISC was organized by the Petra Christian University, Surabaya, Indonesia, and was held entirely online (due to the COVID-19 pandemic) during November 10–12, 2021. Willy Susilo (University of Wollongong, Australia) and Rolly Intan (Petra Christian University, Indonesia) served as the general chairs, whilst we—Joseph Liu (Monash University, Australia) and Sokratis K. Katsikas (Norwegian University of Science and Technology, Norway)—served as the program co-chairs. The Program Committee comprised 54 members from top institutions around the world. Out of 87 submissions, the Program Committee eventually selected 21 papers for presentation at the conference and publication in the proceedings, resulting in an acceptance rate of 24.1%. The review process was double-blind, and it was organized and managed through the EasyChair online reviewing system, with all papers receiving at least three reviews. The final program was quite balanced in terms of topics, containing both theoretical/cryptography papers and more practical/systems security papers.

A successful conference is the result of the joint effort of many people. We would like to express our appreciation to the Program Committee members and external reviewers for the time spent reviewing papers and participating in the online discussion. We deeply thank our invited speakers for their willingness to participate in the conference, especially during the difficult times in the middle of the global pandemic. Further, we express our appreciation to Weizhi Meng (Technical University of Denmark, Denmark), who served as the publication chair. Finally, we thank Springer for publishing these proceedings as part of their LNCS series, and the ISC Steering Committee for their continuous support and assistance.

ISC 2021 would not have been possible without the authors who submitted their work and presented their contributions, as well as the attendees who joined the conference sessions. We would like to thank them all, and we look forward to their future contributions to ISC.

October 2021

Joseph Liu
Sokratis Katsikas

Organization

Steering Committee

Zhiqiang Lin	The Ohio State University, USA
Javier Lopez	University of Malaga, Spain
Masahiro Mambo	Kanazawa University, Japan
Eiji Okamoto	University of Tsukuba, Japan
Michalis Polychronakis	Stony Brook University, USA
Jianying Zhou	Singapore University of Technology and Design, Singapore

General Chairs

Willy Susilo	University of Wollongong, Australia
Rolly Intan	Petra Christian University, Indonesia

Program Chairs

Joseph Liu	Monash University, Australia
Sokratis K. Katsikas	Norwegian University of Science and Technology, Norway

Publication Chair

Weizhi Meng	Technical University of Denmark, Denmark

Technical Program Committee

Masayuki Abe	NTT Secure Platform Laboratories, Japan
Cristina Alcaraz	University of Malaga, Spain
Man Ho Au	University of Hong Kong, Hong Kong
Liqun Chen	University of Surrey, UK
Xiaofeng Chen	Xidian University, China
Mauro Conti	University of Padua, Italy
Frédéric Cuppens	Polytechnique Montreal, Canada
Josep Domingo-Ferrer	Universitat Rovira i Virgili, Spain
Dung Hoang Duong	University of Wollongong, Australia
Steven Furnell	University of Nottingham, UK
Joaquin Garcia-Alfaro	Institut Polytechnique de Paris, France
Vasileios Gkioulos	Norwegian University of Science and Technology, Norway
Stefanos Gritzalis	University of Piraeus, Greece
Fuchun Guo	University of Wollongong, Australia

Additional Reviewers

Mohsen Ali
Marius Anagnostopoulos
Michael Bamiloshin
Thomas Baumer
Cailing Cai
Yanmei Cao
Eyasu Getahun Chekole
Long Chen
Yonghui Chen
Chengjun Lin
Liron David
Fuyang Deng
Vasiliki Diamantopoulou
Philip Empl
Ludwig Englbrecht
Sabrina Friedl
Sebastian Groll
Rami Haffar
Fadi Hassan
Shen Hua
Li Huilin
Najeeb Jebreel
Pallavi Kaliyar
Maria Karyda
Sascha Kern
Ashneet Khandpur Singh
Chhagan Lal
Minghang Li
Yumei Li
Trupil Limbasiya
Chao Lin
Eleonora Losiouk
Jiqiang Lu

Katerina Mavroeidi
Mohamed-Amine Merzouk
Reza Mohammadi
Antonio Muñoz
Vinod P. Nair
Jianting Ning
Jean-Yves Ouattara
Jing Pan
Shimin Pan
Pavlos Papadopoulos
Argyri Pattakou
Baodong Qin
Xianrui Qin
Tian Qiu
Yanli Ren
Rahul Saha
Jun Shen
Stavros Simou
Chunhua Su
Teik Guan Tan
Aggeliki Tsohou
Mingming Wang
Mingli Wu
Yi Xie
Lei Xu
S. J. Yang
Xu Yang
Yang Yang
Shang Zefua
Jixin Zhang
Yudi Zhang
Yuexin Zhang
Haibin Zheng

Contents

Network Security

Detection of Malware, Attacks and Vulnerabilities

Machine Learning for Security

Cryptology

Integer LWE with Non-subgaussian Error and Related Attacks

Tianyu Wang[1,2], Yuejun Liu[3(✉)], Jun Xu[1,2], Lei Hu[1,2], Yang Tao[1],
and Yongbin Zhou[3]

[1] State Key Laboratory of Information Security, Institute of Information
Engineering, Chinese Academy of Sciences, Beijing 100093, China
{wangtianyu,xujun,HuLei,taoyang}@iie.ac.cn
[2] School of Cyber Security, University of Chinese Academy of Sciences,
Beijing 100093, China
[3] Nanjing University of Science and Technology, Nanjing 210094, Jiangsu, China
{liuyuejun,zhouyongbin}@njust.edu.cn

Abstract. This paper focuses on the security of lattice based Fiat-Shamir signatures in leakage scenarios. More specifically, how to recover the complete private key after obtaining a large number of noisy linear equations without modular about the private key. Such a set of equations can be obtained, for example, in [5], by attacking the rejecting sampling step with a side-channel attack. The paper refers to the mathematical problem of recovering the secret vector from this structure as the ILWE problem and proves that it can be solved by the least squares method. A similar mathematical structure has been obtained in [13] by leaking a single bit at certain specific locations of the randomness.

However, the ILWE problem requires the error term to be subgaussian, which is not always the case in practice. This paper therefore extends the original ILWE problem by presenting the non-subgaussian ILWE problem, proving that it can be solved by the least squares method combined with a correction factor, and giving two attack scenarios: an attack with lower bits leakage of randomness than in [13], and a careless implementation attack on the randomness. In the lower bit randomness leakage case, we are able to attack successfully with 2 or 3 bits leakage lower than those in [13] experimentally, and in the careless implementation attack, we are able to recover the private key successfully when the rejection sampling partially fails.

Keywords: Lattice-based cryptography · Fiat-Shamir signature ·
ILWE problem · Least squares method · Statistical analysis

This work is supported in part by National Natural Science Foundation of China (No. U1936209, No. 61632020, No. 62002353 and No. 61732021) and Beijing Natural Science Foundation (No. 4192067).

J. K. Liu et al. (Eds.): ISC 2021, LNCS 13118, pp. 3–25, 2021.
https://doi.org/10.1007/978-3-030-91356-4_1

1 Introduction

When evaluating the concrete security of a public key scheme, we should not only analyze the hardness of mathematical problems the scheme relies on, but also consider the leakage of some sensitive information in the scheme due to implementation, communication or other reasons. Many existing works show that the leakage of some sensitive information will lead to the complete attack of the scheme. For example, Heninger and Shacham [10] showed that the RSA secret key with small public parameters can be efficiently recovered given its 27% random bits. Even if we have not selected some sensitive parameters correctly, we can still transform the originally difficult mathematical problem the scheme based on into a much easier problem with the extra information. For example, when the secret key $d < n^{0.292}$, the RSA problem is no longer difficult, and d can be completely recovered by Coppersmith method in polynomial time [3].

This paper mainly discusses the potential risk of the extra information of the randomness (or nonce) in lattice based Fiat-Shamir signatures. Aiming at the problem of randomness leakage of Fiat-Shamir signature such as DSA and ECDSA, many impressive results have been achieved [6,11,16,17]. The framework of these attacks is to transform the leakage attack into a hidden number problem (HNP) problem [4], which can be further solved by the lattice method or the Bleichenbacher method. The lattice method is suitable for the situation that the number of leaked bits is large but the number of signatures is small [4,16], while the Bleichenbacher method is suitable for the situation where the number of leaked bits is small but the number of signatures is large [2,6].

In recent years, in order to prevent possible attacks of quantum computers in the future, many lattice based schemes resisting quantum attacks have been proposed. Dilithium and qTesla are lattice based Fiat-Shamir signatures and Dilithium has been selected as a candidate for the third round of NIST post quantum standardization competition due to its excellent performance. At present, in addition to the algorithms of the difficult problems on lattice, there are a series of side channel attacks against the specific implementation of lattice based Fiat-Shamir signatures [5,8,9,18,19], but the sensitivity of randomness leakage in lattice signatures has not been analyzed until [13]. Liu et al. first observed that if one bit of specific position of the randomness is leaked, the adversary will get a noisy linear equation of the low bit of signature and secret without modular, that is, $z_{low} + d * 2^l = y_{low} + \langle \mathbf{s}, \mathbf{c} \rangle$, where d represents if there is an overflow and is decided according to the leakage. Recovering $\mathbf{s}$ with enough equations is abstracted as an integer LWE (ILWE) problem [5] and has been extended to the FS-ILWE problem to adjust this attack in their work. Despite the tiny difference between these two problems, we can simply obtain $\mathbf{s}$ simply by the least squares method. Take Dilithium IV for example, around 2^{20} signatures are needed to recover the secret key when leaking the 7-th lower bit of randomness.

1.1 Our Contribution

Although Liu et al. recovered the secret key effectively, their attack has a limitation that it is not suitable for the lower-bit-leakage case, because in order to guess the value d correctly, $|\langle \mathbf{s}, \mathbf{c} \rangle|$ must be smaller than 2^{l-1} and the leakage position must be higher than l. If the leakage position is lower than l, additional error related to the value $\langle \mathbf{s}, \mathbf{c} \rangle$ is introduced. In view of this limitation, we expand the ILWE problem. Instead of requiring randomness to be independent of $\langle \mathbf{s}, \mathbf{c} \rangle$, we relax this requirement into that the expectation of error term is only related to the value $\langle \mathbf{s}, \mathbf{c} \rangle$ and satisfies the tail property of subgaussian. We have proved that solving this new problem with the least squares method will result in a certain multiple of $\mathbf{s}$ and the related conclusion is Theorem 2 (Page 6).

As for λ, we can not only estimate it with $\|\mathbf{s}\|_2$ according to Proposition 1 (Page 7), but also search for its true value without knowing the exact value of $\|\mathbf{s}\|_2$. As a result, we can recover $\mathbf{s}$ by rounding each component of the vector $\frac{1}{\lambda}\tilde{\mathbf{s}}$.

In the past, we only knew the ILWE problem with subgaussian randomness could be solved directly by the least squares method, while knowing little if the randomness is related to $\langle \mathbf{s}, \mathbf{c} \rangle$. With this theorem, we can deal with more abundant scenarios than those in the past. This paper analyzes the following cases:

1. Lower-bit Randomness Leakage Attack. We use Liu et al.'s attack method into the lower-bit randomness leakage case, and then we can get a coefficient multiple of the private key $\lambda\mathbf{s}$. With this change, we can treat the case that the leakage position is 2–3 bits lower than before. We can not handle lower leakage case as there is too little effective information of the secret key to recover it in practice.

2. Careless Implementation Attack. The careless implementation of randomness may lead to the inconsistency of randomness distribution, which may make the rejection sampling invalid or partially invalid for the original signature scheme, resulting in the distribution of signatures contains the information of $\langle \mathbf{s}, \mathbf{c} \rangle$. In Sect. 5, we provide a general approach to extract the secret by the least squares method.

By using the Proposition 1, we can further obtain the number of required signatures and the approximate value of λ in these scenarios. The analysis of these two scenarios shows that the randomness in lattice based Fiat-Shamir signature needs to be protected very carefully, and the detection of signature distribution needs to be added in the implementation of signature algorithm to prevent possible statistical attacks caused by different outputted signatures.

1.2 Organization of the Paper

The rest of this paper will be organized as follows. Section 2 is the preliminaries of this paper. In Sect. 3 we introduce a new extension of the ILWE problem, which we call non-subgaussian ILWE problem, and proves that non-subgaussian

ILWE problem can also be solved directly by the least squares method. In Sect. 4 and 5, we heuristically reduce two attack scenarios of lattice based Fiat-Shamir signatures to the non-subgaussian ILWE problem: lower-bit randomness leakage attack and randomness implementation mistakes attack. In Sect. 6 we show the experimental results of these two attack scenarios and further verified the rationality of our heuristic reduction. In Sect. 7 we summarize our work.

2 Preliminaries

2.1 Notation

For $x \in \mathbb{R}$, rounding the number x is denoted by $\lceil x \rfloor$. Rounding up and rounding down the number x is denoted by $\lceil x \rceil$ and $\lfloor x \rfloor$ respectively. We denote column vectors by bold lowercase (e.g. $\mathbf{x}$) and matrices in bold uppercase (e.g. $\mathbf{A}$). The p-norm of the vector $\mathbf{x} = (x_1, \ldots, x_n)^T \in \mathbb{R}^n$ is denoted by $\|\mathbf{x}\|_p^{1/p} = (|x_1|^p + \ldots + |x_n|^p)^{1/p}$, and the infinity norm by $\|\mathbf{x}\|_\infty = \max(|x_1|, |x_2|, \ldots, |x_n|)$. For a matrix $\mathbf{A} \in \mathbb{R}^{m \times n}$, we denote the i-th column of $\mathbf{A} \in \mathbb{R}^{m \times n}$ by $\mathbf{a}_i$. The operator norm $\|\mathbf{A}\|_p^{op}$ of $\mathbf{A}$ with respect to the p-norm, $p \in [1, \infty]$, is given by:

$$\|\mathbf{A}\|_p^{op} = \sup_{\mathbf{x} \in \mathbb{R}^n \setminus \{0\}} \frac{\|\mathbf{A}\mathbf{x}\|_p}{\|\mathbf{x}\|_p} = \sup_{\|\mathbf{x}\|_p = 1} \|\mathbf{A}\mathbf{x}\|_p. \tag{1}$$

In this paper, $\mathcal{R} \triangleq \mathbb{Z}[x]/(x^n+1)$ is a polynomial ring and $\mathcal{R}_q \triangleq \mathbb{Z}_q[x]/(x^n+1)$, where n is a power of 2. For an element $\mathbf{a} = \sum_{i=0}^{N-1} a_i x^i \in \mathcal{R}$, this element can also be represented as a vector $(a_{n-1}, a_{n-2}, \ldots, a_0)^T$. For two polynomials $\mathbf{a}, \mathbf{b} \in \mathcal{R}$, the inner product is denoted by $\langle \mathbf{a}, \mathbf{b} \rangle = \sum_{i=0}^{d} a_i b_i = \mathbf{a}^T \mathbf{b}$. The polynomial multiplication is represented as $\mathbf{ab}$ and can also be denoted as matrix multiplication $\mathbf{Ab}$ or $\mathbf{Ba}$ where $\mathbf{A}, \mathbf{B}$ are the rotation matrices related to $\mathbf{a}$ and $\mathbf{b}$. The rotation matrix $\mathbf{A}$ of $\mathbf{a}$ is the following Toeplitz matrix:

$$\mathbf{A} = \begin{bmatrix} a_0 & a_1 & a_2 & \cdots & a_{N-1} \\ -a_{N-1} & a_0 & a_1 & \cdots & a_{N-2} \\ \vdots & \vdots & \vdots & \ddots & \vdots \\ -a_1 & -a_2 & -a_3 & \cdots & a_0 \end{bmatrix}. \tag{2}$$

2.2 Gaussian and Subgaussian

For any random variable X, $\mathbb{E}[X]$ denotes the expectation of X and $\mathbb{D}[X] = \mathbb{E}[X^2] - \mathbb{E}[X]^2$ denotes the variance. We write $X \sim \chi$ to denote that X follows the distribution χ. If χ is a discrete distribution over some countable set S, then for any $s \in S$, we denote by $\chi(s)$ the probability that a sample from χ equals to s. In particular, if $f : S \to \mathbb{R}$ is any function and $X \sim \chi$, we have: $\mathbb{E}[f(s)] = \sum_{s \in S} f(s) \cdot \chi(s)$.

Let $\rho(x) = \exp(-\pi x^2)$ for all $x \in \mathbb{R}$. We define $\rho_{\mu, \sigma}(x) = \rho((x - \mu)/\sigma)$ the Gaussian function of parameters μ, σ and we call that a random variable

$\xi \sim N(\mu, \sigma)$ if its probability density function is $\frac{1}{\sqrt{2\pi}\sigma}\rho((x - \mu)/\sigma)$. For any subset $S \subset \mathbb{R}$ such that the sum converges, we let:

$$\rho_{\mu,\sigma}(S) = \sum_{s \in S} \rho_{\mu,\sigma}(s).$$

The discrete Gaussian distribution $D_{\mu,\sigma}$ centered at μ and of parameter σ is the distribution on $\mathbb{Z}$ defined by

$$D_{\mu,\sigma}(x) = \frac{\rho_{\mu,\sigma}(x)}{\rho_{\mu,\sigma}(\mathbb{Z})} = \frac{\exp(-\pi(x - \mu)^2/\sigma^2)}{\rho_{\mu,\sigma}(\mathbb{Z})}$$

for all $x \in \mathbb{Z}$. We omit the subscript c in $\rho_{\mu,\sigma}$ and $D_{\mu,\sigma}$ when $\mu = 0$.

Next we recall the notion of subgaussian distributions in [5] and list some properties of subgaussian distributions.

Definition 1 (Subgaussian random variable [5]). *A random variable X over $\mathbb{R}$ is said to be τ-subgaussian for some τ if the following bound holds for all $s \in \mathbb{R}$:*

$$\mathbb{E}[\exp(sX)] \leq \exp(\frac{\tau^2 s^2}{2}).$$

Lemma 1 (Lemma 2.4 in [5]). *A τ-subgaussian random variable X satisfies:*

$$\mathbb{E}(X) = 0 \quad and \quad \mathbb{E}(X^2) \leq \tau^2.$$

Lemma 2 (Lemma 2.5 in [5]). *Any distribution over $\mathbb{R}$ of mean zero and supported over a bound interval $[a, b]$ is $\frac{(b-a)}{2}$-subgaussian.*

2.3 The ILWE Problem

The ILWE problem is first introduced in [5], their main motivation for studying the ILWE problem is a side-channel attack against the BLISS lattice-based signature [7]. The definition of the ILWE is given below.

Definition 2 (ILWE Distribution [5]). *For any vector $\mathbf{s} \in \mathbb{Z}^n$ and any two probability distribution χ_a, χ_e over $\mathbb{Z}$, the ILWE distribution $\mathcal{D}_{\mathbf{s},\chi_a,\chi_e}$ is the probability distribution over $\mathbb{Z}^n \times \mathbb{Z}$ defined as follows: samples from $\mathcal{D}_{\mathbf{s},\chi_a,\chi_e}$ are of the form*

$$(\mathbf{a}, b) = (\mathbf{a}, \langle \mathbf{a}, \mathbf{s} \rangle + e)$$

where $\mathbf{a} \leftarrow \chi_a^n$ and $e \leftarrow \chi_e$.

Definition 3 (ILWE Problem [5]). *Given m samples $\{(\mathbf{a}_i, b_i)\}_{1 \leq i \leq m}$ from the ILWE distribution $\mathcal{D}_{\mathbf{s},\chi_a,\chi_e}$ for some $\mathbf{s} \in \mathbb{Z}^n$, one is asked to recover the vector $\mathbf{s}$.*

Let σ_e and σ_a be the standard deviation of χ_e and χ_a respectively. Bootle et al. [5] showed the ILWE problem with m samples can be solved in polynomial time using statistical learning techniques when $m \geq \Omega(\sigma_e/\sigma_a)^2$ and σ_e is not superpolynomially larger than σ_a.

Theorem 1 (Theorem 4.5 in [5]). *Suppose that χ_a is a τ_a-subgaussian and χ_e is τ_e-subgaussian, and let $(\mathbf{A}, \mathbf{b} = \mathbf{As} + \mathbf{e})$ the data constructed from m samples of the ILWE distribution $\mathcal{D}_{\mathbf{s},\chi_a,\chi_e}$, for some $\mathbf{s} \in \mathbb{Z}^n$. There exist constants $C_1, C_2 > 0$ such that for all $\eta \geq 1$, if:*

$$m \geq 4\frac{\tau_a^4}{\sigma_a^4}(C_1 n + C_2 \eta) \quad and \quad m \geq 32\frac{\tau_e^2}{\sigma_a^2}\ln(2n),$$

then the least squares estimator $\tilde{\mathbf{s}} = (\mathbf{A}^T\mathbf{A})^{-1}\mathbf{A}^T\mathbf{b}$ satisfies $\|\mathbf{s} - \tilde{\mathbf{s}}\|_\infty < 1/2$, and hence $\lceil \tilde{\mathbf{s}} \rfloor = \mathbf{s}$ with probability at least $1 - \frac{1}{2n} - 2^{-\eta}$. Furthermore, one can choose $C_1 = 2^8 \ln 9$ and $C_2 = 2^9 \ln 2$.

Notice $\tilde{\mathbf{s}} = (\mathbf{A}^T\mathbf{A})^{-1}\mathbf{A}^T\mathbf{b} = \mathbf{s} + (\mathbf{A}^T\mathbf{A})^{-1}\mathbf{A}^T\mathbf{e}$, thus the theorem states that when the number of samples is sufficiently large, the norm $(\mathbf{A}^T\mathbf{A})^{-1}\mathbf{A}^T\mathbf{e}$ is small enough.

2.4 Lattice Based Fiat-Shamir Signatures

Fiat-Shamir signatures is transformed from a Σ-protocol through the famous Fiat-Shamir transform. The first lattice based Fiat-Shamir signature is given by [14] and several improvements have been made. The security of lattice based Fiat-Shamir signatures are based on hard lattice problems such as LWE, SIS and their variants.

The signature in the lattice based Fiat-Shamir paradigm can usually be written as $\mathbf{z} = \mathbf{y} + \mathbf{sc}$, where $\mathbf{s}$ is a matrix and $\mathbf{c}$ is a vector if the scheme is based on LWE and SIS [14]. If the scheme is based on RLWE and RSIS then s, c are polynomials in $\mathcal{R}_q$ [1], while $s \in \mathcal{R}_q^r$ and $c \in \mathcal{R}_q$ if the scheme is based on MLWE and MSIS [15]. As the polynomial multiplication can be represented as matrix multiplication, so no matter what the scheme is, we can always write several signatures as the matrix form $\mathbf{z} = \mathbf{y} + \mathbf{Cs}$, where every component of $\mathbf{z}$ is $z_i = y_i + \langle \mathbf{c}_i, \mathbf{s} \rangle$.

3 The Non-subgaussian ILWE Problem

In this section, we will extend the original ILWE problem to the non-subgaussian ILWE problem. The difference is the expectation of the randomness is a function only related to $\langle \mathbf{s}, \mathbf{a} \rangle$ and the definition is as follows:

Definition 4 (The Non-subgaussian ILWE Distribution). *For any vector $\mathbf{s} \in \mathbb{Z}^n$ and any two probability distribution χ_a, χ_e over $\mathbb{Z}$, $f(x)$ is a continuous function defined on $\mathbb{R}$, the ILWE distribution $\mathcal{D}_{\mathbf{s},\chi_a,\chi_e,f}$ is the probability distribution over $\mathbb{Z}^n \times \mathbb{Z}$ defined as follows: samples from $\mathcal{D}_{\mathbf{s},\chi_a,\chi_e,f}$ are of the form*

$$(\mathbf{a}, b) = (\mathbf{a}, \langle \mathbf{a}, \mathbf{s} \rangle + e + f(\langle \mathbf{a}, \mathbf{s} \rangle))$$

where $\mathbf{a} \leftarrow \chi_a^n$ and $e \leftarrow \chi_e$.

Compared with the ILWE distribution, the non-subgaussian ILWE distribution has an additional term f. The function f is defined to be continuous to ensure we can estimate λ in the next step. Now we give the definition of the non-subgaussian ILWE problem.

Definition 5 (The Non-subgaussian ILWE Problem). *Given m samples $\{(\mathbf{a}_i, b_i)\}_{1 \leq i \leq m}$ from the non-subgaussian ILWE distribution $\mathcal{D}_{\mathbf{s}, \chi_a, \chi_e, f}$ for some $\mathbf{s} \in \mathbb{Z}^n$, one is asked to recover the vector $\mathbf{s}$.*

The analysis in the rest of this paper is based on an assumption that if an n dimensional random vector $\mathbf{a}$ is sampled as $\mathbf{a} \leftarrow \chi_a^n$ and χ_a is τ_a-subgaussian, then for any fixed orthogonal transformation $\mathbf{P} \in O_n(\mathbb{R})$, the random vector $\mathbf{Pa}$ can also be treated as a τ_a-subgaussian random vector distributed on χ_a^n statistically. We make this assumption because the distribution χ_a^n seems close to isotropic. For example, if the vector $\mathbf{a}$ follows a spherical gaussian distribution, then this assumption clearly holds. In Theorem 2, we will show that given enough non-subgaussian ILWE samples, the result of the least squares method is a constant multiple of the secret vector.

Theorem 2. *Suppose that χ_a is a τ_a-subgaussian and χ_e is τ_e-subgaussian, and let $(\mathbf{A}, \mathbf{b})$ be m samples from the non-subgaussian ILWE distribution $\mathcal{D}_{\mathbf{s}, \chi_a, \chi_e, f}$, for some $\mathbf{s} \in \mathbb{Z}^n$. If the least squares estimator $\tilde{\mathbf{s}}$ of $(\mathbf{A}, \mathbf{b})$ converges to some vector $\mathbf{s}'$ when m tend to infinity, then there exist $\lambda \in \mathbb{R}$ such that $\mathbf{s}' = \lambda\mathbf{s}$.*

Proof. Let $\mathbf{A} = (\mathbf{a_1}, \mathbf{a_2}, \ldots, \mathbf{a_m})^T$, $\mathbf{f(As)} = (f(\langle \mathbf{a_1}, \mathbf{s}\rangle), f(\langle \mathbf{a_2}, \mathbf{s}\rangle), \ldots, f(\langle \mathbf{a_m}, \mathbf{s}\rangle))^T$ and $\mathbf{e}' = \mathbf{e} + \mathbf{f(As)}$. Now we select an orthogonal transformation $\mathbf{P} \in O_n(\mathbb{R})$ such that $\{\mathbf{x} \in \mathbb{R}^n | \mathbf{Px} = \mathbf{x}\} = Span\{\mathbf{s}\}$, the two sets of samples $(\mathbf{b} = \mathbf{As} + \mathbf{e}' = \mathbf{AP}^T\mathbf{Ps} + \mathbf{e}', \mathbf{A})$ and $(\mathbf{b} = \mathbf{AP}^T\mathbf{s} + \mathbf{e}', \mathbf{AP}^T)$ behaves almost the same[1], so the least squares estimator of these two sets of samples are equal. In other words, $\tilde{\mathbf{s}} = (\mathbf{A}^T\mathbf{A})^{-1}\mathbf{A}^T\mathbf{b} \approx ((\mathbf{AP}^T)^T\mathbf{AP}^T)^{-1}(\mathbf{AP}^T)^T\mathbf{b} = \mathbf{P}(\mathbf{A}^T\mathbf{A})^{-1}\mathbf{A}^T\mathbf{b} = \mathbf{P}\tilde{\mathbf{s}}$, so $\mathbf{P}\tilde{\mathbf{s}} \approx \tilde{\mathbf{s}} \approx \mathbf{s}'^{2}$, which concludes that $\mathbf{s}' \in Span\{\mathbf{s}\}$ thus $\mathbf{s}' = \lambda\mathbf{s}$. ∎

Now we have explained why $\tilde{\mathbf{s}} = \lambda\mathbf{s}$ intuitively. In the next step, we will estimate the value of λ when knowing the exact Euclidean norm of the secret $\mathbf{s}$:

Proposition 1. *Suppose that χ_a is a τ_a-subgaussian and χ_e is τ_e-subgaussian, and let $(\mathbf{A}, \mathbf{b})$ be m samples from the non-subgaussian ILWE distribution $\mathcal{D}_{\mathbf{s}, \chi_a, \chi_e, f}$, for some $\mathbf{s} = (s_1, 0, \ldots, 0) \in \mathbb{Z}^n$ and a continuous function f. Let $r(a_i^{(1)}) = \frac{f(a_i^{(1)} s_1) + a_i^{(1)} s_1}{a_i^{(1)} s_1}$ where $a_i^{(1)}$ denotes the first component of the vector a_i. If $\mathbb{D}[\chi_a] = \sigma_a^2$, $\mathbb{E}[r(a_i^{(1)})(a_i^{(1)})^2] \neq 0$, $\sigma_1^2 = \mathbb{E}[r(a_i^{(1)})(a_i^{(1)})^2]$, $\sigma_2^2 = \mathbb{E}[r(x_i^{(1)})]$, and*

$$m > M = \max(\frac{4\tau_a^4}{\sigma_a^4}(C_1 n + C_2 \eta), \ 2^7 \frac{\tau_e^2}{\sigma_a^2} \ln(2n), \ 2^{13}(n \ln 9 + \ln 8n)\sigma_a^2 |s_1|^2 \cdot C_3),$$

---

[1] According to our assumption, the distribution of $\mathbf{Pa}$ can also be treated as χ_a, so the latter set of samples can also be treated as sampled from the non-sugbaussian ILWE distribution $\mathcal{D}_{\mathbf{s}, \chi_a, \chi_e, f}$.

[2] "$\approx$" means "converges to" when m tend to infinity.

where $C_1 = 2^8 \ln 9, C_2 = 2^9 \ln 2, C_3 = \max\{\frac{\max\{\sigma_1,\sigma_2\}^2}{\sigma_a^8}, \frac{K^2 \max\{\sigma_1,\sigma_2\}^4}{\min\{\sigma_1,\sigma_2\}^2}\}$, *then* $\Pr[\|\tilde{\mathbf{s}} - \sigma_1^2/\sigma_a^2 \mathbf{s}\|_\infty < 1/2] > 1 - \frac{1}{n} + \frac{1}{4n^2}$.

The proof of Proposition 1 is relatively complex and the details can be found in the Appendix A. What's more, the secret in Proposition 1 has a special form $\mathbf{s} = (s_1, 0, \ldots, 0)^T$, so we have only obtained the conclusion for the special case now. In fact, this special case can be extended to the general case, and all the details can be found in Appendix A. What's more, λ can also be searched by finding $\arg\max_\lambda\{(\lceil \frac{1}{\lambda}\tilde{\mathbf{s}} \rfloor - \frac{1}{\lambda}\tilde{\mathbf{s}})^2\}$ when enough samples have been obtained.

4   Low-Bit's Randomness Leakage Attack

In this section, we introduce the randomness leakage attack in [13] and extend it to the lower-bit leakage. The original attack can be applied to most known Fiat-Shamir signatures and we only introduce Dilithium as an example. The Dilithium scheme is built via the "Fiat-Shamir with aborts" structure and can be seen as a variant of the Bai-Galbraith scheme with a public key compression. Dilithium is based on the hardness of Module-LWE and Module-SIS problems and the secret keys consist of two parts $\mathbf{s}_1 \in \mathcal{R}_q^r$ and $\mathbf{s}_2 \in \mathcal{R}_q^s$, where $\mathcal{R}_q = \mathbb{Z}_q[X]/(X^n+1)$. The signature is computed as $\mathbf{z} = \mathbf{y} + \mathbf{sc}$, where $\mathbf{c} \in \mathcal{R}_q$ and every component of $\mathbf{y}$ is uniformly distributed on $[-\gamma, \gamma]$. Although the public key has been compressed so we cannot recover $\mathbf{s}_2$ only knowing $\mathbf{s}_1$, the work [19] showed that just knowing $\mathbf{s}_1$ is sufficient for existential forgery attack. One polynomial component of $\mathbf{s}_1$ is omitted as $\mathbf{s}$ in the rest of the paper, then the multiplication between $\mathbf{s}$ and $\mathbf{c}$ is a polynomial multiplication, so we can rewrite it as a matrix multiplication $\mathbf{Cs}$, where $\mathbf{C}$ is the rotation of c. The key generation and signing algorithms of Dilithium without public key compression are presented in Algorithm 1. In order to recover the full secret key, we need to solve several independent noisy linear systems independently.

4.1   The Randomness Leakage Attack

Assume that $|\langle \mathbf{c}_i, \mathbf{s} \rangle| < 2^l$, and we have got the $l + 1$-th bit of y_i, then the l least significant bits of y_i, which is denoted as $[y_i]_{2^l}$, can be regarded as an independent subgaussian variable with $\mathbf{c}_i$ and $\mathbf{s}$.[3] The low bits of z_i can be expressed as follows: $[z_i]_{2^l} + d_i \cdot 2^l = [y_i]_{2^l} + \langle \mathbf{c}_i, \mathbf{s} \rangle$, where d_i reflects if the carry or borrow occurs between the sum of $[y_i]_{2^l}$ and $\langle \mathbf{c}_i, \mathbf{s} \rangle$. So the first step of this attack is guessing the value of d_i. If the $(l + 1)$-th bit of z_i and the $(l + 1)$-th bit of y_i are the same, then $d_i = 0$; otherwise $d_i \neq 0$. Furthermore:

$$[z_i]_{2^l} \in (-2^l, -2^{l-1}) \cup (0, 2^{l-1}), \qquad then \quad d_i = 1;$$
$$[z_i]_{2^l} \in (-2^{l-1}, 0) \cup (2^{l-1}, 2^l), \qquad then \quad d_i = -1;$$
$$[z_i]_{2^l} = 0, z_i > 0, \qquad then \quad d_i = 1;$$
$$[z_i]_{2^l} = 0, z_i < 0, \qquad then \quad d_i = -1.$$

---

[3] In fact $\mathbb{E}([y]_{2^l}) = -\frac{2^l}{2^{\gamma+1}-1}\langle \mathbf{s}, \bar{\mathbf{c}} \rangle$ is close to 0, where $2^\gamma \gg 2^l$. So $[y_i]_{2^l}$ can be regarded as subgaussian.

Algorithm 1. Simplified Version of Dilithium

Gen:
$\mathbf{A} \leftarrow \mathcal{R}_q^{k \times l}$
$(\mathbf{s}_1, \mathbf{s}_2) \leftarrow S_\eta^l \times S_\eta^k$
$\mathbf{t} := \mathbf{A}\mathbf{s}_1 + \mathbf{s}_2$
return $pk = (\mathbf{A}, \mathbf{t}), sk = (\mathbf{A}, \mathbf{t}, \mathbf{s}_1, \mathbf{s}_2)$

Sign(sk, M):
$\mathbf{t} := \perp$
while $\mathbf{z} = \perp$ **do**
  $\mathbf{y} \leftarrow S_{\gamma_1 - 1}^l$
  $\mathbf{w}_1 := \mathbf{HighBits}(\mathbf{A}\mathbf{y}, 2\gamma_2)$
  $c \in B_\tau := H(M \| \mathbf{w}_1)$
  $\mathbf{z} := \mathbf{y} + c\mathbf{s}_1$
  if $\|\mathbf{z}\|_\infty \geq \gamma_1 - \beta$ or $\|\mathbf{LowBits}(\mathbf{A}\mathbf{y} - c\mathbf{s}_2, 2\gamma_2)\|_\infty \geq \gamma_2 - \beta$, **then** $\mathbf{z} := \perp$
end while
return $\sigma = (\mathbf{z}, c)$

Assume that we can always guess d correctly, then the sample $(\mathbf{c}_i, [z_i]_{2^l} + d_i \cdot 2^l = [y_i]_{2^l} + \langle \mathbf{c}_i, \mathbf{s} \rangle)$ is in fact follows the ILWE, so finding s given sufficient equations of the low bits of signatures is in fact an ILWE problem[4]. After judging the value of d_i, we can simply apply the least squares method to the low-bits samples and then rounding the output

$$\tilde{\mathbf{s}} = (\mathbf{C}^T \mathbf{C})^{-1} \mathbf{C}^T ([\mathbf{z}]_{2^l} + 2^l \cdot \mathbf{d}).$$

Due to Theorem 1, $\lceil \tilde{\mathbf{s}} \rfloor = \mathbf{s}$ with high probability. In summary, if the $l+1$-th bit of the randomness is leaked, the attack can be divided into the following steps.

1. Guess the value of d, the result relies on whether the $l+1$-th bit of y' equals to the $l+1$-th bit of z' and the value of $[z_i]_{2^l}$,
2. Establish the linear system with randomness $[z_i]_{2^l} + d_i \cdot 2^l = [y_i]_{2^l} + \langle \mathbf{c}_i, \mathbf{s} \rangle$ and compute the least squares estimator $\tilde{\mathbf{s}} = (\mathbf{C}^T \mathbf{C})^{-1} \mathbf{C}^T ([\mathbf{z}]_{2^l} + 2^l \cdot \mathbf{d})$,
3. $\mathbf{s} = \lceil \tilde{\mathbf{s}} \rfloor$.

In summary, if $|\langle \mathbf{c}_i, \mathbf{s} \rangle| < 2^{l-1}$ and the leakage position is higher than $l+1$, we can always guess the value d correctly, thus getting an ILWE sample. With plenty of ILWE instances, the secret can be easily found by the least squares method.

4.2 Extend to Lower Bits

An obstacle of the original attack is that when $|\langle \mathbf{c}_i, \mathbf{s} \rangle| < 2^{l-1}$, the leakage position of y_i must be higher than $l+1$, otherwise we can not obtain the true

---

[4] More precisely, it is an FS-ILWE problem presented in [13], but due to their similarity, we view this problem as ILWE.

value of d with nearly 100% accuracy. Let the information of carry or borrow we guess is denoted by d', then the equation of lower bits we get is

$$[z_i]_{2^l} + d'_i \cdot 2^l = [y_i]_{2^l} + (d'_i - d_i) \cdot 2^l + \langle \mathbf{c}_i, \mathbf{s} \rangle.$$

Actually, the error in the linear system we build after guessing d is $[y_i]_{2^l} + (d'_i - d_i) \cdot 2^l$, which is no longer subgaussian. However, take the l-th-bit's leakage case as an example, we will show that the expectation of the error term is only related to $|\langle \mathbf{c}_i, \mathbf{s} \rangle|$.

After the l-th bit of y_i is leaked, the first step is guessing d. When $|\langle \mathbf{c}_i, \mathbf{s} \rangle| < 2^{l-2}$, then $d' = d$. When $\langle \mathbf{c}_i, \mathbf{s} \rangle < [2^{l-2}, 2^{l-1})$, the judgment of d is shown in the following Table 1.

Table 1. Determine the value of d

z	$z^{(l)} = y^{(l)}$	$[z]_{2^{l-1}}$	Judge d'	True d	$d = d'$
>0	Y	$[0, 2^{l-2})$	0	0	Y
		$[2^{l-2}, 2 \times 2^{l-2})$	0	0	Y
	N	$[0, 2^{l-2})$	1	1	Y
		$[2^{l-2}, 2 \times 2^{l-2})$	-1	1	N
<0	Y	$[0, 2^{l-2})$	0	0	Y
		$[2^{l-2}, 2 \times 2^{l-2})$	0	0	Y
	N	$[0, 2^{l-2})$	-1	1	N
		$[2^{l-2}, 2 \times 2^{l-2})$	1	1	Y

After dealing with different values of $x = \langle \mathbf{c}_i, \mathbf{s} \rangle$, we get the expectation of the randomness is the following function:

$$f(x) = \begin{cases} -2^{l-1} - 2x, & x \in (-2 \cdot 2^{l-2}, -2^{l-2}] \\ 0, & x \in (-2^{l-2}, 2^{l-2}) \\ 2^{l-1} - 2x, & x \in [2^{l-2}, 2 \cdot 2^{l-2}) \end{cases}$$

That is to say, all the equation of the lower bits can be transformed into the following form

$$[z]_{2^l - 1} + d' \cdot 2^{l-1} = \langle \mathbf{c}_i, \mathbf{s} \rangle + ([y]_{2^l - 1} - f(\langle \mathbf{c}_i, \mathbf{s} \rangle)) + f(\langle \mathbf{c}_i, \mathbf{s} \rangle).$$

Now $([y]_{2^l - 1} - f(\langle \mathbf{c}_i, \mathbf{s} \rangle)$ is τ_y-subgaussian and $f(\langle \mathbf{c}_i, \mathbf{s} \rangle)$ is a function only related to $\langle \mathbf{c}_i, \mathbf{s} \rangle$, so the samples $(c_i, [y]_{2^l - 1})$ follow a non-subgaussian ILWE distribution. According to Theorem 2, the least squares estimator $\tilde{\mathbf{s}} = \lambda \mathbf{s}$. In practice, we need to search an approximate value $\lambda' \approx \lambda$ and calculate the rounding vector $\lfloor \frac{1}{\lambda'} \tilde{\mathbf{s}} \rceil$. So the smaller λ is, the larger the error between $\lfloor \frac{1}{\lambda'} \tilde{\mathbf{s}} \rceil$ and $\mathbf{s}$, and it is more difficult to find $\mathbf{s}$. In Sect. 6, we set up several experiments on the Dilithium-5 and this attack works well leaking the 4-th bit of randomness. As a contrast, when there is no correction factor, we can only attack the case leaking the 7-th bit or above. When the leakage position is lower than 4, λ becomes extremely small. As we need to ensure that $\|\lfloor \frac{1}{\lambda}\tilde{\mathbf{s}} \rceil - \mathbf{s}\|_\infty \leq 1/2$ but a smaller λ will expand the left end of the inequality, so more signatures are necessary to find s.

5   The Careless Implementation Attack

In a Fiat-Shamir signature scheme, in order to prevent the leakage of any information of the secret $\mathbf{s}$ through the distribution of the signature $\mathbf{z} = \mathbf{y} + \langle \mathbf{s}, \mathbf{c} \rangle$, rejection sampling is applied to remodeling the distribution of $\mathbf{z}$ to a public distribution. However, a well constructed cryptosystem might be carelessly applied or implemented. Specifically, when some parameters related to the nonce $\mathbf{y}$ are implemented mistakenly, the rejection sampling will lose its effects and thus the signatures will leak some information of the secret $\mathbf{s}$. In this section, according to the error distribution, we abstract different cases for further discussions. We find that no matter what the distribution of $\mathbf{y}$ is, the solution vector obtained by the least squares method is also a constant multiple of the real secret $\mathbf{s}$.

5.1   Gaussian Randomness

Among the lattice based Fiat-Shamir signature schemes, [14] choose to instantiate the error as a Gaussian distribution.[5] The signature is generated by $\mathbf{z} = \mathbf{Sc} + \mathbf{y}$, where the secret key $\mathbf{S} \in \mathbb{Z}_q^{k \times n}$. After generating signatures, these signatures will finally be output with probability $\min(D_\sigma^k(\mathbf{z})/(M \cdot D_{\mathbf{Sc},\sigma}), 1)$. The parameter M is chosen to be the maximum real number such that $D_\sigma^k(\mathbf{z})/(M \cdot D_{\mathbf{Sc},\sigma}) \leq 1$. When the cryptosystem is running normally, the distribution of the signature $\mathbf{z}$ is clearly $D_\sigma^k(\mathbf{z})$, which is a public distribution which is independent with $\mathbf{Sc}$.

When the distribution of $\mathbf{y}$ changes to $D_{\sigma'}^k$, as the output probability of the signature is still $\min(D_\sigma^k(\mathbf{z})/(M \cdot D_{\mathbf{Sc},\sigma}), 1)$, the distribution of the output signature is $D_{\mathbf{Sc},\sigma'} \cdot D_\sigma^k(\mathbf{z})/(M \cdot D_{\mathbf{Sc},\sigma})$, which is in fact a gaussian distribution. Let $\sigma' = \eta\sigma$, then for one component of $\mathbf{z}$, its probability density function is

$$D_{\langle \mathbf{s}, \mathbf{c} \rangle, \sigma'} \cdot D_\sigma^k(z)/(M \cdot D_{\langle \mathbf{s}, \mathbf{c} \rangle, \sigma})$$

$$= K \cdot \exp(-\frac{(z - \langle \mathbf{s}, \mathbf{c} \rangle)^2(\sigma^2 - \sigma'^2)}{2\sigma^2\sigma'^2}) \cdot \exp(-\frac{z^2}{2\sigma^2})$$

$$= K' \cdot \exp(-\frac{(z - \mu)^2}{2\Sigma^2}),$$

where $\mu = (1 - \eta^2)\langle \mathbf{s}, \mathbf{c} \rangle$, $\Sigma = \eta\sigma$ and K, K' are constant real numbers. So the signature $\mathbf{z}$ is gaussian with $\mathbb{E}(\mathbf{z}) = (1 - \eta^2)\mathbf{Sc}$ and $\mathbb{D}(\mathbf{z}) = \eta^2\sigma^2$.

---

[5] In fact, the nonce in [7] is also gaussian, but the signature is of the form $z = y + (-1)^b sc$, which is different with our case.

Now the i-th coefficient of $\mathbf{z}$, which is denoted as z_i, follows the equation $z_i = \langle \mathbf{s}_i, \mathbf{c} \rangle + y_i$. Let $f(\langle \mathbf{s}_i, \mathbf{c} \rangle) = -\eta^2 \langle \mathbf{s}_i, \mathbf{c} \rangle$, then

$$z_i = \langle \mathbf{s}_i, \mathbf{c} \rangle + y_i' + f(\langle \mathbf{s}_i, \mathbf{c} \rangle)$$

and y_i' become a gaussian variable. We can transform these samples to an ILWE form: $z_i = \langle (1 - \eta^2)\mathbf{s}_i, \mathbf{c} \rangle + y_i'$. As a result, when collecting enough samples about the same row of the secret $\mathbf{S}$, the result of the least squares method $\tilde{\mathbf{s}}$ will be close to $(1 - \eta^2)\mathbf{s}$. In order to find out the secret vector $\mathbf{s}_i$, the amount of the signatures we get should be large enough so that $\| \lceil \tilde{\mathbf{s}}/(1 - \eta^2) \rfloor - \mathbf{s}_i \|_\infty < 1/2$. Other rows of $\mathbf{S}$ can be obtained using the same approach.

5.2 Uniform Randomness

In this section, we will deal with the uniform case. Take Dilithium for an example, we take one part of the secret key $\mathbf{s}_1$ be $\mathbf{s}$, then the corresponding signature is $\mathbf{z} = \mathbf{y} + \mathbf{sc}$. The randomness y is chosen uniformly at random among γ-short polynomials in $\mathcal{R}_q$. Rewrite $\mathbf{cs}$ by the matrix multiplication $\mathbf{Cs}$, where $\mathbf{C}$ is the rotation of $\mathbf{c}$. The signature $\mathbf{z}$ will finally be output when $\mathbf{z} \in \{-\gamma + \beta, \dots, \gamma - \beta\}^n$, where $\mathbf{Cs} \in (-\beta, \beta)^n$ and $\mathbf{y} \in (-\gamma, \gamma)$. If the bound γ of the randomness $\mathbf{y}$ is implemented to a different parameter γ' such that the rejection sampling lose its efficacy, we will illustrate that the least squares method can also solve the secret vector $\mathbf{s}$.

It is clear when $\gamma' \geq \gamma$, all the coefficient of $\mathbf{z}$ are uniformly distributed on $(-\gamma + \beta, \gamma - \beta) \cap \mathbb{Z}$, so the distribution of $\mathbf{z}$ is independent of $\mathbf{c}$. In other words, there is no information of the secret $\mathbf{s}$ contained in the distribution of $\mathbf{z}$. When $\gamma' \leq \gamma - 2\beta$, then $\| \mathbf{y} + \mathbf{sc} \|_\infty \leq \gamma + \beta$, which means the rejection sampling completely lose its effectiveness. In this case, $\mathbf{y}$ is a subgaussian vector regardless of $\mathbf{C}$, then recovering s can be reduced to the ILWE problem.

If $\gamma' \in (\gamma - 2\beta, \gamma)$, we write the linear equations $\mathbf{z} = \mathbf{y} + \mathbf{Cs}$ as before, then the i-th coefficient z_i of $\mathbf{z}$ can be represented as $z_i = \langle \mathbf{c}_i, \mathbf{s} \rangle + y_i$, where $\mathbf{c}_i$ is the i-th row of $\mathbf{C}$. After the rejection sampling, the distribution of z_i can be easily obtained, which is related to the value of $\langle \mathbf{c}_i, \mathbf{s} \rangle$. Then the expectation $\mathbb{E}(y_i)$ is related to $\langle \mathbf{c}_i, \mathbf{s} \rangle$, so we can regard $\mathbb{E}(y_i)$ as a function of $\langle \mathbf{c}_i, \mathbf{s} \rangle$ thus $\mathbb{E}(y_i) = f(\langle \mathbf{c}_i, \mathbf{s} \rangle)$, where $f(x)$ is

$$f(x) = \begin{cases} -\dfrac{1}{2}(\gamma - \gamma' - \beta), & x \in (-\beta, -(\gamma - \gamma' - \beta)) \\ 0, & x \in [-(\gamma - \gamma' - \beta), \gamma - \gamma' - \beta] \\ \dfrac{1}{2}(\gamma - \gamma' - \beta), & x \in [\gamma - \gamma' - \beta, \beta). \end{cases}$$

If $\gamma' \in (\gamma - \beta, \gamma)$, then $\mathbb{E}(y_i)$ can also be regarded as a function $\langle \mathbf{c}_i, \mathbf{s} \rangle$, so the samples $(\mathbf{z} = \mathbf{y} + \mathbf{Cs}, \mathbf{C})$ follow a non-subgaussian distribution. After given enough *partially rejected* signatures, we can obtain a vector $\tilde{\mathbf{s}}$ and $\tilde{\mathbf{s}} \approx \lambda \mathbf{s}$ by the least square method with samples $(\mathbf{z} = \mathbf{y} + \mathbf{Cs}, \mathbf{C})$.

A similar problem to the implementation mistakes of randomness is how high the risk is if the rejection bound is relaxed. This is a practical problem because the efficiency of signature scheme is related to the expected number of repetitions due to the rejection sampling. This number is not to be neglected when considering the efficiency of the scheme. If we try to change the original rejection boundary $\|z\|_\infty \leq \gamma - \beta$ to $\|z\|_\infty \leq \gamma' - \beta$, where $0 < \gamma' < \gamma$, then with the similar analysis as Sect. 5.2, it is also a non-subgaussian ILWE problem. The corresponding experimental results are given in Sect. 6.

It takes extremely many samples to recover $\mathbf{s}$ due to the large scale of randomness in the lattice based Fiat-Shamir signatures. However, when given the public key, we can recover the majority of the components of the private key using a smaller number of signatures, and then determine the remaining components of the secret key by exhaustive search or lattice method.

6   Experimental Results

In this section, we have carried out three sets of experiments: lower-bit randomness leakage attack, careless implementation attack with uniform randomness and careless implementation attack with gaussian randomness. We refer to λ as the correction factor.

6.1   Lower-Bit Randomness Leakage Attack

Our discussion is based on the highest security level parameter set, Dilithium-5, of the third round candidate Dilithium. Before carrying out the specific experiment, the leakage boundary l should be determined. 10000 signatures (corresponding to 2.56 million samples) are randomly generated to count the probability of $|\langle \mathbf{s}, \mathbf{c} \rangle|$ falling in the interval $(-2^l, 2^l)$. The probability of $|\langle \mathbf{s}, \mathbf{c} \rangle| < 2^5$ is required to be larger than 99%, so the leakage bound of Dilithium-5 is 6.

Next, try to recover the private key of Dilithium-5 when the 5-th bit, the 4-th bit or even lower bit is leaked. The private key recovery is tested when the fixed number of signatures is given and different correction coefficients are selected. Among them, 7 groups of experiments were carried out for each leakage position.

The first case is leaking the fifth bit. Randomly generate 1000 signatures and 11 different correction factors such as 1, 1.1, 1.2, ..., 2, were selected to attack with 1000 signatures. The experimental results are shown in Fig. 1. The horizontal coordinate in the figure is the correction coefficient, and the vertical coordinate is the number of components in $\lambda\tilde{\mathbf{s}}$ different from components in the private key. Obviously, the vertical coordinate of 0 indicates the recovery of the complete private key. It can be seen from the figure that the optimal correction coefficient is between 1.3 and 1.5 when the fifth bit of the leakage randomness is leaked. What's more, we have give an estimation of the correction factor based on Proposition 1 and the results are in the Table 2.

Next, consider the case of leaking the fourth bit. Since 5000 signatures are given since 1000 signatures are not enough. Besides, 401 different correction factors such as 0, 0.05, 0.1,..., 20 are selected. The experimental results are shown in Fig. 1. It can be seen from the figure that when the fourth bit of randomness is leaked, the optimal correction coefficient is between 6 and 12. We have also give an estimation of the correction factor and the results are in the Table 2. We find that the gap between the theoretical value and the experimental value is very small, which further verifies that the assumptions used to prove Proposition 1 are reasonable.

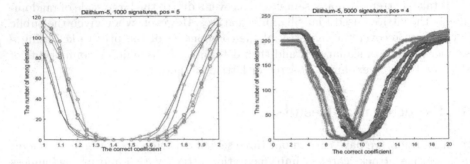

Fig. 1. Attack on Dilithium-5 with 5-th and 4-th bit's leakage

Table 2. Estimation of the correction factor

$\|\mathbf{s}\|_2$	22.181	23.600	23.152	21.977	23.600	22.293	23.302
Position $= 5$	1.374	1.475	1.442	1.362	1.475	1.381	1.453
Position $= 4$	7.411	9.444	8.939	6.959	9.444	7.459	9.220

Finally, the results show that even given 500000 signatures, the secret key of Dilithium-5 can not be recovered when leaking the third bit as the correction factor is extremely large. The estimation of the correction factor is about 1000, which explains why we can't recover the secret key by the least squares method.

6.2   Careless Implementation Attack with Uniform Randomness

We also take Dilithium-5 as an example in this section. In the case of uniform distribution, the change of rejection condition is equivalent to the change of the range of randomness. In practice, in order to reduce the number of rejection times of signature to improve the efficiency of a scheme, we may try to relax the reject condition. Therefore, it is more meaningful to analyze the attacks that signature schemes may suffer under this situation. Now we consider two rejection conditions: $\|\mathbf{z}\|_\infty \leq \gamma + \beta$ and $\|\mathbf{z}\|_\infty \leq \gamma$. In each case, seven groups of experiments are carried out to test the influence of the number of rejected signatures and the correction coefficient on the attack results.

First of all, if the rejection condition is $\|\mathbf{z}\|_\infty \leq \gamma + \beta$, the attacker can obtain all the rejected signatures. Intuitively, the secret key can be recovered without the correction factor, which is confirmed in the following experiment. We have randomly generated 10 million and 20 million messages to obtain the corresponding signatures and 81 different correction coefficients of 0, 0.05, 0.1,..., 4 are selected to attack. The results are shown in Fig. 2.

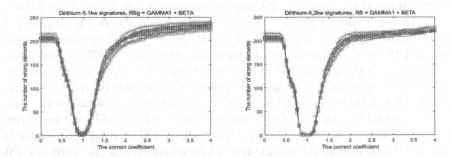

Fig. 2. Attack on Dilithium-5 with the rejection bound $\gamma + \beta$

Secondly, when the rejection condition is γ_1, the attacker can only obtain a part of rejected signatures. Similar to the first case, we test the influence of the number of rejected signatures and the correction factor on the attack result. At this time, 81 different correction coefficients, such as 0, 0.05, 0.1, ..., 4, are still selected. However, because more rejection signatures are needed in this case, the number of messages is increased from 40 million to 50 million. The attack results are shown in Fig. 3. It can be seen from the experimental results that when the rejection condition is γ_1, the optimal correction coefficient is between 1.5 and 2.

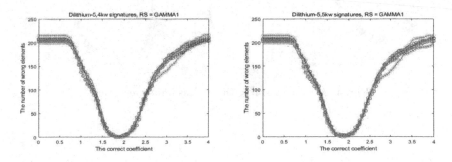

Fig. 3. Attack on Dilithium-5 with the rejection bound γ

Furthermore, we note that the signature does not actually leak any information of $\mathbf{s}$ when $|z| < \gamma - \beta$, so this part of the signature actually reduces the speed of convergence of the least squares method. In our experiments, we remove these signatures and then do the least squares method on the remaining signatures after reducing their size, which can greatly save data complexity and time complexity.

6.3 Careless Implementation Attack with Gaussian Randomness

The signature [14], in which the randomness is Gaussian, is used for analysis. For experimental convenience, the scheme parameters are adjusted as follows: the dimension of the lattice $m = 1024$, the infinite norm of the private key $\|s\|_\infty = 1$, the number of non-zero elements in the output of the random oracle is 44, and the standard deviation of the randomness is $\sigma = 6721$. Two scales of randomness are implemented in this section and the standard deviation are $\sigma' = \frac{1}{2}\sigma, \frac{1}{11}\sigma$ respectively. Four sets of experiments are conducted for each case to test the effect of the correction factor. We randomly generate 1 million of signatures correspond to 1 million of different messages, and 2001 different correction coefficients, such as 0, 0.001, 0.002,..., 2, are selected. The results are shown in Fig. 4. The correction factor are about 0.5, 1 respectively, and the secret key can be completely recovered when $\sigma' = \frac{1}{11}\sigma$.

In this group of experiments, there is a phenomenon that the theoretical value of λ is inconsistent with the experimental value. One possible explanation is that after the careless implementation of the randomness, $\min(D_\sigma^k(\mathbf{z})/(M \cdot D_{\mathbf{Sc},\sigma}), 1) \neq D_\sigma^k(\mathbf{z})/(M \cdot D_{\mathbf{Sc},\sigma})$, so we can't treat the distribution of the signatures as gaussian.

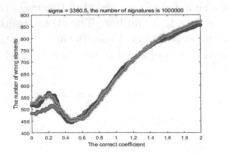 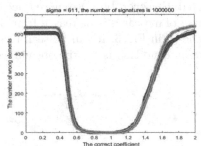

Fig. 4. Attack on [14] with careless implementation

7 Conclusion

In this paper we extend the ILWE problem to the non-subgaussian ILWE problem, and prove the non-subgaussian ILWE problem can still be solved by the least squares method. Then, we give two practical attack scenarios against lattice based Fiat-Shamir signatures: a lower-bit of randomness leakage attack and a careless implementation attack, and finally carry out a series of experiments to verify that the attacks are feasible for a concrete scheme. The above facts show that in lattice based Fiat-Shamir signatures, the secret s can theoretically be recovered just using the least squares method as long as the distribution of signature leaks any information about the private key. Therefore, we should check the distribution of the actual output of signatures in order to avoid the implementation errors that could lead to the leakage of private key information.

In practice, a large number of signatures are often required in order to recover the complete private key. In the future, we will look for algorithms that require less signatures for different attack scenarios by taking into account the known relationship between the public and private keys. Another direction that needs to be improved is to remove the heuristic assumptions in this paper, although the experimental results are very close to the theoretical prediction.

A Proof of Proposition 1

Reduce the General Case to the Special Case. This step is reducing any nonlinear ILWE problem to a special nonlinear ILWE problem where the secret satisfies $\mathbf{s} = (s_1, 0, \ldots, 0)^T$. Let $(\mathbf{A}, \mathbf{b})$ be m samples from the non-subgaussian ILWE distribution $\mathcal{D}_{\mathbf{s}, \chi_a, \chi_e, f}$, $\mathbf{e}' = \mathbf{e} + \mathbf{f}(\mathbf{As})$ and $\mathbf{P} = (\mathbf{p}_1, \mathbf{p}_2, \ldots, \mathbf{p}_m)^T \in O_n(\mathbb{R})$, then $\mathbf{b} = (\mathbf{A}\mathbf{P}^T)(\mathbf{Ps}) + \mathbf{e}'$. In particular, there exists an orthogonal transformation $\mathbf{P}$ such that $\mathbf{Ps} = (\|\mathbf{s}\|_2, 0, \ldots, 0)^T.$[6] As we have illustrated above, the result of the least squares method is

$$(\mathbf{A}^T \mathbf{A})^{-1} \mathbf{A}^T \mathbf{b} = \mathbf{P}^T ((\mathbf{A}\mathbf{P}^T)^T \mathbf{A}\mathbf{P}^T)^{-1} (\mathbf{A}\mathbf{P}^T)^T \mathbf{b}.$$

If we can prove $((\mathbf{A}\mathbf{P}^T)^T \mathbf{A}\mathbf{P}^T)^{-1} (\mathbf{A}\mathbf{P}^T)^T \mathbf{b} \approx \lambda \mathbf{Ps} = (\lambda \|\mathbf{s}\|_2, 0, \ldots, 0)^T$, then $(\mathbf{A}^T \mathbf{A})^{-1} \mathbf{A}^T \mathbf{b} \approx \mathbf{P}^T (\lambda \|\mathbf{s}\|_2, 0, \ldots, 0)^T = \lambda \mathbf{s}$.

Notice that $((\mathbf{A}\mathbf{P}^T)^T \mathbf{A}\mathbf{P}^T)^{-1} (\mathbf{A}\mathbf{P}^T)^T \mathbf{b}$ is the least squares estimator of the samples $(\mathbf{b} = \mathbf{e} + \mathbf{A}\mathbf{P}^T \mathbf{Ps}, \mathbf{A}\mathbf{P}^T)$ where $\mathbf{Ps} = (\|\mathbf{s}\|_2, 0, \ldots, 0)^T$. As the distribution of the random vector $\mathbf{Pa}$ can be treated as the distribution of $\mathbf{a}$, so we have transferred a general non-subgaussian ILWE problem into a special one that only the first component of $\mathbf{s}$ is nonzero. In the rest of this paper, $\mathbf{s} = (s_1, 0, \ldots, 0)^T$ and $\mathbf{a}_i$ is represented as $(a_i^{(1)}, a_i^{(2)}, \ldots, a_i^{(m)})^T$.

Next, combine the terms $\langle \mathbf{a}_i, \mathbf{s} \rangle$ and $f(\langle \mathbf{a}_i, \mathbf{s} \rangle)$ together and rewrite $\langle \mathbf{a}_i, \mathbf{s} \rangle + f(\langle \mathbf{a}_i, \mathbf{s} \rangle)$ as $\langle r(a_i^{(1)}) \mathbf{a}_i, \mathbf{s} \rangle$. Now $b_i = \langle r(a_i^{(1)}) \mathbf{a}_i, \mathbf{s} \rangle + e_i$ and the error becomes subgaussian, where $r_i = \frac{f(a_i^{(1)} s_1) + a_i^{(1)} s_1}{a_i^{(1)} s_1}$. Let $\mathbf{R} = diag(r_1, r_2, \ldots, r_m)$, then these samples can be rewrite as the following matrix form

$$(\mathbf{A}, \mathbf{b} = \mathbf{RAs} + \mathbf{e}). \tag{3}$$

---

[6] "$\mathbf{P} = (\mathbf{p}_1, \mathbf{p}_2, \ldots, \mathbf{p}_m)^T$" can be constructed as the following way: $\mathbf{p}_1 = (s_1/\|\mathbf{s}\|_2, s_2/\|\mathbf{s}\|_2, \ldots, s_m/\|\mathbf{s}\|_2)^T$, $\mathbf{p}_2, \mathbf{p}_3, \ldots, \mathbf{p}_m$ are any set of orthonormal basis on the vector space $Span\{\mathbf{p}_1\}^\perp$.

Estimate λ. We restate that the result of the least squares method is

$$(\mathbf{A}^T\mathbf{A})^{-1}\mathbf{A}^T\mathbf{b} = (\mathbf{A}^T\mathbf{A})^{-1}\mathbf{A}^T\mathbf{e} + (\mathbf{A}^T\mathbf{A})^{-1}(\mathbf{A}^T\mathbf{R}\mathbf{A})\mathbf{s}.$$

According to Theorem 1, $(\mathbf{A}^T\mathbf{A})^{-1}\mathbf{A}^T\mathbf{e}$ tend to zero, so what remains unsettled now is

$$(\mathbf{A}^T\mathbf{A})^{-1}(\mathbf{A}^T\mathbf{R}\mathbf{A})\mathbf{s}.$$

Let $(\mathbf{A}^T\mathbf{A})^{-1} = \mathbf{M}_1$ and $\mathbf{A}^T\mathbf{R}\mathbf{A} = \mathbf{M}_2$ and next we will analyze $\mathbf{M}_2$. As the matrix $\mathbf{R} = diag(r_1, r_2, \ldots, r_m)$, so $\mathbf{R}^{\frac{1}{2}} = diag(\sqrt{r_1}, \sqrt{r_2}, \ldots, \sqrt{r_m})$ and $\mathbf{M}_2 = (\mathbf{R}^{\frac{1}{2}}\mathbf{A})^T(\mathbf{R}^{\frac{1}{2}}\mathbf{A})$. The components of each row of $\mathbf{R}^{\frac{1}{2}}\mathbf{A} = \mathbf{V}$ are no longer obey the same distribution as χ_a^n. In order to get the tail inequalities of the spectral radius of $\mathbf{V}^T\mathbf{V}$, we split $\mathbf{V}^T\mathbf{V}$ as $\sum_{k=1}^m \mathbf{v}_k\mathbf{v}_k^T$, where $\mathbf{V} = (\mathbf{v}_1, \mathbf{v}_2, \ldots, \mathbf{v}_m)^T$ and $\mathbf{v}_k = r_k^{\frac{1}{2}}\mathbf{a}_m$. The elements in row i and column j of the matrix $\mathbf{V}^T\mathbf{V}$ can be expressed as $\sum_{k=1}^m v_k^{(i)} v_k^{(j)} = \sum_{k=1}^m r_k^{(1)} a_k^{(i)} a_k^{(j)}$, then

$$\mathbb{E}[r_k^{(1)} a_k^{(i)} a_k^{(j)}] = 0 \qquad\qquad i \neq j$$

$$\mathbb{E}[r_k^{(1)} a_k^{(i)} a_k^{(j)}] = \mathbb{E}[r_k^{(1)}]\sigma_a^2 = \sigma_2^2 \qquad\qquad i = j \neq 1$$

$$\mathbb{E}[r_k^{(1)} a_k^{(1)} a_k^{(1)}] = \mathbb{E}[r_k^{(1)} a_k^{(1)} a_k^{(1)}] = \sigma_1^2 \qquad\qquad i = j = 1.$$

According to the central limit theorem, the matrix $m\mathbf{M}_1$ will converge to $\sigma_a^2\mathbf{I}_n$ and $\frac{1}{m}\mathbf{M}_2$ will converge to an n-dimensional diagonal matrix $diag(\sigma_1^2, \sigma_2^2, \ldots, \sigma_2^2)$. We claim that $\mathbf{M}_1\mathbf{M}_2\mathbf{s}$ will converge to

$$(\frac{1}{m}\sigma_a^{-2}\mathbf{I}_n)(m \cdot diag(\sigma_1^2, \sigma_2^2, \ldots, \sigma_2^2))\mathbf{s} = (\sigma_1/\sigma_a)^2\mathbf{s}.$$

Formally speaking, we want to prove the following proposition:

Proposition 2. *Let $\mathbf{x}_1, \mathbf{x}_2, \ldots, \mathbf{x}_m$ be random vectors in $\mathbb{R}^n$. All the components of these vectors are independently and identically distributed with the standard deviation be σ_x, $\mathbf{s} = (s_1, 0, \ldots, 0) \in \mathbb{Z}^n$. If for some $\gamma \geq 0$,*

$$\mathbb{E}[\exp(\alpha^T\mathbf{x}_i)] \leq \exp(\|\alpha\|_2^2\gamma/2), \quad \forall\alpha \in \mathbb{R}^n$$

for all $i = 1, 2, \ldots, m$, then for any $a > 0$ and $t > 0$, when

$$m > M = 2^9 \cdot (n\ln 9 + t)\gamma^2 a^2 |s_1|^2 \max\{\frac{\max\{\sigma_1, \sigma_2\}^2}{\sigma_x^8}, \frac{K^2\max\{\sigma_1, \sigma_2\}^4}{\min\{\sigma_1, \sigma_2\}^2}\},$$

$$\Pr[\|(\sum_{i=1}^m \mathbf{x}_i\mathbf{x}_i^T)^{-1}(\sum_{i=1}^m r(x_i^{(1)})\mathbf{x}_i\mathbf{x}_i^T)\mathbf{s} - \frac{\sigma_1^2}{\sigma_x^2}\mathbf{s}\|_2 > 1/a] \leq 1 - 4e^{-t}$$

where $x_i^{(1)}$ is the first component of the random vector $\mathbf{x}_i$, r is a bounded function satisfies $\mathbb{E}[r(x_i^{(1)})(x_i^{(1)})^2] \neq 0$ and $|r| < K > 0$, $\sigma_1^2 = \mathbb{E}[r(x_i^{(1)})(x_i^{(1)})^2]$ and $\sigma_2^2 = \mathbb{E}[r(x_i^{(1)})]$.

The proof will be given at the end of this section. Using this theorem, we can prove Proposition 1.

Proof. According to Theorem 1 and Proposition 2, we can choose $m \geq M$ and $t = \ln(8n)$, then

$$\Pr[\|(\mathbf{A}^T\mathbf{A})^{-1} \cdot \mathbf{A}^T\mathbf{e}'\|_\infty < 1/4] \qquad\qquad \leq 1 - 1/2n$$

$$\Pr[\|(\sum_{i=1}^m \mathbf{a}_i\mathbf{a}_i^T)^{-1}(\sum_{i=1}^m r(a_i^{(1)})\mathbf{a}_i\mathbf{a}_i^T)\mathbf{s} - \frac{\sigma_1^2}{\sigma_a^2}\mathbf{s}\|_2 < 1/4] \qquad \leq 1 - 1/2n,$$

where each component of $\mathbf{e}'$ satisfies $e' = e - f(\langle \mathbf{a}, \mathbf{s}\rangle)$, thus the least squares estimator satisfies

$$\|\tilde{\mathbf{s}} - \sigma_1^2/\sigma_a^2\mathbf{s}\|_\infty = \|(\mathbf{A}^T\mathbf{A})^{-1}\cdot\mathbf{A}^T\mathbf{b} - \sigma_1^2/\sigma_a^2\mathbf{s}\|_\infty$$

$$\leq \|(\mathbf{A}^T\mathbf{A})^{-1}\cdot\mathbf{A}^T\mathbf{e}'\|_\infty + \|(\sum_{i=1}^m \mathbf{a}_i\mathbf{a}_i^T)^{-1}(\sum_{i=1}^m r(a_i^{(1)})\mathbf{a}_i\mathbf{a}_i^T)\mathbf{s} - \sigma_1^2/\sigma_a^2\mathbf{s}\|_\infty$$

then $\Pr[\|\tilde{\mathbf{s}} - \sigma_1^2/\sigma_a^2\mathbf{s}\|_\infty < 1/2]$

$$\leq \Pr[\|(\mathbf{A}^T\mathbf{A})^{-1}\mathbf{A}^T\mathbf{e}'\|_\infty + \|(\mathbf{A}^T\mathbf{A})^{-1}(\sum_{i=1}^m r(a_i^{(1)})\mathbf{a}_i\mathbf{a}_i^T)\mathbf{s} - \frac{\sigma_1^2}{\sigma_a^2}\mathbf{s}\|_\infty < 1/2]$$

$$\leq \Pr[\|(\mathbf{A}^T\mathbf{A})^{-1}\mathbf{A}^T\mathbf{e}'\|_\infty < \frac{1}{4}]\cdot \Pr[\|(\mathbf{A}^T\mathbf{A})^{-1}(\sum_{i=1}^m r(a_i^{(1)})\mathbf{a}_i\mathbf{a}_i^T)\mathbf{s} - \frac{\sigma_1^2}{\sigma_a^2}\mathbf{s}\|_\infty < \frac{1}{4}]$$

$$\leq (1 - 1/2n)^2 = 1 - \frac{1}{n} + \frac{1}{4n^2}. \qquad \blacksquare$$

The bound of Proposition 1 is relatively loose. In fact, when the function f is close to a zero function, the samples required in practice is almost the same as the bound in Theorem 1.

To prove Proposition 2, we should measure the operator norm of the sum of random matrix. Fortunately, the following lemma in [12] provided a method to solve this problem.

Lemma 3 (Lemma A.1 in [12]). *Let* $\mathbf{x}_1, \mathbf{x}_2, \ldots, \mathbf{x}_m$ *be random vectors in* $\mathbb{R}^n$ *such that, for some* $\gamma \geq 0$,

$$\mathbb{E}[\mathbf{x}_i\mathbf{x}_i^T|\mathbf{x}_1, \mathbf{x}_2, \ldots, \mathbf{x}_{i-1}] = \mathbf{I}_n \quad and$$

$$\mathbb{E}[\exp(\alpha^T\mathbf{x}_i)|\mathbf{x}_1, \mathbf{x}_2, \ldots, \mathbf{x}_{i-1}] \leq \exp(\|\alpha\|_2^2\gamma/2), \quad \forall \alpha \in \mathbb{R}^n$$

for all $i = 1, 2, \ldots, m$, *almost surely. For all* $\epsilon_0 \in (0, 1/2)$ *and* $t > 0$,

$$\Pr[\|(\sum_{i=1}^m \frac{1}{m}\mathbf{x}_i\mathbf{x}_i^T) - \mathbf{I}_n\|_2^{op} > \frac{1}{1 - 2\epsilon_0}\cdot\varepsilon_{\epsilon_0,t,m}] \leq 2e^{-t}$$

where

$$\varepsilon_{\epsilon_0,t,m} := \gamma\cdot(\sqrt{\frac{32(n\ln(1 + 2/\epsilon_0) + t)}{m}} + \frac{2(n\ln(1 + 2/\epsilon_0) + t)}{m}).$$

We can get two corollaries below using the Lemma 3.

Corollary 1. *Let* $\mathbf{x}_1, \mathbf{x}_2, \ldots, \mathbf{x}_m$ *be random vectors in* $\mathbb{R}^n$ *such that, for some* $\gamma \geq 0$,

$$\mathbb{E}[\mathbf{x}_i \mathbf{x}_i^T | \mathbf{x}_1, \mathbf{x}_2, \ldots, \mathbf{x}_{i-1}] = \sigma_x^2 \mathbf{I}_n \quad and$$

$$\mathbb{E}[\exp(\alpha^T \mathbf{x}_i) | \mathbf{x}_1, \mathbf{x}_2, \ldots, \mathbf{x}_{i-1}] \leq \exp(\|\alpha\|_2^2 \gamma / 2), \quad \forall \alpha \in \mathbb{R}^n$$

for all $i = 1, 2, \ldots, m$, *almost surely. For all* $\epsilon_0 \in (0, 1/2)$ *and* $t > 0$,

$$\Pr[\|(\sum_{i=1}^m \frac{1}{m} \mathbf{x}_i \mathbf{x}_i^T)^{-1} - \sigma_x^{-2} \mathbf{I}_n\|_2^{op} > \frac{\sigma_x^{-2}}{1 - 2\epsilon_0} \cdot \varepsilon_{\epsilon_0, t, m}] \leq 2e^{-t}$$

where

$$\varepsilon_{\epsilon_0, t, m} := \sigma_x^{-2} \gamma \cdot \left(\sqrt{\frac{32(n \ln(1 + 2/\epsilon_0) + t)}{m}} + \frac{2(n \ln(1 + 2/\epsilon_0) + t)}{m} \right).$$

Proof. Let $\mathbf{y}_i = \frac{1}{\sigma_x} \mathbf{x}_i$ for $i \in \{1, 2, \ldots, m\}$, $\mathbf{A}_1 = \sum_{i=1}^m \mathbf{y}_i \mathbf{y}_i^T$ so $\mathbb{E}[\frac{1}{m} \mathbf{A}_1] = \mathbf{I}_n$ and $\mathbf{y}_i$ is $\sqrt{\gamma}/\sigma_x$-*subgaussian*. Let $\boldsymbol{\Delta A}_1 = \frac{1}{m} \mathbf{A}_1 - \mathbf{I}_n$, then $(\mathbf{I}_n + \boldsymbol{\Delta A}_1) = \frac{1}{m} \mathbf{A}_1$. Notice that $\mathbf{I}_n = (m \cdot \mathbf{A}_1^{-1})(\mathbf{I}_n + \boldsymbol{\Delta A}_1) = m \cdot \mathbf{A}_1^{-1} + m \cdot \mathbf{A}_1^{-1} \boldsymbol{\Delta A}_1$, so it is clear that

$$\|\mathbf{I}_n - m \cdot \mathbf{A}_1^{-1}\|_2^{op} \leq m \|\mathbf{A}_1^{-1}\|_2^{op} \|\boldsymbol{\Delta A}_1\|_2^{op}. \tag{4}$$

Furthermore,

$$m \|\mathbf{A}_1^{-1}\|_2^{op} = \|\mathbf{I}_n - m \cdot \mathbf{A}_1^{-1} \boldsymbol{\Delta A}_1\|_2^{op} \leq \|\mathbf{I}_n\|_2^{op} + m \|\mathbf{A}_1^{-1}\|_2^{op} \|\boldsymbol{\Delta A}_1\|_2^{op}$$

so

$$m \|\mathbf{A}_1^{-1}\|_2^{op} \leq \frac{1}{1 - \|\boldsymbol{\Delta A}_1\|_2^{op}}. \tag{5}$$

Combine Eq. 4 and 5, we have

$$\|\mathbf{I}_n - m \cdot \mathbf{A}_1^{-1}\|_2^{op} \leq \frac{\|\boldsymbol{\Delta A}_1\|_2^{op}}{1 - \|\boldsymbol{\Delta A}_1\|_2^{op}}. \tag{6}$$

According to Lemma 3, we have:[7]

$$\Pr[\|(\sum_{i=1}^m \frac{1}{m} \mathbf{x}_i \mathbf{x}_i^T)^{-1} - \sigma_x^{-2} \mathbf{I}_n\|_2^{op} > \frac{\sigma_x^{-2}}{1 - 2\epsilon_0} \cdot \varepsilon_{\epsilon_0, t, m}]$$

$$\leq \Pr[\|\boldsymbol{\Delta A}_1\|_2^{op} > \frac{1}{1 - 2\epsilon_0} \cdot \varepsilon_{\epsilon_0, t, m}] \leq 2e^{-t}. \qquad \blacksquare$$

---

[7] We have omit an infinitesimal, which only have tiny impact. Similar simplifications are applied in other proofs.

Corollary 2. *Let* $\mathbf{x}_i = (x_i^{(1)}, x_i^{(2)}, \ldots, x_i^{(n)}), i \in 1, \ldots, m$ *be* m *random vectors and all the components are independent random variables with standard deviation be* σ *and*

$$\exists \gamma \geq 0, \quad \mathbb{E}[\exp(\alpha^T \mathbf{x}_i)|\mathbf{x}_1, \mathbf{x}_2, \ldots, \mathbf{x}_{i-1}] \leq \exp(\|\alpha\|_2^2 \gamma / 2), \quad \forall \alpha \in \mathbb{R}^n$$

for all $i = 1, 2, \ldots, m$, *almost surely. For all* $\epsilon_0 \in (0, 1/2)$ *and* $t > 0$,

$$\Pr[\|(\sum_{i=1}^{m} \frac{1}{m} r(x_i^{(1)}) \mathbf{x}_i \mathbf{x}_i^T) - diag(\sigma_1^2, \sigma_2^2, \ldots, \sigma_2^2)\|_2^{op} > \frac{\max\{\sigma_1, \sigma_2\}^2}{(1 - 2\epsilon_0)} \cdot \varepsilon_{\epsilon_0, t, m}] \leq 2e^{-t}$$

where r *is a function satisfies* $\mathbb{E}[r(x_i^{(1)})(x_i^{(1)})^2] \neq 0$, $|r(x_i^{(1)})| < K$, $\sigma_1^2 = \mathbb{E}[r(x_i^{(1)})(x_i^{(1)})^2]$, $\sigma_2^2 = \mathbb{E}[r(x_i^{(1)})]$ *and*

$$\varepsilon_{\epsilon_0, t, m} := K\gamma / \min\{\sigma_1, \sigma_2\}^2 \cdot (\sqrt{\frac{32(n \ln(1 + 2/\epsilon_0) + t)}{m}} + \frac{2(n \ln(1 + 2/\epsilon_0) + t)}{m}).$$

Proof. Let $\mathbf{v}_i = r(x_i^{(1)})^{1/2} \cdot \mathbf{x}_i$, we can prove $\mathbb{E}[\mathbf{v}_i \mathbf{v}_i^T] = diag(\sigma_1^2, \sigma_2^2, \ldots, \sigma_2^2) = \mathbf{\Lambda}$. Then $\mathbb{E}[\mathbf{\Lambda}^{-1/2} \mathbf{v}_i (\mathbf{\Lambda}^{-1/2} \mathbf{v}_i)^T] = m \mathbf{I}_n$ and

$$\mathbb{E}[\exp(\alpha^T \mathbf{\Lambda}^{-1/2} \mathbf{v}_i)|] = \mathbb{E}[\exp(\alpha^T \mathbf{\Lambda}^{-1/2} r(x_i^{(1)})^{1/2} \mathbf{x}_i)|]$$

$$\leq \exp((\|\alpha^T \mathbf{\Lambda}^{-1/2}\|_2^{op})^2 K\gamma / 2) \leq \exp(\|\mathbf{\Lambda}^{-1}\|_2^{op} \|\alpha\|_2^2 K\gamma / 2), \quad \forall \alpha \in \mathbb{R}^n.$$

This implies that $\mathbf{\Lambda}^{-1/2} \mathbf{v}_i$ is a $\|\mathbf{\Lambda}^{-1/2}\|_2^{op} \sqrt{K\gamma} - subgaussian$ random vector. Let $\mathbf{A}_2 = \sum_{i=1}^{m} r(x_i^{(1)}) \mathbf{x}_i \mathbf{x}_i^T$, then the rest is the similar with Corollary 2. ■

Now we can prove Proposition 2.

Proof. Let $\mathbf{A}_1 = \sum_{i=1}^{m} \mathbf{x}_i \mathbf{x}_i^T$ and $\mathbf{A}_2 = \sum_{i=1}^{m} f(x_i^{(1)}) \mathbf{x}_i \mathbf{x}_i^T$, then $\mathbb{E}[\mathbf{x}_i \mathbf{x}_i^T] = \sigma_x^2 \mathbf{I}_n$, $\mathbb{E}[f(x_i^{(1)}) \mathbf{x}_i \mathbf{x}_i^T] = diag(\sigma_1^2, \sigma_2^2, \ldots, \sigma_2^2) = \mathbf{\Lambda}$, and

$$\|(m\mathbf{A}_1^{-1}) \cdot (\frac{1}{m} \mathbf{A}_2) \mathbf{s} - \sigma_x^{-2} \mathbf{I}_n \cdot \mathbf{\Lambda} \mathbf{s}\|_2$$

$$= \|(m\mathbf{A}_1^{-1}) \cdot (\frac{1}{m} \mathbf{A}_2) \mathbf{s} - (m\mathbf{A}_1^{-1}) \cdot \mathbf{\Lambda} \mathbf{s} + (m\mathbf{A}_1^{-1}) \cdot \mathbf{\Lambda} \mathbf{s} - \sigma_x^{-2} \mathbf{I}_n \cdot \mathbf{\Lambda} \mathbf{s}\|_2$$

$$\leq (\|m\mathbf{A}_1^{-1}\|_2^{op} \cdot \|\frac{1}{m} \mathbf{A}_2 - \mathbf{\Lambda}\|_2^{op} + \|m\mathbf{A}_1^{-1} - \sigma_x^{-2} \mathbf{I}_n\|_2^{op} \cdot \|\mathbf{\Lambda}\|_2^{op}) \cdot |s_1|.$$

Use Corollary 1 and 2, we choose $\epsilon_0 = 1/4$ and M in the proposition, we have

$$\Pr[\|m\mathbf{A}_1^{-1} - \sigma_x^{-2} \mathbf{I}_n\|_2^{op} < \frac{1}{2a \max\{\sigma_1, \sigma_2\}|s_1|}] > 1 - 2e^{-t}$$

$$\Pr[\|\frac{1}{m} \mathbf{A}_2 - \mathbf{\Lambda}\|_2^{op} < \frac{1}{2a \min\{\sigma_1, \sigma_2\}|s_1|}] > 1 - 2e^{-t},$$

so $\Pr[\|(m\mathbf{A}_1^{-1})\cdot(\frac{1}{m}\mathbf{A}_2)\mathbf{s}-\sigma_x^{-2}\mathbf{I}_n\cdot\Lambda\mathbf{s}\|_2<\frac{1}{a}]$

$>\Pr[\|m\mathbf{A}_1^{-1}\|_2^{op}\|\frac{1}{m}\mathbf{A}_2-\Lambda\|_2^{op}|s_1|<\frac{1}{2a}]\times\Pr[\|m\mathbf{A}_1^{-1}-\sigma_x^{-2}\mathbf{I}_n\|_2^{op}\|\Lambda\|_2^{op}|s_1|<\frac{1}{2a}]$

$>\Pr[\|\frac{1}{m}\Lambda^{-1/2}\mathbf{A}_2\Lambda^{-1/2}-\mathbf{I}_n\|_2^{op}<\frac{1+\|\Delta\mathbf{A}_1\|_2^{op}}{2a\min\{\sigma_1,\sigma_2\}|s_1|}]$

$\times\Pr[\|m\mathbf{A}_1^{-1}-\sigma_x^{-2}\mathbf{I}_n\|_2^{op}<\frac{1}{2a\max\{\sigma_1,\sigma_2\}|s_1|}]$

$>(1-2e^{-t})^2>1-4e^{-t}.$ ∎

References

1. Bindel, N., et al.: qTESLA. Submission to the NIST Post-Quantum Cryptography Standardization (2017). https://tesla.informatik.tu-darmstadt.de/de/tesla/
2. Bleichenbacher, D.: On the generation of one-time keys in DL signature schemes. In: Presentation at IEEE P1363 Working Group Meeting, p. 81 (2000)
3. Boneh, D., Durfee, G.: Cryptanalysis of RSA with private key d less than $N^{0.292}$. In: Stern, J. (ed.) EUROCRYPT 1999. LNCS, vol. 1592, pp. 1–11. Springer, Heidelberg (1999). https://doi.org/10.1007/3-540-48910-X_1
4. Boneh, D., Venkatesan, R.: Hardness of computing the most significant bits of secret keys in Diffie-Hellman and related schemes. In: Koblitz, N. (ed.) CRYPTO 1996. LNCS, vol. 1109, pp. 129–142. Springer, Heidelberg (1996). https://doi.org/10.1007/3-540-68697-5_11
5. Bootle, J., Delaplace, C., Espitau, T., Fouque, P.-A., Tibouchi, M.: LWE without modular reduction and improved side-channel attacks against BLISS. In: Peyrin, T., Galbraith, S. (eds.) ASIACRYPT 2018. LNCS, vol. 11272, pp. 494–524. Springer, Cham (2018). https://doi.org/10.1007/978-3-030-03326-2_17
6. De Mulder, E., Hutter, M., Marson, M.E., Pearson, P.: Using Bleichenbacher"s solution to the hidden number problem to attack nonce leaks in 384-bit ECDSA. In: Bertoni, G., Coron, J.-S. (eds.) CHES 2013. LNCS, vol. 8086, pp. 435–452. Springer, Heidelberg (2013). https://doi.org/10.1007/978-3-642-40349-1_25
7. Ducas, L., Durmus, A., Lepoint, T., Lyubashevsky, V.: Lattice signatures and bimodal Gaussians. In: Canetti, R., Garay, J.A. (eds.) CRYPTO 2013. LNCS, vol. 8042, pp. 40–56. Springer, Heidelberg (2013). https://doi.org/10.1007/978-3-642-40041-4_3
8. Espitau, T., Fouque, P.A., Gérard, B., Tibouchi, M.: Side-channel attacks on BLISS lattice-based signatures: exploiting branch tracing against strongswan and electromagnetic emanations in microcontrollers. In: CCS, pp. 1857–1874. ACM, New York (2017)
9. Groot Bruinderink, L., Hülsing, A., Lange, T., Yarom, Y.: Flush, gauss, and reload – a cache attack on the BLISS lattice-based signature scheme. In: Gierlichs, B., Poschmann, A.Y. (eds.) CHES 2016. LNCS, vol. 9813, pp. 323–345. Springer, Heidelberg (2016). https://doi.org/10.1007/978-3-662-53140-2_16
10. Heninger, N., Shacham, H.: Reconstructing RSA private keys from random key bits. In: Halevi, S. (ed.) CRYPTO 2009. LNCS, vol. 5677, pp. 1–17. Springer, Heidelberg (2009). https://doi.org/10.1007/978-3-642-03356-8_1
11. Howgrave-Graham, N.A., Smart, N.P.: Lattice attacks on digital signature schemes. Des. Codes Crypt. **23**(3), 283–290 (2001)

12. Hsu, D., Kakade, S.M., Zhang, T.: Tail inequalities for sums of random matrices that depend on the intrinsic dimension. Electron. Commun. Probab. **17**(14), 1–13 (2012)
13. Liu, Y., Zhou, Y., Sun, S., Wang, T., Zhang, R., Ming, J.: On the security of lattice-based Fiat-Shamir signatures in the presence of randomness leakage. IEEE Trans. Inf. Forensics Secur. **16**, 1868–1879 (2020)
14. Lyubashevsky, V.: Lattice signatures without trapdoors. In: Pointcheval, D., Johansson, T. (eds.) EUROCRYPT 2012. LNCS, vol. 7237, pp. 738–755. Springer, Heidelberg (2012). https://doi.org/10.1007/978-3-642-29011-4_43
15. Lyubashevsky, V., et al.: CRYSTALS-Dilithium. Submission to the NIST Post-Quantum Cryptography Standardization (2017). https://pq-crystals.org/dilithium
16. Nguyen, S.: The insecurity of the digital signature algorithm with partially known nonces. J. Cryptol. **15**(3), 151–176 (2002)
17. Nguyen, P.Q., Shparlinski, I.E.: The insecurity of the elliptic curve digital signature algorithm with partially known nonces. Des. Codes Crypt. **30**(2), 201–217 (2003)
18. Pessl, P., Bruinderink, L.G., Yarom, Y.: To BLISS-B or not to be: attacking strongswan's implementation of post-quantum signatures. In: CCS, pp. 1843–1855. ACM, New York (2017)
19. Ravi, P., Jhanwar, M.P., Howe, J., Chattopadhyay, A., Bhasin, S.: Side-channel assisted existential forgery attack on Dilithium - a NIST PQC candidate. Cryptology ePrint Archive, Report 2018/821 (2018). https://eprint.iacr.org/2018/821

Layering Quantum-Resistance into Classical Digital Signature Algorithms

Teik Guan Tan$^{(\boxtimes)}$ and Jianying Zhou

Singapore University of Technology and Design, Singapore, Singapore
teikguan_tan@mymail.sutd.edu.sg

Abstract. It is proven that asymmetric key cryptographic systems that rely on Integer Factorization or Discrete Logarithm as the underlying hard problem are vulnerable to quantum computers. Using Shor's algorithm on a large-enough quantum computer, an attacker can cryptanalyze the public key to obtain the private key in $O(logN)$ time complexity. For systems that use the classical Digital Signature Algorithm (DSA), Rivest-Shamir-Adleman (RSA) algorithm or Elliptic-Curve Digital Signature Algorithm (ECDSA), it means that authentication, data integrity and non-repudiation between the communicating parties cannot be assured in the post-quantum era.

In this paper, we present a novel approach using zero-knowledge proofs on the pre-image of the private signing key to layer in quantum-resistance into digital signature deployments that require longer-term post-quantum protection while maintaining backward compatibility with existing implementations. We show that this approach can extend the cryptographic protection of data beyond the post-quantum era and is also easy to migrate to. An implementation of this approach applying a ZKBoo zero-knowledge proof on ECDSA signatures is realized using a RFC3161-compatible time-stamp server with OpenSSL and an Adobe Acrobat Reader DC.

Keywords: Digital signature · Elliptic Curve Digital Signature Algorithm (ECDSA) · Zero-knowledge proof · Post-quantum security

1 Introduction

Asymmetric key cryptography is the tool used by systems worldwide to preserve trust amongst parties in the digital realm. The use of digital signatures allow communicating parties to authenticate each other, check the integrity of the data exchanged, and prove the origin of the data in situations of repudiation. Under National Institute of Standards and Technology's (NIST) Digital Signature Standards FIPS 186-4 [26], three signature algorithms are described. These are i) Digital Signature Algorithm (DSA) which is based on discrete logarithm cryptography first introduced by Diffie and Hellman [15]; ii) Rivest-Shamir Adelman (RSA) [34], and iii) Elliptic-Curve Digital Signature Algorithm (ECDSA)

© Springer Nature Switzerland AG 2021
J. K. Liu et al. (Eds.): ISC 2021, LNCS 13118, pp. 26–41, 2021.
https://doi.org/10.1007/978-3-030-91356-4_2

which is based on Elliptic Curve Cryptography (ECC) [8] and together we call them classical digital signature algorithms. The security of DSA and ECDSA are based on the hard problem of solving discrete logarithm over a finite field of very large numbers, while the security of RSA is based on the difficulty of integer factorization over a finite field of very large numbers.

The advent of large fault-tolerant quantum computers poses a big risk to systems that use these digital signature algorithms. Shor's [35] algorithm is able to solve both the discrete logarithm problem and integer factorization problem in $O(logN)$ polynomial time. This means that any adversary in possession of a large-enough quantum computer will be able to compute a user's private signing key when given the user's public key in a matter of hours, and generate valid digital signatures to impersonate the user. In addition, data that was previously signed by the user no longer can be proven to be authentic and trustworthy. As a reference post-quantum deadline, NIST has provided a report [13] mentioning that by year 2030, it is likely that a quantum computer capable of cryptanalyzing RSA-2048 can be built with a budget of one billion dollars. To address this, NIST is embarking on a post-quantum standardization exercise [29,30] to select suitable quantum-secure digital signature and key-exchange algorithms. The final selection is expected to complete soon with the new standards slated to be published by year 2024. Separately, NIST has also recommended two stateful hash-based signatures, namely Leighton-Micali Signatures and eXtended-Merkle Signature Scheme, for post-quantum use under conditions [14].

While the industry is likely to encourage new system implementations post-2024 to consider adopting the new digital signature standards, we expect different challenges for existing or upcoming systems. NIST has published some challenges they explored with post-quantum cryptography replacement and migration [4,12], and we supplement it with additional questions specific to digital signatures. Should system operators using digital signatures embark on a cryptographic migration to the stateful hash-based signatures [14] instead of waiting for the post-quantum standardization? How about documents that are already digitally signed, and are required to remain trustworthy beyond year 2030? Do these documents need to be counter-signed with new algorithms? Since the counter-signer may be a non-interested third party to the transaction, what liability does the counter-signer bear for the verifying party? How about legacy systems that cannot be migrated? When are the verifying parties expected to be ready to verify the new algorithms since the migrations are happening at a different pace? What are the legal implications for the verifying party if the existing non-quantum-secure signature passes verification, but the verifying party is unable to verify the new quantum-secure signature? These are questions with no straightforward answers and seeking a proper resolution may require more time than afforded by the impending post-quantum deadline.

Our approach is different. If the existing digital signatures can remain quantum-resistant even after large-enough quantum computers are built, then many of the transition-related questions can be avoided. Existing systems will not face compatibility issues, migration timelines to the new algorithms are less counter-party dependent, and existing digitally signed documents retain their authenticity in the post-quantum era. This is possible by layering a quantum-secure zero-knowledge proof of the pre-image of the private signing key along with the signature. Our contributions are as follows:

- Extend the digital signature scheme to construct a quantum-resistant digital signature scheme with backward-compatibility properties.
- Realize the quantum-resistant digital signature scheme using a zero-knowledge proof to be included with digital signatures to make them quantum-resistant.
- Deploy a real-world implementation of a RFC3161-compatible [2] time-stamp server to issue quantum-resistant ECDSA timestamp digital signatures with X.509v3 certificates that are compatible with the existing Adobe PDF Acrobat Reader DC v2021.x.

The rest of this paper is organized as follows. Section 2 covers the background of digital signatures and zero-knowledge proofs. Section 3 describes the proposed signature scheme, covers the description of the algorithms and provides measurements made on execution timings and proof sizes. Section 4 describes the real-line deployment of the proposed signature scheme and covers the migration strategy. Section 5 discusses some of the related works and Sect. 6 concludes the paper.

2   Background

2.1   Digital Signature Basics

We describe a simple scenario for two communicating parties Alice and Bob, where Alice has a message M to be sent to Bob. Alice wants to ensure that Bob receives the message unchanged (integrity) and knows that it is from Alice (authenticity). Bob wants to be able to prove to a third-party that the message is indeed from Alice (non-repudiation).

Definition 1. *We define a digital signature scheme as a triple of polynomial-time algorithms KeyGen, Sign, Verify with the following parameters:*

KeyGen(1^n) $\Rightarrow$ $\{K_s, K_p\}$ takes in a security parameter 1^n which defines the cryptographic key strength of n, and outputs a private key K_s and corresponding public key K_p.
Sign(M, K_s) $\Rightarrow$ $\{\sigma\}$ takes in a message M and the private key K_s, and outputs a signature σ.
Verify(M, K_p, σ) $\Rightarrow$ $\{result\}$ takes in a message M, the public key K_p and signature σ, and outputs accept if and only if σ is a valid signature generated by Sign(M, K_s).

In this case, Alice, the signing party, calls *KeyGen* to generate $\{K_s, K_p\}$. K_p is published where Bob and other parties have access to. Alice then calls *Sign* with her private key K_s to sign the message M, generating a signature

σ. Alice transmits $\{M, \sigma\}$ to Bob. Bob, the verifying party, calls $Verify$ with Alice's public key K_p to verify the signature σ for message M. If $Verify$ returns accept, then Bob has successfully received a message M unchanged and the signature proof σ from Alice.

2.2 Zero-Knowledge Proof

Goldwasser et al. [20] provided the concept of zero-knowledge proofs where the proof conveys no additional knowledge besides the correctness of the proposition. While there has been many concrete realizations of zero-knowledge proofs, quantum-resistant non-interactive zero-knowledge proofs are either ZKStark [6] or MPC-in-the-head (Multi-party computation in-the-head) [24] based proofs.

For MPC-in-the-head proofs, a prover has to create a boolean computational circuit of n branches with commitment, of which $n - 1$ views can be revealed to the verifier as proof of knowledge. To make the proof non-interactive, the prover can use Fiat-Shamir's heuristic [17] to deterministically, yet unpredictably decide which $n - 1$ views to send to the verifier. The verifier then walks through the $n - 1$ views with a $\frac{1}{n}$ chance that the proposition is incorrect. By increasing the number of rounds (with different random input parameters) that the prover has to compute the circuit and provide the views, it exponentially reduces the statistical probability that the prover is making a false claim.

3 Proposed Quantum-Resistant Digital Signatures

Since Shor's algorithm on quantum computers break the integer factorization problem [35], discrete logarithm problem [35] and elliptic-curve discrete logarithm problem [32], we can safely assume that adversaries can feasibly compute all RSA/DSA/ECDSA private keys K_s given the public key K_p when large enough quantum computers are built. On the other hand, symmetric key and hash-based cryptography remain relatively quantum-resistant. Grover's algorithm [21] on quantum computers can only achieve a quadratic speedup of $O(\sqrt{N})$ when performing a brute-force search, and this has been proven to be optimal [7].

Therefore, our proposal is to extend the signing process to layer in a zero-knowledge proof of knowledge of the pre-image of the private key to protect the signature. The extended verifying process can then verify this proof to ascertain that the signature is genuinely created by the owner of the private key and not a quantum-capable adversary. For backward-compatibility, the existing verifying process can still verify the digital signature without the proof, albeit losing the quantum-resistant assurance.

3.1 Quantum-Resistant Digital Signature Scheme

We start by extending the classical digital signature scheme (Definition 1) described in Sect. 2.1.

Definition 2. *The extended quantum-resistant digital signature scheme is as follows:*

$KeyGen_q(1^n) \Rightarrow \{\rho, K_p\}$ *takes in a security parameter 1^n which defines the cryptographic key strength of n, and outputs a secret pre-image ρ and a public key K_p. K_p is the associated public key to the private key $H(\rho)$ where $H()$ is a collapsing hash function [38].*

$Sign_q(M, \rho) \Rightarrow \{\sigma, \pi\}$ *takes in a message M and the secret pre-image ρ, and outputs a signature σ computed using $Sign(M, H(\rho))$ as well as a quantum-resistant zero-knowledge proof π that i) $H(\rho)$ is computed from ρ and ii) σ is computed from $H(\rho)$.*

$Verify_q(M, K_p, \sigma, \pi) \Rightarrow \{result\}$ *takes in a message M, the public key K_p and signature σ, and outputs accept if and only if $Verify(M, K_p)$ returns accept and π is a valid zero-knowledge proof that σ is computed from ρ.*

Intuitively, Definition 2 inherits the classical security properties of Definition 1 with an additional layer of quantum-resistance placed on the private key. A classical adversary will not be able to compromise the soundness of $Verify_q$ when interacting with the signing party since the additional information obtained from $Sign_q$ is a zero-knowledge proof that does not reveal the secret pre-image ρ or private key $K_s = H(\rho)$.

Lemma 1 (Quantum Resistance). *Definition 2 offers additional quantum-resistance for digital signatures generated using $Sign_q$ provided $Verify_q$ is used to verify the signature σ and proof π.*

Proof. We assume that a quantum-capable adversary is able to use Shor's algorithm [35] to recover $H(\rho)$ from K_p. Using $H(\rho)$, the adversary is then able to arbitrarily generate valid signatures σ using $Sign$ which will be accepted by $Verify$. However, the adversary will not be able generate the proof π since the value of ρ is not recoverable from $H(\rho)$ as $H()$ is a collapsing hash function and resistant to pre-image attacks even from quantum computers [38]. Thus, $Verify_q$ is resistant to quantum-capable adversaries. □

Lemma 2 (Backward Compatibility). *A signing party using $KeyGen_q$ and $Sign_q$ of Definition 2 generates signatures σ that are backward compatible with verifying parties using $Verify$ of Definition 1.*

Proof. Signatures σ returned by $Sign_q$ are generated using the same algorithm $Sign$ where $H(\rho)$ is effectively equal to K_s. Hence, any verifying party in this case using $Verify$ will be able to ignore π, and continue to call $Verify$ to check the validity of the signature σ with respect to M and K_p. A demonstration of the backward compatibility can be seen in Sect. 4. □

3.2   Realizing the Proposed Digital Signature Scheme

We use the following algorithms to realize our quantum-resistant digital signature scheme:

- *Digital signing algorithm.* Either DSA or ECDSA can be easily used as the digital signing algorithm. This is because the private key generator for DSA and ECDSA is essentially an unpredictable random number generated over a finite field. This matches nicely with the output of a one-way hash function $H()$. Using RSA as the signing algorithm is more complex and tedious since key generation involves the matching the output of a hash function to two or more unpredictable prime numbers used to compute the RSA modulus. Possible techniques include mapping the hash output into an ordered list of very large primes [25] or repeatedly hashing (or mining) random numbers till a prime is found. For our reference implementation, ECDSA is used as it has the smallest key size which translates to the smallest proof size. The curve chosen is secp256r1 (or prime256v1) [8].
- *Hash function.* The hash function to be used in our reference implementation is SHA-256 [18] as it is collapsing [38] and the output fits well with the secp256r1 curve.
- *Zero-knowledge proof system.* The zero-knowledge proof system to be used has to be post-quantum secure. We have chosen ZKBoo [19] as it is a 3-branch MPC-in-the-head realization and already has a ready SHA-256 implementation. ZKBoo is also used as the underlying proof system to create ZKB++ for Picnic [10], an alternative finalist candidate in NIST's post-quantum standardization exercise [30].

Realization of $KeyGen_q$. The function $KeyGen_q$ shown in Algorithm 1 works very similarly to $KeyGen$. An additional step (see Step 5 of Algorithm 1) is performed to hash the secret pre-image ρ prior to computing public key K_p.

Algorithm 1: Quantum-resistant ECDSA Key Generation $KeyGen_q$.

---
1 **begin**
2 | $G \leftarrow$ ECC base point; $P \leftarrow$ ECC order;
3 | Generate secret pre-image ρ;
4 | Compute private key $K_s = H(\rho)$;
5 | Compute public key $K_p = (x, y)$ where $K_p \equiv K_s \cdot G \bmod P$;
6 | destroy K_s;
7 | return ρ, K_p;
8 **end**

Algorithm 2: Quantum-resistant ECDSA signing $Sign_q$.

1	**begin**
2	$\quad$ $G \leftarrow$ ECC base point; $P \leftarrow$ ECC order;
3	$\quad$ $\rho \leftarrow$ secret pre-image;
4	$\quad$ $M \leftarrow$ message;
5	$\quad$ Generate signature random r;
6	$\quad$ Compute r^{-1} where $r * r^{-1} \equiv 1 \bmod P$;
7	$\quad$ Compute $R = (R_x, R_y)$ where $R \equiv r \cdot G \bmod P$;
8	$\quad$ Compute hash of message $H(M)$;
9	$\quad$ Enumerate ZKBoo proof $\pi =$ **begin**
10	$\quad\quad$ Zero-knowledge computation of private key K_s where $K_s = H(\rho)$;
11	$\quad\quad$ Zero-knowledge computation of public key K_p where $K_p \equiv K_s \cdot G \bmod P$;
12	$\quad\quad$ Compute s where $s \equiv r^{-1} * (H(M) + R_x * K_s) \bmod P$;
13	$\quad\quad$ Commit R_x, s in the proof;
14	$\quad$ **end**
15	$\quad$ destroy r, r^{-1}, K_s;
16	$\quad$ return $\sigma = \{R_x, s\}, \pi$;
17	**end**

Algorithm 3: Quantum-resistant ECDSA verification $Verify_q$.

1	**begin**
2	$\quad$ $G \leftarrow$ ECC base point; $P \leftarrow$ ECC order;
3	$\quad$ $K_p \leftarrow$ ECC public key;
4	$\quad$ $R_x, s \leftarrow$ signature σ; $\pi \leftarrow$ proof; $M \leftarrow$ message;
5	$\quad$ Compute s^{-1} where $s * s^{-1} \equiv 1 \bmod P$;
6	$\quad$ Compute hash of message $H(M)$;
7	$\quad$ Compute $u_1 = s^{-1} * H(M) \bmod P$;
8	$\quad$ Compute $u_2 = s^{-1} * R_x \bmod P$;
9	$\quad$ Compute $V = (V_x, V_y)$ where $V = u_1 \cdot G + u_2 \cdot K_p \bmod P$;
10	$\quad$ **if** $V_x \neq R_x$ **then**
11	$\quad\quad$ return "Failed Signature Verification"
12	$\quad$ **end**
13	$\quad$ **else**
14	$\quad\quad$ Verify ZKBoo proof $\pi =$ **begin**
15	$\quad\quad\quad$ Check that R_x, s is committed in the proof;
16	$\quad\quad\quad$ Check that zero-knowledge computation of K_p from unknown pre-image is correct;
17	$\quad\quad\quad$ **if** *Check Failed* **then**
18	$\quad\quad\quad\quad$ return "Failed Proof Verification"
19	$\quad\quad\quad$ **end**
20	$\quad\quad$ **end**
21	$\quad$ **end**
22	$\quad$ return success;
23	**end**

Realization of $Sign_q$. The $Sign_q$ function is shown in Algorithm 2. Besides computing the ECDSA signature using the private key $H(\rho)$, the $Sign_q$ function returns the ZKBoo proof π which includes: i) zero-knowledge proof of knowledge of pre-image of $H(\rho)$; ii) zero-knowledge proof that public key K_p is computed from $H(\rho)$; and iii) commitment that $H(M)$ is the message being signed.

The implementation in Step 10 of Algorithm 2 uses Giacomelli et al.'s [19] SHA-256 code. Special care has to be taken to code Step 11 of Algorithm 2 as the number of computational steps in the proof π could reveal the private key K_s. When performing elliptic-curve multiplication, we use the double-and-add always technique which is effective against side channel power analysis timing attacks [27].

Realization of $Verify_q$. The function $Verify_q$ shown in Algorithm 3 consists of two parts where the first part (from Steps 5 to 12) is the ECDSA signature verification similar to $Verify$ while the second part (from Steps 14 to 20) is the additional verification of the quantum-resistant zero-knowledge proof.

3.3 Performance Measurement

The proposed digital signature scheme is implemented in C^1 and tested on an Intel I5-8250U 8th Gen machine with 8 CPU cores and 8 GB RAM, running a Cygwin terminal on 64-bit Microsoft Windows 10. No operating system level CPU scheduling or adjustments are done. We measure the execution times of $Sign_q$ and $Verify_q$ as well as the proof sizes when we vary the number of ZKBoo rounds from 50 to 250, in increments of 50. Increasing the number of rounds increases the bit-strength of the proof, but inadvertently also increases the proof sizes and execution times. The measurements are found in Table 1.

Table 1. Measurement of proof sizes and execution times of $Sign_q$ and $Verify_q$

ZKBoo rounds	50	100	150	200	250
Size of proof (in KBytes)	1,978	3,956	5,934	7,912	9,890
$Sign_q$ execution time (in seconds)	20.9	45.9	72.9	95.1	118.2
$Verify_q$ execution time (in seconds)	19.6	45.0	71.0	93.2	115.7

At first glance, the measured overheads for a 250-bit strength proof show a very large proof of about 10 MB in size and takes almost two minutes to either carry out $Sign_q$ or $Verify_q$. However, when we implement a real-life deployment in Sect. 4, we are able to reduce the impact to the user experience as the proof could be generated asynchronously and stored separately from the certificate.

4 Real-Life Deployment

To study issues related to backward-compatibility and migration to quantum-resistance, we deploy the proposed digital signature scheme into a time-stamp

---

[1] Source codes can be made available upon request.

server while using an existing (unchanged) Adobe Acrobat Reader DC to request for quantum-resistant time-stamped signed PDFs. The deployment is carried out on a laptop with an Intel I5-8250U 8th Gen machine with 8 CPU cores and 8 GB RAM, running 64-bit Microsoft Windows 10 for both the client and server. The setup is as follows:

- *Time-stamp client.* We use an Adobe Acrobat Reader DC v2021.x. This client already supports ECDSA [3] and is used unmodified.
- *Time-stamp server.* We use an open-source time-stamp server (from https:// github.com/kakwa/uts-server) by Pierre-Francois Carpentier. This server is used with codes unmodified.
- *Cryptographic library.* The time-stamp server makes use of OpenSSL v1.1.x to carry out the operations of Certification Authority (CA) issuance of server certificates, as well as to carry out digital signing according to RFC3161 [2]. We modify the version of OpenSSL v1.1.1b to carry out the extended digital signature scheme for both X.509 certificate issuance and time-stamping. An optimization done is to make OpenSSL return the ECDSA signature, while generating the ZKBoo proofs asynchronously. This allows the ECDSA-signed time-stamp to be returned to the client without waiting for the ZKBoo proof to be completely generated. The proofs are thus stored separately from the certificate.
- *Repository.* Since the quantum-resistant 256-round ZKBoo proofs for the certificates and time-stamps are 10 MB each, they could not be easily transmitted to the client. Our modified version of OpenSSL will write the proofs into Dropbox (www.dropbox.com), while embedding the URL link in the signed X.509 certificate or the PKCS#7 time-stamp that is returned to the calling program.

4.1 Deployment Summary

Figure 1 describes the use-cases of the real-life implementation that is tested.

In the setup phase (done once), OpenSSL is used to generate the keys and certify for both the root CA certificate and time-stamp server certificate. We adopt a simple certificate hierarchy where the root CA will certify the server certificate without the need for an intermediate CA (see Fig. 2). Both certificates include the link under the X.509 Authority-Information-Access extension to point to the quantum-resistant proof in Dropbox. The root CA certificate is imported into the Adobe Acrobat to establish the root-to-trust.

In the RFC3161 phase, PDF documents can be timestamped be initiating the request from the Adobe Acrobat which contacts the Time-stamp Server and receives an ECDSA-signed PKCS#7 time-stamp. The time-stamp signature proof is similarly stored in Dropbox with the URL link embedded in the time-stamp. This time-stamp can be verified by the Adobe Acrobat (see Fig. 3) and saved in the PDF. Note that the unmodified Adobe Acrobat only verifies the ECDSA-signed time-stamp and certificate chain and not the ZKBoo proof, resulting in no changes in wait-time experienced by the end-user.

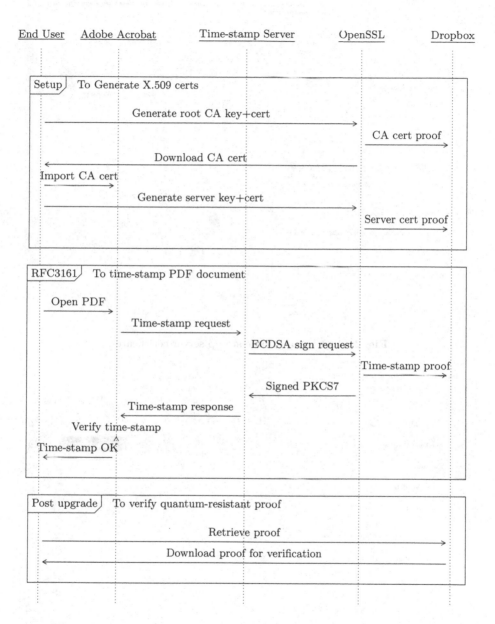

Fig. 1. Real-life deployment of quantum-resistant time-stamp service.

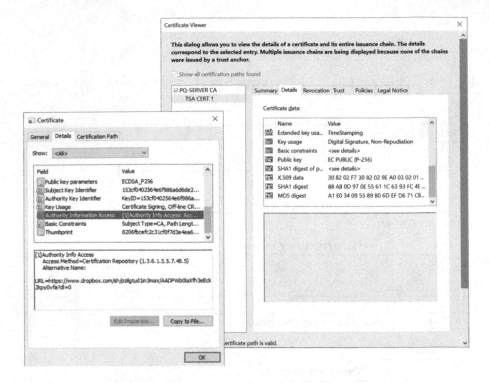

Fig. 2. Root CA and time-stamp server certificates.

Fig. 3. Time-stamp verification by Adobe Acrobat unaffected by extension.

In the Post upgrade phase, any verifying party capable of running $Verify_q$ can follow the link found in the certificates/signature block to download the quantum-resistant proofs for complete signature verification as per Algorithm 3.

4.2 Exploring Migration

To understand the impact to systems which are gradually migrating to the quantum-resistant digital signature scheme, we list the different outcomes in Table 2 for the signing and verifying parties at different stages of migration.

Table 2. Outcomes for parties at different stages of migration

		Verifying party	
		Definition 1[a]	Definition 2[b]
Signing party	Definition 1[a]	This is the "as-is" scenario. Signed documents are vulnerable to forgery in the post-quantum era.	Signed documents do not include the quantum-resistant proof. Verifying parties have the choice to either reject the document or use $Verify$ to check the signature while informing the signing party to perform the migration
	Definition 2[b]	This is the appropriate "Step 1" of the migration process. Signed documents include the quantum-resistant proof. Signing parties do not need to wait for verifying parties to migrate before carrying out this step. Verifying parties continue to verify the signature while ignoring the quantum-resistant proof	This is the "to-be" state, and the appropriate "Step 2" of the migration process. After the signing parties have migrated and started sending signed documents that include the quantum-resistant proof, the verifying parties can update their systems to verify the signature and proof to complete the migration process

[a]Not yet migrated. Still using Definition 1's $KeyGen$, $Sign$ and $Verify$.
[b]Migration done. Upgraded using Definition 2's $KeyGen_q$, $Sign_q$ and $Verify_q$.

The appropriate migration strategy to layer in quantum-resistance would therefore be to firstly upgrade the signing parties to include the quantum-resistant proof with the signature, before upgrading the verifying parties to be able to verify the proofs. For verifying parties who choose to upgrade early, it is recommended that they include Definition 1's $Verify$ function to maintain compatibility with signing parties who may not have upgraded yet.

5 Related Work

The instinctive approach to make digital signatures quantum-secure is to use a replacement or an additional quantum-secure algorithm. At this point of writing, NIST's post-quantum standardization exercise [29, 30] has identified two lattice-based algorithms, Dilithium and Falcon, and one multivariate-based algorithm, Rainbow, as the three finalist digital signature algorithms. Three alternative algorithms, namely multivariate-based GeMSS, zero-knowledge-based Picnic and stateless hash-based SPHINCS$^+$, have been shortlisted but will undergo further evaluation beyond the year 2024 deadline. Ideally, a "drop-in replacement" in the form of a software library or hardware security module, would be used to swap out or augment RSA/DSA/ECDSA with the new algorithm being standardized. But since each of these algorithms have unique resource, performance and platform considerations [33, 36, 37], coupled with different key ceremony processes and protocols, it is more likely that a migration playbook [4] needs to be designed and carried out.

Another approach is to use a backup key that can override the regular signing key in the event of compromise. In Chaum et al. [11], the authors propose the use a quantum-resistant stateful hash-based W-OTS$^+$ backup key which is created during the key generation process, and can be used as a fall-back procedure in the event the original key is compromised or lost. While such backup digital signing key approaches can work as an account-recovery mechanism for authentication-related protocols, they are not suitable for routine non-interactive digital signing use-cases where longer-term non-repudiation protection of data is required.

Specific to the time-stamping use-case, the use of a sequence of hashes, chaining them in either a forward or backward direction, is a well-researched approach to provide long-term, possibly quantum-secure, time-stamping. Digital time-stamping by linking the sequence of documents to be time-stamped through a linear hash-chain is first proposed by Haber and Stornetta in 1991 [23]. This is improved by Bayer et al. [5] to use Merkle trees [28] instead of a linear hash-chain. Fast forward to the present where blockchains such as Ethereum already support time-stamping smart contracts [16, 31]. Abadi et al. [1] further provided a decentralized time-stamp protocol on blockchains that can prevent pre/post-dating. As these techniques typically rely on a public verifiable chain to determine a specific time of occurrence, they are not applicable as a quantum-resistant mechanism to protect digital signatures in general. Public blockchains also face privacy-related concerns since the number of transactions performed and the timings that they were transacted are publicly available.

6   Conclusion

In this paper, we have taken a different approach in implementing post-quantum digital signing. Instead of replacing or adding on a different quantum-secure digital signing algorithm, we have shown that it is possible to continue to use the classical RSA, DSA or ECDSA digital signing algorithms while achieving longer-term quantum resistance. This is achieved by layering in a zero-knowledge proof of knowledge of the pre-image of the private key in addition to the digital signature. With our approach, digital signature implementations wanting to move ahead in quantum readiness continue to maintain backward-compatibility to existing applications. This is important since different systems may have different timelines and schedules on when the migration to quantum readiness happens, and our approach is able to ensure the seamless operations between upgraded and non-upgraded applications.

But the work is not yet complete. The current implementation is neither computational-efficient nor space-efficient. We envision future work in:

- *Optimizing the zero-knowledge proof.* Both the size of the zero-knowledge proof and execution times for $Sign_q$ and $Verify_q$ can be significantly improved. There are other MPC-in-the-head based zero-knowledge proofs such as ZKB++ [9], TurboIKOS [22] which achieve better performance and/or space efficiencies. Our implementation can be updated to use them.
- *Increasing the spectrum of applications.* Beyond time-stamping PDF documents, there are other applications such as blockchain, Secure Email, and Transport Layer Security that can use this approach to layer in quantum resistance.
- *Updating standards.* In our implementation, the X.509 Authority Information Access extension is used to store the link for the zero-knowledge proof. This may clash with other applications already using this extension and hence may not be the most appropriate use of the extension. A standardized extension can be established for storing such zero-knowledge proofs.

Acknowledgement. This project is supported by the Ministry of Education, Singapore, under its MOE AcRF Tier 2 grant (MOE2018-T2-1-111).

References

1. Abadi, A., Ciampi, M., Kiayias, A., Zikas, V.: Timed signatures and zero-knowledge proofs—timestamping in the blockchain era—. In: Conti, M., Zhou, J., Casalicchio, E., Spognardi, A. (eds.) ACNS 2020. LNCS, vol. 12146, pp. 335–354. Springer, Cham (2020). https://doi.org/10.1007/978-3-030-57808-4_17
2. Adams, C., Cain, P., Pinkas, D., Zuccherato, R.: RFC 3161: Internet x. 509 public key infrastructure time-stamp protocol (TSP) (2001)
3. Adobe: Adobe DC Digital Signatures Guide - Supported Standards (2018). https://www.adobe.com/devnet-docs/acrobatetk/tools/DigSigDC/standards.html. Accessed Apr 2021
4. Barker, W., Polk, W., Souppaya, M.: Getting ready for post-quantum cryptography: explore challenges associated with adoption and use of post-quantum cryptographic algorithms. The Publications of NIST Cyber Security White Paper (DRAFT), CSRC, NIST, GOV 26 (2020)
5. Bayer, D., Haber, S., Stornetta, W.S.: Improving the efficiency and reliability of digital time-stamping. In: Capocelli, R., De Santis, A., Vaccaro, U. (eds.) Sequences II, pp. 329–334. Springer, New York (1993). https://doi.org/10.1007/978-1-4613-9323-8_24
6. Ben-Sasson, E., Bentov, I., Horesh, Y., Riabzev, M.: Scalable, transparent, and post-quantum secure computational integrity. IACR Cryptology ePrint Archive 2018/46 (2018)
7. Bennett, C.H., Bernstein, E., Brassard, G., Vazirani, U.: Strengths and weaknesses of quantum computing. SIAM J. Comput. **26**(5), 1510–1523 (1997)
8. Certicom: SEC 2: Recommended elliptic curve domain parameters. Technical Report SEC2-Version-1.0, Certicom Research, Mississauga, ON, Canada (2000)
9. Chase, M., et al.: The picnic digital signature algorithm: update for round 2 (2019)
10. Chase, M., et al.: Post-quantum zero-knowledge and signatures from symmetric-key primitives. In: Proceedings of the 2017 ACM SIGSAC Conference on Computer and Communications Security, pp. 1825–1842. ACM (2017)

11. Chaum, D., Larangeira, M., Yaksetig, M., Carter, W.: W-OTS$^+$ up my sleeve! a hidden secure fallback for cryptocurrency wallets. In: Sako, K., Tippenhauer, N.O. (eds.) ACNS 2021. LNCS, vol. 12726, pp. 195–219. Springer, Cham (2021). https://doi.org/10.1007/978-3-030-78372-3_8

12. Chen, L.: Cryptography standards in quantum time: new wine in old wineskin? IEEE Secur. Priv. **15**(4), 51 (2017)

13. Chen, L., et al.: NISTIR 8105: Report on post-quantum cryptography. US Department of Commerce, National Institute of Standards and Technology (2016)

14. Cooper, D.A., Apon, D.C., Dang, Q.H., Davidson, M.S., Dworkin, M.J., Miller, C.A.: Recommendation for stateful hash-based signature schemes. NIST Special Publication 800-208 (2020)

15. Diffie, W., Hellman, M.: New directions in cryptography. IEEE Trans. Inf. Theory **22**(6), 644–654 (1976)

16. Estevam, G., Palma, L.M., Silva, L.R., Martina, J.E., Vigil, M.: Accurate and decentralized timestamping using smart contracts on the Ethereum blockchain. Inf. Process. Manag. **58**(3), 102471 (2021)

17. Fiat, A., Shamir, A.: How to prove yourself: practical solutions to identification and signature problems. In: Odlyzko, A.M. (ed.) CRYPTO 1986. LNCS, vol. 263, pp. 186–194. Springer, Heidelberg (1987). https://doi.org/10.1007/3-540-47721-7_12

18. FIPS PUB: 180-4. Secure Hash Standard (SHS). Information Technology Laboratory, National Institute of Standards and Technology (NIST), Gaithersburg (2015)

19. Giacomelli, I., Madsen, J., Orlandi, C.: ZKBoo: faster zero-knowledge for Boolean circuits. In: 25th USENIX Security Symposium (USENIX Security 2016), pp. 1069–1083 (2016)

20. Goldwasser, S., Micali, S., Rackoff, C.: The knowledge complexity of interactive proof systems. SIAM J. Comput. **18**(1), 186–208 (1989)

21. Grover, L.K.: Quantum mechanics helps in searching for a needle in a haystack. Phys. Rev. Lett. **79**(2), 325 (1997)

22. Gvili, Y., Ha, J., Scheffler, S., Varia, M., Yang, Z., Zhang, X.: TurboIKOS: improved non-interactive zero knowledge and post-quantum signatures. In: Sako, K., Tippenhauer, N.O. (eds.) ACNS 2021. LNCS, vol. 12727, pp. 365–395. Springer, Cham (2021). https://doi.org/10.1007/978-3-030-78375-4_15

23. Haber, S., Stornetta, W.S.: How to time-stamp a digital document. In: Menezes, A.J., Vanstone, S.A. (eds.) CRYPTO 1990. LNCS, vol. 537, pp. 437–455. Springer, Heidelberg (1991). https://doi.org/10.1007/3-540-38424-3_32

24. Ishai, Y., Kushilevitz, E., Ostrovsky, R., Sahai, A.: Zero-knowledge from secure multiparty computation. In: Proceedings of the Thirty-Ninth Annual ACM Symposium on Theory of Computing, pp. 21–30. ACM (2007)

25. Jones, J.P., Sato, D., Wada, H., Wiens, D.: Diophantine representation of the set of prime numbers. Am. Math. Mon. **83**(6), 449–464 (1976)

26. Kerry, C., Gallagher, P.: FIPS PUB 186-4: Digital signature standard (DSS). Federal Information Processing Standards Publication, National Institute of Standards und Technology (2013)

27. Kocher, P.C.: Timing attacks on implementations of Diffie-Hellman, RSA, DSS, and other systems. In: Koblitz, N. (ed.) CRYPTO 1996. LNCS, vol. 1109, pp. 104–113. Springer, Heidelberg (1996). https://doi.org/10.1007/3-540-68697-5_9

28. Merkle, R.C.: One way hash functions and DES. In: Brassard, G. (ed.) CRYPTO 1989. LNCS, vol. 435, pp. 428–446. Springer, New York (1990). https://doi.org/10.1007/0-387-34805-0_40

29. Moody, D.: NIST Status Update on the 3rd Round (2021). https://csrc.nist. gov/CSRC/media/Presentations/status-update-on-the-3rd-round/images-media/ session-1-moody-nist-round-3-update.pdf. Accessed July 2021
30. NIST: Post-Quantum Cryptography: Round 3 Submissions (2019). https://cs rc.nist.gov/projects/post-quantum-cryptography/round-3-submissions. Accessed July 2021
31. Pastor, M., dela Eva, R.: TimeStamp Smart Contract (2021). https://ec.europa.eu/ cefdigital/wiki/display/EBSIDOC/TimeStamp+Smart+Contract. Accessed July 2021
32. Proos, J., Zalka, C.: Shor's discrete logarithm quantum algorithm for elliptic curves. arXiv preprint quant-ph/0301141 (2003)
33. Raavi, M., Wuthier, S., Chandramouli, P., Balytskyi, Y., Zhou, X., Chang, S.-Y.: Security comparisons and performance analyses of post-quantum signature algo-rithms. In: Sako, K., Tippenhauer, N.O. (eds.) ACNS 2021. LNCS, vol. 12727, pp. 424–447. Springer, Cham (2021). https://doi.org/10.1007/978-3-030-78375-4_17
34. Rivest, R.L., Shamir, A., Adleman, L.: A method for obtaining digital signatures and public-key cryptosystems. Commun. ACM 21(2), 120–126 (1978)
35. Shor, P.W.: Polynomial-time algorithms for prime factorization and discrete loga-rithms on a quantum computer. SIAM Rev. 41(2), 303–332 (1999)
36. Sikeridis, D., Kampanakis, P., Devetsikiotis, M.: Post-quantum authentication in TLS 1.3: a performance study. In: 27th Annual Network and Distributed System Security Symposium, NDSS 2020, San Diego, California, USA, 23–26 February 2020. The Internet Society (2020)
37. Tan, T.G., Szalachowski, P., Zhou, J.: SoK: challenges of post-quantum digital signing in real-world applications. Cryptology ePrint Archive, Report 2019/1374 (2019). https://eprint.iacr.org/2019/1374
38. Unruh, D.: Collapse-binding quantum commitments without random oracles. In: Cheon, J.H., Takagi, T. (eds.) ASIACRYPT 2016. LNCS, vol. 10032, pp. 166–195. Springer, Heidelberg (2016). https://doi.org/10.1007/978-3-662-53890-6_6

Cryptanalysis of RSA Variants with Primes Sharing Most Significant Bits

Meryem Cherkaoui-Semmouni[1], Abderrahmane Nitaj[2(✉)], Willy Susilo[3], and Joseph Tonien[3]

[1] ICES Team, ENSAIS, Mohammed V University in Rabat, Rabat, Morocco
meryem.semmouni@um5s.net.ma
[2] Normandie University, UNICAEN, CNRS, LMNO, 14000 Caen, France
abderrahmane.nitaj@unicaen.fr
[3] Institute of Cybersecurity and Cryptology, School of Computing and Information Technology, University of Wollongong, Wollongong, Australia
{willy.susilo,joseph.tonien}@uow.edu.au

Abstract. We consider four variants of the RSA cryptosystem with an RSA modulus $N = pq$ where the public exponent e and the private exponent d satisfy an equation of the form $ed - k\left(p^2 - 1\right)\left(q^2 - 1\right) = 1$. We show that, if the prime numbers p and q share most significant bits, that is, if the prime difference $|p - q|$ is sufficiently small, then one can solve the equation for larger values of d, and factor the RSA modulus, which makes the systems insecure.

Keywords: RSA variants · Continued fractions · Coppersmith's method · Lattice reduction

1 Introduction

The RSA cryptosystem [16] is one of the most used public key cryptosystems. The arithmetic of RSA is based on a few parameters, namely a modulus of the form $N = pq$ where p and q are large primes, a public exponent e satisfying $\gcd(e, \phi(N)) = 1$ where $\phi(N) = (p - 1)(q - 1)$, and a private exponent d satisfying $ed \equiv 1 \pmod{\phi(N)}$. To encrypt a message m, one simply computes the ciphertext $c \equiv m^e \pmod{N}$, and to decrypt it, one computes $m \equiv c^d \pmod{N}$.

To ease the exponentiation in the decryption phase, a natural way is to choose a mall private exponent. Unfortunately, Wiener [21] showed that if $d < \frac{1}{3}N^{\frac{1}{4}}$, then one can factor N by computing the convergents of the continued fraction expansion of $\frac{e}{N}$. Later on, Boneh and Durfee [1] extended the bound up to $d < N^{0.292}$ by applying Coppersmith's method [7] and lattice reduction techniques. Also, there are plenty of attacks on RSA that depend on the arithmetical structure of its parameters [2,10]. A typical attack on RSA with a specific structure, presented by de Weger [20] in 2002, exploits the size of the difference of the prime factors $|p - q|$. It notably improves the attack of Wiener, as well as the attack of Boneh and Durfee when $|p - q|$ is suitably small.

© Springer Nature Switzerland AG 2021
J. K. Liu et al. (Eds.): ISC 2021, LNCS 13118, pp. 42–53, 2021.
https://doi.org/10.1007/978-3-030-91356-4_3

Since its invention by Rivest, Shamir and Adleman in 1978, many variants of RSA have been proposed such as Multi-prime RSA [6], Rebalanced RSA [21], and RSA-CRT [19]. These variants use more or less the same arithmetic. However, some variants of RSA with notably different structures have been proposed in the literature. In the following, we present four of such variants having similar moduli and key equations.

1) In 1993, Smith and Lennon [17] proposed a system, called LUC, based on Lucas sequences. The modulus is $N = pq$, and the public and the private exponents are positive integers e and d satisfying $ed \equiv 1$ (mod $(p^2 - 1)(q^2 - 1)$).

2) In 1995, Kuwakado et al. [12] presented a cryptosystem based on the singular cubic curve with the equation $y^2 \equiv x^3 + ax^2$ (mod N) where $N = pq$ is an RSA modulus, and $a, x, y \in \mathbb{Z}/N\mathbb{Z}$. In this system, the public exponent e and the private exponent d satisfy $ed \equiv 1$ (mod $(p^2 - 1)(q^2 - 1)$).

3) In 2002, Elkamchouchi et al. [8] proposed a cryptosystem in the ring of Gaussian integers. The operations are performed modulo $N = PQ$ where P and Q are two Gaussian primes. The public exponent e and the private exponent d are positive integers satisfying $ed \equiv 1$ (mod $(|P|^2 - 1)(|Q|^2 - 1)$) where $|P|$ and $|Q|$ are prime integers.

4) In 2006, Castagnos [5] presented a probabilistic cryptosystem over quadratic field quotients. As in LUC, this cryptosystem uses Lucas sequences, and the modulus is in the form $N = pq$. As in the previous cryptosystems, the public exponent e, and the private exponent d are positive integers satisfying $ed \equiv 1$ (mod $(p^2 - 1)(q^2 - 1)$).

A common characteristic of the former cryptosystems is that they share the key equation $ed \equiv 1$ (mod $(p^2 - 1)(q^2 - 1)$). The cryptanalysis of such systems started in 2016 with the work of Bunder et al. [3]. They transformed the key equation into an equation of the form $ed - k(p^2 - 1)(q^2 - 1) = 1$, and showed that $\frac{k}{d}$ can be computed by a convergent of the continued fraction expansion of $\frac{e}{N^2 - \frac{9}{4}N+1}$ if $d < \sqrt{\frac{2N^3 - 18N^2}{e}}$. Then, in 2017, Bunder et al. [4] studied the case when $N = pq$, and the public exponent e satisfies an equation of the form $ex - (p^2 - 1)(q^2 - 1)y = z$. They combined Coppersmith's technique, and the continued fraction method and showed that one can factor N if $xy < 2N - 4\sqrt{2}N^{\frac{3}{4}}$ and $|z| < |p - q|N^{\frac{1}{4}}y$. For $z = 1$, the equation becomes $ed - k(p^2 - 1)(q^2 - 1) = 1$, and the bound on d is $d < \sqrt{2N - 4\sqrt{2}N^{\frac{3}{4}}}$. The same equation $ex - (p^2 - 1)(q^2 - 1)y = z$ was later considered by Nitaj et al. [15]. For $e = N^\alpha$, and $d = N^\delta$, they showed that the equation $ed - k(p^2 - 1)(q^2 - 1) = 1$ can be solved and N can be factored if $\delta < \frac{7}{3} - \frac{2}{3}\sqrt{1 + 3\alpha}$. In [18], Peng et al. obtained the better bound $\delta < 2 - \sqrt{\alpha}$ by mixing Coppersmith's method and unravelled linearization techniques. Finally, Zheng et al. [22] reconsidered the key equation $ed - k(p^2 - 1)(q^2 - 1) = 1$, and obtained a similar bound on d which is applicable for $1 \leq \alpha < 4$.

In this paper, we study the cryptanalysis of the former four variants of RSA if the RSA modulus $N = pq$ is such that $q < p < 2q$, and $p - q = N^\beta$. We note here that, for $q < p < 2q$, we have always $0 < \beta < \frac{1}{2}$. However, if $\beta < \frac{1}{4}$, then one can find p and q by Fermat's method (see [20]), or by Coppersmith's method [7]. Our starting point is the key equation $ed - k\left(p^2 - 1\right)\left(q^2 - 1\right) = 1$ which is common to the four variants. More precisely, for $q < p < 2q$, we set $e = N^\alpha$, $p - q = N^\beta$, $d = N^\delta$. Then, by applying the continued fraction algorithm, we show that, under the condition $\delta < 2 - \beta - \frac{1}{2}\alpha$, the rational number $\frac{k}{d}$ is a convergent of the continued fraction expansion of $\frac{e}{(N-1)^2}$. This leads us to find p and q, and break the system. Also, we show that the key equation can be transformed to a modular polynomial equation of the form $f(x,y) = xy + Ax + 1 \equiv 0 \pmod{e}$, with $A = -(N-1)^2$, where $(x, y) = \left(-k, (p - q)^2\right)$ is a solution. Then by applying Coppersmith's method and lattice reduction techniques, we show that, under the condition $\delta < 2 - \sqrt{2\alpha\beta}$, one can factor the RSA modulus N. If we apply our attacks to the case where p and q are randomly chosen, that is $p - q = \mathcal{O}\left(N^\beta\right)$ with $\beta = \frac{1}{2}$, then our bounds on δ and d retrieve the existing bounds in the previous attacks in [3, 15, 18, 22].

The paper is organized as follows. Section 2 presents the preliminaries to the next sections. In Sect. 3, we present our first attack based on the continued fraction algorithm. In Sect. 4, we present our second attack based on Coppersmith's method and lattice reduction techniques. In Sect. 5, we compare the new results to existing ones in the literature. We conclude the paper in Sect. 6.

2 Preliminaries

In this section, we present some fundamental concepts and results relevant to our methods.

2.1 A Useful Lemma

We start by the following result (see [3]).

Lemma 1. *Let $N = pq$ be an RSA modulus with $q < p < 2q$. Then*

$$N^2 - \frac{5}{2}N + 1 < \left(p^2 - 1\right)\left(q^2 - 1\right) < N^2 - 2N + 1.$$

2.2 Continued Fractions

Let ξ be real number. The continued fraction expansion of ξ is an expression of the form

$$\xi = a_0 + \cfrac{1}{a_1 + \cfrac{1}{a_2 + \cfrac{1}{a_3 + \cdots}}},$$

where $a_0 \in \mathbb{Z}$, and $a_i \in \mathbb{N}^*$ for $i \geq 1$. If ξ is a rational number, the list $[a_0, a_1, a_2, \ldots]$ of partial quotients is finite and can be computed in polynomial time. For $n \geq 0$, $[a_0, a_1, a_2, \ldots, a_n]$ is a rational number and is called a convergent of the continued fraction expansion of ξ. There are various properties of the continued fraction expansion of real numbers, and the following is useful to check whether a rational number $\frac{a}{b}$ is a convergent of a real number ξ [9].

Theorem 1. *Let ξ be a positive real number. If a and b are integers satisfying $\gcd(a, b) = 1$ and*

$$\left| \xi - \frac{a}{b} \right| < \frac{1}{2b^2},$$

then $\frac{a}{b}$ is a convergent of the continued fraction expansion of ξ.

2.3 Lattice Reduction

Let $b_1, b_2, \ldots, b_\omega$ be ω linearly independent vectors of $\mathbb{R}^n$ with $n \geq \omega$. The lattice $\mathcal{L}$ spanned by the vectors $b_1, b_2, \ldots, b_\omega$ is the set of their integer linear combinations, that is

$$\mathcal{L} = \left\{ \sum_{i=1}^{\omega} x_i b_i, \ x_1, \ldots, x_\omega \in \mathbb{Z} \right\}.$$

The list $(b_1, b_2, \ldots, b_\omega)$ is called a basis of the lattice $\mathcal{L}$, ω is its dimension, and n is its rank. When $\omega = n$, the lattice is called full-rank. A basis matrix B for the lattice can be constructed by expanding the vectors b_i in the rows. The lattice determinant is then defined by $\det(\mathcal{L}) = \sqrt{\det(BB^t)}$, where B^t is the transpose of B. When the lattice if full-rank, B is a square matrix and $\det(\mathcal{L}) = |\det(B)|$.

Lattices are used in several domains, especially in cryptography for creating new systems and for cryptanalysis. As a lattice has infinitely many bases, it is crucial to find a basis with good properties, typically with short vectors. In 1982, Lenstra, Lenstra, and Lovász [13] proposed an algorithm, called LLL, to find a good basis and short vectors in a lattice. A useful property of the LLL algorithm is the following result [14].

Theorem 2. *Let $\mathcal{L}$ be a lattice spanned by a basis $(u_1, u_2, \ldots, u_\omega)$. The LLL algorithm produces a new basis $(b_1, b_2, \ldots, b_\omega)$ satisfying*

$$\|b_1\| \leq \cdots \leq \|b_i\| \leq 2^{\frac{\omega(\omega-1)}{4(\omega+1-i)}} \det(\mathcal{L})^{\frac{1}{\omega+1-i}}, \quad i = 1, \ldots, \omega.$$

Let e be an integer and $f(x_1, x_2, \ldots, x_n) = \sum_{i_1, i_2, \ldots, i_n} a_{i_1, i_2, \ldots, i_n} x_1^{i_1} x_2^{i_2} \cdots x_n^{i_n}$ with $a_{i_1, i_2, \ldots, i_n} \in \mathbb{Z}$. The Euclidean norm of the polynomial f is defined by $\|f(x_1, x_2, \ldots, x_n)\| = \sqrt{\sum a_{i_1, i_2, \ldots, i_n}^2}$. In 1997, Coppersmith [7] developed a technique to find the small solutions of the modular polynomial equation $f(x_1) \equiv 0 \pmod{N}$ with one variable, and the small roots of the polynomial $f(x_1, x_2) = 0$ with two variables, by applying lattice reduction. Later, the technique has been extended to more variables, especially to find the small solutions of the modular polynomial equation $f(x_1, x_2, \ldots, x_n) \equiv 0 \pmod{e}$. The following result, due to Howgrave-Graham [11], is a cornerstone in Coppersmith's method.

Theorem 3 (Howgrave-Graham). *Let $f(x_1, x_2, \ldots, x_n) \in \mathbb{Z}[x_1, x_2, \ldots, x_n]$ be a polynomial with at most ω monomials, and e a positive integer. Suppose that*

$$f(x_1', x_2', \ldots, x_n') \equiv 0 \pmod{e} \text{ and } \|f(x_1 X_1, x_2 X_2, \ldots, x_n X_n))\| < \frac{e}{\sqrt{\omega}},$$

where $|x_1'| < X_1, |x_2'| < X_2, \ldots, |x_n'| < X_n$. Then $f(x_1', x_2', \ldots, x_n') = 0$ holds over the integers.

The starting step in Coppersmith's method for finding the small solutions of the modular polynomial equation $f(x_1, x_2, \ldots, x_n) \equiv 0 \pmod{e}$ is to generate ω polynomials $g_i(x_1, x_2, \ldots, x_n)$ satisfying $g_i(x_1', x_2', \ldots, x_n') \equiv 0 \pmod{e}$ for $1 \leq i \leq \omega$. The coefficients of the polynomials $g_i(x_1, x_2, \ldots, x_n)$ are then used to build a matrix of a lattice $\mathcal{L}$. Applying the LLL algorithm to the lattice produces a new matrix from which ω new polynomials $h_i(x_1, x_2, \ldots, x_n)$ are extracted such that $h_i(x_1', x_2', \ldots, x_n') \equiv 0 \pmod{e}$. If, in addition, at least n of such polynomials satisfy Theorem 3, then using resultant techniques or Gröbner basis method, one can extract the small solution $(x_1', x_2', \ldots, x_n')$. We note that for $n \geq 3$, Coppersmith's method to extract the solutions is heuristic. It depends on the assumption that the polynomials derived from the reduced basis are algebraically independent. In this paper, we always successfully extracted the solutions by Gröbner basis computation.

3   The Attack Based on Continued Fraction Algorithm

In this section, we present our first attack which is based on the continued fraction algorithm.

Theorem 4. *Let $N = pq$ be an RSA modulus with $q < p < 2q$ and $|p - q| = N^\beta$. Let $e = N^\alpha$ be a public exponent satisfying the equation $ed - k\left(p^2 - 1\right)\left(q^2 - 1\right) = 1$ with $d = N^\delta$. If*

$$\delta < 2 - \beta - \frac{1}{2}\alpha.$$

then one can find p and q in polynomial time.

Proof. Suppose that $N = pq$ with $q < p < 2q$ and that a public exponent e satisfies the key equation $ed - k\left(p^2 - 1\right)\left(q^2 - 1\right) = 1$. Then

$$
\begin{aligned}
ed - (N - 1)^2 k &= k\left(p^2 - 1\right)\left(q^2 - 1\right) + 1 - (N - 1)^2 k \\
&= 1 + k\left(\left(p^2 - 1\right)\left(q^2 - 1\right) - (N - 1)^2\right) \\
&= 1 - k(p - q)^2.
\end{aligned}
$$

This leads to

$$\left|\frac{e}{(N-1)^2} - \frac{k}{d}\right| = \frac{\left|1 - k(p-q)^2\right|}{d(N-1)^2} < \frac{k(p-q)^2}{d(N-1)^2}.$$

Using the key equation, we get $k\left(p^2 - 1\right)\left(q^2 - 1\right) = ed - 1 < ed$. Then

$$\frac{k}{d} < \frac{e}{(p^2 - 1)(q^2 - 1)},$$

and

$$\left|\frac{e}{(N-1)^2} - \frac{k}{d}\right| < \frac{e(p-q)^2}{(N-1)^2\left(p^2-1\right)\left(q^2-1\right)}.$$

By Lemma 1, we have

$$(N-1)^2\left(p^2-1\right)\left(q^2-1\right) > (N-1)^2\left(N^2 - \frac{5}{2}N + 1\right)$$

$$= N^4 - \frac{9}{2}N^3 + 7N^2 - \frac{9}{2}N + 1$$

$$> \frac{1}{2}N^4,$$

where the last inequality is valid for $N \geq 8$. Hence using $e = N^\alpha$, $|p - q| = N^\beta$, and $d = N^\delta$, we get

$$\left|\frac{e}{(N-1)^2} - \frac{k}{d}\right| < \frac{e(p-q)^2}{(N-1)^2\left(p^2-1\right)\left(q^2-1\right)} < 2N^{\alpha+2\beta-4}.$$

If $2N^{\alpha+2\beta-4} < \frac{1}{2}N^{-2\delta}$, that is $\delta < 2 - \beta - \frac{1}{2}\alpha$, then

$$\left|\frac{e}{(N-1)^2} - \frac{k}{d}\right| < \frac{1}{2}N^{-2\delta} = \frac{1}{2d^2}.$$

It follows that one can find $\frac{k}{d}$ amongst the convergents of the continued fraction expansion of $\frac{e}{(N-1)^2}$. Then, using the values of k and d in the key equation $ed - k\left(p^2 - 1\right)\left(q^2 - 1\right) = 1$, we get $p^2 + q^2 = N^2 + 1 - \frac{ed-1}{k}$. Combining this with $N = pq$, we find p and q. $\qquad\square$

We note that if p and q are such that $p - q \approx N^{\frac{1}{2}}$, then $\beta \approx \frac{1}{2}$, and the bound on δ in Theorem 4 is $\delta < \frac{3}{2} - \frac{\alpha}{2}$. This retrieves the results of [3].

4   The Attack Based on Coppersmith's Method

In this section, we apply Coppersmith's method and lattice reduction techniques to launch an attack on the RSA variants with a modulus $N = pq$ where the prime difference $|p - q|$ is sufficiently small, and the exponents e and d satisfy the equation $ed - k\left(p^2 - 1\right)\left(q^2 - 1\right) = 1$.

Theorem 5. *Let (N, e) be a public key for the RSA variants where $N = pq$ with $q < p < 2q$, and $e = N^\alpha$. Suppose that e satisfies the equation $ed - k\left(p^2 - 1\right)\left(q^2 - 1\right) = 1$ with $d = N^\delta$ and $|p - q| < N^\beta$. If*

$$\delta < 2 - \sqrt{2\alpha\beta} - \varepsilon.$$

for a small positive constant ε, then one can factor N in polynomial time.

Proof. Suppose that $N = pq$ and $e = N^\alpha$ satisfy the equation $ed - k\left(p^2 - 1\right)\left(q^2 - 1\right) = 1$ with $d = N^\delta$ and $|p - q| = N^\beta$. By Lemma 1, for $N \geq 5$, we have

$$\left(p^2 - 1\right)\left(q^2 - 1\right) > N^2 + 1 - \frac{5}{2}N > \frac{1}{2}N^2.$$

Then

$$k = \frac{ed - 1}{\left(p^2 - 1\right)\left(q^2 - 1\right)} < \frac{2ed}{N^2} = 2N^{\alpha+\delta-2},$$

which gives an upper bound for k. On the other hand, the key equation can be rewritten as

$$(-k)(p - q)^2 - (N - 1)^2(-k) + 1 \equiv 0 \pmod{e}.$$

Consider the polynomial $f(x, y) = xy + Ax + 1$, with $A = -(N - 1)^2$. Then $(x, y) = (-k, (p - q)^2)$ is a solution of the modular polynomial equation $f(x, y) \equiv 0 \pmod{e}$. To find the small solutions, we apply Coppersmith's method [7] to the polynomial $F(x, u) = u + Ax$ where $u = xy + 1$ with the bounds

$$|x| < 2N^{\alpha+\delta-2}, \quad |y| < N^{2\beta}, \quad |u| < 2N^{\alpha+\delta+2\beta-2}.$$

Let m and t be two positive integers to be specified later. Consider the polynomials

$$G_{k,i_1,i_2,i_3}(x, y, u) = x^{i_1} F(x, u)^k e^{m-k},$$

with $k = 0, \ldots m$, $i_1 = 0, \ldots, m - k$, $i_2 = 0$, $i_3 = k$,

$$H_{k,i_1,i_2,i_3}(x, y, u) = y^{i_2} F(x, u)^k e^{m-k},$$

with $i_1 = 0, i_2 = 1, \ldots t$, $k = \left\lfloor \frac{m}{t} \right\rfloor i_2, \ldots, m$, $i_3 = k$.

In the expansion of the polynomial $H_{k,i_1,i_2,i_3}(x, y, u)$, each term xy is replaced by $u - 1$. The monomials of $G_{k,i_1,i_2,i_3}(x, y, u)$ and $H_{k,i_1,i_2,i_3}(x, y, u)$ are ordered by the following rule

- A monomial of $G_{k,i_1,i_2,i_3}(x, y, u)$ is prior to every monomial of $H_{k,i_1,i_2,i_3}(x, y, u)$.
- The monomials of $G_{k,i_1,i_2,i_3}(x, y, u)$ are ordered following the output of the procedure
  for $k = 0, \ldots m$, for $i_1 = 0, \ldots, m - k$, for $i_2 = 0$, for $i_3 = k$, output $x^{i_1} y^{i_2} u^{i_3}$.
- The monomials of $H_{k,i_1,i_2,i_3}(x, y, u)$ are ordered following the output of the procedure
  for $i_1 = 0$, for $i_2 = 1, \ldots t$, for $k = \left\lfloor \frac{m}{t} \right\rfloor i_2, \ldots, m$, for $i_3 = k$, output $x^{i_1} y^{i_2} u^{i_3}$.

The polynomials are ordered by similar rules. We set

$$X = 2N^{\alpha+\delta-2}, \ Y = N^{2\beta}, \ U = 2N^{\alpha+\delta+2\beta-2}. \tag{1}$$

We consider the lattice $\mathcal{L}$ where the rows of the basis matrix is built by considering the coefficients of the monomials of the polynomials $G_{k,i_1,i_2,i_3}(Xx, Yy, Uu)$ and $H_{k,i_1,i_2,i_3}(Xx, Yy, Uu)$. We note that the lattice $\mathcal{L}$ is different from the lattices used in [15, 18, 22]. Table 1 shows the lattice basis matrix generated by $m = 2$ and $t = 2$.

Table 1. The lattice basis matrix for $m = 2$ and $t = 2$.

	1	x	x^2	u	xu	u^2	yu	yu^2	y^2u^2
$G_{0,0,0,0}(x,y,u)$	e^2	0	0	0	0	0	0	0	0
$G_{0,1,0,0}(x,y,u)$	0	Xe^2	0	0	0	0	0	0	0
$G_{,2,0,0}(x,y,u)$	0	0	X^2e^2	0	0	0	0	0	0
$G_{1,0,0,1}(x,y,u)$	0	Xa_1e	0	Ue	0	0	0	0	0
$G_{1,1,0,1}(x,y,u)$	0	0	X^2a_1e	0	XUe	0	0	0	0
$G_{2,0,0,2}(x,y,u)$	0	0	$X^2a_1^2$	0	$2UXa_1$	U^2	0	0	0
$H_{1,0,1,1}(x,y,u)$	$-a_1e$	0	0	Ua_1e	0	0	UYe	0	0
$H_{2,0,1,2}(x,y,u)$	0	$-a_1^2X$	0	$-2Ua_1$	a_1^2UX	$2U^2a_1$	0	U^2Y	0
$H_{2,0,2,2}(x,y,u)$	a_1^2	0	0	$-2Ua_1^2$	0	$U^2a_1^2$	$-2Ua_1Y$	$2U^2a_1Y$	U^2Y^2

The lattice basis matrix is triangular and the determinant of the lattice is of the form

$$\det(\mathcal{L}) = X^{n_X} Y^{n_Y} U^{n_U} e^{n_e}, \tag{2}$$

and the dimension is ω with

$$n_X = \sum_{k=0}^{m} \sum_{i_1=0}^{m-k} i_1 = \frac{1}{6}m^3 + o(m^3),$$

$$n_Y = \sum_{i_2=1}^{t} \sum_{k=\lfloor \frac{m}{t} \rfloor}^{m} i_2 = \frac{1}{2}mt^2 - \frac{1}{3}\left\lfloor \frac{m}{t} \right\rfloor t^3 + o(mt^2),$$

$$n_U = \sum_{k=0}^{m} \sum_{i_1=0}^{m-k} k + \sum_{i_2=1}^{t} \sum_{k=\lfloor \frac{m}{t} \rfloor}^{m} k = \frac{1}{6}m^3 + \frac{1}{2}m^2t - \frac{1}{6}\left\lfloor \frac{m}{t} \right\rfloor^2 t^3 + o(m^3),$$

$$n_e = \sum_{k=0}^{m} \sum_{i_1=0}^{m-k} (m-k) + \sum_{i_2=1}^{t} \sum_{k=\lfloor \frac{m}{t} \rfloor}^{m} (m-k)$$

$$= \frac{1}{3}m^3 + \frac{1}{2}m^2t + \frac{1}{6}\left\lfloor \frac{m}{t} \right\rfloor^2 t^3 - \frac{1}{2}\left\lfloor \frac{m}{t} \right\rfloor mt^2 + o(m^3).$$

$$\omega = \sum_{k=0}^{m} \sum_{i_1=0}^{m-k} 1 + \sum_{i_2=1}^{t} \sum_{k=\lfloor \frac{m}{t} \rfloor}^{m} 1 = \frac{1}{2}m^2 + mt - \frac{1}{2}\left\lfloor \frac{m}{t} \right\rfloor t^2 + o(m^2).$$

If we set $t = m\tau$ and replace $\lfloor \frac{m}{t} \rfloor$ by $\frac{1}{\tau}$ in the above approximations, we get

$$n_X = \frac{1}{6}m^3 + o(m^3),$$

$$n_Y = \frac{1}{6}\tau^2 m^3 + o(m^3),$$

$$n_U = \frac{1}{6}(2\tau + 1)m^3 + o(m^3), \tag{3}$$

$$n_e = \frac{1}{6}(\tau + 2)m^3 + o(m^3),$$

$$\omega = \frac{1}{2}(\tau + 1)m^2 + o(m^2).$$

Applying the LLL algorithm to the lattice $\mathcal{L}$, we get a new matrix satisfying the inequalities of Theorem 2. To combine it with Theorem 3, we set

$$2^{\frac{\omega(\omega-1)}{4(\omega-2)}} \det(\mathcal{L})^{\frac{1}{\omega-2}} < \frac{e^m}{\sqrt{\omega}},$$

or equivalently $\det(\mathcal{L}) < 2^{-\frac{\omega(\omega-1)}{4}} (\sqrt{\omega})^{2-\omega} e^{m(\omega-2)}$. Using (2), we get

$$X^{n_X} Y^{n_Y} U^{n_U} e^{n_e} < 2^{-\frac{\omega(\omega-1)}{4}} (\sqrt{\omega})^{2-\omega} e^{m(\omega-2)}.$$

Then, using (3), and by a straightforward calculation, we get the inequality

$$\frac{1}{6}(\alpha + \delta - 2) + \frac{1}{6}\tau^2(2\beta) + \frac{1}{6}(2\tau + 1)(\alpha + \delta + 2\beta - 2)$$

$$+ \frac{1}{6}(\tau + 2)\alpha - \frac{1}{2}(\tau + 1)\alpha < -\varepsilon_1,$$

where ε_1 is a small positive constant that depends only on N and m. The left side is optimized for $\tau_0 = \frac{2-\delta-2\beta}{2\beta}$. Plugging τ_0 in the former inequality, we get

$$-\delta^2 + 4\delta + 2\alpha\beta - 4 < -\varepsilon_2,$$

with a small positive constant ε_2. This leads to the inequality

$$\delta < 2 - \sqrt{2\alpha\beta} - \varepsilon,$$

where ε is a small positive constant. Note that we also need $\tau_0 \geq 0$, that is $2 - \delta - 2\beta \geq 0$ and $\delta \leq 2 - 2\beta$. Consequently, δ should satisfy

$$\delta < \min\left(2 - \sqrt{2\alpha\beta} - \varepsilon, 2 - 2\beta\right).$$

For $\alpha \geq 2\beta$, that is $e \geq |p - q|^2$, we have $2 - \sqrt{2\alpha\beta} \leq 2 - 2\beta$, and the condition becomes $\delta < 2 - \sqrt{2\alpha\beta} - \varepsilon$. Under these conditions, the reduced lattice has three polynomials $h_1(x, y, u)$, $h_2(x, y, u)$ and $h_2(x, y, u)$ sharing the root $(x, y, u) = (-k, (p-q)^2, -k(p-q)^2 + 1)$. Then, applying Gröbner basis or resultant computations, we can extract the solution from which we deduce $p - q = \sqrt{y}$. Combining with the equation $pq = N$, this leads to the factorization of $N = pq$, and terminates the proof.   □

5   Comparison with Former Attacks

Before starting comparing our results to existing ones, we notice that the bound on δ in Theorem 5 is always better than the bound in Theorem 4. To ease the comparison, we neglect the term ε in Theorem 5. For the same parameters α and β, the difference between the bounds in Theorem 5 and Theorem 4 is

$$2 - \sqrt{2\alpha\beta} - \left(2 - \beta - \frac{1}{2}\alpha\right) = \beta + \frac{1}{2}\alpha - \sqrt{2\alpha\beta}$$

$$= \frac{\left(\beta + \frac{1}{2}\alpha\right)^2 - 2\alpha\beta}{\beta + \frac{1}{2}\alpha + \sqrt{2\alpha\beta}}$$

$$= \frac{\left(\beta - \frac{1}{2}\alpha\right)^2}{\beta + \frac{1}{2}\alpha + \sqrt{2\alpha\beta}}$$

$$\geq 0,$$

which implies that $2 - \sqrt{2\alpha\beta} \geq 2 - \beta - \frac{1}{2}\alpha$.

In [3], Bunder et al. studied the key equation $ed - k\left(p^2 - 1\right)\left(q^2 - 1\right) = 1$ by the method of the continued fractions. They showed that if d satisfies $d < \sqrt{\frac{2N^3 - 18N^2}{e}}$, then $\frac{k}{d}$ is a convergent of the continued fraction expansion of $\frac{e}{N^2 - \frac{9}{4}N+1}$, the key equation can be solved and N can be factored. If we set $d = N^\delta$, and $e = N^\alpha$, then the former inequality gives $\delta < \frac{3}{2} - \frac{1}{2}\alpha$ which is the same than the bound of Theorem 4 with $|p - q| = N^\beta$ and $\beta = \frac{1}{2}$. As a consequence, the results of [3] can be retrieved by our method as in Theorem 4.

In [15], Nitaj et al. studied the variant equation $eu - \left(p^2 - 1\right)\left(q^2 - 1\right)v = w$ with $e = N^\alpha$, $u < N^\delta$, $|w| < N^\gamma$, and showed that under the conditions $\delta < \frac{7}{3} - \gamma - \frac{2}{3}\sqrt{1 + 3\alpha - 3\gamma}$, one can factor the RSA modulus $N = pq$. If we take $\gamma = 0$, then the equation becomes $eu - \left(p^2 - 1\right)\left(q^2 - 1\right)v = 1$, and the condition is $\delta < \frac{7}{3} - \frac{2}{3}\sqrt{1 + 3\alpha}$. To compare it with the bound of Theorem 5, we take $|p - q| = N^\beta$ with $\beta = \frac{1}{2}$, and the bound becomes $\delta < 2 - \sqrt{\alpha}$. Then

$$2 - \sqrt{\alpha} - \left(\frac{7}{3} - \frac{2}{3}\sqrt{1 + 3\alpha}\right) = \frac{2}{3}\sqrt{1 + 3\alpha} - \sqrt{\alpha} - \frac{1}{3}$$

$$= \frac{\frac{4}{9}(1 + 3\alpha) - \left(\sqrt{\alpha} + \frac{1}{3}\right)^2}{\frac{2}{3}\sqrt{1 + 3\alpha} + \sqrt{\alpha} + \frac{1}{3}}$$

$$= \frac{\frac{1}{3} + \frac{1}{3}\alpha - \frac{2}{3}\sqrt{\alpha}}{\frac{2}{3}\sqrt{1 + 3\alpha} + \sqrt{\alpha} + \frac{1}{3}}$$

$$= \frac{\frac{1}{3}\left(1 - \sqrt{\alpha}\right)^2}{\frac{2}{3}\sqrt{1 + 3\alpha} + \sqrt{\alpha} + \frac{1}{3}}$$

$$\geq 0,$$

which shows that our bound in Theorem 5 is always better than the bound of [15].

In [18], Peng et al. studied the key equation $ed - k\left(p^2 - 1\right)\left(q^2 - 1\right) = 1$ by Coppersmith's method, with $e = N^\alpha$, and $d = N^\delta$. The key equation is first transformed to the modular equation $k\left(N^2 + 1 - p^2 - q^2\right) + 1 \equiv 0 \pmod{e}$, and then to the modular equation $x(y + A) + 1 \equiv 0 \pmod{e}$ with $A = N^2 + 1$, $x = k$, and $y = -\left(p^2 + q^2\right)$. They showed that one can factor the RSA modulus if $\delta < 2 - \sqrt{\alpha}$. In Theorem 5, if we set $|p - q| = N^\beta$ with $\beta = \frac{1}{2}$, we get the same condition. This shows that our method can be considered as an extension of the work in [18].

In [22], Zheng et al. studied the key equation $ed - k\left(p^2 - 1\right)\left(q^2 - 1\right) = 1$ and transformed it to $k\left((N + 1)^2 - (p + q)^2\right) + 1 \equiv 0 \pmod{e}$, and also to $x(y + A) + 1 \equiv 0 \pmod{e}$ with $A = (N + 1)^2$, $x = k$, and $y = -(p + q)^2$. They showed that one can solve the equation and factor N if $d = N^\delta$, $e = N^\alpha$, and $\delta < 2 - \sqrt{\alpha}$. As specified before, this result can be retrieved by our method of Theorem 5.

6   Conclusion

In this paper, we studied the key equation $ed - k\left(p^2 - 1\right)\left(q^2 - 1\right) = 1$ derived from four variants of the RSA cryptosystem with a modulus $N = pq$, a public exponent e, and a private exponent d. Moreover, we considered the situation where the prime factors p and q are of equal bitsize, and share an amount of their most significant bits. We presented two different attacks on such variants. The first attack is based on the continued fraction algorithm, and the second attack is based on lattice reduction. For both attacks, we showed that the variants are insecure if the prime difference $p - q$, and the private exponent d are suitably small. Finally, we compared our new attacks to existing ones, and showed that our methods are more suitable for the cryptanalysis of the RSA variants.

References

1. Boneh, D., Durfee, G.: Cryptanalysis of RSA with private key d less than $N^{0.292}$. In: Advances in Cryptology-Eurocrypt 1999, Lecture Notes in Computer Science, vol. 1592, Springer-Verlag, pp. 1–11 (1999)
2. Boneh, D.: Twenty years of attacks on the RSA cryptosystem. Notices Amer. Math. Soc. **46**(2), 203–213 (1999)
3. Bunder, M., Nitaj, A., Susilo, W., Tonien, J.: A new attack on three variants of the RSA cryptosystem. In: Liu, J.K., Steinfeld, R. (eds.) ACISP 2016. LNCS, vol. 9723, pp. 258–268. Springer, Cham (2016)
4. Bunder, M., Nitaj, A., Susilo, W., Tonien, J.: A generalized attack on RSA type cryptosystems. Theoretical Comput. Sci. **704**, 74–81 (2017)
5. Castagnos, G.: An efficient probabilistic public-key cryptosystem over quadratic field quotients, 2007, Finite Fields and Their Applications, 13(3–13), p. 563–576 (2007). http://www.math.u-bordeaux1.fr/~gcastagn/publi/crypto_quad.pdf
6. Collins, T., Hopkins, D., Langford, S., Sabin, M.: Public key cryptographic apparatus and Method. US Patent 5,848,159, Jan 1997

7. Coppersmith, D.: Small solutions to polynomial equations, and low exponent RSA vulnerabilities. J. Crypt. **10**(4), 233–260 (1997)
8. Elkamchouchi, H., Elshenawy, K., Shaban, H.: Extended RSA cryptosystem and digital signature schemes in the domain of Gaussian integers. In: Proceedings of the 8th International Conference on Communication Systems, pp. 91–95 (2002)
9. Hardy, G.H., Wright, E.M.: An Introduction to Theory of Numbers, 5th edn. The Clarendon Press, Oxford University Press, New York (1979)
10. Hinek, M.: Cryptanalysis of RSA and Its Variants. Chapman & Hall/CRC, Cryptography and Network Security Series, Boca Raton (2009)
11. Howgrave-Graham, N.: Finding small roots of univariate modular equations revisited. In: Darnell, M. (ed.) Cryptography and Coding 1997. LNCS, vol. 1355, pp. 131–142. Springer, Heidelberg (1997). https://doi.org/10.1007/BFb0024458
12. Kuwakado, H., Koyama, K. Tsuruoka, Y.: A new RSA-type scheme based on singular cubic curves $y^2 = x^3 + bx^2$ (mod n). IEICE Transactions on Fundamentals, vol. E78-A, pp. 27–33 (1995)
13. Lenstra, A.K., Lenstra, H.W., Lovász, L.: Factoring polynomials with rational coefficients. Math. Ann. **261**, 513–534 (1982)
14. May, A.: New RSA Vulnerabilities Using Lattice Reduction Methods, PhD Thesis, University of Paderborn (2003)
15. Nitaj, A., Pan, Y., Tonien, J.: A generalized attack on some variants of the RSA cryptosystem. In: Cid, C., Jacobson, M., Jr. (eds.) SAC 2018. LNCS, vol. 11349, pp. 421–433. Springer, Cham (2018). https://doi.org/10.1007/978-3-030-10970-7_19
16. Rivest, R., Shamir, A., Adleman, L.: A Method for obtaining digital signatures and public-key cryptosystems. Commun. ACM **21**(2), 120–126 (1978)
17. Smith, P.J., Lennon, G.J.J.: LUC: A New Public-Key Cryptosystem, pp. 103–117. Elsevier Science Publishers, Ninth IFIP Symposium on Computer Science Security (1993)
18. Peng, L., Hu, L., Lu, Y., Wei, H.: An improved analysis on three variants of the RSA cryptosystem. In: Chen, K., Lin, D., Yung, M. (eds.) Inscrypt 2016. LNCS, vol. 10143, pp. 140–149. Springer, Cham (2017)
19. Quisquater, J.J., Couvreur, C.: Fast decipherment algorithm for RSA public key cryptosystem. Electron. Lett. **18**, 905–907 (1982)
20. de Weger, B.: Cryptanalysis of RSA with small prime difference. Appl. Algebra Eng. Commun. Comput. **13**(1), 17–28 (2002)
21. Wiener, M.: Cryptanalysis of short RSA secret exponents. IEEE Trans. Inf. Theory **36**, 553–558 (1990)
22. Zheng, M., Kunihiro, N., Hu, H.: Cryptanalysis of RSA Variants with Modified Euler Quotient. In: Joux A., Nitaj A., Rachidi T. (eds.) Progress in Cryptology-AFRICACRYPT 2018. AFRICACRYPT 2018. Lecture Notes in Computer Science, vol. 10831. Springer, Cham (2018)

Cryptanalysis of Two White-Box Implementations of the SM4 Block Cipher

Jiqiang Lu[1,2,3(✉)] and Jingyu Li[1]

[1] School of Cyber Science and Technology, Beihang University, Beijing, China
lijingyu98@buaa.edu.cn
[2] Guangxi Key Laboratory of Cryptography and Information Security, Guilin, China
[3] HangZhou Innovation Institute, Beihang University, Beijing, China
lvjiqiang@buaa.edu.cn

Abstract. The SM4 block cipher has a 128-bit block length and a 128-bit user key, formerly known as SMS4. It is a Chinese national standard and an ISO international standard. White-box cryptography aims primarily to protect the secret key used in a cryptographic software implementation in the white-box scenario that assumes an attacker to have full access to the execution environment and execution details of an implementation. Since white-box cryptography has many real-life applications nowadays, a few white-box implementations of the SM4 block cipher has been proposed, in particular, in 2009 Xiao and Lai presented the first white-box SM4 implementation based on traditional way, which has been attacked with the lowest currently published attack complexity of about 2^{32} using affine equivalence technique; and in 2020 Yao and Chen presented a white-box SM4 implementation based on state expansion, and got the lowest attack complexity of about 2^{51} among a variety of attack techniques. In this paper, we present collision-based attacks on Yao and Chen's and Xiao and Lai's white-box SM4 implementations with a time complexity of about 2^{23} for recovering a round key, and thus show that their security is much lower than previously published.

Keywords: White-box cryptography · Block cipher · SM4 (SMS4) · Collision attack

1 Introduction

In 2002, Chow et al. [8,9] introduced white-box cryptography and proposed white-box implementations to the AES [26] and DES [27] block ciphers. White-box cryptography works under the white-box security model, which assumes an attacker has full access to the execution environment and execution details (such as intermediate values, CPU calls, memory registers, etc.) of a software implementation, giving the attacker more power than the black-box and grey-box security models. Nowadays, white-box cryptography has many real-life application scenarios like TV boxes, mobile phones and game consoles, and some white-box cryptography solutions have been in use.

© Springer Nature Switzerland AG 2021
J. K. Liu et al. (Eds.): ISC 2021, LNCS 13118, pp. 54–69, 2021.
https://doi.org/10.1007/978-3-030-91356-4_4

The primary security threat for white-box cryptography is key extraction attack, which aims to extract the key used in white-box implementation. Chow et al.'s white-box AES implementation has been cryptanalysed extensively [5,18,23,29], and the main attack results are as follows. In 2004, Billet et al. [5] presented an attack with a time complexity of 2^{30} (referred to below as BGE attack). In 2013, Lepoint et al. [18] improved the BGE attack to have a time complexity of 2^{22}, and presented a collision-based attack with a time complexity of 2^{22}. There are also a few attacks [14,15,21,32] on Chow et al.'s white-box DES implementation. On the other hand, a number of different white-box implementation designs have been proposed [1,3,7,16,22,33], but almost all of them have been broken with a practical or semi-practical time complexity [3,10,18,24,25]. Generally speaking, it has been well understood that the line of white-box implementation for an existing cryptographic algorithm is hardly impossible to achieve the full security under the black-box model, but it is expected that it can still provide some protection with realistic significance.

The SM4 block cipher was first released in 2006 as the SMS4 [11] block cipher used in the Chinese WLAN national standard WAPI (WLAN Authentication and Privacy Infrastructure), which has a 128-bit block length and a 128-bit user key. SMS4 became a Chinese cryptographic industry standard in 2012, labeled with SM4, which then became a Chinese national standard [12] in 2016 and an ISO international standard in 2021 [13]. The main white-box implementation results of SMS4/SM4 are as follows. In 2009, Xiao and Lai [34] proposed the first white-box SM4 implementation with a series of lookup tables and affine transformation operations. In 2013, Lin and Lai [19] attacked Xiao and Lai's white-box SM4 implementation with a time complexity of around 2^{47}, by combining the BGE attack with a few other techniques like differential cryptanalysis. In 2015, Shi et al. [28] proposed a lightweight white-box SM4 implementation based on the idea of dual cipher [4]. In 2016, Bai and Wu [2] proposed a white-box SM4 implementation with complicated encoding and decoding processes. In 2018, Lin et al. [20] attacked Shi et al.'s white-box SM4 implementation with a time complexity of 2^{49}, basing it on Biryukov et al.'s affine equivalence technique [6]. In 2020, Yao and Chen [35] proposed a white-box SM4 implementation with some original internal states expanded by dummy states under the control of a secret random number, and finally got the lowest attack complexity of about 2^{51} after an extensive security analysis. Most recently, Wang et al. [31] applied Lepoint et al.'s collision-based attack idea to attack Shi et al.'s white-box SM4 implementation with a time complexity of around 2^{23} (note that collision-based attacks on Shi et al.'s and Yao and Chen's white-box SM4 implementations appeared earlier in Wang's thesis [30], however, due to the distinctions among the white-box AES and SM4 implementation operations, there is a fundamental flaw on the collision principle of the attacks described in [30], which makes the attacks invalid; besides, Wang dealt with those dummy states by enumerating the associated 4-bit random vector for Yao and Chen's white-box SM4 implementation).

In this paper, we apply Lepoint et al.'s collision-based idea to attack Yao and Chen's white-box SM4 implementation with a time complexity of about

2^{23}, in particular, we find that the effect of those dummy states can be bypassed without any workload by first devising an appropriate collision function and then using a trick to recover the linear parts of the concerned affine output encodings. The attack significantly reduces the estimated security of Yao and Chen's white-box SM4 implementation, from the designers' semi-practical level 2^{51} to a very practical level. The attack can be similarly applied to Xiao and Lai's white-box SM4 implementation with a time complexity of about 2^{23} too, reducing much the best previously published attack complexity of 2^{32} based on affine equivalence technique. These suggest that Yao and Chen's white-box SM4 implementation does not improve on Xiao and Lai's white-box SM4 implementation in the sense of security, and their realistic significance is reduced.

The remainder of the paper is organised as follows. In the next section, we describe the notation and the SM4 block cipher. We describe our attack on Yao and Chen's white-box SM4 implementation in Sect. 3, and briefly describe our attack on Xiao and Lai's white-box SM4 implementation in Sect. 4. Section 5 concludes this paper.

2 Preliminaries

In this section, we give the notation used throughout this paper, and briefly describe the SM4 block cipher.

2.1 Notation

We use the following notation throughout this paper.

$\oplus$ bitwise exclusive OR (XOR)
$\lll$ left rotation of a bit string
$\|$ bit string concatenation
$\circ$ functional composition

2.2 The SM4 Block Cipher

SM4 [11,12] is a unbalanced Feistel cipher with 32 rounds, a 128-bit block size and a 128-bit key length. Denote by $(X_i, X_{i+1}, X_{i+2}, X_{i+3})$ the 128-bit input to the i-th round, by rk_i the 32-bit i-th round key, where $i = 0, 1, \ldots, 31$ and $X_i \in GF(2)^{32}$.

Define the nonlinear function $\tau : GF(2)^{32} \to GF(2)^{32}$ that applies the same 8-bit S-box $\mathbf{S}$ four times in parallel as

$$x \mapsto \left(\mathbf{S}(x_{[31\ldots24]}), \mathbf{S}(x_{[23\ldots16]}), \mathbf{S}(x_{[15\ldots8]}), \mathbf{S}(x_{[7\ldots0]}) \right);$$

and define the linear function $\mathbf{L} : GF(2)^{32} \to GF(2)^{32}$ as

$$x \mapsto x \oplus (x \lll 2) \oplus (x \lll 10) \oplus (x \lll 18) \oplus (x \lll 24). \tag{1}$$

Then, the invertible transformation $\mathbf{T} : \mathrm{GF}(2)^{32} \times \mathrm{GF}(2)^{32} \to \mathrm{GF}(2)^{32}$ is defined to be

$$(x, rk_i) \to \mathbf{L}(\tau(x \oplus rk_i)),$$

and the round function $\mathbf{F} : \mathrm{GF}(2)^{128} \times \mathrm{GF}(2)^{32} \to \mathrm{GF}(2)^{128}$ under round key rk_i is

$$((X_i, X_{i+1}, X_{i+2}, X_{i+3}), rk_i) \mapsto (X_{i+1}, X_{i+2}, X_{i+3}, X_i \oplus$$
$$\mathbf{T}(X_{i+1} \oplus X_{i+2} \oplus X_{i+3}, rk_i)). \tag{2}$$

The encryption procedure of SM4 consists of the 32 round functions $\mathbf{F}$'s and finally a reverse transformation $R : \mathrm{GF}(2)^{128} \to \mathrm{GF}(2)^{128}$ defined as

$$(X_{32}, X_{33}, X_{34}, X_{35}) \mapsto (X_{35}, X_{34}, X_{33}, X_{32}).$$

It is depicted in Fig. 1.

The decryption process of SM4 is the same as the encryption process, except that the round keys are used in the reverse order. We refer the reader to [11,12] for detailed specifications.

Particularly, it is easy and worthy to note that the linear transformation $\mathbf{L}$ (as described in Eq. (1)) of SM4 can also be represented as an invertible 32×32-bit matrix

$$\begin{bmatrix} B_1 & B_2 & B_2 & B_3 \\ B_3 & B_1 & B_2 & B_2 \\ B_2 & B_3 & B_1 & B_2 \\ B_2 & B_2 & B_3 & B_1 \end{bmatrix}, \tag{3}$$

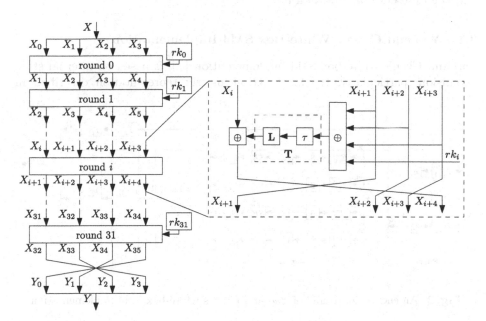

Fig. 1. SM4 encryption procedure

with B_1, B_2 and B_3 being 8×8-bit block matrices as follows.

$$B_1 = \begin{bmatrix} 1&0&1&0&0&0&0&0 \\ 0&1&0&1&0&0&0&0 \\ 0&0&1&0&1&0&0&0 \\ 0&0&0&1&0&1&0&0 \\ 0&0&0&0&1&0&1&0 \\ 0&0&0&0&0&1&0&1 \\ 0&0&0&0&0&0&1&0 \\ 0&0&0&0&0&0&0&1 \end{bmatrix}, \ B_2 = \begin{bmatrix} 0&0&1&0&0&0&0&0 \\ 0&0&0&1&0&0&0&0 \\ 0&0&0&0&1&0&0&0 \\ 0&0&0&0&0&1&0&0 \\ 0&0&0&0&0&0&1&0 \\ 0&0&0&0&0&0&0&1 \\ 1&0&0&0&0&0&0&0 \\ 0&1&0&0&0&0&0&0 \end{bmatrix}, \ B_3 = \begin{bmatrix} 1&0&0&0&0&0&0&0 \\ 0&1&0&0&0&0&0&0 \\ 0&0&1&0&0&0&0&0 \\ 0&0&0&1&0&0&0&0 \\ 0&0&0&0&1&0&0&0 \\ 0&0&0&0&0&1&0&0 \\ 1&0&0&0&0&0&1&0 \\ 0&1&0&0&0&0&0&1 \end{bmatrix}.$$

Let x_0, x_1, x_2, x_3 be four byte variables, represent $\mathbf{L}$ as four 32×8-bit matrices $[\mathbf{L}_0 \ \mathbf{L}_1 \ \mathbf{L}_2 \ \mathbf{L}_3]$, and define

$$\mathbf{L}_0(x) = x \cdot [B_1 \ B_3 \ B_2 \ B_2]^T, \ \mathbf{L}_1(x) = x \cdot [B_2 \ B_1 \ B_3 \ B_2]^T,$$
$$\mathbf{L}_2(x) = x \cdot [B_2 \ B_2 \ B_1 \ B_3]^T, \ \mathbf{L}_3(x) = x \cdot [B_3 \ B_2 \ B_2 \ B_1]^T,$$

then we have $\mathbf{L}(x_0 || x_1 || x_2 || x_3) = \mathbf{L}_0(x_0) \oplus \mathbf{L}_1(x_1) \oplus \mathbf{L}_2(x_2) \oplus \mathbf{L}_3(x_3)$.

3   Collision-Based Attack on Yao and Chen's White-Box SM4 Implementation

In this section, we first describe Yao and Chen's white-box SM4 implementation, and then present our attack on it.

3.1   Yao and Chen's White-Box SM4 Implementation

Yao and Chen's white-box SM4 implementation [35] is based on internal state expansion, particularly, the 32×32-bit matrix representation described in

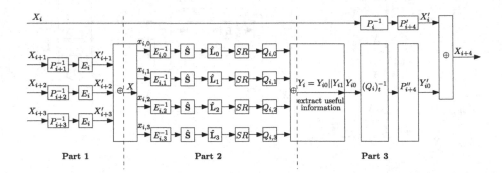

Fig. 2. An encryption round of Yao and Chen's white-box SM4 implementation

Eq. (3) of the linear transformation $\mathbf{L}$ is expanded to the following 64×64-bit matrix $\widehat{\mathbf{L}}$ with the 8×8-bit zero matrix $\mathbf{0}$:

$$\widehat{\mathbf{L}} = \begin{bmatrix} B_1 & \mathbf{0} & B_2 & \mathbf{0} & B_2 & \mathbf{0} & B_3 & \mathbf{0} \\ \mathbf{0} & B_1 & \mathbf{0} & B_2 & \mathbf{0} & B_2 & \mathbf{0} & B_3 \\ B_3 & \mathbf{0} & B_1 & \mathbf{0} & B_2 & \mathbf{0} & B_2 & \mathbf{0} \\ \mathbf{0} & B_3 & \mathbf{0} & B_1 & \mathbf{0} & B_2 & \mathbf{0} & B_2 \\ B_2 & \mathbf{0} & B_3 & \mathbf{0} & B_1 & \mathbf{0} & B_2 & \mathbf{0} \\ \mathbf{0} & B_2 & \mathbf{0} & B_3 & \mathbf{0} & B_1 & \mathbf{0} & B_2 \\ B_2 & \mathbf{0} & B_2 & \mathbf{0} & B_3 & \mathbf{0} & B_1 & \mathbf{0} \\ \mathbf{0} & B_2 & \mathbf{0} & B_2 & \mathbf{0} & B_3 & \mathbf{0} & B_1 \end{bmatrix}.$$

Represent the matrix $\widehat{\mathbf{L}}$ as four 64×16-bit matrices, that is, $\widehat{\mathbf{L}} = \begin{bmatrix} \widehat{\mathbf{L}}_0 & \widehat{\mathbf{L}}_1 & \widehat{\mathbf{L}}_2 & \widehat{\mathbf{L}}_3 \end{bmatrix}$. Then, an encryption round of Yao and Chen's white-box SM4 implementation consists of the following three parts according to Eq. (2), as depicted in Fig. 2. Note first that X_j is the corresponding original value protected with an affine output encoding $P_l(x) = A_l \cdot x \oplus a_l$, where x is a 32-bit variable, a_l is a secret (randomly generated) 32-bit vector, A_l is a secret (randomly generated) general invertible 32×32-bit matrix, and $l = 0, 1, \cdots, 35$.

Part 1: Implement $X_{i+1} \oplus X_{i+2} \oplus X_{i+3} \mapsto X$. In order to obtain the original value of $X_{i+1} \oplus X_{i+2} \oplus X_{i+3}$ from the protected forms X_{i+1}, X_{i+2} and X_{i+3}, apply first the inverses P_{i+1}^{-1}, P_{i+2}^{-1} and P_{i+3}^{-1} of the three output encodings respectively to X_{i+1}, X_{i+2} and X_{i+3}, followed by an identical diagonal output encoding $E_i = \mathrm{diag}(E_{i,0}, E_{i,1}, E_{i,2}, E_{i,3})$, where $E_{i,0}, E_{i,1}, E_{i,2}, E_{i,3}$ are four general invertible 8×8-bit affine transformations $(i = 0, 1, \ldots, 31)$.

This part can be summarised as

$$X'_{i+j} = E_i \circ P_{i+j}^{-1}(X_{i+j}), \quad j = 1, 2, 3;$$
$$X = X'_{i+1} \oplus X'_{i+2} \oplus X'_{i+3},$$

where X is a 32-bit variable. Observe that the final result of this part $X = E_i \circ (P_{i+1}^{-1}(X_{i+1}) \oplus P_{i+2}^{-1}(X_{i+2}) \oplus P_{i+3}^{-1}(X_{i+3}))$ is the original value of $X_{i+1} \oplus X_{i+2} \oplus X_{i+3}$ protected with the output encoding E_i in such a way that its four bytes are protected respectively with the four 8-bit encodings $E_{i,0}, E_{i,1}, E_{i,2}, E_{i,3}$.

Part 2: Implement $\mathbf{T}(X \oplus rk_i) \mapsto Y_i (= Y_{i0}||Y_{i1})$. The input X of the second part is the output of the first part, represent X as 4 bytes $X = (x_{i,0}, x_{i,1}, x_{i,2}, x_{i,3})$, and represent the round key rk_i as 4 bytes $rk_i = (rk_{i,0}, rk_{i,1}, rk_{i,2}, rk_{i,3})$, where $i = 0, 1, \ldots, 31$. Next, construct four lookup tables that map from 8-bit input to 64-bit output each, as follow:

$$Table_{i,0} = G_{i,0} \circ \widehat{\mathbf{L}}_0[\widehat{\mathbf{S}}(E_{i,0}^{-1}(x_{i,0}), rk_{i,0}, \alpha_{i,0})_{t_{i,0}}],$$

$$Table_{i,1} = G_{i,1} \circ \widehat{\mathbf{L}}_1[\widehat{\mathbf{S}}(E_{i,1}^{-1}(x_{i,1}), rk_{i,1}, \alpha_{i,1})_{t_{i,1}}],$$

$$Table_{i,2} = G_{i,2} \circ \widehat{\mathbf{L}}_2[\widehat{\mathbf{S}}(E_{i,2}^{-1}(x_{i,2}), rk_{i,2}, \alpha_{i,2})_{t_{i,2}}],$$

$$Table_{i,3} = G_{i,3} \circ \widehat{\mathbf{L}}_3[\widehat{\mathbf{S}}(E_{i,3}^{-1}(x_{i,3}), rk_{i,3}, \alpha_{i,3})_{t_{i,3}}],$$

where

- $\alpha_{i,j}$ is an 8-bit random number ($j = 0, 1, 2, 3$);
- $\widehat{L}_j$ is the corresponding j-th 64×16-bit part of $\widehat{L}$;
- $(t_{i,0}, t_{i,1}, t_{i,2}, t_{i,3})$ is a 4-bit random vector ($t_{i,j} \in \{0, 1\}$), and

$$\widehat{S}(E_{i,j}^{-1}(x_{i,j}), rk_{i,j}, \alpha_{i,j})_{t_{i,j}}$$

$$= \begin{cases} S(E_{i,j}^{-1}(x_{i,j}) \oplus rk_{i,j}) \; || \; S(E_{i,j}^{-1}(x_{i,j}) \oplus \alpha_{i,j}), & t_{i,j} = 0; \\ S(E_{i,j}^{-1}(x_{i,j}) \oplus \alpha_{i,j}) \; || \; S(E_{i,j}^{-1}(x_{i,j}) \oplus rk_{i,j}), & t_{i,j} = 1. \end{cases}$$

That is, the $\widehat{S}$ operation is constructed by expanding the original S operation with a dummy S operation under the control of the 1-bit $t_{i,j}$ parameter.
- $G_{i,j}$ is the composition of a shift matrix SR and an output encoding $Q_{i,j}$. The shift matrix SR transforms the expanded 64-bit value after $\widehat{L}_j$ into such a 64-bit value that the former half is the original 32-bit part (without expansion) and the latter half consists only of some dummy bits. $Q_{i,j}$ is of the affine form $Q_{i,j}(x) = L_Q \cdot x \oplus C_{Q_{i,j}}$, here x is a 64-bit variable, the linear part L_Q is a block diagonal matrix being composed of eight 8×8-bit matrices, and the constant part $C_{Q_{i,j}}$ consists of eight concatenated 8-bit vectors.

The final output of this part is the XOR of the four 64-bit outputs of the four lookup tables, which is denoted by $Y_i = Y_{i0}||Y_{i1}$ with Y_{i0} being supposed to be the original useful 32-bit value.

Part 3: Implement $Y_{i0} \oplus X_i \mapsto X_{i+4}$. This part first extracts the original useful 32-bit value from the 64-bit expanded output of the second part, and then calculates X_{i+4}, as follows.

$$Y_{i0}' = P_{i+4}'' \circ (Q_i)_t^{-1}(Y_{i0}),$$
$$X_i' = P_{i+4}' \circ P_i^{-1}(X_i),$$
$$X_{i+4} = Y_{i0}' \oplus X_i',$$

where $(Q_i)_t^{-1}$ represents the corresponding part of the inverse of the encodings $L_Q \cdot x \oplus (C_{Q_{i,0}} \oplus C_{Q_{i,1}} \oplus C_{Q_{i,2}} \oplus C_{Q_{i,3}})$ of the second part, and P_{i+4}' and P_{i+4}'' are new affine output encodings of the forms $P_{i+4}'(x) = P_{i+4} \oplus a_{i+4}'$ and $P_{i+4}''(x) = P_{i+4} \oplus a_{i+4}''$, respectively, so that X_{i+4} is a protected form with an affine output encoding $P_{i+4}(x) = A_{i+4} \cdot x \oplus a_{i+4}$, like X_i.

As a result, the whole white-box SM4 implementation can be obtained by iterating the above process for all the 32 rounds with possibly independent encodings.

Yao and Chen analysed its security against a variety of attack techniques like BGE, and got that the attack complexity using affine equivalence technique was 2^{97}, and the lowest attack complexity was 2^{51} among all used attack techniques.

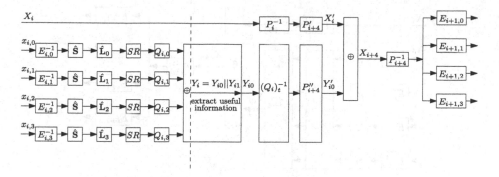

Fig. 3. Our collision function at a high level

3.2 Attacking Yao and Chen's White-Box SM4 Implementation

In this subsection, we apply Lepoint et al.'s collision-based idea to attack Yao and Chen's white-box SM4 implementation with a time complexity of about 2^{23}. AES and SM4 have different structures, and Yao and Chen's white-box SM4 implementation is distinct from Chow et al.'s white-box AES implementation: there are dummy states with indeterminate positions and the encoding used in X_{i+4} involves a general 32×32-bit matrix, which does not allow us to apply Lepoint et al.'s attack idea efficiently within one round, as done on Chow et al.'s white-box AES implementation. However, after a detailed investigation we find an appropriate collision function by considering two consecutive rounds in Yao and Chen's white-box SM4 implementation, plus a trick that can recover the linear parts of the concerned encodings, to bypass the effects due to the dummy states and etc.

3.2.1 Devising a Collision Function

As illustrated in Fig. 3 at a high level, the collision function used in our attack takes as input the two 32-bit input parameters $(x_{i,0}||x_{i,1}||x_{i,2}||x_{i,3}, X_i)$ in the second part of an encryption round of Yao and Chen's white-box SM4 implementation, and ends with the output of an $E_{i+1,j}$ operation of the X_{i+4} branch in the first part of the next encryption round ($j = 0, 1, 2, 3$). Observe that E_i and E_{i+1} are diagonal affine transformations, $E_{i,j}$ and $E_{i+1,j}$ are invertible 8×8-bit affine transformations, and $x_{i,j}$ is the original input byte to the j-th original S-box of the i-th encryption round in a protected form with $E_{i,j}$.

The collision function is functionally equivalent and can be simplified to the one depicted in Fig. 4. Without loss of generality, we set $X_i = 0$ in our attack and all subsequent descriptions, and denote the constant $P_{i+4}^{-1} \circ P'_{i+4} \circ P_i^{-1}(X_i) \oplus A_{i+4}^{-1} \cdot a''_{i+4} = P_{i+4}^{-1} \circ P'_{i+4} \circ P_i^{-1}(0) \oplus A_{i+4}^{-1} \cdot a''_{i+4}$ by ε. We now explain where the value ε comes from. Let $\widehat{X}$ denotes the original 32-bit value immediately after the **L** operation under the input $X = (x_{i,0}, x_{i,1}, x_{i,2}, x_{i,3})$, then we have

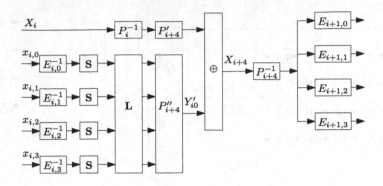

Fig. 4. Equivalent of our collision function

$$P_{i+4}^{-1} \circ (Y'_{i0} \oplus P'_{i+4} \circ P_i^{-1}(X_i))$$
$$= P_{i+4}^{-1}(Y'_{i0}) \oplus P_{i+4}^{-1} \circ P'_{i+4} \circ P_i^{-1}(X_i)$$
$$= P_{i+4}^{-1} \circ P''_{i+4}(\widehat{X}) \oplus P_{i+4}^{-1} \circ P'_{i+4} \circ P_i^{-1}(X_i)$$
$$= P_{i+4}^{-1} \circ (P_{i+4}(\widehat{X}) \oplus a''_{i+4}) \oplus P_{i+4}^{-1} \circ P'_{i+4} \circ P_i^{-1}(X_i)$$
$$= P_{i+4}^{-1} \circ (A_{i+4}(\widehat{X}) \oplus a_{i+4} \oplus a''_{i+4}) \oplus P_{i+4}^{-1} \circ P'_{i+4} \circ P_i^{-1}(X_i)$$
$$= A_{i+4}^{-1} \circ (A_{i+4}(\widehat{X}) \oplus a_{i+4} \oplus a''_{i+4} \oplus a_{i+4}) \oplus P_{i+4}^{-1} \circ P'_{i+4} \circ P_i^{-1}(X_i)$$
$$= \widehat{X} \oplus A_{i+4}^{-1} \cdot a''_{i+4} \oplus P_{i+4}^{-1} \circ P'_{i+4} \circ P_i^{-1}(X_i),$$

which is equal to $\widehat{X} \oplus \varepsilon$ when $X_i = 0$.

As a consequence, the collision function denoted by $f(x_{i,0}, x_{i,1}, x_{i,2}, x_{i,3}, X_i)$, or simply $f(x_{i,0}, x_{i,1}, x_{i,2}, x_{i,3})$ under $X_i = 0$, is

$$f(x_{i,0}, x_{i,1}, x_{i,2}, x_{i,3}) = \begin{bmatrix} E_{i+1,0} \\ E_{i+1,1} \\ E_{i+1,2} \\ E_{i+1,3} \end{bmatrix} \circ \oplus_\varepsilon \circ L \circ \begin{bmatrix} \mathbf{S} \circ \oplus_{rk_{i,0}} \circ E_{i,0}^{-1}(x_{i,0}) \\ \mathbf{S} \circ \oplus_{rk_{i,1}} \circ E_{i,1}^{-1}(x_{i,1}) \\ \mathbf{S} \circ \oplus_{rk_{i,2}} \circ E_{i,2}^{-1}(x_{i,2}) \\ \mathbf{S} \circ \oplus_{rk_{i,3}} \circ E_{i,3}^{-1}(x_{i,3}) \end{bmatrix}.$$

Furthermore, we express f as a concatenation of four byte functions f_0, f_1, f_2 and f_3:

$$f(x_{i,0}, x_{i,1}, x_{i,2}, x_{i,3}) = (f_0(x_{i,0}, x_{i,1}, x_{i,2}, x_{i,3}), f_1(x_{i,0}, x_{i,1}, x_{i,2}, x_{i,3}),$$
$$f_2(x_{i,0}, x_{i,1}, x_{i,2}, x_{i,3}), f_3(x_{i,0}, x_{i,1}, x_{i,2}, x_{i,3}));$$

and define $\mathbf{S}_j$ function as

$$\mathbf{S}_j(\cdot) = \mathbf{S} \circ \oplus_{rk_{i,j}} \circ E_{i,j}^{-1}(\cdot) = \mathbf{S}(rk_{i,j} \oplus E_{i,j}^{-1}(\cdot)), \quad j = 0, 1, 2, 3. \quad (4)$$

3.2.2   Recovering $\mathbf{S}_j$ Functions

Next we try to recover the functions $\mathbf{S}_0$, $\mathbf{S}_1$, $\mathbf{S}_2$ and $\mathbf{S}_3$ by exploiting collisions on the output of the functions f_j. We first use the following collision to recover $\mathbf{S}_0$ and $\mathbf{S}_1$:

$$f_0(\alpha, 0, 0, 0) = f_0(0, \beta, 0, 0), \tag{5}$$

where $\alpha, \beta \in \mathrm{GF}(2^8)$. By the linear transformation $\mathbf{L}$ in Eq. (3), Eq. (5) immediately means the following equation:

$$E_{i+1,0} \circ \oplus_{\varepsilon_0} \circ \left(B_1 \circ \mathbf{S}_0(\alpha) \oplus B_2 \circ \mathbf{S}_1(0) \oplus B_2 \circ \mathbf{S}_2(0) \oplus B_3 \circ \mathbf{S}_3(0)\right)$$
$$= E_{i+1,0} \circ \oplus_{\varepsilon_0} \circ \left(B_1 \circ \mathbf{S}_0(0) \oplus B_2 \circ \mathbf{S}_1(\beta) \oplus B_2 \circ \mathbf{S}_2(0) \oplus B_3 \circ \mathbf{S}_3(0)\right),$$

where ε_0 is the corresponding byte of the constant ε. Since $E_{i+1,0}$ is a bijection, we have the following equation:

$$B_1 \circ \mathbf{S}_0(\alpha) \oplus B_2 \circ \mathbf{S}_1(0) = B_1 \circ \mathbf{S}_0(0) \oplus B_2 \circ \mathbf{S}_1(\beta).$$

For convenience, define $u_m = \mathbf{S}_0(m)$ and $v_m = \mathbf{S}_1(m)$, then we have

$$B_1 \circ (u_0 \oplus u_\alpha) = B_2 \circ (v_0 \oplus v_\beta). \tag{6}$$

Since $\alpha \mapsto f_0(\alpha, 0, 0, 0)$ and $\beta \mapsto f_0(0, \beta, 0, 0)$ are bijections, we can find 256 collisions. After removing $(\alpha, \beta) = (0, 0)$, we get 255 pairs (α, β) satisfying Eq. (5), each providing an equation of the form of Eq. (6). In the same way, we use other f_j functions ($j \in \{1, 2, 3\}$) to generate similar equations with different coefficients in $\{B_1, B_2, B_3\}$. Finally, we get 4×255 linear equations with all 512 unknowns, as follows:

$$\begin{cases} B_1 \circ (u_0 \oplus u_\alpha) = B_2 \circ (v_0 \oplus v_\beta); \\ B_2 \circ (u_0 \oplus u_\alpha) = B_3 \circ (v_0 \oplus v_\beta); \\ B_3 \circ (u_0 \oplus u_\alpha) = B_1 \circ (v_0 \oplus v_\beta); \\ B_2 \circ (u_0 \oplus u_\alpha) = B_2 \circ (v_0 \oplus v_\beta). \end{cases} \tag{7}$$

Define $u'_m = u_0 \oplus u_m$ and $v'_m = v_0 \oplus v_m$, with $m \in \{1, 2, \ldots, 255\}$, so that the number of unknowns is reduced to $2 \times 255 = 510$. Thus, Eq. (6) can be rewritten as

$$B_1 \circ u'_\alpha = B_2 \circ v'_\beta,$$

meaning that the linear system of Eq. (7) can be represented with 510 unknowns as

$$\begin{cases} B_1 \circ u'_\alpha = B_2 \circ v'_\beta, \\ B_2 \circ u'_\alpha = B_3 \circ v'_\beta, \\ B_3 \circ u'_\alpha = B_1 \circ v'_\beta, \\ B_2 \circ u'_\alpha = B_2 \circ v'_\beta. \end{cases}$$

The 4×255 equations yield a linear system of rank 509; and in such a linear equation system, all other unknowns can be expressed as a function of one of them, say u'_1, that is, there exist coefficients a_i and b_i such that $u'_m = a_m \cdot u'_1$ and $v'_m = b_m \cdot u'_1$. That is,

$$u_m = a_m \cdot (u_0 \oplus u_1) \oplus u_0,$$
$$v_m = b_m \cdot (u_0 \oplus u_1) \oplus v_0. \tag{8}$$

Next we can recover the $\mathbf{S}_0$ function by exhaustive search on the pair (u_0, u_1), and at last we use the following equation from the definition of the $\mathbf{S}_0$ function to verify whether the obtained $\mathbf{S}_0$ function is right or not:

$$\mathbf{S}^{-1} \circ \mathbf{S}(\cdot) = rk_{i,0} \oplus E_{i,0}^{-1}(\cdot).$$

Since $E_{i,0}^{-1}$ is an 8×8-bit invertible affine transformation, the above function has an algebraic degree of at most 1. For a wrong pair (u_0, u_1), a wrong candidate function $\mathbf{S}_0^*$ would be got which is an affine equivalent to $\mathbf{S}_0$, namely there exists an 8×8-bit matrix a and an 8-bit vector b such that $\mathbf{S}_0^*(\cdot) = a \cdot \mathbf{S}_0(\cdot) \oplus b$, with $a \neq 0$ and $(a, b) \neq (0, 1)$. The function $\mathbf{S}^{-1} \circ \mathbf{S}_0^*(\cdot)$ satisfies

$$\mathbf{S}^{-1} \circ \mathbf{S}_0^*(\cdot) = \mathbf{S}^{-1}\big(a \cdot \mathbf{S}_0\big(rk_{i,0} \oplus E_{i,0}^{-1}(\cdot)\big) \oplus b\big).$$

In this case, $\mathbf{S}^{-1} \circ \mathbf{S}_0^*(\cdot)$ has an algebraic degree greater than 1 with an overwhelming probability. More specifically, we set the function $\hat{g}(\cdot) = \mathbf{S}^{-1} \circ \mathbf{S}^*(\cdot)$, used Lai's higher-order derivative concept [17] to calculate the 1st-order derivative of $\hat{g}$, and finally ran ten thousand tests without obtaining a function with an algebraic degree of 1 or less. For instance, the 1st-order derivative $\hat{\varphi}$ at (01) is set to

$$\hat{\varphi}(x) = \hat{g}(x \oplus 01) \oplus \hat{g}(x),$$

and we verify $\bigoplus_{i=0}^{255} \hat{\varphi}(x_i) = 0$ with 2^7 inputs of x, since $\hat{\varphi}(x) = \hat{\varphi}(x \oplus 01)$. For each wrong pair, the probability of getting $\bigoplus_{i=0}^{255} \hat{\varphi}(x_i) = 0$ is roughly 2^{-8}, so wrong guesses can be quickly removed.

After recovering $\mathbf{S}_0$, we can use Eq. (8) to recover $\mathbf{S}_1$ by exhaustive search on v_0, and similarly recover $\mathbf{S}_2$ and $\mathbf{S}_3$ with other equations finally.

3.2.3   Recovering the Linear Parts of Output Encodings $E_{i+1,j}$

After the $\mathbf{S}_j$ functions have been recovered $(j = 0, 1, 2, 3)$, however it is not as easy to recover the output encodings $E_{i+1,j}$ as Lepoint et al.'s attack on Chow et al.'s white-box AES implementation, because of the existence of the unknown constant ε, which is partially due to the different structures of Feistel and SPN ciphers and the design of Yao and Chen's white-box SM4 implementation. Anyway, we find a trick to recover the linear part of the output encodings $E_{i+1,j}$. Since $E_{i+1,j}$ is an invertible affine transformation, we write $E_{i+1,j}(\cdot) = C_{i+1,j}(\cdot) \oplus c_{i+1,j}$, where $C_{i+1,j}$ is a general invertible 32×32-bit matrix and $c_{i+1,j}$ is an 8-bit constant.

Given a 32-bit input $(x_{i,0}, x_{i,1}, x_{i,2}, x_{i,3})$ to the f collision function, denote the original 32-bit value immediately after the $\widehat{\mathbf{L}}$ operation as follows:

$$Y = \begin{bmatrix} Y_0 & Y_1 & Y_2 & Y_3 \end{bmatrix}^T = \mathbf{L}_0 \circ \mathbf{S}_0(x_{i,0}) \oplus \mathbf{L}_1 \circ \mathbf{S}_1(x_{i,1}) \oplus \mathbf{L}_2 \circ \mathbf{S}_2(x_{i,2}) \oplus \mathbf{L}_3 \circ \mathbf{S}_3(x_{i,3}).$$

As $\mathbf{L}$ is public and we have recovered $\mathbf{S}_j$ above $(j = 0,1,2,3)$, we can compute Y_j. The output of the f collision function is

$$f = \begin{bmatrix} f_0 & f_1 & f_2 & f_3 \end{bmatrix}^T = \begin{bmatrix} E_{i+1,0}(Y_0 \oplus \varepsilon_0) \\ E_{i+1,1}(Y_1 \oplus \varepsilon_1) \\ E_{i+1,2}(Y_2 \oplus \varepsilon_2) \\ E_{i+1,3}(Y_3 \oplus \varepsilon_3) \end{bmatrix},$$

where $(\varepsilon_0, \varepsilon_1, \varepsilon_2, \varepsilon_3) = \varepsilon$.

Subsequently, to recover $E_{i+1,j}$, we need to know the 8-bit unknown constant ε_j. A straightforward way is to try by exhaustive search, which would cause an additional time complexity of 2^8. However, we can recover the linear part $C_{i+1,j}$ at ease, as follows.

First, we choose the 32-bit input $X0 = (\hat{x}_{i,0}, \hat{x}_{i,1}, \hat{x}_{i,2}, \hat{x}_{i,3})$ to the f collision function, so that the original 32-bit value immediately after the $\mathbf{L}$ operation is 0; this can be done easily by choosing $X0$ such that $(\mathbf{S}_0(\hat{x}_{i,0}), \mathbf{S}_1(\hat{x}_{i,1}), \mathbf{S}_2(\hat{x}_{i,2}), \mathbf{S}_3(\hat{x}_{i,3})) = \mathbf{L}^{-1}(0) = 0$. Thus, its corresponding output under the f_0 collision function is

$$f_0(X0) = C_{i+1,0}(\varepsilon_0) \oplus c_{i+1,0}. \tag{9}$$

Next, we select an arbitrary 32-bit input $X = (x_{i,0}, x_{i,1}, x_{i,2}, x_{i,3})$ to the f collision function, and its corresponding output under the f_0 collision function is

$$f_0(X) = E_{i+1,0}(\widehat{X} \oplus \varepsilon) = C_{i+1,0}(\widehat{X}) \oplus C_{i+1,0}(\varepsilon_0) \oplus c_{i+1,0}, \tag{10}$$

where $\widehat{X} = \mathbf{L}(\mathbf{S}_0(x_{i,0}), \mathbf{S}_1(x_{i,1}), \mathbf{S}_2(x_{i,2}), \mathbf{S}_3(x_{i,3}))$, which denotes the original 32-bit value immediately after the $\mathbf{L}$ operation under the input X.

At last, XORing Eq. (9) and Eq. (10), we get $f_0(X) \oplus f_0(X0) = C_{i+1,0}(\widehat{X})$. As a consequence, we can recover the linear part $C_{i+1,0}$ of the output encodings $E_{i+1,j}$. The linear parts of other output encodings $E_{i+1,j}$ can be recovered similarly.

3.2.4   Recovering Round Key rk_i

We first show how to recover the key byte $rk_{i,j}$. According to Eq. (4) and Eq. (5), we define the function g as follows:

$$g = f_0\big(E_{i,0}^{-1}(\mathbf{S}^{-1}(\cdot) \oplus rk_{i,0}), 0, 0, 0\big),$$

which satisfies

$$g(x) = E_{i+1,0}(B_1 \circ x \oplus c) = C_{i+1,0}(B_1 \circ x \oplus c) \oplus c_{i+1,0},$$

where $c = B_2 \circ \mathbf{S}_1(0) \oplus B_2 \circ \mathbf{S}_2(0) \oplus B_3 \circ \mathbf{S}_3(0) \oplus \varepsilon_0$, and $C_{i+1,0}(\varepsilon_0) \oplus c_{i+1,0}$ has been calculated in Eq. (9). Because of the 8×8-bit invertible affine transformation

$E_{i+1,0}$, the function g has algebraic degree at most 1. For a wrong guess $\hat{rk}_{i,0} \neq rk_{i,0}$, the function $\hat{g}$ is defined as:

$$\hat{g}(x) = f_0\big(E_{i,0}^{-1}(\mathbf{S}^{-1}(x) \oplus \hat{rk}_{i,0}), 0, 0, 0\big)$$
$$= E_{i+1,0}\big(B_1 \cdot \mathbf{S}(\mathbf{S}^{-1}(x) \oplus \hat{rk}_{i,0} \oplus rk_{i,0}) \oplus c\big).$$

In this case, with a similar test, $\hat{g}$ has an algebraic degree of more than 1 with an overwhelming probability. We extract $rk_{i,0}$ by exhaustive search, that is, we verify $\bigoplus_{i=0}^{255} \hat{\varphi}(x_i) = 0$ for each guess $\hat{rk}_{i,0}$, where $\hat{\varphi}(x) = \hat{g}(x \oplus 01) \oplus \hat{g}(x)$. For a wrong guess $\hat{rk}_{i,0}$, $\bigoplus_{i=0}^{255} \hat{\varphi}(x_i) = 0$ roughly occurs with probability 2^{-8}, so wrong guesses can be quickly removed.

The other three key bytes $rk_{i,1}$, $rk_{i,2}$ and $rk_{i,3}$ can be similarly recovered by changing the definition of the function g. For instance, we define $g = f_j\big(0, E_{i,1}^{-1}(\mathbf{S}^{-1}(\cdot) \oplus rk_{i,1}), 0, 0\big)$ to retrieve the key byte $rk_{i,1}$. Finally, the full sectet key of SM4 can be easily recovered by inverting the key schedule scheme from the second round.

3.2.5   Time Complexity

In the phase of recovering $\mathbf{S}_0$, there are 2^{16} candidates (u_0, u_1) for exhaustive search, and to verify $\bigoplus_{i=0}^{255} \hat{\varphi}(x_i) = 0$ we need to calculate $\hat{\varphi}(x_i)$ for 2^7 inputs. For a wrong guess (u_0, u_1), the probability of $\bigoplus_{i=0}^{255} \hat{\varphi}(x_i) = 0$ is 2^{-8} roughly. Thus, the expected value of the test is $1 + 1/256 + \cdots + 1/(256^{15}) \leq 1.004$. The time complexity of recovering $\mathbf{S}_0$ is hence of $2^{16} \cdot 1.004 \cdot 2^7 \approx 2^{23}$.

We recover $\mathbf{S}_1$, $\mathbf{S}_2$ and $\mathbf{S}_3$ by exhaustive search on v_0 and produce the complexity of $3 \cdot (2^8 \cdot 1.004 \cdot 2^7) \approx 3 \cdot 2^{15}$. Thus, the total complexity of the recovery of $\mathbf{S}_j$ is $2^{23} + 3 \cdot 2^{15} \approx 2^{23}$.

The time complexity for recovering the linear part of output encoding $E_{i+1,j}$ is negligible. We divide the 32-bit round key into four bytes. The time complexity of recovering one key byte is rough $2^8 \cdot 1.004 \cdot 2^7 \approx 2^{15}$, so the complexity of recovering a round key is $4 \cdot 2^{15} = 2^{17}$. To sum up, the total time complexity of recovering one round key is $2^{23} + 2^{17} \approx 2^{23}$.

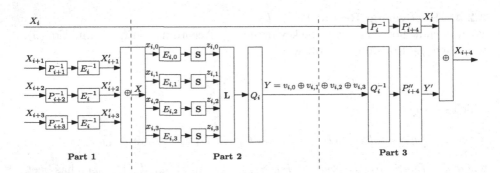

Fig. 5. An encryption round of Xiao and Lai's white-box SM4 implementation

4 Collision-Based Attack on Xiao and Lai's White-Box SM4 Implementation

Xiao and Lai's white-box SM4 implementation [34] is similar to Yao and Chen's white-box SM4 implementation at a high level, except that there is no state expansion to the S-box layer and thus the original $\mathbf{L}$ operation is used. Figure 5 depicts an encryption round of Xiao and Lai's white-box SM4 implementation, where Q_i is a general invertible affine output encoding.

Therefore, we can apply the above collision-based attack to Xiao and Lai's white-box SM4 implementation in the same way, and the attack's time complexity is also around 2^{23} for recovering a round key.

5 Concluding Remarks

The SM4 block cipher is a Chinese national standard and an ISO international standard, first released as SMS4 in 2006. In 2009 Xiao and Lai presented the first white-box SM4 implementation with the best currently published attack complexity of about 2^{32} using affine equivalence technique, and in 2020 Yao and Chen presented a new white-box SM4 implementation with the best self-estimated attack complexity of about 2^{51} among a variety of attack techniques. In this paper, we have presented collision-based attacks on Yao and Chen's and Xiao and Lai's white-box SM4 implementations with a time complexity of about 2^{23}, and thus their security is much lower than previously published and their realistic significance is reduced. Our attacks indicate to some degree that a white-box SM4 implementation following a similar protection line is hardly secure generally as long as the inputs to the original S-box layers of two consecutive rounds can be known, and thus we have to explore a different design way.

Acknowledgement. This work was supported by National Natural Science Foundation of China (No. 61972018) and Guangxi Key Laboratory of Cryptography and Information Security (No. GCIS202102). Jiqiang Lu is Qianjiang Special Expert of Hangzhou.

References

1. Baek, C.H., Cheon, J.H., Hong, H.: White-Box AES implementation revisited. J. Commun. Netw. **18**(3), 273–287 (2016)
2. Bai, K., Wu, C.: A secure White-Box SM4 implementation. Secur. Commun. Netw. **9**(10), 996–1006 (2016)
3. Bai, K., Wu, C., Zhang, Z.: Protect White-Box AES to resist table composition attacks. IET Inf. Secur. **12**(4), 305–313 (2018)
4. Barkan, E., Biham, E.: In how many ways can you write Rijndael? In: Zheng, Y. (ed.) ASIACRYPT 2002. LNCS, vol. 2501, pp. 160–175. Springer, Heidelberg (2002). https://doi.org/10.1007/3-540-36178-2_10

5. Billet, O., Gilbert, H., Ech-Chatbi, C.: Cryptanalysis of a White Box AES implementation. In: Handschuh, H., Hasan, M.A. (eds.) SAC 2004. LNCS, vol. 3357, pp. 227–240. Springer, Heidelberg (2004). https://doi.org/10.1007/978-3-540-30564-4_16

6. Biryukov, A., De Cannière, C., Braeken, A., Preneel, B.: A Toolbox for cryptanalysis: linear and affine equivalence algorithms. In: Biham, E. (ed.) EUROCRYPT 2003. LNCS, vol. 2656, pp. 33–50. Springer, Heidelberg (2003). https://doi.org/10.1007/3-540-39200-9_3

7. Bringer, J., Chabanne, H., Dottax, E.: White box cryptography: another attempt. IACR Cryptol. ePrint Arch. **2006**, 468 (2006)

8. Chow, S., Eisen, P., Johnson, H., Van Oorschot, P.C.: White-Box cryptography and an AES implementation. In: Nyberg, K., Heys, H. (eds.) SAC 2002. LNCS, vol. 2595, pp. 250–270. Springer, Heidelberg (2003). https://doi.org/10.1007/3-540-36492-7_17

9. Chow, S., Eisen, P., Johnson, H., van Oorschot, P.C.: A White-Box DES implementation for DRM applications. In: Feigenbaum, J. (ed.) DRM 2002. LNCS, vol. 2696, pp. 1–15. Springer, Heidelberg (2003). https://doi.org/10.1007/978-3-540-44993-5_1

10. Derbez, P., Fouque, P., Lambin, B., Minaud, B.: On recovering affine encodings in white-box implementations. IACR Trans. Cryptogr. Hard. Embed. Syst. **2018**(3), 121–149 (2018)

11. Office of State Commercial Cryptography Administration of China: The SMS4 Block Cipher (2006). (in Chinese)

12. Standardization Administration of China: Information Security Technology - SM4 Block Cipher Algorithm (2016)

13. International Standardization of Organization (ISO), International Standard - ISO/IEC 18033–3:2010/AMD1:2021, Amendment 1 - Information technology - Security techniques - Encryption algorithms - Part 3: Block ciphers - SM4 (2021)

14. Goubin, L., Masereel, J.-M., Quisquater, M.: Cryptanalysis of White Box DES implementations. In: Adams, C., Miri, A., Wiener, M. (eds.) SAC 2007. LNCS, vol. 4876, pp. 278–295. Springer, Heidelberg (2007). https://doi.org/10.1007/978-3-540-77360-3_18

15. Jacob, M., Boneh, D., Felten, E.: Attacking an obfuscated cipher by injecting faults. In: Feigenbaum, J. (ed.) DRM 2002. LNCS, vol. 2696, pp. 16–31. Springer, Heidelberg (2003). https://doi.org/10.1007/978-3-540-44993-5_2

16. Karroumi, M.: Protecting White-Box AES with dual ciphers. In: Rhee, K.-H., Nyang, D.H. (eds.) ICISC 2010. LNCS, vol. 6829, pp. 278–291. Springer, Heidelberg (2011). https://doi.org/10.1007/978-3-642-24209-0_19

17. Lai, X.: Higher order derivatives and differential cryptanalysis. In: Blahut, R.E., Costello, D.J., Maurer, U., Mittelholzer, T. (eds.) Communications and Cryptography. The Springer International Series in Engineering and Computer Science (Communications and Information Theory), vol. 276, pp. 227–233. Springer, Boston, MA (1994). https://doi.org/10.1007/978-1-4615-2694-0_23

18. Lepoint, T., Rivain, M., De Mulder, Y., Roelse, P., Preneel, B.: Two attacks on a White-Box AES implementation. In: Lange, T., Lauter, K., Lisoněk, P. (eds.) SAC 2013. LNCS, vol. 8282, pp. 265–285. Springer, Heidelberg (2014). https://doi.org/10.1007/978-3-662-43414-7_14

19. Lin, T., Lai, X.: Efficient attack to White-Box SMS4 implementation. J. Softw. **24**(9), 2238–2249 (2013).(in Chinese)

20. Lin, T., Yan, H., Lai, X., Zhong, Y., Jia, Y.: Security evaluation and improvement of a White-Box SMS4 implementation based on affine equivalence algorithm. Comput. J. **61**(12), 1783–1790 (2018)
21. Link, H.E., Neumann, W.D.: Clarifying obfuscation: improving the security of White-Box DES. In: International Symposium on Information Technology: Coding and Computing, pp. 679–684. IEEE (2005)
22. Luo, R., Lai, X., You, R.: A new attempt of White-box AES implementation. In: Proceedings of IEEE International Conference on Security, pp. 423–429. IEEE (2014)
23. Michiels, W., Gorissen, P., Hollmann, H.D.L.: Cryptanalysis of a generic class of White-Box implementations. In: Avanzi, R.M., Keliher, L., Sica, F. (eds.) SAC 2008. LNCS, vol. 5381, pp. 414–428. Springer, Heidelberg (2009). https://doi.org/10.1007/978-3-642-04159-4_27
24. De Mulder, Y., Roelse, P., Preneel, B.: Cryptanalysis of the Xiao – Lai White-Box AES implementation. In: Knudsen, L.R., Wu, H. (eds.) SAC 2012. LNCS, vol. 7707, pp. 34–49. Springer, Heidelberg (2013). https://doi.org/10.1007/978-3-642-35999-6_3
25. De Mulder, Y., Wyseur, B., Preneel, B.: Cryptanalysis of a perturbated White-Box AES implementation. In: Gong, G., Gupta, K.C. (eds.) INDOCRYPT 2010. LNCS, vol. 6498, pp. 292–310. Springer, Heidelberg (2010). https://doi.org/10.1007/978-3-642-17401-8_21
26. National Institute of Standards and Technology (NIST): Advanced Encryption Standard (AES), FIPS-197 (2001)
27. National Bureau of Standards (NBS): Data Encryption Standard (DES), FIPS-46 (1977)
28. Shi, Y., Wei, W., He, Z.: A lightweight white-box symmetric encryption algorithm against node capture for WSNs. Sensors **15**(5), 11928–11952 (2015)
29. Tolhuizen, L.: Improved cryptanalysis of an AES implementation. In: Proceedings of the 33rd WIC Symposium on Information Theory in the Benelux, pp. 68–71 (2012)
30. Wang, R.: Security analysis of lightweight white-box cryptography algorithm . Master's thesis, Beihang University (2021). (in Chinese)
31. Wang, R., Guo, H., Lu, J., Liu, J.: Cryptanalysis of a White-Box SM4 implementation based on collision attack. IET Inf. Secur. (to appear)
32. Wyseur, B., Michiels, W., Gorissen, P., Preneel, B.: Cryptanalysis of White-Box DES implementations with arbitrary external encodings. In: Adams, C., Miri, A., Wiener, M. (eds.) SAC 2007. LNCS, vol. 4876, pp. 264–277. Springer, Heidelberg (2007). https://doi.org/10.1007/978-3-540-77360-3_17
33. Xiao, Y., Lai, X.: A secure implementation of white-box AES. In: Proceedings of the Second International Conference on Computer Science and its Applications, pp. 1–6. IEEE (2009)
34. Xiao, Y., Lai, X.: White-Box cryptography and a SMS4 implementation . In: Proceedings of 2009 Annual Conference of the Chinese Association of Cryptologic Research, pp. 24–34 (2009). (in Chinese)
35. Yao, S., Chen, J.: A new method for White-Box implementation of SM4 algorithm (in Chinese). J. Cryptol. Res. **7**(3), 358–374 (2020)

A Non-interactive Multi-user Protocol for Private Authorised Query Processing on Genomic Data

Sara Jafarbeiki[1,2]([✉]), Amin Sakzad[1], Shabnam Kasra Kermanshahi[3],
Ron Steinfeld[1], Raj Gaire[2], and Shangqi Lai[1]

[1] Monash University, Melbourne, Australia
sara.jafarbeiki@monash.edu
[2] CSIRO, Canberra, Australia
[3] RMIT University, Melbourne, Australia

Abstract. This paper introduces a new non-interactive multi-user model for secure and efficient query executions on outsourced genomic data to the cloud. We instantiate this model by leveraging searchable symmetric encryption (SSE). This new construction supports various types of queries (i.e., count, Boolean, k'-out-of-k match queries) on encrypted genomic data, and we call it NIMUPrivGenDB. Most importantly, it eliminates the need for the data owner and/or trusted entity to be online and avoids per-query interaction between the data owner and/or trusted entity and users. This is achieved by introducing a new mechanism called QUAuth to enforce access control based on the types of queries (Q) each user (U) is authorised (Auth) to submit. To the best of our knowledge, this is the first paper proposing an authorisation mechanism based on queries on genomic data. Moreover, QUAuth offers user management by supporting authorisation updates. We proved that our construction achieves strong security against malicious behaviour among authorised users, where a malicious user pretends to be other users by using others' unique IDs, and colluding attacks among these users are also considered. Finally, our proposed protocol's implementation and evaluation demonstrate its practicality and efficiency in terms of search computational complexity and storage cost.

Keywords: Genomic data privacy · Searchable encryption · Secure outsourcing · Cloud security · Non-interactive · Multi-user · Authorisation

1 Introduction

The rapid improvements in the generation and availability of genomic data have had an influence on related scientific studies. These massive genomic datasets aid our understanding of the connection between many of the diseases and genes. The most prevalent form of genetic variation is single nucleotide polymorphisms

© Springer Nature Switzerland AG 2021
J. K. Liu et al. (Eds.): ISC 2021, LNCS 13118, pp. 70–94, 2021.
https://doi.org/10.1007/978-3-030-91356-4_5

(SNPs), and many genetic studies include finding interactions between SNPs and traits or diseases (phenotypes). Genomic data are highly sensitive, notably, because they are irrevocable and have stigmatising implications for both individuals and their families [1].

Various types of queries on a genomic dataset can help users of a genome system providing search functionalities, e.g., count query, Boolean query, k'-out-of-k matches query [2–5]. These users are normally analysts to conduct research or clinicians to get information of a patient. Given the multiple users involved in such a system to do analysis or provide care, the concern of who retrieves what information has to be considered with subtlety. For instance, clinicians are allowed to retrieve information of a particular person as their patient, which is considered as the primary purpose of genomic data collection. However, analysts are not allowed to get the data of particular records for research, which can be identified unless an exception applies [6–8].

Cloud computing services provide a promising way to store vast volumes of data and delivers great advantages to consumers. Undoubtedly, large-scale genomic data storage and query processing would receive cost and speed benefit from using cloud computing infrastructures. However, placing sensitive genomic dataset in a public cloud system without implementing any cybersecurity measures raises privacy and security concerns [9,10].

Different cryptographic solutions have been used to provide confidentiality and secure query executions on genomic data [2–5,11–14]. For a detailed comparison on what features each of these schemes bring to the table, please see Table 1. Interactive access control mechanism causes delays and query submission dependency on data owner/trusted entity. Other works [15,16] gave authorisation mechanisms for different purposes such as allowing authorised queries of a list of specific SNPs or computing weighted average test over SNPs stored on data owner's device. A non-interactive authorisation mechanism based on submitted queries has not been studied yet. As extra merit to non-interactivity, updating a user's search permission based on types of queries without affecting other users has not been investigated. These schemes, while supporting various types of queries on genomic data, either do not provide an access control mechanism or require data owner and/or trusted entity to interactively control the access of the system.

A naive solution would use different servers for different categories of users, e.g., clinicians would be allowed to submit their queries to server 1, analysts would be allowed to execute queries using server 2 and so on. However, such naive solution would increase the storage cost and initialisation computational cost by approximately a factor of the number of types of users. Furthermore, only with non-colluding servers' assumption will this simplistic approach be seen as a model that can fulfill authorisation requirements based on submitted queries. Otherwise, if servers collude, different users can submit queries to different servers and authorisation based on types of queries will not take place. Moreover, this naive solution does not support/offer authorisation update functionality (see Table 1).

Table 1. Comparison of existing schemes for query executions on genomic data

Scheme	Method		Functionality		Authorisation		Storage cost for outsourced data
	Primitive	Solution	Dataset	Queries	Yes/No	Non/Interactive	
[15]	Asymmetric	Software	SNP	N/A	Yes (Weights)	Interactive	N/A
[16]	Asymmetric	Software	SNP	N/A	Yes (Functions)	Interactive	N/A
[11]	Asymmetric	Software	SNP	C	No	N/A	$r(4xb)$
[12]	Symmetric	Hybrid	SNP, PH	C	No	N/A	$rx\ell_E$
[13]	Asymmetric	Hybrid	SNP, PH	C	No	N/A	$3b(3^x - 1)$
[2]	Asymmetric	Software	SNP, PH$^+$	C	No	N/A	$1.5(3^x - 1)(m + 2b)$ **
[3]	Asymmetric	Software	SNP, PH$^+$, M	C	No	N/A	$1.5(3^x - 1)(m + 4b)$ **
[4]	Asymmetric	Software	SNP, PH	C, top k	No	N/A	$2rx + 2rb$
[5]	Asymmetric	Software	SNP	C, N, k'	No	N/A	$r(8xb)$
[14]	Symmetric	Software	SNP, PH$^+$, M	C, N, k', B	Yes (Queries)	Interactive	$rx(\ell_E + \ell_P) + m$
Naive solution	Symmetric	Software	SNP, PH$^+$, M	C, N, k', B	Yes (Queries)	Non-Interactive	$urx(\ell_E + \ell_P) + um$
NIMUPrivGenDB	Symmetric	Software	SNP, PH$^+$, M	C, N, k', B	Yes† (Queries)	Non-Interactive	$rx(\ell_E + \ell_P) + m + q|\mathcal{U}|(\ell_F)$

Notations: PH: Phenotype; M: Metadata; C: Count; N: Negation; k': k'-out-of-k match; B: Boolean; x: Number of columns in the original database; r: Number of records in DB; u: Number of categories of users in the system; q: Number of types of supported queries; $|\mathcal{U}|$: Number of all the users of the system; $^+$: Phenotype includes the exact disease/trait, not just positive/negative signs to show whether that record has one particular phenotype or not; b: Public key modulus size in bits; ℓ_p: Size of an element from $\mathbb{Z}_p$ (p is a prime number); ℓ_E: Size of the block of SE; ℓ_F: Size of the output of a Pseudorandom Function (PRF); m: Bloom Filter (BF) size; **: This depends on the distribution of genotypes in the dataset; †: It also supports authorisation update; $- - - -$: Separates the works on top of it as the ones that are not in the exact context of this work (they either do not support different queries, or authorise based on different parameters).

In contrast, an efficient system would allow users to submit queries to a server and receive authorised results back without interacting with intermediate entities and without replicating the database onto multiple servers. The model in [14] utilises searchable symmetric encryption (SSE) influenced by oblivious cross-tags (OXT) protocol in [17], which provides a method for searching encrypted data efficiently and securely. It also supports different types of queries on encrypted genomic data; however, it is an interactive model with a middle trusted entity checking each submitted query.

1.1 Our Contributions

We present a new non-interactive multi-user model, NIMUPrivGenDB, for different query executions (Table 1-Functionality) on genomic data. Our model leverages SSE scheme inspired by OXT scheme of Cash et al. [17] to provide data confidentiality. Motivated by NIMC-SSE-Π_2 in [18], this paper proposes a new authorisation mechanism, QUAuth, to achieve authorised queries submission in a non-interactive fashion. To the best of our knowledge, this is the first paper proposing a non-interactive multi-user model utilising SSE, that controls the users' access based on submitted queries. The proposed model in [18] authorises users based on search keywords whereas QUAuth is based on query types. In addition, QUAuth eliminates per-query authorisation by granting the user a query-authorised private key associated with the types of queries the user is allowed to submit (Table 1-Authorisation)[1]. Therefore, it does not require the online presence of a trusted entity in the query submission process. Moreover, this query-authorised key is also dependent on the user ID, which makes it unique for each user. Hence, the authorisation can be updated and a user management mechanism can take into place to add/revoke each user's access. NIMUPriv-GenDB is also proved to be secure against malicious users that try to forge other users' key using those users' unique ID. Moreover, it is secure against users collusion attack. All the above advantages are achieved without relying on non-colluding servers. This in turn results in enforcing access policy in our model with newly proposed mechanism, QUAuth, without multiplying the storage cost to the number of categories of users (Table 1-Storage cost) as opposed to the navie solution. Furthermore, our experimental evaluations indicates the low communication, computation, and storage costs, which makes NIMUPrivGenDB suitable in practice for real-world applications. It is demonstrated that besides all above-mentioned added functionalities, our protocol's search time complexity is still approximately the same as [14] without sacrificing much storage. It is also approximately 100 and 22 times faster than [2] and [4] for a query with 10 keywords, respectively. Please see Appendix 1 for more details on our technique.

---

[1] We used/tested this model for query processing on genomic data. However, this proposed mechanism may be of independent interest. It can be utilised in other applications where access to the data is essential based on the types of queries.

2   Preliminaries

2.1   Biology Background

Genome is the complete set of genetic information of an organism. The genome is encoded in double-stranded deoxyribonucleic acid (DNA) molecules, which are made up of two long and complementary polymer chains of four basic units called nucleotides, which are represented by the letters A (Adenine), C (Cytosine), G (Guanine), and T (Thymine) in humans and many other species. The human genome consists of approximately 3 billion such letters (base pairs).

Single nucleotide polymorphisms (SNPs) are the most common form of DNA variation, and they occur where a single nucleotide (A, C, G, or T) varies between members of the same species. The majority of SNPs are biallelic, with only two possible variants (alleles) observed. The set of specific alleles carried by an individual is called their genotype. Together, SNPs account for a large proportion of the genetic variation underlying many human traits such as height and predisposition to disease [19,20].

Phenotype refers to an individual's manifestation of a characteristic or trait. SNP variations are often associated with the trait in question and how individuals develop diseases and respond to drugs, vaccines and other agents. Thus, they help in the discovery of the genetic mechanisms that underlying these characteristics (called phenotypes).

Table 2 illustrates one type of data representation in a database of SNP genotypes for a number of individuals with the individuals' phenotype and other information. The genotypes of each SNP are listed in a single column [2,12].

Table 2. Data representation with SNPs

Record	SNP$_1$	SNP$_2$	SNP$_3$	SNP$_4$	...	Phenotype	Gender	Ethnicity
1	AG	CC	TT	AA	...	Cancer A	Female	White
2	AA	CC	CT	AG	...	Cancer B	Male	White
3	AG	CT	CC	AA	...	Cancer A	Female	Black

Queries on genomic data have different types that can help researchers analyse genomic and phenotype data and find their correlations, or help clinicians in finding patients' genomic related information, such as reaction to a medicine, or their potential diseases. Some different query types on this dataset are[2]:

Count Query: A count query measures the number of records in the database that match the query predicates and assists in the calculation of many statistical algorithms, which is especially useful in genetic association studies. Some statistical tests are performed by computing a series of count queries [21]. The

---

[2] In all of these queries, negation terms can be added as predicates. Other information like gender and ethnicity can also be added as predicates in the query.

total number of SNPs specified in the query predicate is called the query size. Example of count query on dataset in Table 2: Select count from sequences where phenotype = Cancer B AND $SNP_2 \neq CT$ AND $SNP_4 = AG$, Result: 1.

Boolean Query: Apart from finding the number of matches, we may need to extract the data owners' details in order to assist them with treatment or to warn them about a drug allergy or vaccine. As a consequence, clinicians can ask for the IDs or other details of patients with unique genotypes so that they can contact them. This can be accomplished by first extracting the IDs whose genotypes match the question symbols, and then using those IDs to extract any additional information required by the clinician. Of necessity, since this sort of information can be risky, access control has to be considered.

k'-out-of-k Match Query: A threshold (k') is used to decide if at least k' number of the SNPs out of k number of the query predicates' characteristics (except the first predicate) matches for the records. This can be used to retrieve IDs with this threshold matching to check their information like diseases/medications. If this is being checked for one record, the answer is either yes or no. Example: Retrieve IDs from sequences where at least $k' = 2$ matches out of $k = 3$ SNP predicates: phenotype = Cancer A AND $SNP_2 = CC$ AND $SNP_3 = CC$ AND $SNP_4 = AA$, Result: $\{1, 3\}$.

2.2 Cryptographic Background

Frequently used notations in this paper are listed in Table 3. The required cryptographic preliminaries are described as follows.

Pseudorandom Function (PRF). A PRF [22] is a collection of functions in which no efficient algorithm can tell the difference between a randomly chosen PRF function and a random oracle (a function whose outputs are fixed entirely at random) with a substantial advantage.

Let X and Y be sets, $F: \{0,1\}^\lambda \times X \to Y$ be a function, $s \xleftarrow{\$} S$ be the operation of assigning to s an element of S chosen at random, $F(X,Y)$ denote the set of all functions from X to Y, λ denote the security parameter for the PRF, and $negl(\lambda)$ represent a negligible function. We say that F is a pseudorandom function (PRF) if for all efficient adversaries $\mathcal{A}$, $\mathrm{Adv}_{F,\mathcal{A}}^{\mathrm{prf}}(\lambda) = \Pr[\mathcal{A}^{F(K,\cdot)}(1^\lambda) = 1] - \Pr[\mathcal{A}^{f(\cdot)}(1^\lambda) = 1] \leq negl(\lambda)$, where the probability is over the randomness of $\mathcal{A}$, $K \xleftarrow{\$} \{0,1\}^\lambda$, and $f \xleftarrow{\$} \mathrm{Fun}(X,Y)$.

Set-Constrained Pseudorandom Function (SC-PRF). In this subsection, a specific class of constrained pseudorandom functions [18,23,24], called set-constrained PRFs (SC-PRFs) is discussed. (We use the SC-PRF presented and utilised in [18]) Let $F : \mathcal{K} \times \mathcal{X} \to \mathcal{Y}$ be a keyed-function from domain $\mathcal{X}$ to range $\mathcal{Y}$, and key space $\mathcal{K}$. The function F itself can be computed by a deterministic algorithm, which on input $(k, x) \in \mathcal{K} \times \mathcal{X}$ outputs the value $F(k, x) \in \mathcal{Y}$. A PRF $F : \mathcal{K} \times \mathcal{X} \to \mathcal{Y}$ is called set-constrained if there exists an additional key space $\mathcal{K}_c$ and two poly-time algorithms F.Eval and F.Cons:

Table 3. Notations

Notation	Description
ID_O	Data Owner's unique ID
ID'_O	Encrypted Data Owner's ID
$\mathcal{S}$	The set of all SNP indeices s
Θ_s	The set of all genotypes appeared in SNP_s
$\mathsf{G}_s = \{g = s \| \theta_s : \theta_s \in \Theta_s\}$	The set of all keywords g formed by concatanating a SNP index to all genotypes of that particular SNP
G_ρ	The set of all keywords g related to phenotypes
G_Δ	The set of all keywords g related to other information such as gender and ethnicity
$g \in \mathsf{G} = \{\mathsf{G}_s\}_{s \in \mathcal{S}} \cup \mathsf{G}_\rho \cup \mathsf{G}_\Delta$	List of all keywords g in the database
$\mathsf{G}_{\mathsf{ID}_O}$	List of keywords ID_O has, which defines the genotypes, phenotypes and other information related to a particular Data Owner
$\mathsf{MUGDB}(g) = \{\mathsf{ID}_O : g \in \mathsf{G}_{\mathsf{ID}_O}\}$	The set of Data Owner IDs that contain that particular g, which is either genotype or phenotype or information like gender
MUGDB	Multi-User Genotype-Phenotype DataBase
EMUGDB	Encrypted Multi-User Genotype-Phenotype DataBase
γ	Type of a query
Γ	List of the types of queries
$\Gamma_{\mathsf{ID}_{O_i}}$	List of the types of queries ID_{O_i} is allowed to submit
$\mathcal{U}_i$	A unique certificate for i-th user
Enc, Dec	Encryption, Decryption
sterm	The least frequent term among predicates in the query
xterm	Other predicates in the query (except sterm)

-F.Cons (k, S) : on input a function key $k \in \mathcal{K}$ and the description of a set $S \subseteq \mathcal{X}$, it outputs a set-constrained key k_S.

-F.Eval (k_S, x) : on input a constrained key k_S for set $S \subseteq \mathcal{X}$ and an element $x \in S$, it outputs $y \in \mathcal{Y}$. For correctness, it is required that:

$$\mathsf{F.Eval}\,(k_S, x) = \begin{cases} F(k, x), & x \in S \\ \bot, & \text{otherwise.} \end{cases}$$

It is now obvious that the key k_S enables us to evaluate $F(k, x)$ on any $x \in S$ but no other x. Intuitively, it's secure if no poly-time adversary can tell the difference between a totally random string and the PRF value of one point not in the queried subsets. The security is given in Appendix 2.

Searchable Symmetric Encryption (SSE) and Overview of OXT. SSE allows searchable ciphertext and search tokens to be generated by the secret key holder. One notable work in the area of Searchable Encryption is the scheme proposed by Cash et al. [17] called Oblivious Cross Tag (OXT). It supports conjunctive search and general Boolean queries. For single keyword searches, a specific data structure known as tuple-set or TSet is utilised. For multiple keyword searches, an additional dataset called XSet is utilised to see if the documents found for the first keyword also satisfy the remaining query. Even though the search query is of a Boolean type rather than a single keyword, the OXT scheme achieves sublinear search time. The amount of time required is related to the number of documents containing the least common keyword. The OXT scheme syntax consists of EDBSetup, TokenGen, Search, and Retrieve algorithms. In the EDBSetup, it generates the encrypted database (TSet and XSet data structures) using security parameter. In the TokenGen, it generates search tokens based on query predicates. In the Search, it uses the search token to search through the encrypted database and outputs the search results. In the Retrieve, it decrypts the encrypted results output from the search process. Below are the algorithms in more details:

EDB $\leftarrow$ EDBSetup(λ, DB): It first takes the security parameter λ as input and outputs the secret key K = $\{K_X, K_I, K_Z, K_S, K_T\}$, where K_X, K_I, K_Z and K_S, K_T are secret keys for PRF F_p (with range in $\mathbb{Z}_p^*$) and PRF F, respectively. Then, it initialises the TSet T to an empty array indexed by keywords from W and initialises the XSet to an empty set. For each $w \in$ W, it performs as follows: Initialise $\mathbf{t}$ to be an empty list and initialise a counter c to 0. Set $K_e \leftarrow F(K_S, w)$ and for each ind $\in$ DB(w): (i) Set xind $\leftarrow F_p(K_I, \text{ind})$, $z \leftarrow F_p(K_Z, w\|c)$, $y \leftarrow$ xind $\cdot z^{-1}$, and $e \leftarrow$ Enc(K_e, ind). (ii) Append (y, e) to $\mathbf{t}$ and set $c \leftarrow c + 1$. (iii) Set xtag $\leftarrow g^{F_p(K_X, w) \cdot \text{xind}}$ and add xtag to XSet. Then, it sets T[w] $\leftarrow \mathbf{t}$, runs TSet.Setup(T) and outputs TSet. The encrypted database is set as EDB = (TSet, XSet).

Tok $\leftarrow$ TokenGen(K, Q): This algorithm inputs a query Q with included keywords ($\overline{w}$), where $\overline{w} = (\overline{w}_1, \ldots, \overline{w}_n)$, and keys. It then chooses the keyword with lowest-frequency as the sterm and considers the remaining keywords as xterms. Assume $\overline{w}_1$ is the sterm (least frequent keyword). This algorithm generates the search token Tok = (stag, xtoken[1], xtoken[2], $\ldots$, xtoken[n]) as follows: Set stag $\leftarrow$ TSet.GetTag($K_T, \overline{w}_1$). For $c = 1, 2, \ldots$ and until the server sends stop do: (i) For $i = 2, \ldots, n$, set xtoken[c, i] $\leftarrow g^{F_p(K_Z, \overline{w}_1\|c) \cdot F_p(K_X, \overline{w}_i)}$. (ii) Set xtoken[$c$] $\leftarrow$ (xtoken[$c, 2$], $\ldots$, xtoken[c, n]).

Res $\leftarrow$ Search(Tok, EDB): This algorithm first sets $\mathbf{t} \leftarrow$ TSet.Retrieve (TSet, stag). For each (e, y) pairs in $\mathbf{t}$, it tests whether $\forall i = 2, \ldots, n$, such that xtoken[c, i]$^y \in$ XSet. If so, it adds e into Res. When the last tuple in $\mathbf{t}$ is reached, it sends stop to the client and halts, and returns Res as search results.

IND $\leftarrow$ Retrieve(Res, $K_S, \bar{w}_1$): This algorithm creates an empty set IND, then sets $K_e \leftarrow F(K_S, \bar{w}_1)$; and for each e received, computes ind $\leftarrow$ Dec (K_e, e) and puts it in IND.

The TSet instantiation proposed and utilised in OXT scheme is described here, which is a hash table with B buckets of size S each. Each keyword in a database is associated with a list of fixed-length data tuples in a special data structure known as TSet (Each keyword w has a list of ids that have that particular w). It is an inverted index that is used to search for single keywords. A database DB = (ind$_i$, w$_i$) is a list of (id, keyword) pairs. W is a list of all keywords.

TSet.Setup(S): The input to this algorithm is an array S of lists of equal-length bit strings indexed by the elements of W. It outputs a pair TSet, K$_T$. For each w $\in$ W, S[w] is a list of strings and contains one tuple per each document which matches w.

TSet.GetTag(K$_T$, w): The input to this algorithm is K$_T$ and w and it outputs stag that can be used for search (retrieving the documents that match w).

TSet.Retrieve(TSet, stag): This algorithm inputs TSet, stag and outputs a list of strings, t = S[w].

3   Proposed Solution

3.1   System Model Overview

The proposed model consists of different components, including data provider (trustee), data owner, data server (genomic data database), and users (analysts or clinicians). Their roles are discussed below:

Data Owner (O): A data owner is an individual who visits a medical facility (trustee) as a study participant or patient. Therefore, her information is gathered and preserved, and she gives the trustee permission to use her genomic data for potential analysis or care.

Trustee ($\mathcal{T}$): It is a medical facility, that collects genomic data for analysis/care purposes and sends this information in a specific format to the data server. The main tasks of this entity are: (i) encoding gathered data, generating an inverted index, and encrypting it, (ii) managing the cryptographic keys, and (iii) authenticating users and authorising them for submitting different types of queries based on the access list for different categories of users.

Users ($\mathcal{U}$): Analysts who want to analyse/conduct research on genomic data, or physicians who want to learn more about their patients, are the two types of users in this system. They submit specific requests to the data server and wait for the execution results. Different queries are allowed for different users (for example, analysts may run count queries, whereas clinicians may run count/Boolean/k'-out-of-k match queries). Therefore, in our solution, users have to use their query-authorised key, that does not let them process a query that they are not allowed to. The number of types of users and the association of queries to users can change based on the application requirements without changing the model.

Data Server ($\mathcal{D}$): It stores genomic data, phenotypes, and other details that $\mathcal{T}$ provides. $\mathcal{D}$ runs encrypted queries on encrypted data and returns the results.

The system model is depicted in Appendix 3, and the syntax of our proposed non-interactive multi-user searchable encryption is given in Appendix 4.

3.2   Threat Model

Our ultimate aim with the cloud-based genomic data outsourcing solution is that the Data Server ($\mathcal{D}$) to learn nothing about the shared genomic data or the query conducted by the analysts/clinicians. However, in our model and construction, we allow a small well-defined leakage to the server, as in [18], to make the system performance practical. Since the trustee is in charge of index generation and data encryption, we assume it is a trustworthy entity. Users are assumed to be malicious and attempt to perform queries that reveal more information about the database than that which can be revealed by the user's authorised queries. In our proposed model, we assume that $\mathcal{D}$ is honest-but-curious, which means that it follows the protocol honestly and has no dishonest intent to produce an incorrect result. However, $\mathcal{D}$ may attempt to obtain more data than is intended to be extracted during or after the protocol's execution. We assume that $\mathcal{D}$ does not collude with the users, and the users receive the correct keys from $\mathcal{T}$. $\mathcal{T}$ is aware of the types of queries users are allowed to submit, but it has no means to learn the exact keywords searched by the users. Users may collude to submit a new query type or use other user's ID to search.[3]

4   NIMUPrivGenDB Construction

This section provides a detailed construction of NIMUPrivGenDB with four algorithms: Π_{MUG} = (NIMUPrivGenDB.{Initialisation, TokenGeneration, Search, Retrieve}). The idea in our protocol is to generate different QSets for each query that the system supports. For each user of the system, different qtags are generated based on the user unique ID and the query type that particular user is allowed to submit. For example, in Table 4, the first user with id $\mathcal{U}_1$ is allowed to submit queries $\gamma_1, \gamma_2, \gamma_3$. Therefore, a related qtag has been generated dependening on the γ and $\mathcal{U}_1$ in three QSets$_1$, QSets$_2$, and QSets$_3$. However, the second user, $\mathcal{U}_2$ is only allowed to submit γ_2 type query. The number of QSets can change by the number of different queries our model supports. QUAuth mechanism is now defined by introduction of QSets, qtags via **User.Auth** algorithm, and the way the authorisation/search process takes place using qtags.

---

[3] The proposed model in [14] adds a middle entity called vetter to the system model to control the access of users to the system. Our model does not have a trusted middle entity and hence, provide the control on users in a non-interactive way. Moreover, we add user management functionality to our system without the need of per-query interaction with a trusted entity (vetter). In terms of security, we demonstrate that NIMUPrivGenDB does not leak much more information than [14] to the data server and also it is secure against malicious colluding users.

Table 4. Different QSets for different query types.

QSet$_1$		QSet$_2$		QSet$_3$	
qtag$_{\mathcal{U}_1,1}$	$\gamma = 1$	qtag$_{\mathcal{U}_1,2}$	$\gamma = 2$	qtag$_{\mathcal{U}_1,3}$	$\gamma = 3$
qtag$_{\mathcal{U}_4,1}$	$\gamma = 1$	qtag$_{\mathcal{U}_2,2}$	$\gamma = 2$	qtag$_{\mathcal{U}_4,3}$	$\gamma = 3$
...	...	qtag$_{\mathcal{U}_3,2}$	$\gamma = 2$	...	...

We now put forward detailed explanations of our protocol. Let $\hat{\mathsf{F}} : \mathcal{K} \times \mathcal{X} \to \mathcal{Y}$ be a SC-PRF with algorithms $(\hat{\mathsf{F}} \cdot \mathsf{Cons}, \hat{\mathsf{F}} \cdot \mathsf{Eval})$, and assume that the query set $\Gamma = \bigcup_{i=1}^{r} \Gamma_{\mathsf{ID}_{O_i}}$ for ACL $= (\mathsf{ID}_{O_i}, \Gamma_{\mathsf{ID}_{O_i}})_{i=1}^{r}$ is contained in the domain $\mathcal{X}$ of $\hat{\mathsf{F}}$. Then, the phases are described as follows:

1) NIMUPrivGenDB.Initialisation$(\lambda, \mathsf{MUGDB}, \Gamma, \mathsf{ACL}, \mathcal{U})$ This process is illustrated in Algorithm 1. The Trustee $\mathcal{T}$ runs this algorithm. Given security parameter λ and a genotype-phenotype database MUGDB containing genotypes Θ for each SNP$_s$, phenotypes $\in \mathsf{G}_\rho$, other information $\in \mathsf{G}_\Delta$, this algorithm outputs the encrypted database EMUGDB. Furthermore, on input $\Gamma, \mathsf{ACL}, \mathcal{U}$, it generates a key, sk$_{\Gamma_i}$, for each user $\mathcal{U}_i$ of the system using the ACL and based on the queries that $\mathcal{U}_i$ is allowed to submit. This algorithm uses the below sub-algorithms:

MUGeEncode(MUGDB): In this algorithm, $\mathcal{T}$ generates the list of keywords, G_s for genotypes for different SNPs, G_ρ for phenotype column and G_Δ for other columns containing more information or metadata, like gender and ethnicity. It creates G_s by concatenating the index of a SNP to each $\theta_s \in \Theta_s$, $g = s || \theta_s$ for each $g \in \mathsf{G}_s$. For example, considering Table 2, there would be three defined keywords for SNP$_3$, those are: 3CC, 3CT, 3TT.

MUBInv(G, MUGDB): $\mathcal{T}$ generates an inverted index [25] IINX by running this algorithm which inputs the keywords in G and the database MUGDB. The pairs of (g, ID_O) for all the keywords $g \in \mathsf{G} = \{\mathsf{G}_s\}_{s \in \mathcal{S}} \cup \mathsf{G}_\rho \cup \mathsf{G}_\Delta$ is generated. In inverted indexing data structure, a keyword points to the records that contain the considered keyword.

EMUGDB.Setup$(\lambda, \mathsf{IINX}, \mathsf{MUGDB}, \Gamma, \mathcal{U}_i, \mathsf{ACL})$: On input the security parameter λ, generated inverted index IINX, set of different queries Γ, users $\mathcal{U}_i$, related ACL and the database MUGDB, $\mathcal{T}$ executes this algorithm and outputs the encrypted database EMUGDB $= (\mathsf{Inv}_\mathsf{G}, \mathbb{S}_\mathsf{G}, \mathsf{QSet}_j)$ and the set of keys, K. It chooses random key K_S for PRF F and keys $\mathsf{K}_X, \mathsf{K}_I, \mathsf{K}_Z$ for PRF F_p and K_q for set-constrained PRF $\hat{\mathsf{F}}$ and the generator $h \in \mathbb{G}$. Then, it generates the EMUGDB. In more details, for each user $\mathcal{U}_i$, based on the access list, the queries she is allowed to submit are extracted. Then, a qtag$_{\mathcal{U}_i,j}$ dependent on $\mathcal{U}_i$ for each type of query γ_j (computing SC-PRF of concatenation of query type and $\mathcal{U}_i$) is generated and stored in QSet. For each $g \in \mathsf{G}$ it computes value of K_e and then for the c-th $\mathsf{ID}_O \in \mathsf{MUGDB}[g]$, the trustee generates a value y and a ciphertext $\mathsf{ID}'_O \leftarrow \mathsf{Enc}\,(k_e, \mathsf{ID}_O)$, and adds (ID'_O, y) to inv (a list of (ID'_O, y) pairs related to each g). Also, it computes τ_G associated with the keyword/record (g, ID_O), and adds it to an initially empty set $\mathbb{S}_\mathsf{G}$. Then, by using TSet.Setup algorithm, it generates Inv_G and outputs K_T. The EMUGDB is stored in the data server, and the keys, K, are sent to the users to generate tokens for the search.

User.Auth$(\gamma, \text{ACL}, \mathcal{U}_i, \text{K}_q)$: When a legitimate user $\mathcal{U}_i$ is allowed to perform query types $\Gamma_i = \{\gamma_1, \ldots, \gamma_j\}$, the trustee produces a corresponding private key sk_{Γ_i} for this $\mathcal{U}_i$ and each query types, and returns it to the user along with Γ_i (refer to Algorithm 1). This key is used for generating token for the search.

Algorithm 1. NIMUPrivGenDB.Initialisation

NIMUPrivGenDB.Initialisation$(\lambda, \text{MUGDB}, \Gamma, \text{ACL}, \mathcal{U})$

Input : $\lambda, \text{MUGDB}, \Gamma, \text{ACL}, \mathcal{U}$
Output : EMUGDB, K, sk_{Γ_i}
The $\mathcal{T}$rustee performs:
1: G $\leftarrow$ **MUGeEncode**(MUGDB)
2: IINX $\leftarrow$ **MUBInv**(G, MUGDB)
3: (EMUGDB, K, K$_q$) $\leftarrow$ **EMUGDB.Setup** $(\lambda, \text{IINX}, \text{MUGDB}, \Gamma, \mathcal{U}_i, \text{ACL})$
4: $\text{sk}_{\Gamma_i} \leftarrow$ **User.Auth**$(\Gamma, \text{ACL}, \mathcal{U}_i, \text{K}_q)$
5: $\mathcal{T}$rustee outsources EMUGDB to the $\mathcal{D}$.
6: $\mathcal{T}$rustee sends K $= (\text{K}_S, \text{K}_X, \text{K}_I, \text{K}_Z, \text{K}_T), \text{sk}_{\Gamma_i}$ to the $\mathcal{U}$ser $\mathcal{U}_i$.

EMUGDB.Setup$(\lambda, \text{IINX}, \text{MUGDB}, \Gamma, \mathcal{U}_i, \text{ACL})$

Input : $\lambda, \text{IINX}, \text{MUGDB}, \Gamma, \mathcal{U}_i, \text{ACL}$
Output : EMUGDB, K, K$_q$
1: Select keys K$_S$ for PRF F and keys K$_X$, K$_I$, K$_Z$ for PRF F_p and K$_q$ for SC-PRF $\hat{\text{F}}$ using security parameter λ, and $\mathbb{G}$ a group of prime order p and generator h.
2: **for** each $\mathcal{U}_i$ **do**
3:     based on the ACL, extract $\Gamma_{\mathcal{U}_i}$
4:     **for** $\gamma_j \in \Gamma_{\mathcal{U}_i}$ **do**
5:         $\text{qtag}_{\mathcal{U}_i,j} \leftarrow \hat{\text{F}}(\text{K}_q, \gamma_j || \mathcal{U}_i)$
6:         QSet$_j$($\text{qtag}_{\mathcal{U}_i,j}) \leftarrow \gamma_j$
7:     **end for**
8: **end for**
9: Parse MUGDB as (ID_O, g) and $\mathbb{S}_G \leftarrow \{\}$
10: **for** $g \in$ G **do**
11:     Initialise inv $\leftarrow \{\}$; let K$_e \leftarrow F(\text{K}_S, g)$.

12:     **for** $\text{ID}_O \in \text{MUGDB}(g)$ **do**
13:         Set a counter $c \leftarrow 1$
14:         Compute $\text{XID}_O \leftarrow F_p(\text{K}_I, \text{ID}_O)$, $z \leftarrow F_p(\text{K}_Z, g||c); y \leftarrow \text{XID}_O.z^{-1}, \text{ID}'_O \leftarrow \text{Enc}(\text{K}_e, \text{ID}_O)$.
15:         Set $\tau_G \leftarrow h^{F_p(\text{K}_X, g) \cdot \text{XID}_O}$ and $\mathbb{S}_G \leftarrow \mathbb{S}_G \cup \tau_G$
16:         Append (y, ID'_O) to inv and $c \leftarrow c+1$.
17:     **end for**
18:     IINX[g] $\leftarrow$ inv
19: **end for**
20: Set (Inv$_G$, K$_T$) $\leftarrow$ TSet.Setup(IINX)
21: EMUGDB $= (\text{Inv}_G, \mathbb{S}_G, \text{QSet}_j)$ $j = 1, 2, 3$.
22: **return** EMUGDB and K $= (\text{K}_S, \text{K}_X, \text{K}_I, \text{K}_Z, \text{K}_T)$

User.Auth$(\Gamma, \text{ACL}, \mathcal{U}_i, \text{K}_q)$
//based on the access list ACL for each user and type of queries data owner decides for each user, $\mathcal{U}_i$ which can submit different γ_j, ($\Gamma_{\mathcal{U}_i} =$ all γ_j that $\mathcal{U}_i$ can submit):
1: **for** each $\mathcal{U}_i$ of the system **do**
2:     $\Gamma_i \leftarrow \{\}$
3:     **for** each $\gamma_j \in \Gamma_{\mathcal{U}_i}$ **do**
4:         $\gamma_j \leftarrow \gamma_j || \mathcal{U}_i$
5:         $\Gamma_i \leftarrow \Gamma_i \cup \gamma_j$
6:     **end for**
7:     $\text{sk}_{\Gamma_i} \leftarrow \hat{\text{F}}.\text{Cons}(\text{K}_q, \Gamma_i)$ for each $\mathcal{U}_i$
8:     **return** sk_{Γ_i} to user $\mathcal{U}_i$
9: **end for**

---

2) NIMUPrivGenDB.TokenGeneration$(\text{q}, \text{K}, \text{sk}_{\Gamma_i})$: $\mathcal{U}$ runs this algorithm (see Algorithm 2), which takes the query $\text{q}(g_1, \ldots, g_n)$, the key set K, and query-authorised key of the user sk_{Γ_i} as inputs and outputs the search tokens $\text{qtag}_{\mathcal{U}_i,j}$, that is based on the type of the query γ_j and $\mathcal{U}_i$, alongside gToK. Follow the blue and black lines for Boolean/Count queries, and the black and red lines for k'-out-of-k match queries. Before computing tokens, $\mathcal{U}_i$ generates the keywords related to the genotypes for SNPs by using the encoding mechanism used in initialisation phase, and the new query will be generated as $\text{q}(g_1, \ldots, g_n)$. For example, g_i can be cancer B, or Female, or 1AA, or 3CT, or 4AG,... for $i = 1, \ldots, n$.

In particular, $\mathcal{U}$ generates tokens as follows: $\text{qtag}_{\mathcal{U}_i,j}$ is generated based on the query type which is going to be submitted and $\mathcal{U}_i$, using the key sk_{Γ_i}. Then,

---

Algorithm 2. NIMUPrivGenDB.TokenGeneration

Input : $q(g_1, \ldots, g_n), K, sk_{\Gamma_i}$
Output : $qtag_{\mathcal{U}_i,j}$, gToK
//based on the type of query q, $\mathcal{U}$ chooses γ
1: **if** Query=Boolean **then**
2:     $\gamma \leftarrow 1$
3:   **elseif** Query=Count
4:     $\gamma \leftarrow 2$
5:   **else**
6:     $\gamma \leftarrow 3$
7: **end if**
8: Computes $qtag_{\mathcal{U}_i,j} \leftarrow \hat{\mathsf{F}}.\mathsf{Eval}(sk_{\Gamma_i}, \gamma_j \| \mathcal{U}_i)$.
9: $\mathcal{U}$ser sends $qtag_{\mathcal{U}_i,j}$ and γ_j to $\mathcal{D}$.
10: Computes $\tau_\rho \leftarrow \mathsf{TSet.GetTag}(K_T, g_1)$.
11: $\mathcal{U}$ser sends τ_ρ to $\mathcal{D}$.
   // Based on the type of the query allowed to

submit, $\mathcal{U}$ generates gToK:
–Boolean/Count, k'-out-of-k match Query–
12: **for** $c = 1, 2, \ldots$ until $\mathcal{D}$ stops **do**
13:     **for** $i = 2, \ldots, n$ **do**
14:         $\mathcal{G}$token$[c, i] \leftarrow h^{F_P(K_Z, g_1 \| c) \cdot F_P(K_X, g_i)}$
15:     **end for**
16:     $\mathcal{G}$token$_1[c] \leftarrow (\mathcal{G}$token$[c, i], \ldots)$
   //for non-negated terms
17:     $\mathcal{G}$token$_2[c] \leftarrow (\mathcal{G}$token$[c, i], \ldots)$
   //for negated terms
18:     $\mathcal{G}$token$[c] \leftarrow (\mathcal{G}$token$[c, 2], \ldots, \mathcal{G}$token$[c, n])$
   //for all terms
19: **end for**
20: gToK $\leftarrow (\tau_\rho, \mathcal{G}$token$_1, \mathcal{G}$token$_2)$
21: gToK $\leftarrow (\tau_\rho, \mathcal{G}$token$, k')$
22: **return** $qtag_{\mathcal{U}_i,j}$, gToK

---

it is sent to $\mathcal{D}$, that checks if it is a valid token. In particular, if user $\mathcal{U}_i$ is allowed to submit that particular γ_j, the generated token $qtag_{\mathcal{U}_i,j}$ is a valid token, otherwise, it is not valid and the user cannot perform the query. The τ_ρ is generated based on the least frequent predicate, considering it as g_1 (the $\mathsf{TSet.GetTag}(K_T, g_1)$ from TSet in OXT [17] is utilised here). To compute gToK, for count/Boolean queries, one token is generated for non-negated requested predicates such as genotypes, phenotypes, gender, ethnicity, and one token is generated for negated terms. For k'-out-of-k match query, since there are no negated terms and the procedure is only to verify the number of matches based on some threshold (k'), one token is created.

3) NIMUPrivGenDB.Search($qtag_{\mathcal{U}_i,j}$ gToK, EMUGDB, T): This algorithm inputs the search tokens $qtag_{\mathcal{U}_i,j}$ and gToK and the encrypted database EMUGDB, then outputs the search result. First, if the submitted $qtag_{\mathcal{U}_i,j}$ is valid, the data server will proceed by retrieving all the (ID'_O, y) invoking $\mathsf{TSet.Retrieve}(\mathsf{Inv_G}, \tau_\rho)$ algorithm. Then, based on different tokens as the input for different queries (Boolean/Count/k'-out-of-k), the $\mathcal{D}$ performs different processes and outputs the result of the query. The search process starts when the qtag is submitted. Afterwards, if that particular qtag exists in the related QSet, the submitted stag will be used for continuing the search process. The whole process is described in Algorithm 3 (the blue and black lines are for Boolean/Count queries, and the red and black lines for k'-out-of-k match). For checking whether the retrieved IDs for submitted τ_ρ satisfy the rest of non-negated or negated terms in the query, the $\mathcal{G}$token^y will be checked to be in the set or not, respectively. When the Data Owner IDs need to be retrieved (like in Boolean or k'-out-of-k match queries), $\mathcal{D}$ creates an empty set, named RSet to put the related encrypted IDs (ID'_O) in it. For the count query, it also creates that empty set and puts the IDs in it, but later the $|\mathsf{RSet}|$ will be returned. A threshold T can be defined to check the output of count query, such that if it is less than T, do not reveal the result.

4) NIMUPrivGenDB.Retrieve(RSet, g_1, K): As given in Algorithm 4, the user uses K and g_1 to generate the key for decrypting the retrieved $ID'_O \in$ RSet, where Dec is the decryption algorithm.[4]

Algorithm 3. NIMUPrivGenDB.Search

Input : $\text{qtag}_{\mathcal{U}_{i},j}$, gToK, EMUGDB, T
Output : RSet/|RSet|
$\mathcal{D}$ performs the search based on input γ
1: RSet $\leftarrow$ {}
2: if $\text{qtag}_{\mathcal{U}_{i},j} \notin \text{QSet}_j$ then
3:     reject the query
4:   else
5:     RSet $\leftarrow$ {}
6:     inv $\leftarrow$ TSet.Retrieve(Inv_G, τ_p)
7:     for $c = 1, \ldots, |\text{inv}|$ do
8:         Retrieve (ID'_O, y) from the c−th tuple in inv
        –Boolean/Count, k'-out-of-k match Query–
9:         if $\gamma = 1$ or 2 then
10:             if $\mathcal{G}\text{token}_1[c, i]^y \in \mathbb{S}_G$ for all $i = 2, \ldots, n$ in $\mathcal{G}\text{token}_1$ and $\mathcal{G}\text{token}_2[c, i]^y \notin \mathbb{S}_G$ for all i in $\mathcal{G}\text{token}_2$ then
11:                 RSet $\leftarrow$ RSet$\cup\{ID'_O\}$
12:             else
13:                 m $\leftarrow$ 0
14:                 for $i = 2, \ldots, n$ do
15:                     if $\mathcal{G}\text{token}[c, i]^y \in \mathbb{S}_G$ then
16:                         m $\leftarrow$ m+1
17:                     end if
18:                 end for
19:                 if m $\geq k'$ then
20:                     RSet $\leftarrow$ RSet $\cup \{ID'_O\}$
21:                 end if
22:             end if
23:         end if
24:     end for
25:     if $\gamma = 1$ or 3 then
26:         return RSet
27:     else
28:         if |RSet| $\geq$ T then
29:             return |RSet|
30:         end if
31:     end if
32: end if

Algorithm 4. NIMUPrivGenDB.Retrieve

Input : RSet, g_1, K
Output : IDSet
1: IDSet $\leftarrow$ {}
2: $\mathcal{U}$ser sets $K_e \leftarrow F(K_S, g_1)$
3: for each $ID'_O \in$ RSet received do
4:     Compute $ID_O \leftarrow \text{Dec}(K_e, ID'_O)$
5:     IDSet $\leftarrow$ IDSet $\cup \{ID_O\}$
6: end for
7: return IDSet

---

5   Security Definitions and Analysis

Definition 1 (Leakage to Data Server). *We define* $\mathcal{L}_{\mathcal{D}}(\text{MUGDB}, \text{q})$ *of our scheme for* $\text{MUGDB} = \{(ID_O, g)\}$, *$r$ equals number of Data Owners (records) and* $\text{q} = (g_1[i], g_x[i])$, *where g_1 is the* sterm *and g_x is the* xterms *in the query, as a tuple* $(N, \bar{s}, \bar{q}, \text{SP}, \text{RP}, \text{IP}, \text{XP}, \text{QT}, \text{NP})$[5], *where* N *represents the total number of* (g, ID_O) *pairs which is* $\sum_{i=1}^{r} \text{G}_{ID_{Oi}}$, *$\bar{s}$ indicates which queries have the same* sterm, *$\bar{q}$ indicates which queries have the same* qtag *(the type of the query and the user are the same),* SP *represents the number of records (data owners) matching the first predicate in the query,* RP *is the result pattern and indicates the intersection of sterm $g_1[i]$ with any xterm $g_x[i]$ in the same query* $(\text{RP}[i] = \text{MUGDB}(g_1[i]) \cap$

---

[4] Attribute-Based Encryption [26] can also be utilised to let the $\mathcal{T}$ realise fine-grained access control on the encrypted data, but it is not the main point of this work.

[5] All components are the same as [17], except $\bar{q}$, NP, QT, and same as [14], except $\bar{q}$.

MUGDB($g_x[i]$)), XP *indicates the number of xterms in the query,* QT *is the query threshold, k',* NP *represents the number of negated and non-negated terms in the query,* IP *is the conditional intersection pattern. Formally,* IP *is indexed by (i, j, α, β) where $1 \le i, j \le Q$ (a sequence of queries) and $1 \le \alpha, \beta \le n$ (where n is the maximum number of xterms in any query) and defined as follows:*

$$IP[i, j, \alpha, \beta] = \begin{cases} \mathsf{MUGDB}(g_1[i]) \cap \mathsf{MUGDB}(g_1[j]), & \text{if } i \neq j \text{ and } g_{x_\alpha}[i] = g_{x_\beta}[j] \\ \emptyset, & \text{otherwise} \end{cases}$$

$\mathcal{D}$'s view in an adaptive attack (database and queries are selected by $\mathcal{D}$) can be simulated using only the output of $\mathcal{L}_\mathcal{D}$. Below, we define a real experiment Real $_\mathcal{A}^{\Pi_{\mathsf{MUG}}}(\lambda)$ and an ideal experiment Ideal $_{\mathcal{A},Sim}^{\Pi_{\mathsf{MUG}}}(\lambda)$ for an adversary $\mathcal{A}$ and a simulator Sim, respectively:

Real $_\mathcal{A}^{\Pi_{\mathsf{MUG}}}(\lambda)$: $\mathcal{A}(1^\lambda)$ chooses MUGDB and a list of queries q. The experiment then runs (EMUGDB, K, sk$_{\Gamma_i}$) ← Initialisation(λ, MUGDB, Γ, ACL, $\mathcal{U}$) and gives EMUGDB to $\mathcal{A}$. Then $\mathcal{A}$ repeatedly chooses a query q. The experiment runs the algorithm TokenGeneration on inputs (q(g), K, sk$_{\Gamma_i}$), and returns search tokens to $\mathcal{A}$. Eventually, $\mathcal{A}$ returns a bit that experiment uses as its output.

Ideal $_{\mathcal{A},Sim}^{\Pi_{\mathsf{MUG}}}(\lambda)$: The game starts by setting a counter $i = 0$ and an empty list q. $\mathcal{A}(1^\lambda)$ chooses a GDB and a query list q. The experiment runs EGDB ← $Sim(\mathcal{L}_\mathcal{D}(\mathsf{GDB}))$ and gives EGDB to $\mathcal{A}$. Then, $\mathcal{A}$ repeatedly chooses a search query q. To respond, the experiment records this query as q[i], increments i and gives the output of $Sim(\mathcal{L}_\mathcal{D}(\mathsf{GDB}, q))$ to $\mathcal{A}$, where q consists of all previous queries as well as the latest query issued by $\mathcal{A}$. Eventually, the experiment outputs the bit that $\mathcal{A}$ returns.

Definition 2 (Security w.r.t. Data Server). *The protocol Π_{MUG} is called $\mathcal{L}_\mathcal{D}$-semantically-secure against adaptive attacks if for all adversaries $\mathcal{A}$ there exists an efficient algorithm Sim such that*

$$| \Pr[Real_\mathcal{A}^{\Pi_{\mathsf{MUG}}}(\lambda) = 1] - \Pr[Ideal_{\mathcal{A},Sim}^{\Pi_{\mathsf{MUG}}}(\lambda) = 1]| \le \mathrm{negl}(\lambda).$$

Definition 3 (Unforgeable search tokens through colluding corrupted users). *We define a game,* Expt$_{\mathcal{A},\mathsf{qtag}}^{\mathrm{UF}}(\lambda)$, *specified below to capture security against token forgery attacks by a collusion of malicious users: 1) The adversary $\mathcal{A}$ chooses different $\mathcal{U}_i$'s with different permitted query sets $\Gamma_{\mathcal{U}_i}$'s as ACL and sends to the challenger. 2) The challenger selects K$_q$ using security parameter and runs EMUGDB.Setup(λ, Γ, $\mathcal{U}_i$, ACL) to generate QSets. 3) The challenger runs User.Auth(K$_q$, $\mathcal{U}_i$, ACL, Γ) for different users received from adversary and returns sk$_{\Gamma_i}$ for different requested users to $\mathcal{A}$. 4) The adversary returns a search token qtag* for query Q* with type γ^* and user $\mathcal{U}_i^*$. 5) The experiment outputs 1 if (a) γ^* is a new query type $\gamma^* \in \Gamma^* \backslash \bigcup_{i \in [q]} \gamma_i$ (b) $\mathcal{U}_i^*$ is one of the adversary's selected users at the beginning, and (c) qtag* is valid.*

Definition 4 (Security w.r.t. Users). *The search token in Π_{MUG} is unforgeable against (i) malicious users pretending to be other users by using those users' IDs, (ii) colluding users trying to generate a valid search token for a query* *type they are not allowed to submit, if for all PPT adversary $\mathcal{A}$, it holds that* $\Pr\left[\text{Expt}_{\mathcal{A},qtag}^{\text{UF}}(\lambda) = 1\right] \leq \text{negl}(\lambda)$.

Security Analysis: We state the security of our protocol against data server and compromised users, respectively. The proofs of the following theorems are given in Appendix 5.

Theorem 1. *Let $\mathcal{L}_{\mathcal{D}}$ be the leakage function defined in Sect. 5. Then, our protocol is $\mathcal{L}_{\mathcal{D}}$-semantically-secure against adaptive data server (Definition 2) , if OXT [17] is secure and under the assumption of the security of regular PRFs and SC-PRF.*

Theorem 2. *Under the security of regular PRFs and set-constrained PRF $\hat{\mathsf{F}}$, our scheme Π_{MUG} is secure against malicious users in terms of search token in Π_{MUG} is unforgeable against (i) malicious users pretending to be other users by using those users' IDs and (ii) adaptive colluding attacks among users to generate a search token for a query type they are not allowed to submit (Definition 4)[6].*

6   Implementation and Evaluation

This section presents the evaluation results of our protocol. The source code is written in Java programming language, and our machine used to run the code is Intel(R) Core(TM) i7-8850H CPU @ 2.60 GHz processors with 32 GB RAM, running Ubuntu Linux 18.04. We use an in-memory key-value storage Redis [27] to store the generated Inv_G and QSets for querying purposes. In addition, we use Alexandr Nikitin's Bloom filter [28] to store $\mathbb{S}_G$, which is the fastest Bloom filter implementation for JVM, and we set the false-positive rate of the bloom filter to 10^{-6}. We used the JPBC [29] in our implementation.

Real-life and synthetic datasets are used for evaluating NIMUPrivGenDB. The real-life data are from The Harvard Personal Genome Project (PGP) [30], and we extracted data of 58 participants with $2,000$ SNPs, their phenotype, gender, and ethnicity. These participants have had different types of cancer such as breast, brain, thyroid, uterine, kidney, melanoma, colon, prostate as the phenotype, or they were Covid-19 positive/negative recently. Then, using the above-mentioned actual dataset as a basis, we generated multiple synthetic datasets with varying number of records (5,000–40,000) and SNPs (500–2,000) to test NIMUPrivGenDB. To evaluate our protocol's performance, we use the well-known tree-based GGM PRF [31] and implement NIMUPrivGenDB, which shows that our protocol has low communication and computation costs and is suitable for real-world applications. We remark that the size of secret key sk_{Γ_i} is dependent on the size of the set Γ_i. In our application, since the size of this

---

[6] The security against malicious users in Theorem 2 is a generic characteristic, which can be utilised in scenarios with more supported types of queries. In other words, the designed protocol and the security proof against unforgeability by a collusion of users can be generalised to handle more than three queries.

set is three for each user, this is not a bottleneck or drawback. However, for applications with a larger set size, constrained PRF of Brakerski et al. [32] can be considered, which has a short constrained key.

We show the storage cost in Table 5, which is in the order of $rx + q|\mathcal{U}|$. Although storage cost in our model increases when the number of users and their supported queries increases, we show that to support submitting different queries with a defined access list, extra storage overhead is not costly. Hence, our solution is practical when different queries are allowed for different types of users rather than having different databases (naive solution explained in Introduction), which leads to more storage cost. The quantity |QSets| grows approximately linearly with the number of users and their authorised queries and does not depend on the number of SNPs or the number of records. For example, for around 1,000 users, |QSets| is approximately 50 KB. Therefore, the storage overhead (expansion factor) of NIMUPrivGenDB is still around 80, while it is 180 in [2], and in the order of 1024 in [5,11] (without supporting user authorisation). Note that it is 160 in naive solution.

Table 5. Size of original and encrypted database.

#Records(r)	#SNPs = 500		#SNPs = 1,000	
	Original	Encrypted	Original	Encrypted
5,000	14 MB	1.12 GB +|QSets|	28.9 MB	2.22 GB +|QSets|
10,000	28.5 MB	2.27 GB +|QSets|	57.8 MB	4.50 GB +|QSets|
20,000	57 MB	4.43 GB +|QSets|	115.6 MB	8.89 GB +|QSets|
40,000	114 MB	8.92 GB +|QSets|	224 MB	17.8 GB +|QSets|

Next, we evaluated the initialisation phase of our protocol. From Fig. 1 we can see that the initialisation time grows linearly with the number of records and the number of SNPs, as we expected it is in the order of rx. It is worth mentioning that generating QSets does not take much time and is considered negligible with respect to MUBInv and EMUGDB.Setup time. The key generation time for the users is also negligible compared to the time takes to encrypt the dataset.

To show the benefit of non-interactive protocol, we compare the communication overhead in interactive protocol, PrivGenDB, and our protocol, NIMUPriv-GenDB here. In PrivGenDB, there is a middle entity involved to check every query submitted to the system. So, there might be delays in response. Moreover, the communication overhead in interactive protocol is around 150B + 2 KB (depends on the result being sent back to the user). 150B is the size of a plain text query sent to the middle entity, that has to be sent for each desired query. However, in our solution, a one-time key is generated and sent to the user with the size of approximately 142B. Therefore, communication overhead in our non-interactive model is around 142B for each user (does not depend on the number of submitted queries by a user) plus around 16B for each qtag. This is in contrast to the interactive protocol that is around (150B + 2 KB) ∗ (number of queries).

Finally, we present the search time of our protocol in Fig. 2. Search time increases linearly with the number of records satisfying the first predicate in the query (α), not the total number of records, hence achieves sublinear search time. Moreover, number of SNPs does not affect the search complexity of our protocol. Adding QSets or users does not add much search complexity, since it is just a lookup table. NIMUPrivGenDB query execution time for 5,000 records and 500 SNPs, is around 1.3 s, 2.3 s with query sizes of 10 and 20 respectively. The query execution time is somehow the same as that of naive solution, with the use of proposed QUAuth. Whereas, the storage overhead in naive solution is multiplied by the number of categories of users (if user management is not considered), or multiplied by the number of users which is not practical. However, NIMUPrivGenDB provides the efficient query submission functionality and user management for multi-user scenario with small amount of storage overhead. With all the functionalities added to NIMUPrivGenDB compared to the state-of-the-art, it still provides less search time complexity, e.g., for a query with 10 keywords on a dataset of 5,000 records and 500 SNPs, NIMUPrivGenDB takes 1.3 s; whereas, e.g., it takes approximately 77.8 s and 29 s for [2] and [4] to respond, respectively.

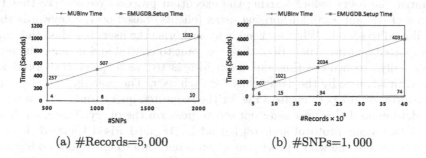

(a) #Records=5,000   (b) #SNPs=1,000

Fig. 1. Initialisation time for datasets with different number of SNPs and records.

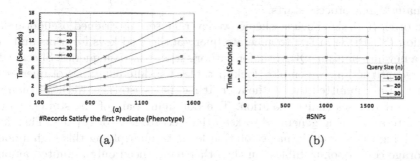

(a)   (b)

Fig. 2. (a) Query execution time on dataset with 40,000 records in total (different number of records satisfy the phenotype in the query). (b) Query execution time on datasets with $r = 5,000$ and different number of SNPs, with different query sizes.

7 Conclusion

The proposed non-interactive multi-user model/protocol, NIMUPrivGenDB, enables efficient query executions on outsourced genomic data at low storage cost. This new protocol avoids the per-query interaction between the data owner and the user. With the newly proposed mechanism, QUAuth, users are autho-rised based on the query types, and their access to the system is managed and can be revoked. Our protocol is secure against colluding malicious users. Apart from that, it protects user privacy so that the trustee only learns the types of queries the user is allowed to submit and has no means to learn the exact search keywords. Finally, the implementation results demonstrate its practicality due to low communication, computation and storage costs.

Appendix

Appendix 1
Our Techniques: Following the idea of authorising different users for submit-ting different types of queries, the main task is to develop a scheme that can authorise the users before starting the execution process. We observe that the scheme of [18] supports authorising users (clients) based on the keywords they are allowed to search. What we need is to authorise the users based on the types of supported queries. Apart from that, we want to control and manage the users individually. To achieve this, our main idea is to use a query-authorised key created in advance by the data owner for each user. The user then employs this query-authorised key to create a tag for the requested query, and the data server may determine if this user is authorised to perform the query. The main differ-ence between our protocol and [18] is that in [18] authorised keywords have to be considered in the whole process of token generation to make sure no keyword other than those of authorised is submitted. However, in our protocol, a new mechanism is proposed to make sure an authorised query is submitted before the main search process starts.

In order to design such a scheme, we leverage set-constrained pseudorandom function (SC-PRF) in [18] to generate query-authorised keys for users and pro-pose a new mechanism, QUAuth, for authorisation based on queries. Specifically, in our construction, we employ lookup tables for different types of queries for checking the submitted tag by the user. It incurs less storage overhead than the multiple databases (naive) solution. The dominant part of the storage cost is related to a set being generated to keep the (record, keyword) pairs. Therefore, multiplying the storage in naive solution leads to multiplying this high amount of storage cost. Lookup tables, on the other hand, need only a limited amount of storage. Therefore, for each query submission, the data server checks the sub-mitted tag against the related lookup table, and if that particular user is allowed to execute the submitted query, the server processes the query. To incorporate extra features, such as authorisation updates, the users' ID has been exploited in QUAuth, while a naive solution would need one storage per user, which is highly impractical. QUAuth, on the other hand, provides this by increasing the minimal amount of storage overhead as the number of users grows.

In addition, our construction achieves an enhanced security against untrusted clients in comparison to [18]. It is proved that our construction is secure not only against colluding attacks among untrusted users, but also against search token forgery using other users' unique IDs through untrusted users. This is achieved by considering user's unique ID in key generation, and the need for using that key and unique ID to generate search token in the next phase for starting search.

Appendix 2

The security of SC-PRF is officially captured by the game outlined below.

- Setup: Challenger selects $k \xleftarrow{\$} \mathcal{K}$ and $b \xleftarrow{\$} \{0,1\}$, and initialises empty sets $E, \mathcal{Q}$ and C.
- Query Phase: In this phase, the adversary adaptively issues the following queries: (i) Evaluation query: on input $x \in \mathcal{X}$, the challenger returns $F(k, x)$ and adds x to E. (ii) Key query: on input a set $S \subseteq \mathcal{X}$, the challenger returns a set-constrained key F.Cons (k, S), and adds S to $\mathcal{Q}$.
- Challenge Phase: on input a challenge query $x^* \in \mathcal{X}$, the challenger outputs $F(k, x^*)$ if $b = 1$, otherwise returns $u \xleftarrow{\$} \mathcal{Y}$, and then adds x^* to C.
- Guess: the adversary outputs a guess b' of b.

$\mathcal{A}$ wins in the above game if all the following conditions hold: (1) $b' = b$; (2) $E \cap C = \emptyset$; (3) for all $x^* \in C$, $x^* \notin \bigcup_{S \in \mathcal{Q}} S$.

Definition 5. *(Secure Set-Constrained PRF). A set-constrained PRF $F : \mathcal{K} \times \mathcal{X} \leftarrow \mathcal{Y}$ is secure if for all PPT adversary $\mathcal{A}$, the advantage of $\mathcal{A}$ winning in the above game is negligible in λ.*
That is, $Adv_{\mathcal{A},F}^{SC-PRF}(\lambda) = | \Pr[\mathcal{A} \ wins] - \frac{1}{2} | \leq negl(\lambda)$

Appendix 3
System Design Overview of NIMUPrivGenDB See Fig. 3.

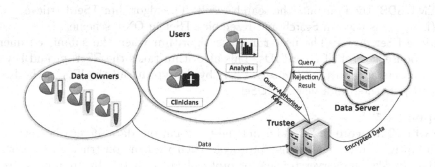

Fig. 3. System design overview of NIMUPrivGenDB

Appendix 4
Syntax of Our Proposed Non-interactive Multi-user SSE

Initialisation(λ, MUGDB, Γ, ACL, $\mathcal{U}$): Trustee runs this algorithm. Given the security parameter λ, the multi-user genomic database MUGDB, types of the queries Γ, the access list ACL, and the users $\mathcal{U}$, this algorithm outputs the encrypted database EMUGDB and a key sk_{Γ_i} for each user $\mathcal{U}_i$. Trustee uses below sub-algorithms to complete the initialisation:

- G $\leftarrow$ **MUGeEncode**(MUGDB): To encode the genotypes in the database, trustee runs this algorithm that constructs keywords related to genotypes by concatenating each SNP index to all genotypes of that particular SNP.
- IINX $\leftarrow$ **MUBInv**(G, MUGDB): This algorithm gets as input the keywords in G and generates an inverted index.
- (EMUGDB, K, K_q) $\leftarrow$ **EMUGDB.Setup**(λ, IINX, MUGDB, Γ, $\mathcal{U}_i$, ACL): The inputs to this algorithms are the security parameter λ, the generated inverted index IINX, types of queries Γ, the access list ACL, and the users $\mathcal{U}$, and outputs are the encrypted multi-user database EMUGDB = (Inv$_G$, $\mathbb{S}_G$, QSets), and a set of keys K, K_q. TSet.Setup(IINX) is used in **EMUGDB.Setup** algorithm and resembles TSet in OXT scheme.
- sk_{Γ_i} $\leftarrow$ **User.Auth**(Γ, ACL, $\mathcal{U}_i$, K_q): Trustee runs this algorithm by using K_q, types of queries and access list for a particular user $\mathcal{U}_i$ to generate a specific key sk_{Γ_i} for each user of the system. Each user has its own key and can later submit the queries using this key.

TokenGeneration(q($g_1, \ldots, g_n$), K, sk_{Γ_i}): A user runs this algorithm with inputs being the desired query (with encoded keywords, if they are genotype-related keywords), the set of key K, and its own specific key sk_{Γ_i}, and outputs being the tokens $qtag_{\mathcal{U}_i,j}$ and gToK. The input threshold T is used for limiting the number of records returned as the result of the submitted count query. TSet.GetTag(K_T, g_1) is used in TokenGeneration algorithm and resembles TSet in OXT scheme.

Search($qtag_{\mathcal{U}_i,j}$, gToK, EMUGDB, T): This algorithm inputs the search tokens $qtag_{\mathcal{U}_i,j}$ (that specifically lets the server to authorise the user and the type of the query submitted through this user), gToK and the encrypted database EMUGDB, then outputs the search result. The algorithm TSet.Retrieve (Inv$_G$, τ_ρ) is used in Search and resembles TSet in OXT scheme.

Retrieve(RSet, g_1, K): The user runs this algorithm when the submitted query response is a set of record IDs. This algorithm takes the RSet, g_1 and key K as inputs and outputs the set of ID$_O$ by decrypting all the ID$'_O$ in the RSet and puts them in a new set IDSet.

Appendix 5
Proof of Theorem 1. Let $\mathcal{A}$ be an honest-but-curious data server who performs an adaptive attack against our protocol. Then we can construct an algorithm $\mathcal{B}$ that breaks the server privacy of protocol OXT in [17] by running $\mathcal{A}$ as a subroutine with non-negligible probability.

- Algorithm $\mathcal{B}$ passes the selected GDB by $\mathcal{A}$ to the OXT challenger.

- The OXT challenger runs (K,EDB) ← OXT.Setup(GDB) and returns EDB to the algorithm $\mathcal{B}$. Then, algorithm $\mathcal{B}$ chooses a random key, K_q and runs lines 2 to 9 of algorithm EMUGDB.Setup to generate QSet and sets EMUGDB = {EDB, QSets}.
- The algorithm $\mathcal{B}$ sends EMUGDB to an adversary $\mathcal{A}$.
- For each q query issued by the adversary $\mathcal{A}$, the algorithm $\mathcal{B}$ defines NIMUPrivGenDB.TokenGeneration(K; q[i]), where q[i] = (s[i], x[i, ·]), which computes qtag, (by first computing the key sk_{Γ_i}, and then computing the lines 1 to 9 of algorithm NIMUPrivGenDB.TokenGeneration or simply generating qtag by running line 5 of EMUGDB.Setup for requested query type), and then uses the xtoken output of the TokenGeneration oracle of OXT. For count and Boolean queries, it categorises negated/non-negated terms and runs the TokenGeneration algorithm of OXT twice. For k'-out-of-k matches, it just omits the k' from query sent by $\mathcal{A}$, pass the rest to TokenGeneration algorithm of OXT and generate the token by using that output and including k' to send it to $\mathcal{A}$.
- Finally, the adversary $\mathcal{A}$ outputs a bit that the algorithm $\mathcal{B}$ returns.

Since the core construction of our scheme is exploited from OXT in [17], we use the oracle of OXT to reduce the security of it to that of OXT protocol. Thus, if the security of OXT holds, the security of our scheme is guaranteed.

Simulator 1 *(for Count and Boolean queries) By considering $\mathcal{A}$ as an honest-but-curious server against our protocol, Π_{MUG}, we construct an algorithm $\mathcal{B}$ that breaks the server privacy of OXT protocol [17] by running $\mathcal{A}$. Let S_{OXT} be the simulator for OXT; then we construct a simulator S_{MUG} for our scheme. The algorithm $\mathcal{B}$ uses S_{OXT} to construct the simulator S_{MUG} in order to answer the queries issued by $\mathcal{A}$. Simulator for the initialisation phase, perform the following algorithm apart from using the simulator of OXT. It selects a key, K_q and calculates qtag for different queries $\mathcal{A}$ may submit, and generates QSet.*

A sequence of T conjunctive queries is represented by q = (s, x), where the i-th query is written as q[i] = (s[i], x[i, ·]) for $i \in [T]$, and s[i], x[i, ·] denote the sterm and xterms in the i -th query, respectively. Then, for the token generation, it first generates query-qtag by using that K_q and knowing the type of query $\mathcal{A}$ submitted. It can use the leakage $\bar{q}$ to send the relative qtag back to $\mathcal{A}$. For count and Boolean queries, such a simulator can be constructed by using S_{OXT}, a simulator for OXT protocol. By using added NP, the S_{MUG} can simulate the two $\mathcal{G}$tokens, for negated terms and non-negated terms. Then, it combines them as the gToK.

For k'-out-of-k match queries, by using S_{OXT}, $\mathcal{G}$token is constructed and then the extra QT component is added and gToK is simulated. Now we just need to use the simulator of OXT for $\mathcal{A}_{OXT}$, to construct the simulator of our scheme for $\mathcal{A}_{MUG}$. By running S_{OXT} for EDBSetup and TokenGen queries, we can construct a simulator S_{MUG} for EDBSetup and TokenGen queries of our scheme.

$$\Pr(Real_{\mathcal{A}}^{\Pi_{MUG}} = 1) - \Pr(Ideal_{\mathcal{A},S_{MUG}}^{\Pi_{MUG}} = 1) \leq$$
$$[\Pr(Real_{\mathcal{B}}^{\Pi_{OXT}} = 1) - \Pr(Ideal_{\mathcal{B},S_{OXT}}^{\Pi_{OXT}} = 1)] + \mathrm{Adv}_{F,\mathcal{B}}^{SC-PRF}(\lambda)$$

Since OXT is secure, its advantage is negligible. The advantage of SC-PRF is also negligible. Hence, the advantage of our protocol, Π_{MUG} is negligible.

Proof of Theorem 2. Suppose that there is an efficient adversary $\mathcal{A}$ that can generate a new valid search token for a new query type γ_j^*, which implies that $\mathcal{A}$ produces a new qtag, then we show that we can construct an efficient algorithm $\mathcal{B}$ (with $\mathcal{A}$ as the subroutine) to break the security of set-constrained PRF. For the case that $\mathcal{A}$ wins by producing a qtag for the new query type γ^*, the algorithm $\mathcal{B}$ is described as below.

$\mathcal{B}$ has access to constrained key generation oracle $\mathcal{O}_{K_q}^{\hat{\mathsf{F}}}(\cdot)$ of SC-PRF $\hat{\mathsf{F}}$. $\mathcal{A}$ selects different $\mathcal{U}_i$ with different $\Gamma_{\mathcal{U}_i}$. For the i-th key extraction query where $\Gamma_{\mathcal{U}_i} = \{\gamma_{1,i}, \ldots, \gamma_{m,i}\}$, for $\mathcal{U}_i$, the algorithm $\mathcal{B}$ concatenates all γ_j with $\mathcal{U}_i$ and gets sk_{Γ_i} by querying her own oracle $\mathcal{O}_{K_q}^{\hat{\mathsf{F}}}(\Gamma_i)$, and then returns sk_{Γ_i} for each requested $\mathcal{U}_i$. At last, $\mathcal{A}$ outputs a search token qtag* for a query Q^* with a new type γ^* and user $\mathcal{U}_i$. Then $\mathcal{B}$ forwards $\gamma^*\|\mathcal{U}_i$ to his own challenger and receives the response y^*, such that

$$y^* = \begin{cases} \hat{\mathsf{F}}\left(K_q, \gamma^*\|\mathcal{U}_i\right), b = 1, \\ u, \qquad\qquad\quad b = 0, \end{cases}$$

where u is randomly chosen from $\mathcal{Y}$. After that, $\mathcal{B}$ checks whether or not the event that $y^* =$ qtag* denoted by experiment E happens. If yes, it outputs 1, otherwise returns 0. From the simulation, we get that
$\Pr[b' = 1 \mid b = 1] - \Pr[b' = 1 \mid b = 0]$
$= \Pr[E \mid y^* = \hat{\mathsf{F}}\left(K_q, \gamma^*\|\mathcal{U}_i\right)] - \Pr[E \mid y^* = u]$
$= \Pr[\mathcal{A} \text{ wins} \mid y^* = \hat{\mathsf{F}}\left(K_q, \gamma^*\|\mathcal{U}_i\right)] - \Pr[E \mid y^* = u] \geq \Pr[\mathcal{A} \text{ wins}] - \mathrm{negl}(\lambda)$,
where b is uniformly random and independent of $\mathcal{A}'s$ final output. Therefore, $\Pr[\mathcal{A} \text{ wins}] \leq \mathrm{Adv}_{\hat{\mathsf{F}},\mathcal{B}}^{\mathsf{SC\text{-}PRF}}(\lambda) + \mathrm{negl}(\lambda)$, which indicates that $\mathcal{A}$ can generate a valid search token with a fresh query type for user $\mathcal{U}_i$ except for a negligible probability.

References

1. Kupersmith, J.: The privacy conundrum and genomic research: re-identification and other concerns, Health Affairs. Project HOPE (2013)
2. Hasan, M.Z., Mahdi, M.S.R., Sadat, M.N., Mohammed, N.: Secure count query on encrypted genomic data. J. Biomed. Inform. **81**, 41–52 (2018)
3. Mahdi, M.S.R., Sadat, M.N., Mohammed, N., Jiang, X.: Secure count query on encrypted heterogeneous data. In: 2020 IEEE International Conference on (DASC/PiCom/CBDCom/CyberSciTech), pp. 548–555. IEEE (2020)
4. Ghasemi, R., Al Aziz, M.M., Mohammed, N., Dehkordi, M.H., Jiang, X.: Private and efficient query processing on outsourced genomic databases. IEEE J. Biomed. Health Inform. **21**(5), 1466–1472 (2016)
5. Nassar, M., Malluhi, Q., Atallah, M., Shikfa, A.: Securing aggregate queries for DNA databases. IEEE Trans. Cloud Comp. **7**(3), 827–837 (2017)
6. Krishna, R., Kelleher, K., Stahlberg, E.: Patient confidentiality in the research use of clinical medical databases. Am. J. Public Health **97**(4), 654–658 (2007)

7. Shabani, M., Borry, P.: Rules for processing genetic data for research purposes in view of the new EU general data protection regulation. Eur. J. Hum. Genet. **26**(2), 149–156 (2018)
8. A.G.H. Alliance: Genomic data & privacy law, May 2018. https://www.australiangenomics.org.au/genomics-and-privacy-law/
9. Erlich, Y., et al.: Redefining genomic privacy: trust and empowerment. PLoS Biol. **12**(11), e1001983 (2014)
10. Erlich, Y., Narayanan, A.: Routes for breaching and protecting genetic privacy. Nat. Rev. Genet. **15**(6), 409–421 (2014)
11. Kantarcioglu, M., Jiang, W., Liu, Y., Malin, B.: A cryptographic approach to securely share and query genomic sequences. IEEE Trans. Inform. Tech. Biomed. **12**(5), 606–617 (2008)
12. Canim, M., Kantarcioglu, M., Malin, B.: Secure management of biomedical data with cryptographic hardware. IEEE Trans. Inform. Tech. Biomed. **16**(1), 166–175 (2011)
13. Chenghong, W., et al.: Scotch: secure counting of encrypted genomic data using a hybrid approach. In: AMIA Annual Symposium Proceedings, vol. 2017. American Medical Informatics Association, p. 1744 (2017)
14. Jafarbeiki, S., et al.: PrivGenDB: efficient and privacy-preserving query executions over encrypted SNP-phenotype database (2021). https://arxiv.org/abs/2104.02890
15. Perillo, A.M., De Cristofaro, E.: PAPEETE: Private, Authorized, and Fast Personal Genomic Testing. SciTePress (2018)
16. Naveed, M., et al.: Controlled functional encryption. In: Proceedings of the 2014 ACM SIGSAC Conference on Computer and Communications Security, pp. 1280–1291 (2014)
17. Cash, D., Jarecki, S., Jutla, C., Krawczyk, H., Roşu, M.-C., Steiner, M.: Highly-scalable searchable symmetric encryption with support for Boolean queries. In: Canetti, R., Garay, J.A. (eds.) CRYPTO 2013. LNCS, vol. 8042, pp. 353–373. Springer, Heidelberg (2013). https://doi.org/10.1007/978-3-642-40041-4_20
18. Sun, S.F., et al.: Non-interactive multi-client searchable encryption: realization and implementation. IEEE Trans. Dependable Secur. Comput. (2020)
19. National human genome research institute. https://www.genome.gov/genetics-glossary/Phenotype. No date
20. Gibson, G.: Population genetics and GWAS: a primer. PLoS Biol. **16**(3), e2005485 (2018)
21. Chen, F., et al.: Princess: privacy-protecting rare disease international network collaboration via encryption through software guard extensions. Bioinformatics **33**(6), 871–878 (2017)
22. Katz, J., Lindell, Y.: Introduction to Modern Cryptography. CRC Press, Boca Raton (2020)
23. Boneh, D., Waters, B.: Constrained pseudorandom functions and their applications. In: Sako, K., Sarkar, P. (eds.) ASIACRYPT 2013. LNCS, vol. 8270, pp. 280–300. Springer, Heidelberg (2013). https://doi.org/10.1007/978-3-642-42045-0_15
24. Hohenberger, S., Koppula, V., Waters, B.: Adaptively secure puncturable pseudorandom functions in the standard model. In: Iwata, T., Cheon, J.H. (eds.) ASIACRYPT 2015. LNCS, vol. 9452, pp. 79–102. Springer, Heidelberg (2015). https://doi.org/10.1007/978-3-662-48797-6_4
25. Garcia-Molina, H., Ullman, J.D., Widom, J.: Database System Implementation, vol. 672. Prentice Hall, Upper Saddle River (2000)

26. Goyal, V., Pandey, O., Sahai, A., Waters, B.: Attribute-based encryption for fine-grained access control of encrypted data. In: Proceedings of the 13th ACM Conference on Computer and Communications Security, pp. 89–98 (2006)
27. R. Labs: Redis, vol. 2017. https://redis.io
28. Nikitin, A.: Bloom Filter Scala, vol. 2017. https://alexandrnikitin.github.io/blog/bloom-filter-for-scala/
29. Caro, A.D., Iovino, V.: JPBC: Java pairing based cryptography, pp. 850–855. In: ISCC 2011. IEEE (2011)
30. The Personal Genome Project: Harvard Medical School. Title = PersonalGenomes.org. https://pgp.med.harvard.edu/data
31. Goldreich, O., Goldwasser, S., Micali, S.: How to construct random functions. In: Providing Sound Foundations for Cryptography: On the Work of Shafi Goldwasser and Silvio Micali, pp. 241–264 (2019)
32. Brakerski, Z., Vaikuntanathan, V.: Constrained Key-Homomorphic PRFs from Standard Lattice Assumptions. In: Dodis, Y., Nielsen, J.B. (eds.) TCC 2015. LNCS, vol. 9015, pp. 1–30. Springer, Heidelberg (2015). https://doi.org/10.1007/978-3-662-46497-7_1

Bigdata-Facilitated Two-Party Authenticated Key Exchange for IoT

Bowen Liu[1(✉)], Qiang Tang[1], and Jianying Zhou[2]

[1] Luxembourg Institute of Science and Technology (LIST),
5 Avenue des Hauts-Fourneaux, 4362 Esch-sur-Alzette, Luxembourg
{bowen.liu,qiang.tang}@list.lu
[2] Singapore University of Technology and Design, 8 Somapah Road,
Singapore 487372, Singapore
jianying_zhou@sutd.edu.sg

Abstract. Authenticated Key Exchange (AKE) protocols, by definition, guarantee both session key secrecy and entity authentication. Informally, session key secrecy means that only the legitimate parties learn
the established key and mutual authentication means that one party can
assure itself the session key is actually established with the other party.
Today, an important application area for AKE is Internet of Things (IoT)
systems, where an IoT device runs the protocol to establish a session key
with a remote server. In this paper, we identify two additional security
requirements for IoT-oriented AKE, namely Key Compromise Impersonation (KCI) resilience and Server Compromise Impersonation (SCI)
resilience. These properties provide an additional layer of security when
the IoT device and the server get compromised respectively. Inspired by
Chan et al.'s bigdata-based unilateral authentication protocol, we propose a novel AKE protocol which achieves mutual authentication, session key secrecy (including perfect forward secrecy), and the above two
resilience properties. To demonstrate its practicality, we implement our
protocol and show that one execution costs about 15.19 ms (or, 84.73
ms) for the IoT device and 2.44 ms (or, 12.51 ms) for the server for security parameter $\lambda = 128$ (or, $\lambda = 256$). We finally propose an enhanced
protocol to reduce the computational complexity on the end of IoT by
outsourcing an exponentiation computation to the server. By instantiating the signature scheme with NIST's round three alternate candidate
Picnic, we show that one protocol execution costs about 14.44 ms (or,
58.45 ms) for the IoT device and 12.78 ms (or, 46.34 ms) for the server
for security parameter $\lambda = 128$ (or, $\lambda = 256$).

Keywords: Internet of Things · Authenticated key exchange · Perfect
forward secrecy · Key compromise impersonation resilience · Server
compromise impersonation resilience

1 Introduction

Two-party key exchange is a fundamental cryptographic primitive that enables
two parties to establish secure communication channels over an open network.

© Springer Nature Switzerland AG 2021
J. K. Liu et al. (Eds.): ISC 2021, LNCS 13118, pp. 95–116, 2021.
https://doi.org/10.1007/978-3-030-91356-4_6

Furthermore, an authenticated key exchange protocol not only allows two parties to negotiate a session key but also ensures the authenticity of the involved parties [5]. The basic security property of an AKE protocol is that only the legitimate parties can gain access to the established secret key in every protocol execution (i.e. a session). In addition, some AKE protocols guarantee perfect forward secrecy which preserves the session key secrecy even if the long-term credentials of both parties are compromised. Regarding their construction, most existing AKE protocols employ only a single type of authentication factor (e.g. long-term secret keys or digital certificates). Consequently, if the single authentication factor gets compromised, then the AKE protocol's security will be broken.

In this paper, we are interested in two-party AKE protocols for IoT systems, where an IoT device and a server run the protocol to authenticate each other and establish a session key. We generally assume that the IoT device is standalone and no human user is necessarily present when it is engaged in the protocol execution. Note that we do recognize some exceptional scenarios, e.g. when the IoT device is a smart phone, where a human user is able to involve in the AKE protocol. It is well known that IoT devices are constrained with respect to computation capability, network bandwidth, and battery life. This advocates lightweight AKE designs. Regarding security, we would like to emphasize two observations.

- An IoT device is very likely to be compromised and has the stored credentials leaked, e.g. via side-channel attacks. This motivates us to consider key compromise impersonation resilience (see the definition below) to be a valuable property for IoT-oriented AKE protocols.
- Even less likely, the server could also be compromised. Taking into account the fact that the IoT device can be deployed in a critical infrastructure, it is ideal that an attacker should not be able to impersonate the server to the IoT device even if it has compromised the server.

It is worth noting that we assume the attacker only learns some credentials by compromising an entity. Other types of damage (e.g. installing a trapdoor or disabling the entity) are not directly related to AKE and are beyond the scope of our paper.

As a result, our objective is to construct AKE protocols with the following properties in addition to the standard session key security property.

1. *(Prefect) Forward Secrecy. Forward secrecy* means that if one party's long-term key is compromised, the secrecy of its previous session keys should not be affected. *Perfect forward secrecy* (PFS) requires that previous session keys remain secure even if both parties' long-term keys have been compromised.
2. *Key Compromise Impersonation (KCI) Resilience.* Even if an attacker has obtained one party's long-term private key, then it still cannot impersonate the other party to this party.
3. *Server Compromise Impersonation (SCI) Resilience.* Even if an attacker has compromised the server, then it still cannot impersonate the server to the IoT device.

Our analysis shows that it is very challenging for single-factor-based AKE protocols to achieve all these properties. Hence, in this paper, we will focus on AKE protocols, where the entity authentication is based on two or more factors.

1.1 Related Work

We emphasize that two-party authenticated key exchange is a fruitful research area, with many existing protocols, implementations and standards. For the sake of space, we refer the readers to survey papers/books like [6] for a detailed overview. Regarding Two-Factor Authenticated Key Exchange (2FAKE), Lee et al. [25] proposed a protocol which combines a smart card and a password as authentication factors. Byun [10] proposed a 2FAKE protocol by using a shared common secret and Physical Unclonable Functions (PUFs) as authentication factors. Guo and Chang [21] proposed a chaotic maps-based AKE protocol with password and smart cards as additional authentication factors. Later, Liu and Xue [28] proposed a chaos-based AKE protocol using password as the other authentication factor. Challa et al. [13] proposed an AKE protocol using password, biometric information and a smart card as authentication factors. In 2008, Pointcheval and Zimmer [31] proposed the first Multi-Factor Authenticated Key Exchange (MFAKE) protocol which combines a password, a secret key, and biometric information as the authentication factors. Later, Hao and Clarke [22] pointed out that an adversary can break the protocol by only compromising a single password factor based on the deficiency of its security model (i.e. server impersonation has not been considered). Byun [8,9,11] proposed MFAKE protocols by using PUF, biometric template and long-term secret keys as authentication factors. Li et al. [26] proposed a MFAKE protocol by using password, biometric fingerprint and Personal Identification Number (PIN) as authentication factors. Stebila [34] proposed an MFAKE scheme, where multiple short secrets (e.g. one-time response) are used in addition to a password. Besides, Fleischhacker et al. [20] proposed a modular MFAKE framework by combining any subset of multiple low-entropy (one-time) passwords/PINs, high-entropy private/public keys, and biometric factors.

Since we assume there is no human involvement, PIN, password and biometric factors do not fit into our setting. In addition, PUF-based AKE protocols require special type of IoT devices, e.g. it should have PUF embedded. In order to design general purpose two-factor or multi-factor AKE protocols, we need to find other authentication factors. Regarding entity authentication, authentication factors can be classified into three categories: *something you know, something you have,* and *something you are* [17]. In addition, Brainard et al. proposed a fourth category: *some one you know* which is the social networking information-based authentication factor [7]. Among all, the *something you have* category fits into our IoT setting, and bigdata could be a candidate of good authentication factor. To this end, Chan et al. [14] proposed a bigdata-based unilateral two-factor authentication protocol. In more detail, their protocol uses all available historical data and relevant tags as an authentication factor, where the tags are generated injectively based on the historical data, in addition to the conventional first authentication factor of the shared long-term key. It is shown that, in a bounded storage model [3,19], the protocol remains secure since the adversary can only capture limited records of the large amount of full historical data.

1.2 Our Contribution

In this paper, our contribution is multifold. Firstly, inspired by Chan et al.'s work [14], we introduce a new IoT-oriented AKE setting, where bigdata is used as an additional factor in addition to a shared long-term private key for facilitating mutual authentication. We propose a security model to capture all the desired security properties listed in the previous subsection. To our knowledge, no existing AKE protocol achieves all these properties, as shown in Table 1.

Table 1. Comparison among different AKE protocols

Protocol	Authentication factor	Security property						Communication pass
		P1	P2	P3	P4	P5	P6	
[31]	Biometic, Password and Secret Key	✗	✓	✓	-	-	-	4
[26]	Biometic, Password and PIN	✗	✓	✓	✓	-	-	4
[25]	Password and Secret Key	✓	✓	✓	✗	-	-	2
[34]	Password and Customized Elements	✓	✓	✓	-	-	-	3
[13]	Biometric, Password and Smart Card	✓	✓	✓	-	-	-	3
[8–11,28]	PUF/Chaos and Others	✓	✓	✓	✓	-	-	3
[20]	Multiple Customized Elements	✓	✓	✓	-	-	-	2 * No. of Factors
Ours	Bigdata and Secret Key	✓	✓	✓	✓	✓	✓	3

'P1': Mutual authentication, 'P2': Session key security, 'P3': Forward secrecy, 'P4': Prefect forward secrecy, 'P5': Key compromise impersonation resilience, 'P6': Server compromise impersonation resilience, '✓': Provides the security property, '✗': Does not prevent the attack, '-': The security property has not been considered.

Secondly, we propose a novel AKE protocol, which uses both long-term private keys and bigdata as its authentication factors. Regarding the processing of bigdata, we distribute the relevant credentials to both the IoT and the server. As a result, we avoid one vulnerability of Chan et al.'s scheme, described in the Appendix of the full paper [27]. Under the general assumption that the Pseudo-Random Functions (PRFs) are secure and the attacker can only retrieve a limited amount of data from a compromised server, we further prove that, our AKE protocol achieves all the desired properties based on the Computational Diffie-Hellman (CDH) assumption and the Strong Diffie-Hellman (SDH) assumption in the random oracle model with an appropriate parameter setup.

Thirdly, by using Raspberry Pi 3 Model B+ as the IoT device and a PC as the server, we investigate the parameter configurations for the big dataset held by the server and identify the optimal parameters. We run the experiment and show that one protocol execution takes 15.19 ms (or, 84.73 ms) for the IoT device and 2.44 ms (or, 12.51 ms) for the server for security parameter $\lambda = 128$ (or, $\lambda = 256$). Lastly, we propose an enhanced protocol to reduce IoT's computational complexity by outsourcing an exponentiation computation to the server. The enhanced protocol does not increase round complexity (i.e. it still needs three message passes) and only slightly increases the communication complexity. By instantiating the signature scheme with NIST's round three alternate candidate *Picnic*, we show that one protocol execution costs about 14.44 ms (or, 58.45 ms) for the IoT device and 12.78 ms (or, 46.34 ms) for the server for security parameter $\lambda = 128$ (or, $\lambda = 256$). The running time for the IoT device has become 1.05 and 1.45 times faster for $\lambda = 128$ and $\lambda = 256$, respectively. We notice that the improvement can be further enhanced with techniques from [15].

Table 1 shows that our protocol achieves more security properties than the existing ones in the literature. Nevertheless, we compare its complexity with the protocol from [9] which falls into a similar setting to ours. Moreover, we also resolve the scalability question concerning the server needs to serve a large number of IoT devices and store a huge amount of bigdata.

1.3 Paper Organisation

The rest of the paper is organised as follows. In Sect. 2, we describe the security model. In Sect. 3 and Sect. 4, we describe our novel AKE protocol and provide security analyses respectively. In Sect. 5, we detail our implementation procedure and present the evaluation results, and then present the enhanced protocol and corresponding experimental results. In addition, we make a simple comparison and resolve the scalability question. In Sect. 6, we conclude the paper.

2 IoT-Oriented AKE Security Model

In this section, we first describe our IoT-oriented AKE setting, and then present a security model based on the existing ones, e.g. Bellare-Rogaway [4], Shoup model [32], Canetti-Krawczyk model [12], and particularly that of Pointcheval and Zimmer [31].

2.1 IoT-Oriented AKE Setting

For simplicity, we only consider one IoT device and one server, and denote them as c and s respectively. For entity authentication, we assume two factors.

- One is a long-term shared private key mk between the two parties.
- The other is based on a dataset, which contains a large number of data items denoted as d_i $(1 \leq i \leq L)$ for some L. In the initialisation phase, the server processes the dataset with a set of secret keys, which map each data item to a tag. The server sends a subset of the secret keys (denoted as S_c) to the IoT device, and keeps some secret keys (denoted as S_s) together with the data item and tag tuples (d_i, t_i) $(1 \leq i \leq L)$ locally.

In contrast to Chan et al. [14], the dataset is considered as private information in our design. Furthermore, we assume a bounded retrieval model [2,18], which implies that an attacker can only obtain a small portion of the data item and tag tuples (d_i, t_i) $(1 \leq i \leq L)$ when it compromises the server. To sum up, the long-term private credentials for the IoT device and the server are $(mk, \mathcal{S}_c)$ and $(mk, \mathcal{S}_s, (d_i, t_i)$ $(1 \leq i \leq L))$, respectively.

2.2 Preliminary Notions

For our security model, we will adopt the standard game-based definitions. Below, we briefly introduce the preliminary notions.

For generality, we assume the parties can have concurrent runs of the protocol. Each execution of the protocol is called a session. If the attacker is passive, then a session will be happening between two instances, one from the IoT device c and the other from the server s. For a party $p \in \{c, s\}$, we use π_p^i to denote its i-th instance. Each instance can possess the following essential variables:

- *pid*: the partner identifier, where the server's identifier is denoted as s and c represents the identifier of IoT device.
- *sid*: the session identifier, and each *sid* should be unique.
- *sk*: the session key derived by π_p^i at the end of the protocol execution. It is initialized as $\perp$.
- *acc*: the state of acceptance $acc \in \{\perp, accepted, rejected\}$, which represents the state of π_p^i at the end of the protocol execution. It is initialized as $\perp$, will be set as *accepted* if the instance successfully completes the protocol execution, and will be set as *rejected* otherwise.
- *rev*: the status $rev \in \{revealed, unrevealed\}$ of the session key *sk* of π_p^i. It is initialized as *unrevealed*.

We assume the party p maintains a status variable $cpt \in \{corrupted, uncorrupted\}$ which denotes whether or not it has been compromised or corrupted.

The notion of *partnering*, also called *matching conversation*, happens between two instances: one is the instance of an IoT device π_c^i and the other instance of a server π_s^j, for some i and j. It requires the following conditions to be satisfied:

- $\pi_c^i.acc = \pi_s^j.acc = accepted$
- $\pi_c^i.sid = \pi_s^j.sid$
- $\pi_c^i.sk = \pi_s^j.sk$
- $\pi_c^i.pid = s$ and $\pi_s^j.pid = c$

An instance π_p^i $(p \in \{c, s\})$ is said to be *fresh*, if the following conditions are satisfied: $\pi_p^i.acc = accepted$; $\pi_p^i.rev = unrevealed$, $p.cpt = uncorrupted$; if it has any partner instance $\pi_{p'}^j$, then $p'.cpt = uncorrupted$ and $\pi_{p'}^j.rev = unrevealed$.

Definition 1. *An AKE protocol is* sound *if, in the presence of any passive attacker, a protocol execution always successfully ends and results in a matching conversation between the IoT device c and the server s.*

2.3 Game-Based Security Definitions

For game-based security definitions, an attacker $\mathcal{A}$'s advantage over a security property is evaluated by a game played between the attacker and a challenger $\mathcal{C}$ who simulates the activities of the legitimate players, namely the IoT device c and the server s in our setting. In our security model, we assume that $\mathcal{A}$ is a probabilistic polynomial time (P.P.T.). We further assume that $\mathcal{A}$ fully controls the communication network so that it can intercept, delay, modify and delete the messages sent between any two instances.

Formally, the attacker $\mathcal{A}$'s intervention in a security game is modeled via the following oracle queries submitted to the challenger $\mathcal{C}$.

- $Send(msg, \pi_p^i)$: $\mathcal{A}$ can send any message msg to an instance π_p^i via this query. π_p^i responds according to the protocol specification. For simplicity, we assume the attacker can send a null message for the initiator to start a protocol execution.
- $Corrupt_c()$: After receiving this query, the challenger $\mathcal{C}$ returns the long-term key of c, namely mk and $\mathcal{S}_c$. Simultaneously, the challenger $\mathcal{C}$ sets c's status variable as $c.cpt = corrupted$.
- $Corrupt_s(\mathbb{I}_{\mathcal{A}})$: After receiving this query, the challenger $\mathcal{C}$ returns the long-term key of s, namely mk and $\mathcal{S}_s$, and the (d_i, t_i) whose index i falls inside $\mathbb{I}_{\mathcal{A}}$. In the bounded retrieval model, $\mathbb{I}_{\mathcal{A}}$ has a limited size. Simultaneously, the challenger $\mathcal{C}$ sets s's status variable as $s.cpt = corrupted$.
- $Reveal(\pi_p^i)$: This query can only be issued to an accepted instance π_p^i. After receiving this query, the challenger $\mathcal{C}$ returns the contents of the session key $\pi_p^i.sk$. Simultaneously, the session key status of π_p^i and its partner $\pi_{p'}^j$ are set to $\pi_p^i.rev = \pi_{p'}^j.rev = revealed$.
- $Test(\pi_p^i)$: The instance π_p^i should be fresh. After receiving this query, the challenger $\mathcal{C}$ flips a coin $b \in \{0,1\}$ uniformly at random, and returns the session key if $b = 0$, otherwise, it outputs a random string from the session key space.

Definition 2. *In our security model, an AKE protocol is said to be secure if it is sound and the advantages $Adv^{PFS}(\mathcal{A})$, $Adv_s^{KCI}(\mathcal{A})$, $Adv_c^{KCI}(\mathcal{A})$ and $Adv^{SCI}(\mathcal{A})$ are negligible for any P.P.T. attacker $\mathcal{A}$. These advantages are defined in the security games in following-up subsections.*

2.3.1 Session Key Security and Forward Secrecy

This game is designed for modeling session key security, including the known key security property (i.e., the knowledge of session keys generated in other sessions should not help the attacker to learn anything more about the session key in a target session.). In more detail, it is defined as follows:

1. $\mathcal{C}$ generates parameters and gives the public parameters to $\mathcal{A}$.
2. Once $\mathcal{A}$ has all public parameters, it can issue a polynomial number of $Send$ and $Reveal$ queries in any order.

3. At some point, $\mathcal{A}$ chooses a fresh instance π_c^i for some i or π_s^j for some j, and issues a *Test* query.
4. $\mathcal{A}$ can continue issuing queries as in step 2, but not any *Reveal* query to the tested instance and its partner.
5. Eventually, $\mathcal{A}$ terminates the game and outputs a guess bit b' for b.

$\mathcal{A}$ wins the game if $b' = b$. Formally, $\mathcal{A}$'s advantage is defined as $Adv^{SK}(\mathcal{A}) = |\Pr[b = b'] - \frac{1}{2}|$.

In order to model (perfect) forward secrecy, we only need to slightly modify the above game.

– If $\mathcal{A}$ is allowed to issue one of $Corrupt_c$ and $Corrupt_s$ queries in Step 4 of the above game, then we obtain the security game for *forward secrecy*. The attacker $\mathcal{A}$'s advantage is defined as $Adv^{FS}(\mathcal{A}) = |\Pr[b = b'] - \frac{1}{2}|$.
– If $\mathcal{A}$ is allowed to issue both $Corrupt_c$ and $Corrupt_s$ queries in Step 4 of the above game, then we obtain the security game for *perfect forward secrecy*. The attacker $\mathcal{A}$'s advantage is defined as $Adv^{PFS}(\mathcal{A}) = |\Pr[b = b'] - \frac{1}{2}|$.

It is clear that $Adv^{PFS}(\mathcal{A}) \geq Adv^{FS}(\mathcal{A}) \geq Adv^{SK}(\mathcal{A})$. In other words, if $Adv^{PFS}(\mathcal{A})$ is negligible then the others will also be negligible.

2.3.2   Key Compromise Impersonation Resilience

For the KCI property, we consider two scenarios and propose two security games accordingly. In the first scenario, $\mathcal{A}$ impersonates the IoT device c to the corrupted server s. In the second scenario, $\mathcal{A}$ impersonates the server s to the corrupted IoT device c. Next, we describe the security game for the first scenario.

1. $\mathcal{C}$ generates the parameters and gives the public ones to $\mathcal{A}$.
2. $\mathcal{A}$ sends $Corrupt_s$ to $\mathcal{C}$ for the secret information of s.
3. $\mathcal{A}$ can issue a polynomial number of *Send* and *Reveal* queries in any order.
4. $\mathcal{A}$ terminates the game and outputs a session identifier $sid_{\mathcal{A}}$ for a selected instance π_s^j.

Let $Succ_s$ denote an event, defined by the following two conditions. Formally, $\mathcal{A}$'s advantage is defined as $Adv_s^{KCI}(\mathcal{A}) = \Pr[Succ_s]$.

– π_s^j successfully accepts;
– Not all messages π_s^j receives are identical to what have been sent by some instance π_c^i which also possesses $sid_{\mathcal{A}}$ as its session identifier. This condition excludes the trivial "attack" that $\mathcal{A}$ simply relays the message exchanges between π_c^i and π_s^j.

For the second scenario, we only need to make two changes in the above game. In step 2, $\mathcal{A}$ is allowed to issue $Corrupt_c$ query instead of $Corrupt_s$ query. In step 4, $\mathcal{A}$ outputs a session identifier $sid_{\mathcal{A}}$ for a selected instance π_c^i. Let $Succ_c$ denote an event, defined by the following two conditions. Formally, $\mathcal{A}$'s advantage is defined as $Adv_c^{KCI}(\mathcal{A}) = \Pr[Succ_c]$.

– π_c^i successfully accepts;
– Not all messages π_c^i receives are identical to what has been sent by some instance π_s^j which also possesses $sid_{\mathcal{A}}$ as its session identifier.

2.3.3 Server Compromise Impersonation Resilience

For the SCI resilience property, we require that any attacker $\mathcal{A}$ cannot impersonate the server s to the IoT device c even if it can compromise the server, i.e. issuing a $Corrupt_s$ query in the game. The following security game captures this property.

1. $\mathcal{C}$ generates the parameters and gives the public ones to $\mathcal{A}$.
2. $\mathcal{A}$ can send $Corrupt_s$ to $\mathcal{C}$ for the secret information of s.
3. $\mathcal{A}$ can issue a polynomial number of $Send$ and $Reveal$ queries in any order.
4. $\mathcal{A}$ terminates the game and outputs a session identifier $sid_{\mathcal{A}}$ for a selected instance π_c^i.

Let $Succ$ denote an event defined by the following two conditions. Formally, $\mathcal{A}$'s advantage is defined as $Adv^{SCI}(\mathcal{A}) = \Pr[Succ]$.

- π_c^i successfully accepts;
- Not all messages π_c^i receives are identical to what have been sent by some π_s^j which also possesses $sid_{\mathcal{A}}$ as its session identifier.

3   The Proposed AKE Protocol

To bootstrap the AKE protocol, an initialisation phase is required for the IoT device and the server to configure their credentials. In practice, these entities can be configured in a secure lab, and then the IoT device is deployed in the remote environment, say in a factory site. In this section, we first introduce this phase, and then describe the proposed AKE protocol in detail.

3.1   Initialisation Phase

In this phase, the server s chooses a security parameter λ (e.g. $\lambda = 128$ or $\lambda = 256$) and initializes the following public parameters: a group $\mathbb{G}$ of prime order q, a generator g of $\mathbb{G}$, a cryptographic hash function $\mathsf{H} : \{0,1\}^* \to \mathbb{Z}_q$ and two Pseudo-Random Functions (PRFs) $\mathsf{F} : \{0,1\}^\lambda \times \{0,1\}^* \to \mathbb{Z}_q$, $\mathsf{E} : \{0,1\}^\lambda \times \{0,1\}^\lambda \to \{0,1\}^\lambda$. Furthermore, the server s generates a public/private key pair $(pk = g^{sk}, sk)$, where $sk \in \mathbb{Z}_q$, and also generates $sk_1 = \{mk\}$ where $mk \in \{0,1\}^\lambda$ as the long-term shared key and $sk_2 = \{K, K'\}$ for tag generation and data processing where $K \in \mathbb{Z}_q$ and $K' \in \{0,1\}^\lambda$. Suppose the server s possesses a dataset $\mathbb{D}$ which contains L data items d_i ($1 \leq i \leq L$). For every data item $d_i \in \mathbb{D}$, the server generates its tag as $t_i = K \cdot \mathsf{H}(d_i) + \mathsf{F}_{K'}(i)$, which is computed in the finite field $\mathbb{Z}_q$. We define a dataset $\mathbb{D}^*$ which contains all data item and tag tuples (d_i, t_i) ($1 \leq i \leq L$). In addition, the server also chooses an index parameter z which is an integer. For clarity, we summarize the initialisation phase in Fig. 1.

As a quick remark, referring to our problem setting described in Sect. 2.1 and the security model, the IoT device's long-term credentials $\mathcal{S}_c = \{mk, K'\}$ and the server's long-term credentials $\mathcal{S}_s = \{mk, sk, K, \mathbb{D}^*\}$.

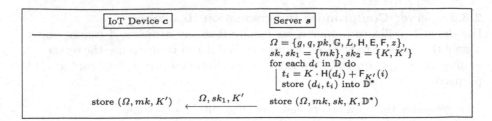

Fig. 1. Initialisation phase

Even though our work is inspired by [14], our initialisation is significantly different in two aspects. Firstly, we assume the dataset $\mathbb{D}$ is pre-configured or randomly generated by the server. This dataset is also treated as secret information for the server. Secondly, the keys for tag generation (namely, sk_2) are split and separately stored in the IoT device c (namely, K) and the server s (namely, K'). Overall, these differences make it impossible for an attacker to forge tags even if it has compromised one party. One specific benefit is that it helps us avoid the vulnerability of Chan et al.'s scheme [14], described in the Appendix of the full paper [27].

3.2 Description of the Proposed AKE Protocol

Intuitively, the proposed AKE protocol is in the Diffie-Hellman style while the mutual authentication is achieved by (1) asking the IoT device and the server to mutually prove the data-tag relationship via the distributed credentials in the *Initialisation Phase*, and (2) asking the server to prove its knowledge about sk via computing a^*. The protocol is summarized in Fig. 2, and its detailed execution is as follows. We use the notation $a \xleftarrow{\$} \mathbb{B}$ to denote selecting a from the set $\mathbb{B}$ uniformly at random.

1. The IoT device c first selects $r_1 \xleftarrow{\$} \mathbb{Z}_q^*$ to compute $a = pk^{r_1}$ and $g' = g^{r_1}$. Then, it selects $r_2 \xleftarrow{\$} \{0,1\}^\lambda$ and a random subset $\mathbb{I}_c$ of z distinct indices for the tuples in $\mathbb{D}^*$, and then sends $g', r_2, \mathbb{I}_c$ and $M_1 = \mathsf{H}(mk||a||g'||r_2||\mathbb{I}_c)$ to the server s.
2. After receiving the message, the server s first computes $a^* = g'^{sk}$ and verifies whether or not $M_1 = \mathsf{H}(mk||a^*||g'||r_2||\mathbb{I}_c)$ holds. If the verification passes, it randomly selects a subset $\mathbb{I}_s$ of z distinct indices which should be disjoint from $\mathbb{I}_c$. Next, it computes $r_2' = \mathsf{E}_{mk}(r_2)$, $X = K \cdot \sum_{i \in \mathbb{I}}^i (\mathsf{H}(d_i) \cdot \mathsf{F}_{r_2'}(i))$ and $Y = \sum_{i \in \mathbb{I}}^i (t_i \cdot \mathsf{F}_{r_2'}(i))$, where $\mathbb{I} = \mathbb{I}_c \cup \mathbb{I}_s$. Note that we assume X, Y are computed in the finite field $\mathbb{Z}_q$. Besides, the server s randomly selects r_3 to compute $b = pk^{r_3}$ and $dh = a^{*r_3}$. Finally, the server s sends $b, \mathbb{I}_s, X$ and $M_2 = \mathsf{H}(a^*||b||dh||\mathbb{I}_s||X||Y||①)$ to the IoT device c. For the sake of space, we use ① to denote the messages sent in the first round, namely, $g', r_2, \mathbb{I}_c, M_1$.

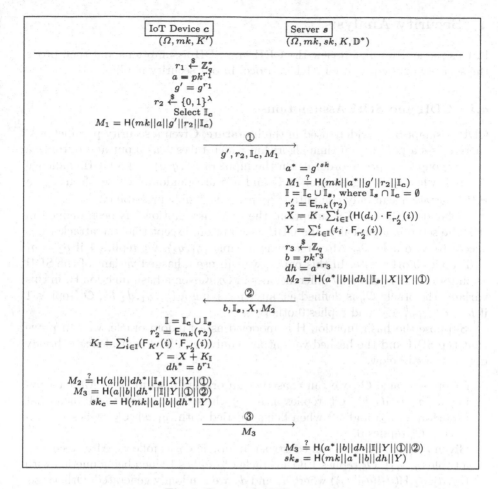

Fig. 2. Proposed AKE protocol

3. After receiving the message, the IoT device c computes $r_2' = \mathsf{E}_{mk}(r_2)$ and $K_\mathbb{I} = \sum_{i\in\mathbb{I}}^i (\mathsf{F}_{K'}(i) \cdot \mathsf{F}_{r_2'}(i))$, where $\mathbb{I} = \mathbb{I}_c \cup \mathbb{I}_s$. Next, it computes $Y = X + K_\mathbb{I}$ and $dh^* = b^{r_1}$, and verifies whether $M_2 = \mathsf{H}(a||b||dh^*||\mathbb{I}_s||X||Y||①)$ holds. If the verification passes, it computes $M_3 = \mathsf{H}(a||b||dh^*||\mathbb{I}||Y||①||②)$ and sends it to the server s. Finally, the IoT device c computes its session key and session identifier as $sk_c = \mathsf{H}(mk||a||b||dh^*||Y)$ and $sid_c = \mathsf{H}(①||②)$ respectively.

4. After receiving the message, the server s verifies whether or not the equality $M_3 = \mathsf{H}(a^*||b||dh||\mathbb{I}||Y||①||②)$ holds. If the verification passes, it computes its session key and session identifier as $sk_s = \mathsf{H}(mk||a^*||b||dh||Y)$ and $sid_s = \mathsf{H}(①||②)$ respectively.

It is straightforward to verify that the above AKE protocol is sound under Definition 1.

4   Security Analysis

In this section, we first review the CDH and SDH assumptions and then prove the security of the proposed AKE protocol in our security model.

4.1   CDH and SDH Assumptions

CDH assumption is widely used in the literature. Given a security parameter λ, there exists a polynomial time algorithm which takes λ as input and outputs a cyclic group $\mathbb{G}$ of prime order q. On the input of $(\mathbb{G}, q, g)$ and a CDH challenge (g^a, g^b), where g is a generator of $\mathbb{G}$ and a, b are randomly chosen from $\mathbb{Z}_q^*$, a P.P.T. attacker can only compute g^{ab} with a negligible probability.

Related to the CDH assumption, the SDH assumption has been defined in [1]. The setup is identical to the CDH assumption, except that the attacker has access to an oracle $\mathcal{O}_b$. After receiving a tuple (g_1, g_2), $\mathcal{O}_b$ replies 1 if $g_2 = g_1^b$ and replies 0 otherwise. In this paper, we will use a hashed variant of the SDH assumption where the only difference lies in $\mathcal{O}_b$. Given a hash function H, in this variant, the oracle $\mathcal{O}_b'$ is defined as: after receiving a (g_1, d_1, d_2, h), $\mathcal{O}_b'$ replies 1 if $h = \mathsf{H}(d_1 || g_1^b || d_2)$ and replies 0 otherwise.

Suppose the hash function H is modeled as a random oracle, we can prove that the SDH and the hashed variant are equivalent. The equivalence is briefly demonstrated below.

- Given an oracle $\mathcal{O}_b$, we can construct an oracle $\mathcal{O}_b'$ as follows. After receiving a (g_1, d_1, d_2, h), $\mathcal{O}_b'$ replies 1 if (1) there is a query to H such that $h = \mathsf{H}(d_1 || x || d_2)$ and (2) when being queried with (g_1, x), $\mathcal{O}_b$ replies 1. Otherwise, $\mathcal{O}_b'$ replies 0.
- Given an oracle $\mathcal{O}_b'$, we can construct an oracle $\mathcal{O}_b$ as follows. After receiving a tuple (g_1, g_2), $\mathcal{O}_b$ replies 1 if the oracle $\mathcal{O}_b'$ replies 1 when being queried with $(g_1, d_1, d_2, \mathsf{H}(d_1 || g_2 || d_2))$ where d_1 and d_2 are randomly generated. Otherwise, $\mathcal{O}_b$ replies 0.

4.2   Security Proofs

We prove the proposed AKE protocol is secure under Definition 2, by showing the advantages $Adv^{PFS}(\mathcal{A})$, $Adv_s^{KCI}(\mathcal{A})$, $Adv_c^{KCI}(\mathcal{A})$ and $Adv^{SCI}(\mathcal{A})$ are negligible in the following Lemmas. Note that we generally assume that the Pseudo-Random Functions (PRFs) are secure and the attacker can only retrieve a limited amount of data from a compromised server (i.e. bounded retrieval model). For the sake of simplicity, we avoid repeating them in each Lemma and the full proofs appear in the full paper [27].

Lemma 1. *The proposed protocol achieves KCI resilience in the first scenario defined in Sect. 2.3.2 (i.e. $\mathcal{A}$ cannot impersonate c to s even after it has compromised s). The security property holds based on the CDH assumption in the random oracle as long as $\frac{\binom{n-z}{z}}{\binom{L-z}{z}}$ is negligible.*

Lemma 2. *The proposed protocol achieves KCI resilience in the second scenario defined in Sect. 2.3.2 (i.e. $\mathcal{A}$ cannot impersonate s to c even after it has compromised c). The security holds based on the SDH assumption in the random oracle.*

Lemma 3. *The proposed protocol achieves SCI resilience property defined in Sect. 2.3.3 (i.e. $\mathcal{A}$ cannot impersonate s to c even after it has compromised s). The security property holds in the random oracle as long as $\frac{\binom{n}{z}}{\binom{L}{z}}$ is negligible.*

It is clear that $\frac{\binom{n}{z}}{\binom{L}{z}} > \frac{\binom{n-z}{z}}{\binom{L-z}{z}}$. To make Lemma 1 and Lemma 3 hold, we (at least) need to make $\frac{\binom{n}{z}}{\binom{L}{z}}$ negligible.

Lemma 4. *The proposed protocol achieves the PFS property based on the SDH assumption in the random oracle as long as $\frac{\binom{n-z}{z}}{\binom{L-z}{z}}$ is negligible.*

5   Performance Evaluation and Enhancements

In Table 2, we summarize the asymptotic complexity (i.e. the number of different types of computations) of the proposed protocol.

Table 2. Complexity of the proposed protocol

	Modular exponentiation	Multiplication	Addition	PRF E	PRF F	Hash H
Tag generation	-	L	L	-	L	L
IoT device	3	$2z$	$2z$	1	$4z$	5
Server	3	$4z + 1$	$4z - 2$	1	$2z$	$2z + 5$

In the rest of this section, we implement our protocol and provide the detailed running time. Furthermore, we show how to reduce the running time for the IoT device. At last, we make a comparison to the protocol from [9] and resolve the scalability question.

5.1   Parameter Selection and Implementation Results

We consider two security levels, namely $\lambda = 128$ and $\lambda = 256$. Next, we first describe how to set up the parameters and then present the implementation results.

5.1.1 Parameter Setup

With respect to the instantiation of group $\mathbb{G}$, we use the Koblitz curve secp256k1 and secp521r1, respectively. These curves are recommended parameters defined in Standards for Efficient Cryptography [33], and the parameters can be found in the Appendix of the full paper [27]. When $\lambda = 256$, we use SHA-256 to implement the function H and use HMAC-SHA256 to instantiate the PRF E. For the PRF F, we can also use HMAC-SHA256 by truncating its output size to q. When $\lambda = 128$, we can further truncate the outputs of these functions to fit into the required domain. We skip the detail here.

Given a security parameter, we take the following approach to determine the parameters L, n, z.

1. Since we rely on the bounded retrieval model, we need to first set a threshold τ, which limits how much data an attacker can retrieve if it has compromised the server. For our implementation, we suppose the attacker can only retrieve $\tau = 100$ MB data. It will be straightforward to adapt our discussions to other τ values.
2. With τ, we enumerate some potential sizes for a single data item in $\mathbb{D}$. Let the sizes be denoted as x_i ($1 \le i \le T$) for some integer T. For every x_i, we do the following.
   (a) Compute $n_i = \frac{\tau}{x_i}$, which represents the number of tuples an attacker can retrieve if it has compromised the server.
   (b) With n_i, we need to try different (z, L) pairs so that $\frac{\binom{n}{z}}{\binom{L}{z}}$ is negligible w.r.t the security parameter. Note that a smaller z requires a larger L.
   (c) Evaluate the obtained (z, L) pairs, and try to find the one which results in a good balance between the size of $\mathbb{D}$ (i.e. $L \times x_i$) and the complexity of $2z$ hash computations. In another word, both z and L should not be too large. It is also worth noting that if z is very large, there is also the cost of multiplications in the computation of X and Y for the server (this makes a difference in our case of $\lambda = 256$, see below).
3. Further evaluate the (z, L) pairs for all x_i ($1 \le i \le T$) obtained at the end of last step, and select the most suitable one.

In the following table, we enumerate five options for the size of a single data item in $\mathbb{D}$ and present the hashing time and the value for n correspondingly. All the computations are done with a PC, with its configurations described in the next subsection.

Table 3. Data item sizes

Data item size (MB)	0.0005	0.001	0.01	0.1	1
Hash one data item (ms)	0.004	0.007	0.068	0.689	6.698
Value of n	10^6	10^5	10^4	10^3	10^2

For the security parameter $\lambda = 128$, we compute the (z, L) pairs shown in Table 4, where the top row lists different data item size and n value tuples.

Each pair guarantees that $\frac{\binom{n}{z}}{\binom{L}{z}} \leq \frac{1}{2^{128}}$. In the table, we have also presented the computation time for $2z$ hashes and the storage for the server. From the table, it seems the most appropriate pair is $(z = 50, L = 5896957)$, which achieves a better balance for hashing time and storage for the server. If storage is more important for the server, then $(z = 50, L = 589588)$ can be the alternative.

Table 4. Determine (z, L) when $\lambda = 128$

	$(0.0005, 10^6)$	$(0.001, 10^5)$	$(0.01, 10^4)$	$(0.1, 10^3)$	$(1, 10^2)$
Value of L when $z = 10$	7131518127	713122933	71283411	7099433	680759
Size of $\mathbb{D}$ (GB)	3565.76	713.12	712.83	709.94	680.76
Hash $2z$ data items (ms)	0.075	0.14	1.38	13.91	134.02
Value of L when $z = 20$	84447713	8444058	843693	83655	7637
Size of $\mathbb{D}$ (GB)	42.22	8.44	8.43	8.37	7.64
Hash $2z$ data items (ms)	0.15	0.27	2.73	26.89	267.91
Value of L when $z = 50$	**5896957**	589588	58851	5777	462
Size of $\mathbb{D}$ (GB)	**2.95**	0.59	0.59	5.78	0.46
Hash $2z$ data items (ms)	**0.36**	0.72	6.77	67.49	669.29
Value of L when $z = 100$	2428319	242769	24214	2357	147
Size of $\mathbb{D}$ (GB)	1.21	0.24	0.24	0.24	0.15
Hash $2z$ data items (ms)	0.73	1.45	13.73	135.31	1342.25

For the security parameter $\lambda = 256$, we compute the (z, L) pairs shown in Table 5. Each pair guarantees that $\frac{\binom{n}{z}}{\binom{L}{z}} \leq \frac{1}{2^{256}}$. It may seem that $(z = 100, L = 5896835)$ is a good choice. However, considering also the costs in multiplications (see our explanation in Step 2. (c)) from the aforementioned approach description, the most appropriate pair is $(z = 50, L = 3476724)$ in this case. In addition, we do not choose $(z = 50, L = 34774689)$ because the storage is too high.

Table 5. Determine (z, L) when $\lambda = 256$

	$(0.0005, 10^6)$	$(0.001, 10^5)$	$(0.01, 10^4)$	$(0.1, 10^3)$	$(1, 10^2)$
Value of L when $z = 10$	50858779596503	5085671978593	508361198100	50629932185	4854873253
Dataset size (GB)	25429389.80	5085671.98	5083611.98	5062993.22	4854873.25
Hash $2z$ data items (ms)	0.081	0.14	1.37	14.11	142.14
Value of L when $z = 20$	7131482474	713087280	71247750	7063691	644102
Size of $\mathbb{D}$ (GB)	3565.74	713.09	712.48	706.37	644.10
Hash $2z$ data items (ms)	0.16	0.29	2.76	25.47	265.13
Value of L when $z = 50$	34774689	**3476724**	346928	33945	2601
Size of $\mathbb{D}$ (GB)	17.39	**3.48**	3.47	3.39	2.60
Hash $2z$ data items (ms)	0.36	**0.89**	6.67	64.22	673.19
Value of L when $z = 100$	5896835	589466	58729	5653	276
Size of $\mathbb{D}$ (GB)	2.95	0.59	0.06	0.57	0.28
Hash $2z$ data items (ms)	0.71	1.44	14.21	139.64	1324.91

5.1.2   Implementation Results

With the selected parameters from the previous subsection, we implement the proposed AKE protocol in C with the MIRACL cryptographic library [30][1]. In the experiment, we use a PC as the server. It has an Intel® Core™ i7-4770 CPU @ 3.4 GHz processor with 16 GB RAM. In the literature, most benchmarks are implemented by using a single-board computer to simulate an IoT device, like Arduino, BeagleBone Black, Raspberry Pi, etc. [14,23,24]. Therefore, we use a Raspberry Pi 3 Model B+ with ARM Cortex-A53 @ 1.4 GHz processor and 1 GB RAM as the IoT device. To obtain fair execution results, we execute the codes ten times and take the average. Table 6 depicts the results. From the table, we observe that the running time of the server is much smaller than that of the IoT device. This may look strange, but it could be preferable in practice given that the server may need to support a large number of IoT devices. For the IoT device, the running time 15.19 ms (when $\lambda = 128$) and 84.73 ms (when $\lambda = 256$) could be acceptable in many application scenarios. But, it will be interesting to reduce this complexity, particularly for IoT devices which have less computing power than the Raspberry Pi.

Table 6. Running time (ms)

	Modular exponentiation	Multiplication	Addition	PRF E	PRF F	Hash H	Total
$\lambda = 128$, Elliptic Curve: secp256k1, $L = 5896957, n = 10^6, z = 50$							
IoT device	13.61	0.16	0.03	0.04	0.66	0.06	**15.19**
Server	1.69	0.04	0.01	0.04	0.06	0.37	**2.44**
$\lambda = 256$, Elliptic Curve: secp521r1, $L = 3476724, n = 10^5, z = 50$							
IoT device	81.96	0.34	0.05	0.04	0.96	0.12	**84.73**
Server	11.08	0.09	0.02	0.02	0.07	0.73	**12.51**

5.2   Efficiency Enhancement for the IoT

Referring to the AKE protocol in Fig. 2 from Sect. 3.2, the values of a and g' can be computed in advance. By doing so, the IoT device can avoid about two-thirds of the computations required in the protocol execution.

Besides the "trivial" pre-computation strategy, we can try to offload one exponentiation from IoT to the server. For the enhanced AKE protocol, the initialisation phase stays the same except the following.

– IoT device is configured with a set $\mathbb{S}$ which contains tuples in the form of (g^u, u) where $u \xleftarrow{\$} \mathbb{Z}_q^*$. This allows us to outsource the computation of g^{r_1} to the server without revealing r_1.
– The original (pk, sk) is discarded and a new key pair (spk, ssk) is generated for a signature scheme (Sign, Verify) which achieves *existential unforgeability under chosen-message attacks* (EUF-CMA). This is necessary to achieve KCI resilience when the attacker compromises the IoT device.

---

[1] Source code is available at https://github.com/n00d1e5/Demo_Bigdata-facilitated_Two-party_AKE_for_IoT.

The Enhanced AKE protocol is summarized in Fig. 3.

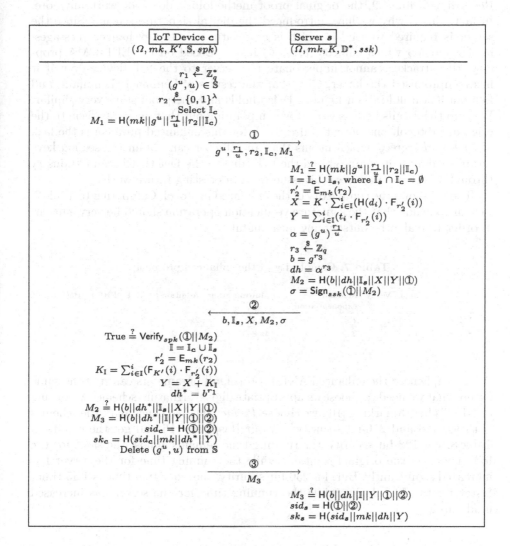

Fig. 3. Enhanced AKE protocol

Regarding the security of the enhanced protocol, we sketch below how the Lemmas from Sect. 4 still hold. First of all, the results of Lemma 1 and Lemma 3 will not be affected because compromising the server does not give the attacker any more privileges. Intuitively, our modification against the original AKE protocol from Sect. 3 does not give any more power to the attacker when it compromises the server, i.e. in the original case, it obtains sk while in the enhanced protocol it obtains ssk. In addition, the security results mainly come from the inability for the attacker to forge bigdata-related information. The new security proofs can be carried out in a very similar manner, we skip the details here. Regarding Lemma 2, the original proof methodology does not work anymore. In fact, this is why we have introduced the digital signature scheme. Since the server is required to send σ which is a signature for the exchanged messages, i.e. ① and M_2 which embeds $(b, \mathbb{I}_s, X)$ inside. Based on the EUF-CMA property, the attacker cannot impersonate the server to the IoT device even if it has compromised the latter. Give that the results of Lemma 1, Lemma 2, and Lemma 3 still hold, then Lemma 4 also holds and the proof stays very similar. We skip the details here as well. It worth pointing out that, in comparison to the original protocol, one potential drawback for this enhanced protocol is the lack of *backward secrecy*, which means that an attacker can obtain the session keys established after it compromised the IoT (due to the fact that it can obtains r_1 through u). How to address this issue is an interesting future work.

Table 7 shows the complexity of the enhanced protocol. Comparing to Table 2, we can conclude that the signature verification operation should be very efficient in order to make the outsourcing meaningful.

Table 7. Complexity of the enhanced protocol

	Sign	Verify	Modular exponentiation	Multiplication	Addition	PRF E	PRF F	Hash H
IoT device	-	1	1	$2z$	$2z$	1	$4z$	5
Server	1	-	3	$4z + 1$	$4z - 2$	1	$2z$	$2z + 5$

To implement the enhanced AKE protocol, all parameters can stay the same except that we need to choose an appropriate digital signature scheme. According to NIST's benchmarking [16], we choose *Picnic* [29]. We benchmark the schemes both for 128 and 256-bit security[2] on our Raspberry Pi and get the results in Table 8. For 128-bit security, the running time remains almost the same for the IoT device as the original solution, while the running time for the server has increased significantly. But, for 256-bit security, the execution time is 1.45 times faster for the IoT device while the running time for the server has increased moderately.

Table 8. Running time (ms)

	Sign	Verify	Modular exp.	Multiplication	Addition	PRF E	PRF F	Hash H	Total
$\lambda = 128$, Elliptic Curve: secp256k1, $L = 5896957$, $n = 10^6$, $z = 50$									
IoT device	-	8.32	4.54	0.16	0.03	0.04	0.66	0.06	**14.44**
Server	10.34	-	1.69	0.04	0.01	0.04	0.06	0.37	**12.78**
$\lambda = 256$, Elliptic Curve: secp521r1, $L = 3476724$, $n = 10^5$, $z = 50$									
IoT device	-	28.36	27.32	0.34	0.05	0.04	0.96	0.12	**58.45**
Server	33.83	-	11.08	0.09	0.02	0.02	0.07	0.73	**46.34**

---

[2] Source code of both schemes picnic-L1-full for 128-bit security and picnic-L5-full for 256-bit security is available at https://github.com/IAIK/Picnic.

Furthermore, it is clear that if there is a more efficient signature scheme, then the efficiency gain will be more for the enhanced AKE protocol. To further improve its efficiency, we can also try to outsource the computation of $dh^* = b^{r_1}$ to the server. To this end, *Protocol 5* from [15] can be employed. A detailed investigation of this direction is an interesting future work.

5.3   Comparison with Existing Protocol(s)

Regarding the setting mentioned in the beginning of Sect. 1, the protocol from [9] is similar to ours, even though it does not achieve the KCI and SCI properties. We choose 128-bit AES to instantiate the encryption algorithm and use the same group to implement this protocol for the security level $\lambda = 128$, and summarize the results in Table 9. In comparison to the results from Table 6, it is clear that the complexities for the IoT device are very close while the complexity for the server is slightly higher in our protocol. Note also the fact that we have not taken into account the PUF operations, which may increase the complexity for the IoT device for the protocol from [9].

Table 9. Complexity and Running time (ms) of [9]

	Modular exponentiation	Encryption	Decryption	Hash H	Total
IoT Device	13.61	0.00006	-	0.06	≈13.67
Server	1.69	0.000006	0.000006	0.02	≈1.71

In this paper, we have assumed a setting with one IoT device and the server. In practice, the server may serve a large number of IoT devices, e.g. thousands of them. In this case, the security properties will not be affected in any manner, but there are potential scalability concerns. From our implementation results, the running time of the server can scale to a considerable number of IoT devices, and the main concern is the storage. Below, we propose a simple solution to resolve this question.

Instead of storing an individual dataset $\mathbb{D}$ for every IoT device, the server can store a global dataset $\tilde{\mathbb{D}}$ which contains L data items $\tilde{d}_i$ $(1 \le i \le L)$. In addition, the server can generate a global secret key gk for dataset configuration. Consider an IoT device, which has the identifier id. For both the *Initialisation Phase* and the AKE protocol, the server can construct a dataset $\mathbb{D}$ for this IoT device on-the-fly, where every element d_i is derived from $\tilde{d}_i$ as follows:

$$d_i = \tilde{H}(id\|gk\|\tilde{d}_i)$$

where $\tilde{H}$ is a hash function. By doing so, the server only needs to store the global dataset $\tilde{\mathbb{D}}$ and ephemerally generate $\mathbb{D}$ when necessary. When the cryptographic hash function $\tilde{H}$ is modeled as a random oracle, it is straightforward to verify that the security properties of the proposed protocols will not be affected. Due to the space limitation, we skip the details here.

6   Conclusion

Motivated by Chan et al.'s unilateral authentication scheme [14], we have proposed a bigdata-facilitated two-party AKE protocol for IoT systems. The proposed protocol achieves a wide range of security properties including PFS, KCI resilience and SCI resilience. In particular, the KCI and SCI resilience properties are well demanded by the IoT environment, and cannot be satisfied by existing AKE protocols. Furthermore, we have presented an enhanced protocol, which can significantly reduce the computation load for the IoT with an appropriate signature scheme. Our work has left a number of future research directions. As mentioned in Sect. 5.2, it is an immediate future work to give a formal proof of the enhanced AKE protocol even if it is almost straightforward. Furthermore, it is worth investigating to further improve the efficiency of the protocol by integrating the *Protocol 5* from [15] and evaluate its efficiency gain vs the added communication complexity. Along this direction, it is also worth exploring other signature schemes which have better verification efficiency.

Acknowledgement. This paper is supported in the context of the project CATALYST funded by Fonds National de la Recherche Luxembourg (FNR, reference 12186579).

References

1. Abdalla, M., Bellare, M., Rogaway, P.: The oracle Diffie-Hellman assumptions and an analysis of DHIES. In: Naccache, D. (ed.) CT-RSA 2001. LNCS, vol. 2020, pp. 143–158. Springer, Heidelberg (2001). https://doi.org/10.1007/3-540-45353-9_12
2. Alwen, J., Dodis, Y., Wichs, D.: Leakage-Resilient public-key cryptography in the bounded-retrieval model. In: Halevi, S. (ed.) CRYPTO 2009. LNCS, vol. 5677, pp. 36–54. Springer, Heidelberg (2009). https://doi.org/10.1007/978-3-642-03356-8_3
3. Aumann, Y., Ding, Y.Z., Rabin, M.O.: Everlasting security in the bounded storage model. IEEE Trans. Inf. Theory **48**(6), 1668–1680 (2002)
4. Bellare, M., Rogaway, P.: Entity authentication and key distribution. In: Stinson, D.R. (ed.) CRYPTO 1993. LNCS, vol. 773, pp. 232–249. Springer, Heidelberg (1994). https://doi.org/10.1007/3-540-48329-2_21
5. Blake-Wilson, S., Menezes, A.: Authenticated Diffie-Hellman key agreement protocols. In: Tavares, S., Meijer, H. (eds.) SAC 1998. LNCS, vol. 1556, pp. 339–361. Springer, Heidelberg (1999). https://doi.org/10.1007/3-540-48892-8_26
6. Boyd, C., Mathuria, A., Stebila, D.: Protocols for Authentication and Key Establishment. Springer, Heidelberg (2020). https://doi.org/10.1007/978-3-662-58146-9
7. Brainard, J., Juels, A., Rivest, R.L., Szydlo, M., Yung, M.: Fourth-factor authentication: somebody you know. In: Proceedings of the 13th ACM Conference on Computer and Communications Security, pp. 168–178 (2006)
8. Byun, J.W.: A generic multifactor authenticated key exchange with physical unclonable function. Secur. Commun. Networks **2019** (2019)
9. Byun, J.W.: An efficient multi-factor authenticated key exchange with physically unclonable function. In: 2019 International Conference on Electronics, Information, and Communication (ICEIC), pp. 1–4. IEEE (2019)

10. Byun, J.W.: End-to-end authenticated key exchange based on different physical unclonable functions. IEEE Access **7**, 102951–102965 (2019)
11. Byun, J.W.: PDAKE: a provably secure PUF-based device authenticated key exchange in cloud setting. IEEE Access **7**, 181165–181177 (2019)
12. Canetti, R., Krawczyk, H.: Analysis of key-exchange protocols and their use for building secure channels. In: Pfitzmann, B. (ed.) EUROCRYPT 2001. LNCS, vol. 2045, pp. 453–474. Springer, Heidelberg (2001). https://doi.org/10.1007/3-540-44987-6_28
13. Challa, S., et al.: Secure signature-based authenticated key establishment scheme for future IoT applications. IEEE Access **5**, 3028–3043 (2017)
14. Chan, A.C.-F., Wong, J.W., Zhou, J., Teo, J.: Scalable two-factor authentication using historical data. In: Askoxylakis, I., Ioannidis, S., Katsikas, S., Meadows, C. (eds.) ESORICS 2016. LNCS, vol. 9878, pp. 91–110. Springer, Cham (2016). https://doi.org/10.1007/978-3-319-45744-4_5
15. Chevalier, C., Laguillaumie, F., Vergnaud, D.: Privately outsourcing exponentiation to a single server: cryptanalysis and optimal constructions. Algorithmica **83**(1), 72–115 (2020). https://doi.org/10.1007/s00453-020-00750-2
16. Dang, V.B., Farahmand, F., Andrzejczak, M., Mohajerani, K., Nguyen, D.T., Gaj, K.: Implementation and benchmarking of round 2 candidates in the NIST post-quantum cryptography standardization process using hardware and software/hardware co-design approaches. Cryptology ePrint Archive: Report 2020/795 (2020)
17. Davies, S.G.: Touching Big Brother: how biometric technology will fuse flesh and machine. Inf. Technol. People **7**(4), 38–47 (1994)
18. Di Crescenzo, G., Lipton, R., Walfish, S.: Perfectly secure password protocols in the bounded retrieval model. In: Halevi, S., Rabin, T. (eds.) TCC 2006. LNCS, vol. 3876, pp. 225–244. Springer, Heidelberg (2006). https://doi.org/10.1007/11681878_12
19. Dziembowski, S.: Intrusion-Resilience via the bounded-storage model. In: Halevi, S., Rabin, T. (eds.) TCC 2006. LNCS, vol. 3876, pp. 207–224. Springer, Heidelberg (2006). https://doi.org/10.1007/11681878_11
20. Fleischhacker, N., Manulis, M., Azodi, A.: A modular framework for multi-factor authentication and key exchange. In: Chen, L., Mitchell, C. (eds.) SSR 2014. LNCS, vol. 8893, pp. 190–214. Springer, Cham (2014). https://doi.org/10.1007/978-3-319-14054-4_12
21. Guo, C., Chang, C.C.: Chaotic maps-based password-authenticated key agreement using smart cards. Commun. Nonlinear Sci. Numer. Simul. **18**(6), 1433–1440 (2013)
22. Hao, F., Clarke, D.: Security analysis of a multi-factor authenticated key exchange protocol. In: Bao, F., Samarati, P., Zhou, J. (eds.) ACNS 2012. LNCS, vol. 7341, pp. 1–11. Springer, Heidelberg (2012). https://doi.org/10.1007/978-3-642-31284-7_1
23. Kruger, C.P., Hancke, G.P.: Benchmarking Internet of Things devices. In: 2014 12th IEEE International Conference on Industrial Informatics (INDIN), pp. 611–616. IEEE (2014)
24. Krylovskiy, A.: Internet of things gateways meet linux containers: performance evaluation and discussion. In: 2015 IEEE 2nd World Forum on Internet of Things (WF-IoT), pp. 222–227. IEEE (2015)
25. Lee, Y., Kim, S., Won, D.: Enhancement of two-factor authenticated key exchange protocols in public wireless LANs. Comput. Electr. Eng. **36**(1), 213–223 (2010)
26. Li, Z., Yang, Z., Szalachowski, P., Zhou, J.: Building low-interactivity multi-factor authenticated key exchange for industrial Internet-of-Things. IEEE Internet of Things J. **8**(2), 844–859 (2020)

27. Liu, B., Tang, Q., Zhou, J.: Bigdata-facilitated Two-party Authenticated Key Exchange for IoT (full paper) (2021). https://eprint.iacr.org/2021/1131. Accessed 10 Sept 2021
28. Liu, Yu., Xue, K.: An improved secure and efficient password and chaos-based two-party key agreement protocol. Nonlinear Dyn. **84**(2), 549–557 (2015). https://doi.org/10.1007/s11071-015-2506-2
29. Microsoft: The Picnic Signature Algorithm. https://github.com/microsoft/Picnic/
30. MIRACL Ltd.: Multiprecision Integer and Rational Arithmetic Cryptographic Library – the MIRACL Crypto SDK (2019). https://github.com/miracl/MIRACL
31. Pointcheval, D., Zimmer, S.: Multi-factor authenticated key exchange. In: Bellovin, S.M., Gennaro, R., Keromytis, A., Yung, M. (eds.) ACNS 2008. LNCS, vol. 5037, pp. 277–295. Springer, Heidelberg (2008). https://doi.org/10.1007/978-3-540-68914-0_17
32. Shoup, V.: On Formal Models for Secure Key Exchange. Cryptology ePrint Archive, Report 1999/012 (1999). https://eprint.iacr.org/1999/012
33. Standards for Efficient Cryptography (SEC): SEC 2: Recommended elliptic curve domain parameters (2000)
34. Stebila, D., Udupi, P., Chang Shantz, S.: Multi-factor password-authenticated key exchange. Inf. Secur. **2010**, 56–66 (2010)

Randomized Component Based Secure Secret Reconstruction in Insecure Networks

Xinyan Wang and Fuyou Miao(✉)

School of Computer Science and Technology, University of Science and Technology of China, Hefei 230026, China
mfy@ustc.edu.cn

Abstract. In Shamir (t, n) secret sharing scheme, the secret can be recovered by any t or more than t shareholders. However, in insecure networks, if the number of participants is greater than t, a participant who does not own a valid share can also recover the secret by collecting components from other honest shareholders. Harn proposed the first secure secret reconstruction scheme, which used linear combination of shares to solve this problem, but this scheme is vulnerable to linear subspace attack. Miao used randomized component to disrupt the linear relationship and protect the share from being exposed. However, it can also be attacked by lattice. In this paper, we propose two randomized component based secure secret reconstruction schemes in insecure networks. The first scheme uses a random element whose distribution range at least equals to the share to protect the secrecy of share. Furthermore, the scheme is ideal and perfect. The second scheme is an improved scheme using bivariate polynomial, which is not only used for share and randomized component generation, but for secure channel construction. We don't need to establish the secure channel for each pairwise shareholders in advance. s-box transmission breaks the linear relationship among randomized components and guarantee the perfect secrecy of our scheme.

Keywords: Secret sharing · Insecure networks · Secure secret reconstruction · Randomized component · Bivariate polynomial

1 Introduction

(t, n) secret sharing (SS) was first introduced respectively by Shamir [22] and Blakley [4] in 1979. It is mainly divided into share distribution and secret reconstruction these two parts. In distribution phase, a mutually trusted dealer divides the secret s into n shares and distributes them to n shareholders through secure channel. Then threshold t or more than t shareholders cooperate in the secret reconstruction to reconstruct the secret, while less than t shareholders cannot

Supported by National Key R&D Program of China 2018YFB0803405.

J. K. Liu et al. (Eds.): ISC 2021, LNCS 13118, pp. 117–138, 2021.
https://doi.org/10.1007/978-3-030-91356-4_7

get any information about the secret. Different from Shamir scheme of recovering secret using interpolation polynomials, Bloom [3] also proposed a secret sharing scheme using Chinese Remainder Theorem (CRT) in 1983. Then many secret sharing schemes (i.e. [5,6,10,20,24]) based on Chinese Remainder Theorem were proposed.

Shamir (t,n) secret sharing scheme can realize that any t or more than t shareholders can recover the secret. However, when the communication among shareholders is in an insecure network, it may lead to some threats. We show the two models of active attack and passive attack in Fig. 1.

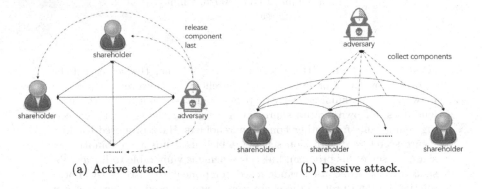

(a) Active attack.   (b) Passive attack.

Fig. 1. Model of attacks in insecure networks.

(a) **Active attack:** If the number of participants is larger than t, there may exist an active attack adversary who does not own a valid share participating in secret reconstruction and releasing his components last. In this case, he can recover the secret or forge a legal share by collecting enough components from other honest shareholders.

(b) **Passive attack:** Since all components are sent in insecure networks, even a passive attack adversary who does not participate in the secret reconstruction directly, he can eavesdrop all components sent in secret reconstruction and recover the secret himself.

1.1   Related Work

One potential method against passive attack is establishing secure channels for each pair of shareholders. Many proposed secret sharing schemes are based on the assumption that secure channels have been established in advance. Then in order to resist active attack, Chor [7] proposed verifiable secret sharing (VSS) to verify other participants' shares before secret reconstruction. In a VSS scheme, each shareholder verifies the authenticity of received shares rather than uses them to recover the secret directly. There are also many research papers (i.e. [2,8,15, 21,25]) based on VSS. However, VSS scheme requires more calculation processes. Furthermore, the adversary still gets valid shares from honest shareholders even though his illegal behaviour can be detected.

Harn [9] proposed secure secret reconstruction (SSR) using linear combination of shares to protect the privacy of shares and prevent the adversary from obtaining secret by releasing his share last. Then more schemes based on secure secret reconstruction were proposed. Xiao [27] modified the scheme [9] by changing the degree of polynomial. Harn [12] proposed an asynchronously rational secret sharing scheme to solve the problem, in which a dishonest shareholder can release a fake share at last to make the correct secret recoverable only by himself when shares are released asynchronously. Using bivariate polynomial, Hsu [14] proposed a secure secret reconstruction scheme which can verify all shares at once; Meng [18] proposed a threshold changeable secret sharing, which can increase the threshold of the scheme to the exact number of the participants. Then Harn [13] proposed a secure secret reconstruction scheme which claimed to be information theoretical secure. He [11] also proposed a dynamic threshold secret sharing scheme using bivariate polynomial, which can make the threshold equal to the exact number of participants.

However, a participant who does not own a valid share can also forge a legal share in secure secret reconstruction schemes [9,11] by using linear subspace cryptanalysis [1,16]. Since the schemes [12–14,18,27] employ the same idea as scheme [9] to protect the share, all these schemes can be attacked by subspace linear attack. Ahmadian [1] found that $t + k - 1$ valid released components are sufficient to forge any number of components in scheme [9]. Then Jamshidpour [16] found that no matter how large the threshold is, any $t + 1$ released components can recover the secret and forge a legal share in scheme [11]. Xia [26] also analyzed the linear subspace attack in schemes [9,11] and introduced a game-based model that can be used to formally analyze secret sharing schemes.

The main drawback in Harn scheme [9] is that $t + k - 1$ components expand a linear subspace of components. That is, an adversary can forge a legal share if he knows $t + k - 1$ linearly independent components. In order to prevent this attack, Miao [19] proposed a randomized component based secure secret sharing scheme. Compared to scheme [9], this scheme uses random integers to break the linear relationship among components. Furthermore, each shareholder only needs to own one share. Based on Miao scheme, Meng [17] also proposed a novel threshold changeable secret sharing scheme. However, as the distribution range of random integers in Miao scheme is smaller than share, it leads to short vectors consisting these random integers. The scheme is vulnerable to lattice attack.

1.2 Our Contribution

Based on the idea of randomized component in Miao scheme [19], we propose two secure secret reconstruction schemes in insecure networks, one is based on Chinese Remainder Theorem for polynomial and the other is based on bivariate polynomial. We add random element in our schemes to break the relationship among components. Then different from Miao scheme, the distribution range of our random element is no less than that of shares. As a result, both schemes can well protect the secrecy of shares and resist lattice attack.

We summarize contributions as follows:

- A (t, n) secure secret reconstruction scheme based on Chinese Remainder Theorem for polynomial is proposed. Using a novel randomized polynomial whose distribution range is no less than that of shares, the scheme can prevent the participant who does not own a valid share from recovering the secret and forging a legal share. This scheme can resist both the linear subspace attack and lattice attack. Furthermore, it is perfect and ideal.
- A (t, n) secure secret reconstruction scheme based on bivariate polynomial is proposed, in which bivariate polynomial is used to generate shares, secure channel key and randomized components. Shareholders don't need to establish secure channels in advance. s-boxes are used during the generation of randomized components to enable the scheme to be resistant to both linear subspace and lattice attack.

1.3   Organization

The rest of this paper is organized as follows. Section 2 introduces some preliminaries and analyzes the problems of secure secret reconstruction schemes [9,19]. Section 3 introduces the model and security goals. In Sect. 4, a basic SSR scheme based on CRT for polynomial is proposed. In Sect. 5, an improved SSR scheme using bivariate polynomial is also proposed. Section 6 describes our schemes' properties and compares our schemes with other SSR schemes. Conclusion is included in Sect. 7.

2   Preliminaries

Some definitions are introduced in this section. Then description of Asmuth-Bloom (t, n) secret sharing and secure secret reconstruction schemes [9,19] are also given.

Definition 1. *Information entropy*

Suppose X is a discrete-time discrete valued random variable with a sample space SP. Let $H(\cdot)$ be the information entropy function, then the entropy of X is denoted as:

$$H(X) = E(-\log_2 P(X)) = \sum_{x \in SP} -P(x)\log_2 P(x),$$

where E is the expectation operator and $P(\cdot)$ is the probability distribution function of X.

Definition 2. *Perfect secrecy [23]*

For any distribution on plaintext space M and the corresponding distribution on ciphertext space C, the condition of perfect secrecy for an encryption scheme $\Pi = (Gen, Enc, Dec)$ is that

$$\Pr(M = m | C = c) = \Pr(M = m),$$

where m is a plaintext and c is a ciphertext.

Perfect Secrecy Necessary Condition: If an encryption scheme with message space M and key space K satisfies perfect secrecy, then $|K| \geq |M|$. From the view of information entropy, a perfect secrecy scheme satisfies $H(K) \geq H(M)$.

Definition 3. *Perfect secret sharing scheme*
   Let P be a set of participants, Γ be an access structure on P and S be the set of secrets. A perfect secret sharing scheme $PS(\Gamma, S)$ satisfies:

1. *any qualified subset can reconstruct the secret:* $\forall_{X \in \Gamma} H(S|X) = 0$;
2. *any non-qualified subset has no information on secret:* $\forall_{X \notin \Gamma} H(S|X) = H(S)$.

Definition 4. *Information Rate*
   Information rate is the size ratio of secret to share. Let s be the secret and $S = \{s_1, s_2, \dots s_n\}$ be the share set, then the information rate is

$$\rho = \frac{\log_2 |s|}{\max_{s_i \in S}(\log_2 |s_i|)}.$$

Ideal Secret Sharing Scheme: If a perfect scheme has the information rate 1, it's an ideal scheme.

2.1   Asmuth-Bloom (t, n) SS Scheme

Asmuth-Bloom (t, n) SS Scheme is a secret sharing scheme based on Chinese Remainder Theorem (CRT). First, dealer selects a large prime p and a secret $s < p$. Then dealer selects n pairwise coprime integers $m_1, m_2, \dots m_n$ satisfying:

1. $m_1 < m_2 < \dots < m_n$;
2. $\gcd(m_i, p) = 1, 1 \leq i \leq n$ and $\gcd(m_i, m_j) = 1, 1 \leq j \leq n, j \neq i$;
3. $m_1 m_2 \dots m_t > p m_{n-t+2} m_{n-t+3} \dots m_n$.

Share Generation. Let $m = m_1 m_2 \dots m_t$, then dealer selects a random integer r in $[0, \frac{m}{p} - 1]$ and calculates $s' = s + rp$. Each shareholder's share is $s_i = s' \bmod m_i (i = 1, 2, \dots, n)$, where m_i is the public identity of shareholder U_i.
Secret Reconstruction. If $h(h \geq t)$ shareholders try to recover the secret, the following system of congruence equations can be obtained:

$$\begin{cases} s' = s_1 \bmod m_1 \\ s' = s_2 \bmod m_2 \\ \dots \\ s' = s_h \bmod m_h \end{cases}.$$

According to the Chinese Remainder Theorem, because of $m_1 m_2 \dots m_h \geq m$, the system has a unique solution s' and the secret $s = s' \bmod p$.

2.2 Harn (t,n) Secure Secret Reconstruction Scheme

In order to prevent the participant who does not own a valid share from recovering the secret, Harn proposed a (t,n) secure secret reconstruction scheme. Shareholders need to compute a linear combination of multiple shares as Lagrange component. Then on the basis of this scheme, Harn also modified it to a secure multi-secret sharing scheme with h shares. The following is a detailed description of Harn (t,n) secure multi-secret sharing scheme with h shares.

Share Generation. To reconstruct h secrets $s_i(i = 1, 2, \ldots, h)$ for n shareholders, dealer selects k random polynomials $f_l(x)(l = 1, 2, \ldots, k)$ of degree $t-1$, where $kt > h(n+1) - 2$ and $k > (h-1)(n-t+2)$. Dealer sends k shares $f_l(x_r)$ to each shareholder U_r secretly, where x_r is the public identity of U_r. Then dealer finds public integers w_l, $d_{i,l}$ in $GF(p)$ for each secret s_i, such that: $s_i = \sum_{i=1}^{k} d_{i,l} f_l(w_l)(l = 1, 2, \ldots, k)$, where $w_i \neq w_j$, $w_i \notin \{x_1, x_2, \ldots x_n\}$.

Secret Reconstruction. If $h(h \geq t)$ shareholders try to reconstruct the secret s_i, each participant U_r computes

$$c_r = \sum_{i=1}^{k} d_{i,l} f_l(x_r) \prod_{v=1, v\neq r}^{h} \frac{w_l - x_v}{x_r - x_v} \bmod p$$

and sends it to other participants. Then the secret $s_i = \sum_{r=1}^{h} c_r \bmod p$.

Vulnerable to Linear Subspace Attack. Linear subspace attack is an algebraic-based analysis for linear released components. If the released components are modelled as a linear system with a structured matrix, adversary can use the rank property to mount attacks through rank analysis.

The main drawback in Harn scheme is that it is not sufficient only to hide the polynomials' coefficients for information protection. Since the Lagrange components are generated by the linear combination of the shares, all released components are in a linear subspace of dimension of $t + k - 1$. Consequently, a non-shareholder is able to forge a new component after collecting up to $t + k - 1$ components by using linear subspace attack.

2.3 Miao Randomized Component Based (t,n) SSR Scheme

Miao proposed an improved randomized component based SSR scheme to break the linear relationship among components. Suppose that there are n shareholders $U = \{U_1, U_2, \ldots, U_n\}$ and each shareholder U_i has a public identity x_i.

Share Generation. Dealer selects two large primes p, q satisfying $p > q + nq^2$. He also selects a polynomial over F_p: $f(x) = a_0 + a_1 x + \ldots a_{t-1} x^{t-1} \bmod p$, where $a_0 \in F_q$, $a_i \in F_p$, $i = 1, 2, \ldots t - 1$, $a_{t-1} \neq 0$. The secret $s = a_0$. Then dealer sends the share $s_i = f(x_i) \bmod p$ to each shareholder U_i secretly.

Randomized Component Computation. If $h(h \geq t)$ shareholders try to recover the secret, each participant P_i randomly selects $r_i \in_R F_q$ and constructs the randomized components:

$$RC_i = (f(x_i) \prod_{v=1, v \neq i}^{m} \frac{-x_v}{x_i - x_v} + r_i q) \bmod p.$$

Secret Reconstruction. Then each participant releases $RC_i (1 \leq i \leq h)$ and the secret can be recovered by $s = (\sum_{i=1}^{h} RC_i \bmod p) \bmod q$.

Vulnerable to Lattice Attack. Lattice attack is used to analyze a series of adding short vectors linear components such as $\{f_1 + v_1, f_2 + v_2, \ldots, f_n + v_n\}$, where $f_1, f_2, \ldots f_n$ are linear related and $v_1, v_2, \ldots v_n$ are short vectors added to $f_i (i = 1, 2, \ldots n)$. The adversary can find these short vectors by constructing lattice base and using LLL reduction algorithm.

In Miao scheme, RC_i can be regarded as the encryption of $f(x_i)$ with r_i as the encryption key. Since $f(x_i)$ is uniformly distributed over F_p and r_i is uniformly distributed over F_q, $q < p$, then $|K| < |M|$. From the view of perfect secrecy, r_i cannot protect the secrecy of $f(x_i)$. When adversary collects multiple randomized components, he constructs lattice base and each r_i consisting short vectors can be found by LLL reduction algorithm. Then the adversary obtains share $f(x_i)$ from RC_i and recover the secret.

In order to specifically show the relationship among these related work in Sect. 2, we summarize them in Fig. 2.

Scheme	Method	Problem
Shamir[22]	Interpolation polynomials	Active attack
Asmuth-Bloom[3]	Chinese Remainder Theorem	Active attack

Use linear combination of shares to resist active attack

Scheme	Method	Problem
Harn[9]	Interpolation polynomials	Linear subspace attack

Use randomized component to break the relationship

Scheme	Method	Problem
Miao[19]	Chinese Remainder Theorem	Lattice attack

Fig. 2. Summary of related work.

3 Scheme Model and Security Goals

This section presents the model and security goals of our secure secret reconstruction schemes in insecure networks.

3.1   Scheme Model

Our proposed secure secret reconstruction schemes adopt the same model as Harn [9], which includes three types of entities: dealer, shareholder and adversary.

Dealer: Dealer is trusted by all shareholders. He sets up parameters and distributes shares to shareholders.

Shareholder: A shareholder receives valid share from the dealer. Then he uses share to generate the component and sends it to other shareholders through secure channel. Only t or more than t shareholders can recover the secret, while less than t shareholders cannot get any information about the secret.

Adversary: In our scheme, adversary is divided into two types:
   - **Inside adversary:** Less than threshold t legal shareholders use their shares and conspire to recover the secret.
   - **Outside adversary:** A participant who does not own a valid share participates in secret reconstruction and tries to recover the secret or forge a legal share by collecting components from honest shareholders.

The two models of adversary are shown in Fig. 3.

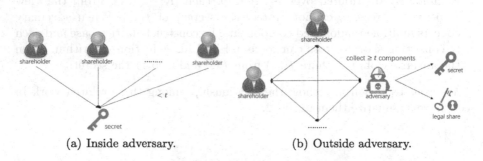

(a) Inside adversary.   (b) Outside adversary.

Fig. 3. Model of adversary.

3.2   Security Goals

Generally, in order to achieve the security of secure secret sharing scheme, we need to ensure that only t or more than t honest shareholders can recover the secret. In insecure networks, shareholders cannot identify other participants and the components sent among shareholders may be captured by outside adversary. As a result, we need to thwart both the inside shareholder conspiracy attack and the outside adversary attack. The security goals of our model are as follows:

   - **Resist attack from inside adversary:** Only t or more than t shareholders can recover the secret, while less than t shareholders cannot.
   - **Resist attack from outside adversary:** If a participant who does not own a valid share collects components from other honest participants, he cannot recover the secret. Even using linear subspace attack and lattice attack, he cannot get any information about the share and secret.

4   Basic Proposed SSR Scheme

4.1   Scheme

First, we propose a (t, n) randomized component based secure secret reconstruction scheme in insecure networks, which is an improvement of Miao scheme [19]. Different from Miao scheme, the random element in our scheme can cover up the information of share and resist lattice attack. Furthermore, this scheme is perfect and ideal.

The scheme is divided into three parts, including initialization, share generation and secret reconstruction.

Initialization: Assume that there are n shareholders $U = \{U_1, U_2, ..., U_n\}$ and
a trusted dealer.
Step 1: Dealer randomly chooses a large prime p and threshold t publicly. The secret $s(x)$ is a polynomial of degree $d - 1$ over F_p.
Step 2: Dealer selects $m_0(x)$ and n public monic and irreducible polynomials of degree d over F_p as each shareholder's identity: $m_i(x)(i = 1, 2, \ldots, n)$.
Share Generation: In order to distribute shares for shareholders to recover the secret $s(x)$:
Step 1: Dealer constructs polynomials $F(x) = s(x) + k(x) \cdot m_0(x)$, where $k(x)$ is a random polynomial over F_p and $\deg(k(x)) = (t - 1)d - 1$.
Step 2: Dealer computes and distributes the share $s_i(x) = F(x) \bmod m_i(x)$ for each shareholder U_i.
Secret Reconstruction: Suppose that there are $h(h \geq t)$ shareholders trying to recover the secret.
Step 1: Before secret reconstruction, each participant $P_i(1 \leq i \leq h)$ randomly selects a polynomial $r_i(x)$, which is uniformly distributed over F_p and satisfies $d - 1 \leq \deg(r_i(x)) \leq (h - 1)d - 1$.
Step 2: Randomized component RC_i is computed by each participant as

$$RC_i(x) = (s_i(x) \cdot c_i(x) + r_i(x) \cdot m_0(x)) \bmod M(x),$$

where $c_i(x) = M_i(x)M_i'(x)$, $M_i(x) = \frac{M(x)}{m_i(x)}$, $M(x) = \prod_{i=1}^{h} m_i(x)$ and $M_i(x)M_i'(x) = 1 \bmod m_i(x)$.
Step 3: Each participant P_i sends $RC_i(x)$ to other $h - 1$ participants through secure channel. After receiving $h - 1$ components, the secret can be computed by $s(x) = (\sum_{i=1}^{h} RC_i(x) \bmod M(x)) \bmod m_0(x)$.

4.2   Correctness Analysis

Suppose that there are $h(h \geq t)$ shareholders trying to recover the secret.

Lemma 1. *The sum of all the adding random polynomials equals to 0, in other words,* $\sum_{i=1}^{h} r_i(x) \cdot m_0(x) \bmod M(x) \bmod m_0(x) = 0$.

Proof. Since $\deg(r_i(x)) \leq (h-1)d-1$, $M(x) = \prod_{i=1}^{h} m_i(x)$ and $\deg(m_i(x)) = d$, for $i = 0, 1, \ldots, n$, then we have $\deg(r_i(x) \cdot m_0(x)) \leq hd-1 < \deg(M(x))$. Therefore, $\sum_{i=1}^{h} r_i(x) \cdot m_0(x) \bmod M(x) \bmod m_0(x) = 0$.

Theorem 1. *The secret $s(x)$ can be recovered by $h(h \geq t)$ shareholders.*

Proof. On account of Lemma 1, we have:

$$\sum_{i=1}^{h} RC_i(x) \bmod M(x) \bmod m_0(x)$$

$$= (\sum_{i=1}^{h} s_i(x) \cdot c_i(x) + \sum_{i=1}^{h} r_i(x) \cdot m_0(x)) \bmod M(x) \bmod m_0(x)$$

$$= \sum_{i=1}^{h} (s_i(x) \cdot c_i(x)) \bmod M(x) \bmod m_0(x) \tag{1a}$$

$$= F(x) \bmod m_0(x) = s(x). \tag{1b}$$

Since $s_i(x) = F(x) \bmod m_i(x)$ and $c_i(x) = M_i(x)M_i'(x)$, step (1a) is equivalent to step (1b) on the basis of Chinese Remainder Theorem. Therefore, $h(h \geq t)$ shareholders can recover the secret by $s(x) = \sum_{i=1}^{h} RC_i(x) \bmod M(x) \bmod m_0(x)$.

4.3   Security Analysis

Lemma 2. *The distributed share $s_i(x)$ is uniformly distributed over F_p.*

Proof. A map σ from $F_p[x]$ to its quotient ring $F_p[x]/\langle m_i(x) \rangle$ can be constructed:

$$\sigma : F_p[x] \to F_p[x]/\langle m_i(x) \rangle, \quad F(x) \mapsto s_i(x) \equiv F(x) \bmod m_i(x). \tag{2}$$

Then given $F(x), G(x) \in F_p[x]$, the above Eq. (2) satisfies:

$$\sigma(F(x) + G(x)) = (F(x) + G(x)) \bmod m_i(x)$$
$$= (F(x) \bmod m_i(x)) + (G(x) \bmod m_i(x))$$
$$= \sigma(F(x)) + \sigma(G(x)).$$

Therefore, σ is a group homomorphism. For any $s_i(x) \in F_p[x]/\langle m_i(x) \rangle$, there exists $F(x) \in F_p[x]$ such that $\sigma(F(x)) = s_i(x)$. Thus, σ is an epimorphism. As a result, if $F(x)$ is uniformly distributed over F_p, then the distributed share $s_i(x) = F(x) \bmod m_i(x)$ is also uniformly distributed over F_p.

Theorem 2. *The proposed scheme can resist attack from inside adversary. In detail, the secret $s(x)$ cannot be recovered by less than t legal shareholders.*

Proof. We consider the worst case of $t-1$ shareholders with valid shares trying to recover the secret illegally. Any $t-1$ inside adversaries can generate $t-1$ congruence equations based on modular of d degree, which can only recover a unique polynomial $F'(x)$ of degree not higher than $d(t-1)-1$. They need to use this polynomial $F'(x)$ to recover the secret $s(x) = F(x) \bmod m_0(x)$.

However, $F'(x)$ satisfies $F'(x) = F(x) \bmod \prod_{i=1}^{t-1} m_i(x)$. They have $F(x) = F'(x) + k(x) \cdot \prod_{i=1}^{t-1} m_i(x)$, where $\deg(k(x)) = d-1$. From the view of information entropy, let $H(s)$ represents the information entropy of the secret and $H(s|\{s_1, s_2, \ldots, s_{t-1}\}$ represents the information entropy of knowing $t-1$ shareholders' shares to recover the secret. Since both $k(x)$ and $s(x)$ are polynomials of degree $d-1$ over F_p, then $H(s) = H(s|\{s_1, s_2, \ldots, s_{t-1}\}) = d\log_2 p$. Thus, $t-1$ inside adversaries cannot get any information about the secret.

Lemma 3. *Given a randomized component $RC_i(x)$, it is impossible to derive the share $s_i(x)$.*

Proof. The randomized component $RC_i(x) = s_i(x) \cdot c_i(x) + r_i(x) \cdot m_0(x)$, where $r_i(x)$ is randomly selected over F_p by shareholder. According to Lemma 2, $s_i(x)$ is uniformly distributed over F_p and $\deg(s_i(x)) = d-1$, the probability of inferring $s_i(x)$ directly is d^p. Then since $\deg(r_i(x)) \geq d-1$, the probability of deriving $s_i(x)$ from RC_i by inferring $r_i(x)$ at least equals to d^p. Thus, given a randomized component $RC_i(x)$, it is impossible to derive the share $s_i(x)$.

Theorem 3. *The proposed scheme can resist attack from outside adversary. In detail, when $h(h \geq t)$ participants try to recover the secret, a participant who does not own a valid share cannot get any information about secret and share by collecting $h-1$ randomized components from other honest participants.*

Proof. Suppose adversary is the hth participant who releases his component last, he can collect $h-1$ randomized components from other participants.

1. First, we prove the outside adversary cannot get any information about the secret. The secret $s(x) = (\sum_{i=1}^{h-1} RC_i(x) + RC_h(x)) \bmod M(x) \bmod m_0(x)$, where $RC_h(x) = s_h(x) \cdot c_h(x) + r_h(x) \cdot m_0(x)$. If the outside adversary wants to compute $RC_h(x)$, he needs to know the share $s_h(x)$. Both $s(x)$ and $s_h(x)$ are unknown polynomials of $d-1$ degree over F_p in x. From the view of information entropy, let $H(s)$ represents the information entropy of the secret and $H(s|\{RC_1, RC_2, \ldots RC_{h-1}\})$ represents the information entropy of knowing $h-1$ shareholders' randomized components to recover the secret. $H(s) = H(s|\{RC_1, RC_2, \ldots RC_{h-1}\}) = d\log_2 p$, then outside adversary cannot get any information about the secret by collecting $h-1$ randomized components from other honest participants.

2. Next, we prove the outside adversary cannot get any information about the share. On account of Lemma 3, it is impossible for outside adversary to derive

the original share s_i from the randomized component RC_i.

Then we discuss whether the outside adversary can obtain the share through linear subspace attack and lattice attack. Since $r_i(x)$ is randomly selected and separated from $F(x)$, adversary cannot find any relationship among randomized components by linear subspace cryptanalysis. In randomized component $RC_i(x)$, $r_i(x)$ can be regarded as the key K to protect the message $s_i(x)$. The degree of $r_i(x)$ is at least $d-1$, which satisfies $\deg(r_i(x)) \geq \deg(s_i(x)) = d-1$ and guarantee $|K| \geq |M|$. Our scheme satisfies perfect secrecy and can resist both linear subspace attack and lattice attack.

5 Improved Bivariate Polynomial Based SSR Scheme

5.1 Scheme

This scheme is an improved randomized component based secure secret reconstruction scheme using bivariate polynomial, which can generate both the share and the randomized component. Furthermore, we don't need to establish the secure channel for each pairwise shareholders in advance. Each shareholder owns two shares, where the additional share is used for secure channel key generation.

The second scheme is divided into six parts, including initialization, share generation, calculation of pairwise key, establishment of secure channel, calculation of randomized component and secret reconstruction.

Here we use $\deg_x(F(x,y))$ to represent the degree of bivariate polynomial $F(x,y)$ in x and use $\deg_y(F(x,y))$ to represent the degree of $F(x,y)$ in y.

Initialization: Assume that there are n shareholders $U = \{U_1, U_2, ..., U_n\}$ and a trusted dealer.

Step 1: Dealer randomly chooses a large prime p, a integer d, the threshold t and makes them public.

Step 2: Dealer selects $a_{i,j} \in Z_p (1 \leq i, j \leq dt - 1)$ and construct a matrix A as:

$$A = \begin{bmatrix} a_{0,0} & a_{0,1} & \cdots & a_{0,dt-1} \\ a_{1,0} & a_{1,1} & \cdots & a_{1,dt-1} \\ \vdots & \vdots & \ddots & \vdots \\ a_{dt-1,0} & a_{dt-1,1} & \cdots & a_{dt-1,dt-1} \end{bmatrix}.$$

Then the bivariate polynomial $F(x,y)$ with degree $dt - 1$ can be constructed as: $F(x,y) = \begin{bmatrix} x^0 & x^1 & \cdots & x^{dt-1} \end{bmatrix} \cdot A \cdot \begin{bmatrix} y^0 & y^1 & \cdots & y^{dt-1} \end{bmatrix}^T \bmod p$.

Step 3: Dealer chooses public polynomials $m_0(x)$ and $m_0(y)$ of degree d over F_p and public non-linear mapping $s1$-box and $s2$-box: $F_p \to F_p$. The secret

$$s(x,y) = F(x,y) \bmod m_0(x) \bmod m_0(y).$$

Share Generation:

Step 1: Shareholders pick coprime polynomials $m_i(x)(1 \leq i \leq n)$ of degree d over F_p as their public identity.

Step 2: Dealer computes and distributes two shares $s_{i,1}(x,y) = F(x,y) \bmod m_i(x)$ and $s_{i,2}(x,y) = F(x,y) \bmod m_i(y)$ for each shareholder $U_i(1 \le i \le n)$ secretly. $m_i(y)$ is the polynomial which uses variable y to replace the variable x in $m_i(x)$.

Calculation of Pairwise Key: We use function sgn to describe the relationship of shareholder's identity.

$$\mathrm{sgn}(m_i(x) - m_j(x)) = \begin{cases} 1; \ if \ m_i(x) > m_j(x) \\ -1; \ if \ m_i(x) < m_j(x) \end{cases}.$$

Shareholder U_i computes the pairwise key $k_{i,j}(x,y)$ with U_j as follows:

$$k_{i,j}(x,y) = \begin{cases} s_{i,1}(x,y) \bmod m_j(y); \ if \ \mathrm{sgn}(m_i(x) - m_j(x)) = 1 \\ s_{i,2}(x,y) \bmod m_j(x); \ if \ \mathrm{sgn}(m_i(x) - m_j(x)) = -1 \end{cases}. \qquad (3)$$

We describe $k_{i,j}(x,y)$ as: $k_{i,j}(x,y) = \begin{bmatrix} x^0 \ x^1 \ \dots \ x^{d-1} \end{bmatrix} \cdot E \cdot \begin{bmatrix} y^0 \ y^1 \ \dots \ y^{d-1} \end{bmatrix}^T$, where E is the coefficient matrix of $k_{i,j}(x,y)$:

$$E = \begin{bmatrix} e_{0,0} & e_{0,1} & \cdots & e_{0,d-1} \\ e_{1,0} & e_{1,1} & \cdots & e_{1,d-1} \\ \vdots & \vdots & \ddots & \vdots \\ e_{d-1,0} & e_{d-1,1} & \cdots & e_{d-1,d-1} \end{bmatrix}.$$

Establishment of Secure Channel: Before secret reconstruction, each pair of participants establish secure channels with each other.

Step 1: To generate the secure channel key with participant P_j, participant P_i calculates $k'_{i,j} = \sum\limits_{i=0,j=0}^{d-1} e_{i,j} \bmod p$, where $e_{i,j}(0 \le i,j \le d-1)$ are parameters of coefficient matrix E in $k_{i,j}(x,y)$.

Step 2: Participant P_i inputs $k'_{i,j}$ into s_1-box and generates the pairwise secure channel key $s_1(k'_{i,j})$ with P_j.

Calculation of Randomized Component: Assume that there are $h(h \ge t)$ shareholders trying to recover the secret.

Step 1: First, participant $P_i(1 \le i \le h)$ computes a new share for secret reconstruction $s_i(x,y) = s_{i,1}(x,y) \bmod m_0(y)$ and generates the component

$$g_i(x,y) = s_i(x,y)M_i(x)M'_i(x), \text{ where } M(x) = \prod_{i=1}^{h} m_i(x), \ M_i(x) = \frac{M(x)}{m_i(x)}$$

and $M_i(x)M'_i(x) = 1 \bmod m_i(x)$.

Step 2: Participant P_i transforms each coefficient in Eq. (3) through s_2-box to gets $s_2(k_{i,j}(x,y))$. Then he generates

$$k_i(x,y) = \sum_{j=1,j\ne i}^{h} (\mathrm{sgn}(m_i(x) - m_j(x)) \cdot s_2(k_{i,j}(x,y))).$$

Step 3: Each randomized component $RC_i(x,y) = g_i(x,y) + k_i(x,y)$ is calculated and sent to other participants through previously established secure channel.

Secret Reconstruction: After receiving $h - 1$ randomized components from other participants, the secret $s(x, y) = \sum_{i=1}^{h} RC_i(x, y) \bmod M(x) \bmod m_0(x)$.

5.2   Correctness Analysis

Suppose that there are $h(h \geq t)$ shareholders trying to recover the secret.

Lemma 4. *Each pair of shareholders can generate the same pairwise key. Specifically, shareholder U_i and U_j can generate $k_{i,j}(x, y) = k_{j,i}(x, y)$.*

Proof. Assume that $m_i(x) > m_j(x)$, then $\mathrm{sgn}(m_i(x) - m_j(x)) = 1$. We have

$$k_{i,j}(x, y) = F(x, y) \bmod m_i(x) \bmod m_j(y); \tag{4}$$

$$k_{j,i}(x, y) = F(x, y) \bmod m_j(x) \bmod m_i(y), \tag{5}$$

where $m_i(x)$, $m_j(x)$ are polynomials only in x and $m_i(y)$, $m_j(y)$ are polynomials only in y. Since the order of modular operation of polynomials based on different variables does not affect the result of computation, Eq. (4) equals to Eq. (5). For any pairwise shareholders U_i and U_j, we have $k_{i,j}(x, y) = k_{j,i}(x, y)$. Therefore, each pair of shareholders can generate the same pairwise key.

Lemma 5. *The sum of adding random polynomials equals to 0, in other words,* $\sum_{i=1}^{h} k_i(x, y) = 0$.

Proof. According to Lemma 4, for any pairwise shareholders U_i and U_j, we have $k_{i,j}(x, y) = k_{j,i}(x, y)$ and $s_2(k_{i,j}(x, y)) = s_2(k_{j,i}(x, y))$. Thus,

$$\mathrm{sgn}(m_i(x) - m_j(x)) \cdot s_2\left(k_{i,j}(x, y)\right) + \mathrm{sgn}(m_j(x) - m_i(x)) \cdot s_2\left(k_{j,i}(x, y)\right)$$
$$= (\mathrm{sgn}(m_i(x) - m_j(x)) + \mathrm{sgn}(m_j(x) - m_i(x))) \cdot s_2\left(k_{i,j}(x, y)\right) \tag{6a}$$
$$= 0, \tag{6b}$$

where step (6a) equals to step (6b) due to for any pairwise shareholders U_i and U_j: $\mathrm{sgn}(m_i(x) - m_j(x)) + \mathrm{sgn}(m_j(x) - m_i(x)) = 1 + (-1) = 0$.

For any pairwise shareholders U_i and U_j, there is:

$$\sum_{i=1}^{h} k_i(x, y) = \sum_{i=1}^{h} \sum_{j=1, j \neq i}^{h} (\mathrm{sgn}(m_i(x) - m_j(x)) \cdot s_2(k_{i,j}(x, y))) = 0.$$

Therefore, the sum of adding random polynomials equals to 0.

Theorem 4. *The secret $s(x, y)$ can be recovered by $h(h \geq t)$ shareholders.*

Proof. According to Lemma 5, we have

$$\sum_{i-1}^{h} RC_i(x,y) \bmod M(x) \bmod m_0(x)$$

$$= (\sum_{i=1}^{h} g_i(x,y) + \sum_{i=1}^{h} k_i(x,y)) \bmod M(x) \bmod m_0(x)$$

$$= \sum_{i=1}^{h} g_i(x,y) \bmod M(x) \bmod m_0(x)$$

$$= \sum_{i=1}^{h} s_i(x,y) M_i(x) M'_i(x) \bmod M(x) \bmod m_0(x) \tag{7a}$$

$$= F(x,y) \bmod m_0(x) \bmod m_0(y) = s(x,y). \tag{7b}$$

Since $s_i(x,y) = F(x,y) \bmod m_i(x) \bmod m_0(y)$, step (7a) is equivalent to step (7b) on the basis of Chinese Remainder Theorem. Therefore, $h(h \geq t)$ shareholders can recover the secret by $s(x) = \sum_{i=1}^{h} RC_i(x,y) \bmod M(x) \bmod m_0(x)$.

5.3 Security Analysis

Lemma 6. *The distributed shares $s_{i,1}(x)$, $s_{i,2}(x)$ and share for secret reconstruction $s_i(x)$ are uniformly distributed over F_p.*

Proof. Since for any bivariate polynomial $F(x,y) \in F_p[x,y]$, there exists unique $s_{i,1}(x,y) \in F_p[x,y]/\langle m_i(x) \rangle$ such that $s_{i,1}(x,y) \equiv f(x,y) \bmod m_i(x)$. A map σ from $F_p[x,y]$ to its quotient ring $F_p[x,y]/\langle m_i(x) \rangle$ can be constructed as follows:

$$\sigma : F_p[x,y] \to F_p[x,y]/\langle m_i(x) \rangle$$
$$F(x,y) \mapsto s_{i,1}(x,y) \equiv F(x,y) \bmod m_i(x). \tag{8}$$

Given $F(x,y), G(x,y) \in F_p[x,y]$, Eq. (8) satisfies

$$\sigma(F(x,y) + G(x,y)) = (F(x,y) + G(x,y)) \bmod m_i(x)$$
$$= (F(x,y) \bmod m_i(x)) + (G(x,y) \bmod m_i(x))$$
$$= \sigma(F(x,y)) + \sigma(G(x,y)).$$

Thus, σ is a group homomorphism. For any $s_{i,1}(x,y) \in F_p[x,y]/\langle m_i(x) \rangle$, there exists $F(x,y) \in F_p[x,y]$ such that $\sigma(F(x,y)) = s_{i,1}(x,y)$. σ is an epimorphism. As a result, if $F(x,y)$ is uniformly distributed over F_p, then $s_{i,1}(x,y) = F(x,y) \bmod m_i(x)$ is also uniformly distributed over F_p. Similarly, we also have $s_{i,2}(x,y) = F(x,y) \bmod m_i(y)$ and $s_i(x,y) = s_{i,1}(x,y) \bmod m_0(y)$ uniformly distributed over F_p.

Theorem 5. *The proposed scheme can resist attack from inside adversary. In detail, the secret $s(x,y)$ cannot be recovered by less than t legal shareholders.*

Proof. We consider the worst case of $t-1$ shareholders trying to recover the secret illegally. Any $t - 1$ inside adversaries can generate $t - 1$ congruence equations based on modular of d degree in x, which can only recover a unique bivariate polynomial $F'(x, y)$ with $\deg_x(F'(x, y)) \geq d(t-1) - 1$. We use $\theta(x, y)$ to represent $F(x, y) \bmod m_0(y)$ and $\omega(x, y)$ to represent $F'(x, y) \bmod m_0(y)$. Inside adversaries need to use $\omega(x, y)$ to recover the secret $s(x, y) = \theta(x, y) \bmod m_0(x)$.

However, $\omega(x, y)$ satisfies $\omega(x, y) = \theta(x, y) \bmod \prod_{i=1}^{t-1} m_i(x)$. Then they have

$\theta(x, y) = \omega(x, y) + k(x, y) \cdot \prod_{i=1}^{t-1} m_i(x)$, where $\deg_x(k(x, y)) = \deg_y(k(x, y)) = d - 1$. From the view of information entropy, let $H(s)$ represents the information entropy of the secret and $H(s|\{s_1, s_2, \ldots, s_{t-1}\})$ represents the information entropy of knowing $t - 1$ shareholders' shares to recover the secret. Since $\deg_x(k(x, y)) = \deg_x(s(x, y)) = d - 1$ and $\deg_y(k(x, y)) = \deg_y(s(x, y)) = d - 1$, then $H(s) = H(s|\{s_1, s_2, \ldots, s_{t-1}\}) = d\log_2 2p$. Thus, $t - 1$ inside adversaries cannot get any information about the secret.

Lemma 7. *Given a randomized component $RC_i(x, y)$, it is impossible to derive the share $s_i(x, y)$.*

Proof. The randomized component $RC_i(x, y) = g_i(x, y) + k_i(x, y)$, where $g_i(x, y) = s_i(x, y)M_i(x)M'_i(x)$ and $k_i(x, y)$ is generated by s2-box transmission. s2-box breaks the linear relationship between $s_i(x, y)$ and $k_i(x, y)$ and makes the transformed bivariate polynomial $k_i(x, y)$ distributed uniformly over F_p.

On account of Lemma 6, the share $s_i(x, y)$ is uniformly distributed over F_p and $\deg_x(s_i(x, y)) = \deg_y(s_i(x, y)) = d - 1$, the probability of inferring $s_i(x, y)$ is d^{2p}. Since $\deg_x(k_i(x, y)) = \deg_y(k_i(x, y)) = d - 1$, the probability of deriving $s_i(x, y)$ from $RC_i(x, y)$ by inferring $k_i(x, y)$ also equals to d^{2p}. Thus, given a randomized component $RC_i(x, y)$, it is impossible to derive the share $s_i(x, y)$.

Theorem 6. *The proposed scheme can resist attack from outside adversary. In detail, when $h(h \geq t)$ participants try to recover the secret, a participant who does not own a valid share cannot get any information about secret and share by collecting $h - 1$ randomized components from other honest participants.*

Proof. Suppose that the adversary is the hth participant who releases his component last, he can collect $h-1$ randomized component from other participants.

1. First, we prove the outside adversary cannot get any information about the secret. After collecting $h - 1$ randomized components, the secret $s(x, y) = (\sum_{i=1}^{h-1} RC_i(x, y) + RC_h(x, y)) \bmod M(x) \bmod m_0(x)$, where $\deg_x(s(x, y)) = \deg_y(s(x, y)) = d - 1$. However, each participant uses $k_i(x, y)$ to cover up the original component and $RC_h(x, y) = g_h(x, y) + k_h(x, y)$, where $RC_h(x, y)$ is generated by $s_{h,1}(x, y)$ and $s_{h,2}(x, y)$. If the outside adversary want to recover the secret, he has to use these two shares to calculate $RC_h(x, y)$ and eliminate other participants' disrupted information added. The shares are generated by

$s_{h,1}(x,y) = F(x,y) \bmod m_h(x)$ and $s_{h,2}(x,y) = F(x,y) \bmod m_h(y)$, where both the degree of shares in x and y at least equals to the secret $s(x,y)$. From the view of information entropy, let $H(s)$ represents the information entropy of the secret and $H(s|\{RC_1, RC_2, \ldots RC_{h-1}\})$ represents the information entropy of knowing $h-1$ shareholders' randomized components to recover the secret, then there is $H(s) = H(s|\{RC_1, RC_2, \ldots RC_{h-1}\}) = d\log_2 2p$. As a result, the adversary cannot get any information about the secret by collecting $h-1$ randomized components.

2. Next, we prove the outside adversary cannot get any information about the share. On account of Lemma 7, it is impossible for outside adversary to derive the original share $s_i(x,y)$ from the randomized component $RC_i(x,y)$.

   Then we discuss whether the outside adversary can obtain the share through linear subspace attack and lattice attack. s-boxes are used to disrupt the linear relationship among randomized components. In randomized component $RC_i(x,y)$, $k_i(x,y)$ can be regarded as the key K to protect the message $s_i(x,y)$. Both $k_i(x,y)$ and $s_i(x,y)$ are polynomials of degree $d-1$ in x and y over F_p, which can guarantee $|K| = |M|$. Our scheme satisfies perfect secrecy and can resist linear subspace attack and lattice attack.

Theorem 7. *Our proposed scheme can resist passive attack with each pair of shareholders generating the same secure channel key.*

Proof. On account of Lemma 4, for any pairwise shareholders U_i and U_j with $m_i(x) > m_j(x)$, we have $k_{i,j}(x,y) = k_{j,i}(x,y)$. Since $k'_{i,j} = \sum\limits_{i=0,j=0}^{d-1} e_{i,j} \bmod p$, where $e_{i,j} (0 \le i,j \le d-1)$ are parameters of coefficient matrix E in $k'_{i,j}(x,y)$, then $k'_{i,j} = k'_{j,i}$ and $s_1(k'_{j,i}) = s_1(k'_{i,j})$. As a result, each pair of shareholders can generate the same secure channel key.

If a passive adversary want to compute the key $s_1(k'_{j,i})$, he needs to know at least one of the shares $s_{i,1}(x,y)$. Since $\deg_x(s_{i,1}(x,y)) = \deg_x(s(x,y))$ and $\deg_y(s_{i,1}(x,y)) > \deg_y(s(x,y))$, the probability of guessing key is larger than guessing the secret. Our proposed scheme can resist passive attack.

6   Properties and Comparisons

We analyze the properties of our schemes in three aspects: active attack, passive attack and information rate. The active attack can be divided into inside adversary attack and outside adversary attack these two parts. Linear subspace attack and lattice attack are two attack strategies of outside adversary.

6.1   Properties

Our first secure secret reconstruction scheme can resist both the inside and outside adversary attack in insecure networks. The random element $r_i(x)$ added in the component can prevent the outside adversary from obtaining the secret and share by collecting randomized components from other honest participants. Since $r_i(x)$ is randomly selected, there is no linear relationship among randomized components. As a result, our first scheme can resist linear subspace attack. In addition, the degree of $r_i(x)$ at least equals to the share, which can guarantee perfect secrecy and prevent lattice attack. This scheme is based on the assumption that the secure channel is well established to resist passive attack.

The second secure secret reconstruction scheme uses bivariate polynomial, which can generate both the share and randomized component. This scheme can also prevent the inside and outside adversary from recovering secret illegally. Particularly, it establishes the secure channel for each pairwise shareholders before secret reconstruction and can resist passive attack in insecure networks. Each shareholder owns two shares, where the additional share is used for pairwise key and randomized component generation. s-boxes are used to disrupt the linear relationship and resist linear subspace attack. Then, because both share for secret reconstruction and random element are bivariate polynomials with the same degree in x and y, this scheme can protect the share in perfect secrecy and resist lattice attack.

Next, we analyze our schemes' information rate according to Definition 4 and show their properties in Table 1.

Table 1. Properties of our schemes.

Scheme	Secret size	Number of share	Each share size	Information rate
Scheme 1	p^d	1	p^d	1
Scheme 2	p^{d^2}	2	$p^{d^2 t}$	$\frac{1}{t}$

In the first scheme, both the secret and share are polynomials with degree $d-1$ over F_p. The information rate of our first scheme can be computed as:

$$\rho = \frac{\log_2 |s|}{\max_{s_i \in S}(\log_2 |s_i|)} = \frac{\log_2 p^d}{\log_2 p^d} = 1.$$

In the second scheme, the secret is a bivariate polynomial with degree $d-1$ in both x and y over F_p. Each shareholder owns two shares, where $\deg_x(s_{i,1}(x,y)) = \deg_y(s_{i,2}(x,y)) = d-1$ and $\deg_y(s_{i,1}(x,y)) = \deg_x(s_{i,2}(x,y)) = dt-1$. The information rate of our second scheme can be computed as:

$$\rho = \frac{\log_2 |s|}{\max_{s_i \in S}(\log_2 |s_i|)} = \frac{\log_2 p^{d^2}}{\log_2 p^{d^2 t}} = \frac{1}{t}.$$

The information rate of our first scheme is 1, while the second scheme is $\frac{1}{t}$. Thus, our first scheme is perfect and ideal. The lower information rate in the second scheme is the price of establishing secure channel and generating randomized component effectively by distributing more information to each shareholder.

6.2   Comparisons

We compare our schemes with other secure secret reconstruction schemes [9,11, 17–19] and the result is shown in Table 2.

Since information rate is the size ratio of secret to share, which can denote the efficiency of a shareholder sharing a secret, we mainly use information rate to describe the scheme performance bellow. For a secure secret sharing scheme, the information rate is generally not more than 1. The higher information rate is, the more efficiently the scheme works.

Table 2. Comparison of different SSR schemes.

Scheme	Resist IAA[a]	Resist LSA[b]	Resist LA[c]	Secure channel	Information rate
Harn [9]	✓	✗	✓	✗	1
Harn [11]	✓	✗	✓	✓	$\frac{1}{t}$
Meng [17]	✓	✓	✓	✗	$(\frac{1}{6},\frac{1}{4})$
Meng [18]	✓	✗	✓	✗	$\frac{1}{t}$
Miao [19]	✓	✓	✗	✗	$(\frac{1}{3},\frac{1}{2})$
Our scheme 1	✓	✓	✓	✗	1
Our scheme 2	✓	✓	✓	✓	$\frac{1}{t}$

[a]IAA is inside adversary attack.
[b]LSA is linear subspace attack.
[c]LA is lattice attack.

From the table, we know that scheme [17,19] and our schemes can resist linear subspace attack, but scheme [19] is vulnerable to lattice attack. Only scheme [11] and our scheme 2 don't need to establish secure channel in advance and can resist passive attack in insecure networks. The information rate of scheme [9] and our first scheme is 1. Although the information rate of our second scheme is $\frac{1}{t}$, it can resist all attacks we analyzed in insecure networks.

7   Conclusion

In this paper, we first point two common attacks: active and passive attack on secret sharing in insecure networks. Then we introduce secure secret reconstruction scheme, which can prevent the participant who does not own a valid share from obtaining the secret and share by collecting other participants' components. We also analyze the possible attacks on Harn and Miao proposed SSR scheme. Using linear subspace cryptanalysis, adversary can obtain the secret by analyzing the relationship among sending components. Due to the adding randomized integer cannot protect the share in an information theoretically secure manner, Miao scheme is vulnerable to lattice attack.

In order to solve these problems, we describe the model and security goals of our secure secret reconstruction scheme in insecure networks. Based on the same idea of randomized component in Miao scheme, we propose two novel secure secret reconstruction schemes. The first scheme is based on Chinese Remainder Theorem for polynomial. The adding random element in this scheme breaks the relationship among components and can protect the secrecy of share. Furthermore, this scheme is perfect and ideal. Then we also propose an improved secure secret reconstruction scheme based on bivariate polynomial. The bivariate polynomial is used for share and randomized component generation. Specifically, this scheme can resist passive attack and establish the secure channel for each pairwise shareholders in advance. Each shareholder owns two shares, where the additional share can generate the secure channel key and randomized component. s-boxes disrupt the linear relationship and randomized component can enable our scheme to satisfy perfect secrecy. Both of our schemes are resistance to linear subspace attack and lattice attack. The inside and outside adversary in insecure networks cannot get any information about the secret and share in our two schemes.

References

1. Ahmadian, Z., Jamshidpour, S.: Linear subspace cryptanalysis of harn's secret sharing-based group authentication scheme. IEEE Trans. Inf. Forensics Secur. **13**, 1 (2017). https://doi.org/10.1109/TIFS.2017.2757454
2. Ao, J., Liao, G., Ma, C.: A novel non-interactive verifiable secret sharing scheme. In: 2006 International Conference on Communication Technology. pp. 1–4 (2006). https://doi.org/10.1109/ICCT.2006.342026
3. Asmuth, C., Bloom, J.: A modular approach to key safeguarding. IEEE Trans. Inf. Theory **29**(2), 208–210 (1983). https://doi.org/10.1109/TIT.1983.1056651
4. Blakley, G.: Safeguarding cryptographic keys (pdf). In: International Workshop on Managing Requirements Knowledge, p. 313 (1979)
5. Chanu, O.B., Tentu, A.N., Venkaiah, V.C.: Multi-stage multi-secret sharing schemes based on Chinese remainder theorem. In: ICARCSET 2015 (2015). https://doi.org/10.1145/2743065.2743082
6. Chen, Z., Li, S., Zhu, Y., Yan, J., Xu, X.: A cheater identifiable multi-secret sharing scheme based on the Chinese remainder theorem. Secur. Commun. Networks **8**(18), 3592–3601 (2015). https://doi.org/10.1002/sec.1283, https://onlinelibrary.wiley.com/doi/abs/10.1002/sec.1283
7. Chor, B., Goldwasser, S., Micali, S., Awerbuch, B.: Verifiable secret sharing and achieving simultaneity in the presence of faults. In: 26th Annual Symposium on Foundations of Computer Science (SFCS 1985), pp. 383–395 (1985). https://doi.org/10.1109/SFCS.1985.64
8. Ersoy, O., Pedersen, T.B., Kaya, K., Selçuk, A.A., Anarim, E.: A CRT-based verifiable secret sharing scheme secure against unbounded adversaries. Secur. Commun. Networks **9**(17), 4416–4427 (2016). https://doi.org/10.1002/sec.1617
9. Harn, L.: Secure secret reconstruction and multi-secret sharing schemes with unconditional security. Secur. Commun. Networks **7**(3), 567–573 (2014). https://doi.org/10.1002/sec.758
10. Harn, L., Fuyou, M., Chang, C.C.: Verifiable secret sharing based on the Chinese remainder theorem. Secur. Commun. Networks **7**(6), 950–957 (2014). https://doi.org/10.1002/sec.807

11. Harn, L., Hsu, C.F.: Dynamic threshold secret reconstruction and its application to the threshold cryptography. Inf. Process. Lett. **115**, 851–857 (2015). https://doi.org/10.1016/j.ipl.2015.06.014

12. Harn, L., Lin, C., Li, Y.: Fair secret reconstruction in (t, n) secret sharing. J. Inf. Secur. Appl. **23**, 1–7 (2015). https://doi.org/10.1016/j.jisa.2015.07.001, https://www.sciencedirect.com/science/article/pii/S2214212615000344

13. Harn, L., Xia, Z., Hsu, C., Liu, Y.: Secret sharing with secure secret reconstruction. Inf. Sci. **519**, 1–8 (2020). https://doi.org/10.1016/j.ins.2020.01.038, https://www.sciencedirect.com/science/article/pii/S0020025520300402

14. Hsu, C., Harn, L., Wu, S., Ke, L.: A new efficient and secure secret reconstruction scheme (SSRS) with verifiable shares based on a symmetric bivariate polynomial. Mobile Inf. Syst. **2020**, 1039898 (2020). https://doi.org/10.1155/2020/1039898

15. Imai, J., Mimura, M., Tanaka, H.: Verifiable secret sharing scheme using hash values. In: 2018 Sixth International Symposium on Computing and Networking Workshops (CANDARW), pp. 405–409 (2018). https://doi.org/10.1109/CANDARW.2018.00081

16. Jamshidpour, S., Ahmadian, Z.: Security analysis of a dynamic threshold secret sharing scheme using linear subspace method. Inf. Process. Lett. **163**, 105994 (2020). https://doi.org/10.1016/j.ipl.2020.105994

17. Meng, K.: A novel and secure secret sharing algorithm applied to insecure networks. Wirel. Pers. Commun. **115**(2), 1635–1650 (2020). https://doi.org/10.1007/s11277-020-07647-x

18. Meng, K., Miao, F., Huang, W., Xiong, Y.: Threshold changeable secret sharing with secure secret reconstruction. Inf. Process. Lett. **157**, 105928 (2020). https://doi.org/10.1016/j.ipl.2020.105928, https://www.sciencedirect.com/science/article/pii/S0020019020300156

19. Miao, F., Xiong, Y., Wang, X., Badawy, M.: Randomized component and its application to (t, m, n)-group oriented secret sharing. IEEE Trans. Inf. Forensics Secur. **10**(5), 889–899 (2015). https://doi.org/10.1109/TIFS.2014.2384393

20. Ning, Yu., Miao, F., Huang, W., Meng, K., Xiong, Y., Wang, X.: Constructing ideal secret sharing schemes based on Chinese remainder theorem. In: Peyrin, T., Galbraith, S. (eds.) ASIACRYPT 2018. LNCS, vol. 11274, pp. 310–331. Springer, Cham (2018). https://doi.org/10.1007/978-3-030-03332-3_12

21. Pedersen, T.P.: Non-Interactive and information-theoretic secure verifiable secret sharing. In: Feigenbaum, J. (ed.) CRYPTO 1991. LNCS, vol. 576, pp. 129–140. Springer, Heidelberg (1992). https://doi.org/10.1007/3-540-46766-1_9

22. Shamir, A.: How to share a secret. Commun. ACM **22**, 612–613 (1979). https://doi.org/10.1145/359168.359176

23. Shannon, C.E.: Communication theory of secrecy systems*. Bell Syst. Tech. J. **28**(4), 656–715 (1949). https://doi.org/10.1002/j.1538-7305.1949.tb00928.x

24. Verma, O.P., Jain, N., Pal, S.K.: A hybrid-based verifiable secret sharing scheme using Chinese remainder theorem. Arabian J. Sci. Eng. **45**(4), 2395–2406 (2020). https://doi.org/10.1007/s13369-019-03992-7

25. Wang, N., Cai, Y., Fu, J., Chen, X.: Information privacy protection based on verifiable (t, n)-threshold multi-secret sharing scheme. IEEE Access **8**, 20799–20804 (2020). https://doi.org/10.1109/ACCESS.2020.2968728

26. Xia, Z., Yang, Z., Xiong, S., Hsu, C.-F.: Game-Based security proofs for secret sharing schemes. In: Yang, C.-N., Peng, S.-L., Jain, L.C. (eds.) SICBS 2018. AISC, vol. 895, pp. 650–660. Springer, Cham (2020). https://doi.org/10.1007/978-3-030-16946-6_53
27. Xiao, M., Xia, Z.: Security analysis of a multi-secret sharing scheme with unconditional security. In: Wang, G., Chen, B., Li, W., Di Pietro, R., Yan, X., Han, H. (eds.) SpaCCS 2020. LNCS, vol. 12383, pp. 533–544. Springer, Cham (2021). https://doi.org/10.1007/978-3-030-68884-4_44

Transparency Order of (n, m)-Functions—Its Further Characterization and Applications

Yu Zhou[1]([✉]), Yongzhuang Wei[2], Hailong Zhang[3], Luyang Li[4], Enes Pasalic[5], and Wenling Wu[6]

[1] Science and Technology on Communication Security Laboratory, Chengdu 610041, China
zhouyu.zhy@tom.com
[2] Guilin University of Electronic Technology, Guilin 541004, China
walker_wei@msn.com
[3] State Key Laboratory of Cryptology, P.O. Box 5159, Beijing 100878, China
zhanghailong@iie.ac.cn
[4] National Engineering Laboratory for Wireless Security, Xi'an University of Post and Telecommunications, Xi'an 710061, China
luyang_li@foxmail.com
[5] FAMNIT & IAM, University of Primorska, Koper, Slovenia
[6] TCA Laboratory, SKLCS, Institute of Software, Chinese Academy of Sciences, Beijing 100190, China
wwl@tca.iscas.ac.cn

Abstract. The concept of transparency order is a useful measure for the robustness of (n, m)-functions (cryptographic S-boxes as mappings from $GF(2)^n$ to $GF(2)^m$) to multi-bit Differential Power Analysis (DPA). The recently redefined notion of transparency order ($\mathcal{RTO}$), based on the cross-correlation coefficients, uses a very delicate assumption that the adversary has a priori knowledge about the so called pre-charged logic value (a constant register value set by a system) used in DPA-like attacks. Moreover, quite contradictorily, this constant value is used as a variable when maximizing $\mathcal{RTO}$. To make the attack scenario more realistic, the notion of *differential transparency order* ($\mathcal{DTO}$) is defined for (n, m)-functions, which can efficiently eliminate the impact posed by this pre-charged logic value. By considering $(4, 4)$ S-boxes which are commonly used in the design of lightweight block ciphers, we deduce in the simulated scenario that the information leakage using $\mathcal{DTO}$ is usually larger compared to the standard indicator. Towards its practical applications, we illustrate that the correlation power analysis (CPA) based on the novel notion of $\mathcal{DTO}$ performs better than that uses the classical notion of $\mathcal{RTO}$. This conclusion is confirmed in two cases, i.e. CPA against MARVIN and CPA against PRESENT-128.

Keywords: (n, m)-functions · Transparency order · Differential transparency order · Auto-correlation · Cross-correlation

© Springer Nature Switzerland AG 2021
J. K. Liu et al. (Eds.): ISC 2021, LNCS 13118, pp. 139–157, 2021.
https://doi.org/10.1007/978-3-030-91356-4_8

1   Introduction

Differential Power Analysis (DPA) [14,17] is one of the strongest forms of side-channel attacks. In order to minimize information leakage, the substitution boxes (S-boxes), the only nonlinear part of block ciphers, should be resistant to higher-order differential cryptanalysis which is closely related to DPA-like attacks. In a particular context of linear cryptanalysis and its relation to DPA, in [14] the authors analyzed the S-boxes of AES and DES in terms of signal-to-noise ratio ($\mathcal{SNR}$).

In 2005, Prouff [21] introduced a useful characterization of S-boxes in terms of their robustness to DPA-like attacks and proposed the definition of the transparency order ($\mathcal{TO}$) based on the auto-correlation coefficients of (n,m)-functions, where this term stands for a common representation of S-boxes that map n binary inputs to m binary outputs. The main conclusion is that S-boxes with smaller $\mathcal{TO}$ offer a higher resistance to DPA attacks, and additionally both a lower bound and an upper bound on $\mathcal{TO}$ were deduced in [21].

Even though, the whole approach of defining the resistance to DPA, as given in [21], was questioned recently in [9] by identifying certain limitations and inconsistency of the original definition. Accordingly, a revised definition of the transparency order ($\mathcal{RTO}$), based on the cross-correlation coefficients of (n,m)-functions (thus not only auto-correlation), was introduced in [9]. This definition appears to capture better the resistance to DPA attacks in the Hamming weight model and in particular address better the case when the so-called hardware implementation with pre-charged logic is used. This redefinition also motivated several attempts [9] to find small size S-boxes that apart from satisfying other cryptographic criteria such as high degree, high nonlinearity, good differential properties also have a good transparency order. And some analysis and constructions of $\mathcal{RTO}$ for Boolean function were obtained in [24]. Some transparency order relationships between one Boolean function and its decomposition functions were obtained in [26].

In practice, the accuracy of the leakage model and the noise level significantly influence the efficiency of CPA [4,15], which is also confirmed in this work. In a similar fashion, other forms of side-channel cryptanalysis can be efficiently applied to encryption algorithms such as an DPA attack performed on the well-known stream ciphers Grain and Trivium in [12]. The sensitivity of a proper choice of the indicator of information leakage was further investigated in [11, 13], where Fei *et al.* introduced the so-called confusion coefficient ($\mathcal{CC}$) as a useful measure of the robustness of encryption algorithms against side-channel cryptanalysis. Experimental results related to the DPA attacks mounted on DES and AES confirmed that this leakage model has a high accuracy and it ensures a larger success rate compared to classical models.

Nevertheless, it turns out that both definitions of the transparency order, based either on auto-correlation [21] or cross-correlation coefficients [9], still have certain shortcomings. For instance, these definitions heavily depend on the so called pre-charged (constant) logic value β which cannot be efficiently predicted by an adversary in the Hamming distance model. Moreover, the estimate of both essential indicators (absolute and sum-of-square) is performed using maximization over β. This basically contradicts the fact that this parameter is considered to be a constant, namely it is system dependent and commonly corresponds to the initial register value. For these reasons, we introduce the notion of differential transparency order ($\mathcal{DTO}$), which is not affected by the pre-charged logic value β at all and might even better capture the robustness of S-boxes to DPA attacks. In accordance to this new definition, the information leakage of many $(4, 4)$ S-boxes used in lightweight block ciphers are determined. Our simulations indicate that the information leakage of these S-boxes measured through the new indicator is larger than that of $\mathcal{RTO}$. A theoretical upper and lower bounds on $\mathcal{DTO}$ are also derived.

In particular, it is illustrated that the correlation power analysis (CPA) [4] attack that uses this novel notion of $\mathcal{DTO}$ is more efficient compared to the same attack than implemented with respect to $\mathcal{RTO}$. This conclusion is experimentally confirmed when applying CPA attack to encryption algorithms MARVIN and PRESENT since the correlation coefficients of power traces achieve larger values in the context of $\mathcal{DTO}$ than those of $\mathcal{RTO}$.

This article is organized as follows. In Sect. 2, we introduce some relevant notations and definitions related to Boolean functions and briefly discuss two different notions of transparency order. A new measure of information leakage, also including differential aspects of S-boxes and denoted $\mathcal{DTO}$, is proposed in Sect. 3. In Sect. 4, the affine invariance of $\mathcal{DTO}$ is analyzed, and the lower and upper bounds on $\mathcal{DTO}$ are given in Sect. 5. Finally, some concluding remarks are given in Sect. 6.

2   Preliminaries

We denote by $\mathbb{F}_2$ the finite field with two elements: 0,1. $\mathbb{F}_2^n$ is the n-dimensional vector space over $\mathbb{F}_2$. A function $F : \mathbb{F}_2^n \to \mathbb{F}_2^m$ is called an (n, m)-function (or S-box), where n and m are two positive integers. F can be viewed as a collection of its coordinate Boolean functions, $F(x) = (f_1(x), \ldots, f_m(x))$, where $f_i : \mathbb{F}_2^n \to \mathbb{F}_2$ is a Boolean function. For shortness, we usually use the notation $F = (f_1, \ldots, f_m)$. Every Boolean function $f \in \mathbb{B}_n$ admits a unique representation called the algebraic normal form (ANF) which is a multivariate polynomial over $\mathbb{F}_2$:

$$f(x_1, \ldots, x_n) = a_0 \oplus \bigoplus_{1 \leq i \leq n} a_i x_i \oplus \bigoplus_{1 \leq i < j \leq n} a_{i,j} x_i x_j \oplus \cdots \oplus a_{1,\ldots,n} x_1 x_2 \cdots x_n,$$

where the coefficients $a_0, a_i, a_{i,j}, \cdots, a_{1,\ldots,n} \in \mathbb{F}_2$. The algebraic degree, $deg(f)$, is the largest length of the monomial(s) with non-zero coefficients. A Boolean function $f \in \mathbb{B}_n$ is said to be balanced if its truth table contains equal number of ones and zeros, that is, $|\{x \in \mathbb{F}_2^n : f(x) = 1\}| = |\{x \in \mathbb{F}_2^n : f(x) = 0\}| = 2^{n-1}$. An (n, m)-function F is called balanced if every image value in $\mathbb{F}_2^m$ is taken exactly 2^{n-m} times when the input ranges through $\mathbb{F}_2^n$.

In this paper, $\mathbf{0}^n, \mathbf{1}^n \in \mathbb{F}_2^n$ will denote the all-zero and all-one vectors, respectively.

Before giving Definition 1, we need to give the definition of cross-correlation function. The cross-correlation function between $f, g \in \mathbb{B}_n$ is defined as

$$\triangle_{f,g}(\alpha) = \sum_{x \in \mathbb{F}_2^n} (-1)^{f(x) \oplus g(x \oplus \alpha)}, \alpha \in \mathbb{F}_2^n.$$

In particular, when $f = g$, then the auto-correlation function of $f \in \mathbb{B}_n$ is given by

$$\triangle_f(\alpha) = \sum_{x \in \mathbb{F}_2^n} (-1)^{f(x) \oplus f(x \oplus \alpha)}, \alpha \in \mathbb{F}_2^n.$$

Two functions $f, g \in \mathbb{B}_n$ are said to be perfectly uncorrelated if $\triangle_{f,g}(\alpha) = 0$, for any $\alpha \in \mathbb{F}_2^n$. The following definition is proved useful in the remainder of this article.

Definition 1. *Let $f, g \in \mathbb{B}_n$. f and g are almost perfectly uncorrelated, if $\triangle_{f,g}(\alpha) = 0$ for any $\alpha \in \mathbb{F}_2^{n*}$, where $\mathbb{F}_2^{n*} = \mathbb{F}_2^n \setminus \mathbf{0}^n$.*

Apparently, when f and g are perfectly uncorrelated it implies that they are almost perfectly uncorrelated.

In 2005, Prouff [21] gave the original definition of the transparency order in Definition 2.

Definition 2. *[21] Let $F = (f_1, \ldots, f_m)$ be an (n, m)-function. The transparency order $(\mathcal{TO})$ is defined by:*

$$\mathcal{TO}(F) = \max_{\beta \in \mathbb{F}_2^m} \{ | m - 2wt(\beta) | - \frac{1}{2^{2n} - 2^n} \sum_{a \in \mathbb{F}_2^{n*}} | \sum_{i=1}^m (-1)^{\beta_i} \triangle_{f_i}(a) | \}. \quad (1)$$

In 2017, the revised definition was given recently in [9].

Definition 3. *[9] Let $F = (f_1, \ldots, f_m)$ be a balanced (n, m)-function. The redefining transparency order $(\mathcal{RTO})$ of F is defined by:*

$$\mathcal{RTO}(F) = \max_{\beta \in \mathbb{F}_2^m} \{ m - \frac{1}{2^{2n} - 2^n} \sum_{a \in \mathbb{F}_2^{n*}} \sum_{j=1}^m | \sum_{i=1}^m (-1)^{\beta_i \oplus \beta_j} \triangle_{f_i, f_j}(a) | \}. \quad (2)$$

Remark 1. *Recently, the notion of modified transparency order $(\mathcal{MTO})$ was introduced in [18]. To calculate $\mathcal{MTO}$, the term $\sum_{a \in \mathbb{F}_2^{n*}} \sum_{j=1}^m | \sum_{i=1}^m (-1)^{\beta_i \oplus \beta_j} \triangle_{f_i, f_j}(a) |$ in (2) is simply replaced by $\sum_{a \in \mathbb{F}_2^{n*}} | \sum_{j=1}^m \sum_{i=1}^m (-1)^{\beta_i \oplus \beta_j} \triangle_{f_i, f_j}(a) |$. The authors then claimed that the notion of $\mathcal{MTO}$ captures better the multi-bit DPA in Hamming weight leakage model than $\mathcal{RTO}$. However, our experimental results (fixing the success rate to be at least 0.8) indicate that there is only a marginal improvement (in certain cases) in the number of traces needed when performing multi-bit DPA attack using the $\mathcal{MTO}$ measure compared to $\mathcal{RTO}$.*

3 Differential Transparency Order—A Novel DPA Concept

In this section, we introduce a new measure of the information leakage relevant to DPA type of cryptanalysis. Notice that both original definitions employ the Hamming distance model to quantify the possibility of deducing (a portion of) the secret key K used in the computation of the form $F(x \oplus \dot{K})$. In brief, both approaches are based on the measuring of the number of changed bits (using the corresponding power traces) in $F(x \oplus \dot{K})$ through $H(F(x \oplus \dot{K}) \oplus \beta)$, where $H(\cdot)$ measures the Hamming weight of a given input. The parameter β is the so-called precharge logic value specific to a given system (namely the initial register value), which can be treated as a fixed constant, see [9]. Then, $\mathcal{TO}$ and $\mathcal{RTO}$ respectively employ the auto- and cross-correlation properties of $F(x \oplus \dot{K})$.

In difference to both these definitions which are very sensitive to the unknown constant β, using the similar idea of differential attacks [19], the adversary may consider the differential output of the cryptographic S-box so that $G(x \oplus \dot{K}) = F(x \oplus \dot{K}) \oplus F(x \oplus \gamma \oplus \dot{K})$, where $(x, x \oplus \gamma)$ is a pair of input plaintext blocks and γ is a nonzero constant. Moreover,

$$H(G(x \oplus \dot{K})) = H(F(x \oplus \dot{K}) \oplus F(x \oplus \gamma \oplus \dot{K})) = H(F(x \oplus \dot{K}) \oplus \beta \oplus F(x \oplus \gamma \oplus \dot{K}) \oplus \beta).$$

More specifically, the adversary can use the correlation property of $H(G(x \oplus \dot{K}))$ and the value of $|H(F(x \oplus \dot{K}) \oplus \beta) - H(F(x \oplus \gamma \oplus \dot{K}) \oplus \beta)|$, where $|\cdot|$ denotes the absolute value. This observation has been described and efficiently used in attack by Oswald et al. [20]. The main problem with the current concept of transparency order is the fact that $\mathcal{RTO}$ is an estimated (maximum) value that depends on β rather than the exact value which can be computed for a given constant β that is system dependent.

This is indeed important since $H(G(x \oplus \dot{K}))$ can be efficiently measured by the adversary and $H(G(x \oplus \dot{K}))$ is actually not directly affected by the parameter β^* in the Hamming distance model, i.e. it is equivalent to observe $H(G(x \oplus \dot{K}) \oplus \beta^*)$, where the precharge logic value β^* is set to zero.

This essentially means that $F(x)$ is replaced by $G(x)$ in the definition of $\mathcal{RTO}$ and additionally $\beta^* = \mathbf{0}^m$ in Eq. (2). To thwart DPA attack in this model, the leakage information of a given S-box should be small enough for every possible value γ. This leads us to a yet another revision of the concept of transparency order which we refer to as *differential transparency order (DTO)*.

3.1 Differential Transparency Order

Definition 4. *Let $F = (f_1, \ldots, f_m) \in \mathbb{F}_2^n$ be an (n, m)-function. The differential transparency order (DTO) is defined by:*

$$\mathcal{DTO}(F) = \max_{\gamma \in \mathbb{F}_2^{n*}} \{ m - \frac{1}{2^{2n} - 2^n} \sum_{a \in \mathbb{F}_2^{n*}} \sum_{j=1}^{m} | \sum_{i=1}^{m} \triangle_{G_i, G_j}(a) | \}, \qquad (3)$$

where $G_i(x) = f_i(x) \oplus f_i(x \oplus \gamma)$ for some $\mathbf{0}^n \neq \gamma \in \mathbb{F}_2^n$ and $1 \leq i \leq m$.

Example 1. *The S-box of Prince [3] block cipher is given in Table 1. It can be easily verified that $\mathcal{RTO}(F) = 2.333$, whereas $\mathcal{DTO}(F) = 2.533 > \mathcal{RTO}(F)$. It means that the information leakage of this S-box is larger using our new indicator $\mathcal{DTO}(F)$ compared to the leakage evaluated using $\mathcal{RTO}(F)$.*

Table 1. S-box of Prince

x	0	1	2	3	4	5	6	7	8	9	10	11	12	13	14	15
$S(x)$	11	15	3	2	10	12	9	1	6	7	8	0	14	5	13	4

We further notice that there are eight S-boxes in Lblock cipher having this property (similar to S-box in Prince), whereas all S-boxes used in Midori have larger $\mathcal{DTO}$ than $\mathcal{RTO}$. Tables 2 and 3 illustrate that the information leakage based on $\mathcal{DTO}$ is larger than the value of original $\mathcal{RTO}$ for most of the $(4,4)$ S-boxes (except the S-box in Piccolo) that are practically used as the core component in lightweight block ciphers.

Table 2. Comparison of $\mathcal{RTO}(F)$ with $\mathcal{DTO}(F)$ for the first group of $(4,4)$ S-boxes

S-boxes	PRESENT [6]	Lblock [25]	Piccolo [23]	Marvin [16]
$\mathcal{RTO}(F)$	2.467	2.567	2.567	2.667
$\mathcal{DTO}(F)$	3.000	3.133	3.533	4.000

Table 3. Comparison of $\mathcal{RTO}(F)$ with $\mathcal{DTO}(F)$ for the second group of $(4,4)$ S-boxes

S-boxes	Skinny [5]	Pride [1]	Midori [2]	Gift [7]
$\mathcal{RTO}(F)$	2.567	2.467	2.167	2.200
$\mathcal{DTO}(F)$	3.533	3.067	2.800	3.000

3.2 CPA Efficiency Using $\mathcal{RTO}$ and $\mathcal{DTO}$—A Comparison

We now illustrate that under Hamming weight leakage model, the CPA attack that utilizes the concept of $\mathcal{DTO}$ can be more efficient (in terms of the success rate) than the same attack that employs the classical $\mathcal{RTO}$ measure. For this purpose we have performed simulations by implementing Marvin [16] and PRESENT-128 [6] encryption algorithms and applying the CPA attack on their S-boxes. The correlation coefficients derived using only 16 power traces are calculated using $\mathcal{RTO}$ and $\mathcal{DTO}$ respectively and the success rate of the attack is then compared.

In more detail, our targeted intermediate value v (where the power traces are taken from) is selected to be the output of S-box of the first round of either PRESENT-128 or MARVIN algorithm. It is furthermore assumed that different bits of v leak the information independently and identically, in which case the signal part leakages essentially follow the Hamming weight model. In more detail, the Hamming weight of v is used to denote the power leakage of v. Then, electronic noise of a crypto device need to be embedded (simulated) which is assumed to follow the Gaussian distribution. We denote the noise and signal part contained in the ith power trace by n_i and s_i, respectively. Then, the power consumption of the ith power trace can be expressed as $t_i = s_i + n_i$.

In our experiments, the signal-to-noise ratio ($\mathcal{SNR}$) is varied to evaluate the correctness of the theoretical analysis. The $\mathcal{SNR}$ is defined as the ratio between the variance of signal part leakages VAR_s and the variance of noise part leakages VAR_n, i.e., $\mathcal{SNR} = \frac{\text{VAR}_s}{\text{VAR}_n}$. First, the value of VAR_s can be computed. For example, when the target is an implementation of the PRESENT-128 algorithm, the values of v are randomly chosen as integers in the interval $[0,15]$ which gives the Hamming weight of v. With the Hamming weight of all possible values of v, the variance of signal part leakages VAR_s can be obtained. More specifically, the Hamming weight of 16 possible values of v can be denoted as $HW_0, \ldots, HW_{15}$. Using these values, the variance of signal part leakages VAR_s can be calculated by using equation $\text{VAR}_s = \frac{1}{16} \sum_{i=0}^{15} (HW_i - \frac{1}{16} \sum_{j=0}^{15} HW_i)^2$. Then, the power traces obtained form the implemented algorithm can be used to recover a portion of the secret key, say k_c, when the same key is repeatedly used by the targeted device e times. For this purpose, we employ CPA as the attack method. Averaging the results when applying the CPA attack e times to a particular target (PRESENT-128 or MARVIN), the success rate (SR) of CPA can be empirically estimated. In order to get accurate estimates of SR_{CPA}, the value of e is empirically set to $1,000$.

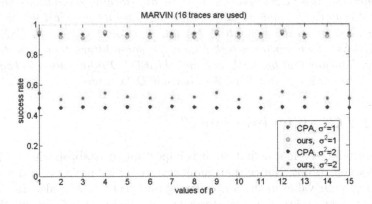

Fig. 1. Success rate of CPA against MARVIN with the noise level $\sigma^2 \in \{1, 2\}$

The simulation results of CPA attack applied to MARVIN and PRESENT-128 are given in Fig. 1 and Fig. 2, respectively. Notice that only 16 power traces are used in both cases and the success rate of CPA performed using $\mathcal{DTO}$ is significantly higher than the same attack that employs the classical $\mathcal{RTO}$ concept. The main reason for this behaviour is that the influence of the difference between two S-Box inputs is embedded in the leakage model based on $\mathcal{DTO}$ which is not the case when the leakage model that uses $\mathcal{RTO}$ is considered. Moreover, the β value that depicts the maximum success rate of CPA with $\mathcal{DTO}$ in Fig. 1 and Fig. 2 is consistent with the value of γ that maximizes $\mathcal{DTO}(F)$, see equation (3). This further illustrates that the indicator $\mathcal{DTO}$ is more accurate parameter when evaluating the resistance of cryptographic S-boxes against CPA attacks.

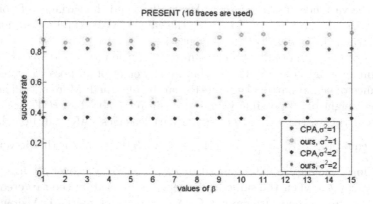

Fig. 2. Success rate of CPA against PRESENT-128 with the noise level $\sigma^2 \in \{1, 2\}$

Remark 2. *To achieve the success rate of 0.8 in the case of PRESENT-128, the multi-bit DPA attack proposed by Li et al. [18] requires at least 30 power traces when the noise level equals to 1. It is confirmed by simulations that $\mathcal{DTO}$ in general achieves a smaller value than $\mathcal{RTO}$ and its practical use is justified by its employment in the simulated CPA attack on block ciphers PRESENT-128 and MARVIN which performs better than the same attack that uses the $\mathcal{RTO}$ indicator. It means that the CPA with embedded $\mathcal{DTO}$ information leakage model appears to be more efficient than the multi-bit DPA attack.*

4   Is $\mathcal{DTO}$ Affine Invariance?

Having introduced a new definition, it is important to establish whether $\mathcal{DTO}$ is affine invariant or not. Notice that many cryptographic notions (such as nonlinearity, maximum value in the auto-correlation spectrum and algebraic degree) remain invariant under affine transformation applied to input/output. We show that $\mathcal{DTO}$ is affine invariant when only the input is affected by this transformation, whereas when both the input and output are subjected to affine transformation we illustrate (by specifying examples) that the affine invariance of $\mathcal{DTO}$ is not generally true.

For two balanced (n, n)-functions S_1 and S_2, if there exists a pair of invertible affine mappings A and B such that $B^{-1} \circ S_1 \circ A = S_2$ then S_1 and S_2 are called affine equivalent. Each of these affine mappings can be expressed as a linear transform followed by an addition, which leads to an affine equivalence relation of the form

$$S_1(x) = B^{-1} \cdot S_2(A \cdot x \oplus a) \oplus b, x \in \mathbb{F}_2^n,$$

with A and B invertible $n \times n$-bit linear mappings, and a and b n-bit constants.

A partial affine invariance (applying affine transformation to the input) of the $\mathcal{DTO}$ criterion is stated in the following theorem.

Theorem 1. *Let $F = (f_1, \ldots, f_n) \in \mathbb{F}_2^n$ be a balanced (n, n)-function. Then, for any affine permutation $A \in \mathbb{A}_n$ and $c \in \mathbb{F}_2^n$ we have $\mathcal{DTO}(F(A \cdot x \oplus c)) = \mathcal{DTO}(F(x))$.*

Proof. For convenience, let $h_i(x) = f_i(A \cdot x \oplus c)$ for $1 \leq i \leq n$ and $L_i(x) = h_i(x) \oplus h_i(x \oplus \gamma)$ for some $\mathbf{0}^n \neq \gamma \in \mathbb{F}_2^n (1 \leq i \leq n)$, we will prove $\mathcal{DTO}(F) = \mathcal{DTO}(H)$ for $H = (h_1, \ldots, h_n)$.

From Definition 4, let

$$\mathcal{DTO}(H, \gamma) = n - \frac{1}{2^{2n} - 2^n} \sum_{a \in \mathbb{F}_2^{n*}} \sum_{j=1}^{n} \left| \sum_{i=1}^{n} \triangle_{L_i, L_j}(a) \right|.$$

Since A is an affine permutation over $\mathbb{F}_2^n$,

$$\mathcal{DTO}(H, \gamma) = n - \frac{1}{2^{2n} - 2^n} \sum_{a \in \mathbb{F}_2^{n*}} \sum_{j=1}^{n} \left| \sum_{i=1}^{n} \sum_{x \in \mathbb{F}_2^n} (-1)^{f_i(A \cdot x \oplus c) \oplus f_i(A \cdot (x \oplus \gamma) \oplus c)} \right.$$

$$\left. (-1)^{f_j(A \cdot (x \oplus a) \oplus c) \oplus f_j(A \cdot ((x \oplus a) \oplus \gamma) \oplus c)} \right|$$

$$= n - \frac{1}{2^{2n} - 2^n} \sum_{a \subset \mathbb{F}_2^{n*}} \sum_{j=1}^{n} \left| \sum_{i=1}^{n} \sum_{x \in \mathbb{F}_2^n} (-1)^{f_i(A \cdot x \oplus c) \oplus f_i(A \cdot x \oplus A \cdot \gamma \oplus c)} \right.$$

$$\left. (-1)^{f_j(A \cdot x \oplus A \cdot a \oplus c) \oplus f_j(A \cdot x \oplus A \cdot a \oplus A \cdot \gamma \oplus c)} \right|$$

$$= n - \frac{1}{2^{2n} - 2^n} \sum_{a \in \mathbb{F}_2^{n*}} \sum_{j=1}^{n} \left| \sum_{i=1}^{n} \sum_{\substack{y = A \cdot x \oplus c \\ x \in \mathbb{F}_2^n}} (-1)^{f_i(y) \oplus f_i(y \oplus A \cdot \gamma)} \right.$$

$$\left. (-1)^{f_j(y \oplus A \cdot a) \oplus f_j(y \oplus A \cdot a \oplus A \cdot \gamma)} \right|$$

$$= n - \frac{1}{2^{2n} - 2^n} \sum_{\substack{r = A \cdot a \\ a \in \mathbb{F}_2^{n*}}} \sum_{j=1}^{n} \left| \sum_{i=1}^{n} \triangle_{G_i, G_j}(r) \right|$$

(where $G_i(x) = f_i(x) \oplus f_i(x \oplus A \cdot \gamma)$)

$$= \mathcal{DTO}(F, A \cdot \gamma).$$

Since $\gamma \in \mathbb{F}_2^{n*}$, $\mathcal{DTO}(F(A \cdot x \oplus c)) = \mathcal{DTO}(F(x))$. ∎

Similarly as for $\mathcal{RTO}$ [9], we can only prove that $\mathcal{DTO}$ of F and $F \circ A$ are the same for any affine permutation $A \in \mathbb{A}_n (c \in \mathbb{F}_2^n)$. On the other hand, $\mathcal{DTO}$ of F and $B \circ F \circ A$ are not the same under affine transformation A and B which is illustrated through the following examples found by computer search:

1. We consider the output values of the $(4, 4)$-function S-box, denoted by F and used in LBlock [25], given by $F = E9F0D4AB128376C5$ (the output values are given in hexadecimal format for the inputs sorted lexicographically). By applying the affine transformation so that $G = B \circ F \circ A$ where

$$A = \begin{pmatrix} 1\,0\,0\,0 \\ 0\,1\,0\,0 \\ 0\,0\,1\,0 \\ 0\,0\,0\,1 \end{pmatrix} \qquad B = \begin{pmatrix} 1\,1\,0\,0 \\ 0\,1\,0\,0 \\ 0\,0\,1\,0 \\ 0\,0\,0\,1 \end{pmatrix}$$

   one can verify that $G = 69705CAB1283FE4D$. Then, we have $\mathcal{DTO}(F) = 3.133$ and $\mathcal{DTO}(G) = 3.000$ and consequently $\mathcal{DTO}(F) \neq \mathcal{DTO}(G)$.
2. Similarly, for the $(4, 4)$ S-box of Marvin [16] whose output values are given by $F = 021B83ED46F5C79A$, using the same A and B as above one can verify that $G = B \circ F \circ A$ gives $G = 021B8365CE7D4F9A$. We have $\mathcal{DTO}(F) = 4$ and $\mathcal{DTO}(G) = 3.067$ and hence $\mathcal{DTO}(F) \neq \mathcal{DTO}(G)$.
3. Also for the $(4, 4)$ S-box of Midori cipher [2] given by $F = CAD3EBF78915\ 0246$, by applying $G = B \circ F \circ A$ one obtains $G = 4A536B7F891D02CE$. Then, $\mathcal{DTO}(F) = 2.800$ and $\mathcal{DTO}(G) = 2.867$, so that $\mathcal{DTO}(F) \neq \mathcal{DTO}(G)$.

We conclude this section by considering representatives of 302 affine equivalence classes of $(4, 4)$ S-boxes specified in [8] (applying affine transformation to the input only) and comparing their $\mathcal{DTO}$ and $\mathcal{RTO}$ value. The simulation results are given in Appendix and the main conclusion is that approximately 94 % of these S-boxes have a larger $\mathcal{DTO}$ than their corresponding $\mathcal{RTO}$ value (see Tables 5, 6 and 7).

Remark 3. *A similar behaviour is noted for $(8, 8)$ S-boxes regarding the comparison between the transparency order indicators. In most of the cases, our simulations show that $\mathcal{RTO}(F) < \mathcal{DTO}(F)$. For instance, for the S-box of Midori-128 cipher [2] one obtains $\mathcal{RTO}(F) = 4.267$ and $\mathcal{DTO}(F) = 5.753$. Nevertheless, the inverse S-box of AES [10] has $\mathcal{RTO}(F) = 6.916$ and $\mathcal{DTO}(F) = 6.573$, thus $\mathcal{RTO}(F) > \mathcal{DTO}(F)$, which is possibly due to good differential properties of the inverse function.*

5   Lower and Upper Bounds on $\mathcal{DTO}$

In this section we derive some upper and lower bounds related to the $\mathcal{DTO}$ indicator. It will be demonstrated that for certain sizes of S-boxes these bounds are tight.

Theorem 2. *Let $F = (f_1, \ldots, f_m)$ be an (n, m)-function. If G_i and G_j are almost perfectly uncorrelated functions for $1 \leq i \neq j \leq m$, then*

$$0 \leq \mathcal{DTO}(F) \leq m,$$

where $G_i(x) = f_i(x) \oplus f_i(x \oplus \gamma)$ for some $\mathbf{0}^n \neq \gamma \in \mathbb{F}_2^n$ and $1 \leq i \leq m$.

Especially, $\mathcal{DTO}(F) = m$ if and only if $\mid \triangle_{G_j}(a) \mid = 0$ for any $\alpha \in \mathbb{F}_2^{n*}$ and $1 \leq j \leq m$. Also, $\mathcal{DTO}(F) = 0$ if and only if $\mid \triangle_{G_j}(\alpha) \mid = 2^n$, for any $\alpha \in \mathbb{F}_2^n \setminus \mathbf{0}^n$ and $1 \leq j \leq m$.

Proof. Since $G_i(x)$ and $G_j(x)$ are almost perfectly uncorrelated, then $\triangle_{G_i,G_j}(a) = 0$ for any $a \in \mathbb{F}_2^{n*}$ and $1 \leq i \neq j \leq m$. Thus,

$$\mathcal{DTO}(F) = \max_{\gamma \in \mathbb{F}_2^m} \{ m - \frac{1}{2^{2n} - 2^n} \sum_{a \in \mathbb{F}_2^{n*}} \sum_{j=1}^{m} \mid \sum_{i=1}^{m} \triangle_{G_i,G_j}(a) \mid \}$$

$$= \max_{\gamma \in \mathbb{F}_2^m} \{ m - \frac{1}{2^{2n} - 2^n} \sum_{a \in \mathbb{F}_2^{n*}} \sum_{j=1}^{m} \mid \triangle_{G_j,G_j}(a) \mid \}.$$

For any $G_j(x) = f_j(x) \oplus f_j(x \oplus \gamma)$, with $1 \leq j \leq m$, we know that $0 \leq \mid \triangle_{G_j,G_j}(a) \mid = \mid \triangle_{G_j}(a) \mid \leq 2^n$. This implies that $0 \leq \mathcal{DTO}(F) \leq m$.

In particular, we have $\mathcal{DTO}(F) = m$ if and only if $\mid \triangle_{G_j}(a) \mid = 0$ for any $\alpha \in \mathbb{F}_2^{n*}$ and $1 \leq j \leq m$. Similarly, $\mathcal{DTO}(F) = 0$ if and only if $\mid \triangle_{G_j}(\alpha) \mid = 2^n$, for any $\alpha \in \mathbb{F}_2^n \setminus \mathbf{0}^m$ and $1 \leq j \leq m$. ∎

Example 2. *To demonstrate the tightness of our lower and upper bounds, we give two examples.*

1) *Let $F = (f_1, f_2)$, where $f_1(x_1, \ldots, x_4) = x_1 x_2 \oplus x_3 x_4$ and $f_2(x_1, \ldots, x_4) = x_1 x_3 \oplus x_2 x_4 \oplus 1$ are 4-variable bent functions. Then, $G_1(x_1, \ldots, x_4) = \gamma_2 x_1 \oplus \gamma_1 x_2 \oplus \gamma_4 x_3 \oplus \gamma_3 x_4 \oplus \gamma_1 \gamma_2 \oplus \gamma_3 \gamma_4$, $G_2(x_1, \ldots, x_4) = \gamma_3 x_1 \oplus \gamma_4 x_2 \oplus \gamma_1 x_3 \oplus \gamma_2 x_4 \oplus \gamma_1 \gamma_3 \oplus \gamma_2 \gamma_4$. It can be easily verified that both G_1 and G_2 are balanced functions for some $\mathbf{0}^4 \neq \gamma = (\gamma_1, \ldots, \gamma_4) \in \mathbb{F}_2^4$. Thus, $\mid \triangle_{G_1}(\alpha) \mid = \mid \triangle_{G_2}(\alpha) \mid = 2^4$ and $\mid \triangle_{G_1,G_2}(\alpha) \mid = 0$ for $\mathbf{0}^4 \neq \alpha \in \mathbb{F}_2^4$. Thus, $\mathcal{DTO}(F) = 0$.*

2) *Using computer simulations, we find that the $(4, 4)$ S-box of block cipher MARVIN [16], given in Table 4, reaches the upper bound on $\mathcal{DTO}$.*

Table 4. S-box of MARVIN

x	0	1	2	3	4	5	6	7	8	9	10	11	12	13	14	15
$S(x)$	0	2	1	11	8	3	14	13	4	6	15	5	12	7	9	10

The algebraic normal forms of the coordinate functions f_i of this S-box $F = (f_1, f_2, f_3, f_4)$ are given as: $f_1(x_1, \ldots, x_4) = x_1 x_3 \oplus x_1 x_4 \oplus x_2$, $f_2(x_1, \ldots, x_4) = x_3 x_4 \oplus x_1$, $f_3(x_1, \ldots, x_4) = x_1 x_3 \oplus x_3 x_4 \oplus x_4$, $f_4(x_1, \ldots, x_4) = x_2 x_3 x_4 \oplus x_1 x_2 x_3 \oplus x_2 x_4 \oplus x_3$. Let $G_j(x) = f_j(x) \oplus f_j(x \oplus \gamma)(1 \leq i \leq 4, \mathbf{0}^4 \neq \gamma \in \mathbb{F}_2^4)$, then we have $\mathcal{DTO}(F) = 4$.

Lemma 1. *Let* $F = (f_1, \ldots, f_m)$ *be an* (n, m)-*function, and* $G_i(x) = f_i(x) \oplus f_i(x \oplus \gamma)$ *for some* $0^n \neq \gamma \in \mathbb{F}_2^n$ *and* $1 \leq i \leq m$. *Then*

$$\sum_{a \in \mathbb{F}_2^n} \triangle_{G_i, G_j}(a) = \triangle_{f_i}(\gamma) \triangle_{f_j}(\gamma).$$

Proof.

$$\sum_{a \in \mathbb{F}_2^n} \triangle_{G_i, G_j}(a) = \sum_{a \in \mathbb{F}_2^n} \Big[\sum_{x \in \mathbb{F}_2^n} (-1)^{f_i(x) \oplus f_i(x \oplus \gamma) \oplus f_j(x \oplus a) \oplus f_j(x \oplus \gamma \oplus a)} \Big]$$

$$= \sum_{a \in \mathbb{F}_2^n} \Big[\sum_{x \in \mathbb{F}_2^n} (-1)^{f_i(x) \oplus f_i(x \oplus \gamma)} (-1)^{f_j(x \oplus a) \oplus f_j(x \oplus \gamma \oplus a)} \Big]$$

$$= \sum_{x \in \mathbb{F}_2^n} (-1)^{f_i(x) \oplus f_i(x \oplus \gamma)} \sum_{a \in \mathbb{F}_2^n} (-1)^{f_j(x \oplus a) \oplus f_j(x \oplus a \oplus \gamma)}$$

$$= \sum_{x \in \mathbb{F}_2^n} (-1)^{f_i(x) \oplus f_i(x \oplus \gamma)} \triangle_{f_j}(\gamma)$$

$$= \triangle_{f_i}(\gamma) \triangle_{f_j}(\gamma). \blacksquare$$

Based on Lemma 1, we give an upper bound on $\mathcal{DTO}(F)$ for (n, m)-functions.

Theorem 3. *Let* $F = (f_1, \ldots, f_m)$ *be an* (n, m)-*function,* $G_i(x) = f_i(x) \oplus f_i(x \oplus \gamma)$ *for some* $0^n \neq \gamma \in \mathbb{F}_2^n$ *and* $1 \leq i \leq m$. *Then,*

$$\mathcal{DTO}(F) \leq \max_{\gamma \in \mathbb{F}_2^{n*}} \{ m - \frac{1}{2^{2n} - 2^n} \mid \sum_{j=1}^{m} \sum_{i=1}^{m} [\triangle_{f_i}(\gamma) \triangle_{f_j}(\gamma) - \triangle_{G_i, G_j}(0^n)] \mid \}.$$

Proof. By Lemma 1 and using the inequality $\sum_{i=1}^{m} \mid a_i \mid \geq \mid \sum_{i=1}^{m} a_i \mid$ for any $a_i \in \mathbb{R}$, then

$$\mathcal{DTO}(F) = \max_{\gamma \in \mathbb{F}_2^{n*}} \{ m - \frac{1}{2^{2n} - 2^n} \sum_{a \in \mathbb{F}_2^{n*}} \sum_{j=1}^{m} \sum_{i=1}^{m} \mid \sum \triangle_{G_i, G_j}(a) \mid \}$$

$$\leq \max_{\gamma \in \mathbb{F}_2^{n*}} \{ m - \frac{1}{2^{2n} - 2^n} \sum_{a \in \mathbb{F}_2^{n*}} \mid \sum_{j=1}^{m} \sum_{i=1}^{m} \triangle_{G_i, G_j}(a) \mid \}$$

$$\leq \max_{\gamma \in \mathbb{F}_2^{n*}} \{ m - \frac{1}{2^{2n} - 2^n} \mid \sum_{a \in \mathbb{F}_2^{n*}} \sum_{j=1}^{m} \sum_{i=1}^{m} \triangle_{G_i, G_j}(a) \mid \}$$

$$= \max_{\gamma \in \mathbb{F}_2^{n*}} \{ m - \frac{1}{2^{2n} - 2^n} \mid \sum_{j=1}^{m} \sum_{i=1}^{m} [\sum_{a \in \mathbb{F}_2^{n*}} \triangle_{G_i, G_j}(a)] \mid \}$$

$$= \max_{\gamma \in \mathbb{F}_2^{n*}} \{ m - \frac{1}{2^{2n} - 2^n} \mid \sum_{j=1}^{m} \sum_{i=1}^{m} [\triangle_{f_i}(\gamma) \triangle_{f_j}(\gamma) - \triangle_{G_i, G_j}(0^n)] \mid \},$$

which is an upper bound on $\mathcal{DTO}(F)$. $\blacksquare$

Remark 4. *According to Theorem 3, the upper bound on $\mathcal{DTO}(F)$ can be obtained provided the knowledge of the autocorrelation distributions of f_i ($1 \leq i \leq m$) with respect to $\mathbf{0}^n \neq \gamma \in \mathbb{F}_2^n$. This computation is therefore essential for the evaluation of differential transparency order.*

Note that an (n, m)-function $F = (f_1, \ldots, f_m)$ is bent [22] if and only if all of the component functions $v \cdot F$ are bent function for any $v \in \mathbb{F}_2^n$ and $wt(v) > 0$. From this fact and Theorem 3 we can give an upper bound on $\mathcal{DTO}(F)$ for (n, m)-bent function.

Corollary 1. *Let $F = (f_1, \ldots, f_m)$ be an (n, m)-bent function (with $m \leq \frac{n}{2}$), and $\mathbf{0}^n \neq \gamma \in \mathbb{F}_2^n$. Then*

$$\mathcal{DTO}(F) \leq m - \frac{m}{2^n - 1}.$$

Proof. Because $F = (f_1, \ldots, f_m)$ is an (n, m)-bent function, we know that f_i and $f_i \oplus f_j$ are all bent functions for $1 \leq i < j \leq m$. Moreover, we have $\triangle_{f_i}(a) = 0$ and $\triangle_{f_i \oplus f_j}(a) = 0$ for any $a \in \mathbb{F}_2^n$ and $wt(a) > 0$.

By Theorem 3, we have

$$\mathcal{DTO}(F) \leq \max_{\gamma \in \mathbb{F}_2^{n*}} \{ m - \frac{1}{2^{2n} - 2^n} \mid \sum_{j=1}^{m} \sum_{i=1}^{m} [\triangle_{f_i}(\gamma) \triangle_{f_j}(\gamma) - \triangle_{G_i, G_j}(\mathbf{0}^n)] \mid \}$$

$$= \max_{\gamma \in \mathbb{F}_2^{n*}} \{ m - \frac{1}{2^{2n} - 2^n} \mid \sum_{j=1}^{m} \sum_{i=1}^{m} [\triangle_{G_i, G_j}(\mathbf{0}^n)] \mid \}$$

$$= \max_{\gamma \in \mathbb{F}_2^{n*}} \{ m - \frac{1}{2^{2n} - 2^n} \mid [\sum_{i=1}^{m} \triangle_{G_i, G_i}(\mathbf{0}^n) + 2 \sum_{1 \leq i < j \leq m} \triangle_{G_i, G_j}(\mathbf{0}^n)] \mid \}$$

$$= \max_{\gamma \in \mathbb{F}_2^{n*}} \{ m - \frac{1}{2^{2n} - 2^n} \mid [m \times 2^n + 2 \sum_{1 \leq i < j \leq m} \triangle_{f_i \oplus f_j}(\gamma)] \mid \}$$

$$= m - \frac{m}{2^n - 1}. \blacksquare$$

Table 5. Distribution of differential transparency order for $(4, 4)$ S-boxes (I)

$\mathcal{RTO}$	Number	$\mathcal{DTO}$	Number
0.000	1	4.000	1
0.467	1	2.000	1
0.800	1	4.000	1
1.067	1	4.000	1
1.133	1	3.533	1
1.267	1	2.000	1
1.333	3	2.000	1
		3.533	1
		4.000	1
1.400	1	2.800	1
1.533	1	2.000	1
1.600	1	4.000	1
1.733	2	2.533	1
		2.800	1
1.800	4	2.000	1
		2.533	1
		2.800	1
		3.533	1
1.833	1	2.600	1
1.867	5	2.000	1
		2.600	1
		3.067	1
		3.533	1
		4.000	1
1.900	1	2.533	1
1.933	8	2.467	1
		2.533	1
		2.800	2
		3.067	3
		3.533	1
1.967	3	2.800	2
		3.000	1
2.000	2	3.067	1
		3.533	1
2.033	1	2.800	1
2.067	3	2.800	1
		3.067	1
		4.000	1
2.100	2	2.800	2
2.133	6	2.600	1
		3.067	1
		3.267	1
		3.533	1
		4.000	2
2.167	2	3.000	1
		3.267	1
2.200	2	2.800	1
		3.067	1
2.233	1	2.800	1

Table 6. Distribution of differential transparency order for $(4, 4)$ S-boxes (II)

$\mathcal{RTO}$	Number	$\mathcal{DTO}$	Number
2.267	6	2.533	1
		2.600	1
		3.000	3
		3.267	1
2.300	5	2.533	1
		2.600	1
		2.733	1
		2.800	1
		3.267	1
2.333	22	2.533	3
		2.600	4
		2.667	1
		2.733	2
		2.800	1
		2.867	1
		3.000	2
		3.067	2
		3.133	1
		3.267	2
		3.533	3
2.367	15	2.533	2
		2.600	3
		2.733	1
		2.800	2
		2.867	1
		3.000	3
		3.067	1
		3.267	2
2.400	22	2.533	2
		2.600	2
		2.800	3
		3.000	5
		3.067	6
		3.267	3
		4.000	1
2.433	21	2.533	2
		2.600	1
		2.733	2
		2.800	3
		3.000	5
		3.067	3
		3.133	1
		3.267	2
		3.533	2
2.467	30	2.533	8
		2.600	3
		2.733	1
		2.800	3
		3.000	6
		3.067	4
		3.267	4
		3.533	1

Table 7. Distribution of differential transparency order for $(4,4)$ S-boxes (III)

$\mathcal{RTO}$	Number	$\mathcal{DTO}$	Number
2.500	31	2.533	2
		2.600	4
		2.733	2
		2.800	5
		3.000	4
		3.067	6
		3.267	7
		3.533	1
2.533	30	2.533	2
		2.600	2
		2.733	2
		2.800	6
		3.000	5
		3.067	5
		3.267	7
		4.000	1
2.567	26	2.533	3
		2.600	3
		2.667	1
		2.733	1
		2.800	1
		2.867	1
		3.000	9
		3.067	5
		3.533	2
2.600	20	2.267	1
		2.533	2
		2.600	5
		2.733	2
		2.800	2
		3.000	2
		3.067	4
		3.267	1
		3.533	1
2.633	9	2.533	2
		2.600	1
		2.733	2
		2.800	2
		3.000	1
		3.533	1
2.667	7	2.600	1
		2.733	1
		2.800	2
		3.000	1
		3.533	2
2.700	1	3.200	1
2.733	1	2.800	1
2.767	1	3.000	1

6   Conclusions

This article further addresses some relevant concepts related to multi-bit differential power cryptanalysis in the Hamming distance model. Motivated by certain shortcomings of the previous definitions (most importantly avoiding the dependency on the pre-charged constant logic value), we (once again) revise this notion and introduce a novel concept of differential transparency order $\mathcal{DTO}$. It is illustrated through examples and simulations that $\mathcal{DTO}$ is not affine invariant (under affine action on both input and output) and furthermore that $\mathcal{DTO}$ attains larger value than $\mathcal{RTO}$ in general. Most notably, we demonstrate that the CPA attacks perform better when the novel concept is embedded in the information leakage model. In the next step, we will focus on the $\mathcal{DTO}$ of $(8, 8)$-functions, and discuss the relationship between $\mathcal{DTO}$ and other cryptographic indicators.

Acknowledgments. Yu Zhou is supported in part by the Sichuan Science and Technology Program (2020JDJQ0076). Yongzhuang Wei is supported by the National Natural Science Foundation of China (61872103), the Guangxi Science and Technology Foundation (Guike AB18281019) and the Guangxi Natural Science Foundation (2019GXNS-FGA245004). Hailong Zhang is supported by the National Natural Science Foundation of China (61872040). Enes Pasalic is supported in part by the Slovenian Research Agency (research program P1-0404 and research projects J1-9108, J1-1694, N1-0159, J1-2451). Luyang Li is supported by the Natural Science Foundation of Shaanxi Provincial Department of Education (20JK0911).

References

1. Albrecht, M.R., Driessen, B., Kavun, E.B., Leander, G., Paar, C., Yalçın, T.: Block ciphers – focus on the linear layer (feat. PRIDE). In: Garay, J.A., Gennaro, R. (eds.) CRYPTO 2014, Part I. LNCS, vol. 8616, pp. 57–76. Springer, Heidelberg (2014). https://doi.org/10.1007/978-3-662-44371-2_4
2. Banik, S., et al.: Midori: a block cipher for low energy. In: Iwata, T., Cheon, J.H. (eds.) ASIACRYPT 2015, Part II. LNCS, vol. 9453, pp. 411–436. Springer, Heidelberg (2015). https://doi.org/10.1007/978-3-662-48800-3_17
3. Borghoff, J., et al.: PRINCE – a low-latency block cipher for pervasive computing applications - extended abstract. In: Wang, X., Sako, K. (eds.) ASIACRYPT 2012. LNCS, vol. 7658, pp. 208–225. Springer, Heidelberg (2012). https://doi.org/10.1007/978-3-642-34961-4_14
4. Brier, E., Clavier, C., Olivier, F.: Correlation power analysis with a leakage model. In: Joye, M., Quisquater, J.-J. (eds.) CHES 2004. LNCS, vol. 3156, pp. 16–29. Springer, Heidelberg (2004). https://doi.org/10.1007/978-3-540-28632-5_2
5. Beierle, C., et al.: The SKINNY family of block ciphers and its low-latency variant MANTIS. In: Robshaw, M., Katz, J. (eds.) CRYPTO 2016. LNCS, vol. 9815, pp. 123–153. Springer, Heidelberg (2016). https://doi.org/10.1007/978-3-662-53008-5_5
6. Bogdanov, A., et al.: PRESENT: an ultra-lightweight block cipher. In: Paillier, P., Verbauwhede, I. (eds.) CHES 2007, Part II. LNCS, vol. 4727, pp. 450–466. Springer, Heidelberg (2007). https://doi.org/10.1007/978-3-540-74735-2_31

7. Banik, S., Pandey, S.K., Peyrin, T., Sasaki, Yu., Sim, S.M., Todo, Y.: GIFT: a small present - towards reaching the limit of lightweight encryption. In: Fischer, W., Homma, N. (eds.) CHES 2017. LNCS, vol. 10529, pp. 321–345. Springer, Cham (2017). https://doi.org/10.1007/978-3-319-66787-4_16
8. De Cannière, C.: Analysis and design of symmetric encryption algorithms (Ph.D.), Katholieke Universiteit Leuven (2007)
9. Chakraborty, K., Sarkar, S., Maitra, S., Mazumdar, B., Mukhopadhyay, D., Prouff, E.: Redefining the transparency order. Des. Codes Cryptogr. 82(1–2), 95–115 (2017)
10. Daemen, J., Rijmen, V.: The Design of Rijndael: AES-the Advanced Encryption Standard. Springer, Heidelberg (2013). https://doi.org/10.1007/978-3-662-04722-4
11. Fei, Y., Adam Ding, A., Lao, J., Zhang, L.: A Statistics-based Fundamental Model for Side-channel Attack Analysis. Cryptology ePrint Archive, report 2014/152 (2014). http://eprint.iacr.org/2014/152
12. Fischer, W., Gammel, B.M., Kniffler, O., Velten, J.: Differential power analysis of stream ciphers. In: Abe, M. (ed.) CT-RSA 2007. LNCS, vol. 4377, pp. 257–270. Springer, Heidelberg (2006). https://doi.org/10.1007/11967668_17
13. Fei, Y., Luo, Q., Ding, A.A.: A statistical model for DPA with novel algorithmic confusion analysis. In: Prouff, E., Schaumont, P. (eds.) CHES 2012. LNCS, vol. 7428, pp. 233–250. Springer, Heidelberg (2012). https://doi.org/10.1007/978-3-642-33027-8_14
14. Guilley, S., Hoogvorst, P., Pacalet, R.: Differential power analysis model and some results. In: Quisquater, J.-J., Paradinas, P., Deswarte, Y., El Kalam, A.A. (eds.) CARDIS 2004. IIFIP, vol. 153, pp. 127–142. Springer, Boston, MA (2004). https://doi.org/10.1007/1-4020-8147-2_9
15. Guillot, P., Millérioux, G., Dravie, B., El Mrabet, N.: Spectral approach for correlation power analysis. In: El Hajji, S., Nitaj, A., Souidi, E.M. (eds.) C2SI 2017. LNCS, vol. 10194, pp. 238–253. Springer, Cham (2017). https://doi.org/10.1007/978-3-319-55589-8_16
16. Simplício, M.A., Jr., Barbuda, P.D.F.F.S., Barreto, P.S.L.M.: The MARVIN message authentication code and the LETTERSOUP authenticated encryption scheme. Secur. Commun. Netw. 2(2), pp. 165–180 (2009)
17. Kocher, P., Jaffe, J., Jun, B.: Differential power analysis. In: Wiener, M. (ed.) Advances in Cryptology - CRYPTO 1999, pp. 388–397. Springer, Heidelberg (1999)
18. Li, H., Zhou, Y., Ming, J., Yang, G., Jin, C.: The notion of transparency order, revisited. Comput. J. (2020). https://doi.org/10.1093/comjnl/bxaa069
19. Nyberg, K., Knudsen, L.R.: Provable security against a differential attack. J. Cryptol. 8(1), 27–37 (1995)
20. Oswald, E., Mangard, S., Herbst, C., Tillich, S.: Practical second-order DPA attacks for masked smart card implementations of block ciphers. In: Pointcheval, D. (ed.) CT-RSA 2006. LNCS, vol. 3860, pp. 192–207. Springer, Heidelberg (2006). https://doi.org/10.1007/11605805_13
21. Prouff, E.: DPA attacks and S-boxes. In: Gilbert, H., Handschuh, H. (eds.) FSE 2005. LNCS, vol. 3557, pp. 424–441. Springer, Heidelberg (2005). https://doi.org/10.1007/11502760_29
22. Rothaus, O.S.: On bent functions. J. Comb. Theory A 20, 300–305 (1976)
23. Shibutani, K., Isobe, T., Hiwatari, H., Mitsuda, A., Akishita, T., Shirai, T.: Piccolo: an ultra-lightweight blockciphe. In: Preneel, B., Takagi, T. (eds.) CHES 2011. LNCS, vol. 6917, pp. 342–357. Springer, Heidelberg (2011). https://doi.org/10.1007/978-3-642-23951-9_23

24. Wang, Q., Stănică, P.: Transparency order for Boolean functions: analysis and construction. Des. Codes Crypt. **87**(9), 2043–2059 (2019). https://doi.org/10.1007/s10623-019-00604-1
25. Wu, W., Zhang, L.: LBlock: a lightweight block cipher. In: Lopez, J., Tsudik, G. (eds.) ACNS 2011. LNCS, vol. 6715, pp. 327–344. Springer, Heidelberg (2011). https://doi.org/10.1007/978-3-642-21554-4_19
26. Zhou, Yu., Dong, X., Wei, Y.: On the transparency order relationships between one Boolean function and its decomposition functions. J. Inf. Secur. Appl. **58**, 1–9 (2021)

Web and OS Security

Browserprint: An Analysis of the Impact of Browser Features on Fingerprintability and Web Privacy

Seyed Ali Akhavani[1(✉)], Jordan Jueckstock[2], Junhua Su[2],
Alexandros Kapravelos[2], Engin Kirda[1], and Long Lu[1]

[1] Northeastern University, 360 Huntington Ave, Boston, MA 02115, USA
{sadatakhavani.s,e.kirda,l.lu}@northeastern.edu
[2] North Carolina State University, Raleigh, NC 27695, USA
{jjuecks,jsu6,akaprav}@ncsu.edu

Abstract. Web browsers are indispensable applications in our daily lives. Millions of users use web browsers for a wide range of activities such as social media, online shopping, emails, or surfing the web. The evolution of increasingly more complicated web applications relies on browsers constantly adding and removing features. At the same time, some of these web services use browser fingerprinting to track and profile their users with clear disregard for their web privacy. In this paper, we perform an empirical analysis of browser features evolution and aim to evaluate browser fingerprintability. By analyzing 33 Google Chrome, 31 Mozilla Firefox, and 33 Opera major browser versions released through 2016 to 2020, we discover that all of these browsers have unique feature sets which makes them different from each other. By comparing these features to the fingerprinting APIs presented in literature that have appeared in this field, we conclude that all of these browser versions are uniquely fingerprintable. Our results show an alarming trend that browsers are becoming more fingerprintable over time because newer versions contain more fingerprintable APIs compared to older ones.

Keywords: Browser security · Fingerprinting · Privacy · Web security

1 Introduction

Web browsers have become indispensable in our daily lives. The majority of the online activity of many Internet users comprises of using a browser to access social media, online shopping, surfing the web, messaging, and accessing stored information in the cloud. Unfortunately, many companies are interested in collecting the private browser activities of end-users for marketing and sales purposes. To achieve their data collection objectives, some web services use "browser fingerprinting" to track and profile their users with clear disregard for their web privacy.

© Springer Nature Switzerland AG 2021
J. K. Liu et al. (Eds.): ISC 2021, LNCS 13118, pp. 161–176, 2021.
https://doi.org/10.1007/978-3-030-91356-4_9

As browsers increasingly supplant traditional operating systems as the application publishing platforms of choice, many unique details of a user's browser such as its hardware, operating system, browser configuration and preferences can be exposed through the browser. An attacker who collects and sums these outputs can create a unique "fingerprint" for tracking and identification purposes. In addition, browsers have also been increasing in complexity as more and more new features are being integrated into them, raising concerns that the attack surface offered by this software "bloating" (i.e., the increase in the number of components and code not needed by every user) is contributing to making browsers more difficult to secure against attacks.

Browser fingerprinting has been determined to be an important problem by previous research (e.g., [4,7,20,23]) as well as browser vendors themselves (e.g., [8,22,28]). To date, however, no studies have looked at popular browsers historically and have attempted to determine how their fingerprintability has evolved over the years. Past work has demonstrated that the ability to simply fingerprint a browser's precise version without relying on possibly spoofed User-Agent strings can be useful to attackers [26]. In the further light of web privacy research showing the potential and/or real-world exploitation of novel APIs for fingerprinting [6,15,24], we consider the raw volume of implemented APIs to be a rough but useful proxy estimate of a browser's potential fingerprintability.

In this paper, we perform an empirical analysis of a large number of browser features that have been integrated or phased out of the popular Mozilla Firefox, the Google Chrome, and the Opera browsers between the years 2016 and 2020. We consider browser features to be all functionality that is available to attackers directly through JavaScript, since these are the root problem of most web attacks. Our aim is to answer a number of research questions about the *fingerprintability* and security of these browsers over this time period. We propose a new metric for quantifying the fingerprintability of browser versions that rely on the number of browser features that are associated with fingerprinting. This metric is based on previous research and current fingerprinting techniques discovered in the wild (see Sect. 3.2 for more details). By analyzing 33 Google Chrome, 31 Mozilla Firefox, and 33 Opera major browser versions, our results suggest that these popular browsers have unique feature sets that make them significantly different from each other. Hence, by comparing these features to the fingerprinting APIs presented in literature, we conclude that all of these browser versions are uniquely fingerprintable. Our results suggest the alarming trend that browsers are becoming more fingerprintable over time as newer versions of popular browsers have more fingerprintable APIs embedded in them.

This paper makes the following key contributions:

- We show that all major Mozilla Firefox, Google Chrome, and Opera browser versions between 2016 until 2020 are uniquely fingerprintable based exclusively on the presence or absence of browser features.
- We analyze Mozilla Firefox, Google Chrome, and Opera and report major differences between feature introduction and removal trends. While Firefox tends to keep a steady number of features in the browser (i.e., introducing

new features while removing older ones), Chrome, in contrast, is growing and more features are kept as the browser evolves. Opera, similar to Chrome, seems to be adding lots of features and not interested in removing the older ones.

- We show that although Google Chrome and Opera are both based upon Chromium and share the same codebase, there are still differences in their feature introduction and removal patterns. But this shared codebase makes them very similar in our fingerprintability analysis.
- We provide all the source code and datasets that we have collected in our experiments to the community[1].

2   Research Questions

In this paper, by performing an automated analysis, we attempt to answer the following research questions:

1. *Are major versions of Firefox, Chrome, and Opera browsers fingerprintable?* Our results suggest that the feature set for each browser version is unique. There exist multiple APIs in every browser version that we have analyzed that can be used for fingerprinting. By extracting all the features supported by a browser and exposed via API calls, we can uniquely identify each browser version.

2. *Are Firefox, Chrome, and Opera becoming more fingerprintable over time?* One of the major conclusions of our study is that the number of APIs one can use in the newer versions of Chrome, Opera, and Firefox is larger than the older versions. Hence, newer browser versions are even more fingerprintable than previous versions, and our findings suggest that this trend is likely to continue. As a result, privacy might be an even more significant concern in the future for browser users.

3. *What "lifespan profiles" can we cluster browser features into? Are there any "permanently removed" features? If so, how does their life cycle look like?* Our results suggest that we can categorize browser features based on their lifespan into three main categories (i.e., persistent features, non persistent features, and recurring features). We observe that most of the features are added permanently, and are not removed over time – indicating that browsers are indeed becoming more "bloated" as they evolve.

4. *With respect to browser bloating, how does Firefox compare to Chrome and Opera?* In our study, we were able to map the number of unique features for major versions of Firefox, Chrome, and Opera. The results suggest that Chrome and Opera are introducing more features over time than Firefox, but that all of these browser vendors have shown a significant increase in the total number of features they support per version since 2016. Compared to Firefox, Chrome and Opera tend to introduce more new features and keep them around longer.

---

[1] https://github.com/sa-akhavani/browserprint.

5. *Could the incognito mode in Chrome and the private window mode in Firefox and Opera reduce the possibility of being fingerprinted by websites?* Our analysis suggests that the incognito and private window modes have negligible impact on reducing fingerprinting. That is, almost all fingerprinting APIs are accessible in these modes the same way that they are available in non-private mode.

6. *Although Opera and Chrome are both Chromium-based and share the same codebase, is there any noticeable difference between these two browsers in case of fingerprintability?* In our analysis, we found out that Opera and Chrome have very similar sets of fingerprintable APIs and there is not much difference between these two browsers in case of fingerprintability. But there exist differences in some browser-specific features between these two browsers. Additionally, Opera and Chrome follow almost the same pattern in feature adding and removal as a result of their shared codebase. These browsers tend to keep a majority of their features untouched.

3   Methodology

To be able to determine how fingerprintable a browser is, we need to determine the features it supports when a webpage is visited by a user. Similarly, we need to understand which features are supported by a specific version because attackers typically target such features in attacks (e.g., a bug in the video access functionality might be exploited). Hence, to answer the research questions we pose in this study, we need to be able to figure out exactly what features are supported by each browser version under analysis. In this section, we describe the methodology we followed in this work, and explain how we created the datasets we used in our analyses.

3.1   Feature Gathering

In order to collect *browser feature* sets from Firefox, Opera, and Chrome, we crafted a special JavaScript-instrumented webpage that analyzes the visiting browser. We use the term *feature* to describe JavaScript objects, methods, and property values built into the global namespace of the browser's JavaScript implementation (i.e., the `window` object). Clearly, this definition is JavaScript-centric. However, it is unambiguous and naturally scalable, as we can automate the collection of features from many different browser implementations using standard scripting and crawling techniques. When our instrumented page is loaded by the browser, our JavaScript is executed. This code probes and iterates through the features supported by the browser. This is done by using JavaScript to traverse the tree of non-cyclic JavaScript object references accessible from a pristine (i.e., unmodified by polyfills or other prototype-chain modifications) `window` object, and collecting the full feature names encountered during the traversal. Each feature name comprises the sequence of property names leading from the global object to a given built-in JavaScript value. The traversal code is careful to not modify this object (which doubles as the global variable namespace) in any way, to avoid contaminating the resulting set of feature names. Captured feature sets are then stored in a database, tagged with identifying metadata such as the browser's User-Agent string.

We use the terms *browser features*, as defined in this section, and *JavaScript APIs* interchangeably in our work.

3.2 Browser Fingerprinting APIs

We conduct an in-depth analysis in order to determine which browser features are associated with fingerprinting. Our analysis generates a list of suspicious APIs that we use in our measurements in Sect. 4 to quantify *fingerprintability*: the ratio of browser features in a browser version that are associated with fingerprinting techniques. We describe in the following how we determine which browser features are related to browser fingerprinting.

Our list of suspicious browser fingerprinting APIs contains a total of 313 JavaScript APIs. These APIs are considered suspicious because the purpose of using these API depends on the intent of the programmer who writes the code. We call this list *suspicious fingerprinting APIs* in this paper. In Panopticlick's research [4], browser fingerprinting is achieved through a combination of APIs that seem innocent, such as `Navigator.plugins`, `Navigator.userAgent`, and `Screen.colorDepth`. These APIs provide functionality that matches their original objectives. However, they can be abused by creating a unique fingerprint of the client's browser due to exposing information that narrows down the diversity of visited users. We use two methods to assemble the list of fingerprinting APIs: literature review and experimental analysis.

Literature Review. The foundation of the API list is composed of four core fingerprinting papers, Panopticlick [4], AmIUnique [1], Hiding in the Crowd [18], and FPDetective [7]. This analysis resulted in approximately 10% of the list of suspicious fingerprinting APIs. Some of the APIs are directly mentioned in these papers and the others are modified to match standard APIs[2] with the same functionality. The concepts of Canvas, WebGL, Font fingerprinting are introduced among these APIs. These concepts lead to the next turn of investigation of papers which are Cookieless Monster [23] and Pixel Perfect [20]. This investigation does not bring more APIs but a direction to experimental analysis.

Experimental Analysis. The experimental analysis consists of two stages, collecting APIs by crawling websites and extracting suspicious APIs from the crawling data. In terms of data collecting, the workflow is the same as the one in VisibleV8 [19]. A customized crawler was driven to visit all websites in the Easylist [2] domain file that contains 13,241 domains. Then, the raw logs generated by VisibleV8 were gathered and the VisibleV8 post processor was applied

---

[2] https://developer.mozilla.org/en-US/docs/Web/API.

to process the raw data. After removing duplicate and non-standard APIs, the APIs usage of 8,682 domains with 56,828 origins was collected. Non-standard APIs indicate ones that are not listed in the WebIDL [5] data package. In other words, VisibleV8 and its post processor were adopted to aggregate and summarize standard JS API usage of the target domains.

While collecting APIs from the wild, the API suspicious list was extended through crawling on panopticlick.eff.org, amiunique.org, and browserleaks.com websites. These websites are explicitly marked as browser fingerprinting websites. Therefore, augmenting suspicious fingerprinting APIs among these websites is more efficient than a random walk on the enormous JS API pool.

The next step is to perform a manual analysis to check every API utilized by these three websites. First, we search for information and usage of an API on Mozilla's MDN Web Docs [21]. Then, we determine whether an API fingerprints users based on the information the API conveys. That is to say, an API is classified as a suspicious fingerprinting API if it can provide the information to filter certain users out. For example, there are two users with distinct user agents. By calling Navigator.userAgent, the programmer should be able to distinguish between these two users. Navigator.userAgent can be recognized as a fingerprinting API in this case. The majority of suspicious fingerprinting APIs comes from manual analysis and the idea of categorizing fingerprinting APIs is incited by the browserleaks.com website.

The last step is to manually search for more fingerprinting APIs with the keyword. Namely, in Canvas fingerprinting, most APIs include the "Canvas" or "CanvasRendering". A program was created to filtrate APIs that contain "Canvas" or "CanvasRendering" among APIs of 8k crawled domains. The same pattern also applies to BatteryManager, WebGLRenderingContext, and Speech-Synthesis. Meanwhile, the fingerprint2.js [16] was reviewed to supplement the suspicious fingerprinting API list.

There are limitations to the methods we used for constructing a suspicious fingerprinting API list. First and foremost, this list only provides a partial view of full fingerprinting APIs. To the best of our knowledge, there is no complete table of fingerprinting APIs and more research is needed in this direction. The second limitation is during the manual analysis. There could be misconceptions between the API usage provided by Mozilla web APIs page and the way programmers exploit them. Lastly, part of JS APIs is filtered out by the VisibleV8 post processor. This can be improved by using a larger set of WebIDL data or precisely use the aggregated raw APIs.

As a service to the community, we have made our list of fingerprinting APIs publicly available.

3.3   Browser Testing Platform

In this work, we target Google Chrome, Mozilla Firefox, and Opera browsers as they are well-known, popular browsers that have millions of users. Firefox possesses a distinct codebase unlike Chrome and Opera which are both based on Chromium. We gathered a copy of every major Firefox, Chrome, and Opera version that was released during the March 2016 to April 2020 timeframe, i.e., Chrome versions 49–81, Firefox versions 45–75, and Opera versions 36–68.

To individually connect each browser version to our instrumented feature gathering web application, we mainly used the BrowserStack web service [10]. BrowserStack is a cloud-based web and mobile testing platform that enables developers to test their websites and mobile applications across on a wide range of browsers, operating systems, and real mobile devices. If a specific browser version or configuration was not available on BrowserStack, we developed and used automation scripts to instrument and run the browser instances on a desktop computer running Windows 10.

4   Analysis

In this section, we describe the analysis we performed on the datasets that we collected, and the insights that we distilled from the analysis. We leverage the browser features dataset and the suspicious fingerprinting APIs dataset in our analysis.

4.1   Analysis of the Browser Features

The first analysis we performed on the dataset we collected was to understand how browser features have evolved over time. As we describe in Sect. 3, we consider *browser features* all functionality exposed to JavaScript as objects, methods, and property values. This definition of browser features reflects on 1) how attackers craft web attacks (i.e., creating a unique fingerprint using such features, or exploiting vulnerabilities) and 2) a measurable metric across browser versions. Understanding and gaining insights into how browsers are dealing with new as well as older features is important to be able to distill conclusions about how secure and fingerprintable browsers are becoming as they evolve. Hence, our analysis looked at specific browser features that were introduced, what the typical lifespan of features looks like.

After extracting feature information for all of the browsers under analysis, we automatically parsed the generated reports and analyzed them to see if the features in these browsers fall into specific categories. Our analysis suggested that the features in Firefox, Opera, and Chrome can be categorized into three main categories:

- **Persistent Features**: These are features that are added to a specific version, and that continue to exist in every version that is released after the feature was introduced. We consider a feature to be "persistent" if it appears in at least two distinct browser versions.
- **Non-Persistent Features**: These are features that existed in older versions of the browser, but were removed, and never appeared in newer versions of the browser again. We consider a feature to be "non-persistent" if it is absent in at least two distinct versions of the browser versions under analysis.

– **Recurring Features**: These are features that are added and removed from the browser from time to time. That is, they are introduced, they are removed, and they might appear again at some point. Such features are typically being tested by the vendors, and it is not clear if they will become persistent, or non-persistent.

Our analysis suggests that Chrome possesses 9,718 persistent, 711 non-persistent, and 3,161 recurring features that it supports. Similarly, Opera contains 9,674 persistent, 711 permanently removed, and 3,219 recurring features. On the other hand, Firefox supports 6,274 persistent, 809 non-persistent, and 115 recurring features. Note that Firefox, overall, supports significantly fewer features than Chrome and Opera. Also, our analysis suggests that Firefox, compared to Chrome and Opera, is keeping fewer features (i.e., they are removing more) over time. Figure 1 illustrates the feature categories for each browser vendor. It can be seen that Opera and Chrome are having similar patterns since lots of their features are related to Chromium which is their shared codebase. Besides, Chrome and Opera have a greater portion of recurring features compared to Firefox. This means that Chrome and Opera tend to do more experiments on adding and removing specific features through time.

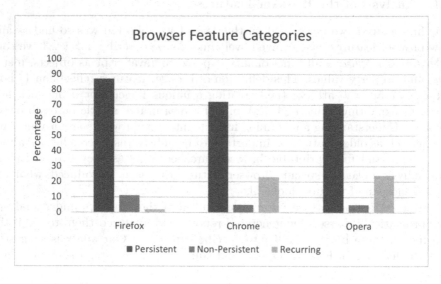

Fig. 1. Feature category distribution for browsers.

In this work, we also performed an analysis of the common features between Firefox, Chrome, and Opera. Since 2016, the total number of features introduced by these browsers is 15,945. Among all these features, there exist only 4,843 common features among Firefox and Chrome – which is approximately 30% of the total number of features that these vendors support. This number is the same between Firefox and Opera too, with 4,843 common features between them.

On the other hand, Chrome and Opera have a bigger set of common features. There exists 13,558 common features between Opera and Chrome – which is approximately 85% of the total number of features that these vendors support. The impact of this huge common features set on fingerprintability between two browsers are analyzed in the next section.

We can conclude that Firefox does not have a high feature overlap with Chrome and Opera. Note that although these browsers often offer very similar functionality, unsurprisingly, their codebase might be very different from each other. We are aware that Firefox's codebase is very different from Chrome's and Opera's. Hence the API names through which these features are available are also often significantly different. To the contrary, Chrome and Opera share the same codebase. This leads to having a bigger set of common features between these two browsers.

Figures 2 and 3 show the feature addition and removal trends for Firefox and Chrome. The data shows that Chrome is adding and removing many more features than Firefox in each version that is released if one looks at the overall numbers of features. However, Firefox seems to be more constant with respect to the number of new features added, and older features removed. Hence, Firefox seems to be more aggressive with respect to removing older features from the browser, "debloating" this way the browser. Chrome and Opera share the same trend, so we omit a separate figure for Opera and leave Fig. 3 as a representative visualization of feature introduction and removal for Chromium-based browsers.

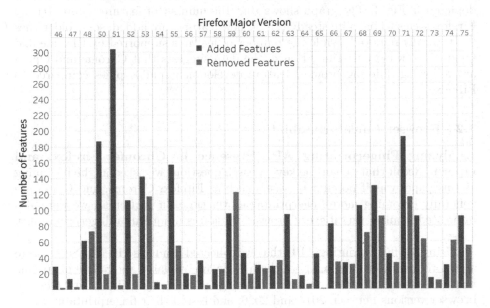

Fig. 2. Feature introduction and removal in Firefox.

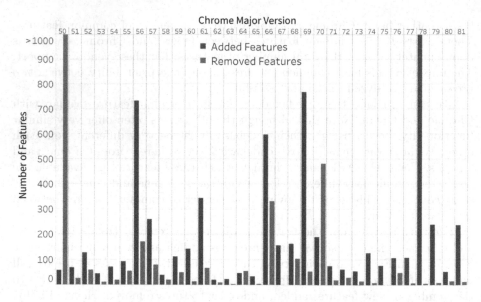

Fig. 3. Feature introduction and removal in Chrome.

By using the feature datasets we extracted from the Firefox, Opera, and Chrome versions, we compared feature trends for these browsers. The trends are depicted in Fig. 4. The graph shows that the number of features supported by Firefox seems to be quite steady (i.e., if new features are added, some older ones are typically removed) while the number of features supported by Chrome and Opera is growing over time. Hence, the data suggests that Chrome and Opera are following differing browser feature development philosophies compared to Firefox.

4.2   Browser Fingerprintability

Analyzing Fingerprinting API Presence in Chrome, Firefox, and Opera. Recall that one of the key research questions we asked at the beginning of this paper was if popular browsers such as Firefox, Chrome, and Opera are generally becoming more fingerprintable over time. In particular, we were also interested in answering if every browser version is unique in a fingerprintability sense.

Using the fingerprinting APIs that we collected (and described in Sect. 3), we aimed to determine how many of these APIs are available and active in specific browser versions. That is, we iterated through all the major Firefox and Chrome browser versions between 2016 and 2020, and tested their fingerprintability.

In Chrome 49 (i.e., the oldest Chrome version in our analysis), there exist 139 APIs from the suspicious fingerprinting APIs list. Which means they could be used for fingerprinting. In Chrome 81 (the newest Chrome version in our analysis), there exist 274 APIs from the suspicious fingerprinting APIs list. In

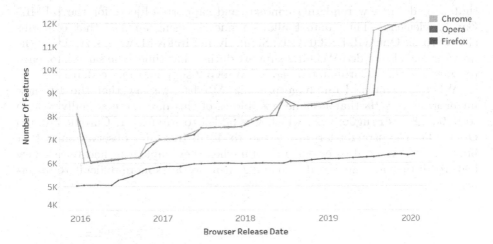

Fig. 4. Feature trends in Firefox, Opera, and Chrome when compared to each other.

short, the number of APIs that could be used for fingerprinting Chrome versions are increasing over time. That is, the data suggest that Chrome is becoming easier to fingerprint as it evolves over time.

Compared to Chrome, Firefox 45 (i.e., the oldest version in our study) has 147 APIs from the suspicious fingerprinting APIs list. In contrast, Firefox 75 (which is the latest Firefox version in our study) has 271 fingerprinting APIs from the suspicious fingerprinting APIs list. Interestingly, though, Firefox 71 has 276 APIs from the suspicious fingerprinting APIs list. Our data analysis suggests that Firefox has become more fingerprintable over time, but that lately, although more features are added to it, its fingerprintability might have started to decline. In fact, Firefox has indeed started to take the fingerprinting problem seriously and has been increasingly taking steps to prevent it (e.g., [22]).

In addition, Opera 36 (i.e., the oldest version in our study) contains 139 suspicious fingerprinting APIs. On the other hand, Opera 68 (the latest Opera version in our measurement) is consist of 274 suspicious fingerprinting APIs. The trend is very similar to Google Chrome but there are minor differences at some points which could be seen in Fig. 5.

Figure 5 depicts, in detail, the presence of fingerprinting APIs in Chrome, Firefox, and Opera that we measured. Note that in January 2017, there is a significant increase in the number of fingerprinting APIs that each browser supports. More than 100 fingerprinting APIs were added to both browsers. To determine what caused this spike, we investigated and analyzed the release notes of both Firefox 51 [17], Chrome 56 [13], and Opera 43 which is based on Chromium 56 [3].

The release notes indicate that HTML5 was enabled for all users by default in Chrome 56. As of this version, Adobe Flash Player was disabled and only allowed to run with specific user permissions. Chrome also enabled the WebGL 2.0 API that provides a new rendering context, and supports objects for the HTML5 Canvas elements. This context allows rendering using an API that conforms closely to the OpenGL ES 3.0 API[3]. Similarly, in Firefox 51, we observed that the browser had also added WebGL2 support during that time. The same happened to Opera 43 since Chromium 56 added WebGL2 support to its codebase.

When we analyzed our fingerprinting API list, we saw that the 107 new fingerprinting APIs that became possible as of this date were actually related to `WebGL2RenderingContext` which was added to Firefox 51, Chrome 56, and Opera 43. The straight-forward lesson to distill from our observation is that browser vendors need to be extra careful when they implement and release new features if they are interested in making their browsers more difficult to fingerprint.

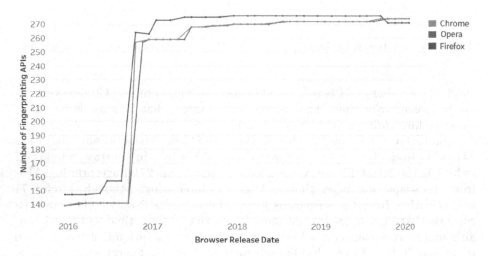

Fig. 5. Presence of fingerprinting APIs in Chrome, Firefox, and Opera.

As part of our experiments, we also collected the feature sets for Firefox's Private Window, Google Chrome's Incognito, and Opera's Private Window. We measured the fingerprintability of the browsers in these modes. For Chrome, our results show that there is a small difference between the total number of features in regular mode versus the total number of features in incognito mode. For instance, Chrome 80's regular mode has 11,946 features while it has 11,936 features available in Incognito mode. The results were similar for Firefox's regular mode versus its Private Window Mode. For example, Firefox 75's regular mode has 6,370 total features while its Private Window Mode has 6,358 features available. Besides, Opera's private window had the same fingerprinting APIs compared to the regular mode and had zero impact on reducing fingerprintability.

---

[3] https://www.khronos.org/registry/webgl/specs/latest/2.0/.

Hence, we conclude that the incognito and private window modes do not help users against browser fingerprinting since every fingerprinting API that exists in a version's normal mode also appears in the same browser version's Incognito (or Private Window) mode.

Unique Feature Set. In our analyses, we automatically deduced a "feature set" for each browser version that we analyzed. A feature set is a set of (i.e., the list of) browser features that exist in that specific browser version under analysis. When we compared the features sets for each browser version to each other (e.g., Firefox 54 versus 55), we observed that each feature set was unique for all the browser versions that we tested. That is, there exist no two browsers that possess the same feature set. Hence, from this observation, we can deduce that all the browser versions that we analyzed are uniquely fingerprintable.

The reason why the feature sets are unique among different browser versions is that each browser, as we described before, have recurring as well as non-persistent features. As a result, the fact that vendors continuously add, remove, and sometimes re-add features into their browsers also make them more fingerprintable.

One interesting trend is that the differences between the feature sets of Chrome, Firefox, and Opera in their newer versions is becoming smaller. That is, we observed much more intersections with each other than in older versions. Our data suggest that the feature sets for all Firefox, Chrome, and Opera are converging towards homogeneity of browser features.

5   Related Work

Our work focuses on the intersection of browser evolution and browser fingerprinting.

Browser Evolution. The first web browser, WorldWideWeb [9], was developed in 1990 by Tim Berners-Lee. That browser did not have JavaScript, did not support cookies and users could not adapt their browser with extensions. All these features and thousands more were introduced in browsers over time, matching the needs of the ever-evolving web.

Synder et al. [27] use a similar method to us to collect browser features by using the web API and extracting different kinds of JavaScript functions. They measure browser feature usage among Alexa's popular websites and also how many security vulnerabilities have been associated with related browser features. However, they do not aim to measure fingerprintability of different browsers which is one of the main goals of our paper. In another work by Snyder [29], a cost-benefit approach to improving browser security was conducted. Our work focuses on how browsers have become more fingerprintable over time based on the features they introduce, taking a new perspective on the privacy and security costs that the browser evolution brings.

Recent work has focused on methods to automatically reduce the functionality of the browser at the binary level. Chenxiong et al. [12] propose a debloating framework for the browser that removes unused features. Our work is complementary to debloating efforts of the browser, as we focus on which browser features affect the users' privacy the most. Also, our work suggests that the debloating of browsers might not really be necessary as there does not seem to exist a correlation between the number of features added to the browsers over time, and how insecure they become.

Browser Fingerprinting. There have been a number of studies on browser fingerprinting and browser bloating. The first large-scale study on browser fingerprinting was conducted by Eckersley [14]. Eckersley showed that a wide range of properties in a user's browser and the installed plugins can be combined to form a unique fingerprint. His study made us eager to see what is happening in the world of browser features, and to try to analyze the impact of different browser features on creating unique user fingerprints.

Browser fingerprinting can be done by using different methods. Cao et al. [11] created user fingerprints by using OS-level features from screen resolution to the number of CPU cores. They also measure the uniqueness of different browser types by analyzing its OS-level features.

Olejnik et al. [25] show that one way of fingerprinting a browser is using web history. In this method, there is no need for a client-side state. However, note that this method is no longer possible because browser vendors have fixed this issue and (i.e., extracting user history is not possible as before).

Nikiforakis et al. [23] showed how tracking has moved from using cookies (stateful) to browser fingerprinting (stateless) on the web. Mowery et al. [20] demonstrated how the `canvas` HTML5 feature can be abused for browser fingerprinting based on the differences in rendering images on different GPUs. Starov et al. [30] measured how bloated browser extensions are in terms of the artifacts that they inject in visited pages, and can be used to identify the presence of the users' installed extensions. Trickel et al. [31] proposed a defense mechanism against identifying installed browser extensions in users' browsers based on artifacts that reveal their presence on the visited pages.

In light of the prior research on browser fingerprinting, our aim was to collect data and analyze the trends, and to see whether we are becoming better at managing browser fingerprinting (or if this privacy issue is becoming worse as new features are being introduced in new browser versions).

6   Conclusion

The evolution of the web relies on browsers adding new features that drive innovation in web applications. Yet, this innovation comes at a significant cost to the end users' privacy, since browser fingerprinting techniques abuse certain browser features. In this paper, we analyzed the impact of browser features on browser fingerprinting. We investigated more than 30 major browser versions for Google Chrome, Mozilla Firefox, and Opera between 2016 and 2020.

First, we extracted every browser feature that existed in these browser versions using the browser APIs. Then, we analyzed the feature sets for these browsers and compared them. One key observation was that the feature numbers are overall increasing in modern browsers, and they are indeed becoming more "bloated" in general.

Next, we compared the feature reports for these browsers to the already listed fingerprinting APIs in browsers that are presented in the literature. Our findings suggested that each browser version between 2016 and 2020 was uniquely fingerprintable, and that the fingerprintablity of the browsers has been increasing over the years.

We envision our research to affect how browser vendors introduce new features and take into consideration the effects that these have on browser fingerprintability. Our goal is to highlight the concerning trend of "bloating" in the browser and encourage browser vendors to remove abused features in order to improve privacy on the web.

References

1. Am IUnique. https://amiunique.org. Accessed 20 June 2021
2. EasyList. https://easylist.to/. Accessed 20 June 2021
3. Opera version history. https://help.opera.com/en/opera-version-history/. Accessed 30 June 2021
4. Panopticlick. https://panopticlick.eff.org. Accessed 10 Jan 2021
5. WebIDL Level 1. https://www.w3.org/TR/WebIDL-1/. Accessed 20 July 2021
6. Acar, G., Eubank, C., Englehardt, S., Juarez, M., Narayanan, A., Diaz, C.: The web never forgets: persistent tracking mechanisms in the wild. In: Proceedings of the ACM SIGSAC Conference on Computer and Communications Security (2014)
7. Acar, G., et al.: Fpdetective: dusting the web for fingerprinters. In: Proceedings of the 2013 ACM SIGSAC Conference on Computer & Communications Security. CCS 2013, pp. 1129–1140. Association for Computing Machinery, New York, NY, USA (2013). https://doi.org/10.1145/2508859.2516674
8. Apple: Safari privacy overview (2019). https://www.apple.com/safari/docs/.pdf
9. Berners-Lee, T.: The worldwideweb browser (1990). https://www.w3.org/People/Berners-Lee/WorldWideWeb.html
10. BrowserStack: App & Browser Testing Made Easy (2021). https://www.browserstack.com/
11. Cao, Y., Li, S., Wijmans, E.: (cross-)browser fingerprinting via OS and hardware level features (2017). https://doi.org/10.14722/ndss.2017.23152
12. Chenxiong, Q., Koo, H., Oh, C., Kim, T., Lee, W.: Slimium: debloating the chromium browser with feature subsetting. In: Proceedings of the ACM Conference on Computer and Communications Security (CCS) (2020)
13. Google Chrome: New in Chrome 56 — Web (2017). https://developers.google.com/web/updates/2017/01/nic56. Accessed 20 June 2021
14. Eckersley, P.: How unique is your web browser? In: Atallah, M.J., Hopper, N.J. (eds.) PETS 2010. LNCS, vol. 6205, pp. 1–18. Springer, Heidelberg (2010). https://doi.org/10.1007/978-3-642-14527-8_1
15. Englehardt, S., Narayanan, A.: Online tracking: a 1-million-site measurement and analysis. In: Proceedings of the 2016 ACM SIGSAC Conference on Computer and Communications Security, pp. 1388–1401 (2016)

16. fingerprintjs: fingerprintjs.   https://github.com/fingerprintjs/fingerprintjs. Accessed 15 July 2021
17. Mozilla Firefox: Firefox 51.0, See All New Features, Updates and Fixes (2017). https://www.mozilla.org/en-US/firefox/51.0/releasenotes/. Accessed 20 June 2021
18. Gómez-Boix, A., Laperdrix, P., Baudry, B.: Hiding in the crowd: An analysis of the effectiveness of browser fingerprinting at large scale. In: Proceedings of the 2018 World Wide Web Conference. WWW 2018, pp. 309–318. International World Wide Web Conferences Steering Committee, Republic and Canton of Geneva, CHE (2018). https://doi.org/10.1145/3178876.3186097
19. Jueckstock, J., Kapravelos, A.: Visible V8: in-browser monitoring of JavaScript in the wild. In: Proceedings of the ACM Internet Measurement Conference (IMC), October 2019
20. Mowery, K., Shacham, H.: Pixel perfect: fingerprinting canvas in HTML5. In: Proceedings of W2SP (2012)
21. Mozilla: MDN Web Docs - Web APIs. https://developer.mozilla.org/en-US/docs/Web/API
22. Mozilla: How to block fingerprinting with Firefox (2020). https://blog.mozilla.org/firefox/how-to-block-fingerprinting-with-firefox/
23. Nikiforakis, N., Kapravelos, A., Joosen, W., Kruegel, C., Piessens, F., Vigna, G.: Cookieless monster: exploring the ecosystem of web-based device fingerprinting. In: Proceedings of the IEEE Symposium on Security and Privacy (2013)
24. Olejnik, L., Englehardt, S., Narayanan, A.: Battery status not included: assessing privacy in web standards. In: Proceedings of the International Workshop on Privacy Engineering (IWPE) (2017)
25. Olejnik, A., Castelluccia, C., Janc, A.: Why Johnny can't browse in peace: On the uniqueness of web browsing history patterns (2012)
26. Schwarz, M., Lackner, F., Gruss, D.: JavaScript template attacks: automatically inferring host information for targeted exploits. In: NDSS (2019)
27. Snyder, P., Ansari, L., Taylor, C., Kanich, C.: Browser feature usage on the modern web. In: Proceedings of the Internet Measurement Conference (IMC) (2016)
28. Snyder, P., Livshits, B.: Brave, fingerprinting, and privacy budgets (2019). https://brave.com/brave-fingerprinting-and-privacy-budgets/
29. Snyder, P., Taylor, C., Kanich, C.: Most websites don't need to vibrate: a cost-benefit approach to improving browser security. In: Proceedings of the ACM SIGSAC Conference on Computer and Communications Security (2017)
30. Starov, O., Laperdrix, P., Kapravelos, A., Nikiforakis, N.: Unnecessarily Identifiable: Quantifying the fingerprintability of browser extensions due to bloat. In: Proceedings of the World Wide Web Conference (WWW) (2019)
31. Trickel, E., Starov, O., Kapravelos, A., Nikiforakis, N., Doupe, A.: Everyone is different: client-side diversification for defending against extension fingerprinting. In: Proceedings of the USENIX Security Symposium (2019)

TridentShell: A Covert and Scalable Backdoor Injection Attack on Web Applications

Xiaobo Yu[1], Weizhi Meng[2], Lei Zhao[3], and Yining Liu[1(✉)]

[1] School of Computer Science and Information Security, Guilin University of
Electronic Technology, Guilin 541004, China
ynliu@guet.edu.cn

[2] Department of Applied Mathematics and Computer Science, Technical University
of Denmark, 2800 Kongens Lyngby, Denmark

[3] School of Cyber Science and Engineering, Wuhan University, Wuhan 430072, China

Abstract. Web backdoor attack is a kind of popular network attack, which can cause a serious damage to websites. In practice, cyber attackers often exploit vulnerabilities in the system or web applications to implant a backdoor to a web server. To address this challenge, static feature detection is believed to be an effective solution. However, it may also leave a potential security "hole" that could be exploited by intruders. In this paper, we propose a novel backdoor attack method called TridentShell, which can inject a webshell into the memory of web application server without leaving attack traces. Our attack is able to bypass almost all types of static detection methods. In particular, it attempts to blend itself into the web server and erase attack traces automatically, instead of encrypting or obfuscating the content of webshell to avoid detection. Besides, TridentShell can still be executed even when the webmasters restrict the access to web directory. In the evaluation, we showcase how TridentShell can successfully inject a webshell into five different types of Java application servers (covering around 87% Java application servers in the market), and can remove the attack traces on the server (increasing the detection difficulty).

Keywords: Backdoor attack · Webshell · Web security · Java application · Static feature detection

1 Introduction

With the rapid development of web applications and the ever-increasingly enlargement of users, more attention has been given on how to make web services more secure and reliable. According to the semiannual safety report issued by CNCERT/CC [3], the first six months in 2019 had a 20% year-over-year growth rate in the amount of web backdoor attacks. Web backdoor, often referred to as webshell, has become the main threat for web security, which is a popular cyber-attack to obtain the privilege of a victim's server. It provides a web interface that

© Springer Nature Switzerland AG 2021
J. K. Liu et al. (Eds.): ISC 2021, LNCS 13118, pp. 177–194, 2021.
https://doi.org/10.1007/978-3-030-91356-4_10

enables cyber attackers to remotely control the server, such as intelligence gathering, command execution, file transferring, network traffic forwarding, lateral movement and so forth.

Due to the wide usage of webshell in cyber attacks, there have been many previous research studies in this field. Generally, webshell detection methods can be divided into two types: static detection [10,20], and dynamic detection [21,22]. Static detection mainly focuses on identifying script files containing malicious codes using different algorithms. Different from the static detection, dynamic detection focuses on analyzing the features of webshell during the execution time. While for dynamic detection, when being run on a cluster scale, the cost of development time is high and numerous false positives may occur [13]. Because of these challenges in dynamic detection, the static detection naturally becomes a popular webshell detection.

Static detection has been widely studied in recent years. Hu et al. [15] developed a webshell detection method based on decision tree, they extracted different static features of script files to classify and detect webshell. Hu et al. [14] proposed a detection model based on Naive Bayesian theory, which can effectively detect the confused webshell and improve the classification accuracy rate. Sun et al. [19] proposed a webshell detection method based on matrix decomposition and machine learning methods. It could effectively predict webshell and finally achieve the purpose of classification.

However, after investigating a large number of static detection methods, we observe that most existing methods focus mainly on the features of a script file or log file, while ignoring the diverse forms of attacks, such as fileless attack [18]. Fileless attack as a kind of new attack conception enables to carry out intrusions successfully where no executable file is written to disk. This type of attack provides characteristics of higher concealment, longer latency, and greater harm. Due to these characteristics, fileless attack has drawn increasing attention and penetrated into many links of attack activities in recent years.

Motivated by the above observations, in this paper, we propose a novel backdoor attack method called TridentShell, which can inject webshell into the memory of web application server without leaving attack traces, and is able to detour almost all types of static detection methods. Instead of encrypting or obfuscating the content of webshell, our attack can blend itself into the web server and erase attack traces automatically to avoid being detected. Moreover, it is generic and flexible, which not only can attack different types of Java application servers but also can be executed even when the webmasters restrict access to web directory. To summarize, we have made the following contributions.

- By investigating a large number of static detection methods, we observe that most static detection methods focus mainly on the features of file contents while ignoring the existing forms of webshell. This observation poses a new angle to design a backdoor attack.
- We propose a generic and covert backdoor attack by injecting webshell into the memory of web application server, without leaving any attack traces. The webshell can be executed even when the access to web directory is restricted.

– We evaluate the effectiveness and run-time performance of our webshell. The experimental results indicate that our webshell can compromise five different types of Java application servers (covering about 87% Java application servers in the current market) and remain no traces on the server. We also show that TridentShell is resistant to antivirus software, access control policy and static detection methods to some extent.

The rest of this paper is structured as follows: Sect. 2 describes the background and the related work. Our proposed attack - TridentShell is described in Sect. 3, including attack vector, its methodology and the implementation details. Section 4 evaluates the effectiveness and run-time performance of our attack with a series of experiments, as well as discusses the limitations and future work. We conclude the paper in Sect. 5.

2 Background and Related Work

2.1 Static Webshell Detection

Static webshell detection mainly focuses on identifying script files containing malicious codes using different algorithms. Due to the classification nature of webshell detection, feature selection will make a determining impact on the detection result, including text feature selection and syntax feature selection. Regular expression detection method has been widely applied in the field of text feature, but this detection method can be easily bypassed by obfuscated webshell for the sake of its limited expression ability and the rapid development of current obfuscation technology.

To make up the shortcomings of regular expression, researchers began to use statistical analysis to detect malicious files. Statistical analysis technique focuses on identifying obfuscated webshell based on statistical features including information entropy, if the webshell is being encrypted. 1) The longest word, which means that the file content appears to be obfuscated via coding technique such as Base64 to form a long string. 2) Index of coincidence, if the coincidence index is low, the file might be encrypted or obfuscated. 3) The compression ratio, as the character within obfuscated webshell distributes more evenly than normal, compression ratio would thus become much larger. NeoPI [10] is a very popular webshell detection tool based on statistical analysis, and it can detect obfuscated or encrypted contents within text and script files. Cui et al. [12] proposed a PHP webshell detecting model, which is a combination of random forest classifier and GBDT classifier. Furthermore, they extracted both common statistical features and opcode sequence features from PHP source files.

Although statistical analysis is good at identifying obfuscated webshell in a holistic mode, it would be ineffective if attackers insert obfuscated malicious codes into a big chunk of normal code. To solve this problem, syntax feature selection has attracted attention and becomes widely acceptable. This kind of detection methods were used to explore all possible execution paths of script files, so it can complete some difficult detection tasks. Li et al. [16] proposed a webshell detection system called ShellBreaker, which detects malicious script files by correlating syntactical and semantic features. Then they used a statistical classifier to analyze these features. Experimental results demonstrated that their system can achieve the detection rate of 91.7%, and a false positive rate of 1%.

Besides, Shi et al. [17] proposed a log-based lightweight webshell detection method, and the webshell can be detected from three angles: text feature, statistical feature and correlation feature. The experiments indicated that this method is able to discover backdoor attacks either underway or already completed.

2.2   Java Bytecode Instrumentation Technique

Java bytecode instrumentation technique was firstly introduced in Java SE 5. It assists developers using an independent agent program to monitor Java application before application runs. This monitoring method can not only get status of JVM but also modify Java class definitions. In Java SE 6, this technique was further updated and makes it possible to load an agent program into an already running JVM. Owing to its good performance, it has already been practiced in the field of network security. Runtime Application Self-Protection Technology (RASP) [8] is one of the many applications of Java instrumentation technique. RASP is a new application security protection technique, which injects a protection program into an application or application runtime environment and enables to detect and prevent real-time attacks. Besides, when protection program incorporated in the application execution environment, this incorporation is noninvasive and requires no modification to application code [11]. Based on this observation, an attractive insight to make covert backdoor attack is to inject malicious codes into application server at run-time. More importantly, as most of detection methods focus on the static features of file contents, an "invisible" webshell can escape detection easily. By injecting a webshell into an application server, we can design a hard-to-spot web backdoor attack.

2.3   Webshell Backdoor

Webshell is a malicious web-based command execution environment existing in multiple forms, especially written in some scripting language like ASP, PHP, JSP or CGI. It enables attackers to remotely control a web server and provide various functionalities such as intelligence gathering, command execution, file transferring, network traffic forwarding, etc. The webshell attack flow chart can be described in Fig. 1. First, the attacker implants a webshell to victim's server by exploiting the relevant vulnerabilities. Then the attacker can remotely access to the webshell through a browser or a webshell management tool and get command execution environment. All these actions aim to finally obtain the control of the web server.

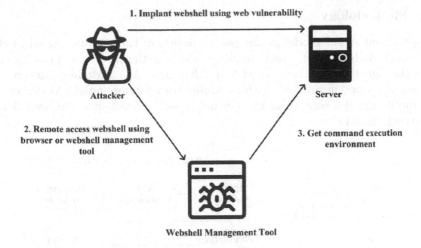

Fig. 1. Webshell attack flowchart

3 Our Proposed Attack: TridentShell

3.1 Attack Vector

Target Scope and Presupposition. Before introducing our attack in more detail, we need to firstly discuss the target scope and presupposition of our attack. In particular, the prime attack targets are Java application servers such as Apache Tomcat, JBoss, WebLogic, Jetty and Resin. Besides, to enable attackers to execute our webshell in a target server, we presuppose that an attacker has obtained the normal user permissions on the server before implementing a backdoor (this is common in practice).

Attack Characteristics. By using Java instrumentation technology, TridentShell could hook specified class within the Java application in order to control the whole HTTP request process. Moreover, it can provide the feature of *noninvasion*, that is, there is no need for attackers to add or modify any configuration files and application code on the server. Nevertheless, almost all webshell attacks may face the following two challenges in a practical attacking scenario.

– **Challenge 1: How to be scalable to different application platforms.** In most realistic attacking scenarios, there are different kinds of Java application servers, and the Java class within each of these servers is also diverse. How to locate hooked Java class is thus undoubtedly a difficult task. There is a need to find a solution to extend the scalability of webshell attacks.
– **Challenge 2: How to clean the traces of our attack remained on a server.** In most cases, attacking traces will be left on a server. For example, the Windows OS has the file locking mechanism, when a webshell is executed, the attack file will be occupied and could not be deleted. Hence, it is very essential to find a solution to erase traces before being discovered.

3.2 Methodology

The proposed attack model in this paper consists of two modules: Load Module and Agent Module. First, Load Module connects to the Java virtual machine and loads the Agent Module into target VM. After that, Agent Module can complete a series of actions in the VM, such as adding transformer, getting loaded classes and modifying the content of the normal class. Figure 2 shows an overview of the attack model.

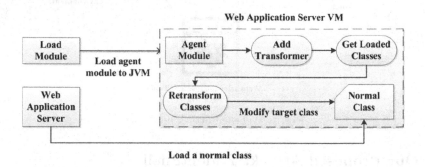

Fig. 2. Attack model

Load Module. For each Java program, Java Virtual Machine (JVM) will create a corresponding instance of the virtual machine after startup. The main task is to load the Agent Module into Java application server virtual machine. Firstly, it invokes the method *listVirtualMachines* in order to get a list of the Java virtual machine descriptors. Then, it attempts to match the currently running Java web application server according to the display name of the virtual machine descriptor. Once it successfully completes the matching, it will connect to the virtual machine instance of the application server by calling the method *attach* and invoking the method *LoadAgent* to load our crafted agent JAR file [7].

Agent Module. Since we aim to generate a covert webshell, an intuitive approach to remotely control the victim machine is to send a malicious command through Uniform Resource Locator (URL). As shown in Fig. 3(a), the normal procedure for HTTP request in Java application server is: a user's browser sends the URL to the target server, then the server parses this URL and hands it off to the Filter and Servlet. During this process, if a match is found, then the server will send back a response to the browser.

As shown in Fig. 3(b), if we tamper with a key Java class for handling the HTTP requests, then an "intangible" webshell can be implemented. Specifically, the main task of Agent Module is to hook the key class and modify it. When the Agent Module has been loaded into an application server virtual machine,

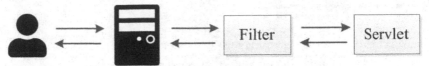

(a) The procedure for HTTP request in the Java application server

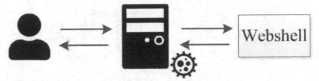

(b) The procedure for HTTP request in an infected server

Fig. 3. The procedure for an HTTP request

it will register supplied transformer by invoking a method *addTransformer* at first. Afterwards, Agent Module calls the method *getAllLoadedClasses* to achieve all classes loaded by the current virtual machine. Thus, during the normal request process, once the key class is called, it would be hooked, and a backdoor will be inserted. Listing 1.1 describes the code illustration of backdoor. First, we accept two arguments including HTTP requests and responses. Then, we define the input parameters of *password* and *cmd*. Only when the user inputs a correct password, the backdoor can execute the command properly.

Listing 1.1. A code illustration of backdoor

```
1  Javax.servlet.http.HttpServletRequest request = $1;
2  Javax.servlet.http.HttpServletResponse response = $2;
3  String password = request.getParameter('password');
4  String cmd = request.getParameter('cmd');
5  String output = '';
6  if (password.equals('backdoor')) {
7      output = execmd(cmd);
```

3.3   Implementation

Based on the understanding of our attack model, in this part, we introduce how to address the two challenges in our implementation.

Challenge and Solution 1: Extending the Application Platform of Our Webshell. To apply our attack model in a practical attacking scenario, it is important to extend our attack capability to compromise different types of servers. The key to this challenge is to locate the corresponding classes that will handle HTTP requests before the requests flow into the Filter and Servlet in different Java application servers. However, almost all application servers contain a large number of class files, it is not an easy task to find such class.

Fig. 4. The invocation chain of FilterChain (the TRACE command can help search the invocation path of FilterChain and count all performance overhead in this invocation chain. Each of these rows starts with the elapsed time overhead followed by the invocation method).

FilterChain is an object provided by the servlet container, which can offer a view into the invocation chain of a filtered request for a resource, and filters use *FilterChain* to invoke the next filter in the chain [6]. Thus, if we can control the entrance of the filter chain, we can direct the HTTP requests to go through our malicious logic flow rather than the normal filter. To achieve this goal, we carefully investigate relevant Java classes and find that *Arthas* can help locate Java classes. *Arthas* is an open-source Java diagnostic tool provided by Alibaba middleware team [1], which can help developers dynamically trace Java programs and monitor the state of JVM in real-time. It can be used to trace the specific class and view the full request trees. Below we can take the Tomcat for example:

```
77      private void internalDoFilter(ServletRequest request, ServletResponse response) throws IOException, ServletException {
78          if (this.pos < this.n) {
79              ApplicationFilterConfig filterConfig = this.filters[this.pos++];
80                                                          Encapsulating HTTP request and response.
81              try {
82                  Filter filter = filterConfig.getFilter();
83                  if (request.isAsyncSupported() && "false".equalsIgnoreCase(filterConfig.getFilterDef().getAsyncSupported())) {
84                      request.setAttribute( "org.apache.catalina.ASYNC_SUPPORTED", Boolean.FALSE);
85                  }
86
87              if (Globals.IS_SECURITY_ENABLED) {
88                  Principal principal = ((HttpServletRequest)request).getUserPrincipal();
89                  Object[] args = new Object[]{request, response, this};
90                  SecurityUtil.doAsPrivilege( "doFilter", filter, classType, args, principal);
91              } else {
92                  filter.doFilter(request, response, this);    ◄── The entrance of the filter chain.
93              }
```

Fig. 5. The part code of internalDoFilter

- **Tracing the Filter.** As shown in Fig. 3, the HTTP requests should enter the filters after being sent to the server; thus, an intuitive approach to locate the key class is to trace the Filter. Specifically, we can trace the interface *javax.Servlet.FilterChain* and view the entire invocation process. As shown in Fig. 4, we can observe that the HTTP requests should first enter *ApplicationFilterChain*, which is the implementation class of *FilterChain*, and finally reach *service* in the Servlet.

– **Looking for the Hook Point.** After carefully reviewing the class code of *ApplicationFilterChain*, we can find that *internalDoFilter* satisfies our need. As shown in Fig. 5, *ServletRequest* and *ServletResponse* as parameters of this method can encapsulate HTTP requests and responses. Besides, this method contains the entrance of the filter chain. For these reasons, we construct a backdoor function in this method and force the HTTP request into our function before it goes through filter chain.

Based on such approach, we eventually identify the key Java classes and their hook methods for five different types of Java application servers, as shown in Table 1.

Table 1. List of hook methods in different Java middleware

Java middleware	Hook method
Tomcat	org.apache.catalina.core.ApplicationFilterChain:internalDoFilter()
JBoss	org.apache.catalina.core.ApplicationFilterChain:internalDoFilter()
Resin	com.caucho.server.dispatch.ServletInvocation:service()
Jetty	org.eclipse.jetty.server.handler.HandlerWrapper:handle()
WebLogic	weblogic.wsee.server.servlet.BaseWSServlet:service()

Challenge and Solution 2: Cleaning the Traces of Our Attack Remained and Achieving Fileless Webshell. As Windows has the file locking mechanism, when Load Module is executed to load Agent Module into JVM, it cannot be deleted because the *DeleteFile* function on Windows fails if an application attempts to delete a file that has other handler open for normal I/O [5]. Due to this, most backdoor attacks will leave obvious attack traces. To clean the traces of our attack, there is a need to figure out which process is holding the Load Module and preventing from deletion. Then we need to get the file handler and release it. To achieve this goal, we design the following approach:

– **Getting Debug Privilege.** Before we enumerate all current system processes, we must get debug privilege at first. Debug privilege is a security policy setting that allows someone to debug a process that they would not otherwise have access to. For example, a process running as a user with the debug privilege enabled on its token can debug a service running as the local system [4]. Listing 1.2 shows the code illustration of enabling the debug privilege in the process. First, we invoke the function *OpenProcessToken* to get the token of current process. Then, we attempt to activate the debug privilege of current token by calling the function *LookupPrivilegeValue*. When *Attributes*

is set to *SE_PRIVILEGE_ENABLED*, debug privilege has been successfully
activated.

Listing 1.2. A code illustration of enabling the debug privilege

```
1   BOOL EnableDebugPrivilege(BOOL fEnable){
2       BOOL fOk = FALSE;
3       HANDLE hToken;
4       if (OpenProcessToken(GetCurrentProcess(),
            TOKEN_ADJUST_PRIVILEGES, &hToken)){
5           TOKEN_PRIVILEGES tp;
6           Tp.PrivilegeCount = 1;
7           LookupPrivilegeValue(NULL, SE_DEBUG_NAME, &tp
                .Privileges[0].Luid);
8           tp.Privileges[0].Attributes = fEnable ?
                SE_PRIVILEGE_ENABLED : 0;
9           AdjustTokenPrivileges(hToken, FALSE, &tp,
                sizeof(tp), NULL, NULL);
10          fOk = (GetLastError() == ERROR_SUCCESS);
11          CloseHandle(hToken);
12          }
13      return(fOk);
14  }
```

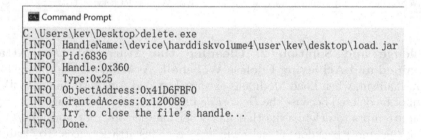

Fig. 6. The result of releasing target handler (after executing 'delete.exe', the file handler of 'load.jar' can be released at runtime. Then we can delete 'load.jar' to make sure
that no attack traces will be left on the disk).

– **Enumerating System Processes and Getting File Handler.** After ele-
vating permission, we can call a kernel function *NtQuerySystemInformation*
to get handlers for all processes. By invoking kernel function *NtDuplicateOb-
ject*, we can get more detailed information about these handlers, including
handler name, process ID, object address and more. By matching the handler name, we can eventually figure out the process that is holding the Load
Module open.

– **Releasing File Handler.** Even though we get the corresponding process handler by the approach above, it is still a pseudo handler that could not be directly operated. Thus, we may need to invoke kernel function *DuplicateHandle* and convert this pseudo handler to a real handler. In addition, *dwOptions* - the parameter of *DuplicateHandle* also needs to be set as *DUPLI-CATE_CLOSE_SOURCE*, as this handler will be closed in the source process. Hence we can finally release the target handler, and an instance is depicted in Fig. 6.

4 Evaluation

4.1 Experimental Design and Settings

We assess our webshell based on the following criteria: (1) We examine the effectiveness of our attack with **five** distinct types of Java application servers, including Tomcat, JBoss, Resin, Jetty, and WebLogic. All of them can be downloaded from their official website. (2) We evaluate the run-time performance of our attack with **four** types of security policies, including static webshell detection methods, access control policy, antivirus engines and Windows Defender. (3) All Java application servers were running on Windows 10, with Intel(R) Core (TM) i5-7360 CPU@2.30 GHz and 512 GB RAM.

Table 2. The effectiveness evaluation

	Tomcat	JBoss	WebLogic	Jetty	Resin
Directly display	✓	✓	✓	✗	✗
Executable	✓	✓	✓	✓	✓

✓: The requirement (left) is satisfied on the corresponding server (top).
✗: The requirement (left) is not satisfied on the corresponding server (top).

4.2 Effectiveness of Our Approach

To evaluate the effectiveness of our attack under different Java application servers, we selected five commonly used servers including Tomcat, JBoss, WebLogic, Jetty, Resin. By using Java bytecode instrumentation technique, we can inject the backdoor function into a normal Java class. The experimental results are shown in Table 2. It is observed that for the first three servers, we could directly interact with the webshell on the webpage. For the latter two servers, our attack cannot display correctly on the webpage because of the default settings for page redirection on the server. However, it does not affect the function of our TridentShell, it can still compromise the target server through HTTP request. We explain the result as follows.

Figure 7 and Fig. 8 respectively shows the attack effect on the first three and latter two servers. As shown in Fig. 7, we can interact with our TridentShell directly through URL on the first three web servers and make them display the system command 'systeminfo' on the webpage. However, the system command we executed cannot be correctly displayed on the latter two servers. Hence we aim to verify the validity of our webshell through DNSLog, which is a platform to help verify no-echo command execution. More specifically, we can get a random subdomain in this platform. Then we execute the command *'ping SUBDOMAIN'* through URL on the target web server. If this command has been executed by the target server, we can receive this DNS query record in this platform. As shown in Fig. 8, we could successfully receive two records from the target server. This proves that our TridentShell can still be used on Jetty and Resin. To demonstrate the effectiveness of our attack on each of the servers, we print out the word of *'[SERVER_NAME] Attack Success'* to the console, as shown in Fig. 9.

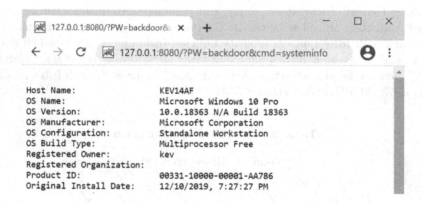

Fig. 7. Executing the command 'systeminfo' with our TridentShell through browser

Fig. 8. DNS query record in DNSLog

(a) Tomcat & JBoss (since Tomcat and JBoss have the same hook methods, we only show the attack result on Tomcat)

(b) WebLogic

(c) Resin

(d) Jetty

Fig. 9. The result of attack on five different servers

4.3   Robustness of TridentShell

Resistance to Static Feature Detection. Static webshell detection includes regular expression detection method, statistical feature detection method, syntax feature detection method and log-based webshell detection method, etc. The first three detection methods mainly rely on matching potential malicious codes in source files. As our TridentShell will be injected into server memory and leave no attack files on the server, these approaches are naturally not effective at recognising our attack.

Moreover, log analysis technique mainly detects abnormal files from a huge amount of web log files. For example, Shi et al. [17] proposed a webshell detection method based on the server log text file. They matched the file access path and the parameters that are submitted, and detected webshell via a comparison regarding the access frequency to the webpage file. However, we find that their pre-processing stage could be compromised by our TridentShell. To be more specific, before detecting any abnormal files, they need to firstly clean records about static files from web log, e.g., the files with the suffix '.html'. While we could trigger our backdoor attack from arbitrary URL path since we hook the method that handles HTTP requests in a Java application server. Thus, if we construct a malicious URL that ends with the '.html' suffix, we could bypass this detection method. As shown in Fig. 10, we constructed a backdoor URL ended with 'index.html' and could trigger our webshell successfully. The experimental results demonstrate that such detection method is ineffective to defeat our attack.

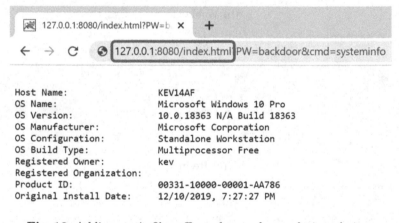

Fig. 10. Adding static file suffix to bypass log analysis technique

```
   C:\Windows\system32\cmd.exe

C:\Users\test\Desktop>move agent.jar C:\Tomcat\webapps\ROOT
Access is denied.
          0 file(s) moved.

C:\Users\test\Desktop>java -jar agent.jar
[+]Current Container: Apache Tomcat
[+]Try to hook internalDoFilter ...
[+]Done.
```

Fig. 11. To evaluate our attack under access control

Fig. 12. The scanning result by VirusTotal

Access Control. We then demonstrate the flexibility of our attack at the deployment phase. Traditional webshell is a malicious script file, which must be saved under the Web directory; otherwise it will not work correctly. In some practical attacking scenarios, the server administrator often prevents web backdoor attack by forbidding *Web directory write permission*. That is, a normal user is prohibited from creating or updating file in this directory. Although this measure can defend against traditional webshell, but it is not workable to our TridentShell. This is because our webshell can be executed on any arbitrary path as long as the Java runtime environment installed and configured on the server. The experimental results are shown in Fig. 11. It shows that our webshell cannot be moved to Web directory, but it can still perform a backdoor attack.

Antivirus Software. We then evaluate the concealment of our attack under antivirus engines and the Windows defender. More specifically, we first use Virus-Total [9], which is a popular antivirus website allowing to scan malicious files with more than 70 antivirus tools.

As shown in Fig. 12, all the antivirus engines in VirusTotal cannot identify our TridentShell as a backdoor. We analyze the potential reasons as follows. (1) The file format of our TridentShell is JAR, which is different from script files that can be called remotely. Hence most antivirus engines would not regard it as a potential threat. (2) The main function of our TridentShell is just adding or substituting java codes, thus it was only treated as a normal programming behavior. For instance, we compare a general backdoor (e.g., Chopper webshell [2]) with our proposed webshell at the pre-attack stage. At this stage, we try to implant the backdoor to the target server. As shown in Fig. 13(a) and Fig. 13(b), the general webshell was detected by the Windows Defender immediately whereas our TridentShell would not trigger any alarm.

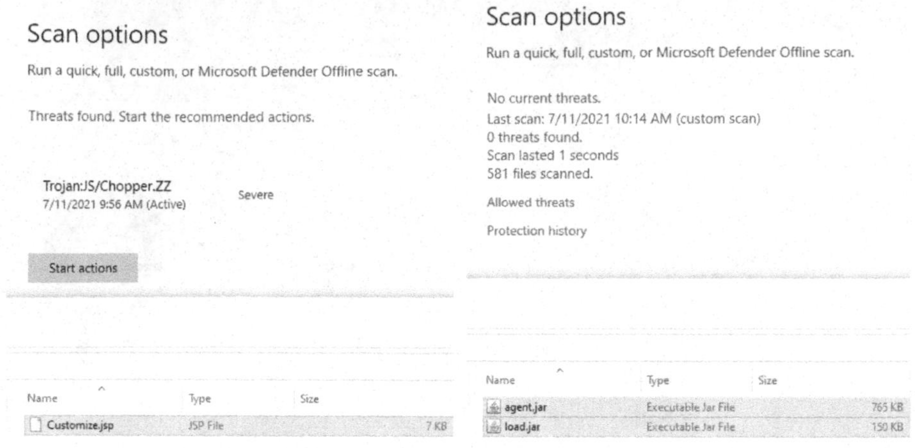

Scan options

Run a quick, full, custom, or Microsoft Defender Offline scan.

Threats found. Start the recommended actions.

Trojan:JS/Chopper.ZZ
7/11/2021 9:56 AM (Active)   Severe

Start actions

Name	Type	Size
Customize.jsp	JSP File	7 KB

Scan options

Run a quick, full, custom, or Microsoft Defender Offline scan.

No current threats.
Last scan: 7/11/2021 10:14 AM (custom scan)
0 threats found.
Scan lasted 1 seconds
581 files scanned.

Allowed threats

Protection history

Name	Type	Size
agent.jar	Executable Jar File	765 KB
load.jar	Executable Jar File	150 KB

(a) General webshell   (b) Our webshell

Fig. 13. The scanning result by Windows Defender

4.4   Limitations and Future Work

Although our proposed TridentShell has shown the high concealment and robustness against the antivirus software and static detection, we aware that our attack may have two main limitations. First, it lacks enough capability to completely withstand dynamic webshell detection, which often uses the network traffic, system commands and state exceptions to identify a malicious backdoor. Second, when our TridentShell runs on the Resin and Jetty, it cannot display correctly on the webpage.

In our future work, we plan to investigate the performance of dynamic detection methods and analyze dynamic features in order to enhance our proposed webshell and bypass the detection. Besides, we intend to improve the display function of our TridentShell on Resin and Jetty. Also, we plan to explore our attack impact on other servers.

5   Conclusion

In this paper, we observe that most of existing methods focus mainly on the features of the script file or log file but ignore the existing form of attack. Motivated by this, we proposed a generic, covert backdoor attack called TridentShell, which can inject a webshell into the memory of web application server, which is able to bypass almost all types of static detection methods. To make our webshell more effective in practice, we address two challenges including how to extend its application platform and clean the traces after the attacks. The experimental results demonstrate that our approach can successfully compromise five different types of Java application servers (covering about 87% Java application servers in the market). In addition, TridentShell is resistant to antivirus software, static detection methods and other security policies to some extent.

Acknowledgments. This work is supported in part by National Natural Science Foundation of China under Grants 62072133 and 61662016 and, in part by the Key Projects of Guangxi Natural Science Foundation under Grant 2018GXNSFDA281040.

References

1. Arthas. https://arthas.aliyun.com/
2. China chopper. https://www.fireeye.com/blog/threat-research/2013/08/breaking-down-the-china-chopper-web-shell-part-i.html
3. CNCERT semiannual safety report. https://www.cert.org.cn/publish/main/upload/File/2019Firsthalfyear.pdf
4. Debug privilege. https://docs.microsoft.com/en-us/windows-hardware/drivers/debugger/debug-privilege
5. Deletefilea function. https://msdn.microsoft.com/library/windows/desktop/aa363915(v=vs.85).aspx
6. Filter chain. http://tomcat.apache.org/tomcat-5.5-doc/servletapi/javax/servlet/FilterChain.html
7. Package com.sun.tools.attach. https://docs.oracle.com/javase/7/docs/jdk/api/attach/spec/com/sun/tools/attach/package-summary.html
8. Runtime application self-protection. https://www.gartner.com/en/information-technology/glossary/runtime-application-self-protection-rasp
9. Virustotal. https://www.virustotal.com/gui/
10. Web shell detection using NeoPI. https://resources.infosecinstitute.com/web-shell-detection
11. Čisar, P., Čisar, S.M.: The framework of runtime application self-protection technology, pp. 000081–000086 (2016)
12. Cui, H., Huang, D., Fang, Y., Liu, L., Huang, C.: Webshell detection based on random forest-gradient boosting decision tree algorithm, pp. 153–160 (2018)
13. Guo, Y., Marco-Gisbert, H., Keir, P.: Mitigating webshell attacks through machine learning techniques. Future Internet **12**(1), 12 (2020)
14. Hu, B.: Research on webshell detection method based on Bayesian theory. Sci. Mosaic **6**, 66–70 (2016)
15. Hu, J., Xu, Z., Ma, D., Yang, J.: Research of webshell detection based on decision tree. J. Network New Media **6**(005) (2012)
16. Li, Y., Huang, J., Ikusan, A., Mitchell, M., Zhang, J., Dai, R.: ShellBreaker: automatically detecting PHP-based malicious web shells. Comput. Secur. **87**, 101595 (2019)
17. Liuyang, S., Yong, F.: Webshell detection method research based on web log. J. Netw. New Media **2**(11) (2016)
18. Mansfield-Devine, S.: Fileless attacks: compromising targets without malware. Network Secur. **2017**(4), 7–11 (2017)
19. Sun, X., Lu, X., Dai, H.: A matrix decomposition based webshell detection method, pp. 66–70 (2017)
20. Tu, T.D., Guang, C., Xiaojun, G., Wubin, P.: Webshell detection techniques in web applications, pp. 1–7 (2014)

21. Yang, W., Sun, B., Cui, B.: A webshell detection technology based on HTTP traffic analysis. In: Barolli, L., Xhafa, F., Javaid, N., Enokido, T. (eds.) IMIS 2018. AISC, vol. 773, pp. 336–342. Springer, Cham (2019). https://doi.org/10.1007/978-3-319-93554-6_31

22. Zhang, H., et al.: Webshell traffic detection with character-level features based on deep learning. IEEE Access **6**, 75268–75277 (2018)

Andromeda: Enabling Secure Enclaves for the Android Ecosystem

Dimitris Deyannis[1,2,3]($\boxtimes$), Dimitris Karnikis[2], Giorgos Vasiliadis[2],
and Sotiris Ioannidis[2,4]

[1] Sphynx Technology Solutions AG, Zug, Switzerland
d.ntegiannis@sphynx.ch
[2] FORTH-ICS, Heraklion, Crete, Greece
{deyannis,dkarnikis,gvasil}@ics.forth.gr
[3] University of Crete, Heraklion, Crete, Greece
deyannis@csd.uoc.gr
[4] Technical University of Crete, Chania, Crete, Greece
sotiris@ece.tuc.gr

Abstract. The Android OS is currently used in a plethora of devices that play a core part of our everyday life, such as mobile phones, tablets, smart home appliances, entertainment systems and embedded devices. The majority of these devices typically process and store a vast amount of security-critical and privacy-sensitive data, including personal contacts, financial accounts and high-profile enterprise assets. The importance of these data makes these devices valuable attack targets.

In this paper we propose Andromeda, a framework that provides secure enclaves for Android OS to mitigate attacks that target sensitive or critical code, data and communication channels. Andromeda offers the first SGX interface for Android OS (to the best of our knowledge), as well as services that enhance its security and offer protection schemes for several applications that deal with sensitive or secret data. Andromeda is also able to securely execute SGX-enabled code on behalf of external devices that are not equipped with SGX-capable CPUs. Moreover, Andromeda protects cryptographic keys from memory dump attacks with less than 16% overhead on the corresponding cryptographic operations and provides secure, end-to-end encrypted, communication and computation channels for external devices paired with the Android device.

1 Introduction

Android has become a very popular open-source operating system that targets a large set of devices [11], including mobile phones, tablets, smart home appliances, entertainment systems and embedded devices. All these devices play a core part of our everyday life and usually process and store a vast amount of privacy-sensitive data, such as personal info, financial accounts, cryptographic keys and high-profile enterprise assets. The importance of this data makes these devices

© Springer Nature Switzerland AG 2021
J. K. Liu et al. (Eds.): ISC 2021, LNCS 13118, pp. 195–217, 2021.
https://doi.org/10.1007/978-3-030-91356-4_11

a valuable target for attacks and forces enterprises and device owners to be concerned about the security of the data stored on them.

Furthermore, Android is also used as a hub for a diverse set of smaller devices, such as wearables, web-cams, sensors, control and automation systems, etc. These external devices act as data producers (e.g., image/video capturing, motion sensors, temperature/humidity sensors, activity trackers etc.), sending all of their data to a corresponding application that runs on Android. Several different application frameworks do currently exist, such as Samsung SmartThings [12] and Android Sensor API [4], that enable third-party developers to build apps that compute on such, typically sensitive, data. Even though such applications allow the user to easily access the data, still at the same time they are being posed to significant risks as data is usually left unprotected and prone to misuse/abuse by unverified processes. As such, enabling applications to compute on sensitive data that external devices generate (such as surveillance material, heart rates, activities performed, motion patterns), while preserving the integrity of data and preventing any unwanted or malicious abuse, is an important problem. The protection of sensitive data is even more difficult to be achieved in such use cases, since external and wearable devices are not equipped with trusted components. In most cases, the only option available to protect the sensitive data they produce is to use the TEE offered by other (remote) devices, if available.

To mitigate such attacks and protect user data, many operating systems or frameworks that target such devices deploy permission-based access control mechanisms, such as authentication and disk encryption. For instance, IoT frameworks, such as Bosch's IoT [6] and Amazon's AWS [1], use permission-based access control for data sources and sinks, however they do not control the flows between the authorized sources and sinks [26]. Many approaches leverage hardware-based trusted computing techniques to isolate the execution of applications [17,23,33,38]. For instance, several works utilize ARM TrustZone [14] to run security-sensitive code or protect security-critical data, such as cryptographic keys and payment information [31,32,39]. However, TrustZone is shared simultaneously by all applications since there is only one TEE provided by the hardware. Thus, by design, it can not provide isolation between the applications that utilize the TEE, as they all co-reside in the same secure space. As a result, if one of the trusted applications goes rogue, any other application that runs in the secure world can possibly be affected. This prevents it from being universally leveraged simultaneously across different applications, either in user-space (e.g., banking applications, etc.) or kernel-space (security monitors, device keystore, etc.). In addition, TrustZone does not protect against attackers with physical DRAM access. Moreover, although TrustZone is provided by almost all ARM processors, it can not be directly used by application developers; it requires control of the device and its firmware, which is not the case in many cases.

In this paper we introduce Andromeda, a framework that provides secure enclaves for Android OS so Android developers can explicitly use them for their applications, either by using the native API in C/C++ or our Java interface that provides access to the secure enclaves through JNI bindings. In contrast to previous approaches, Andromeda has the potential for multiple enclaves in a system simultaneously, making it more flexible for general-purpose security-critical operations, offering per-application or per-function isolated secure environments. In addition, Andromeda implements popular Android services, enhanced with secure enclaves capabilities, hence securing and protecting their functionalities. We offer two representative services (i.e., a secure key management system, and a data protection scheme for data flows) that enhance the security of Android OS and offer protection schemes for several applications that deal with sensitive data (such as cipher keys, personal data, medical data, etc.). These services enable Andromeda to support an efficient and robust end-to-end encrypted data flow model in which external devices that pair with Android can securely transfer and process their data in the Android device, or even with a remote cloud-service.

We have currently implemented Andromeda prototype for Intel CPU processors with SGX support; any device that is equipped with a SGX-enabled processor can run Andromeda natively, out of the box, including handheld devices, convertibles, set-top boxes, and car entertainment units. However, we have to point out that Andromeda is not bound to Intel SGX; instead the proposed mechanisms could be implemented on top of other architectures offering secure user-level enclaves. For instance, there are approaches that implement user-level secure enclaves, compatible to SGX, either independent of the underlying CPU (such as Komodo [27]) either on top of ARM TrustZone (such as Sanctuary [20]); Andromeda is not fundamentally tight to Intel SGX and, as such, could be implemented on top of such approaches instead. Besides that, we note that a number of vendors are developing similar hardware protection mechanisms, including AMD SEV [2] and IBM's SecureBlue++ [19]. Even though these mechanisms are not identical, many of the proposed techniques of Andromeda can be adapted to use these hardware features, the need of which will increase in the future.

The contributions of our paper are the following:

- We present a systematic methodology to port the SGX framework for the Android OS, including the SGX kernel driver, the required libraries and background services needed for its operation and a custom cross-compiler (Sect. 5). This allows Android developers to explicitly use SGX for their applications either by using the native API in C/C++ (Sect. 6.2), or our proposed Java interface that provides access to the secure enclaves through JNI bindings (Sect. 6.3).
- We implement popular Android services, enhanced with SGX capabilities, hence securing and protecting their functionalities (Sect. 4.2). The SGX enclaves enable multiple secure spaces that can be used simultaneously by different applications, in contrast with other TEE ecosystems, such as ARM TrustZone, that allow only a single secure space that is shared for everyone and often times requires control of the device and its firmware.
- We implement a programming paradigm tailored for externally paired devices, that enables a robust, efficient, and trusted data flow between external devices that pair with the Android OS (Sect. 4.2). Such devices can securely offload

data storage and computations to the Android OS in a trustworthy manner, without necessarily being equipped with TEE-enabled CPUs.

2 Background

2.1 Intel SGX

Intel SGX [8] is a technology for application developers who are seeking to protect selected code and data from disclosure attacks or modifications. Intel SGX makes such protections possible through the use of enclaves, which are trusted execution environments for applications. Enclave code and data reside in enclave page cache (EPC), which is a region of protected physical memory. Both enclave code and data are guarded by CPU access controls, and are also cache-resident. Every time the data are moved to DRAM, they are encrypted via an extra on-chip memory encryption engine (MEE), at the granularity of cache lines. For Intel Skylake CPUs [9], the EPC size is between 64 MB and 128 MB and SGX provides a paging mechanism for swapping pages between the EPC and untrusted DRAM.

Enclave memory is also protected against memory modifications and rollbacks, using integrity checking. Non-enclave code cannot access enclave memory, however enclave code can access untrusted DRAM outside the EPC directly. It is the responsibility of the enclave code, however, to verify the integrity of all untrusted data. Application code can be put into an enclave by special instructions and software made available to developers via the Intel SGX SDK. The Intel SGX SDK is a collection of APIs, libraries, documentation, sample source code, and tools that allows software developers to create and debug Intel SGX enabled applications in C and C++ and is targeted for ×86_64 computer systems.

2.2 The Android OS

Android is an operating system mainly designed for small handheld smart devices, including but not limited to mobile phones, tablets and watches. It is being developed by Google LLC, was first released in 2007 and is currently the most widespread OS for smart devices [10,13]. Android's backbone is based on the Linux kernel, thus granting it extensively tested security features and stability, and also allowing developers and manufacturers alike to develop hardware drivers for a well known kernel. Google also had to make a few additions in order to provide a more customised kernel functionality for Android's requirements. A few key additions are the wakelocks, a power management component crucial for mobile devices, a unique out of memory (OOM) handling also informally known as 'Viking Killer', the ashmem, a new shared memory allocator for low-memory devices, pmem a process memory allocator and also Binder an Android specific interprocess communication mechanism and remote method invocation system essential to Android, due to the fact that it does not support the use of the Linux SysV IPC.

Android is built on top of the Linux kernel with components such as the hardware abstraction layer (HAL), which provides various standard interfaces that allow higher Java APIs and code to make use of a device's hardware components, and the Android Runtime (ART), a special virtual machine similar to Java's JVM, designed to run on low-memory devices. There are also Native C/C++ Libraries and both HAL and ART are written in C/C++, however these native libraries do not provide the same functionality as they would in a native Linux machine. On the top layer of the Android architecture, there is the Java API Framework, which provides applications a means to access the other layers in a constant way throughout different machines. All Android applications, while able to use native C/C++ code, are developed in Java, enabling them to be executed on multiple and different devices.

The majority of cryptographic operations in Android, including encryption, decryption, message authentication (MAC), key generation and agreement, are handled by the Android Keystore [3], that also provides a central place for storing cryptographic keys for all applications. Keymaster is a part of the Android Keystore service and responsible for generating new keys for encrypting, decrypting and hashing data. It supports various cryptographic functions like AES, RSA, SHA and more. In order to generate such an encrypted key for an application and perform cryptographic operations, one has to generate a `SecretKey`, initialize a `Cipher` with the desired mode (encrypt, decrypt or other) and choose the appropriate algorithm and its properties for the current operation. Android defines an abstract programming interface that can be used for the third-party implementations, plugged in seamlessly as needed. Therefore application developers may take advantage of any number of provider-based implementations without having to add or rewrite code.

3 Threat Model and Assumptions

In this work, we assume a powerful and active adversary who has root privileges and access to the physical hardware (with the exception of the CPU) as well. The adversary can control the entire software stack, including the OS kernel and other system software. However, we explicitly exclude denial-of-service (DoS) attacks on enclaves, given that the design of SGX allows the host OS to control an enclave's life cycles anyway. As a result, an attacker can prevent or abort the execution of enclaves, but should not gain any knowledge by doing so. Moreover, side-channel attacks [21] that exploit timing or page faults or based on vulnerabilities of the application running inside the enclave are proven to be feasible on SGX enclaves. However, protecting SGX enclaves from side-channel attacks that either focus on software or hardware bugs is orthogonal to Andromeda and thus we consider that it is out of scope of our work. However, any successful attempt to protect SGX-enabled code/hardware has a direct benefit to our framework. Finally, we assume the design and implementation of SGX itself, including all cryptographic operations, is secure and does not contain any vulnerabilities.

4 Andromeda Architecture

Our objective is to offer secure enclaves for the Android OS which must protect sensitive services from the threats defined in Sect. 3. This will enable Android developers to explicitly leverage them for their applications. We also want to utilize secure enclaves inside Android services that operate on sensitive data (such as Keystore), so they can be used transparently by applications. Overall, Android developers should be able to build their applications and make use of the secure enclaves as transparently as possible, ideally without writing extra code or heavily modifying existing applications.

An enclave cannot be initiated on its own but instead the Intel Launch enclave must be used to generate the appropriate launch token. In addition, an enclave's code always has to be executed in Ring-3 with a reduced set of allowed instructions and a limited amount of available memory. Thereby, we decide to build an architecture that runs solely on the user-space, providing the interface and the services that Android applications can use in an expressive and flexible way. Figure 1 gives an overview of the Andromeda architecture. It comprises of different layers that can be used by different kinds of applications for different purposes. Using these mechanisms, we enhance popular Android services, such as the Device Pairing and Keystore service, to leverage secure enclaves internally in order to increase their security in a robust and transparent way. Finally, we also implement an environment, within SGX, so external devices that have paired with Android can securely transfer and store sensitive data on the Android device. Andromeda is responsible to protect all sensitive data by encrypting them across the full path from the external device to the Android OS. Further, Andromeda optionally enables the processing of these data via functions that the data-publishing application has submitted for execution in the SGX enclaves.

4.1 Trusted Execution and Storage

Andromeda provides a trusted execution and data storage service on top of SGX. The service can be used by local Android apps, as well as from remotely paired devices, as described in Sect. 4.2. At the lowest level, applications can use the native API provided by the SGX runtime libraries, in order to achieve the maximum performance. The process of utilising secure enclaves in an application developed in native C/C++ code remains the same as for every other native C/C++ Android application. The developer needs to prepare and integrate the Intel SGX counterpart of the application (similar to the Linux environment) and then cross-compile the application with our custom Android tool-chain, which is able to handle the compilation of both trusted and untrusted parts of the code. Developing Intel SGX enclaves for an APK implemented using Java requires the use of JNI bindings. For this reason, we provide a Java API (described in Sect. 6.3, which wraps the SGX functionalities in appropriate classes. The developer needs to extend these classes with methods that will be eventually executed in the SGX enclave of the application and perform the code compilation using the Andromeda tool-chain which also provides JNI bindings for each

SGX-enabled function requested. In this way, the developer can easily interface with the enclaves from the APK level. Moreover, Andromeda provides the implementation of a secure data vault system and exposes a simple Java API for Android applications. Using the data vault service, applications can securely store data inside the SGX enclaves or seal them for secure file system storage.

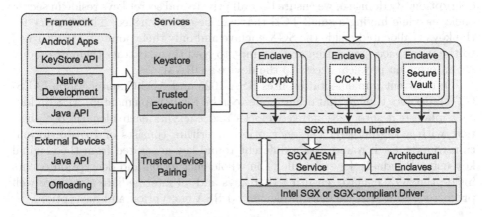

Fig. 1. Architecture of Andromeda

4.2   Andromeda Services

Keystore Service. The main purpose of Android Keystore is to store cryptographic keys and offer cryptographic operations in a secure container, protecting them from tampering. However, if not implemented with secure hardware support, it is vulnerable to a broad set of attacks, as described in Sect. 3. Having the secret and private keys stored in clear-text makes them an easy target for a malicious software running on the device. Andromeda offers the mechanisms to keep the secret keys in a protected space, within secure enclaves, thus solving and overcoming leakage scenarios.

The Keystore is implemented in C/C++ while Android uses a binder to communicate with the Java part. Internally, Android Keystore can handle different type of entries. Some of them are PrivateKey, SecretKeyEntry and TrustedCertificateEntry. Each one of these entries is identified by an alias name which corresponds to the Keystore entry. When generating such an entry, it is possible to choose from a range of cryptographic algorithms available in the Keystore or use the default. In this way, the Android Keystore is able to store multiple keys simultaneously, regardless of type, name and algorithm. At the same time, different running programs can utilize the Keystore and store their keys without having to deal with collisions.

An overview of our SGX-enabled Keystore operation is illustrated in Fig. 2. A major advantage of Andromeda Keystore is that it can be used even by legacy apps without any code modifications or recompilation. The simplest way is to have the entire Keystore inside a single enclave. However, this design leads to a large TCB that is generally harder to review, or possibly verify, and is assumed to have more vulnerabilities. To overcome this problem, we place in secure enclaves only three core operations, which are used by the majority of cryptographic algorithms: (i) the key generation, (ii) the data encryption, and (iii) the data decryption. By doing so, we ensure that all private and secret keys reside in secure enclaves while having a small TCB that can be easily verified. The memory for the keys is allocated inside the SGX enclave and only their pointers are returned to the user-space, preventing any attempt to read them, extract them or modify them, even via physical access to the device's DRAM.

Our current implementation uses RSA-1024 and AES Counter Mode (AES-CTR); we note though that other modes can be easily implemented. AES divides each plain-text into 128-bit fixed blocks and encrypts each block into cipher-text with a 128-bit key. The encryption algorithm consists of 10 transformation rounds. Each round uses a different round key generated from the original key using Rijndael's key schedule. The whole encryption and decryption occurs inside the SGX enclave, ensuring that keys and all intermediate states are well protected. Similarly, we have implemented RSA encryption and decryption.

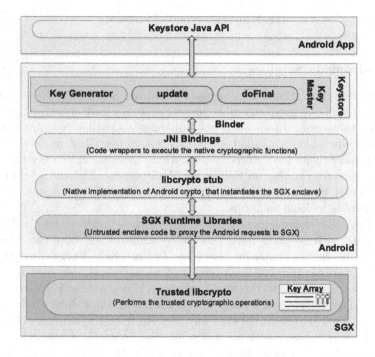

Fig. 2. The Keystore Architecture. The cipher keys are stored only in SGX enclaves. Developers can encrypt and decrypt their data using the default Keystore API, which internally redirects to Andromeda's trusted implementation.

Trusted Device Pairing. Andromeda provides secure device pairing between devices, even when only one (i.e., the Android device) is equipped with an SGX-enabled processor. Such scenarios are typical when small external devices, such as sensors and wearables with limited security capabilities, need to be paired with more powerful Android devices (i.e., a phone or gateway). To accomplish secure device pairing and attestation in such use cases, Andromeda offers the functionality that enables the external devices to securely connect with the SGX-capable Android device. The main concept is that data-publishing wearable or external devices can protect their sensitive data, so it will only reside or processed within designated functions that run in SGX-provided enclaves.

First, Andromeda generates a key pair and distributes the public key to the external device and the corresponding private key to a local secure enclave. Each external device has its own secure enclave, to ensure isolation between each other. These keys can be used later to establish a session key via Diffie-Hellman. The process of establishing and storing the keys is performed entirely inside SGX enclaves in the case of the Android device. We assume that the external device runs on a minimal code base with limited I/O, thus the integrity of the key management can be attested and preserved. While this end-to-end encryption of the I/O channel ensures data protection during transfers, the need of attestation between the two devices remains a critical point in order to prevent malicious users impersonating as one of the two devices. In cases where the external device is capable to execute the Intel Remote Attestation process it is able to verify that it is indeed communicating with a secure enclave, running on SGX-capable hardware without emulation. However, in some cases, Intel Remote Attestation can not be performed due to the limited computing capabilities of many external devices. To overcome this, we utilize one-time passwords (OTP) instead, which are an essential part for our remote attestation alternative procedure. More specifically, we use Google key generator to create an arbitrary key that we can then register with a secure SGX enclave. The registration is performed at the first connection and Andromeda (optionally) prompts the user to verify the registration. Once the key has been successfully registered, the attestation procedure starts by the external device demanding a 6-digit OTP to be exchanged. The generated OTPs are based on the RFC 6238. Upon receiving the OTP, the external device calculates an OTP with the same key. If both match, the external device can be certain that it communicate with the SGX enclave, since the entire OTP process is performed inside the enclave. Once the OTP is verified, the secure communication channel is established as described above.

5   Implementation

5.1   Setting up SGX for Android

Cross-compiling Intel SGX for Android OS is a challenging task. Due to the complexity of the software and the many differences between a Linux distribution and Android, we have to split the porting process in several smaller tasks in order to constantly proving the potential and validity of our goal. For this reason we perform the Android port in the following steps. First, we compile the SGX SDK for a different Linux distribution than Ubuntu, which is the officially supported, namely Arch Linux. Since Android is also based on Linux, this process lets us understand how different compiler and library versions affect the possibility of porting SGX on Android. Second, we validate that we can build the Android Open Source Project (AOSP) form scratch and successfully install and run it on an SGX-capable x86 machine. Finally, we integrate the SGX functionality into the AOSP source tree by cross-compiling and providing the necessary libraries for its correct operation.

The whole process of building the SGX environment for a non supported Linux distribution is a quite tedious procedure due to the kernel, compiler and library version incompatibilities. While analyzing the dependencies of SGX SDK we find the following to be essential for a standard enclave execution: (i) the SGX kernel driver, (ii) `aesm_service` which is a background daemon serving as a management agent for SGX enabled applications, (iii) the `libsgx_urts.so` and `libsgx_uae_service.so`, needed for executing enclaves in hardware mode, the `libsgx_urts_sim.so` and `libsgx_uae_service_sim.so`, needed for the software emulation mode, and finally (iv) the `le_prod_css.bin` and `libsgx_le.signed.so`. This analysis allowed us to understand the software requirements and the process of building the SGX environment for an unsupported platform.

Porting SGX on Android is an even more complicated process. First, AOSP has to be built from scratch and be installed on an SGX-enabled x86 machine. Then, porting the SGX environment is a time-consuming process since each change to the source tree requires to (i) build the Android image, (ii) flash it on the host machine and (iii) verify the correctness of each change as well as the stability of the system. The SGX SDK is designed to be build on desktop-based Linux distributions using GCC > v5 while Google's NDK (Native Development Kit for Android) offers `GCC-4` and `clang` that are not able to compile the SGX source tree. For this reason, we use CrystaX NDK [7] which acts as a drop-in replacement for Google's Android NDK, offering GCC-5.3 compatibility. Also, the SGX SDK contains a group of libraries that must be compiled for Android in order for the environment to execute properly, such as `protobuf`, `ssl`, `libssp`, `curl`, `gperftools` and `libunwind`. To cross-compile them, we need to export and set the corresponding flags for the Makefile and configuration files of each project to link to the CrystaX compiler by setting the `cross_compiling` field to `true`. Then, all references to `lpthread` have to be removed from the Makefiles, since it is automatically linked at the Android version of the standard library. Moreover, due to the stripped down kernel version that is used by the Android OS, the `RDRAND` instruction that is used by `sgx_read_rand` to perform random number generation is not available. To overcome this issue we use a software based implementation for random number generation that is fully compatible with the existing API and works on Android and SGX.

After successfully cross-compiling the SGX source tree, the final step is to cross-compile the kernel driver and port it to Android. Unfortunately, there are inconsistencies between the supported kernel used by Ubuntu and the Android kernel headers and the signatures of several kernel functions are different. For this reason, some patches are required in order to build the driver which also requires to be built in-source with Android. Once the SGX porting is completed, we build a demo application that utilizes SGX enclaves in both hardware and simulation mode. Finally, in order to execute Intel SGX enclave code, the application must be signed using Intel's sgx_sign tool, which we rebuild and use in order to compile Android applications as needed. The problem is that cross compiling the whole Intel SGX source developing tools (SDK) and platform software (PSW), would produce the sgx_sign binary that is only executable on Android; this would be quite inflexible to build an application and then sign it at the Android using the application. Instead, we rebuild the source but this time using only the Ubuntu default tools, store the sgx_sign, and then use it to compile our applications when needed.

5.2 Running an SGX Application

An SGX application can run either in hardware or simulation mode. To make use of the underlying hardware and leverage Intel SGX as a service, we compile SGX applications using make SGX_MODE=HW which links against libsgx_urts.so. Of course, since these libraries are not available in the source tree of Android they must be provided to the LD_LIBRARY_PATH of the corresponding application by exporting the paths of each one of them. Apart from the required SGX dependencies, the libraries that were linked during the SDK compilation must be also provided and exported to the LD_LIBRARY_PATH of the given application. Additionally, we use insmod to load the driver and then start the aesm_service. The Android service system has several differences compared to Linux; editing a system service file like init.d is not enough for Android to deploy a new system service. Instead, a new application, marked as a service, has to be created and meet specific code requirements [5]; i.e., all native functions of aesm_service need to be wrapped with JNI calls for it to be accessible by the Java part.

To overcome this issue, we simply adjust the aesm_service source code to run as a daemon in the background and interact directly with the native part. The other solution would be to discard the whole Android application part and interact with the native part directly. By examining the source code of aesm_service we manage to run the application as daemon (which is essentially a service) so the app would start and stay alive. Whereas, if we start it without the specified input it would just terminate with no output. Also, the aesm_service requires the le_prod_css.bin and libsgx_le.signed.so binaries to properly execute so we transfer these binaries from the Intel SGX output directory to the aesm_service directory in Android before its execution. Finally, running an application in Android requires it to be built with the -pie and -fPIE flags. These flags instruct the linker that the program's code can be executed regardless its absolute address. After all the aforementioned requirements are met, we are able to cross-compile and execute SGX-enabled Android applications.

Enclaves can be created using the ECREATE instruction, which initializes an SGX enclave control structure (SECS) in the EPC. The EADD instruction adds pages to the enclave, which are further tracked and protected by the SGX (i.e., the virtual address and its permissions). The EINIT instruction creates a cryptographic measurement, after the loading of all enclave pages. The cryptographic measurement can be used by remote parties for attestation. After the enclave has been initialized, enclave code can be executed through the EENTER instruction, which switches the CPU to enclave mode and jumps to a predefined enclave offset. The EEXIT instruction causes execution to leave the enclave.

6 Andromeda Framework

The Andromeda framework is split in three parts: (i) the enclave-enhanced Android Keystore, which can be utilized transparently, (ii) the native API, used to initialize and configure SGX using native code, and (iii) the Java API, which provides a set of building blocks for APKs.

6.1 Andromeda Keystore

The Android apps can transparently utilize the Andromeda Keystore service to securely perform cryptographic operations. Private keys and other sensitive information are kept in encrypted form in an array that resides in SGX memory and cannot be accessed in any way by the host. To perform a cryptographic operation: (i) the required (encrypted) key is fetched from the array, (ii) it is decrypted inside the enclave, and (iii) the actual operation is performed on the input data. This extension of the Android Keystore, provided by Andromeda, is completely transparent to the developer. All necessary modifications are performed at the native C/C++ part of Android's Keystore while the corresponding Java API remains unmodified, rendering it completely backwards compatible with legacy applications. Persistent secure storage of keys and important metadata can be achieved using the sealing technique. The Keystore service will seal and export the contents of the secure enclaves to the specified file-system locations, protecting them during unexpected execution termination or device power-off. The exported data are encrypted and accompanied with the necessary metadata that ensure their validity. Once Keystore's enclaves need to be re-enabled, the service will repopulate them by loading and unsealing the data. If the data is invalid or tampered, the service provides the necessary exceptions.

6.2 Native Development

Using the Andromeda SGX tool-chain, developers can create their own SGX enclaves for their Android applications. To do so, native code in C/C++ has to be developed for the enclave functionality as well as the respective ECALLs and OCALLs that manipulate the data (sensitive or not) in the trusted and the untrusted part. In order to access the SGX code and functions, JNI bindings must be provided to the Java part of the APK to connect it with the native C/C++ and SGX counterpart. These JNI functions must be written in order to initialize the enclave instance, setup the environment and access the secure enclave code, functions and data. The process is quite similar with a Linux environment; the basic difference with SGX-enabled Android applications is that all native C/C++ code that implements the SGX enclaves and the native C/C++ code that handles their execution should be cross-compiled with the Andromeda Android tool-chain which handles all the steps required to build the source tree.

6.3   Andromeda Java API

In order to assist the development of SGX-enabled Android applications, Andromeda also offers an API that developers can use to offload specific parts of the code into secure enclaves. The Andromeda Java API provides a set of building blocks for APKs and automates the generation process of secure enclaves that execute only minimal parts of the application logic in the trusted environment. The Andromeda Java API are shown in Table 1 and allows the creation of enclaves, the configuration of input and output between enclaves, and the execution of user-defined functions.

Secure Execution. The Java functions provided by the Andromeda API offer the following functionality: The developer can create a new secure enclave Java class instance using the `TrustedEnvironment()` constructor. To make the establishment of the trusted environment, the secure enclave Java class provides the `load()` method that passes configuration settings and user-defined configuration extensions to the enclave. This operation will generate a new enclave using the C/C++ layer of the Andromeda API and provide the necessary handles to the Java counterpart in order to interface with the enclave. The enclave and its metadata can be securely erased using the `destroy()` method, which optionally passes finalization data to the enclave. Developers can use the `run()` method to perform a trusted execution in the secure enclave. The `run()` method is extensible and includes the code that performs the desired computations inside the SGX enclave. Andromeda also provides the option to implement multiple functions to be executed in the trusted environment which can be invoked using their respective index (using the corresponding `run()` method argument). The `run()` method can be called an arbitrary number of times with different inputs.

In contrast to the manual development of SGX-enabled Android applications, when using the Andromeda Java API the Andromeda tool-chain will generate the appropriate native C/C++ SGX code that implements the functionality defined in the `run()` method. Moreover, the tool-chain will generate the enclave driver code, that handles I/O and function calling, as well as establish connection with the Java API by creating the necessary JNI bindings.

Secure Vault API. The Java functions provided by the Andromeda secure vault API enable both short term and persistent secure storage functionality.

Table 1. Andromeda Java API for SGX enclave utilization.

Constructor summary	
Constructor	Description
TrustedEnvironment()	Creates a new secure enclave class instance
Method summary	
Modifier and Type	Method description
void	**load**(EnclaveConfig config) Initializes the secure enclave
EnclaveOutput	**run**(int index, EnclaveInput i) Performs the trusted execution
int	**store**(byte[] data) Stores the data and returns its index
byte[]	**retrieve**(int index) Retrieves the data using its index
SealedData	**seal**(Object d) Seals the enclave data and stores to file-system
Object	**unseal**(SealedData d) Unseals the data and populates the enclave
void	**pair**(ChannelConfig config) Creates a secure connection with the external device
void	**transmit**(ChannelConfig config, byte[] data) Securely transmits data to the external device
byte[]	**receive**(ChannelConfig config) Securely receives data from the external device
void	**terminate**() Disconnects the external
void	**destroy**() Destroys the secure enclave

The developer can use the `store()` function in order to store a data object within a secure enclave. The data object can be of any kind, such as cryptographic keys, certificates, fingerprints, tokens or any other data considered sensitive in the scope of the application. Upon successful data storage, the API will return an index which can be used to retrieve the actual data through the `retrieve()` function. Moreover, the Andromeda Java API provides access to the SGX sealing and unsealing functionality, via the `seal()` and `unseal()` methods respectively. Using the `seal()` function, the developer can encrypt the data within the enclave using a secret key derived within SGX. Once the data are sealed, they can be stored in main memory or storage with assurances of integrity and authenticity and can only be unsealed using `unseal()`. These functions can also be used to periodically generate backups of the secure storage in order to prevent data loss (e.g., from unpredictable execution termination).

Secure Pairing API. The secure device pairing functionality is provided by dedicated Andromeda API methods. These methods can be utilized by the Android application controlling the external device, as long as the external device includes Andromeda's connection libraries, which do not require SGX support, in its software stack. The developer is able to establish a secure communication channel with an external device using the `pair()` method. The external device can be connected either via Bluetooth or Wi-Fi. Andromeda will then perform the attestation procedure for both devices. The configuration data passed to this method indicate the device ID, the attestation procedure (Remote Attestation or OTP), the option of notifying the user with a verification pop-up and other metadata, essential for initiating the connection. Once the attestation process is completed, Andromeda will perform the communication channel establishment automatically, as described in Sect. 4.2. Once communication is initiated, the devices are able to exchange data using the `transmit()` and `receive()` functions respectively. Finally, the developer can execute the `terminate()` function for a `TrustedEnvironment` instance in order to disconnect the external device.

7 Evaluation

7.1 Security Analysis

We now evaluate the security properties of Andromeda by describing possible attacks and showing how our proposed design protects against them.

Memory Attacks. We implement Andromeda in a way that nothing but a pointer to enclave memory is ever written into host memory. The pointer's content can not be read or modified since it resides into the enclave. When Andromeda performs the desired operations, the output is transferred back to Android memory. In the meantime, we keep the enclave execution alive completely isolated from the Android system, without being affected by side effects of the OS or hardware, such as interrupt handling, scheduling, swapping, and ACPI suspend modes.

Controlling the Kernel. In cases where the attackers have successfully taken full control of the Android OS kernel, any sensitive data manipulated by Andromeda is still sound and safe. Once again, even though the attackers may have full read/write/execute rights in the whole system, they cannot read/write/execute code inside the enclave. As a result, any attempt to modify or read enclave code will result in a Segmentation violation since this memory is not mappable outside the enclave code, keeping the data secured.

Integrity of Data. In a typical scenario, attackers can exploit software vulnerabilities and manage to inject code of their choice to a running service. Sensitive data, such as secret keys and checksums, stored in the address space of the process, can be easily acquired. In contrast, hiding sensitive data in a secure enclave prevents access even to fully privileged processes. To verify this, we attach our process with `gdb` in order to check the allocated pointers in the enclave code and trace the calls. However, no such data can be extracted since the enclave code and data are inaccessible from non-enclave code nor the function calls or memory stack. Such operations always result in Segmentation violations.

7.2 Performance Analysis

We now assess the performance of Andromeda and the extra overhead introduced for the execution of the secure enclaves. For our experiments we use an Intel NUC 8i5BEK kit with an SGX-enabled Intel i5-8259U CPU at 2.3 GHz and 8 GB of DDR4 RAM. The system is running Android x86 version 7.1.2_r33.

AES Evaluation. We compare the performance of the AES-128 crypto algorithm, as achieved by the vanilla Android Keystore system, versus the SGX-enabled implementation provided by Andromeda, using a custom benchmarking tool. In each processing loop, the tool generates a random secret key and a random stream of data. The data vary in size from 32 B up to 32 MB. To avoid any potential caching effects that may result in inaccurate results, we generate a new key and data stream in each processing loop. Once an AES key and a stream of data are prepared in memory, the tool performs cryptographic operations on the data using AES-128 in CTR mode, using both the vanilla and the SGX-enhanced Keystore system, provided by Andromeda. Figure 3(a) shows the performance characteristics of the native AES code execution. We achieve this by monitoring only the AES functions found in the native C code part of the Android Keystore system. Our evaluation indicates that the overhead introduced by the

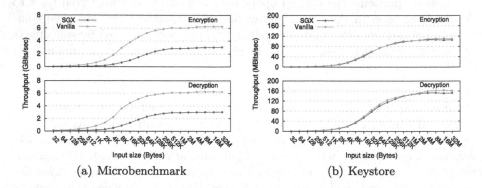

(a) Microbenchmark   (b) Keystore

Fig. 3. Throughput comparison between the AES-128 CTR found in Android's Keystore and the SGX-enabled version provided by Andromeda's Keystore.

SGX-enabled implementation ranges between 51% and 84% for the encryption operations and from 51% to 78% for the decryption.

In the next experiment we explore the throughput sustained in the APK scope. We achieve this by performing the same experiment but in this case we monitor the execution time of the Java cryptographic functions provided to the APK by the Keystore system (Fig. 3(b)). The execution time includes the entire execution path and the overhead introduced by the various layers of the Android architecture, including the IPC, the binder and the numerous function calls until the actual cryptographic operations are performed. We notice that the sustained throughput perceived by the APK is one order of magnitude lower (compared to Fig. 3(a)), due to the overhead introduced by the various layers of the software stack involved in the process (i.e., JNI, IPC, and the binder). Similarly, the perceived overhead introduced by the SGX enclaves is minimised, between 0.6% to 13% for encryption and 0.6% to 11% for decryption.

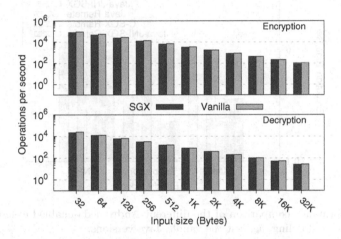

Fig. 4. Sustained throughput achieved for the vanilla and the SGX-enabled implementation of the RSA-1024 cryptographic algorithm.

RSA Evaluation. We now present the performance comparison between the vanilla and our SGX-enabled implementation of the RSA algorithm. We perform the evaluation as follows. We develop a benchmarking application capable to perform RSA key generation, encryption and decryption. In each processing loop, the tool generates a new RSA key-pair and performs cryptographic operations against a set of input data. The data set consist of 10,000 random data chunks, varying in size from 32 B up to 32 KB, with each set containing chunks of the same size. We choose to generate a new set of random data in each processing loop in order to eliminate any caching effects. We execute the benchmarking application for every data set, each time monitoring the number of sustained cryptographic operations per second. The outcome of this experiment is displayed in Fig. 4.

We notice that the SGX-enabled implementation introduces a maximum overhead of 16%, observed when processing 64 B long data, with the lowest introduced overhead being 2.3% during the encryption of 2 KB long data. The maximum sustained decryption rate is observed for the vanilla implementation during the encryption of 32 B long data with the introduced overhead being 12.6%. The minimum observed overhead introduced by the use of SGX enclaves is 0.9%, encountered during the decryption of 2 KB long values. For both crypto operations, we observe that the perceived overhead introduced by the I/O between the benchmarking application and the SGX-enclave is minimised due to the processing complexity of the RSA algorithm.

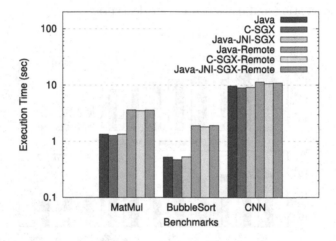

Fig. 5. Performance comparison of the different Andromeda-enabled execution methods, including offloading, against the vanilla Java versions.

Computation Offloading. We present the performance of three benchmarking applications, executed, using the different methods provided by the Andromeda framework, as well as the overhead introduced by executing them remotely. In particular, we compare the execution of the vanilla Java implementation against their secure implementation using C and SGX natively, compiled with our custom cross-compiler, and their implementation using the Andromeda Java API for SGX. These benchmarks consist of some typical operations that external devices or wearables may perform on sensitive data (e.g., for analytics on finance or health data, image processing, etc.) and also exhibit different performance characteristics (i.e., IO-bound, memory-intensive, computational-intensive). The first benchmark performs matrix multiplication on two tables with 10K rows and columns. The second benchmark performs bubble sort on an array of 20K random integers. Finally, the third benchmark is a convolutional neural network that performs image classification using as input images with size 800×600 pixels, generated by an external device.

As we can see in Fig. 5, the vanilla Java implementation requires 5.4% to 11.2% more time to finish its execution than the respective SGX-enabled implementations (developed either in native C or using the Andromeda SGX Java API) whereas the time needed for code offloading ranges from 5.13% to 7.5% for Java. The reason for this is that in both SGX-enabled versions, the functions are executed natively using C. The overhead introduced by the I/O with the secure enclave, the JNI layer (in the SGX-enabled Java implementation) and the data offloading on the socket level are minimal in these cases and does not overshadow the speedup gained by the native execution.

8   Discussion and Limitations

Misusing Andromeda Keystore for Encrypting/Decrypting Messages. Intel SGX cannot verify whether a request for an operation has been received from a benign or a malicious user. As a result, an attacker who has managed to gain access to the base Android system or the Keystore service could leverage Intel SGX to encrypt and decrypt messages. Still, the adversary cannot steal any key stored in secure enclaves.

Denial-of-Service. Adversaries who have compromised the Android system can easily disrupt the operation of Intel SGX. For example, they can delete or modify input or output data by hooking the functions that communicate with the SGX application or even kill or suspend the execution of enclaves. As the main purpose of Intel SGX is to protect sensitive data and perform trusted operations, defending against these attacks is out of the scope of this work.

Portability. Andromeda is currently implemented on Intel SGX-equipped CPUs. Even though this prevents us from adopting it to other CPU models, we note that Andromeda is not fundamentally bound to Intel SGX; instead our proposed architecture could be implemented on top of other approaches that offer secure user-level enclaves. For instance, there are recently proposed approaches that implement user-level secure enclaves, similar to SGX, either independent of the underlying CPU [27] either on top of ARM TrustZone [20]; porting Andromeda to these approaches is part of our future work.

9   Related Work

ARM TrustZone [14] enables the development of two separate environments, the trusted and the untrusted world. This split enables the execution of the rich OS (that runs in the untrusted world) and the system software that controls basic operations that must be protected and runs in the trusted world. Santos et al. [33] use TrustZone for securing mobile applications, by establishing and isolating trusted components. However, their approach requires a trusted language runtime in the TCB, due to the fact that there is only a single trusted world. DroidVault [29] presents a security solution for storing and manipulating sensitive data. The data are stored in an encrypted form on the filesystem and are only processed (decrypted) in TrustZone. TZ-RKP implements a low-TCB system level safe security monitor on top of the TrustZone architecture [16] that provides a real-time OS kernel protection. The monitor routes privileged system functions through secure world for examination. Samsung KNOX [32] is a secure container framework, leveraging ARM TrustZone, that offers protection from both the software and the hardware. However, KNOX is primarily a closed-source system and its architecture is not well documented in the open literature. A major limitation of all these TrustZone-based approaches is that they do not protect against attackers with physical DRAM access. Moreover, TrustZone is not best suited to be securely shared by multiple applications, as there is only one shared TEE provided by the hardware, offering limited isolation granularity compared to SGX. This prevents it from being leveraged simultaneously by different applications, either in user-space (e.g., banking applications, etc.) or kernel-space (security monitors, device keystore, etc.).

Intel SGX [8] offers fine-grained confidentiality and integrity at the enclave level. Haven [18] aims to execute unmodified legacy Windows applications inside SGX enclaves by porting a Windows library OS into SGX. TrustAV [25] offloads malware analysis operations within secure enclaves to shield the transfer and processing of private user data in untrusted environments. Graphene-SGX [37] encapsulates the entire libOS, including the unmodified application binary, supporting libraries, and a trusted runtime with a customized C library and ELF loader inside an SGX enclave. VC3 [34] uses SGX to achieve confidentiality and integrity for the Map Reduce framework. SCONE [15] is a shielded execution framework that enables developers to compile their C applications into Docker containers. SGX-Mon [24] is a host-based kernel integrity monitor that resides in SGX enclaves to prevent attackers from tampering its execution and operation-critical data. In contrast with these works, Andromeda is the first approach, to the best of our knowledge, that enables SGX enclaves for the Android OS. Moreover, there are recently proposed approaches that implement user-level enclaves, similar to SGX, either independent of the underlying CPU [27] or on top of ARM TrustZone [20]; Andromeda is not fundamentally tight to Intel SGX and, as such, could be implemented on top of such approaches instead.

Finally, several improvements for SGX have been recently developed in order to protect against memory bugs [28,30,35] or controlled-channel attacks [36]. SGXBOUNDS [28] enables bounds-checking with low memory overheads, in order to fit within the limited EPC size. SGX-Shield [35] implements Address Space Layout Randomization (AS-LR) in enclaves, with a scheme to maximize the entropy, and the ability to hide and enforce ASLR decisions. Eleos [30] proposes to reduce the number of enclave exits by asynchronously servicing system calls outside of the enclaves, and enabling user-space memory paging. T-SGX [36] is an approach that combines SGX with Transactional Synchronization Extensions, in order to mitigate controlled-channel attacks. All these works are orthogonal to our approach and can be integrated to Andromeda.

10   Conclusion

In this work, we present the design, implementation, and evaluation of Andromeda, a framework that provides the first SGX interface for Android OS. Using Andromeda, developers can explicitly use SGX for their applications via the native API in C/C++ or the Java interface that provides access to the secure enclaves through JNI bindings. Also, Andromeda offers services that enhance Android's security and provides protection schemes for applications that deal with sensitive data.

As part of our future work, we plan to port Andromeda to SGX-compliant approaches that do not depend on specific CPU models though, either using software-only techniques [27], either on top of ARM TrustZone [20]. Also, we plan to enhance our secure pairing mechanism by utilizing protocols that offer mutually trusted secure communication channels between enclaves that reside in different physical devices, similar to [22].

Acknowledgments. The research work was supported by the Hellenic Foundation for Research and Innovation (HFRI) and the General Secretariat for Research and Technology (GSRT), under the HFRI PhD Fellowship grant (GA. No. 2767). This work was also supported by the projects CONCORDIA, C4IIoT and COLLABS, funded by the European Commission under Grant Agreements No. 830927, No. 833828, and No. 871518. This publication reflects the views only of the authors, and the Commission cannot be held responsible for any use which may be made of the information contained therein.

References

1. Amazon's AWS permission managements. https://aws.amazon.com/iam/details/manage-permissions/
2. AMD Secure Encrypted Virtualization (SEV). https://developer.amd.com/amd-secure-memory-encryption-sme-amd-secure-encrypted-virtualization-sev/
3. Android Keystore. https://developer.android.com/training/articles/keystore.html
4. Android Sensor API. https://developer.android.com/guide/topics/sensors/sensors_overview
5. Android Services. https://developer.android.com/guide/components/services.html
6. Bosch IoT. https://www.bosch-iot-suite.com/permissions/
7. Crystax NDK. https://www.crystax.net/android/ndk/
8. Intel Software Guard Extensions (SGX). https://software.intel.com/en-us/sgx
9. Intel's Skylake Processors. https://www.intel.com/content/dam/www/public/us/en/documents/white-papers/ia-introduction-basics-paper.pdf
10. International Data Corporation. https://www.idc.com/promo/smartphone-market-share/os

11. Mobile Operating System Market Share Worldwide. https://gs.statcounter.com/os-market-share/mobile/worldwide
12. Samsung SmartThings. https://www.samsung.com/us/smart-home/smartthings/
13. Statista. https://www.statista.com/statistics/266136/global-market-share-held-by-smartphone-operating-systems/
14. ARM LIMITED: ARM Security Technology - Building a Secure System using TrustZone Technology (2009)
15. Arnautov, S., et al.: SCONE: secure linux containers with Intel SGX. In: OSDI (2016)
16. Azab, A.M., et al.: Hypervision across worlds: real-time kernel protection from the ARM TrustZone secure world. In: CCS (2014)
17. Azab, A.M., Ning, P., Wang, Z., Jiang, X., Zhang, X., Skalsky, N.C.: Hypersentry: enabling stealthy in-context measurement of hypervisor integrity. In: CCS (2010)
18. Baumann, A., Peinado, M., Hunt, G.: Shielding applications from an untrusted cloud with haven. ACM Trans. Comput. Syst. **33**(3), 8:1–8:26 (2015)
19. Boivie, R., Williams, P.: Secureblue++: CPU support for secure execution. Technical Report (2012)
20. Brasser, F., Gens, D., Jauernig, P., Sadeghi, A.R., Stapf, E.: Sanctuary: Arming TrustZone with user-space enclaves (2019)
21. Caddy Tom: Side-channel attacks (2011). https://link.springer.com/referencework/10.1007%2F0-387-23483-7
22. Chalkiadakis, N., Deyannis, D., Karnikis, D., Vasiliadis, G., Ioannidis, S.: The million dollar handshake: secure and attested communications in the cloud. In: CLOUD (2020)
23. Colp, P., et al.: Protecting data on smartphones and tablets from memory attacks. In: ASPLOS (2015)
24. Deyannis, D., Karnikis, D., Vasiliadis, G., Ioannidis, S.: An enclave assisted snapshot-based kernel integrity monitor. In: EdgeSys (2020)
25. Deyannis, D., Papadogiannaki, E., Kalivianakis, G., Vasiliadis, G., Ioannidis, S.: TrustAV: practical and privacy preserving malware analysis in the cloud. In: CODASPY (2020)
26. Fernandes, E., Paupore, J., Rahmati, A., Simionato, D., Conti, M., Prakash, A.: FlowFence: practical data protection for emerging IoT application frameworks. In: Proceedings of the 25th USENIX Security Symposium. USENIX Security (2016)
27. Ferraiuolo, A., Baumann, A., Hawblitzel, C., Parno, B.: Komodo: using verification to disentangle secure-enclave hardware from software. In: SOSP (2017)
28. Kuvaiskii, D., et al.: SGXBOUNDS: memory safety for shielded execution. In: Proceedings of the Twelfth European Conference on Computer Systems. EuroSys (2017)
29. Li, X., Hu, H., Bai, G., Jia, Y., Liang, Z., Saxena, P.: DroidVault: a trusted data vault for android devices. In: ICECCS (2014)
30. Orenbach, M., Lifshits, P., Minkin, M., Silberstein, M.: Eleos: ExitLess OS services for SGX enclaves. In: EuroSys (2017)
31. Pirker, M., Slamanig, D.: A framework for privacy-preserving mobile payment on security enhanced ARM TrustZone platforms. In: TrustCom (2012)
32. Samsung: White Paper : An Overview of Samsung KNOX (2013). http://www.samsung.com/my/business-images/resource/white-paper/2013/11/Samsung_KNOX_whitepaper_An_Overview_of_Samsung_KNOX-0.pdf
33. Santos, N., Raj, H., Saroiu, S., Wolman, A.: Using ARM TrustZone to build a trusted language runtime for mobile applications. In: ASPLOS (2014)

34. Schuster, F., et al.: VC3: trustworthy data analytics in the cloud using SGX. In: Proceedings of the 2015 IEEE Symposium on Security and Privacy. S&P (2015)
35. Seo, J., et al.: SGX-Shield: enabling address space layout randomization for SGX programs. In: NDSS (2017)
36. Shih, M.W., Lee, S., Kim, T., Peinado, M.: T-SGX: eradicating controlled-channel attacks against enclave programs. In: NDSS (2017)
37. Tsai, C.C., Porter, D.E., Vij, M.: Graphene-SGX: A practical library OS for unmodified applications on SGX. In: USENIX ATC (2017)
38. Wang, J., Stavrou, A., Ghosh, A.: HyperCheck: a hardware-assisted integrity monitor. In: Jha, S., Sommer, R., Kreibich, C. (eds.) RAID 2010. LNCS, vol. 6307, pp. 158–177. Springer, Heidelberg (2010). https://doi.org/10.1007/978-3-642-15512-3_9
39. Zheng, X., Yang, L., Ma, J., Shi, G., Meng, D.: TrustPAY: trusted mobile payment on security enhanced ARM TrustZone platforms. In: ISCC (2016)

Network Security

FEX – A Feature Extractor for Real-Time IDS

Andreas Schaad[✉] and Dominik Binder[✉]

Offenburg University of Applied Sciences, Badstrasse 24, 77652 Offenburg, Germany
{andreas.schaad,dominik.binder}@hs-offenburg.de

Abstract. In the field of network security, the detection of possible intrusions is an important task to prevent and analyse attacks. Machine learning has been adopted as a particular supporting technique over the last years. However, the majority of related published work uses post mortem log files and fails to address the required real-time capabilities of network data feature extraction and machine learning based analysis [1–5]. We introduce the network feature extractor library FEX, which is designed to allow real-time feature extraction of network data. This library incorporates 83 statistical features based on reassembled data flows. The introduced Cython implementation allows processing individual packets within 4.58 μs. Based on the features extracted by FEX, existing intrusion detection machine learning models were examined with respect to their real-time capabilities. An identified Decision-Tree Classifier model was thus further optimised by transpiling it into C Code. This reduced the prediction time of a single sample to 3.96 μs on average. Based on the feature extractor and the improved machine learning model an IDS system was implemented which supports a data throughput between 63.7 Mbit/s and 2.5 Gbit/s making it a suitable candidate for a real-time, machine-learning based IDS.

Keywords: IDS · Machine learning · Real-time · Feature extraction

1 Introduction

1.1 Background

Standard and well-proven network intrusion detection approaches include signature- or anomaly-based detection techniques. Independently of the detection techniques used, appropriate measures must be taken to extract and process valuable information from the raw network data. Early IDS systems used basic statistical methods to process network data, so that simple patterns can be identified. In the meantime, however, these procedures have been largely replaced by machine learning based approaches, as these are able to take more complex relationships in the data into account, which is resulting in an improved intrusion detection rate [1–4]. However, the extraction of proper features from the raw network data before applying any machine-learning based analysis is a challenge in itself. Such a feature extraction should not only be done post mortem on log files but as close as possible to the real-time processing of network data. Such a real-time feature extraction capability would enable both, training IDS models as well as using trained models for real-time intrusion detection.

© Springer Nature Switzerland AG 2021
J. K. Liu et al. (Eds.): ISC 2021, LNCS 13118, pp. 221–237, 2021.
https://doi.org/10.1007/978-3-030-91356-4_12

1.2 Problem Statement and Contribution

A feature extractor, which generates the input values for a machine-learning algorithm from raw network data, should be able to generate these features in real-time. The generated features must be processed immediately by the selected and pre-trained machine learning model and feed the generated result back to the user.

One known openly available academic feature extractor without real-time functionality is the open source tool CICFlowMeter [5], which serves as a reference tool for the real-time feature extractor presented and discussed in this paper.

This paper provides a framework for machine learning based real-time network intrusion detection (we call it FEX). This includes both:

- the design of a performant real-time capable feature extractor; as well as
- the training and implementation of an IDS based on this extractor.

While the implementation of the IDS is intended to prove its practical suitability, the feature extractor is also intended to be able to be used for further academic purposes and is openly available on Github [11]. Due to the optimized runtime and the real-time usability, the feature extractor should open up new possibilities like the use of reinforcement learning techniques and improved support for online- instead of batch learning [16]. The four main contributions of this work are therefore:

- Based on the existing reference tool CICFlowMeter, a new "real-time" feature extractor is designed and developed, including a data flow generation algorithm and computational complexity assessment.
- To prove the correct functionality of the created feature extractor, the produced results are compared with those of the identified reference tool [5].
- Based on a widely used network intrusion dataset [10], our feature extractor is used to create a test/train dataset which is used to train and evaluate a detection model using selected machine learning techniques.
- The feature extractor and the trained model are used for the implementation of an IDS system to enable the calculation of the theoretical data throughput and assess its real-time capability.

1.3 Paper Structure

Section 2 provides a review of the current state of the art in the area of intrusion detection systems using machine learning techniques and in particular the CICFlowMeter system our work uses as a reference benchmark (Sect. 2.3). Section 3 details the architecture, discusses the algorithmic complexity and measures the implementation of our network feature extractor FEX. Section 4 provides details on a model trained for the purposes of detecting intrusions by using FEX. Section 5 demonstrates the real-time network traffic extraction capabilities of FEX combined with the trained IDS model in the context of an IDS implementation. Section 6 concludes the paper and provides a critical discussion.

2   Related Work

2.1   Network Intrusion Detection Techniques

An IDS is a type of software designed to automatically monitor and analyse events on a computer system or network to detect possible intrusions [6]. In general, intrusions can be described as events, which try to compromise certain security goals. These can be analysed on the end device itself, i.e. the host, or can be detected by analysing the network traffic. In case of a host-based IDS possible intrusions are infections through malware, the exploitation of vulnerabilities in applications or general unauthorized access to systems. Since these attacks are usually carried out by an external attacker or, as in the case of a malware infection, are likely dependent on network communication with the attacker, an analysis of the entire network traffic is favorable in order to protect many end devices simultaneously. For all IDS types, different methods of intrusion detection exist. These can be divided into the three fields of anomaly-based, signature-based and specification-based detection techniques. In the context of this paper we only focus on anomaly-based detection techniques [7] which address the properties of normal user behavior. Strong deviations from this benign behavior represent an anomaly. Over the recent years machine learning techniques have been adopted to facilitate such an analysis.

2.2   Machine Learning Based Network Intrusion Detection

Only a limited amount of work appears to address machine learning based intrusion detection focusing on real-time operation. In [1], a real-time flow-based network traffic classification system was introduced. The used reconstruction of data flows is based on the "TCP Session Reconstruct Tool", which uses the TcpRecon algorithm. Based on the reassembled data flows they extracted 14 statistical features to perform a machine learning based classification. The evaluation of this system showed an average delivery delay between 0.49 and 7.50 s. In [2], the authors presented a real-time IDS using a Decision-Tree Classifier. The performed classification is based on 12 extracted features. The authors state that the detection takes place within 2 s per record. They also claim the classification itself only takes a few milliseconds, while the rest of the computation time is needed for the performed preprocessing steps. In [3], a real-time IDS system for ultra-high-speed big data environments based on a Hadoop implementation was introduced. The authors claim that the system is highly suitable for real-time operation due to the performance of the multilayered architecture used. The work contains a benchmark to comparable systems, in which their system scored best, but no details regarding the execution time or a processable data throughput can be taken from the work. In [4], a deep learning based approach was introduced for real-time web intrusion detection. The authors also claim the system is capable of real-time predictions, but no information about the required computation time is given.

2.3   CICFlowMeter

In order to use machine learning techniques for the analysis of network data, the data must first be brought into a suitable form through the so-called feature engineering process. For this purpose, the open source network traffic flow generator and analyser CICFlowMeter [1] was developed. This tool processes network data and generates features based on the received network packets. Thereby the CICFlowMeter creates bidirectional data flows, which means that the respective direction of the packets is taken into account. A data flow thereby always describes the communication between two communication partners via the same ports and protocols (similar to the method described in Sect. 3.2). This process can be done online, by receiving network data through a network interface, as well as offline, by reading out stored data in a pcap file. After a data flow is terminated, 83 statistical features are calculated based on the collected information of the respective data flow. These features describe the properties of the data flow to such an extent that they can be used as input values for machine learning models. For example, the first six features describe the metadata of the connection in the form of IPs, ports and the time of creation of the data flow. From the perspective of the TCP/IP stack, data from the transport layer is used, so that these features can be created independently of the respective application. The termination of a data flow is determined in two ways. In the case of a TCP connection, a data flow always ends when a packet with a FIN flag is detected. However, since this option does not work for UDP packets due to the statelessness and since it may happen, for example in the case of port-scans, that a TCP connection is not terminated with a FIN flag, there is an additional timeout which ensures the termination of a data flow.

The CICFlowMeter has already been used in several projects, which prove the functionality of the tool such as classifying traffic for detection of VPN traffic [8] or traffic from the TOR network [9]. In addition, the CICIDS2017 dataset is offered, which is generated on the basis of the CICFlowMeter and of machine learning based IDS [10]. We will use this dataset for evaluating our work in the context of this paper.

While the tool is best suited for research work and the creation of datasets, it reaches its limits when the functionality of real-time operation is required. Because this tool comes in the form of a stand-alone application it is not possible to integrate it into a real time process. The function of processing network data by receiving network data via a network interface also runs in real time, but there is no possibility to process it directly afterwards. Instead the data is stored in a CSV-file and can only be further processed subsequently by an external program. Due to these limitations, the applicability of the tool is very limited. An extension of the functions of this tool to include real-time processing functionality would open up new application possibilities. In addition to real-time IDS on machine learning basis, the said functionalities would also allow the use of techniques like reinforcement learning and other time-dependent areas of application. The following section discussed the design of the new feature extractor FEX based on the CICFlowMeter to overcome the described limitations.

3   FEX - A Feature EXtractor for Machine Learning-Based IDS

As we saw in the previous section, the core functionality of the CICFlowMeter is already highly suited for generating data flow oriented features based on raw network data. However, it was also noted that this tool has major drawbacks with regard to the real-time usage. As the CICFlowGenerator is a stand-alone application it is not possible to use it directly for a real time application. Although the feature extraction can be carried out during operation, there is no possibility to analyse and process the produced features directly. To solve these problems, it would be ideal to provide this functionality in form of a library. This allows the same computations to be carried out during operation and gives the user a high degree of flexibility for the further handling of the generated data. Exactly this was done in the context of this paper by the development of FEX, which is presented in detail in the following. Though the basic structure as well as the generated features are based on the CICFlowMeter, our own packet parsers and extraction algorithms appear to be more suitable for real-time processing. FEX is openly available as a Python/Cython library [11] with an overall design goal to reduce external dependencies to a bare minimum.

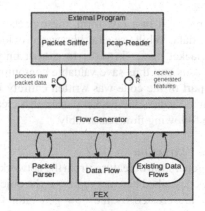

Fig. 1. FEX architecture

3.1 Architecture

The architecture of the FEX library is shown in Fig. 1 as a technical architecture model (TAM). This illustration shows how the library can be used via an external program to perform the feature extraction process. In short, the components fulfil the following function:

- From raw packet data the required information is parsed from the packet fields. The raw packet data is received by the external program.
- Individual packets are assigned to a data flow based on information about the sender and receiver.
- Each data flow contains features that describe the properties of the transported packets. These are returned to the external program as output.

3.2 Design

Packet-Sniffer/pcap-Reader

As a first step to work with network data, it must be retrieved in a proper form. This can be done either during operation by sniffing on a network interface or offline by reading in network data already stored in the form of a pcap-file. Since one of the aims of this library is to provide the most flexible handling possible, the integration of this component within the library has been omitted. The form of the input source can thus be freely determined by the user. The only prerequisites are that the network data is available in raw, unprocessed form and that a timestamp of the packet arrival is available in microseconds.

Packet Parser

Since the packets were received in a raw form, these packet values must be parsed, to access the transmitted data. Whilst several libraries provide such functionality, we implemented a custom packet parser in order to extract only the bare minimum of information from the packets and thus save valuable computing time in terms of real-time functionality. This part of the code was written entirely in Cython and compiled in C. Based on the extracted values the packet parser also creates the 5-tuple Flow-Id which is required for the following flow reassembly.

Data Flows and Feature Extraction

A central element for the generation of features from the network data is the reassembly of data flows. The data flows described here are represent the object of such a reassembled data flow. Those objects are created by the flow generator from individual network packets which have been preprocessed by the packet parser. By reconstructing the data flows from the network data, the packets are assigned to their respective connection between the communication partners involved. Based on these data flows, the actual features are generated for each data flow. The internal state of each data-flow object stores the intermediate values required, which describe the information previously exchanged. When adding further packets, these intermediate states are updated accordingly. The generated features are 79 numerical values, which are used for the later application in the machine learning task. In addition, there is the metadata of the data flow, which enables a unique tuple for addressing the data flow according to the method mentioned in Sect. 3.2.

Since a detailed explanation of the generation of the individual features with 79 values would be too extensive, these are now explained in a summarized form. Generally, the bidirectionality of the connection for all data packets is taken into account during the process of data flow generation. This means that when updating a data flow, the Flow Generator always detects whether the new packet is incoming or outgoing relative to the receiver. Due to the bidirectionality, most of the features occur for each of the two flow directions. These values include very general information describing the packet transfer, such as the duration of the data flow, the number of packets sent per direction, the size of the content of the packets per direction, and the size of the payload and header of those packets. Moreover, all set flags within a data flow are recorded and the summed individually. In addition, it is separately noted whether the PSH and URG flags were set when the connection was initialized. Information about the flags can only be retrieved in a TCP-based connection, which is why in case of an UDP connection they keep the value 0. Besides this simple information, which can be extracted directly by updating a single variable each time a packet arrives, other statistical values are also derived. For the generation of these statistical values, a statistical counter was developed, which is described separately, since special considerations were made with regard to runtime and memory complexity. This generation of values by the statistical counter was used for the following information sources:

- all incoming/outgoing packets
- time between the transmission of all packets
- time between the transmission of incoming and outgoing packets
- active time of the data flow
- idle time within the data flow
- values regarding the length of the contents of the data flow

For all these sources of information, the number of observations, the sum, the minimum, the maximum, the average, the variance and the standard deviation can be extracted by the statistical counter. It should be noted that not all possible values were extracted in every case. Here the format of the CICFlowMeter was strictly followed, so that the same features are generated.

Statistics Summary Generator
As part of the feature extraction, statistical values of certain characteristics are generated. These are updated every time a new packet is added to a data flow. Features such as the number of observations, the sum, the minimum and the maximum could be directly implemented by updating a single variable for each. To calculate the variance and standard deviation West's algorithm was used, which allows this operation in an optimised manner without caching intermediate values [12]. Therefore the operation takes place within a memory and execution complexity of $O(1)$.

Flow Generator
The central component of the architecture is the Flow Generator, as this element controls the interaction of all other components:

- Individual packets must be assigned to the corresponding data flows. If no data flow exists, a new one must be created.
- The termination of a data flow must be recognised and handled. This can be done by the FIN-flag for TCP-connections or by a timeout.
- The features are generated by a data flow as soon as it is finished. Optionally, the status of unfinished data flows can also be read out via the parameter of the output Event.

The algorithm in Fig. 2 shows how the desired tasks are solved by the Flow Generator. The function receives the already parsed packet and processes it. For the explanation of the processes, the pseudo code can be viewed in logical blocks:

Algorithm 1 FEX: Data Flow Generation Algorithm

```
 1: function ADDPACKET(packet, existingDataFlows)
 2:     flowExists ← False
 3:     features ← []
 4:     if packet.forwardId in existingDataFlows then
 5:         flowExists ← True
 6:         flowId ← packet.forwardId
 7:     else if packet.backwardId in existingDataFlows then
 8:         flowExists ← True
 9:         flowId ← packet.backwardId

10:     if flowExists then
11:         flow ← existingDataFlows[flowId]
12:         if packet.timestamp − flow.getStartTime() > timeoutThreshold  then
13:             if flow.packetCount >= minPacketsPerFlow then
14:                 features ← flow.getFeatures()
15:             existingDataFlows.pop(flowId)
16:             newFlow = new DataFlow(packet)
17:             existingDataFlows[flowId] = newFlow
18:         else if packet.finFlagIsSet then
19:             flow.addPacket(packet)
20:             if flow.packetCount >= minPacketsPerFlow then
21:                 features ← flow.getFeatures()
22:             existingDataFlows.pop(flowId)
23:         else
24:             flow.addPacket(packet)
25:             existingDataFlows[flowId] = flow
26:             if outputEvent > 0 then
27:                 if flow.packetCount >= minPacketsPerFlow then
28:                     features ← flow.getFeatures()
29:     else
30:         flow = new DataFlow(packet)
31:         existingDataFlows[flowId] = flow
    return features
```

Fig. 2. Data flow generation algorithm

- After the initial initialisation of the variable (line 2–3), a check is first made to see whether the packet to be processed can be assigned to an existing data flow (line 4–9). Since these are bidirectional data flows, the 5-tuple of the data Flow-id is checked for both the incoming and outgoing direction.
- Lines 10–17 handle the case in which the appropriate data flow exists and a timeout was triggered by exceeding the given threshold. The features are therefore generated for the previous state of the data flow. This data flow is then deleted and a new data flow is initialized with the current packet.
- Lines 18–22 describe the case in which an existing data flow is terminated by receiving a FIN-flag. The data flow is updated a last time and the features are generated afterwards.

- Lines 23–28 cover the case in which a data flow exists but is not terminated. Optionally it is possible to receive features of an intermediate stage by specifying the outputEvent.
- Finally, lines 29–31 deal with the case where no existing data flow exists and a new data flow is added to the set of existing data flows.
- At the end of the algorithm the array of features is always returned.

3.3 Evaluation

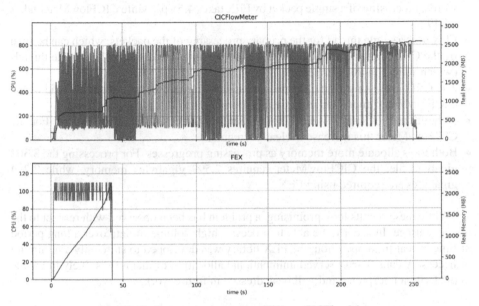

Fig. 3. Performance comparison FEX vs. CICFlowMeter

A critical aspect of the development, which also served as motivation for the development of the FEX library, is the runtime performance. In this step, this performance of the feature extraction process was measured in terms of runtime, CPU usage and memory usage for the FEX library and the CICFlowMeter respectively (Quad Core Intel i5-8250U 8 Threads 64 bit @3,4 GHz, 24 GB RAM). In this test setup, both tools were used in offline mode to process an identical pcap file. Since for the later machine learning process (Sect. 4) it is necessary to create training data anyway, this comparison is carried out directly on the basis of the dataset which will be used in that step. This dataset consists of five individual files, each of which describes the network data of a weekday on which attacks were carried out within the test network.

More details on this dataset are presented in Sect. 4.1. Since the CICFlowMeter tool is only able to process a single file at a time, the decision was made to perform this test only on one of the five pcap-files. Here the file was used which contains the data from Thursday 06.07.2017. This file has a size of about 8.302 gigabytes and contains about 9.322 million individual network packets. The processing by both tools took place successively, whereby the tool psrecord was used in parallel to record CPU and memory usage in intervals of 100 μs. The recorded data are visualized in Fig. 3.

Based on the test experiment presented, the following observations are made:

- By using the FEX library the file could be processed within 42.7 s. CICFlowMeter needed 256.3 s and thus six times longer.
- Based on the time measurement and the given number of 9.322 million packets it can be calculated that on average the FEX library is able to process 218,313 packets per second, while the CICFlowMeter can only process 36,371 packets/sec. In other words, processing of a single packet by FEX takes 4.58 μs while CICFlowMeter takes 27.49 μs.
- FEX uses a single thread for the primary processing of the packets, which can be seen by the CPU usage. The CICFlowMeter, on the other hand, uses all available threads (which were 8 in this test setup).
- The CPU load using FEX is almost constantly the same, while the CPU load of the CICFlowMeter fluctuates strongly and even drops to 0% in the meantime.
- In both cases, it can be seen that the memory increases over the runtime. For the CICFlowMeter this increase is clearly irregular.
- Both tools allocate more memory as processing progresses. For processing the 8.302 gigabyte file, the CICFlowMeter requires 2.599 gigabytes memory, while 2.284 gigabytes are required using FEX.

While these results look promising, a problem has been observed with respect to the memory usage. In order to be able to process a high volume of data over a long period of time in real-time operation, the FEX library was developed to store only a minimum of necessary data. The observed unintentional allocation of memory is likely to be due to the Python interpreter and will be addressed in future work.

4   Training a Model for Real-Time Intrusion Detection

This section now details the use of standard machine learning techniques to generate a model for the detection of intrusions, based on features extracted by the FEX library. As a first step, the used training dataset and the performed labelling of the attacks within this dataset are described. Subsequently, the required preprocessing steps and sampling methods are presented. For the training process itself, it was first considered which library would be particularly suitable for real-time application. The machine learning libraries used for this purpose are presented in Sect. 4.3. Using those selected libraries, a comparison of different machine learning models was then carried out. The selected models were examined regarding the quality of their results as well as their prediction time to find a model suitable for real-time applications. For the selected model, a more detailed evaluation of the results is performed. Results are compared with an identical model produced with pre-processed data from the CICFlowMeter context [5].

4.1 Training Data and Labelling

The Intrusion Detection Evaluation Dataset (CICIDS2017) dataset was chosen, which is available at the CIC [10]. This dataset contains recorded network data of a test environment, which consists of a victim network and an attacker network. Over a period of 5 days, various attacks were carried out, which are shown in Table 1. The used dataset is offered both in the raw form of 51.1 gigabytes of raw network data in form of a pcap-file, as well as in an already processed form in the CSV format. Since the specially created feature extractor is used in this step, the raw network data is used for the following feature extraction process. Besides the new generated dataset, the offered pre-processed version of the data processed by the CICFlowMeter will be used in Sect. 4.5, where the results of the models created will be compared on the basis of the two feature extractors.

We label the created dataset using metadata that describes aspects of the various attack scenarios performed, such as the machines involved (the IP of the attacker and the target), the time period of the performed attack, the target port of the attack, and the type of attack [10]. The labelling carried out on the basis of time periods and attack types is also in Table 1. This table also shows how many entries of each attack class are contained in the created dataset and in the dataset provided by CIC. The entries per class were counted in this step to check the correctness of the labelling process. As it can be seen from Table 1, there are only minimal differences in a few cases. Through the shown labelling 13 different classes of attacks were created, which are grouped as presented in [13]. The results of this process are shown in Table 1.

Table 1. Aggregated training data and labelling

New Label	Old Label	Date	Time (UTC)	# CICFlowMeter	# FEX
Benign	Benign	-	-	2,273,097	2,271,881
Brute Force	FTP-Patator	2017-07-04	12:19 - 13:20	7,938	7,937
	SSH-Patator	2017-07-04	17:09 - 19:04	5,897	5,898
DoS	DoS - Slowloris	2017-07-05	12:47 - 13:10	5,796	5,790
	DoS - SlowHttpTest	2017-07-05	13:14 - 13:35	5,499	5,499
	DoS - Hulk	2017-07-05	13:43 - 14:07	231,073	231,052
	DDoS LOIT	2017-07-07	18:56 - 19:17	128,027	128,024
	DoS - GoldenEye	2017-07-05	15:10 - 15:23	10,293	10,293
Web Attack	Web Attack - Brute Force	2017-07-06	12:15 - 13:01	1,507	1,507
	Web Attack - XSS	2017-07-06	13:14 - 13:36	652	652
	Web Attack - Sqli	2017-07-06	13:39 - 13:43	21	21
Bot	Botnet ARES	2017-07-07	12:33 - 16:00	1,966	1,962
Port Scan	Port Scan	2017-07-07	16:06 - 18:24	158,930	158,963

4.2 Sampling

As the classes of the dataset used are highly imbalanced. This is also one of the shortcomings of the used dataset which is described in [13] in more detail. Here it is argued that this imbalance results in a lower accuracy and a high false positive rate. To correct the imbalance, a hybrid-resampling approach is chosen, in which first a partial undersampling and then an oversampling of the remaining classes is performed. In the step of under-sampling the strongly overrepresented classes Benign and DoS are reduced to the size of the DoS class by randomly drawing samples. An oversampling is performed with the remaining classes, so that all classes now contain a size of about 122,000 entries. It is important to note that this process only refers to the training data. The separately generated test dataset remained untouched, since carrying out this process on the test dataset would strongly distort the produced result.

4.3 Library Selection

Since in this work special emphasis was placed on the time of execution, an attempt was made to find suitable libraries for this purpose. We therefore compare the results of the commonly used *scikit − learn* library [14], as well as the lesser known *creme* library [15]. We made this selection because *scikit − learn* performs predictions in batches and *creme* is an online machine learning library. In this context, we want to compare the execution times of both concepts.

Table 2. Model evaluation results

Library	Model	Multi Class	Scaling	Average prediction time	Weighted F1-Score
scikit-learn	LogisticRegression	OvR	standardisation	84μs, 379ns	0.91614
creme	LogisticRegression	OvR	standardisation	214μs 362ns	0.85686
scikit-learn	**DecisionTreeClassifier**	**inherent**	-	**49μs, 605ns**	**0.99848**
creme	DecisionTreeClassifier	inherent	-	10μs, 786ns	0.88620
scikit-learn	PassiveAggressiveClassifier	OvO	standardisation	85μs, 283ns	0.91150
creme	PassiveAggressiveClassifier	OvR	standardisation	211μs, 287ns	0.85926

4.4 Model Selection

Based on the selected libraries, different models were tested for each of the two libraries. Due to the intended real-time application, we take the execution time as well as the quality of our prediction into account. For the selection of suitable models, a benchmark of the *creme* library [15] was considered, in which the execution time of a binary classifier was compared. Since we perform a multi-class-classification, the weighted F1-Score was used to measure the quality of the generated result based on the untouched test dataset. After the training step of the individual models, individual classifications were carried out on the basis of the test dataset, which simulate real-time operation. For this purpose, the required prediction time was measured in nanoseconds. This time measurement, as well as the other results and information on how to carry out the comparison are shown in Table 2. The following observations can be made based on the performed model comparison:

- The average prediction time of the *creme* library's Decision-Tree Classifier is the fastest model at around eleven microseconds and almost five times faster than the second fastest model.
- However, the weighted F1-Score of this fastest model is rather low at 0.88620, which is why this model is almost unusable for the use in an IDS.

- The second fastest model, the Decision-Tree Classifier of the *scikit − learn* library, requires on average about 50 μs for a prediction and shows the best results with a weighted F1-Score of 0.99848.
- A comparison of the weighted F1-Scores between the two libraries shows that the *creme* library performed worse in all cases. This may suggest that the models of this library are not well suited for use in multi-class classification.
- Compared to the benchmark used for model selection [15], the models of the *creme* library perform much slower in this test. A closer look at the implementation of the benchmark showed that the measurement of scaling was not included in the times indicated.
- Besides the scaling, the handling of multi-class classification also seems to play a role in the execution time. The models that provide an inherent multiclass-classification showed the fastest execution times. The OvR or OvO methods require additional computational time.

Despite the worse execution time, the Decision-Tree-Classifier model of the *scikit − learn* library is used in the following as it produces the best results. The computation time a prediction was further optimised by translating the model into C-Code using the *m2gen* library [17]. This C-Code was made accessible under Python using a Cython wrapper. Through this optimisation the duration of a single prediction was further reduced to 3.96 μs on average.

4.5 Evaluation

In the previous model selection, the weighted F1-Score of the selected model was already considered. In this section, a more in-depth evaluation of the model is carried out, which allows further evaluation of the selected models performance as well as comparison to CICFlowMeter.

Confusion Matrix
We evaluate the performance of the model by creating a creating a confusion matrix (Fig. 4) based on untouched test data. As can be observed from the diagonal of the matrix, almost all actual attacks were correctly classified. However notable false-positive misclassifications are present for the Bot and Web Attack fields. We suspect this is due to the small sample size of those classes (see Table 2) and our resampling process.

Comparison with CICFlowMeter
Our evaluation has shown that the produced results based on the data of the FEX library are fairly suitable for an intrusion detection. At this point it is examined whether the results are comparable to those that can be produced by the reference tool [5]. We repeated the machine learning process with the provided training data of the CIC [10] to compare the quality of both feature extractors based on individually trained models. The previously presented training procedure was therefore repeated with the same steps. Since this also includes the process of random sampling and the train-test-split, a certain degree of randomness flows into the results.

Table 3 shows the weighted F1-Score for the models used with both feature extractors, from which we can conclude that both tools perform at least comparably well.

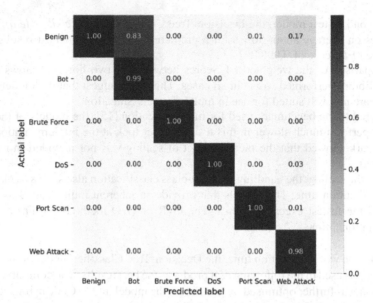

Fig. 4. Normalised confusion matrix

Table 3. Comparison FEX vs. CICFlowMeter

Library	Model	FEX	CICFlowMeter
scikit-learn	LogisticRegression	**0.91614**	0.86402
creme	LogisticRegression	**0.85686**	0.83674
scikit-learn	DecisionTreeClassifier	0.99848	**0.99853**
creme	DecisionTreeClassifier	0.88620	**0.89116**
scikit-learn	PassiveAggressiveClassifier	**0.91150**	0.89103
creme	PassiveAggressiveClassifier	**0.85926**	0.84007

5   Towards a Machine Learning Based Real-Time IDS

We now combine our FEX feature extraction framework with the trained intrusion detection model in order to implement an intrusion detection system that uses real-time traffic. The details of the implementation are provided in [11] and we only report on the test that were carried out and the calculated theoretical throughput of our system.

In order to measure the actual data throughput of the IDS, it is not directly possible to add up the required time periods for processing of packets, feature generation and classification, since each packet is processed by the feature generator, but the classification only takes place at a corresponding end of a data flow. This is also the reason why this measurement of the duration was not carried out directly, but on the basis of two partial measurements. In order to calculate a theoretical data throughput, two possible scenarios are considered. In the first scenario, it is assumed that a classification necessarily takes place after each packet. From a runtime point of view, this scenario represents the worst-case scenario and the absolute minimum data throughput that can be processed with certainty. In a second scenario we try to measure a more realistic behaviour. Within the entire dataset used for the training and evaluation process, it is checked how many packets a dataset consists of on average. To calculate not only the number of packets per second, but also the data throughput, the size of a single packet is considered. Based on the characteristics of the IPv4 and Ethernet v2 protocols we assume a minimum packet size of 68 bytes and a maximum size of 1500 bytes for the following calculations.

In the worst case, we conclude that after each packet has arrived, in addition to the feature extraction a classification is performed. In this worst case, depending on the packet sizes, a data throughput between 63.7 Mbit/s and 1.405 Gbit/s can be processed.

In the realistic case it is assumed that a classification does not necessarily take place after each packet. This case corresponds to the typical use case in which a classification is only made after the completion of a data flow. Since it is not known how many packets a data flow is composed of in real operation, the frequency from the dataset (Sect. 4) is used. The dataset consists of a total of 54.319 million packets, which form 2,829,500 data flows. The result for this realistic scenario is that a data throughput between 113.427 Mbit/s and 2.502 Gbit/s can be processed.

The calculated data throughput is thereby based on the average total processing time per packet and the assumed minimum and maximum sizes of each packet. For the worst-case calculation, the total processing time of 8.54 μs result the feature extraction duration of 4.58 μs and the optimised classification duration of 3.96 μs. For the realistic scenario the classification duration was divided by the frequency of packets per data flow, since it was assumed that the classification takes place after a data flow is terminated, resulting in an average computation time of 4.8 μs.

6 Conclusion

Existing work in the field of machine learning based real-time IDS systems does not adequately address the aspect of time sensitiveness. In [1] and [2] real-time IDS were presented, which took into account the exact duration of data processing, but which were rather slow. In [3, 4] it was further noticed that although a real-time capable architecture was utilized, it is unclear whether this provides the necessary performance to be relevant for real-time operation. In order to solve the identified problem regarding the applicability for a real-time analysis, appropriate methods were presented in this paper to provide such a solution. This includes the creation of a high performance network feature extractor (FEX), which is specially designed for real-time operation. In [2] it was described that this process represents the bottleneck of their architecture, requiring about two seconds computation time. This bottleneck could be avoided in our work by using the performance advantages of a Cython implementation. Despite the larger amount of 83 statistical features in the approach presented, the feature generation process requires only 4.58 μs per packet. Furthermore, it was shown how the data generated by the feature generator can be used to create a suitable machine learning model, producing sufficiently good results. By translating the model into pure C-code, it was shown how the performance could be increased remarkably by a factor of 12.63, which is why it is particularly suitable for real-time operation. Such an optimisation method could not be found in any related

A.

Schaad and D. Binder

work in this area. As a result of these two optimised processes, it was shown how a high-performance, yet very simple IDS was implemented. To underline the performance, a comparison of the computing time with [1] was made, which required between 0.49 and 7.50 s per packet on average. In our work, a similar process requires only between 4.8 and 8.54 μs. The suitability for real-time analysis can therefore be assumed without any doubt. The objective of creating a real-time capable IDS is therefore fulfilled. Among the available feature generators, no comparable alternative with a focus on real-time processing could be found. The created FEX library is available as an open source library [11].

References

1. Santiago, S., Castro e Silva, J., Maia, J.: NTCS: a real time flow-based network traffic classification system. In: Proceedings of the 10th International Conference on Network and Service Management, CNSM 2014, pp. 368–371 (2015)
2. Sangkatsanee, P., Wattanapongsakorn, N., Charnsripinyo, C.: Practical real-time intrusion detection using machine learning approaches. Comput. Commun. **34**, 2227–2235 (2011). https://doi.org/10.1016/j.comcom.2011.07.001
3. Rathore, M.M., Ahmad, A., Paul, A.: Real time intrusion detection system for ultra-high-speed big data environments. J. Supercomput. **72**(9), 3489–3510 (2016). https://doi.org/10.1007/s11227-015-1615-5
4. Kim, A., Park, M., Lee, D.H.: AI-IDS: application of deep learning to real-time web intrusion detection. IEEE Access **8**, 70245–70261 (2020)
5. Canadian Institute for Cybersecurity: Canadian Institute for Cybersecurity - Applications - CICFlowMeter (formerly ISCXFlowMeter). https://www.unb.ca/cic/research/applications.html
6. Mitchell, R., Chen, I.-R.: A survey of intrusion detection in wireless network applications. Comput. Commun. **42**, 1–23 (2014)
7. Bhuyan, M.H., Bhattacharyya, D.K., Kalita, J.K.: Network traffic anomaly detection techniques and systems. In: Network Traffic Anomaly Detection and Prevention. CCN, pp. 115–169. Springer, Cham (2017). https://doi.org/10.1007/978-3-319-65188-0_4
8. Lashkari, A.H., Gil, G.D., Mamun, M.S.I., Ghorbani, A.A.: Characterization of encrypted and VPN traffic using time-related features. In: Proceedings of the 2nd International Conference on Information Systems Security and Privacy - Volume 1: INSTICC, pp. 407–414. SciTePress (2016)
9. Lashkari, A.H., Gil, G.D., Mamun, M.S.I., Ghorbani, A.A.: Characterization of TOR traffic using time based features. In: Proceedings of the 3rd International Conference on Information Systems Security and Privacy - Volume 1 INSTICC, pp. 253–262. SciTePress (2017)
10. Canadian Institute for Cybersecurity: Intrusion Detection Evaluation Dataset (CICIDS2017). https://www.unb.ca/cic/datasets/ids-2017.html
11. https://github.com/dobinder/FEX
12. West, D.H.D.: Updating mean and variance estimates: an improved method. Commun. ACM **22**(9), 532–535 (1979)
13. Panigrahi, I.R., Borah, S.: A detailed analysis of cicids2017 dataset for designing intrusion detection systems. J. Eng. Technol. **7**, 479–482 (2018)
14. Pedregosa, F., et al.: Scikit-learn: machine learning in python. J. Mach. Learn. Res. **12**, 2825–2830 (2011)
15. Halford, M.: Creme - online machine learning in python. https://github.com/creme-ml/creme.

16. Geron, A.: Hands-on Machine Learning with Scikit-Learn, Keras, and TensorFlow: Concepts, Tools, and Techniques to Build Intelligent Systems, 2nd edn. O'Reilly UK Ltd, Newton
17. https://github.com/BayesWitnesses/m2cgen/

Identifying Malicious DNS Tunnel Tools from DoH Traffic Using Hierarchical Machine Learning Classification

Rikima Mitsuhashi[1,2]([envelope]), Akihiro Satoh[3], Yong Jin[4], Katsuyoshi Iida[2], Takahiro Shinagawa[1], and Yoshiaki Takai[2]

[1] The University of Tokyo, Tokyo, Japan
mitsuhashi@os.ecc.u-tokyo.ac.jp, shina@ecc.u-tokyo.ac.jp
[2] Hokkaido University, Hokkaido, Japan
{iida,ytakai}@iic.hokudai.ac.jp
[3] Kyushu Institute of Technology, Fukuoka, Japan
satoh@isc.kyutech.ac.jp
[4] Tokyo Institute of Technology, Tokyo, Japan
yongj@gsic.titech.ac.jp

Abstract. Although the DNS over HTTPS (DoH) protocol has desirable properties for Internet users such as privacy and security, it also causes a problem in that network administrators are prevented from detecting suspicious network traffic generated by malware and malicious tools. To support their efforts in maintaining network security, in this paper, we propose a novel system that identifies malicious DNS tunnel tools through a hierarchical classification method that uses machine-learning technology on DoH traffic. We implemented a prototype of the proposed system and evaluated its performance on the CIRA-CIC-DoHBrw-2020 dataset, obtaining 99.81% accuracy in DoH traffic filtering, 99.99% accuracy in suspicious DoH traffic detection, and 97.22% accuracy in identification of malicious DNS tunnel tools.

Keywords: DNS over HTTPS (DoH) · Network traffic classification · Suspicious DoH traffic · DNS tunnel · Malicious DNS tunnel tool identification

1 Introduction

There is growing momentum to encrypt DNS traffic on the Internet for privacy and security concerns. A promising method to encrypt DNS traffic is DNS over HTTPS (DoH), which uses SSL/TLS protocols for encryption and has been standardized in RFC8484 [5]. DoH has already been implemented in the latest versions of major web browsers, such as Firefox and Google Chrome. In a client system, DoH can be used by installing proxy software such as cloudflared [4], doh-proxy [10], dnscrypt-proxy [8] and doh-client [9] for all DNS domain name

© Springer Nature Switzerland AG 2021
J. K. Liu et al. (Eds.): ISC 2021, LNCS 13118, pp. 238–256, 2021.
https://doi.org/10.1007/978-3-030-91356-4_13

resolutions. For OS support, DoH is available in the insider preview build provided by the Windows Insider Program [15,16]. The structure of domain name resolution using DoH is depicted in Fig. 1. DoH encrypts DNS traffic by using the HTTPS protocol between the client and the DoH server that works as a DNS full-service resolver, and the DoH server uses the conventional DNS protocol with authoritative DNS servers on the Internet for domain name resolutions.

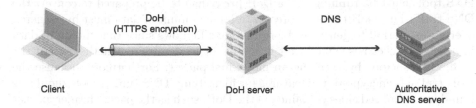

Fig. 1. Domain name resolution using DoH.

By encrypting DNS traffic using DoH technology, Internet users no longer have to worry about privacy violations where someone can eavesdrop on domain name resolutions when they visit websites, and the risk is reduced of their being directed to an unintended website due to tampering by DNS cache poisoning attacks [33]. On the other hand, DoH technology has a problem in that it prevents network administrators from monitoring network traffic for providing network security services. When malware communicates with a command and control (C&C) server on the Internet by using DoH technology, the network administrators cannot detect the communication even if they are monitoring the entire network. The existence of malware that uses DoH to communicate with C&C servers has been confirmed [11]. Many large-scale malware attacks have also been reported [18] and cyber-attacks will not stop on their own. Therefore, the fact that network traffic cannot be monitored because of encryption is a critical issue for network administrators. To deal with this problem, a DoH server could be set up in an organization's network. The network administrator can monitor the DNS traffic as usual since the DNS traffic between the DoH server and the authoritative DNS server uses the conventional DNS protocol without encryption. However, if the clients do not use that DoH server and instead use public DoH servers provided by Internet service providers such as Google and Cloudflare, again the network administrators cannot monitor the DNS traffic.

To determine proper network security solutions, network administrators need to identify the original application programs that generate the malicious DoH traffic, such as malicious DNS tunnel tools. Consequently, it is possible to block traffic to the external websites to which the compromised internal computers access and download the DNS tunnel tools and create rules that prohibit the use of DNS tunnel tools or identify clients in which the DNS tunnel tools are used. In the literature, several approaches have been proposed to detect malicious DoH traffic [29,34]. However, the authors only proposed methods for detecting malicious DoH traffic; their methods cannot identify the programs that generated the traffic. Therefore, network administrators cannot block the particular problematic traffic generated by compromised computers or stop the spread of vulnerabilities within their organization's network.

Machine-learning technology is a useful way to identify DNS tunnel tools, because it can automatically classify DoH traffic according to its characteristics. However, when the technology is learning the features of DNS tunnel tools, the DNS tools must be running and a DoH proxy has to be prepared to convert the DNS traffic into DoH traffic. Moreover, a large amount of data must be gathered over a long period to generate the training traffic flows since the amount of data in a single packet is so small that it is difficult to determine whether or not the traffic is malicious by verifying an individual packet. Furthermore, because the DoH traffic is encrypted, the features for identifying DNS tunnel tools should be found in the limited clues contained in the DoH, such as the packet header, packet number, packet length, packet direction, and arrival interval between packets. Thus, using machine-learning technology to identify DNS tunnel tools takes time and effort. However, once the machine-learning model has been trained and is up and running, it can analyze DoH traffic automatically.

In this paper, we propose a novel system that uses machine-learning technology on DoH traffic to identify malicious DNS tunnel tools that generate encrypted DNS traffic. As shown in Fig. 2, we use a hierarchical network traffic classification. The unique process in the proposed system is the 3rd stage, which is the identification of malicious DNS tunnel tools. We have made parameter-tuned models suitable for each stage of the classification, which enable us to identify DNS tunnel tools with more accuracy.

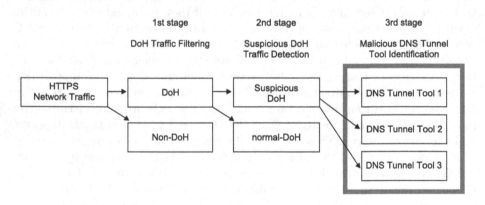

Fig. 2. Concept of hierarchical network traffic classification.

We evaluated the proposed system on the CIRA-CIC-DoHBrw-2020 dataset [3] and found that the DoH traffic filtering had an accuracy and F-score of 99.81% and 99.87%. As far as we know, this F-score is higher than any of the previously reported ones. Regarding detection of suspicious DoH traffic, the accuracy and F-score were 99.99% and 99.99%, respectively. The accuracy of identifying malicious DNS tunnel tools was 97.22% and the F-score was 95.19%. To the best of our knowledge, this is the first report to show the possibility of identifying malicious DNS tunnel tools from an analysis of DoH traffic.

Our contributions are as follows.

- We propose a novel system that uses machine-learning technology on DoH traffic to identify malicious DNS tunnel tools through a hierarchical classification method.
- We show that the proposed system can identify malicious DNS tunnel tools with enough accuracy that it can support security maintenance efforts by network administrators.
- Experiments conducted on the CIC-DoHBrw-2020 dataset indicate that the proposed system can distinguish DoH traffic from other HTTPS traffic more accurately than the previous methods can.

The rest of this paper is organized as follows. Section 2 presents related work on network traffic classification. Section 3 describes the proposed system design of hierarchical network traffic classification. Section 4 shows the experimental evaluation. Section 5 concludes the paper.

2   Related Work

2.1   Network Traffic Classification

Network traffic classification is a very active research area. In particular, a number of approaches to network traffic classification using machine-learning technology have been proposed [30]. As well, there are many reports on classification of encrypted network traffic [19]. However, since DoH technology has a short history and is still in the process of deployment as a practical application, few research reports on DoH traffic classification are included in the survey papers.

Looking at the recently reported research on DoH network classification, D. Vekshin et al. [36] identified DoH network traffic by classifying HTTPS traffic by using machine learning. They also identified DoH clients such as Chrome, Firefox, and Cloudflare by classifying DoH traffic. For both classifications, they used the Ada-boosted decision tree model and obtained a classification accuracy of 99.9%. The dataset they used was the access data to the domain names taken from the top one million websites provided by Alexa [1]. M. MontazeriShatoori et al. [29] used machine-learning technology to classify HTTPS and DoH traffic, then benign and malicious DoH traffic. Both classifications used the random forest model; the former yielded a 99.3% F-score and the latter a 99.9% F-score. They used the CIRA-CIC-DoHBrw-2020 dataset for the evaluation. S. K. Singh et al. [34] improved the accuracy of classifying benign and malicious DoH traffic on the CIRA-CIC-DoHBrw-2020 dataset. They used the gradient boost model and obtained 100% classification accuracy with the holdout method.

2.2 DNS Tunnel Detection

Many studies have been reported on attack methods and countermeasures against DNS [20, 24–26], and the research field of DNS tunnel detection has received particular attention recently. Because domain name resolution based on DNS is one of the most basic and indispensable services on the Internet, attackers exploit the characteristics of DNS to build tunnels. A DNS tunnel is a common technique attackers use to establish C&C nodes and to exfiltrate data from networks [21].

Regarding recent reports on DNS tunnel detection, P. Yang et al. [38] tried to detect DNS covert channels by using a stacking model. The DNS traffic was generated by the collection of tools, including dns2tcp, dnscat2, DeNiSe and Heyoka. They used a stacking model that is an ensemble of three different algorithms (K-nearest neighbors (KNN), support vector machine (SVM) and random forest). A. L. Buczak et al. [21] also detected DNS tunnels by analyzing network traffic. They extracted features from a penetration testing effort and trained random forest classifiers to distinguish normal DNS activity from DNS tunneling activity. D. Lambion et al. [28] detected malicious DNS tunnels by using a convolutional neural network (CNN), random forest, and ensemble classifiers for DNS traffic. They assessed the classifiers' performance and robustness by exposing them to one day of real-traffic data. Y. Chen et al. [22] proposed a framework for DNS tunnel detection using long short-term memory (LSTM), gated recurrent unit (GRU) and CNN. A. Chowdhary et al. [23] presented two methods for detecting DNS tunneling queries. The first method uses cache misses in a DNS full-service resolver and the second method utilizes machine-learning technology to classify a given DNS query. K. Wu et al. [37] introduced a three-stage DNS tunnel detection method based on a character feature extraction, called FTPB, which uses feature extraction to filter out the domain names resolved by the DNS tunnels.

In summary, no studies on either network traffic classification or DNS tunnel detection have reported on DoH traffic classification for identifying malicious DNS tunnel tools. In contrast, in experiments conducted on the CIRA-CIC-DoHBrw-2020 dataset, we have achieved the same or better accuracy than those of previous methods of classification in the 1st and 2nd stage. In addition, we also implemented DNS tunnel tool identification in the 3rd stage.

3   Design

In Sect. 2, we introduced some related work regarding the network traffic classification and investigated the methods of DNS tunnels detection. For network administrators to maintain network security, they need to identify any malicious tools communicating in the DoH traffic. In this section, we describe the design of our system.

3.1   System Overview

To be able to identify the malicious tools used in the DoH communication, it
is necessary to analyze the characteristics of network traffic. We introduce a
hierarchical classification method to identify malicious tools. The key idea is to
determine the best machine-learning model for each stage of the traffic classification. As shown in Fig. 3, the traffic data classification consists of three blocks: 1)
DoH traffic filtering, 2) suspicious DoH traffic detection, and 3) malicious DNS
tunnel tool identification. In the following subsections, we explain the details of
each block.

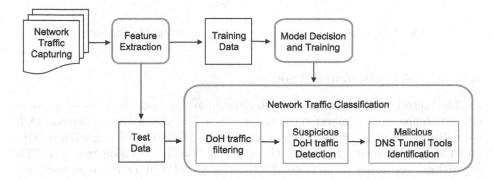

Fig. 3. Overview of proposed system to identify malicious DNS tunnel tools.

3.2   Capturing and Extracting the Features of Network Traffic

As DoH encrypts DNS traffic by using the SSL/TLS protocol, the proposed system takes HTTPS traffic as input data. Although there are likely many different
types of traffic in a network, we can determine if the traffic is generated by
HTTPS from the source or destination port number of the packet. The HTTPS
traffic generated when the client connects to the web server or DoH server is
collected at the capture points shown in Fig. 4. The purpose of the client's connection to the web server is to retrieve web content. The client connects to the
normal DoH server to resolve domain names, but the malicious DNS tunnel
tools on the client might connect with a suspicious DNS server to receive attack
instructions or send sensitive information.

To classify the acquired network traffic with machine-learning models, statistical features are extracted from HTTPS traffic of two-way communications.
Each traffic is determined by the source IP address, destination IP address,
source port number, and destination port number. This information is included
in the header of the packet and can be used because it is not encrypted. Statistical features of the traffic are extracted using a series of packets, e.g., number
of packets, packet direction, packet arrival time, and packet length, etc. The
payload of packets in the HTTPS traffic is encrypted, but these external characteristics can be ascertained.

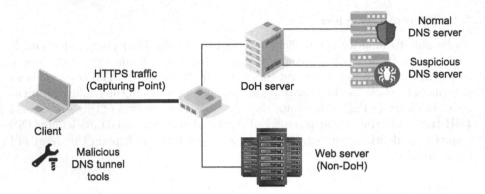

Fig. 4. Network connections and capture point of HTTPS traffic.

3.3   Model Decision and Training

In this subsection, we describe how to determine the model to be used at each stage to implement a hierarchical classification for identifying malicious DNS tunnel tools. In the proposed system, we use the XGBoost [35], LightGBM [27], and CatBoost [31] libraries using the gradient boosting decision tree (GBDT) algorithm. According to S. R et al. [32], these GBDT libraries have substantial flexibility and considerably faster training times compared to other machine learning algorithms at present. They also describe these libraries are widely used in competitive machine learning contests like Kaggle [13] because of their expected high classification accuracy. Generally, boosting is a general ensemble technique that produces a strong classifier from a large number of weak classifiers. As for GBDT, the learning process is as follows. First, a very simple tree that predicts a single number is used. Next, the residual error (observed - predicted) of the tree is calculated. Then, the next decision tree is added to reduce the residual error. If there is still a significant amount of error remaining, another decision tree is added to decrease the error. By repeating this process, a strong classifier is produced.

In addition to the use of high-performance machine-learning libraries, parameter tuning suitable for the dataset is also important to obtain high classification accuracy. We present a method to determine a suitable machine-learning model for traffic classification in Fig. 5. We first train the training data against the parameter-tuned model. Next, we use the trained models to classify the validation data. By comparing the accuracy obtained from the classification of the validation data, we can determine the best parameter-tuned model for the dataset. The determined model is then trained again on the training and validation data and used as a classifier for the test data. This process is carried out in each of the three stages, resulting in the determination of three classifiers. Here we note the problem of overfitting. Overfitting means that a machine-learning model which is closely related to a particular dataset cannot accurately classify additional data. If the parameter tuning overfits the model to the validation data, the model does not classify the test data with sufficient accuracy. Therefore, the results of parameter tuning need to be analyzed by using not only the classification results of the validation data, but also those of the test data.

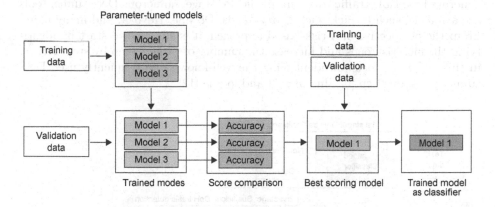

Fig. 5. Model decision process of network traffic classification.

Table 1 shows the parameters used for tuning each model. The parameters are described in the documentation of each model [2,14,17] as being effective in improving classification accuracy. We create specific parameter values by spreading out from the default values in a certain range. We then use a grid search to find the combination that classifies the validation data with the highest accuracy. Here, XGBoost has 35 models, LightGBM has 56 models, and CatBoost has 48 models, so a total of 139 different models are available.

Table 1. Parameters of grid search (underline indicates default parameters).

XGBoost	LightGBM	CatBoost
max_depth: 2, 4, 6, 8, 10, 12, 14	num_leaves: 7, 15, 31, 63, 127, 255, 511	max_depth: 2, 4, 6, 8, 10, 12, 14, 16
max_bin: 128, 256, 512, 1024, 2048	max_bin: 127, 255, 511, 1023, 2047, 4095, 8191, 16383	l2_leaf_reg: 1, 2, 3, 4, 5, 6

3.4 Network Traffic Classification

In order to make it possible to identify malicious tools used in DoH communications, the proposed system classifies network traffic in three stages. Analyzing the network traffic in detail at each stage enhances the possibility of achieving classification with better accuracy. The classifier to be used in each stage is the one determined by the system in Sect. 3.3. Figure 6 shows a diagram of the classification, in which the 1st stage classifies the HTTPS traffic data into DoH and non-DoH; the 2nd stage classifies the DoH traffic into normal DoH and suspicious DoH; and the 3rd stage identifies the suspicious DNS tunnel tools that generated the DoH traffic. In terms of the 3rd stage, numerous DNS tunnel tools are available, such as pick pocket, ozymands, DeNiSe, Heyoka, and many more. From the perspective of a risk-based approach, it is effective to start by identifying the high-risk ones and increase the number of targets step by step. Hence, in this paper, we focus on identifying the well-known and frequently used DNS tunnel tools: dns2tcp [6], dnscat2 [7] and iodine [12].

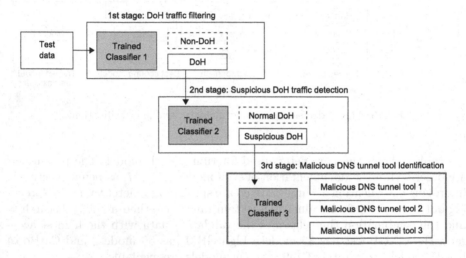

Fig. 6. Hierarchical classification to identify malicious DNS tunnel tools.

4   Evaluation

In Sect. 3, we presented the overall picture of the proposed system, explained how to determine the machine-learning model to be used in the hierarchical classification, and described the classification targets at each stage. In this section, we evaluated the classification performance of an implementation of the proposed system and analyzed the important features.

4.1   Implementation

On the basis of the design proposed in Sect. 3, we implemented the proposed system as follows. In terms of the hardware environment, we used a machine with an Intel Xeon Silver 4210R CPU, 96-GiB memory and Nvidia GeForce RTX 3080 GPU. The software environments were Ubuntu 20.04 with singularity 3.7.3 and Nvidia TensorFlow Release21.02 Container. The machine-learning libraries that we ran and parameter-tuned were XGBoost 1.3.3, LightGBM 3.2.1, and CatBoost 0.25.1. Note that XGBoost and CatBoost were run on the GPU, while LightGBM was run on the CPU.

4.2 Dataset

The experimental evaluations used the CIRA-CIC-DoHBrw-2020 dataset. The number of labels and traffic included in this dataset is shown in Table 2. Since the dataset has a bias in the amount of traffic in each stage, it is important to understand not only the results of the overall classification but also the results of the classifications with a small amount of traffic. We extract 28 statistical traffic features from the dataset as shown in Table 3. We use all the statistical traffic features in each of the three stages.

Table 2. Labels and amount of traffic in the dataset.

	Labels	Traffic
1st stage (HTTPS)	Non-DoH traffic	897494
	DoH traffic	269643
2nd stage (DoH)	Normal DoH traffic	19807
	Suspicious DoH traffic	249836
3rd stage (Malicious DNS tunnel tool)	dns2tcp	167486
	dnscat2	35770
	iodine	46580

We used stratified 10-fold cross-validation to classify the network traffic of the dataset; thus, in each test evaluation, the training and test data were split in the ratio of 9:1. We used accuracy, recall, precision, and F-score as the metrics to measure the overall classification results and those of classifications with a small amount of traffic. The formulas for each of these metrics are as follows. Note that, for the multi-class classification in the 3rd stage, we also used the macro-average of each metric.

$$Accuracy = \frac{TP + TN}{TP + FP + TN + FN} \tag{1}$$

$$Precision = \frac{TP}{TP + FP} \tag{2}$$

$$Recall = \frac{TP}{TP + FN} \tag{3}$$

$$F\text{-}score = \frac{2 \cdot Precision \cdot Recall}{Precision + Recall} \tag{4}$$

where TP means true positive, FP means false positive, FN means false negative, and TN means true negative. Furthermore, we use mean-time-between-false-alarms (MTBFA) as a metric of classification. MTBFA is the average time

Table 3. List of statistical traffic features.

1	Number of flow bytes sent	15	Mode Packet Time
2	Rate of flow bytes sent	16	Variance of Packet Time
3	Number of flow bytes received	17	Standard Deviation of Packet Time
4	Rate of flow bytes received	18	Coefficient of Variation of Packet Time
5	Mean Packet Length	19	Skew from median Packet Time
6	Median Packet Length	20	Skew from mode Packet Time
7	Mode Packet Length	21	Mean Request/response time difference
8	Variance of Packet Length	22	Median Request/response time difference
9	Standard Deviation of Packet Length	23	Mode Request/response time difference
10	Coefficient of Variation of Packet Length	24	Variance of Request/response time difference
11	Skew from median Packet Length	25	Standard Deviation of Request/response time difference
12	Skew from mode Packet Length	26	Coefficient of Variation of Request/response time difference
13	Mean Packet Time	27	Skew from median Request/response time difference
14	Median Packet Time	28	Skew from mode Request/response time difference

between false alarms in monitoring, which is calculated by the following equation. As the number of false alerts (false positives) increases due to the insufficient classification accuracy of the system, MTBFA becomes shorter.

$$MTBFA = \frac{Monitoring\ hours}{Number\ of\ false\ alarms} \tag{5}$$

4.3 Model Decision

Table 4 shows the best accuracy and parameters obtained by performing a grid search on validation data. As all the parameters shown here are larger than the minimum value of the search range and smaller than the maximum value, we concluded that we did not need to extend the search range any further. By comparing the accuracy at each stage, we decided to use the parameter-tuned XGBoost for DoH traffic filtering in the 1st stage, the parameter-tuned Light-GBM for suspicious DoH traffic detection in the 2nd stage, and the parameter-tuned CatBoost for malicious DNS tunnel tool identification in the 3rd stage. Note that, in some of the experiments, the system resources were insufficient. As for the combination of max_depth: 14 and L2_leaf_reg: [1, 2, 3, 4, 5, 6] in the 3rd stage, CatBoost used the CPU because of a shortage of GPU memory.

Table 4. Best score and parameters obtained by grid search.

	1st stage: DoH traffic filtering		2nd stage: Suspicious DoH traffic detection		3rd stage: Malicious DNS tunnel tool identification	
XGBoost	accuracy	0.9981	accuracy	0.99998	accuracy	0.9719
	max_depth	12	max_depth	4	max_depth	6
	max_bin	1024	max_bin	512	max_bin	1024
LightGBM	accuracy	0.9981	accuracy	0.99997	accuracy	0.9721
	num_leaves	255	num_leaves	15	num_leaves	63
	max_bin	511	max_bin	255	max_bin	8191
CatBoost	accuracy	0.9979	accuracy	0.99999	accuracy	0.9690
	max_depth	14	max_depth	4	max_depth	10
	L2_leaf_reg	5	L2_leaf_reg	2	L2_leaf_reg	4

4.4 Results of Malicious DNS Tunnel Tool Identification

The results of network traffic classification using test data and classifiers that were selected in Sect. 4.3 are shown in Table 5. The results of identifying malicious DNS tunnel tools in the 3rd stage were 97.22% in accuracy and 95.19% in F-score. Moreover, the results of filtering DoH traffic in the 1st stage were 99.81% in accuracy and 99.87% in F-score, while the results of detecting suspicious DoH traffic in the 2nd stage were 99.99% in accuracy and 99.99% in F-score. These results indicate that the performance of the proposed system is sufficient to support network administrators in their efforts to maintain network security. In addition, the results of our model were better or equal to those of the other finalist models, which means that the overfitting problem associated with the parameter tuning did not occur.

Looking at MTBFA in the 2nd stage, it was much longer than that in the 1st and 3rd stages. This is due to the high classification accuracy of the 2nd stage, which is acceptable in a large-scale real network environment. In terms of MTBFA in the 3rd stage, it was half an hour and shorter than that in the 2nd stage. To use the proposed system in a real network, it is desirable to be a little longer. This can be achieved by improving the classification accuracy in the 3rd stage. As for the three sequential stages, the metrics were calculated by reflecting the false positives and false negatives of the 1st and 2nd stage to the 3rd stage. The classifiers were XGBoost in the 1st stage, CatBoost in the 2nd stage, and LightGBM in the 3rd stage. Since the accuracy of classification in the 1st and 2nd stage was relatively high, the metrics in the 3rd stage were affected slightly.

Table 5. Results of network traffic classification using test data.

	Classifiers	Accuracy	Precision	Recall	F-score	MTBFA
1st stage: DoH traffic filtering	XGBoost	0.9981	0.9981	0.9994	0.9987	181 min
	LightGBM	0.9981	0.9980	0.9995	0.9987	111 min
	CatBoost	0.9979	0.9978	0.9995	0.9986	101 min
2nd stage: Suspicious DoH traffic detection	CatBoost	0.9999	1.0	0.9999	0.9999	80683 min
	LightGBM	0.9999	0.9999	0.9999	0.9999	48410 min
	XGBoost	0.9999	0.9999	0.9999	0.9999	30256 min
3rd stage: Malicious DNS tunnel tool identification	LightGBM	0.9722	0.9497	0.9543	0.9519	33 min
	XGBoost	0.9706	0.9473	0.9518	0.9495	32 min
	CatBoost	0.9691	0.9446	0.9494	0.9469	29 min
Three sequential stages:		0.9703	0.9487	0.9503	0.9494	31 min

A performance comparison between the proposed system and the systems of the previous studies is shown in Table 6. All previous studies have used the holdout method, which divides the dataset into training and test data, and then evaluates them once. In contrast, the 10 fold cross-validation we used performed 10 evaluations using the training and test data, and then calculated the average of these evaluations. To align the comparisons, we picked the best results from the 10 evaluations. In the 1st stage, which is DoH traffic filtering, our system had the highest precision, recall, and F-score. In the 2nd stage, which is suspicious DoH traffic detection, the results of tour system, like those of the previous studies, reached 1.0 in precision, recall, and F-score. It should be noted that the holdout method may decrease the values of these metrics depending on how the samples are selected when splitting the dataset into training and test data. In the cross-validation results of our system, the precision, recall, and F-score were 1.0, 0.9999 and 0.9999, respectively, with no significant loss in classification accuracy. As far as we know, this is the first attempt to identify malicious DNS tunnel tools; thus, there are no other studies that ours can be compared with.

Table 6. Comparison with previous studies using the holdout method.

	Classifiers	Precision	Recall	F-score
1st stage: DoH traffic filtering	Random Forest [29]	0.993	0.993	0.993
	XGBoost (ours)	**0.9982**	**0.9995**	**0.9989**
2nd stage: suspicious DoH traffic detection	Random Forest [29]	0.999	0.999	0.999
	Gradient Boost [34]	1.0	1.0	1.0
	CatBoost (ours)	**1.0**	**1.0**	**1.0**
3rd stage: malicious DNS tunnel tool identification	LightGBM (ours)	0.952	0.956	0.954

4.5 Consideration of Important Features

To analyze the background that enabled the hierarchical traffic data classification, the most important features used by each classifier are listed in Table 7. For filtering DoH traffic in the 1st stage, XGBoost used "Mode Packet Length" as the most important feature, followed by "Mean Packet Time". "Mode Packet Length" means the packet length that appears most often in the traffic flow, while "Mean Packet Time" refers to the average inter-arrival time of packets in the traffic flow. The value of "Mode Packet Length" is much larger than that of "Mean Packet Time", indicating that the former feature is very important. The average size of "Mode Packet Length" in the 1st stage is 164.0 for the non-DoH traffic and 68.0 for the DoH traffic. This difference is due to the fact that the non-DoH traffic contains a lot of data provided by the web server.

Regarding detecting suspicious DoH traffic in the 2nd stage, CatBoost considered "Mode Packet Length" to be the most important feature, followed by "Median Packet Length". Here, "Median Packet Length" means the packet length that separates the higher half of the traffic flow from the lower half. The average size of "Mode Packet Length" in the 2nd stage is 74.1 for the normal DoH traffic and 67.5 for the suspicious DoH traffic. This difference is due to the fact that normal DoH traffic contains a lot of SSL/TLS key exchange data between the client and DoH server. In contrast, suspicious DoH traffic has less of that data, because most malicious DNS tunnel tools stay connected with the DoH server for a long time.

Regarding identifying DoH tunnel tools in the 3rd stage, LightGBM considered "Median Request/response time difference" to be the most important feature, followed by "Skew from median Request/response time difference", "Mode Request/response time difference", and "Skew from mode Request/response time difference". The top-four features are related to "Request/response time difference", which means the inter-arrival time of received packets in the traffic flow. The remaining part of "Skew from median Request/response time difference" means the value defined by the equation: $3 \cdot (mean - median)/standard\ deviation$, while "Skew from mode Request/response time

Table 7. Most important features in hierarchical traffic data classification.

	Classifiers	Important features	Value
1st stage: DoH traffic filtering	XGBoost	Mode Packet Length	0.7757
		Mean Packet Time	0.0819
2nd stage: suspicious DoH traffic detection	CatBoost	Mode Packet Length	68.9465
		Median Packet Length	13.5604
3rd stage: malicious DNS tunnel tool identification	LightGBM	Median Request/response time difference	3694
		Skew from median Request/response time difference	3304
		Mode Request/response time difference	2963
		Skew from mode Request/response time difference	2290

difference" means the value calculated by the following equation: $(mean - mode)/standard\ deviation$. The average size of "Median Request/response time difference" in the 3rd stage is 0.2 for dns2tcp, 2.7 for dnscat2, and 1.4 for iodine. Since these malicious DNS tunnel tools were developed by separate organizations, we assume that the difference in processing load on the suspicious DNS server caused the difference in response time. We also considered the possibility that the geographical distance from the client to the suspicious DNS servers could be responsible for the difference in response time, but rejected this hypothesis because, according to the description of the CIRA-CIC-DoHBrw-2020 dataset [3], all the malicious DNS tunnel tools used a single suspicious DNS server in common.

4.6   Discussion

We list up some consideration points regarding the evaluation performed. First of all, we used the most popular and famous DNS tunnel tools in the evaluation considering the high possibility of use by attackers. In Sect. 3.4, we have distinguished three DNS tunnel tools with high accuracy. We also agree that there are many other types of malicious DNS tunnel tools, and the number may increase. In this case, even if there are some different factors in the new tools, some similarities may remain. Therefore, we expect that the proposed system will also be effective to those new varieties and the specific evaluation will be performed in future work.

Secondly, we performed the evaluations on a local network environment and confirmed the effectiveness of the proposed system. In Sect. 4.5, we showed that the request-response time feature of network traffic can be used to distinguish between three malicious DNS tunneling tools. It should be noted that in the data we used in our experiments, the malicious DNS servers that each DNS tunnel tool connects to are in a common network and have similar performance specifications. Therefore, we consider that in an environment with similar conditions, the proposed classification using the request-response time feature will work well. Regarding the evaluation in a real network environment, we plan to deploy the proposed system on our campus network and confirm its effectiveness.

On the other hand, in case attackers modify parts of well-known DNS tunnel tools or add new features to them, those tools may be out of the target of the proposed system. Furthermore, the length of connection to the DoH server and the DoH server capacity change based on the different operators. Therefore, we consider that the increase of features specifying these factors will be necessary for the deployment in a real network.

5   Conclusion

DoH technology has been developed to provide security and privacy for Internet users by encrypting the DNS traffic. However, DoH has a significant disadvantage because it prevents network administrators from analyzing network traffic for ensuring network security. Although many studies on encrypted network traffic classification and DNS tunnel detection have been reported, DoH is a new protocol to which previous research results cannot be directly applied.

In this study, we attempted to identify DoH traffic generated by malicious DNS tunnel tools. The payload of DoH traffic is encrypted; thus, its content cannot be accessed. Therefore, we decided to use the statistical features of the packets to analyze the traffic in detail. Our approach is a hierarchical traffic classification in which each stage uses a parameter-tuned model that is suitable for DoH network traffic. We designed, implemented, and evaluated our system with three levels of network traffic classification. For the prototype, we prepared 139 different models by tuning the parameters of the XGBoost, LightGBM, and CatBoost machine-learning libraries, which are expected to have high classification accuracy. To prove that our system can identify malicious DNS tunnel tools and evaluate its performance, we conducted a series of experiments using the CIRA-CIC-DoHBrw-2020 dataset. The results showed that our system can identify malicious DNS tunnel tools with 97.22% accuracy. They also showed that it can filter DoH traffic from normal HTTPS network traffic with 99.81% accuracy and detect suspicious DoH traffic from normal DoH traffic with 99.99% accuracy. We also showed the features that the machine-learning model considered to be important during the classification and discussed the conditions under which high classification accuracy can be achieved by using these features. Then, we discussed several consideration points regarding the evaluation performed.

References

1. Amazon Alexa Voice AI. https://developer.amazon.com/en-US/alexa/. Accessed 17 July 2021
2. CatBoost Documentation - Parameters. https://catboost.ai/docs/concepts/python-reference_parameters-list.html. Accessed 16 June 2021
3. CIRA-CIC-DoHBrw-2020. https://www.unb.ca/cic/datasets/dohbrw-2020.html. Accessed 15 June 2021
4. cloudflared. https://developers.cloudflare.com/cloudflare-one/connections/connect-apps. Accessed 10 July 2021
5. DNS Queries over HTTPS (DoH) - Request For Comments 8484. https://tools.ietf.org/html/rfc8484. Accessed 15 June 2021
6. dns2tcp. https://github.com/alex-sector/dns2tcp. Accessed 3 July 2021
7. dnscat2. https://github.com/iagox86/dnscat2. Accessed 3 July 2021
8. dnscrypt-proxy. https://github.com/DNSCrypt. Accessed 10 July 2021
9. doh-client. https://docs.rs/crate/doh-client/1.1.5. Accessed 10 July 2021
10. doh-proxy. https://github.com/facebookexperimental/doh-proxy. Accessed 10 July 2021
11. First-ever malware strain spotted abusing new DoH (DNS over HTTPS) protocol. https://www.zdnet.com/article/first-ever-malware-strain-spotted-abusing-new-doh-dns-over-https-protocol/. Accessed 10 July 2021
12. iodine. https://code.kryo.se/iodine/. Accessed 3 July 2021
13. Kaggle. https://www.kaggle.com/. Accessed 16 June 2021
14. LightGBM Documentation - Parameters. https://lightgbm.readthedocs.io/en/latest/Parameters.html. Accessed 16 June 2021
15. Windows Insiders can now test DNS over HTTPS. https://techcommunity.microsoft.com/t5/networking-blog/windows-insiders-can-now-test-dns-over-https/ba-p/1381282. Accessed 10 July 2021
16. Windows Insiders gain new DNS over HTTPS controls. https://techcommunity.microsoft.com/t5/networking-blog/windows-insiders-gain-new-dns-over-https-controls/ba-p/2494644. Accessed 10 July 2021
17. XGBoost Documentation - Xgboost Parameters. https://xgboost.readthedocs.io/en/latest/parameter.html. Accessed 16 June 2021
18. Acar, A., Lu, L., Uluagac, A.S., Kirda, E.: An analysis of malware trends in enterprise networks. In: Lin, Z., Papamanthou, C., Polychronakis, M. (eds.) ISC 2019. LNCS, vol. 11723, pp. 360–380. Springer, Cham (2019). https://doi.org/10.1007/978-3-030-30215-3_18
19. Aceto, G., Ciuonzo, D., Montieri, A., Pescapé, A.: Mobile encrypted traffic classification using deep learning: experimental evaluation, lessons learned, and challenges. IEEE Trans. Netw. Serv. Manag. **16**(2), 445–458 (2019)
20. Ajmera, S., Pattanshetti, T.: A survey report on identifying different machine learning algorithms in detecting domain generation algorithms within enterprise network. In: Proceedings of 2020 11th International Conference on Computing, Communication and Networking Technologies (ICCCNT), pp. 1–5 (2020)
21. Buczak, A.L., Hanke, P.A., Cancro, G.J., Toma, M.K., Watkins, L.A., Chavis, J.S.: Detection of tunnels in PCAP data by random forests. In: Proceedings of the 11th Annual Cyber and Information Security Research Conference (2016)
22. Chen, Y., Li, X.: A high accuracy DNS tunnel detection method without feature engineering. In: Proceedings of 2020 16th International Conference on Computational Intelligence and Security (CIS), pp. 374–377 (2020)

23. Chowdhary, A., Bhowmik, M., Rudra, B.: DNS tunneling detection using machine learning and cache miss properties. In: Proceedings of 2021 5th International Conference on Intelligent Computing and Control Systems (ICICCS), pp. 1225–1229 (2021)
24. Ichise, H., Jin, Y., Iida, K.: Analysis of DNS TXT record usage and consideration of botnet communication detection. IEICE Trans. Commun. **E101**(1), 70–79 (2018). https://doi.org/10.1587/transcom.2017ITP0009
25. Ichise, H., Jin, Y., Iida, K., Takai, Y.: NS record history based abnormal DNS traffic detection considering adaptive botnet communication blocking. IPSJ J. Inf. Process. **28**, 112–122 (2020). https://doi.org/10.2197/ipsjjip.28.112
26. Iuchi, Y., Jin, Y., Ichise, H., Iida, K., Takai, Y.: Detection and blocking of DGA-based bot infected computers by monitoring NXDOMAIN responses. In: Proceedings of 2020 7th IEEE International Conference on Cyber Security and Cloud Computing (CSCloud)/2020 6th IEEE International Conference on Edge Computing and Scalable Cloud (EdgeCom), pp. 82–87 (2020)
27. Ke, G., et al.: LightGBM: a highly efficient gradient boosting decision tree. In: Proceedings of Advances in Neural Information Processing Systems, vol. 30 (2017)
28. Lambion, D., Josten, M., Olumofin, F., De Cock, M.: Malicious DNS tunneling detection in real-traffic DNS data. In: Proceedings of 2020 IEEE International Conference on Big Data (Big Data), pp. 5736–5738 (2020)
29. MontazeriShatoori, M., Davidson, L., Kaur, G., Habibi Lashkari, A.: Detection of DoH tunnels using time-series classification of encrypted traffic. In: Proceedings of 2020 IEEE International Conference on Dependable, Autonomic and Secure Computing, International Conference on Pervasive Intelligence and Computing, International Conference on Cloud and Big Data Computing, International Conference on Cyber Science and Technology Congress (DASC/PiCom/CBDCom/CyberSciTech), pp. 63–70 (2020)
30. Pacheco, F., Exposito, E., Gineste, M., Baudoin, C., Aguilar, J.: Towards the deployment of machine learning solutions in network traffic classification: a systematic survey. IEEE Commun. Surv. Tutor. **21**(2), 1988–2014 (2019)
31. Prokhorenkova, L., Gusev, G., Vorobev, A., Dorogush, A.V., Gulin, A.: CatBoost: unbiased boosting with categorical features. In: Proceedings of Advances in Neural Information Processing Systems, vol. 31 (2018)
32. Shyam, R., Ayachit, S.S., Patil, V., Singh, A.: Competitive analysis of the top gradient boosting machine learning algorithms. In: Proceedings of 2020 2nd International Conference on Advances in Computing, Communication Control and Networking (ICACCCN), pp. 191–196 (2020)
33. Siby, S., Juarez, M., Diaz, C., Vallina-Rodriguez, N., Troncoso, C.: Encrypted DNS → privacy? In: Proceedings of Network and Distributed Systems Security (NDSS) Symposium 2020 (2020)
34. Singh, S.K., Roy, P.K.: Detecting malicious DNS over HTTPS traffic using machine learning. In: Proceedings of 2020 International Conference on Innovation and Intelligence for Informatics, Computing and Technologies, pp. 1–6 (2020)
35. Tianqi, C., Carlos, G.: XGBoost: a scalable tree boosting system. In: Proceedings of the 22nd ACM SIGKDD International Conference on Knowledge Discovery and Data Mining, pp. 785–794 (2016)
36. Vekshin, D., Hynek, K., Cejka, T.: DoH insight: detecting DNS over HTTPS by machine learning. In: Proceedings of the 15th International Conference on Availability, Reliability and Security (2020)

37. Wu, K., Zhang, Y., Yin, T.: FTPB: a three-stage DNS tunnel detection method based on character feature extraction. In: Proceedings of 2020 IEEE 19th International Conference on Trust, Security and Privacy in Computing and Communications (TrustCom), pp. 250–258 (2020)
38. Yang, P., Wan, X., Shi, G., Qu, H., Li, J., Yang, L.: Naruto: DNS covert channels detection based on stacking model. In: Proceedings of the 2020 2nd World Symposium on Software Engineering, pp. 109–115 (2020)

Detection of Malware, Attacks and Vulnerabilities

Hybroid: Toward Android Malware Detection and Categorization with Program Code and Network Traffic

Mohammad Reza Norouzian[1(✉)], Peng Xu[1], Claudia Eckert[1], and Apostolis Zarras[2]

[1] Technical University of Munich, Munich, Germany
norouzian@sec.in.tum.de
[2] Delft University of Technology, Delft, The Netherlands

Abstract. Android malicious applications have become so sophisticated that they can bypass endpoint protection measures. Therefore, it is safe to admit that traditional anti-malware techniques have become cumbersome, thereby raising the need to develop efficient ways to detect Android malware. In this paper, we present *Hybroid*, a hybrid Android malware detection and categorization solution that utilizes program code structures as static behavioral features and network traffic as dynamic behavioral features for detection (binary classification) and categorization (multi-label classification). For static analysis, we introduce a natural-language-processing-inspired technique based on function call graph embeddings and design a graph-neural-network-based approach to convert the whole graph structure of an Android app to a vector. For dynamic analysis, we extract network flow features from the raw network traffic by capturing each application's network flow. Finally, *Hybroid* utilizes the network flow features combined with the graphs' vectors to detect and categorize the malware. Our solution demonstrates 97.0% accuracy on average for malware detection and 94.0% accuracy for malware categorization. Also, we report remarkable results in different performance metrics such as F1-score, precision, recall, and AUC.

1 Introduction

Android has become the most popular mobile operating system worldwide. Unfortunately, it has become a primary target platform for attackers using Android to launch millions of malicious applications due to its prominence. Attackers dupe victims to reveal their sensitive information or perform malicious operations, such as spying on users, propagating spam, or launching unwanted advertisements. Simultaneously, investigation of Android malware,

---

M. R. Norouzian and P. Xu—These authors have contributed equally to this work and share first authorship.

© Springer Nature Switzerland AG 2021
J. K. Liu et al. (Eds.): ISC 2021, LNCS 13118, pp. 259–278, 2021.
https://doi.org/10.1007/978-3-030-91356-4_14

which includes malware detection and categorization, has become crucial for security researchers and experts in both academia and industry. As a result, numerous research studies have attempted to detect and categorize Android malware [5,10,17,21,27–29,32].

Numerous approaches leverage the contextual information of Android applications, yet nearly none of them can monitor malware behaviors if we use contextual information statically. For example, Li et al. [14] presented a classifier using the Factorization Machine architecture, which extracts various Android application features from manifest files (e.g., permissions and intents) and source code (API calls). Similarly, Chen et al. [6] proposed an approach that detects Android malware with Android application's static features, such as permissions, components, and sensitive API calls. Although these methods add an extra security level to the Android platform, they come with their limitations, particularly for those obfuscated applications when executed [7]. This problem can be mitigated by introducing dynamic analysis, which monitors malware actions and analyzes the captured behavior when running in a sandboxed environment.

In essence, similar to static analysis, there are two types of dynamic analysis target Android applications. The first focuses on system-level behavior, extracting features from API usage or system calls, whereas the latter extracts features from network-level actions (i.e., data received or sent over the network). Analyzing system-level malware behavior is expensive and slows down the processing speed. In contrast, analyzing network-level activities is scalable and more cost-efficient, while it often exposes the core behavior of malware when trying to communicate with the attacker. Specifically, it can reveal the exfiltrated information and the commands sent or received by the malware. From a network perspective, monitoring and analyzing a system that extracts behavioral information from the user causes less overhead on the end hosts. To detect legitimate and malicious behavior, several approaches utilize the network traffic pattern of Android applications [2,15,16,25,32]. Most of them concentrate on the manual indicated features and build rule-based classifiers for detecting Android malware. Sadly, sophisticated attacks can easily evade network-rule-based methods since rule-based analysis relies on distinguishing expected versus anomalous behavior; these methods may suffer when malware is modified to hide its footprints or behavior. However, one of the main challenges of analyzing network-level activities is related to their offline inspection behavior.

In this paper, we present *Hybroid*, a hybrid framework for Android malware detection and categorization based on static and dynamic features to overcome the drawbacks mentioned above. From the users' point of view, *Hybroid* does not change anything of the Android application itself. We take the program code inside apps as input for static analysis and present a *Natural Language Processing (NLP)* inspired method based on the function call graph, which detects obfuscated applications. In brief, we first design the `opcode2vec`, `function2vec`, and `graph2vec` components to represent instructions, functions, and the entire program's information with vectors. Next, we take network traffic as input and extract 13 features for dynamic analysis. Finally, we combine static and dynamic analysis features and feed them into the machine learning and deep learning

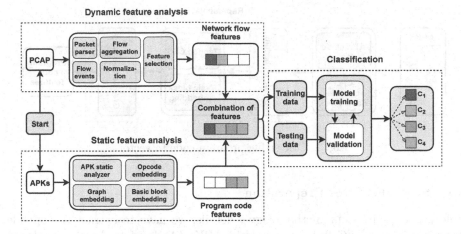

Fig. 1. *Hybroid* architecture

networks for training and prediction. Our results show that *Hybroid* outperforms most existing frameworks, as we get 97.0% accuracy for malware detection and 94.0% accuracy for malware categorization on average.

In summary, we make the following primary contributions:

- We present and open source *Hybroid*,[1] a hybrid framework for Android malware detection and categorization based on static and dynamic features.
- We design and implement automatic extraction of flow-based features from the Android raw network traffic as a dynamic feature.
- We leverage NLP and convert machine codes, functions, and programs to opcode2vec, function2vec, and graph2vec by embedding methods.
- We evaluate the accuracy of our approach using a real-world dataset and show that *Hybroid* outperforms nearly all state-of-the-art solutions.

2   System Design

In this section, we describe the architecture of *Hybroid* (see Fig. 1), which comprises static and dynamic features. We extract static features by studying the *Control Flow Graph (CFG)* of the Android bytecode and the dynamic features by investigating the network flow data. Next, we combine these two groups of features as input vectors to train a machine learning model. Essentially, our approach is divided into three main parts: static features preparation (features from program code), dynamic features preparation (features from network traffic), and machine learning classification.

---

[1] https://github.com/PegX/Hybroid.

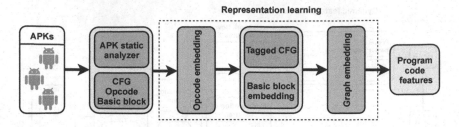

Fig. 2. Converting program code to vector

2.1 Static Features Preparation

Before getting into our methodology's details, we have to extract the opcode, basic block, and CFG from the Android APKs (Android application package). We extract the CFG by utilizing the Androguard framework (APK static analyzer) and iterate each function in the program to get the basic block for each function (method).[2] Furthermore, we analyze each instruction and take opcode as our basic term. After obtaining the opcode, basic block, and CFG, our primary approach is presented as follows. For the packing and obfuscated apps, similar to Xu et al. work [26], Androguard can also help our *Hybroid* to extract CFG and opcode from the apps, and we can also construct our graph structure.

Figure 2 depicts an overview of the steps involved in extracting features from the code graph structure. The entire process includes three main steps: (*i*) opcode embedding that converts the machine instructions into vectors, (*ii*) basic block embedding that transforms a basic block of the program into a vector (basic blocking embedding is done with Tagged CFG, which is used to combine multi-opcode to a vector), and (*iii*) graph embedding that modifies the whole function call graph into a vector. Finally, during the conversion of the opcode, basic block, and function call graph into vectors, we utilize representation learning techniques to learn the essential model parameters for getting the final 64-bit vector.

Representation Learning. To generate the node attribute in the CFG, we leverage representation learning. Representation learning [4], which can learn features from raw data automatically, has increasingly attracted researchers' and engineers' focus. Compared to those manually indicated attributed control flow graph (ACFG) methods, like Xu et al. [30], Adagio [10], and Yan et al. [31], *Hybroid* can extract ACFG automatically without preparing manual features and avoiding the challenge of manual indicated methods (how to pick up the useful features is a challenge) because of the representation learning. Additionally, *Hybroid* borrows ideas from Natural Language Processing to assist the feature engineering. It uses the word2vec to convert instructions to vectors and automatically learns the vector from the basic block's raw instruction.

In brief, *Hybroid* static analysis part introduces representation learning as the fundamental technique to represent code and use the control flow graph as

---

[2] https://github.com/androguard.

fundamental to organize the program. Additionally, it utilizes NLP to convert the byte sequences (instruction and basic block) to vectors, used to replace the manually indicated features [10,31]. *Hybroid* then feeds those generated vectors into a learning-based classifier to extract static features. In other words, *Hybroid* uses the transform learning technique to use the previously trained instruction2vec model to convert the byte sequences to vectors.

Opcode Embedding. To simplify the procedure, we replace instruction (opcode and operands) embedding with opcode embedding. The reason for this replacement is the following. First, the opcode represents Dalvik's instruction behaviors, whereas the operands represent the parameters. Dalvik's operands are virtual registers in a virtual machine. Those values are significantly affected by the underlying usage of Dalvik VM or ART VM. Thus, it is not possible to enumerate them all. Additionally, if various malware samples in the same family use the same malicious pattern, the opcode itself can capture these behaviors.

In theory, our opcode embedding method may suffer from the *operand removal* problem [11]. A significant issue with operand removal is that all the *Invoke-Virtual* instructions have the same embedding vector, no matter what are the targets of the *Invoke-Virtual* instructions.[3] For the opcode embedding method, or `opcode2vec`, we map each opcode $op_i \in$ OP (where OP stands for the whole Dalvik opcodes) to a vector of the real number, using the `word2vec` model with the skip-gram method [18]. `word2vec` is an excellent feature learning technique, which is based on continuous bag-of-word and skip-gram techniques. The skip-gram learning technique uses the current opcode to predict the surrounding opcodes. We train our `opcode2vec` model with a large corpus of opcodes extracted from real applications.

Basic Block Embedding. In this work, we treat the basic block embedding in the control flow graph similarly to the sentence embedding in the natural language processing. Overall, we introduce our method for performing the basic block (nodes in control flow graph) embedding, which are described as follows. We utilize the weighted mean of a non-empty finite multi-set of instruction's opcode to calculate the basic block embedding. Assuming the function f includes n-opcode and a l-dimensional vector represents each opcode, the weight of the corresponding non-negative weights $w_1, w_2, \ldots, w_n$ are given as: $\tilde{f} = \frac{\sum_{i=1}^{n} w_i x_i}{\sum_{i=1}^{n} w_i}$, where x_i represents the l-dimensional opcode embedding and w_i stands for the weighted of each opcode.

Graph Embedding. After deriving the basic block embedding, we take the generated basic block embedding as the node embedding of the control flow graph. In other words, we perform graph embedding on a control flow graph level. The module's ultimate purpose is to convert the graph representation into a vector and then feed it as input for the neural network-based classifier. We take structure2vec [9] graph embedding method to convert one graph to a vector.

---

[3] All the calling instructions such as *invoke-super*, *invoke-direct*, *invoke-static*, and *invoke-interface* suffer from the same problem.

Algorithm 1: Graph embedding

Input: Instruction embedding $v_i : i \in I$, control flow graph insider of a function g_f, parameter α

Output: Graph embedding $v_f : f \in F$

1 Initialize $\mu_v^0 = \vec{Rand}, for all v \in V$

2 **for** $t=1$ **to** T **do**

3   **for** $v \in V$ **do**

4          $l_v = \sum_{u \in N(v)} \mu_u^{(t-1)}$

5          $\mu_v^{(t)} = tanh(W_1 x_v + \sigma(l_v))$

6 $v_f = W_2(\sum_{v \in V} \mu_v^T)/len(V))$

7 **return** v_f

We utilize the Eqs. (1), (2), and (3) to convert a control flow graph to a graph-vector, which stands for the whole Android application. In our work, our graph-based control flow graph embedding includes two components. The first one is the control flow graph extraction, and the other is the graph embedding for each control flow graph, which is adapted from the structure2vec.

The graph vectors (nodes) are basic blocks for graph embedding, and the edges are connections among those basic blocks in the CFG. Each vector (node) contains a set of opcodes inside it. The basic block embedding constructs each node's feature. Finally, a p-dimensional vector μ_i is associated with each vertex v_i. We use adapted structure2vec to dynamically update the p-dimensional vector μ_i^{t+1} during the training of the network. The updating process is executed as follows:

$$\mu_v^{(t+1)} = F(x_v, \sum_{u \in N_v} \mu_u^{(t)}), \forall v \in V. \tag{1}$$

We randomly initialize the $\mu_v^{(0)}$ at each vertex. In practice, we design the function F as follows:

$$F(x_v, \sum_{u \in N_v} \mu_u^{(t)}) = tanh(W_1 x_v + \sigma(\sum_{u \in N(v)} \mu_u)) \tag{2}$$

For an effective nonlinear transformation $\sigma(.)$, we define $\sigma(.)$ itself as an n layer fully-connected neural network and the W_1 is trainable parameter.

$$\sigma(l) = P_1 * ReLU(P_2 * \ldots ReLU(P_n l)) \tag{3}$$

The overall CFG-based embedding algorithm is illustrated in Algorithm 1. The graph embedding generates the vector embedding after all iterations, and we use the average aggregation function as our last step to transform the vector embedding to the graph-based function embedding.

After deriving our graph embedding for the function call graph, we design a two-layer MLP (multilayer perceptron) network as our representation learning network to learn parameters used to convert the program code into vectors.

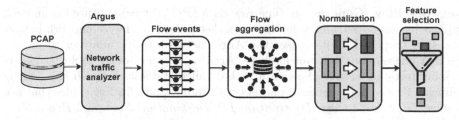

Fig. 3. Dynamic analysis overview

In our network, malware detection is a binary classification issue. We label malware samples as 1 and benign samples as -1 at training. During testing, we treat all predictions less than zero as benign and the rest as malicious.

$$v_{f(G_h)} = \alpha * ((<g_i, w_{i1}> + b_{i1}), w_{i2} + b_{i2}) \tag{4}$$

where the $w_{i1}, w_{i2} \in R^p$ is the weight of the two-layer MLP network and the $b_{i1}, b_{i2} \in R^p$ is the offset from the origin of the vector space. In this setting, a function call graph G_h is classified as malicious if $f(G_h) > 0$ and benign if $f(G_h) < 0$. The vector $v_{f(G_h)}$ that corresponds to $f(G_h)$ is collected as the final representation of the program code. By using the above-stated methods, we finally get a 64-bit vector representing the whole program code and present the static features of program code.

Last but not least, we should mention the transductive and inductive embedding. Our work relies on word2vec to convert instructions to vectors. This requires relying on a large and representative dataset to train the embedding: word2vec is a transductive approach and requires access to the entire alphabet. As our method focuses on instruction mnemonics, our transductive approach of word2vec did not influence the final results since graph embedding (convert the control flow graph to vectors) is an inductive approach in which graphs of the testing dataset are unknown at training time.

2.2 Dynamic Features Preparation

Figure 3 illustrates an overview of dynamic analysis (i.e., extracting features from network traffic). The whole process involves three main steps. The first step is the network flow generation that involves converting raw network traffic into network flow events. Alternatively, we could use deep packet inspection to extract network traffic features to understand the malware behavior better. However, this tactic cannot be applied to most real-world scenarios due to privacy concerns. In contrast, high-level flow features do not necessarily render a correct picture of malware behavior. To address this gap, we leverage static analysis, combining it with dynamic network analysis. In the second step, we normalize the flow features extracted from Argus,[4] and in the last step, we use feature selection mechanisms to reduce and finalize our dynamic feature set.

---

[4] https://openargus.org/.

Network Flow Generation. The raw data (PCAP files) captured from each application network traffic is fed into a packet parser to analyze network behaviors. Our proposed solution uses the Argus network traffic analyzer to handle the first phase of our dynamic analysis. Argus is an open-source tool that generates bidirectional network flow data with detailed statistics for each flow. Argus defines a flow by a sequence of packets with same values for five tuples that are *Source IP, Source Port, Destination IP, Destination Port,* and *Protocol.*

However, the output values of Argus features' are almost numeric, except for two categorical values: direction and flag states. To map them into discrete values, we use the one-hot encoding that encodes categorical features as a one-hot numeric array for our feature generation. The output of Argus involves numerous flow events with around 40 feature sets related to each flow.

Since there are at least more than one flow events for each PCAP file, the next step is to map each bunch of flow events into one data sample. To handle this step, we aggregate the values of network flow features by calculating the mean values, appending them to a single record. These steps mentioned above perform as a preprocessing phase, which converts the raw network data into numeric values that create a dataset ready to train any machine learning model.

Normalization. The extracted features must be normalized before being given to the classification algorithms since their values vary significantly. For example, if we chose Euclidean distance as a distance measure for classification, normalization guarantees that every feature contributes proportionally to the final distance. To achieve normalization, we use min-max scaling as shown below:

$$x^1 = (x - min(x))/(max(x) - min(x)) \tag{5}$$

where $min(x)$ and $max(x)$ represent range values. This method returns feature values within the range $[0, 1]$. An alternative method would be using standard scaling by subtracting the mean values of the features and then scaling them to unit variance. However, this method would mitigate the differences in the values, making the detection harder (we examined this experimentally).

Feature Selection. Selecting features is critical, as it affects the performance of the model. There exist two main reasons to reduce the number of features:

1. *Complexity Reduction:* When the number of features increases, most machine learning algorithms require more computing resources and time for execution. Thus, reducing the number of features is essential for saving time and resources.
2. *Noise Reduction:* Extra features do not always help to improve the algorithm performance. In contrast, they may produce severe problems related to model overfitting. Therefore, selecting a set of useful features reduces the possibility of model overfitting.

Before the training and testing phase, we implemented various feature selection algorithms to find the best set of final features for our analysis. We used three feature selection algorithms: Pearson Correlation, Extra Trees Classifier

Table 1. List of network flow features

Notation	Traffic features
Mean	*Average duration of aggregated records*
sTos	*Source TOS byte value*
dTos	*Destination TOS byte value*
sTtl	*Source to destination TTL value*
dTtl	*Destination to source TTL value*
TotBytes	*Total transaction bytes*
SrcBytes	*Source to destination transaction bytes*
DstWin	*Destination TCP window advertisement*
SrcTCPBase	*Source TCP base sequence number*
DstTCPBase	*Destination TCP base sequence number*
Flgs_er	*State flag for Src loss/retransmissions*
Flgs_es	*State flag for Dst packets out of order*
Dir	*Direction of transaction*

(extremely randomized trees), and a Univariate feature selection (select features according to the highest k scores). At the end of the process, we selected 13 network flow features for our final dynamic analysis feature engineering. These selected features describe the general behavior of the network activity for each data sample and can be found in Table 1.

However, we perform an extra analysis to explore the quality of selected features that are highly related to the target labels. We assume that any two features are independent without being redundant. To investigate the redundancy score, we use Kendall's correlation method (Fig. 4). Notice that any two independent features are interpreted as redundant if the correlation score is extremely high, whereas a high correlation between dependent features is desired.

Observation of Malware Network Communications. We check the type of communication to spot if the applications use secure communication channels or transmit the data on unencrypted flows. We can make observations about the entire encrypted data flows instead of just the handshake or individual packets. This is done by extracting the features of each data record by flow-level instead of packet-level approach. As we can see in Table 2, a relatively small number of applications are using encryption for communication. When we compared malicious to benign applications traffic, we found out that the communications that initially start with more upload than download traffic are more likely to be malicious. The reason is that when malware connects to a control server, it often identifies itself with a client certificate, which is rarely seen during normal TLS usage. Another aspect we notice is that after the initial connection to the control server has been established, the channel is often kept open but idle, with only regular keep-alive packets being sent.

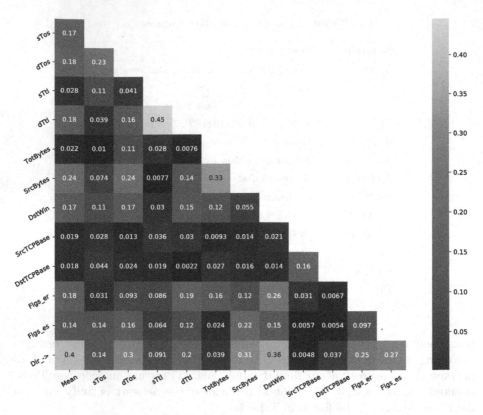

Fig. 4. Dynamic network flow feature correlation scores

When comparing these two aspects with what ordinary TLS traffic created in an HTTPS session in a browser looks like, one can easily see a very different behavior: when requesting a website, the initial upload usually consists only of a GET request (little upload), with a large response in the form of web page content being sent from the server (large download). However, *Hybroid* results (see Sect. 3.5) of malware detection and categorization show that analyzing flow metadata would be effective on encrypted flows too.

2.3   Machine Learning Classification

The classification aims to detect and categorize the APK samples, whether the source APK is a benign application or a specific type of malware. In the beginning, we tested various supervised learning algorithms (support vector machines, naive Bayes, decision tree, random forests, and gradient boosting) to assess classifier performance. The differences of using various learning algorithms confirm our methodology that the selected static and dynamic features help to identify the distinction between benign and malicious APKs. Test results revealed

Table 2. Type of malware category communication networks

Category	HTTP flow	TLS flow
Adware	52.00%	8.00%
Ransomware	29.22%	0.00%
Scareware	61.38%	10.89%
SMSmalware	52.20%	10.28%

that SVM and naive Bayes demonstrated the worst performance and were thus excluded from the tests.

For model validation, we used the cross-validation technique to test whether the model can predict new samples that were not used in previous estimations. The intention for cross-validation is to reduce the chance of overfitting or selection bias and improve the model's generalization to an independent dataset.

3 Evaluation

We use different types of machine learning metrics to test and evaluate *Hybroid*. To do so, we leverage a dataset that contains the original APK files and the mobile network traffic data generated by the applications. Next, we seek to identify the best detection classifier, and based on classifier performance, we try to use different parameter engineering. We compare our solution with other machine learning state-of-the-art related works, such as static and dynamic analyses based detection. The extracted results prove the advantages of our proposed solution, which combines the static and dynamic analysis of Android malware into a unified classification procedure.

3.1 Experimental Setup

We implemented the proposed methods using Python, Scikit-Learn, Tensorflow, and Keras. We set up our experiments on our Euklid server with 32 Core Processor, 128 GB RAM, and 16 GB GPU. Besides, we used 5-fold cross-validation. To obtain a reliable performance, we averaged the results of the cross-validation tests, executed each time with a new random dataset shuffle.

3.2 Evaluation Metrics

Due to the imbalanced nature of the dataset (see Sect. 3.3), accuracy may not be the only reliable indicator of classifier performance. Thus, the performance of detection and categorization will be evaluated with metrics such as precision, recall, and F-measure (F1-score). In general, the accuracy metric is used when true negatives and true positives are crucial; the F1-score is used when false positives and false negatives are more important. When the class distribution

Table 3. Dataset descriptions

Name	Number	Description	Distribution (%)
APK files	2,126	All program code files	100%
PCAP files	2,126	All the raw network traffic files	100%
Benign APKs	1,700	No. of benign APK	80%
Adware APKs	124	No. of Adware category APK	5.9%
Ransomware APKs	112	No. of Ransomware category APK	5.2%
Scareware APKs	109	No. of Scareware category APK	5.2%
SMSmalware APKs	101	No. of SMSmalware category APK	4.7%

is nearly equal, accuracy can be used, whereas the F1-score is a better metric when we have imbalanced classes. However, in most real-life classification problems, the datasets are imbalanced, and therefore, the F1-score is a better metric to evaluate the model. However, since other related studies report accuracy as their primary evaluation metric, we also compare and consider accuracy as a comparison metric. Another metric to evaluate our work is to consider the receiver operating characteristic (ROC) curve, which presents the true positive rate (TPR) against the false positive rate (FPR).

3.3   Dataset

For the dataset, we use the public CICAndMal2017 [13]. The benign applications were collected from the Google play market published in 2015, 2016, and 2017. On the other hand, the malicious ones were collected from various sources such as VirusTotal[5] and Contagio security blog[6]. The dataset includes 426 malware and 1,700 benign samples with their corresponding network traffic raw data, which are delicately captured from physical smartphone devices while running the applications.

In the networking part, the phones' behavior was generated by scripts, which imitated normal phone usage like phone calls and utilized SMS along with GPS spoofing and web browsing. Every phone was also connected to a Gmail, Facebook, Skype, and WhatsApp account. The normal behavior of phones was captured in PCAP files that served as the entry point in our work. After infecting every phone with malware from the malware pool provided with the dataset in the form of APK files, the resulting network communication was collected. Table 3 provides a short description of the CICAndMal2017 dataset.

3.4   Power Law and Opcode Embedding

Before moving to our evaluation tasks, we use the distribution of our opcode to prove the reasonability of using natural processing language techniques in

---
[5] https://virustotal.com.
[6] http://contagiominidump.blogspot.com.

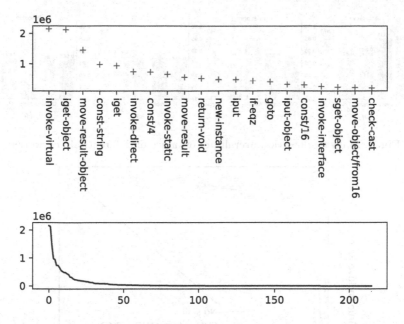

Fig. 5. Power-law distribution for Dalivk opcodes

our works. In order to get the reasonable opcode2vec module, we pre-train the opcode2vec by the AndroZoo dataset. We extract all opcodes by the Androguard tool and obtain 18,240,542 opcodes in total. Then, we take those opcodes as our word corpus to train the opcode2vec model. Figure 5 presents the opcode distribution for the above datasets. More specifically, it shows Dalvik's opcode distribution, which has 216 opcodes, and the top-20 opcodes are presented. They all follow the power-law distribution, which makes borrowing word embedding techniques from natural language processing to do opcode embedding reasonable.

3.5 Performance of Classifiers

In this section, the evaluation of the Android malware detection and categorization algorithms is presented in detail. For the malware detection experiments, we compare *Hybroid* with other related solutions. Figure 6 shows the difference between our solution and the other malware detection schemes. *Hybroid* demonstrates an accuracy of 97.0% (Fig. 6-a), while CIC2017 [13], DREBIN [3], SVM [8], and Adagio [10] demonstrate accuracy of 87.6%, 95.4%, 93.9%, and 89.3%, respectively. Other metrics, such as F1-score, precision, and recall, are also presented in Figs. 6-b, 6-c, and 6-d.

In addition, Fig. 7 shows the ROC curve of our solution and the other compared algorithms, while TPR is plotted against the FPR for the various thresholds of the detection methods. As the ROC curve shows, *Hybroid* demonstrates the best performance (represented by the purple line), which means that the combination of static and dynamic features boosts the classifier performance.

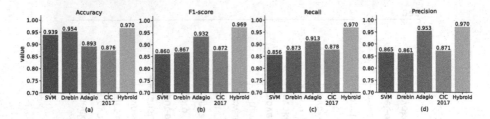

Fig. 6. Malware detection overall performance of different related works

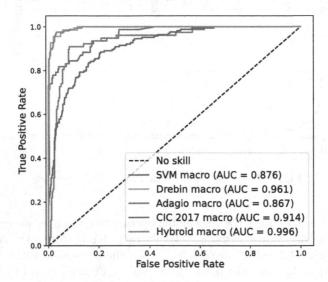

Fig. 7. Malware detection ROC curve of different related works (Color figure online)

Besides, we can observe, *Hybroid* presents the best area under the ROC curve (AUC), which is 99.6%, while the Adagio method shows the worst AUC of 86.7%. The Fig. 7 also presents AUCs of the other compared solution classifiers.

To evaluate our work independently, we tested three various classifiers (decision tree, random forest, and gradient boosting) with static, dynamic, and combined features. We tested these three classifiers to identify differences in the performance of final classifiers. The obtained results confirmed that the combination of static and dynamic features yields the best performance. Moreover, we saw that the decision tree classifier demonstrates the lowest accuracy, precision, and recall compared to the other algorithms. Decision tree is also prone to overfitting. Random forest presented higher accuracy, precision, and recall as a more robust model than decision tree, limiting overfitting without substantially increasing error. On the other hand, compared with random forest, gradient boosting demonstrates the best metric results in our framework, implying that it is the most effective supervised learning algorithm for our experiment.

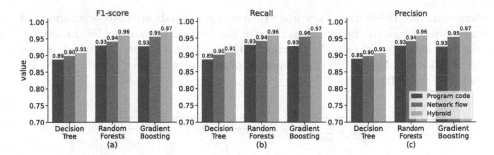

Fig. 8. Malware detection performance of the different classification algorithms

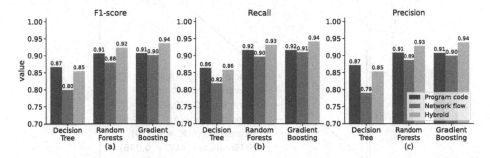

Fig. 9. Malware categorization performance of the different classification algorithms

Gradient boosting is similar to random forest with a set of decision trees but with a main difference. It combines the results of week learners along the way, unlike random forest combines the results by majority rules or averaging at the end of the process. This accounts for the difference in the results.

Figure 8 shows the performance for the malware detection task. In the F1-score of various classifiers, we witness that combined features with gradient boosting achieve the best F1-score, which is 97%. Meanwhile, we only get 93% with static features from the program code and 95% with dynamic features from network flow. On the other hand, among the three classifiers with combined features, the gradient boosting classifier yields the best precision result, which is 97%. Meanwhile, random forest and decision tree demonstrate a precision of 96% and 91%, respectively.

Subsequent to the malware detection, we also evaluated *Hybroid* with the malware categorization, which is a multi-label classification task. We see from Fig. 9 that the gradient boosting classifier receives the best results with combined features, namely 94% precision, 94% recall, and 94% F1-score. With the random forests classifier, our *Hybroid* also demonstrates significant results with a 92% F1-score. Figure 9(a, b, c) depicts the evaluation results with F1-score, recall, and precision in detail.

Also, Fig. 10 illustrates the ROC curves for the malware categorization task. Different curves show the different values of AUC. As it is shown, *Hybroid* demonstrates 97.6% macro accuracy on average for malware categorization, and categorization of the benign class receives the best performance AUC for 99.5%. For SMSware, we obtained the worst AUC, i.e., 94.6%. One potential reason for this issue could be the small number of SMSware in the dataset (only 4.7% samples are SMSware).

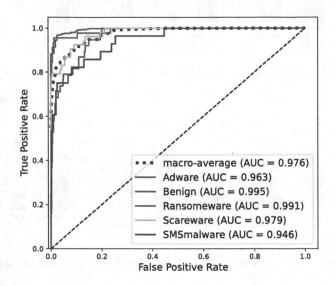

Fig. 10. Malware categorization ROC curve of gradient boosting

4   Limitation and Future Work

Although we combined static and dynamic analysis to improve the performance of *Hybroid*, some issues need to be addressed in the future. The biggest challenge is the lack of labeled data for CICAndMal2017 by Lashkari et al. [13]. They include only 426 malware and 1,700 benign APKs and their corresponding network traffic raw files. The main challenge is not having an alternative good-quality public dataset that covers the network traffic captured on real Android devices. For the malware detection, especially for the static feature-based work, the dataset with 2,126 samples is too small. However, for the networking dynamic feature-based work, 2,126 is a classic number. Actually, most networking dynamic analysis studies evaluate their frameworks with similar numbers, such as Jeon et al. [12] evaluate on 1,401 samples (1,000 malware and 401 benign) or Onwuzurike et al. [20] take 2,336 benign and 1,892 malware samples. Despite the static analysis work that needs more data samples, the number for networking dynamic analysis is normal. To address the lack of enough labeled data in the static analysis, we also separately trained and tested our static graph-based model with 45,592 malware and 90,313 benign samples

following TESSERACT [23] policies (we split 80% of the whole dataset for training and the other 20% for testing). These data samples are captured from the
AndroZoo[7], VirusShare[8], VirusTotal and we achieved the accuracy and F1-score
of 95.0% and 96.0% respectively which shows that our methodology demonstrate
competitive results on much larger dataset too.

Also, for the static analysis, *Hybroid* is affected by the obfuscated APKs,
and we cannot successfully extract graph features from 47 obfuscated APKs. To
further improve the robustness of *Hybroid*, we plan to extend CICAndMal2017
dataset in the near future to have more labeled network traffic data which are
captured from Android real devices.

5   Related Work

Detecting Android malware and categorizing its families have attracted much
attention from researchers as Android smartphones are gaining increasing pop-
ularity. Methods for Android malware detection are generally classified into traditional feature codes and machine learning.

For the traditional feature-based approaches, the detectors inspect the classical malicious behaviors. For example, program code-based malware detection
methods extract features from the code itself. Technically, those features include
permission [2,32], API call [1,3,22,32], N-gram [3], and CFG [10] based methods.
Malware detection methods that use permissions and intents extract them from
manifest files to detect Android malware [3]. In general, DREBIN performs a
comprehensive static analysis, gathering as many application features as possible.
These features are embedded in a joint vector space, such that typical malware
patterns can be automatically identified and used to explain our method's decisions. In contrast with our work, DREBIN takes permissions and intents from
manifest files, which cannot work for the obfuscated APKs. Meanwhile, *Hybroid*
takes the graph structure from the program code, which obfuscation cannot
affect. Additionally, we consider dynamic features from network flow, whereas
DREBIN only considers the static features.

Graph-based malware detection systems use the graph structure for detection purposes, such as the Apk2vec [19] and the Adagio [10]. Adagio [10] shows a
kernel-hashing-based malware detection system on the function call graph, which
is based on the efficient embeddings of function call graphs with an explicit feature map inspired by a linear-time graph kernel. In an evaluation with real
malware samples purely based on structural features, Adagio outperforms several related approaches and detects 89% of the malware with few false alarms,
while it also allows for pinpointing malicious code structures within Android
applications. Both the Adagio and our solution are based on the function call
graph of Android applications. However, we design the graph embedding based
on the function call graph, whereas Adagio uses the kernel-hashing method.

---

[7] https://androzoo.uni.lu.
[8] https://virusshare.com.

In addition, we also take the network flow into our *Hybroid* to obtain the dynamic features.

Machine learning and deep learning techniques are also heavily introduced into the network traffic analysis. Researchers use manual indicated features to recognize a network traffic application pattern with traditional machine learning algorithms, such as traffic classification, network security, and anomaly detection [15,25,32]. Finally, for network traffic analysis, there are three different granularities: raw packet, flow, and session levels [13,16,24,25]. CICAndMal2017 [13] takes network traffic as the dynamic features to detect and categorize the Android malware. Compared to our work, it only considers the network flow rather than other static features, such as program code, permissions, and intents.

6   Conclusion

In this paper, we presented *Hybroid*, a layered Android malware classification framework, which utilizes network traffic as a dynamic and code graph structure as static behavioral features for malware detection. As a hybrid approach, it extracts not only 13 network flow features from the original dumped network dataset but also introduces NLP inspired technique based on function call graph embedding that converts the whole graph structure of an Android application into a vector. *Hybroid* utilizes the network flow features in combination with the graphs vectors to detect and categorize the malware. Overall, it demonstrates an average accuracy of 97.0% and 94.0% in detecting and categorizing the Android malware, respectively. The empirical results imply that our stated solution is effective in the detection of malware applications.

Acknowledgments. This project has received funding from the European Union's Horizon 2020 research and innovation programme under grant agreements No. 830892 (SPARTA), No. 883275 (HEIR), and No. 833115 (PREVISION).

References

1. Aafer, Y., Du, W., Yin, H.: DroidAPIMiner: mining API-level features for robust malware detection in Android. In: Zia, T., Zomaya, A., Varadharajan, V., Mao, M. (eds.) SecureComm 2013. LNICST, vol. 127, pp. 86–103. Springer, Cham (2013). https://doi.org/10.1007/978-3-319-04283-1_6
2. Arora, A., Garg, S., Peddoju, S.K.: Malware detection using network traffic analysis in Android based mobile devices. In: International Conference on Next Generation Mobile Apps, Services and Technologies (2014)
3. Arp, D., Spreitzenbarth, M., Hubner, M., Gascon, H., Rieck, K., Siemens, C.: DREBIN: effective and explainable detection of Android malware in your pocket. In: The Network and Distributed System Security Symposium (NDSS) (2014)
4. Bengio, Y., Courville, A., Vincent, P.: Representation learning: a review and new perspectives. IEEE Trans. Pattern Anal. Mach. Intell. **35**(8), 1798–1828 (2013)

5. Canfora, G., De Lorenzo, A., Medvet, E., Mercaldo, F., Visaggio, C.A.: Effectiveness of opcode ngrams for detection of multi family Android malware. In: International Conference on Availability, Reliability and Security (2015)
6. Chen, C., Liu, Y., Shen, B., Cheng, J.J.: Android malware detection based on static behavior feature analysis. J. Comput. **29**(6), 243–253 (2018)
7. Comparetti, P.M., Salvaneschi, G., Kirda, E., Kolbitsch, C., Kruegel, C., Zanero, S.: Identifying dormant functionality in malware programs. In: 2010 IEEE Symposium on Security and Privacy (2010)
8. Dai, G., Ge, J., Cai, M., Xu, D., Li, W.: SVM-based malware detection for Android applications. In: ACM Conference on Security & Privacy in Wireless and Mobile Networks (WiSec) (2015)
9. Dai, H., Dai, B., Song, L.: Discriminative embeddings of latent variable models for structured data. In: International Conference on Machine Learning (ICML) (2016)
10. Gascon, H., Yamaguchi, F., Arp, D., Rieck, K.: Structural detection of Android malware using embedded call graphs. In: ACM Workshop on Artificial Intelligence and Security (2013)
11. Haq, I.U., Caballero, J.: A survey of binary code similarity. arXiv preprint arXiv:1909.11424 (2019)
12. Jeon, J., Park, J.H., Jeong, Y.S.: Dynamic analysis for IoT malware detection with convolution neural network model. IEEE Access **8**, 96899–96911 (2020)
13. Lashkari, A.H., Kadir, A.F.A., Taheri, L., Ghorbani, A.A.: Toward developing a systematic approach to generate benchmark Android malware datasets and classification. In: International Carnahan Conference on Security Technology (ICCST) (2018)
14. Li, C., Mills, K., Niu, D., Zhu, R., Zhang, H., Kinawi, H.: Android malware detection based on factorization machine. IEEE Access **7**, 184008–184019 (2019)
15. Malik, J., Kaushal, R.: CREDROID: Android malware detection by network traffic analysis. In: ACM Workshop on Privacy-Aware Mobile Computing (2016)
16. Marín, G., Caasas, P., Capdehourat, G.: DeepMAL - deep learning models for malware traffic detection and classification. In: Data Science – Analytics and Applications, pp. 105–112. Springer, Wiesbaden (2021). https://doi.org/10.1007/978-3-658-32182-6_16
17. McLaughlin, N., et al.: Deep Android malware detection. In: ACM Conference on Data and Application Security and Privacy (CODASPY) (2017)
18. Mikolov, T., Sutskever, I., Chen, K., Corrado, G.S., Dean, J.: Distributed representations of words and phrases and their compositionality. In: Advances in Neural Information Processing Systems (2013)
19. Narayanan, A., Soh, C., Chen, L., Liu, Y., Wang, L.: apk2vec: semi-supervised multi-view representation learning for profiling Android applications. In: 2018 IEEE International Conference on Data Mining (ICDM) (2018)
20. Onwuzurike, L., Almeida, M., Mariconti, E., Blackburn, J., Stringhini, G., De Cristofaro, E.: A family of droids-Android malware detection via behavioral modeling: static vs dynamic analysis. In: Annual Conference on Privacy, Security and Trust (PST) (2018)
21. Onwuzurike, L., Mariconti, E., Andriotis, P., Cristofaro, E.D., Ross, G., Stringhini, G.: MaMaDroid: detecting Android malware by building Markov chains of behavioral models (extended version). ACM Trans. Priv. Secur. (TOPS) **22**(2), 1–34 (2019)
22. Peiravian, N., Zhu, X.: Machine learning for Android malware detection using permission and API calls. In: IEEE International Conference on Tools with Artificial Intelligence (2013)

23. Pendlebury, F., Pierazzi, F., Jordaney, R., Kinder, J., Cavallaro, L.: TESSERACT: eliminating experimental bias in malware classification across space and time. In: USENIX Security Symposium (2019)
24. Taheri, L., Kadir, A.F.A., Lashkari, A.H.: Extensible Android malware detection and family classification using network-flows and API-calls. In: International Carnahan Conference on Security Technology (ICCST) (2019)
25. Wang, W., Zhu, M., Zeng, X., Ye, X., Sheng, Y.: Malware traffic classification using convolutional neural network for representation learning. In: International Conference on Information Networking (ICOIN) (2017)
26. Xu, P., Eckert, C., Zarras, A.: Detecting and categorizing Android malware with graph neural networks. In: ACM/SIGAPP Symposium on Applied Computing (SAC) (2021)
27. Xu, P., Eckert, C., Zarras, A.: Falcon: malware detection and categorization with network traffic images. In: Farkaš, I., Masulli, P., Otte, S., Wermter, S. (eds.) ICANN 2021. LNCS, vol. 12891, pp. 117–128. Springer, Cham (2021). https://doi.org/10.1007/978-3-030-86362-3_10
28. Xu, P., Kolosnjaji, B., Eckert, C., Zarras, A.: MANIS: evading malware detection system on graph structure. In: ACM/SIGAPP Symposium on Applied Computing (SAC) (2020)
29. Xu, P., Zhang, Y., Eckert, C., Zarras, A.: HawkEye: cross-platform malware detection with representation learning on graphs. In: Farkaš, I., Masulli, P., Otte, S., Wermter, S. (eds.) ICANN 2021. LNCS, vol. 12893, pp. 127–138. Springer, Cham (2021). https://doi.org/10.1007/978-3-030-86365-4_11
30. Xu, X., Liu, C., Feng, Q., Yin, H., Song, L., Song, D.: Neural network-based graph embedding for cross-platform binary code similarity detection. In: ACM SIGSAC Conference on Computer and Communications Security (CCS) (2017)
31. Yan, J., Yan, G., Jin, D.: Classifying malware represented as control flow graphs using deep graph convolutional neural network. In: IEEE/IFIP International Conference on Dependable Systems and Networks (DSN) (2019)
32. Zulkifli, A., Hamid, I.R.A., Shah, W.M., Abdullah, Z.: Android malware detection based on network traffic using decision tree algorithm. In: Ghazali, R., Deris, M.M., Nawi, N.M., Abawajy, J.H. (eds.) SCDM 2018. AISC, vol. 700, pp. 485–494. Springer, Cham (2018). https://doi.org/10.1007/978-3-319-72550-5_46

A Novel Behavioural Screenlogger Detection System

Hugo Sbai[1]([✉])[iD], Jassim Happa[2][iD], and Michael Goldsmith[1][iD]

[1] University of Oxford, Oxford OX1 3QD, UK
hugo.sbai@balliol.ox.ac.uk
[2] University of London, Royal Holloway, London WC1B 3RF, UK

Abstract. Among the various types of spyware, screenloggers are distinguished by their ability to capture screenshots. This gives them considerable nuisance capacity, giving rise to theft of sensitive data or, failing that, to serious invasions of the privacy of users. Several examples of attacks relying on this screen capture feature have been documented in recent years. Moreover, on desktop environments, taking screenshots is a legitimate functionality used by many benign applications, which makes screenlogging activities particularly stealthy. However, existing malware detection approaches are not adapted to screenlogger detection due to the composition of their datasets and the way samples are executed. In this paper, we propose the first dynamic detection approach based on a dataset of screenloggers and legitimate screenshot-taking applications (built in a previous work), with a particular care given to the screenshot functionality during samples execution. We also propose a tailored detection approach based on novel features specific to screenloggers. This last approach yields better results than an approach using traditional API call and network features trained on the same dataset (minimum increase of 3.108% in accuracy).

Keywords: Screenloggers · Screenshots · Malware detection

1 Introduction

1.1 Context and Motivation

Spyware can be defined as software that gathers information about a person or organisation without their consent or knowledge and sends it to another entity [28]. The software is designed for secrecy and durability. A long-term connection to the victim's machine is established by the adversary, and once spyware is installed on the victim's device, it aims to steal information unnoticed.

Spyware is usually organised in multiple modules, each performing one or more malicious activities, with the ability to use them according to the attacker's purpose [3]. Typical spyware modules include keystroke logging, screen logging,

© Springer Nature Switzerland AG 2021
J. K. Liu et al. (Eds.): ISC 2021, LNCS 13118, pp. 279–295, 2021.
https://doi.org/10.1007/978-3-030-91356-4_15

URL monitoring, turning on the microphone or camera, intercepting sensitive documents and exfiltrating them and collecting location information [28].

Among the aforementioned spyware modules, screenloggers have one of the most dangerous functionalities in today's spyware as they greatly contribute to hackers achieving their goals.

Screenlogger users can be divided into two categories: financially motivated actors and state-sponsored attackers. The first category targets important industrial companies (e.g., BRONZE BUTLER [11]), online banking users (e.g., RTM [25], FIN7 [10], Svpeng [11]), and even banks themselves (e.g., Carbanak [25], Silence [26]). The second category, which is even more problematic, targets critical infrastructure globally. For instance, the malware TinyZbot [8], a variant of Zeus, has targeted critical infrastructure in more than 16 countries. More precisely, the targets can be democratic institutions; for instance, XAgent targeted the US Democratic Congressional Campaign Committee and the Democratic National Committee [19]. In Europe, Regin [26], took screenshots for at least six years in the IT network of the EU headquarters. Diplomatic agencies have also been compromised, for example by the North Korean malware ScarCruft [16]. US defence contractors have also been hit by screenloggers such as Iron Tiger.

Screenloggers have the advantage of being able to capture any information displayed on the screen, offering a large set of possibilities for the attacker compared to other spyware functionalities. Moreover, malware authors are inventive when maliciously using screen captures. Indeed, screen captures have a wide range of purposes. Some malware, such as Cannon and Zebrocy, only take one screenshot during their entire execution as reconnaissance to see if the victim is worth infecting [5,20]. Others hide what is happening on the victim's screen by displaying a screenshot of their current desktop (FinFisher [20,30]) or take numerous screen captures for a close monitoring of the victim's activity. This allows spyware hackers to steal sensitive intellectual property data (BRONZE BUTLER [4]), banking credentials (RTM [25], FIN7 [10], XAgent [19]), or monitor day-to-day activity of banking clerks to understand the banks' internal mechanisms (Carbanak [9], Silence [26]).

The screenshot capability is sometimes the unique functionality used in some phases of an attack to observe while remaining stealthy. For instance, in the Carbanak attack targeting banking employees [28], attackers used the screengrabs to create a video recording of daily activity on employees' computers. The hackers amassed knowledge of internal processes before stealing money by impersonating legitimate local users during the next phase of the attack.

These examples show that the screenshot functionality is widely used today in modern malware programs and can be particularly stealthy, enabling powerful attacks. Even in the case where no specific attack is performed, the simple fact of monitoring and observing all the victims' activity on their device is a serious invasion of privacy. Moreover, screenshots are likely to contain personally identifiable information [24].

What makes the screenlogger threat even more problematic and stealthy is that, on desktop environments, the screenshot functionality is legitimate and, as such, is used by many benign applications (e.g. screen sharing for work or troubleshooting, saving important information, creating figures, monitoring employees). The necessity of capturing the screen has for instance increased with telework, even on sensitive machines. Teleworkers, including bank employees or lawyers, may need to control their office computer remotely from home, or to share their screens during online meetings. Therefore, countering the screenlogger threat cannot 'simply' be done by disabling the screenshot functionality on sensitive machines. Other natural approaches such as white-listing are prone to the ever more sophisticated strategies malware authors can deploy to inject malicious code into legitimate processes or bypass the user's consent.

Paradoxically, no work in the literature proposes a detection methodology adapted to the specifics of screenshot-taking malware. This is what we aim to do in this paper.

1.2 Contributions

More precisely, the contributions brought by this paper are:

- Training and testing of the detection model on a dataset composed exclusively of screenshot-taking malware and legitimate applications representative of the behaviours found in the wild: this allowed to identify the most effective existing detection features for screenlogger detection.
- Creation of features adapted to the screenlogging behaviour using novel techniques: instead of using hundreds of features and trusting a machine learning model to select the most discriminating ones, we propose to use new features that reflect a specific behaviour. The advantage is that malware authors will not be able to misguide the detection system without changing their core functionality. Indeed, existing detection models are prone to overfitting and can easily be misguided by malware authors by acting on features unrelated to the malicious functionalities of their programs.
- Samples execution methodology: in the malware detection field, it is common to automatically run thousands of malware samples in a controlled environment to collect features without interacting with the samples. Such an approach would unfortunately not work for screenloggers, as their malicious functionality needs to be triggered at run time through interaction with the malware program. To collect our features, we paid a particular care to ensure that each malicious or legitimate program worked as intended during its execution (was taking screenshots).

1.3 Paper Outline

In this paper, we start by discussing the relevant literature (Sect. 2) and precising the scope of our work through a system model (Sect. 3) and a threat model (Sect. 4). After that, we outline our experimental setup for screenlogger detection (Sect. 5). Then, we present a detection model based on state of the art features (Sect. 6) and a novel detection model including features specific to the screenlogging behaviour (Sect. 7). Finally, the performances of the two models are compared and discussed (Sect. 8).

2   Literature Review

Several types of malware detection models can be found in the literature.

Signature-based methods give good results for known malware programs with a low false-positive rate. However, they are vulnerable to obfuscation techniques that are more and used by modern malware [31]. Moreover, signature-based methods cannot detect malware integrating polymorphism and metamorphism mechanisms because the signature of the malware changes every time a machine is infected.

The drawback of anomaly-based detection techniques for detecting malware in computer systems is that those systems contain and execute many processes having many possible behaviours. This makes it difficult to define a "normal" behaviour and can result in a high false-positive rate.

Static behaviour-based detection fails to overcome obfuscation techniques [29]. Malware designers can use those techniques to disturb the analysis process and hide the malicious behaviour of the program.

Dynamic behaviour-based detection can overcome obfuscation techniques, as it analyses the runtime behaviour of the malware. Therefore, this technique is widely used in recent malware detection works, which consider diverse types of dynamic features such as API calls [12,13,22] and network traffic [6,18,23]. However, it was shown that the performance of a dynamic behaviour-based detection model greatly depends on the dataset it was trained on. Indeed, the features selected as the most discriminative vary according to the malware type [12,13]. Hence, if the dataset does not contain any screenshot-taking malware or very few, the behaviours related to screenlogging would not be taken into account.

To the best of our knowledge, only one malware detection work explicitly mentions screenloggers [15]. This work focused on detecting spyware and, more specifically, keyloggers, screen recorders, and blockers. The authors proposed a dynamic behavioural analysis through the hooking of kernel-level routines. More precisely, the presented method is designed to detect screenloggers under the Windows operating system. To this end, it hooks the GetWindowDC and BitBilt functions. Then, to classify a screenshot-taking program as spyware or benign, they used a decision tree considering the following features: frequency of repetition, uniqueness of the applicant process, state of the applicant process (hidden or not) and values of parameters in the system calls. The results showed that the proposed method could detect screenloggers with an accuracy of 92% and an error rate of 7%.

However, this method suffers from several weaknesses. Relying exclusively on API calls may not be sufficient to distinguish screenloggers from legitimate screenshot-taking applications. Indeed, by investigating existing screenloggers, it is possible to notice that they may exhibit various behaviours, including the fact that the screenshots frequency may be different from one screenlogger to another. The frequency can be a few seconds, few minutes, or configurable by the adversary. Screenshots can also be taken irregularly at each user event. Legitimate screenshot-taking applications are also diverse. Some of them, such as screensharing applications, need to take screenshots at a high frequency, while others like parental control make take screenshots at a lower frequency, and others like screenshots editing applications may take screenshots occasionally. Therefore, relying only on API calls may lead to high false positives and false negatives rates on an extensive dataset containing different types of screenloggers as well as benign screenshot-taking applications. It is not mentioned whether the dataset used to test the method proposed in [15] contained benign screenshot-taking programs, and there is no information about the nature and diversity of screenloggers. Moreover, the authors perform the hooking on only two functions, namely GetWindowsDC and BitBlt, whereas there are other ways of taking screenshots. For example, it is possible to use the GetDC function instead of GetWindowsDC in order to obtain the device context.

3   System Model

The targeted systems are desktop environments. The main reason why our work focuses on computer operating systems is that the screenshot functionality is a legitimate functionality offered to any application. In contrast, on smartphones, the principle is that apps cannot take screenshots of other apps, and the only way to accomplish this is to exploit specific vulnerabilities or to divert some libraries. However, many limitations exist for these techniques, such as permission required from the user at the beginning of each session, or a recording icon displayed in the notification bar. In sum, the architecture designs of mobile systems and computer systems are fundamentally different, which may lead to different solutions.

Targeted victims may be any individual or organisation, ranging from typical laptop users to small companies or powerful institutions. The victims are not particularly security aware, which implies they are not necessarily cognizant of the existing threats and will not install a specific protection against screenshots, such as a specific viewer to open documents in a secure environment, which prevents screenshots.

4   Threat Model

4.1   General Description

Our threat model is composed of a victim, an attacker and spyware with a screenshot functionality.

In this model, a screenshot is defined as a reproduction in an image format of what is displayed on the screen, even if all pixels may not be visible. Screenloggers must rely on a functionality offered by the operating system to perform their attack.

The adversary's goals are diverse. They can range from general activity monitoring, which requires to see the whole screen, to sensitive data theft, which can be limited to some areas of the screen.

4.2   Operating Process

Attackers may infect a system using common methods such as trojans, social engineering or through a malicious insider. The adversary has no physical access to the victim's device (except in the case of a malicious insider). They have no knowledge about the system and tools installed on it before infection. We also assume they have not compromised the victim's device at a kernel level. Apart from that, the attacker can use any technique to evade detection, including hiding by injecting api calls into system or legitimate processes, dividing its tasks between multiple processes, making the API calls out of sequence, spaced out in time, or interleaved with other API calls.

To reach their objective, attackers take screenshots of the victim's device. The data may be either (1) extracted automatically using OCR tools inside the victim's device locally, then sent to the attacker's server using the victim's network interface or (2) extracted, also using OCR tools, on the attacker's server after screenshots have been transferred from the victim's machine to the attacker's as compressed image files. The screenshots can also be analysed manually by the attacker. Moreover, the screenshots may be taken and sent at regular or irregular rates.

5   Experimental Setup

5.1   Malicious and Benign Datasets

In a previous work [27], we constructed the first dataset dedicated to malicious and legitimate screenshot-taking applications.

To ensure that this dataset was as representative and complete as possible, we included all the behaviours mentioned in the security reports referenced on the MITRE ATT&CK screen capture page [21].

Regarding legitimate applications, we collected samples of five cataegories of legitimate screenshot-taking applications: screen sharing, remote control, children/employee monitoring, screencasting and screenshot editing. Each of these categories exhibits different screenshot-taking and sending behaviours.

Our dataset contains 106 malicious samples and 87 legitimate samples. Although these numbers might seem low compared to the thousands of samples traditionally used in general malware detection works, they correspond to the number of samples used in detection works that target specific categories of malware [17]. Moreover, these numbers are explained by the particular care that must be given for each sample at runtime, as presented in the following section.

5.2   Experimental Framework

In a previous work [27], we realised that none of the screenlogger samples found on available malware datasets (e.g. VirusShare, VirusTotal) were taking screenshots at runtime. This was mainly due to the specificities of screenshot triggering (need to receive a command from the malicious server, need to open certain applications, ...). This means that, even if generalist malware detection works might have been tested on screenlogger samples (among thousands of other malware samples), the screenshot functionality was probably not observed because no attention was paid to screenshot-triggering.

Therefore, the samples we selected for our malicious dataset had to include both the client and server parts.

Our malicious samples were run in two Windows 10 virtual machines to allow the client and server parts to communicate and trigger the screenshot functionality. Legitimate applications were also run in two machines when it was required for screenshot-triggering.

During their execution, the behaviour of malicious and benign samples was monitored using API Monitor and Wireshark.

To implement and test our detection models, we used the Weka framework, which is a collection of machine learning algorithms for solving real-world data mining problems [1].

More precisely, we used it to process the run-time analysis reports, select the best detection features, select the classification algorithms, train and test the models, and visualise the detection results.

6   Basic Detection Approach

To prove the effectiveness of our novel detection model, it was first necessary to construct a model based on features from the malware detection literature. These features were extracted (Sect. 6.1) and transformed (Sect. 6.2). Then a machine learning model was trained and tested (Sect. 6.3) to select the most effective features (Sect. 6.4).

6.1   Feature Extraction

When running the samples from our malicious and benign datasets in a controlled environment, we collected reports on two aspects of their behaviours: API calls (API Monitor reports) and network activity (Wireshark reports).

API Calls. This category of features was extracted from the reports produced by API Monitor.

The first feature we used consisted in counting the number of occurrences of each API call. For each malicious and benign API call report, the numbers of occurrences of the API calls it contains was extracted in a .csv file.

In the literature, we found that malware programs try to dissimulate their malicious functionality by introducing benign API calls to their API call sequences. A popular way of performing malware detection using API calls is to use the number of occurrences of API call sequences rather than API calls taken alone. For this, the concept of N-grams is used. N-grams are sequences of N API calls made successively by the studied program.

As a result, we also extracted features based on the number of occurrences of 2-gram and 3-gram API calls sequences. The values of N were intentionally kept low for two reasons: (1) the number of features increases exponentially with N, and (2) the detection performance often decreases as N increases.

Network Traffic. Using the .pcap files produced by Wireshark and the Argus tool to isolate network flows [2], we extracted 47 network features found in the literature. These features belong to four categories:

- Behaviour-based features [4,6]: these features represent specific flow behaviours. For instance, they include the source and destination IP addresses.
- Byte-based features [18]: these features use byte counts. For instance, they include the average number of bytes from source to destination.
- Packet-based features [4,6,18]: these features are based on packet statistics. For instance, they include the number of small packets (length < 400 bytes) exchanged and the number of packets per second.
- Time-based features [4,6,18]: these features depend on time. For instance, they include the minimum time a flow was idle before becoming active.

6.2   Detection Algorithm

Our detection model uses the Random Forest algorithm [7]. This algorithm trains several decision trees and uses a majority vote to classify observations. Each decision tree is trained on a random subset of the training dataset using a random subset of features.

The main shortcoming of decision trees is that they are highly dependant on the order in which features are used to split the dataset. Random Forest addresses this issue by using multiple trees using different features.

We tested several parameters to optimise the performances of the model:

- Number of trees in the forest (by default 100).
- Number of randomly selected features for each tree.
- Maximum depth of the trees (by default unlimited).
- Minimum number of instance per leaf (by default 1 but can be raised to prevent overfitting).

6.3   Model Training and Testing

To train and test our model, we used the k-fold cross-validation method (with $k = 10$). This method consists in dividing our dataset into k blocks of the same size. The blocks all have the same proportions of malware and legitimate applications. For each block, we train the model on the $k - 1$ other blocks and test it on the current block. The final detection results are obtained by adding the results of each block.

Using cross-validation, we trained and tested our model using first API call features only, then network features only, and, finally, using both categories of features.

6.4   Feature Selection

Due to the high number of features used, to avoid overfitting, it was necessary to select the most useful ones. A features is useful if it is informative enough for our classification task, that is, if it enables to effectively distinguish between malicious and benign behaviours.

For this task we used the Recursive Feature Elimination method [14]. Given a number of features to select, this method iteratively trains our Random Forest model using cross-validation and removes the least important features at each iteration. The importance of a feature is given by the average of its Gini impurity score for each decision tree in which it is used.

The Gini impurity of a feature that splits the samples at a node of a decision tree reflects how 'pure' are the subsets produced by the split. In our case, a subset is purer if it contains mostly screenloggers or mostly legitimate screenshot-taking applications. For instance, a subset containing 75% malware and 25% legitimate applications is purer than a subset that contains 50% malware and 50% legitimate applications. The impurity of a subset is given by the formula:

$$p(malware) * (1 - p(malware)) + p(legitimate) * (1 - p(legitimate))$$

That is: $2 * p(malware) * p(legitimate)$

The Gini impurity of a feature is the weighted average of the impurity scores of the subset it produces. The weights are computed using the number of samples contained in each subset.

When the features are numerical values (which is our case), instead of computing the impurity of the subsets produced by each single value, intervals are used. More precisely, the Gini impurity of the feature is obtained through the following steps:

- Step 1: The values of the feature are sorted.
- Step 2: The averages of each adjacent values are computed.
- Step 3: For each average value from Step 2, the Gini impurity of the feature if the samples were split using this value is computed.
- Step 4: The Gini impurity of the feature is the minimum among the Gini impurities from Step 3.

7   Optimised Detection Approach

The novel detection approach we propose is based on new features specific to the screenlogger behaviour.

Thanks to the comparison made in our previous work between malicious and legitimate screenshot-taking behaviours, we were able to identify promising features for screenlogger detection. These features target specific behaviours that can allow to distinguish between screenloggers and legitimate screenshot taking.

For some of these features, we had to record the times at which screen-shots were taken by the applications. To this end, we used screenshot API call sequences that we had identified in a previous work [27]. Indeed, there does not exist a single API call that can be called to take a screenshot, but rather a succession of API calls that must be called in a given sequence, each one of them accomplishing a different task (e.g. retrieving the Device Context, creating a bitmap, copying the content of one bitmap into another). Different functions can be called at each stage of the sequence, which results in many sequences.

As the functions in the sequences take as parameters the return values of the previous functions, it is impossible for them to be called out-of-order. Moreover, as the return values are kept in memory until they are used as parameters, the screenshot is detected even if the API calls are spaced in time.

For the features where we needed this information, we wrote a script that ran through the API calls reports looking for screenshot sequences and recording their time stamps.

7.1 Interaction with the User

Contrary to screenloggers, a majority of legitimate screenshot-taking applications require an interaction with the user to start taking screenshots.

To extract this feature, we had to identify the API calls which result from user interaction. We found that, on Windows, some API calls involved in user interaction can be called on other applications' windows. As such, they could easily be called by a malware program pretending to interact with the user, whereas in fact, it does not even have a window.

Other API calls, mainly those involved in drawing on the window can only be called by the application that created the window. If they are called by another application, their return value is *false*. Therefore, we monitor this second category of functions and, even if they are called, we verify their return value.

7.2 Visibility of the Screenshot-Taking Process

Unless they infiltrate themselves in legitimate processes, all the malicious samples of our dataset take screenshots through background processes hidden to the user. Legitimate screenshot-taking applications, apart from children/employee monitoring and some applications that create a background process for the screenshot-taking (e.g. TeamViewer), use foreground processes. Thus, the fact that the screenshots are taken by a background process increases the probability of malicious activity.

7.3 Image Sending

A major part of legitimate screenshot-taking applications do not send screenshots over the network, contrary to our malware samples (no malware with the local OCR exploitation feature was found). However, due to the limited monitoring time (3 min), we cannot tell for sure that the screenshots taken by a given application will never be sent. Indeed, some malware can for instance schedule the sending of screenshots. In such a case, even if image packets are not sent during the monitoring time, it can be that these packets will be sent later.

Therefore, our 'Image sending' feature only reflects whether or not screenshots are sent during the monitoring time, and cannot be used to affirm that an application does not send the screenshots it takes. Moreover, determining whether a network packet contains an image is only possible when the packet is not encrypted.

7.4   Remote Command Triggering

An important characteristic shared by almost all screenloggers is that their screenshot-taking activity is triggered by a command received from their C&C server.

Two kinds of screenshot-triggering commands can be distinguished: commands for continuous capture of the screen and punctual commands for a single screenshot. In the first case, only one command is received at the beginning of the screenshot session, whereas in the second case, a command is received before every screenshot event. To cover both cases, we chose to consider that the screenshot-taking activity is triggered by a command even if only one screenshot is preceded by the reception of a network packet.

We had to determine an adequate duration between the reception of the command and the screenshot. Indeed, we only consider that the screenshot was triggered by the network packet if this packet is received within a given time-window T before the screenshot api call sequence. Concretely, for each screenshot taken, we control if:

$$t(screenshot) - t(lastNetworkMessage) < T$$

Note that, to measure this feature accurately, it was necessary that the API calls and network reports be generated at the exact same time.

By analysing our samples, we found that the maximum duration between the command and the screenshot is 46 772 ms, the minimum duration is 0.0059 ms, the average duration is 83.044 ms and the median duration is 33.115 ms. We conducted experiments with these different values for T.

Even if it was not found in our dataset, we account for the case where the process receiving the command is different from the process taking the screenshots.

To the best of our knowledge, our detection model, through this feature, is the first to make a correlation between two kinds of events (reception of a command and screenshot API call sequences) for malware detection.

7.5   Asymmetric Traffic

One of the packet-based network feature we found in the literature is the ratio between the number of incoming packets and the number of outgoing packets.

This feature fails to capture the asymmetric traffic displayed by most screen-loggers as opposed to legitimate screenshot-taking applications (e.g. video call with screen sharing). Indeed, in the case of screenloggers, the asymmetry lies in the quantity of data exchanged, and not necessarily in the number of packets. It may be that the number of incoming and outgoing packets are equal, for example in the case of punctual screenshot commands. In such a case, however, the quantity of data received from the C&C server is significantly lower than the quantity of data sent by the victim machine. Therefore, instead of measuring the ratio between the number of incoming and outgoing packets, we use the ratio between the numbers of bytes exchanged in both directions.

7.6   Captured Area

During our study, we observed that almost all malware capture the full screen as opposed to legitimate applications which may target more specific areas of the screen depending on their purpose. As a result, we implemented a 'captured area' feature which takes three values: full screen, coordinates and target window.

We had to identify, in our screenshot API call sequences, the elements that show what area of the screen is captured. However, there is not only one way to capture a given area of the screen, but several. For instance, to capture a zone with given coordinates, one might get a cropped DC from the beginning using the GetDC function with the desired coordinates as parameters, or take the whole DC and do the cropping afterwards when copying the content of the screen in the destination bitmap using BitBlt's arguments.

Therefore, for each of the three values of the 'captured area' feature, we listed the possible API call sequences which might be used.

Note that we consider that an application capturing more than the three quarters of the screen's area captures the full screen. This is to avoid malware programs pretending that they capture a precise area when, in fact, only few pixels are removed from the whole screen.

7.7   Screenshot Frequency

The last screenlogger-specific feature we created is the frequency of screenshots. We consider that an application takes screenshots at a given frequency if we find the same time interval between ten screenshots. Indeed, some malware programs offer to take punctual screenshot as well as continuous screen capture. Therefore, it is possible that not all the screenshots be taken at the same time interval.

Each time a screenshot API call sequence is found, we record its time stamp. Then, we subtract the timestamps of consecutive sequences and compare the intervals obtained. If more than ten intervals are found to be equal, the feature takes the value of this interval. Screenshots taken using different sequences are accounted for in this frequency calculation.

Some malware programs try to evade detection by dynamically changing the screenshot frequency using random numbers. To cover this case, we consider that the intervals are equal if they are within 15 s of each other.

8   Results and Comparison

8.1   Performance Measurements

Malware detection is a binary classification problem with two classes: malware and legitimate application.

The measures used to assess the performances of our detection models are the following:

- True Positives (TP): Number of malware programs classified as malicious.
- False Positives (FP): Number of legitimate applications classified as malicious.
- True Negatives (TN): Number of legitimate applications classified as legitimate.
- False Negatives (FN): Number of malware programs classified as legitimate.
- Accuracy: Given by the formula $\frac{TP+TN}{TP+TN+FP+FN}$. Accuracy does not discriminate between false positives and false negatives.
- Precision: Given by the formula $\frac{TP}{TP+FP}$. Precision is inversely proportional to the number of false positives.
- Recall: Given by the formula $\frac{TP}{TP+FN}$. Recall is inversely proportional to the number of false negatives.
- F-score: Given by the formula $\frac{2*Precision*Recall}{Precision+Recall}$. Contrary to accuracy, F-score decreases more rapidly if false positives or false negatives are high (i.e. precision or recall are low).

In the case of malware detection, it is crucial that all malware programs be detected, to avoid them causing important damage. On the other hand, classifying a legitimate application as malware, even if it can be inconvenient for the user, might not be as critical. As a result, we give a particular importance to the false negatives and recall metrics.

8.2   Basic Detection Approach

Table 1 contains the results we obtained for the first detection approach using features found in the literature.

Table 1. Detection results for the basic approach using features from the literature

Features	Accuracy	False negatives	False positives	Precision	Recall	F-measure
Network	94.301%	0.038	0.080	0.936	0.962	0.949
1-gram	92.228%	0.038	0.126	0.903	0.962	0.932
2-gram	88.601%	0.104	0.126	0.896	0.896	0.896
3-gram	83.938%	0.123	0.207	0.838	0.877	0.857
(1+2)-gram + network	94.301%	0.038	0.08	0.936	0.962	0.949
1-gram + network	94.301%	0.028	0.092	0.928	0.972	0.949

We can observe that network features seem to give better results overall than API call features. Regarding API calls, using sequences of two and three calls significantly decreases the performances of the model, with more than 10% of malware classified as legitimate (vs 3.8% when individual API calls are used).

Combining network features and API call features does not improves the results compared to using network features alone.

Additionally, using Recursive Feature Elimination, we identified the most relevant API calls for screenlogger detection:

- strcpy_s (Visual C++ Run Time Library)
- ntreleasemutant (NT Native API)
- _isnan (Visual C++ Run Time Library)
- getobjectw (Graphics and Gaming)
- rtltimetotimefields (NT Native API)

We also identified the most relevant state of the art network features:

- Bytes per packet
- Total number of bytes in the initial window from source to destination
- Total number of bytes in the initial window from destination to source
- Total number of bytes from source to destination
- Average number of bytes in a subflow from source to destination

8.3   Optimised Detection Approach

Table 2 contains the results we obtained for the second detection approach using the screenlogger-specific features we implemented.

Table 2. Detection results for the optimised approach using our specific features

Features	Accuracy	False negatives	False positives	Precision	Recall	F-measure
Specific features	97.409%	0.009	0.046	0.963	0.991	0.977

We can see that the detection performance is improved on all metrics: with only 7 features, our model outperforms the first model based on hundreds of standard features. That is because our features capture specific malicious behaviours.

Moreover, a malware author would not be able to act on these features to mislead the classifier without changing the malicious functionality. Indeed, to mislead traditional classifiers based on numerous features, malware authors leverage overfitting by acting on features unrelated the core functionality of their programs. When all the features target a specific behaviour, as in our case, this cannot be done.

9   Conclusion

In this paper, we built a first Random Forest detection model using only API calls and network features from the literature. This model was trained and tested using our malicious and benign datasets. Using Recursive Feature Elimination with Gini importance, we identified the most informative existing features for screenlogger detection.

Then, we built a second model including novel features adapted to the screenlogging behaviour. These features were collected using novel techniques. Particularly, we can cite:

- Using API call sequences to identify specific behaviours. Contrary to existing works which only look at API called in a direct succession using the notion of n-grams, we wrote scripts which keep track of the API calls return values and arguments to characterise some behaviours even if the calls are not made directly one after the other. Numerous different sequences involved in the screenshot-taking process were identified by analysing malware and legitimate applications. These sequences were also divided into three categories depending on the captured area.
- Making a correlations between API calls made by an application and its network activity. During their execution, the API calls and network activity of our samples were simultaneously monitored. This allowed us to extract features such as the reception of a network packet before starting the screenshot activity or the sending of taken screenshots over the network.

When adding these novel features to the detection model, the detection accuracy increased by at least 3.108%. Indeed, it is well known that a detection model based on less features is less likely to fall into overfitting. Moreover, a detection model based on features which have a logical meaning and reflect specific behaviours, is less prone to evasion techniques often used by malware authors.

More generally, our results show that, for some categories of malware, a tailored detection approach might be more effective and difficult to mislead than a generalist approach relying on a great number of seemingly meaningless features fed to a machine learning model.

In the future, we could extend our detection model to infection to allow for an earlier and more effective detection. The detection model could also be integrated into a defense-in-depth solution agaist screenloggers, including prevention mechanisms.

References

1. Albert, B.: Weka 3: Machine learning software in Java. https://www.cs.waikato.ac.nz/ml/weka/
2. Argus, O.: Argus. https://openargus.org
3. Bahtiyar, S.: Anatomy of targeted attacks with smart malware. Secur. Commun. Netw. **9** (2017). https://doi.org/10.1002/sec.1767

4. Beigi, E., Jazi, H., Stakhanova, N., Ghorbani, A.: Towards effective feature selection in machine learning-based botnet detection approaches. In: 2014 IEEE Conference on Communications and Network Security, CNS 2014, pp. 247–255, December 2014. https://doi.org/10.1109/CNS.2014.6997492

5. Bogdan, B.: Six years and counting: inside the complex Zacinlo ad fraud operation, bitdefender. https://labs.bitdefender.com/2018/06/six-years-and-counting-inside-the-complex-zacinlo-ad-fraud-operation/

6. Boukhtouta, A., Mokhov, S., Lakhdari, N.E., Debbabi, M., Paquet, J.: Network malware classification comparison using DPI and flow packet headers. J. Comput. Virol. Hacking Tech. **11**, 1–32 (2015). https://doi.org/10.1007/s11416-015-0247-x

7. Breiman, L.: Random forests. Mach. Learn. **45**(1), 5–32 (2001). https://doi.org/10.1023/A:1010933404324

8. Charline, Z.: Viruses and malware: research strikes back. https://news.cnrs.fr/articles/viruses-and-malware-research-strikes-back

9. The New Jersey Cybersecurity and Communications Integration Cell: Zbot/zeus. https://www.cyber.nj.gov/threat-center/threat-profiles/trojan-variants/zbot-zues

10. Sanger, D.E., Perlroth, N.: Bank hackers steal millions via malware. https://www.nytimes.com/2015/02/15/world/bank-hackers-steal-millions-via-malware.html

11. Ecular, X., Grey, G.: Cyberespionage campaign sphinx goes mobile with anubisspy. https://www.trendmicro.com/enus/research/17/l/cyberespionage-campaign-sphinx-goes-mobile-anubisspy.html

12. Han, W., Xue, J., Wang, Y., Huang, L., Kong, Z., Mao, L.: MalDAE: detecting and explaining malware based on correlation and fusion of static and dynamic characteristics. Comput. Secur. **83**, 208–233 (2019). https://doi.org/10.1016/j.cose.2019.02.007

13. Han, W., Xue, J., Wang, Y., Liu, Z., Kong, Z.: Malinsight: a systematic profiling based malware detection framework. J. Netw. Comput. Appl. **125**, 236–250 (2018). https://doi.org/10.1016/j.jnca.2018.10.022

14. Jason, B.: Recursive feature elimination (RFE) for feature selection in Python. https://machinelearningmastery.com/rfe-feature-selection-in-python/

15. Javaheri, D., Hosseinzadeh, M., Rahmani, A.: Detection and elimination of spyware and ransomware by intercepting kernel-level system routines. IEEE Access **6**, 78321–78332 (2018). https://doi.org/10.1109/ACCESS.2018.2884964

16. Josh, G., Brandon, L., Kyle, W., Pat, L.: SquirtDanger: the swiss army knife malware from veteran malware author thebottle. https://unit42.paloaltonetworks.com/unit42-squirtdanger-swiss-army-knife-malware-veteran-malware-author-thebottle/

17. Stratosphere Labs: The CTU-13 dataset. A labeled dataset with botnet, normal and background traffic. https://www.stratosphereips.org/datasets-ctu13

18. Lashkari, A.H., Kadir, A.F.A., Gonzalez, H., Mbah, K.F., Ghorbani, A.A.: Towards a network-based framework for Android malware detection and characterization. In: 2017 15th Annual Conference on Privacy, Security and Trust (PST), p. 233-23309 (2017). https://doi.org/10.1109/PST.2017.00035

19. Lukas, S.: New telegram-abusing android rat discovered in the wild, welivesecurity by eset. https://www.welivesecurity.com/2018/06/15/new-telegram-abusing-android-rat/

20. Mikey, C.: Xagent malware arrives on Mac, steals passwords, screenshots, iPhone backups. https://appleinsider.com/articles/17/02/14/xagent-malware-arrives-on-mac-steals-passwords-screenshots-iphone-backups

21. Mitre: Screen capture. https://attack.mitre.org/techniques/T1113/
22. Mohaisen, D., Alrawi, O., Mohaisen, M.: AMAL: high-fidelity, behavior-based automated malware analysis and classification. Comput. Secur. **52**, 251–266 (2015). https://doi.org/10.1016/j.cose.2015.04.001
23. Nari, S., Ghorbani, A.: Automated malware classification based on network behavior, pp. 642–647, January 2013. https://doi.org/10.1109/ICCNC.2013.6504162
24. Pan, E., Ren, J., Lindorfer, M., Wilson, C., Choffnes, D.: Panoptispy: characterizing audio and video exfiltration from android applications. Proc. Priv. Enhanc. Technol. **2018**, 33–50 (2018). https://doi.org/10.1515/popets-2018-0030
25. Kaspersky Lab's Global Research and Analysis Team: The great bank robbery: Carbanak cybergang steals $1bn from 100 financial institutions worldwide. https://www.kaspersky.com/about/press-releases/2015-the-great-bank-robbery-carbanak-cybergang-steals-1bn-from-100-financial-institutions-worldwide
26. Symantec Security Response: Regin: top-tier espionage tool enables stealthy surveillance. https://www.databreaches.net/regin-top-tier-espionage-tool-enables-stealthy-surveillance/
27. Sbaï, H., Happa, J., Goldsmith, M., Meftali, S.: Dataset construction and analysis of screenshot malware. In: 2020 IEEE 19th International Conference on Trust, Security and Privacy in Computing and Communications (TrustCom), pp. 646–655 (2020). https://doi.org/10.1109/TrustCom50675.2020.00091
28. Shahzad, R., Haider, S., Lavesson, N.: Detection of spyware by mining executable files, pp. 295–302, February 2010. https://doi.org/10.1109/ARES.2010.105
29. Shijo, P., Salim, A.: Integrated static and dynamic analysis for malware detection. Procedia Comput. Sci. **46**, 804–811 (2015). https://doi.org/10.1016/j.procs.2015.02.149
30. Stefan, O.: The missing piece - sophisticated OS X backdoor discovered, securelist by Kaspersky lab. https://securelist.com/the-missing-piece-sophisticated-os-x-backdoor-discovered/75990/
31. You, I., Yim, K.: Malware obfuscation techniques: a brief survey. In: 2010 International Conference on Broadband, Wireless Computing, Communication and Applications, pp. 297–300 (2010). https://doi.org/10.1109/BWCCA.2010.85

DEVA: Decentralized, Verifiable Secure Aggregation for Privacy-Preserving Learning

Georgia Tsaloli[1](✉), Bei Liang[2], Carlo Brunetta[1], Gustavo Banegas[3], and Aikaterini Mitrokotsa[1,4]

[1] Chalmers University of Technology, Gothenburg, Sweden
{tsaloli,brunetta}@chalmers.se
[2] Beijing Institute of Mathematical Sciences and Applications, Beijing, China
lbei@bimsa.cn
[3] Inria and Laboratoire d'Informatique de l'Ecole polytechnique,
Institut Polytechnique de Paris, Palaiseau, France
gustavo@cryptme.in
[4] School of Computer Science, University of St. Gallen, St. Gallen, Switzerland
katerina.mitrokotsa@unisg.ch

Abstract. Aggregating data from multiple sources is often required in multiple applications. In this paper, we introduce DEVA, a protocol that allows a distributed set of servers to perform secure and verifiable aggregation of multiple users' secret data, while no communication between the users occurs. DEVA computes the sum of the users' input and provides public verifiability, *i.e.,* anyone can be convinced about the correctness of the aggregated sum computed from a threshold amount of servers. A direct application of the DEVA protocol is its employment in the *machine learning* setting, where the aggregation of multiple users' parameters (used in the learning model), can be orchestrated by multiple servers, contrary to centralized solutions that rely on a single server. We prove the security and verifiability of the proposed protocol and evaluate its performance for the execution time and bandwidth, the verification execution, the communication cost, and the total bandwidth usage of the protocol. We compare our findings to the prior work, concluding that DEVA requires less communication cost for a big amount of users.

Keywords: Secure aggregation · Privacy · Verifiability · Decentralization

1 Introduction

Mobile phones, wearables, and other Internet-of-Things (IoT) devices are all connected to distributed network systems. These devices generate a significant amount of data, that often need to remain private. These data in many cases need to be aggregated to compute statistics, or even employed for user modeling and

© Springer Nature Switzerland AG 2021
J. K. Liu et al. (Eds.): ISC 2021, LNCS 13118, pp. 296–319, 2021.
https://doi.org/10.1007/978-3-030-91356-4_16

personalization via federated learning algorithms. Such an application scenario gives rise to the *secure data aggregation* problem, the goal of which is to compute sums of local updated parameters from individual users' devices in a privacy-preserving manner, *i.e.*, any individual user's update is not revealed in the clear.

In the federated learning setting, each *user* maintains her private data on her mobile device, and shares local updated parameters (*e.g.*, gradients) to the server. The central *server* updates the training model using the aggregated updates and performs the appropriate testing of the model. An advantage of federated training is that it diminishes the risk of compromising the user's privacy, since it allows users (mobile devices or organizations) to collaboratively train learning models under the orchestration of a central server, while the data remain located on the sources (*i.e.*, mobile devices or data centers of organizations).

The secure aggregation problem has received significant attention in the literature. Bonawitz *et al.* [13] proposed a practical and secure aggregation protocol for federated learning, which enables a central server to compute the sum of multiple users' parameters and guarantees robustness in a dynamic environment where users may drop out. Even though Bonawitz *et al.* [13] addressed the problem of maintaining user's privacy (i.e., local gradients) in the learning process, Xu *et al.* [21] considered another fundamental issue of data integrity in federated learning, *i.e.*, how to assure the correctness of the aggregated results returned from the central server, since a malicious server might modify the aggregation process [11], bias the final result and cause inferences according to its preferences [6,11,16,22]. To this end, Xu *et al.* provided a privacy-preserving and verifiable aggregation protocol, VerifyNet [21]. The latter enables the users to verify the correctness of the computed sum, while guaranteeing the users' privacy in the training process. In our work, we focus on the verifiability as considered in [21], *i.e.*, guaranteeing the correctness of the aggregated result. Bonawitz *et al.*'s [13] and Xu *et al.*'s [21] solutions adopt a centralized architecture since a *single* central server is responsible for the aggregation of the users' parameters and orchestrates the federated learning process. Even though a central server is an important component of the federated learning process, a single server might attempt to bias the model and cause inferences. For instance, the server may tamper with the learning model so that it always misclassifies a certain pattern in an image recognition system, or allows access to unauthorized users in a biometric authentication system [5]. Decentralized systems have raised considerable interest, since they distribute the storage and the computation among *multiple* servers, thus allowing different organizations to collaboratively perform computations and diminish the security threats incurred by centralized systems.

In this paper, we propose DEVA, a decentralized, verifiable and privacy-preserving aggregation protocol, which enables multiple servers to *jointly* compute the sum of the parameters of multiple users, and further to train and evaluate a global learning model. We stress that although VerifyNet [21] achieves data integrity in the process of training neural networks, it employs a *single central* server for both the aggregation and for returning the verification results. In contrary, our DEVA protocol performs federated learning collaboratively by employing multiple servers for the aggregation process. A single server (hosted by a single organization) might not be trusted by different organizations with similar objectives (*e.g.*, hospitals, banks) that want to **collaboratively** train learning models [7] and thus, multiple cloud servers can resolve this issue. The involvement of multiple servers is challenging, since we need to find a way to obtain the aggregated result from partial outputs, but also need to ensure the correctness of the computed result. In this work, we make the following **contributions**: *(i)* We propose DEVA, a protocol for securely computing the sum (aggregation) of n inputs from multiple users, by employing multiple servers. Our DEVA has a constant number of rounds, low communication cost for each server, and tolerates up to $n-(t_{key}+1)m$ users dropping out during the protocol execution, for t_{key} being a threshold value. Contrary to the setting of only one central server that requires limited trust, in DEVA no server has to be individually trusted and a fraction of the servers can collude. DEVA also handles possible servers' failure as it requires $t+1$ servers to compute the sum. *(ii)* DEVA guarantees the individual user's privacy, *i.e.*, the servers learn only the aggregated result of all users' inputs without knowing any user's input itself. *(iii)* DEVA ensures the correctness of the computed sum by requiring the employed servers to provide a proof about the correctness of their aggregated results. We prove that it is infeasible for any adversary to deceive the users by altering the aggregated results with a valid proof. *(iv)* DEVA is practical and we present experimental results from our prototype implementation. DEVA provides less communication cost for each user participating in the protocol. DEVA also allows to maintain bandwidth cost since increased amount of users can be leveraged by having more servers.

Related Work. To solve the security, accuracy and privacy challenges in learning, some works have been proposed recently [12,13,15,16]. Phong *et al.* [12] proposed a secure deep learning system based on additively homomorphic encryption, Shokri *et al.* [16] proposed a privacy-preserving deep learning protocol focusing on the trade-off between private and accurate learning. Bonawitz *et al.* [13] proposed a secure aggregation protocol tailored for the federated learning process that attempts to achieve a good balance between security, privacy and efficiency, being robust to users dropping out. However, these solutions have multiple limitations: *(i)* they assume a **single** server which is not suitable when different organizations collaboratively train a model; and *(ii)* they provide **no verifiability** guarantees of the learning model. We stress that Bonawitz *et al.* [13] discuss how to address the input verifiability, *i.e.*, verifying that the inputs are in the correct range; however, they **do not** deal with the issue of output verifiability, *i.e.*, verifying that the aggregated result is correct. Some works [4,5,10,17,21] attempted to address the problem of *verifiability* (output correctness), but all of them require a central server and additionally, either they ignore users dropping out [4,5,10] and privacy leakages [5] or require special hardware [17] (thus, placing trust to the hardware manufacturer) or costly computations for verification (low efficiency) [21]. They consider a centralized system, while our goal is to avoid placing the trust to a single server and allow different organizations (hosted by different cloud servers) to collaboratively perform the learning process. Thus, we employ multiple servers and achieve decentralized aggregation.

2 Preliminaries

In this section, we show definitions and assumptions used throughout the paper.

Hash Functions. We employ a collision-resistant homomorphic hash function [23] satisfying additive homomorphism [9], i.e., $H : x \mapsto \mathsf{g}^x$ where g is a generator of the group $\mathbb{G}$ of prime order p.

Key Agreement. Let $\mathbb{G}$ be a cyclic group of order p prime with generator g, e.g., groups based on elliptic curves [8]. Let us report the definition of the Diffie-Hellman key agreement [3] and the related assumptions.

Assumption 1 (Discrete Logarithm Problem). *Consider a cyclic group $\mathbb{G}$ of order p prime with generator g. Given $y \in \mathbb{G}$, the **discrete logarithm problem** (**dLog**) requires to find the value $x \in [0, p{-}1]$ such that $\mathsf{g}^x = y$. We assume the advantage of solving the dLog problem to be negligible, i.e., $\epsilon_{dLog} < \mathsf{negl}$.*

Assumption 2 (Diffie-Hellman Assumptions). *Consider a cyclic group $\mathbb{G}$ of prime order p with generator g and $a, b \in [0, p{-}1]$. Given elements $(A, B) = (\mathsf{g}^a, \mathsf{g}^b)$, the **computation Diffie-Hellman problem (CDH)** requires to compute the element $\mathsf{g}^{ab} \in \mathbb{G}$. The **distinguishing Diffie-Hellman problem** (**DDH**) requires to correctly distinguish between $(\mathsf{g}, A, B, \mathsf{g}^{ab})$ and $(\mathsf{g}, A, B, \mathsf{g}^c)$ for some random $c \in [0, p{-}1]$. We assume the advantage of solving the CDH and the DDH problems to be negligible, i.e., $\epsilon_{CDH} < \mathsf{negl}$ and $\epsilon_{DDH} < \mathsf{negl}$.*

Definition 1 (Diffie-Hellman Key Exchange). *Consider a Diffie-Hellman key agreement scheme with algorithms (Ksetup, Kgen, Kagree) to be defined as:*

- *Ksetup$(1^\lambda) \rightarrow$ pp: the setup algorithm takes as input the security parameter and outputs the public parameters pp which contain a prime p, the description of a cyclic group $\mathbb{G}$ of order p and a generator g for the group $\mathbb{G}$.*
- *Kgen$($pp$, U_i) \rightarrow (sk_i, pk_i)$: the user U_i samples a value $sk_i \in [0, p{-}1]$ and computes $pk_i = \mathsf{g}^a$. The key generation algorithm outputs $(sk_i, pk_i) = (sk_i, \mathsf{g}^{sk_i})$.*
- *Kagree$(sk_i, pk_j) \rightarrow s_{ij}$: the user U_i runs the key agreement algorithm with its own secret sk_i and U_j's public key $pk_j = \mathsf{g}^{sk_j}$ to obtain the agreed secret key $s_{ij} = pk_j^{sk_i} = \mathsf{g}^{sk_j \cdot sk_i}$ between the users U_i and U_j.*

*The key agreement is said to be **correct** if for any pp $\leftarrow$ Ksetup(1^λ), $(sk_i, pk_i) \leftarrow$ Kgen$($pp$, U_i)$, and $(sk_j, pk_j) \leftarrow$ Kgen$($pp$, U_j)$, it holds that $s_{ij} = s_{ji}$. The key agreement scheme is said to be **secure** if for any pp $\leftarrow$ Ksetup(1^λ), $(sk_i, pk_i) \leftarrow$ Kgen$($pp$, U_i)$, as well as $(sk_j, pk_j) \leftarrow$ Kgen$($pp$, U_j)$, it holds that any PPT adversary $\mathcal{A}$ has negligible probability to compute s_{ij} from (pk_i, pk_j). The key agreement's security reduces to the CDH and dLog assumptions.*

Secret Sharing. We provide the definition of a (t, m)-threshold secret sharing scheme in order to achieve additive homomorphism in our protocols. Precisely:

Definition 2. *A (t, m)-threshold secret sharing scheme allows a user U_i to split a secret $x_i \in \mathbb{F}$, where $\mathbb{F}$ is the input domain, into m shares, such that any $t + 1$ shares can be used to reconstruct x_i, while any set of at most t shares gives no information about x_i. Let S be the set such that $|S| = m$ and $T \subseteq S$ with $|T| > t$. Then we consider two algorithms* (SS.share, SS.recon):

- SS.share$(t, x_i, j, S) \to \{x_{ij}\}_{j \in S}$: *for a given threshold t, a secret input $x_i \in \mathbb{F}$, an index j which corresponds to the receiver of the share and the set S, the algorithm outputs a list of shares, namely, $\{x_{i1}, \ldots, x_{im}\}$.*
- SS.recon$(t, \{x_{ij}\}_{j \in T}, T) \to x_i$: *given a threshold t, $|T| > t$ amount of shares x_{ij} and the set T, the algorithm gives x_i.*

Shamir's threshold secret sharing [14], as well as other secret sharing schemes [18–20] have an homomorphic property, as described by Benaloh [1]. More precisely, these schemes allow to combine multiple secrets by performing computations directly on shares. For linear functions, a (t, m) threshold scheme has the additive homomorphic property if the sum of the shares are shares of the sum [1]. Thus, with our notation, if we consider n secret inputs $x_1, \ldots, x_n$ and denote the sum of shares of each $j \in T$ by y_j, then SS.recon$(t, \{y_j\}_{j \in T}, T) \to y$, where

$$y = x_1 + \ldots + x_n. \tag{1}$$

In fact, Shamir's scheme is an additive homomorphic secret sharing scheme and, therefore, we use it in the implementation of our protocol.

Zero-Knowledge Proofs of Discrete Logarithm Knowledge. We will need a zero-knowledge proof of knowledge of a value $\alpha \in [0, p-1]$ such that $A = g^{\alpha}$ and $B = h^{\alpha}$ given the group generators g, h and the corresponding values A, B. We denote the protocol which generates this proof by DLEQ(g, h, A, B, α). Chaum and Pedersen proposed a sigma protocol to perform this proof in [2]. Precisely, the zero knowledge protocol we use is specified as follows: DLEQ(g, h, A, B, α):

- **Proof**.DLEQ(g, h, A, B, α): (i) for the given g, h, compute $s_1 = g^s, s_2 = h^s$ where s is a field element, chosen uniformly at random; (ii) for a hash function Ha such that Ha$(\cdot) \in \{0, 1\}$, compute $c = $ Ha(g, h, A, B, s_1, s_2), (iii) compute $r = s + c \cdot \alpha$, and (iv) output the proof (s_1, s_2, r).
- **Verify**.DLEQ$(g, h, A, B, (s_1, s_2, r))$: (i) for the aforementioned hash function, compute $c = $ Ha(g, h, A, B, s_1, s_2), (ii) check if both $g^r \overset{?}{=} s_1 \cdot A^c$ and $h^r \overset{?}{=} s_2 \cdot B^c$ are satisfied, and (iii) if they are satisfied, accept the proof, otherwise abort.

3   Framework of a DECENTA Problem

In this chapter, we describe the DECENTA problem as well as the required properties that a solution to DECENTA must satisfy.

Problem Statement. Consider n users $U_1, \ldots, U_n$, each with a secret input x_i, and m servers $S_1, \ldots, S_m$. A DECENTA problem aims to **securely** compute the sum of the users' secret inputs, i.e., $y = \sum_{i=1}^{n} x_i$, by aggregating more than a certain amount of partial results; which are computed by the servers. Moreover, the aggregated final result y can be publicly verified, *i.e.*, anyone is able to check if y is the correct sum of all users' inputs without revealing their input itself.

In the setting of a DECENTA problem, no communication is allowed between the users; thus rendering it suitable for application settings where an immense number of users are participating, *e.g.*, this is the case for the federated learning setting, where a very large number of users participate via their mobile devices and thus, cannot establish direct communications channels with other mobile devices (need to rely on a server to play the intermediate communication role). Furthermore, DECENTA supports a dynamic setting, where the participating users (mobile devices) may drop out during the execution of the protocol and the correct aggregation of the values of the remaining users (devices) is still possible. The DECENTA problem captures both features of *decentralization*, since multiple servers are involved in the system instead of a single centralized server, thus, allowing a subset of the servers to be corrupted while still securely computing the sum value; and *verifiability* since it allows the participating users to verify the correctness of the computed result. A protocol solving the DECENTA problem involves the following phases:

Setup: generation of all key pairs that are used during the protocol execution.

Shares and Public Values Generation: each user U_i hides its secret data x_i by splitting it into different shares that are sent to the servers instead of the actual secret users' data. Additionally, each user computes and publishes some values that are used by a verifier to fulfill, later on, the verification process.

Aggregation: it consists of all the steps that are needed to output partial values by each server, which are appropriately used for the generation of the final result y, and the proof (that y is indeed the correct sum), denoted by σ.

Verification: ultimately, combining suitably the result y and the proof σ, this phase performed by a verifier gives out either 1, implying that y is the actual correct sum of all users' secret data x_i, or 0 implying that y is incorrect.

Threat Model and Design Goal. We adopt the threat model proposed by Xu *et al.*, which is used to define the security of VerifyNet [21], a recently proposed privacy-preserving and verifiable federated learning framework. In contrast to the single server (*i.e.* centralized) setting used in VerifyNet, we adjust the threat model to a decentralized multiple-server setting. Precisely, we consider that both the cloud servers and the users follow the protocol's execution as agreed, but they may also try to infer information about other users' data. Additionally to this, in our protocol, we employ multiple servers with the following abilities: *(i)* a threshold of the servers may collude to discover the users' private inputs, and *(ii)* they can modify their computed results and forge proofs in order to provide an incorrect sum to be accepted.

Properties. We require a solution to the DECENTA problem to be *correct*, *secure*, and *verifiable*. Below, we provide the corresponding definitions.

Definition 3 (Correctness). *For all n users $U_1, U_2, \ldots, U_n$ with inputs $x_1, \ldots, x_n$, for all m servers $S_1, \ldots, S_m$, where all U_i and S_j honestly execute the protocol, and for all the partial values output by the servers S_j, the protocol is correct if it satisfies the following requirement:*

$$\Pr\left[\textbf{\textit{Verification}}(\textit{pub\_pars}, \sigma, y) = 1 \wedge y = \sum_{i=1}^{n} x_i\right] = 1.$$

where **pub_pars** *denotes all public parameters necessary for the protocol (if any), y denotes the aggregated final result, which comes from the partial values output by the servers during the protocol, and σ denotes the corresponding proof of y.*

Definition 4 (Verifiability). *For n users $U_1, \ldots, U_n$ with inputs $x_1, \ldots, x_n$, that honestly execute the protocol, and any set of corrupted servers $T = \{S_{j_1}, \ldots, S_{j_{|T|}}\}$ with $|T| < m$ that are controlled by a PPT adversary $\mathcal{A}$, i.e., $\forall j \in [j_1, j_{|T|}]$ such that $S_j \in T$, S_j gives $\{x_{1j}, \ldots, x_{nj}\}$ to $\mathcal{A}$ where x_{ij} is the share given to the server S_j from the user U_i. $\mathcal{A}$ outputs the malicious partial results on behalf of the corrupted servers $S_j \in T$, while the honest servers $S_j \notin T$ output correct partial results. Then, if $\mathcal{A}$ outputs an aggregated result y' together with the corresponding proof σ' such that $y' \neq \sum_{i=1}^{n} x_i$, we require that $\mathcal{A}$ can pass the verification phase with negligible probability. More precisely, for any PPT adversary $\mathcal{A}$, it holds:*

$$\Pr\left[\textbf{\textit{Verification}}(\textit{pub\_pars}, \sigma', y') = 1\right] \leq \varepsilon,$$

for some negligible ε; **pub_pars** *are the public parameters of the protocol.*

Definition 5 (Security). *Let $T = \{S_{j_1}, \ldots, S_{j_{|T|}}\}$ be the set of the corrupted servers with $|T| \leq t$ which are controlled by the adversary $\mathcal{A}$. The goal of the adversary $\mathcal{A}$ is to infer sensitive information about the users' data. We consider security in the setting where all the servers (including the corrupted servers) correctly execute the protocol. A protocol is t-secure if there is no leak of information about the users' data besides what can be derived from publicly available information.*

4 A DECENTA Solution: DEVA

In this section, we present DEVA, an interactive multi-round protocol, inspired by Segal *et al.* [13] work, designed to solve the DECENTA problem.

DEVA Construction. At any point during the protocol, users may drop out, *i.e.*, a user U_i after sending the round-k messages, may not send the consecutive round-$(k + 1)$ messages, where $k \in \{1, 2, 3\}$. By the end of the last round, at least $t + 1$ servers together, where $t \leq m - 1$, will be able to produce an outcome y and a proof σ, which are used to allow anyone to verify if y is indeed the sum of all the inputs of the *"involved"* (active) users.

Briefly, our idea is to split the secret input x_i of each user U_i among m servers via Shamir's threshold secret sharing as described in Sect. 2, and provide x_{ij} to server S_j. Given the property of Shamir's secret sharing scheme to be additive homomorphic, any subset of $t + 1$ servers will be enough to reconstruct y (*i.e.*, the sum of the inputs of the active users) from the given shares x_{ij}. Our main concern is how to prove that the resulted sum y is correct without revealing each user's secret input. A naive way is that each user publishes a value g^{x_i}, and the verification is to check if $\prod_i g^{x_i} = g^y$. We should note that the public value g^{x_i}, probably reveals some information of x_i, but not all x_i (due to the dLog assumption), so we need to randomize g^{x_i} with some random value Ran_i that belongs in the employed group such that $\prod_i Ran_i = 1$, which implies $\prod_i (g^{x_i} \cdot Ran_i) = \prod_i g^{x_i} = g^y$. More precisely, the trick is to generate a randomness Ran_i for each user U_i, and looking ahead, Ran_i consists of a sequence of agreed keys between U_i and each other user $U_{i'}$.

Each user needs to execute a key agreement with the other participating users. Thus, we assign groups of participating users to a unique server to reduce the computational and communication costs. More precisely, we sort n users into m groups, each of which consists of n/m amount of users. Here to simplify the explanation, we assume $m \mid n$, for the general case $m \nmid n$ please refer to our protocol in detail. Next, each group of n/m users generates their own randomness, via their corresponding server, following the trick proposed by Bonawitz *et al.* [13] in which the server plays the role of a bulletin board and coordinates the communications in each group. Later, we address the possible dropouts by suitably adapting the approach in [13] to our case. We assume that, by the end of the last round, there are at least $t_{key} + 1$ users which have not dropped out, in each group of n/m users. Our DEVA protocol is described below:

Setup: all parties are given the security parameter λ, the numbers of users n and servers m, thresholds $t < m$ and $t_{key} < \lceil \frac{n}{m} \rceil$, honestly generated $pp \leftarrow Ksetup(1^\lambda)$, parameter q such that $\mathbb{Z}_q$ is the space from which inputs are sampled, and a group $\mathbb{G}$ of prime order p to be used for key agreement. All n users are partitioned into m disjoint subsets, *i.e.*, $\Gamma_1, \ldots, \Gamma_m$ where for any $j \in [1, m]$, $\Gamma_i \cap \Gamma_j = \emptyset$. Here, we assume n is divided by m, and $\mid \Gamma_j \mid = \frac{n}{m}$ for $j \in [1, m]$.[1]

Round 1 - KeyGeneration for user U_i associated with S_j: U_i generates key pairs $(sk_i^{KA}, pk_i^{KA}) \leftarrow KA.Kgen(pp, U_i)$ along with the pairs $(sk_i^{PKE}, pk_i^{PKE}) \leftarrow PKE.KeyGen(1^\lambda)$; and publish (pk_i^{KA}, pk_i^{PKE}) before moving to the next round;

Round 1 - KeyGeneration for server S_j associated with Γ_j: S_j collects users' public keys (We denote this set of users by Γ_j^1); broadcasts to all users belonging to Γ_j^1 the list of keys $\{(pk_i^{KA}, pk_i^{PKE})\}_{U_i \in \Gamma_j^1}$, and goes to next round;

Round 2 - ShareKeys for user U_i associated with S_j: U_i receives the list $\{(pk_i^{KA}, pk_i^{PKE})\}_{U_i \in \Gamma_j^1}$ broadcasted by the server S_j and proceeds to *sharing keys*:

---

[1] If $m \nmid n$, then $\mid \Gamma_j \mid = \lceil \frac{n}{m} \rceil$ for $j \in [1, m-1]$ and $\mid \Gamma_m \mid = n - (m-1)\lceil \frac{n}{m} \rceil$.

○ using a t_{key}-out-of-$\left|\Gamma_j^1\right|$, with $t_{key} < \left|\Gamma_j^1\right|$, secret sharing scheme, it generates shares of $\mathsf{sk}_i^{\mathsf{KA}}$ for each $\mathsf{U}_{i'} \in \Gamma_j^1$. More precisely, user U_i generates $\mathsf{sk}_{i,i'}^{\mathsf{KA}} \leftarrow \mathsf{SS.share}(t_{key}, \mathsf{sk}_i^{\mathsf{KA}}, \mathsf{U}_{i'}, \Gamma_j^1)$;

○ uses PKE to encrypt shares $\mathsf{sk}_{i,i'}^{\mathsf{KA}}$ under the public key $\mathsf{pk}_{i'}^{\mathsf{PKE}}$ of each other user $\mathsf{U}_{i'} \in \Gamma_j^1$. More precisely, U_i computes $c_{i,i'} \leftarrow \mathsf{PKE.Enc}(\mathsf{pk}_{i'}^{\mathsf{PKE}}, \mathsf{sk}_{i,i'}^{\mathsf{KA}})$;

U_i sends ciphertexts $\{c_{i,i'}\}_{\mathsf{U}_{i'} \in \Gamma_j^1}$ to the server S_j, and goes to the next round;

Round 2 - ShareKeys for server S_j associated with Γ_j^1: S_j collects the list of users U_i which have sent $c_{i,i'}$ (we denote this set of users by Γ_j^2); and sends to each user $\mathsf{U}_{i'} \in \Gamma_j^2$ all ciphertexts under his public key $\mathsf{pk}_{i'}^{\mathsf{PKE}}$, i.e., $\{c_{i,i'}\}_{\mathsf{U}_{i'} \in \Gamma_j^2}$;

Round 3 - ShareInputs for user U_i associated with S_j: U_i receives the list of ciphertexts $\{c_{i',i}\}_{\mathsf{U}_{i'} \in \Gamma_j^2}$ broadcasted by S_j and proceeds to *sharing its input*:

○ with the list $\{\mathsf{pk}_i^{\mathsf{KA}}\}_{\mathsf{U}_i \in \Gamma_j^2}$ broadcasted by the server S_j, uses the key agreement scheme to compute the agreed key between any two users $\mathsf{U}_i, \mathsf{U}_{i'} \in \Gamma_j^2$, i.e., $s_{ii'} \leftarrow \mathsf{KA.Kagree}(\mathsf{sk}_{i'}^{\mathsf{KA}}, \mathsf{pk}_i^{\mathsf{KA}})$;

○ uses a t-out-of-m secret sharing scheme to generate shares of the input x_i for each server $\mathsf{S}_{j'}$ for $j' \in [1, m]$, i.e., $x_{ij'} \leftarrow \mathsf{SS.share}(t, x_i, \mathsf{S}_{j'}, \{\mathsf{S}_{j'}\}_{j' \in [1,m]})$;

○ randomly selects $R_i{}'$ and computes $R_i{}''$ such that

$$R_i' + R_i'' = |\mathbb{G}| \cdot \mathsf{Int} \tag{2}$$

where Int denotes any positive integer, and computes the values

$$\tau_i := \mathsf{g}^{x_i} \cdot \mathsf{g}^{R_i'}, \qquad \rho_i := \mathsf{g}^{R_i''} \cdot \prod_{i' \in \Gamma_j^2 : i < i'} s_{ii'} \cdot \prod_{i' \in \Gamma_j^2 : i > i'} s_{i'i}{}^{-1}.$$

U_i publishes and sends (τ_i, ρ_i) to the specified server S_j and, additionally, sends $x_{ij'}$ to each server $\mathsf{S}_{j'}$ where $j' \in [1, m]$, and goes to the next round;

Round 3 - ShareInputs for server S_j associated with Γ_j^2: S_j collects the list of users U_i which have sent (τ_i, ρ_i) to S_j (denoted by Γ_j^3); then, S_j *collects the shared inputs x_{ij} of all $\mathsf{U}_i \in \bigcup_{j=1}^m \Gamma_j^3$*, i.e., $\{x_{ij}\}_{\mathsf{U}_i \in \Omega}$ where $\Omega := \bigcup_{j=1}^m \Gamma_j^3$;

Round 4 - Aggregation for user U_i associated with S_j: on receiving the ciphertexts $\{c_{i',i}\}_{\mathsf{U}_{i'} \in \Gamma_j^2}$ of each user $\mathsf{U}_{i'}$, with the decryption key $\mathsf{sk}_i^{\mathsf{PKE}}$, U_i decrypts $\{c_{i',i}\}_{\mathsf{U}_{i'} \in \Gamma_j^2}$. More precisely, U_i gets $\mathsf{sk}_{i',i}^{\mathsf{KA}} \leftarrow \mathsf{PKE.Dec}(\mathsf{sk}_i^{\mathsf{PKE}}, c_{i',i})$, and sends a list of shares $\{\mathsf{sk}_{i',i}^{\mathsf{KA}}\}_{\mathsf{U}_{i'} \in \Gamma_j^2 \setminus \Gamma_j^3}$ to the server S_j;

Round 4 - Aggregation for server S_j associated with Γ_j: S_j collects the list of shares $\{\mathsf{sk}_{i',i}^{\mathsf{KA}}\}_{\mathsf{U}_{i'} \in \Gamma_j^2 \setminus \Gamma_j^3}$ from the users U_i (denote this set of users by Γ_j^4) such that $\left|\Gamma_j^4\right| \geq t_{key}$; Consecutively, for each user $\mathsf{U}_{i'} \in \Gamma_j^2 \setminus \Gamma_j^3$, the server S_j:

○ *evaluates the shared keys* $\mathsf{sk}_{i'}^{\mathsf{KA}}$ by running the $\mathsf{SS.recon}(t_{key}, \{\mathsf{sk}_{i',i}^{\mathsf{KA}}\}_{i \in \Gamma_j^4}, \Gamma_j^4)$ reconstruction algorithm, and computes $\mathsf{s}_{ii'} \leftarrow$ $\mathsf{KA.Kagree}(\mathsf{sk}_{i'}^{\mathsf{KA}}, \mathsf{pk}_i^{\mathsf{KA}})$, *i.e., the agreed keys* $\mathsf{s}_{ii'}$;

○ *evaluates the missing values* $z_{i'} := \prod_{i \in \Gamma_j^3 : i < i'} \mathsf{s}_{ii'}^{-1} \cdot \prod_{i \in \Gamma_j^3 : i > i'} \mathsf{s}_{i'i}$, $\forall \mathsf{U}_i \in \Gamma_j^3$;

○ computes $\omega_{i'} := \prod_{i \in \Gamma_j^3 : i < i'} (\mathsf{pk}_i^{\mathsf{KA}})^{-1} \prod_{i \in \Gamma_j^3 : i > i'} \mathsf{pk}_i^{\mathsf{KA}}$ for all users $\mathsf{U}_i \in \Gamma_j^3$, and a proof $\mathbf{Proof}.\mathsf{DLEQ}(g, \omega_{i'}, \mathsf{pk}_{i'}^{\mathsf{KA}}, z_{i'}, \mathsf{sk}_{i'}^{\mathsf{KA}})$ with witness $\mathsf{sk}_{i'}^{\mathsf{KA}}$ using the ZK protocol in [2], described in detail in Sect. 2;

○ computes the partial value $y_j := \sum_{\mathsf{U}_i \in \Omega} x_{ij}$;

The list $(\{\mathsf{pk}_i^{\mathsf{KA}}\}_{\mathsf{U}_i \in \Gamma_j^3}, y_j, \{z_{i'}, \mathbf{Proof}.\mathsf{DLEQ}(g, \omega_{i'}, \mathsf{pk}_{i'}^{\mathsf{KA}}, z_{i'}, \mathsf{sk}_{i'}^{\mathsf{KA}})\}_{\mathsf{U}_{i'} \in \Gamma_j^2 \setminus \Gamma_j^3})$ is finally given as the output by the server S_j;

Public Verification: given a set of servers $\mathcal{T}$ where $|\mathcal{T}| > t$, any verifier:

○ gets from each server S_j the set of active users $\{\mathsf{pk}_i^{\mathsf{KA}}\}_{\mathsf{U}_i \in \Gamma_j^3}$, and computes $\hat{\omega}_{i'} := \prod_{i \in \Gamma_j^3 : i < i'} (\mathsf{pk}_i^{\mathsf{KA}})^{-1} \cdot \prod_{i \in \Gamma_j^3 : i > i'} \mathsf{pk}_i^{\mathsf{KA}}$ for each user $\mathsf{U}_{i'} \in \Gamma_j^2 \setminus \Gamma_j^3$;

○ executes $\mathbf{Verify}.\mathsf{DLEQ}(g, \hat{\omega}_{i'}, \mathsf{pk}_{i'}^{\mathsf{KA}}, z_{i'}, \mathbf{Proof}.\mathsf{DLEQ}(g, \omega_{i'}, \mathsf{pk}_{i'}^{\mathsf{KA}}, z_{i'}, \mathsf{sk}_{i'}^{\mathsf{KA}}))$ to check if it satisfies $g^{\mathsf{sk}_{i'}^{\mathsf{KA}}} = \mathsf{pk}_{i'}^{\mathsf{KA}}$ and $(\hat{\omega}_{i'})^{\mathsf{sk}_{i'}^{\mathsf{KA}}} = z_{i'}$, for each user $\mathsf{U}_{i'} \in \Gamma_j^2 \setminus \Gamma_j^3$. If it fails, abort and output 0.

○ computes the final result $y := \mathsf{SS.recon}(t, \{y_j\}_{j \in \mathcal{T}}, \mathcal{T})$ given $|\mathcal{T}|$ servers, the value σ as $\sigma := \prod_{j=1}^{m} \left(\prod_{\mathsf{U}_i \in \Gamma_j^3} \tau_i \cdot \prod_{\mathsf{U}_i \in \Gamma_j^3} \rho_i \cdot \prod_{\mathsf{U}_{i'} \in \Gamma_j^2 \setminus \Gamma_j^3} z_{i'} \right)$ and checks if

$\sigma \stackrel{?}{=} H(y)$, for H defined to be the hash function described in Sect. 2. If true, output $(y, 1)$. Otherwise output 0.

Below, we state the DEVA's satisfied properties.

Theorem 1 (DEVA Correctness). *The DEVA protocol is correct, i.e., it holds* $Pr\left[\mathbf{Verification}(\sigma, y) = (y, 1)\right] = 1$, *where* σ *and* y *are the outputs of the protocol, honestly executed by all users and servers.*

We present and prove the following lemma which is necessary to prove DEVA's properties. We abuse notation by equivalently denoting $\mathsf{U}_i \in \Gamma_j^3$ as $i \in \Gamma_j^3$.

Lemma 1. *It holds that*

$$\prod_{i \in \Gamma_j^3} \left(\prod_{i' \in \Gamma_j^2 : i < i'} \mathsf{s}_{ii'} \prod_{i' \in \Gamma_j^2 : i > i'} \mathsf{s}_{i'i}^{-1} \right) \cdot \prod_{i' \in \Gamma_j^2 \setminus \Gamma_j^3} \left(\prod_{i \in \Gamma_j^3 : i < i'} \mathsf{s}_{ii'}^{-1} \prod_{i \in \Gamma_j^3 : i > i'} \mathsf{s}_{i'i} \right) \quad (3)$$
$$= \prod_{i \in \Gamma_j^3} \hat{\rho}_i \cdot \prod_{i' \in \Gamma_j^2 \setminus \Gamma_j^3} z_{i'} = 1$$

Proof (DEVA's Lemma 1). Since $\Gamma_j^2 \equiv \Gamma_j^3 \cup (\Gamma_j^2 \setminus \Gamma_j^3)$, for all $i \in \Gamma_j^3$, it holds

$$\hat{\rho}_i = \left(\prod_{i' \in \Gamma_j^3 : i < i'} \mathsf{s}_{ii'} \prod_{i' \in \Gamma_j^2 \setminus \Gamma_j^3 : i < i'} \mathsf{s}_{ii'} \right) \cdot \left(\prod_{i' \in \Gamma_j^3 : i > i'} \mathsf{s}_{i'i}^{-1} \prod_{i' \in \Gamma_j^2 \setminus \Gamma_j^3 : i > i'} \mathsf{s}_{i'i}^{-1} \right)$$

Observe that $\prod_{i \in \Gamma_j^3} \left(\prod_{i' \in \Gamma_j^3 : i < i'} \mathsf{s}_{ii'} \cdot \prod_{i' \in \Gamma_j^3 : i > i'} \mathsf{s}_{i'i}^{-1} \right) = 1$, thus implying,

$$\prod_{i \in \Gamma_j^3} \hat{\rho}_i = \prod_{i \in \Gamma_j^3} \left(\prod_{i' \in \Gamma_j^2 \setminus \Gamma_j^3 : i < i'} \mathsf{s}_{ii'} \prod_{i' \in \Gamma_j^2 \setminus \Gamma_j^3 : i > i'} \mathsf{s}_{i'i}^{-1} \right)$$

$$= \prod_{i' \in \Gamma_j^2 \setminus \Gamma_j^3} \left(\prod_{i \in \Gamma_j^3 : i < i'} \mathsf{s}_{ii'} \prod_{i \in \Gamma_j^3 : i > i'} \mathsf{s}_{i'i}^{-1} \right) = \prod_{i' \in \Gamma_j^2 \setminus \Gamma_j^3} z_{i'}^{-1}$$

$\square$

Proof (DEVA's Correctness - Theorem 1). Let $\Omega = \bigcup_{j=1}^m \Gamma_j^3$ be the set of all users that have sent shared inputs x_{ij} to their corresponding servers. For any T set of servers with $|T| > t$, it holds:

$$y = \mathsf{SS.recon}(t, \{y_j\}_{j \in T}, T) \stackrel{see\ eq.\ (1)}{=} \sum_{i \in \Omega} x_i \tag{4}$$

By construction, we get the following relation that is needed later on:

$$\prod_{\mathsf{U}_i \in \Gamma_j^3} \rho_i = \prod_{i \in \Gamma_j^3} \mathsf{g}^{R_i''} \cdot \prod_{i' \in \Gamma_j^2, i' < i} \mathsf{s}_{ii'} \cdot \prod_{i' \in \Gamma_j^2, i' > i} \mathsf{s}_{ii'}^{-1} \stackrel{Eq.\ (3)}{=} \prod_{i \in \Gamma_j^3} \mathsf{g}^{R_i''} \cdot \prod_{i \in \Gamma_j^3} \hat{\rho}_i \tag{5}$$

Therefore, we can expand σ as follows:

$$\sigma = \prod_{j=1}^m \left[\prod_{\mathsf{U}_i \in \Gamma_j^3} \tau_i \prod_{\mathsf{U}_i \in \Gamma_j^3} \rho_i \prod_{\mathsf{U}_{i'} \in \Gamma_j^2 \setminus \Gamma_j^3} z_{i'} \right]$$

$$\stackrel{Eq.\ (5)}{=} \prod_{j=1}^m \left[\prod_{i \in \Gamma_j^3} \mathsf{g}^{x_i + R_i'} \left(\prod_{i \in \Gamma_j^3} \mathsf{g}^{R_i''} \prod_{i \in \Gamma_j^3} \hat{\rho}_i \right) \prod_{i' \in \Gamma_j^2 \setminus \Gamma_j^3} z_{i'} \right]$$

$$= \prod_{j=1}^m \left[\left(\prod_{i \in \Gamma_j^3} \mathsf{g}^{x_i + R_i'} \prod_{i \in \Gamma_j^3} \mathsf{g}^{R_i''} \right) \cdot \left(\prod_{i \in \Gamma_j^3} \hat{\rho}_i \prod_{i' \in \Gamma_j^2 \setminus \Gamma_j^3} z_{i'} \right) \right] \tag{6}$$

$$\stackrel{Lem.\ 1}{=} \prod_{j=1}^m \left[\prod_{i \in \Gamma_j^3} \mathsf{g}^{x_i + R_i'} \prod_{i \in \Gamma_j^3} \mathsf{g}^{R_i''} \right] = \prod_{i \in \Omega} \mathsf{g}^{x_i + R_i' + R_i''}$$

$$\stackrel{Eq.\ (2)}{=} \mathsf{g}^{\sum_{i \in \Omega} x_i} \stackrel{Eq.\ (4)}{=} \mathsf{g}^y$$

Thus, we get that $\sigma = g^y = H(y)$ which shows that the verification will give 1 with probability 1, *i.e.*, $\Pr[\textbf{Verification}(\sigma, y) = (y, 1)] = 1$.   □

Theorem 2 (DEVA Verifiability). *For n users $\{U_i\}_{i \in [n]}$ with inputs $\{x_i\}_{i \in [n]}$ such that $y - \sum_{i=1}^{n} x_i$, which honestly execute the protocol, consider any set of corrupted servers $T = \{S_{j_1}, \ldots, S_{j_{|T|}}\}$ with $|T| < m$ which are controlled by a PPT adversary $\mathcal{A}$. The verifiability requirement of DEVA follows Definition 4 and it is specified as follows:*

1. *Users and servers run the protocol's setup round 1 and round 2.*
2. *Execute round 3 and, $\forall j \in [j_1, j_{|T|}]$ such that $S_j \in T$, the server S_j gives $\{x_{1j}, \ldots, x_{nj}\}$ to $\mathcal{A}$ where x_{ij} is the share given to S_j from the user U_i.*
3. *Given the tuples output by the corrupted servers $S_j \in T$ at the end of round 4, $\mathcal{A}$ outputs $\left(y_j^*, \{z_{i'}^*, \textbf{Proof}.\text{DLEQ}(g, \omega_{i'}^*, \text{pk}_{i'}^{\text{KA}}, z_{i'}^*, \text{sk}_{i'}^{\text{KA}})\}_{U_{i'} \in \Gamma_j^2 \backslash \Gamma_j^3}\right)$ as a malicious tuple. For honest servers $S_j \notin T$, it honestly computes and publishes $(y_j, \{z_{i'}, \textbf{Proof}.\text{DLEQ}(g, \omega_{i'}, \text{pk}_{i'}^{\text{KA}}, z_{i'}, \text{sk}_{i'}^{\text{KA}})\}_{U_{i'} \in \Gamma_j^2 \backslash \Gamma_j^3}).$*
4. *$\mathcal{A}$ outputs the aggregated result y' and the corresponding proof σ' such that $y' \neq y$.*

For any PPT adversary $\mathcal{A}$, DEVA satisfies $\Pr[\textbf{Verification}(\sigma', y') = 1] \leq \text{negl}.$

Proof (DEVA's Verifiability - Theorem 2). Assume $\textbf{Verification}(\sigma', y') = 1$, where $y' = y + \Delta$ with $\Delta \neq 0$. Due to the property of proof of knowledge, with overwhelming probability $\mathcal{A}$ knows the secret keys (witnesses) $\text{sk}_{i'}^{\text{KA}}$ of all users that dropout at the end of round 2 and before round 3, such that the proof $\textbf{Proof}.\text{DLEQ}(g, \omega_{i'}^*, \text{pk}_{i'}^{\text{KA}}, z_{i'}^*, \text{sk}_{i'}^{\text{KA}})$ is valid, *i.e.*, $g^{\text{sk}_{i'}^{\text{KA}}} = \text{pk}_{i'}^{\text{KA}}$ and $(\omega_{i'}^*)^{\text{sk}_{i'}^{\text{KA}}} - z_{i'}^*$. Let $\Gamma_j^2 \backslash \Gamma_j^3$ be the list of honestly dropped users at the end of round 2 and before round 3. Let us consider the two possible cases:

– $\mathcal{A}$ reports an active user as dropped. *W.l.o.g.*, denote this user as U_{fd} and let z_{fd} denote the related missing value computed[2]. Then, we get:

$$\textbf{Verification}(\sigma', y') = 1 \iff \sigma' = H(y')$$

$$\iff \prod_{j=1}^{m} \left[\left(\prod_{U_i \in \Gamma_j^3} \tau_i \prod_{U_i \in \Gamma_j^3} \rho_i \prod_{U_{i'} \in \Gamma_j^2 \backslash \Gamma_j^3} z_{i'} \right) z_{\text{fd}} \right] = g^{y'}$$

$$\iff \prod_{j=1}^{m} \left[\prod_{U_i \in \Gamma_j^3} \tau_i \prod_{U_i \in \Gamma_j^3} \rho_i \prod_{U_{i'} \in \Gamma_j^2 \backslash \Gamma_j^3} z_{i'} \right] \prod_{j=1}^{m} z_{\text{fd}} = g^{y + \Delta}$$

$$\overset{Eq.\ (6)}{\iff} g^y \prod_{j=1}^{m} z_{\text{fd}} = g^y g^{\Delta} \iff \prod_{j=1}^{m} z_{\text{fd}} = g^{\Delta}$$

---

[2] $\mathcal{A}$ must know the secret key by either breaking the key agreement security **or** by maliciously corrupting the user, *e.g.*, by personally creating it.

– $\mathcal{A}$ reports a dropped out user as active. *W.l.o.g.*, denote this user as U_{fa} and let z_{fa} denote the value computed for this user. Then, we get:

$$\textbf{Verification}(\sigma', y') = 1 \iff \sigma' = H(y') \tag{7}$$

and expanding σ' we have:

$$\sigma' = \prod_{j=1}^{m} \left[\prod_{\mathsf{U}_i \in \Gamma_j^3} \tau_i \prod_{\mathsf{U}_i \in \Gamma_j^3} \rho_i \prod_{\mathsf{U}_{i'} \in \Gamma_j^2 \setminus (\Gamma_j^3 \cup \mathsf{U}_{\mathsf{fa}})} z_{i'} \right]$$

$$\iff \sigma' = \prod_{j=1}^{m} \left[\left(\prod_{\mathsf{U}_i \in \Gamma_j^3} \tau_i \prod_{\mathsf{U}_i \in \Gamma_j^3} \rho_i \prod_{\mathsf{U}_{i'} \in \Gamma_j^2 \setminus (\Gamma_j^3 \cup \mathsf{U}_{\mathsf{fa}})} z_{i'} \right) \left(z_{\mathsf{fa}} z_{\mathsf{fa}}^{-1} \right) \right]$$

$$\iff \sigma' = \prod_{j=1}^{m} \left[\left(\prod_{\mathsf{U}_i \in \Gamma_j^3} \tau_i \prod_{\mathsf{U}_i \in \Gamma_j^3} \rho_i \prod_{\mathsf{U}_{i'} \in \Gamma_j^2 \setminus \Gamma_j^3} z_{i'} \right) z_{\mathsf{fa}}^{-1} \right]$$

$$\iff \sigma' = \prod_{j=1}^{m} \left[\prod_{\mathsf{U}_i \in \Gamma_j^3} \tau_i \prod_{\mathsf{U}_i \in \Gamma_j^3} \rho_i \prod_{\mathsf{U}_{i'} \in \Gamma_j^2 \setminus \Gamma_j^3} z_{i'} \right] \prod_{j=1}^{m} z_{\mathsf{fa}}^{-1}$$

$$\stackrel{Eq.\ (6)}{\iff} \sigma' = g^y \prod_{j=1}^{m} z_{\mathsf{fa}}^{-1}$$

Then, Eq. (7) becomes, equivalently:

$$Eq.\ (7) \iff g^y \prod_{j=1}^{m} z_{\mathsf{fa}}^{-1} = g^{y'} \iff g^y \prod_{j=1}^{m} z_{\mathsf{fa}}^{-1} = g^{y+\Delta}$$

$$\stackrel{Eq.\ (6)}{\iff} g^y \prod_{j=1}^{m} z_{\mathsf{fa}}^{-1} = g^y g^{\Delta} \iff \prod_{j=1}^{m} z_{\mathsf{fa}}^{-1} = g^{\Delta}$$

In both cases, finding Δ requires to solve a dLog problem which is assumed to be hard. Thus, the only two cases that exist are not feasible. Therefore, it holds $\Pr\left[\textbf{Verification}(\sigma', y') = 1\right] \leq \mathsf{negl}$. □

We consider security in the setting where at most t servers are corrupted by the adversary $\mathcal{A}$, namely, assume $T = \{\mathsf{S}_{j_1}, \ldots, \mathsf{S}_{j_{|T|}}\}$ be the set of the corrupted servers such that $|T| \leq t$. All those $|T|$ servers are controlled by $\mathcal{A}$ and all users and servers correctly execute the protocol. $\mathcal{A}$ has the knowledge of at most t_{key} corrupted users' secret inputs. $\mathcal{A}$ attempts to infer the remaining non-corrupted users' secret inputs. We show that the joint view of any set of less than $(t+1)$ corrupted servers and any set of less than $(t_{key}+1)$ corrupted users can be simulated, given the inputs of the corrupted users and only the sum of the inputs of the remaining users. Intuitively, this means that those users and servers learn nothing more than their own inputs, and the sum of the other users' inputs. Consider n users $\mathcal{U} = \{\mathsf{U}_i\}_{i \in [n]}$ along with m servers $\mathcal{S} = \{\mathsf{S}_j\}_{j \in [m]}$, and

$\mathcal{U}$ is partitioned into m disjoint subsets, *i.e.*, $\mathcal{U} = \Gamma_1, \ldots, \Gamma_m$ where for any $j, j' \in [1, m]$, $\Gamma_j \cap \Gamma_{j'} = \emptyset$. Let the input of each user U_i be x_i. For simplicity, we assume m divides n, and $|\Gamma_j| = \frac{n}{m}$ for $j \in [1, m]$. Assume that the group of users Γ_j corresponds to server S_j. Denote by $\Gamma_j^1, \Gamma_j^2, \Gamma_j^3, \Gamma_j^4$ the subsets of users in Γ_j that successfully sent their messages to the corresponding server S_j at round 1, 2, 3 and 4 respectively, such that $\Gamma_j \supseteq \Gamma_j^1 \supseteq \Gamma_j^2 \supseteq \Gamma_j^3 \supseteq \Gamma_j^4$. For example, users in $\Gamma_j^1 \setminus \Gamma_j^2$ are those that abort after completing the execution of round 1 but before sending the message to S_j in round 2. Let $\mathcal{S}'$ be the corrupted servers such that $|\mathcal{S}'| \leq t$, and $\mathcal{U}'$ the corrupted users such that $|\mathcal{U}'| \leq t_{key}$. Let $\mathsf{Real}_{\mathcal{U},\mathcal{S}}^{\mathcal{U}',\mathcal{S}',t,t_{key}}(\{x_i\}_{\mathsf{U}_i \in \mathcal{U}}, \{\Gamma_j^1, \Gamma_j^2, \Gamma_j^3, \Gamma_j^4\}_{j \in [1,m]})$ be a random variable representing the views of all corrupted users in $\mathcal{U}'$ and all corrupted servers in $\mathcal{S}'$ after executing the above instantiated protocol, where the randomness is over their internal randomness and the ones in the setup phase.

Theorem 3 (DEVA Security). *There exists a PPT simulator* Sim *such that for all* $t < m$ *and* $t_{key} < \lceil \frac{n}{m} \rceil$, $\mathcal{U}$, $\mathcal{S}$, $\mathcal{U}'$, $\mathcal{S}'$, $\{x_i\}_{\mathsf{U}_i \in \mathcal{U}'}$, *and* $\{\Gamma_j^1, \Gamma_j^2, \Gamma_j^3, \Gamma_j^4\}_{j \in [1,m]}$, *such that* $|\mathcal{S}'| \leq t$, $|\mathcal{U}'| \leq t_{key}$, $\mathcal{U}' \subseteq \mathcal{U}$, $\mathcal{S}' \subseteq \mathcal{S}$, $\Gamma_j^1 \supseteq \Gamma_j^2 \supseteq \Gamma_j^3 \supseteq \Gamma_j^4$ *for* $j \in [1,m]$, *and* $\mathcal{U}' \subset (\bigcup_{j=1}^m \Gamma_j^4)$, *the output of* Sim *is computationally indistinguishable from the output of* $\mathsf{Real}_{\mathcal{U},\mathcal{S}}^{\mathcal{U}',\mathcal{S}',t,t_{key}}$, *or:*

$$\mathsf{Real}_{\mathcal{U},\mathcal{S}}^{\mathcal{U}',\mathcal{S}',t,t_{key}}(\{x_i\}_{\mathsf{U}_i \in \mathcal{U}}, \{\Gamma_j^1, \Gamma_j^2, \Gamma_j^3, \Gamma_j^4\}_{j \in [1,m]})$$
$$\stackrel{c}{\approx} \mathsf{Sim}_{\mathcal{U},\mathcal{S}}^{\mathcal{U}',\mathcal{S}',t,t_{key}}(\{x_i\}_{\mathsf{U}_i \in \mathcal{U}'}, \mathsf{aux}, \{\Gamma_j^1, \Gamma_j^2, \Gamma_j^3, \Gamma_j^4\}_{j \in [1,m]})$$

where, by considering $\Omega := \bigcup_{j \in [1,m]} \Gamma_j^3$, *and* $\mathsf{aux} := \sum_{\mathsf{U}_i \in \Omega \setminus \mathcal{U}'} x_i$ *if* $|\Gamma_j^4| > t_{key}$ *for* $\forall j \in [1,m]$; *otherwise* $\mathsf{aux} := \perp$.

Proof (DEVA's Security - Theorem 3). Let us construct the simulator Sim by doing a sequence of games from the initial view of the real execution $\mathsf{Real}_{\mathcal{U},\mathcal{S}}^{\mathcal{U}',\mathcal{S}',t,t_{key}}$ such that any two consecutive games are computationally indistinguishable.

Game$_0$: Real is exactly the joint view of the set of corrupted servers $\mathcal{S}'$ and corrupted users $\mathcal{U}'$ in a real execution of the above instantiated protocol.

Game$_1$: given the set of corrupted users $\mathcal{U}'$, let $\Upsilon_j^2 := \mathcal{U}' \cap \Gamma_j^2$ for all $j \in [1, m]$. In Game$_1$, for all $j \in [1, m]$, the ciphertexts that are received by honest users $\mathsf{U}_{i'} \in \Gamma_j^2 \setminus \Upsilon_j^2$ and sent from honest users $\mathsf{U}_i \in \Gamma_j^2 \setminus \Upsilon_j^2$, are replaced with encryptions of 0 instead of $\mathsf{sk}_{i,i'}^{\mathsf{KA}}$, *i.e.*, computing $c_{i,i'} \leftarrow \mathsf{PKE.Enc}(\mathsf{pk}_{i'}^{\mathsf{PKE}}, 0)$ instead of $c_{i,i'} \leftarrow \mathsf{PKE.Enc}(\mathsf{pk}_{i'}^{\mathsf{PKE}}, \mathsf{sk}_{i,i'}^{\mathsf{KA}})$. The IND-CPA security of the PKE encryption scheme guarantees that this game is indistinguishable from the previous one.

Game$_2$: for all $j \in [1, m]$, when the user $\mathsf{U}_i \in (\Gamma_j^2 \setminus \Gamma_j^3) \setminus \Upsilon_j^2$ generates shares of $\mathsf{sk}_i^{\mathsf{KA}}$, we substitute all shares of $\mathsf{sk}_i^{\mathsf{KA}}$ with shares of 0 (every user U_i in the set $(\Gamma_j^2 \setminus \Gamma_j^3) \setminus \Upsilon_j^2$ uses a different sharing of 0), and give those shares to the corrupted users in set $\varUpsilon_j^2$ in Round ShareKeys, *i.e.*, computing $\mathsf{sk}_{i,i'}^{\mathsf{KA}} \leftarrow \mathsf{SS.share}(t_{key}, 0, \mathsf{U}_{i'}, \varUpsilon_j^2)$ for $\mathsf{U}_{i'} \in \varUpsilon_j^2$ instead of computing $\mathsf{sk}_{i,i'}^{\mathsf{KA}} \leftarrow \mathsf{SS.share}(t_{key}, \mathsf{sk}_i^{\mathsf{KA}}, \mathsf{U}_{i'}, \varUpsilon_j^2)$. The properties of Shamir's secret sharing guarantee that the distribution of any $|\mathcal{U}'|$ shares of 0 is identical to the distribution of an equivalent number of shares of $\mathsf{sk}_i^{\mathsf{KA}}$, making this game and the previous one identically distributed.

Game₃: for all $j \in [1, m]$, for each user $\mathsf{U}_i \in (\varGamma_j^2 \setminus \varGamma_j^3) \setminus \varUpsilon_j^2$, instead of computing $\rho_i := \mathsf{g}^{R_i''} \cdot \prod_{i' \in \varGamma_j^2 : i < i'} \mathsf{s}_{ii'} \cdot \prod_{i' \in \varGamma_j^2 : i > i'} \mathsf{s}_{i'i}^{-1}$ and $\tau_i := \mathsf{g}^{x_i} \cdot \mathsf{g}^{R_i'}$, we compute $\rho_i := \mathsf{g}^{\zeta_i} \cdot \prod_{i' \in \varGamma_j^2 : i < i'} \mathsf{s}_{ii'} \cdot \prod_{i' \in \varGamma_j^2 : i > i'} \mathsf{s}_{i'i}^{-1}$ and $\tau_i := \mathsf{g}^{\eta_i}$, where $\zeta_i := -\eta_i$ and η_i is sampled uniformly at random. Since R_i', R_i'' are uniformly random values, this game and the previous one are identically distributed.

Game₄: given the set of corrupted users $\mathcal{U}'$, let $\varUpsilon_j^3 := \mathcal{U}' \cap \varGamma_j^3$ for all $j \in [1, m]$. In Game₄, for all $j \in [1, m]$, when user $\mathsf{U}_i \in \varGamma_j^3 \setminus \varUpsilon_j^3$ generates shares of $\mathsf{sk}_i^{\mathsf{KA}}$, we substitute all shares of $\mathsf{sk}_i^{\mathsf{KA}}$ with shares of 0 (every $\mathsf{U}_i \in \varGamma_j^3 \setminus \varUpsilon_j^3$ uses a different sharing of 0), and give those shares to the corrupted users in set $\varUpsilon_j^3$ in Round 2 - ShareKeys for user U_i, *i.e.*, computing $\mathsf{sk}_{i,i'}^{\mathsf{KA}} \leftarrow \mathsf{SS.share}(t_{key}, 0, \mathsf{U}_{i'}, \varUpsilon_j^3)$ for $\mathsf{U}_{i'} \in \varUpsilon_j^3$. The security of the threshold secret sharing scheme guarantee that Game₄ is identically distributed as Game₃.

Game₅: for a fixed user $\mathsf{U}_{i^*} \in \varGamma_j^3 \setminus \varUpsilon_j^3$ as well as for other users $\mathsf{U}_i \in (\varGamma_j^3 \setminus \varUpsilon_j^3) \setminus \{\mathsf{U}_{i^*}\}$, we substitute $\mathsf{s}_{i^*i} = \mathsf{s}_{ii^*}$ with a uniformly random value, instead of computing the value $\mathsf{s}_{i^*i} = \mathsf{s}_{ii^*} \leftarrow \mathsf{KA.Kagree}(\mathsf{sk}_{i^*}^{\mathsf{KA}}, \mathsf{pk}_i^{\mathsf{KA}})$. More precisely, Sim computes, for any user $\mathsf{U}_i \in (\varGamma_j^3 \setminus \varUpsilon_j^3) \setminus \{\mathsf{U}_{i^*}\}$:

$$\rho_i := \mathsf{g}^{\zeta_i} \underbrace{\left(\prod_{\substack{i' \in \varGamma_j^2 \setminus \{\mathsf{U}_{i^*}\}}}^{i<i'} \mathsf{s}_{ii'} \prod_{\substack{i' \in \varGamma_j^2 \setminus \{\mathsf{U}_{i^*}\}}}^{i>i'} \mathsf{s}_{i'i}^{-1} \right)}_{\vartheta_i} \widetilde{\mathsf{s}_{ii^*}},$$

$$\text{where} \quad \widetilde{\mathsf{s}_{ii^*}} := \begin{cases} \mathsf{s}_{ii^*} & \text{if } i^* > i \\ \mathsf{s}_{ii^*}^{-1} & \text{if } i^* < i \end{cases} \quad \text{and} \quad \mathsf{s}_{ii^*} = \mathsf{s}_{i^*i}$$

is a random element of $\mathbb{G}$, $z_i := \vartheta_i \cdot \widetilde{\mathsf{s}_{ii^*}}$, and

$$\omega_i := \left(\prod_{\substack{i' \in \varGamma_j^2 \setminus \{\mathsf{U}_{i^*}\}}}^{i<i'} \mathsf{pk}_{i'}^{\mathsf{KA}} \prod_{\substack{i' \in \varGamma_j^2 \setminus \{\mathsf{U}_{i^*}\}}}^{i>i'} (\mathsf{pk}_{i'}^{\mathsf{KA}})^{-1} \right) \widetilde{\mathsf{pk}_{i^*}^{\mathsf{KA}}},$$

$$\text{where} \quad \widetilde{\mathsf{pk}_{i^*}^{\mathsf{KA}}} := \begin{cases} \mathsf{pk}_{i^*}^{\mathsf{KA}} & \text{if } i^* > i \\ (\mathsf{pk}_{i^*}^{\mathsf{KA}})^{-1} & \text{if } i^* < i \end{cases}$$

and generates **Proof**.DLEQ$(g, \omega_i, \mathsf{pk}_i^{\mathsf{KA}}, z_i, \mathsf{sk}_i^{\mathsf{KA}})$ using the simulator of the ZK proof. For the fixed user $\mathsf{U}_{i^*} \in \Gamma_j^3 \setminus \Upsilon_j^3$, Sim computes,

$$\rho_{i^*} := g^{\zeta_{i^*}} \underbrace{\left(\prod_{i' \in \Gamma_j^2}^{i^* < i'} \mathsf{s}_{i^* i'} \prod_{i' \in \Gamma_j^2}^{i^* > i'} \mathsf{s}_{i^* i'}^{-1} \right)}_{\vartheta_{i^*}}, \ z_{i^*} := \vartheta_{i^*}, \text{ and}$$

$$\omega_{i^*} := \prod_{i' \in \Gamma_j^2}^{i^* < i'} \mathsf{pk}_{i^*}^{\mathsf{KA}} \prod_{i' \in \Gamma_j^2}^{i^* > i'} (\mathsf{pk}_{i^*}^{\mathsf{KA}})^{-1}$$

and generates **Proof**.DLEQ$(g, \omega_{i^*}, \mathsf{pk}_{i^*}^{\mathsf{KA}}, z_{i^*}, \mathsf{sk}_{i^*}^{\mathsf{KA}})$ using the ZK proof's simulator. The DDH assumption and ZK property assure Game$_5$ to be indistinguishable from Game$_4$.

Game$_6$ or Sim: for all users $\mathsf{U}_i \in \Gamma_j^3 \setminus \Upsilon_j^3$, instead of computing

$$\tau_i := g^{x_i} g^{R_i'}, \quad \rho_i := g^{R_i''} \left(\prod_{i' \in \Gamma_j^2}^{i < i'} \mathsf{s}_{ii'} \prod_{i' \in \Gamma_j^2}^{i > i'} \mathsf{s}_{i'i}^{-1} \right) = g^{R_i''} \tag{8}$$

$$\cdot \left(\prod_{i' \in \Gamma_j^2 \setminus (\Gamma_j^3 \setminus \Upsilon_j^3)}^{i < i'} \mathsf{s}_{ii'} \prod_{i' \in \Gamma_j^2 \setminus (\Gamma_j^3 \setminus \Upsilon_j^3)}^{i > i'} \mathsf{s}_{i'i}^{-1} \right) \left(\prod_{i' \in \Gamma_j^3 \setminus \Upsilon_j^3}^{i < i'} \mathsf{s}_{ii'} \prod_{i' \in \Gamma_j^3 \setminus \Upsilon_j^3}^{i > i'} \mathsf{s}_{i'i}^{-1} \right)$$

we compute

$$\tau_i := g^{\eta_i}, \quad \rho_i := g^{\zeta_i} \prod_{i' \in \Gamma_j^2 \setminus (\Gamma_j^3 \setminus \Upsilon_j^3) : i < i'} \mathsf{s}_{ii'} \prod_{i' \in \Gamma_j^2 \setminus (\Gamma_j^3 \setminus \Upsilon_j^3) : i > i'} \mathsf{s}_{i'i}^{-1} \tag{9}$$

where η_i and ζ_i are sampled uniformly at random and are subject to

$$\sum_{i \in \bigcup_{j=1}^m (\Gamma_j^3 \setminus \Upsilon_j^3)} (\eta_i + \zeta_i) = \mathsf{aux} = \sum_{i \in \left(\bigcup_{j=1}^m \Gamma_j^3 \right) \setminus \mathcal{U}'} x_i$$

To generate the shares of an input for each user $\mathsf{U}_i \in \bigcup_{j=1}^m (\Gamma_j^3 \setminus \Upsilon_j^3)$, given aux, the simulator Sim randomly chooses x_i' such that $\sum_{i \in \bigcup_{j=1}^m (\Gamma_j^3 \setminus \Upsilon_j^3)} x_i' = \mathsf{aux}$, and shares x_i' among m servers using t-out-of-m secret sharing scheme, $i.e.$, for each server S_j for $j \in [1, m]$, $x_{ij} \leftarrow \mathsf{SS.share}(t, x_i', \mathsf{S}_j, \{\mathsf{S}_j\}_{j \in [1,m]})$.

For τ_i and ρ_i generated as in Eq. (9), it implies that, for $\Xi_j := \bigcup_{j=1}^m (\Gamma_j^3 \setminus \Upsilon_j^3)$,

$$\prod_{i \in \Xi_j} \tau_i \cdot \rho_i = \prod_{i \in \Xi_j} \left[g^{\eta_i} \cdot g^{\zeta_i} \cdot \left(\prod_{i' \in \Gamma_j^2 \setminus (\Gamma_j^3 \setminus \Upsilon_j^3)}^{i<i'} s_{ii'} \prod_{i' \in \Gamma_j^2 \setminus (\Gamma_j^3 \setminus \Upsilon_j^3)}^{i>i'} s_{i'i}^{-1} \right) \right]$$

$$= g^{\sum_{i \in \Xi_j}(\eta_i + \zeta_i)} \cdot \left[\prod_{i \in \Xi_j} \left(\prod_{i' \in \Gamma_j^2 \setminus (\Gamma_j^3 \setminus \Upsilon_j^3)}^{i<i'} s_{ii'} \prod_{i' \in \Gamma_j^2 \setminus (\Gamma_j^3 \setminus \Upsilon_j^3)}^{i>i'} s_{i'i}^{-1} \right) \right]$$

$$= g^{\mathsf{aux}} \cdot \left[\prod_{i \in \Xi_j} \left(\prod_{i' \in \Gamma_j^2 \setminus (\Gamma_j^3 \setminus \Upsilon_j^3)}^{i<i'} s_{ii'} \prod_{i' \in \Gamma_j^2 \setminus (\Gamma_j^3 \setminus \Upsilon_j^3)}^{i>i'} s_{i'i}^{-1} \right) \right]$$

while for honestly generated τ_i and ρ_i as Eq. (8),

it holds that $\prod_{i \in \Xi_j} \tau_i \cdot \rho_i$

$$= \prod_{i \in \Xi_j} \left[g^{x_i + R_i' + R_i''} \cdot \left(\prod_{i' \in \Gamma_j^2 \setminus (\Gamma_j^3 \setminus \Upsilon_j^3)}^{i<i'} s_{ii'} \prod_{i' \in \Gamma_j^2 \setminus (\Gamma_j^3 \setminus \Upsilon_j^3)}^{i>i'} s_{i'i}^{-1} \right) \right.$$

$$\left. \cdot \left(\prod_{i' \in \Gamma_j^3 \setminus \Upsilon_j^3}^{i<i'} s_{ii'} \prod_{i' \in \Gamma_j^3 \setminus \Upsilon_j^3}^{i>i'} s_{i'i}^{-1} \right) \right]$$

$$= g^{\sum_{i \in \Xi_j} x_i} \cdot \left[\prod_{i \in \Xi_j} \left(\prod_{i' \in \Gamma_j^3 \setminus \Upsilon_j^3}^{i<i'} s_{ii'} \prod_{i' \in \Gamma_j^3 \setminus \Upsilon_j^3}^{i>i'} s_{i'i}^{-1} \right) \right]$$

$$\cdot \left[\prod_{i \in \Xi_j} \left(\prod_{i' \in \Gamma_j^2 \setminus (\Gamma_j^3 \setminus \Upsilon_j^3)}^{i<i'} s_{ii'} \prod_{i' \in \Gamma_j^2 \setminus (\Gamma_j^3 \setminus \Upsilon_j^3)}^{i>i'} s_{i'i}^{-1} \right) \right]$$

$$= g^{\mathsf{aux}} \cdot \left[\prod_{i \in \Xi_j} \left(\prod_{i' \in \Gamma_j^2 \setminus (\Gamma_j^3 \setminus \Upsilon_j^3)}^{i<i'} s_{ii'} \prod_{i' \in \Gamma_j^2 \setminus (\Gamma_j^3 \setminus \Upsilon_j^3)}^{i>i'} s_{i'i}^{-1} \right) \right]$$

This implies that, choosing η_i and ζ_i uniformly at random to compute τ_i and ρ_i as in Eq. (9) is identically distributed with computing τ_i and ρ_i as in Eq. (8). Since for all $\mathsf{U}_i \in \Gamma_j^3 \setminus \Upsilon_j^3$, η_i and ζ_i are sampled uniformly at random, to generate τ_i and ρ_i, the simulator Sim does not need the knowledge of individual x_i for $\mathsf{U}_i \in \Xi_j$ but, instead, their sum $\sum_{i \in \Xi_j} x_i = \mathsf{aux}$ is sufficient for the simulation. This implies the indistinguishability between Game_5 and Game_6.   □

5 Evaluation

This section describes several experimental results from the implementation of our DEVA protocol. We explain the different findings of DEVA, and provide comparison to prior work of VerifyNet by Xu *et al.* [21]. We got our protocol's experimental results, by implementing a prototype in Python 3.8.3. The execution of the tests was on MacOS 10.14.6 over a MacBookPro (2017) with processor Intel i7-7820HQ CPU @ 2.9 GHz, with 16 GB LPDDR3 2133 MHz RAM, 1 MB L2 cache and 8 MB L3 cache. We used Diffie-Hellman over the elliptic curve secp256k1 for the key agreement, the Shamir's secret sharing scheme as an additive homomorphic secret sharing scheme, and RSA-2048 as a public key encryption scheme. The execution time provided is expressed in milliseconds (ms), while the bandwidth is presented in kilobytes (kB). The source code of our protocol is publicly released[3].

5.1 Implementation Analysis

In this subsection, we explore how our DEVA protocol performs when considering different parameters, *e.g.,* number of users, number of servers or the amount of dropout users and how this affects the communication bandwidth of the protocol and the execution time required.

We are interested in *(i)* each user's execution time and the output data size in relation to the amount of employed servers but also to a different percent of dropout users; *(ii)* each server's execution time and input data size *w.r.t.* the amount of users and the percentage of dropout users; *(iii)* the verification's execution time and the data input size in relation to the amount of users, servers and the number of dropout users considered; and lastly, *(iv)* the total communication bandwidth in relation to the amount of users, servers and number of users that have dropped out.

We describe how our DEVA protocol performs and explain its behavior in each case. The results for the different costs considered per user or per server include all the rounds of the protocol (excluding **Round 1**). Specifically for the server execution time the results contain the cost just from **Round 4** where the aggregation takes place, since no other computation is performed elsewhere by the server.

Execution and Communication Cost Analysis Per User. Our decentralized protocol employs multiple servers for the computation to achieve less computation time per user which is shown to be the case in Fig. 1. In fact, in this figure, it is clear that when the amount of servers is increased, the required execution time for each user decreases. We also observe that when we consider more users, the execution time increases, which is expected since, in that case, each user belongs to a bigger disjoint subset Γ_j; therefore, needs to exchange information within a bigger set of users. Lastly, comparing the two scenarios of dropout, 0% and 30% respectively, we notice minor differences. This happens because the dropout of the users, in the experiments, occurs in **Round 3**, where the computational costly operations that the user performs are already made. We should clarify here that, in our implementation, dropout takes place at that point of the DEVA

---

[3] All code will be released publicly after publication, but is already available to reviewers upon request through the program committee.

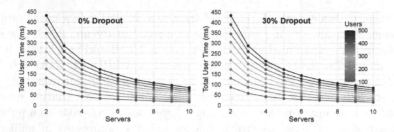

Fig. 1. User execution time for 0% and 30% of dropout users.

protocol with the aim to illustrate the maximum computation time from the user side. Regarding the communication bandwidth that each user has in our DEVA protocol, we expect that the employment of multiple servers results in smaller communication cost for each user. This is because when the protocol uses more servers, less amount of users are connecting to a single server; thus, for *e.g.*, a single user exchanges shares of keys with less users. This expectation is represented in the Fig. 2. Additionally, the figure shows that when dropouts of users occur, less output data are given by each user; which is reasonable since less users are active in that case. Finally, when more users participate in the DEVA protocol, more data communication is required from each user because of the exchange of keys between the users.

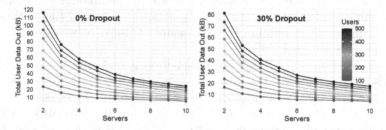

Fig. 2. User output data for 0% and 30% of dropout users.

Execution and Communication Cost Analysis Per Server. The execution time required during the DEVA protocol per server depends on the number of servers that participate in the protocol. More precisely, a big amount of servers participating, offloads the execution time required for each server. On the other hand, the amount of users can affect the time cost of the server in two ways. Firstly, more users require more execution time for the server since each of them handles more computations (since each server handles $\frac{n}{m}$ users when it comes to key sharing (**Round 2**)). Secondly, when there is a user dropout, servers need to compute, among other values, the missing keys from the dropout users as well as the proof **Proof**.DLEQ$(g, \omega_{i'}, \mathsf{pk}_{i'}^{\mathsf{KA}}, z_{i'}, \mathsf{sk}_{i'}^{\mathsf{KA}})$ for each of them; thus, requiring more execution time. The expected behavior of DEVA is illustrated in Fig. 3. The bandwidth cost of each server is easily explained. Less data are received when dropouts of users occur (less users send data to each server). Our experiments show a small difference due to when the dropout happens in the implementation, as we have previously mentioned. Similarly, when more servers are employed, each server receives less data because it handles less users. Our expectations are clearly depicted in Fig. 4.

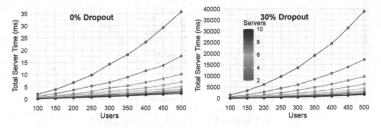

Fig. 3. Server execution time for 0% and 30% of dropout users.

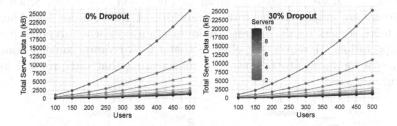

Fig. 4. Server input data for 0% and 30% of dropout users.

DEVA Verification Time and Communication Cost. The verification execution time depends on several parameters that can affect the timing. Surely, a bigger amount of servers should not influence the verification execution time, while *w.r.t.* bigger amount of users or percent of dropout users, the verification time is expected to increase. Figure 5 illustrates the expected behavior of our protocol, considering 500 users and 10 servers for the presented plots, respectively. Regarding the input data needed for the verification, the amount of servers does not affect the input data needed, while bigger dropouts of users require more data. This is because for a smaller number of active users, less public keys are

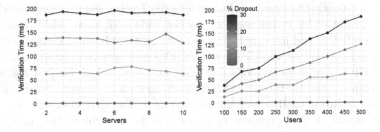

Fig. 5. Verification time of DEVA

received but more zero knowledge proofs need to be checked. In fact, observe our experimental results depicted in Fig. 6.

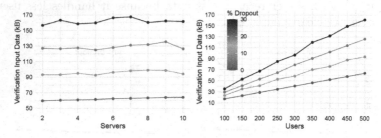

Fig. 6. Verification input data of DEVA.

DEVA Total Communication Cost (Bandwidth). Finally, the total bandwidth of the DEVA protocol is shown in Fig. 7 and shows that when multiple servers are employed the total bandwidth of DEVA decreases. Therefore, using more servers results in less communication cost which reports precisely our expectation. Moreover, we observe that DEVA requires smaller communication cost for more dropout users, demonstrating that our protocol handles dropouts very well.

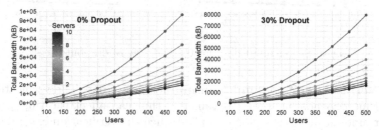

Fig. 7. Total bandwidth of DEVA.

5.2 Comparison

In this subsection, we compare DEVA and the protocol provided by Xu *et al.* VerifyNet [21]. VerifyNet's experiments are conducted on a Intel Xeon E5-2620 CPU @ 2.10 GHz, 16 GB RAM running Ubuntu 18.04. To the best of our knowledge, the authors did not publicly release their source code and, as an additional complication, the CPUs used for running the experiment are hard to compare since Xu *et al.*'s machines are server-CPUs while DEVA's experiments are obtained from a laptop-CPU. For these reasons, we limit our comparison on just the amount of data transmitted by the user. VerifyNet's users have secret *vectors* of length $K = 1000$ as input to the aggregation protocol. To fairly compare, we repeatedly execute our DEVA protocol K times in order to achieve the same amount of aggregated bytes. We execute our experiments in a reasonably distributed setting of $m = 10$ servers, threshold $t = 1$ and key threshold $t_{key} = 1$. In Fig. 8, we compare the amount of data transmitted for each user in executing DEVA or VerifyNet with respect to different amounts of users n or vector sizes K. DEVA is linearly dependent both in the amount of user n and vector size K, while VerifyNet is linear in the vector size but *quadratic* in the amount of users. This different increase factor implies that there will always be, for a fixed vector size K, an amount of users from which our DEVA protocol is more efficient than VerifyNet. As previously discussed, this is due to the fact that in DEVA, the higher the amount of servers, the smaller the amount of data transmitted by each user because it belongs to a smaller subset Γ_j, while the size of this subset depends on the amount of servers. On the other hand, DEVA is clearly not optimal when considering large vector-inputs. It must be observed that VerifyNet is *designed* to work with vectors, key aspect of the specific comparison. DEVA is penalized since multiple executions must be made, thus, posing the DEVA's extension, that allows the usage of vectors as input, an interesting future development.

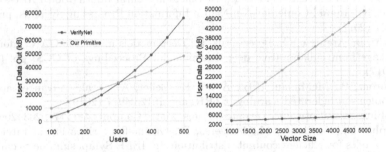

Fig. 8. User's data out comparison for fixed $K = 1000$ and $n = 100$.

6   Conclusion

We proposed DEVA, a secure and practical protocol that allows organizations to collaboratively train their model by employing multiple cloud servers. It protects users' privacy, handles users' dropouts that occur at any round, and provides public output verifiability allowing anyone to check the correctness of the aggregated parameters and thus, it provides greater transparency in the learning process. Servers are *independent* in DEVA and only a threshold amount of them is required to compute the sum. We provided the execution time and bandwidth cost analysis of DEVA for different cases. DEVA is designed to deal well with a large number of users compared to the state of the art, while a future direction would be to extend our work integrating vector size inputs.

Acknowledgement. This work was partially supported by the Wallenberg AI, Autonomous Systems and Software Program (WASP) funded by the Knut and Alice Wallenberg Foundation.

References

1. Benaloh, J.C.: Secret sharing homomorphisms: keeping shares of a secret secret (extended abstract). In: Odlyzko, A.M. (ed.) CRYPTO 1986. LNCS, vol. 263, pp. 251–260. Springer, Heidelberg (1987). https://doi.org/10.1007/3-540-47721-7_19
2. Chaum, D., Pedersen, T.P.: Wallet databases with observers. In: Brickell, E.F. (ed.) CRYPTO 1992. LNCS, vol. 740, pp. 89–105. Springer, Heidelberg (1993). https://doi.org/10.1007/3-540-48071-4_7
3. Diffie, W., Hellman, M.E.: New directions in cryptography. IEEE Trans. Inf. Theory **22**(6), 644–654 (1976)
4. Emura, K.: Privacy-preserving aggregation of time-series data with public verifiability from simple assumptions. In: Pieprzyk, J., Suriadi, S. (eds.) ACISP 2017. LNCS, vol. 10343, pp. 193–213. Springer, Cham (2017). https://doi.org/10.1007/978-3-319-59870-3_11
5. Ghodsi, Z., Gu, T., Garg, S.: SafetyNets: verifiable execution of deep neural networks on an untrusted cloud. In: Advances in Neural Information Processing Systems 30: Annual Conference on Neural Information Processing Systems, pp. 4672–4681 (2017)
6. Hitaj, B., Ateniese, G., Pérez-Cruz, F.: Deep models under the GAN: information leakage from collaborative deep learning. In: Proceedings of CCS, pp. 603–618 (2017)
7. Kairouz, P., McMahan, H.B., Avent, B., Bellet, A., et al.: Advances and open problems in federated learning. CoRR, abs/1912.04977 (2019)
8. Koblitz, N.: Elliptic curve cryptosystems. Math. Comput. **48**(177), 203–209 (1987)
9. Krohn, M., Freedman, M., Mazieres, D.: On-the-fly verification of rateless erasure codes for efficient content distribution. In: IEEE Symposium on Security and Privacy. Proceedings, Berkeley, CA, USA, pp. 226–240 (2004)
10. Leontiadis, I., Elkhiyaoui, K., Önen, M., Molva, R.: PUDA – privacy and unforgeability for data aggregation. In: Reiter, M., Naccache, D. (eds.) CANS 2015. LNCS, vol. 9476, pp. 3–18. Springer, Cham (2015). https://doi.org/10.1007/978-3-319-26823-1_1
11. Liu, Y., et al.: Trojaning attack on neural networks. In: 25th Annual Network and Distributed System Security Symposium, NDSS. The Internet Society (2018)
12. Phong, L.T., Aono, Y., Hayashi, T., Wang, L., Moriai, S.: Privacy-preserving deep learning via additively homomorphic encryption. IEEE Trans. Inf. Forensics Secur. **13**(5), 1333–1345 (2018)
13. Segal, A., et al.: Practical secure aggregation for privacy-preserving machine learning. In: CCS (2017)
14. Shamir, A.: How to share a secret. Commun. ACM **22**(11), 612–613 (1979)
15. Shi, E., Chan, T.-H., Rieffel, E., Chow, R., Song, D.: Privacy-preserving aggregation of time-series data, vol. 2, January 2011
16. Shokri, R., Shmatikov, V.: Privacy-preserving deep learning. In: Ray, I., Li, N., Kruegel, C. (eds.) Proceedings of the 22nd ACM SIGSAC Conference on Computer and Communications Security, pp. 1310–1321. ACM (2015)
17. Tramèr, F., Boneh, D.: Slalom: fast, verifiable and private execution of neural networks in trusted hardware. In: Proceedings of ICLR (2019)
18. Tsaloli, G., Banegas, G., Mitrokotsa, A.: Practical and provably secure distributed aggregation: verifiable additive homomorphic secret sharing. Cryptography **4**(3), 25 (2020)

19. Tsaloli, G., Liang, B., Mitrokotsa, A.: Verifiable homomorphic secret sharing. In: Baek, J., Susilo, W., Kim, J. (eds.) ProvSec 2018. LNCS, vol. 11192, pp. 40–55. Springer, Cham (2018). https://doi.org/10.1007/978-3-030-01446-9_3

20. Tsaloli, G., Mitrokotsa, A.: Sum it up: verifiable additive homomorphic secret sharing. In: Seo, J.H. (ed.) ICISC 2019. LNCS, vol. 11975, pp. 115–132. Springer, Cham (2020). https://doi.org/10.1007/978-3-030-40921-0_7

21. Xu, G., Li, H., Liu, S., Yang, K., Lin, X.: VerifyNet: secure and verifiable federated learning. IEEE Trans. Inf. Forensics Secur. **15**, 911–926 (2020)

22. Xu, W., Evans, D., Qi, Y.: Feature squeezing: detecting adversarial examples in deep neural networks. In: 25th Annual Network and Distributed System Security Symposium, NDSS 2018, San Diego, California, USA. The Internet Society (2018)

23. Yao, H., Wang, C., Hai, B., Zhu, S.: Homomorphic hash and blockchain based authentication key exchange protocol for strangers. In: International Conference on Advanced Cloud and Big Data (CBD), Lanzhou, pp. 243–248 (2018)

DVul-WLG: Graph Embedding Network Based on Code Similarity for Cross-Architecture Firmware Vulnerability Detection

Hao Sun[1], Yanjun Tong[1], Jing Zhao[1(✉)], and Zhaoquan Gu[2]

[1] Dalian University of Technology, Dalian, China
zhaoj9988@dlut.edu.cn
[2] Guangzhou University, Guangzhou, China

Abstract. Vulnerabilities in the firmware of embedded devices have led to many IoT security incidents. Embedded devices have multiple architectures and the firmware source code of embedded devices is difficult to obtain, which makes it difficult to detect firmware vulnerabilities. In this paper, we propose a neural network model called DVul-WLG for cross-architecture firmware vulnerability detection. This model analyzes the similarity between the binary function of the vulnerability and the binary function of the firmware to determine whether the firmware contains the vulnerability. The similarity between functions is calculated by comparing the features of the attribute control flow graph (ACFG) of the functions. DVul-WLG uses Word2vec, LSTM (Long Short-Term Memory) and an improved graph convolutional neural network (GCN) to extract the features of ACFG. This model embeds instructions of different architectures into the same space through canonical correlation analysis (CCA), and expresses instructions of different architectures in the form of intermediate vectors. In this way, the heterogeneity of architectures can be ignored when comparing cross-architecture similarity. We compared DVul-WLG with the advanced method FIT and the basic method Gemini through experiments. Experiments show that DVul-WLG has a higher AUC (Area Under the Curve) value. We also detected vulnerabilities in the real firmware. The accuracy of DVul-WLG is 89%, while FIT and Gemini are 78% and 73%, respectively.

Keywords: Vulnerability detection · Binary code similarity · Graph embedding

1 Introduction

In the era of the Internet of Everything, embedded devices exist in all aspects of daily life. Security issues caused by embedded devices have aroused widespread concern. An embedded device is a closed system that boots into a unified software package called firmware. The lack of security considerations at the beginning of

J. K. Liu et al. (Eds.): ISC 2021, LNCS 13118, pp. 320–337, 2021.
https://doi.org/10.1007/978-3-030-91356-4_17

the firmware design and the reuse of a large amount of code have resulted in many vulnerabilities in the firmware. In addition, vulnerabilities in the firmware can be easily exploited [1]. In July 2020, a research team discovered many serious security vulnerabilities in three different home hubs Fibaro Home Center Lite, Homematic, and eLAN-RF-003. These vulnerabilities can lead to sensitive data leakage, remote code execution, and man-in-the-middle attacks. In December 2020, a hacker used an undiscovered vulnerability to forcibly open the door of a third of PickPoint's lockers, causing thousands of packages throughout Moscow to be at risk of being stolen. From the above-mentioned network attack incidents, it can be found that the vulnerabilities in the firmware have brought great security risks. What's worse is that we cannot use traditional vulnerability scanning tools on PCs and mobile devices to detect firmware vulnerabilities.

The detection of firmware vulnerabilities has become increasingly important. In order to solve this problem, some security researchers have proposed technologies to dynamically detect firmware vulnerabilities [2,3]. However, dynamic detection technology has great limitations. Usually, the firmware is customized for a specific embedded device, so that the detection method of a certain device cannot be universal. The dynamic detection usually adopts the method of firmware simulation. However, the parameters of NVRAM (Non-Volatile Random Access Memory) are usually not available, causing security analysts to repeatedly hijack certain functions to bypass exceptions so that the program can be executed. This process is not always feasible and very time-consuming. Therefore, for large-scale firmware vulnerability detection, static detection methods are more advantageous. The static detection method for firmware vulnerabilities must be universal and lightweight. Traditional static detection techniques such as symbolic execution and stain analysis are not suitable. At present, many static detection methods have solved the problem of detecting vulnerabilities at the source code level [4,5]. However, it is difficult to obtain the source code of the firmware, so these detection methods are not suitable. The detection method of binary code similarity does not require firmware source code, and it is universal and lightweight. Therefore, for firmware vulnerability detection, the detection method of binary code similarity is advantageous and efficient.

As shown in Fig. 1, the binary function can be converted into an attribute control flow graph (ACFG) by the IDA pro disassembly tool [6,7]. When performing binary code similarity detection, first extract the features of ACFG, these features can be used to represent ACFG, thereby representing the binary function. Then the ACFG features are converted into feature vectors through the pre-trained neural network. Finally, the vector distance formula is used to calculate the distance between the feature vectors, and the vector distance is used to express the similarity of the binary function. This paper divides the features of ACFG into three categories: the semantic features of instructions, statistical features and structural features of graphs. FIT [20] uses the method of word embedding in natural language processing to extract the semantic information of instructions. But the traditional word embedding models CBOW (Continuous Bag-of-Words) [8] and Skip-Gram [9] can only consider the semantic relationship of instructions under the same architecture. However, firmwares with different architectures often have the same vulnerabilities, so cross-architecture situations should be considered when comparing similarities with vulnerable functions. When comparing cross-architecture function similarity, it is not only necessary to maintain the semantic association of instructions in the same architecture, but also to maintain similar embeddings for instructions with the same semantics between different architectures, which cannot be achieved by traditional word embedding models. Regarding the structural features of the graph, Gemini [10] designed an aggregation algorithm inspired by Struc2vec, which can aggregate the features of the basic blocks to represent the graphical features of ACFG. However, this method allows the adjacent nodes of each basic block in the graph to have the same influence factor, and then attaches the attributes of the adjacent nodes to the basic block itself through nonlinear changes. In fact, the influence factors of adjacent nodes of the basic block are different, so Gemini's extraction of the structural features of ACFG is not accurate.

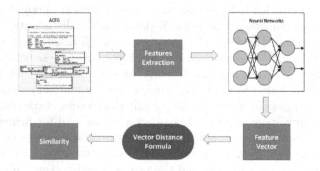

Fig. 1. Schematic diagram of binary code similarity detection.

In view of the above problems, the main challenges of this paper are in two aspects: One is the semantic feature of ACFG. When comparing binary functions of cross-architecture firmware, it is necessary to ensure the similarity of instruction semantics within the same architecture. At the same time, it is necessary to ensure the relevance of instruction semantics under different architectures. The second is the structural feature of ACFG graphics. The traditional GCN cannot extract the structure information of the directed graph, while the ACFG is a directed graph. We need to improve the GCN to be able to accurately extract the structure information of the ACFG.

The main contributions of this paper are as follows:

1 This paper uses code similarity analysis to design a cross-architecture firmware vulnerability detection model. The model combined with deep neural network can accurately extract the semantic and structural features of ACFG.

2 In the process of cross-architecture instruction embedding, this paper compares two classic word embedding models, CBOW and Skip-Gram. At the same time, ARM instructions and MIPS instructions are embedded in the same space through the canonical correlation analysis (CCA) method. When comparing cross-architecture function similarity, the heterogeneity between architectures can be ignored, so that the semantic features of instructions of different architectures are compared in the same dimension, which improves the accuracy of the comparison.

3 This paper uses DGCN [23] to improve the graph embedding aggregation algorithm proposed by Gemini. According to the principle of DGCN, we assign different influence factors to the adjacent nodes of the basic block. Through experimental verification, the method in this paper can better extract the structural features of ACFG.

The remaining organizational structure of this paper is as follows: In the second section, we review more related work. In the third section, we describe the method that Siamese Network embeds the features of ACFG to compare the similarity. In the fourth section, we evaluate the effectiveness of our proposed method through experimental analysis. Finally, summarize all the work of this paper.

2 Relate Work

For our related work, this paper only discusses related technologies for binary vulnerability detection. In 2008, Gao et al. proposed BinHunt [12], a new technique for discovering semantic differences in binary programs. They use techniques such as graph isomorphism and symbolic execution to analyze the control flow graph of the binary program, and can identify the semantic difference between the original program and the patch program, thereby revealing the vulnerabilities eliminated by the patch program. On this basis, Jiang et al. proposed that the semantic differences between binary programs are easily interfered by others using simple obfuscating functions. Therefore, they used deep pollution and automatic input generation techniques to discover the semantic differences of CFG [13]. However, this method of capturing binary vulnerabilities through semantic differences relies on instruction semantics and is only suitable for a single architecture.

In 2013, Martial et al. proposed a polynomial algorithm by fusing the BinDiff algorithm with the Hungarian algorithm of bipartite graph matching [14]. The graph-based edit distance calculates a meaningful similarity measure, which significantly improves the matching accuracy between binary files. Flake proposed a heuristic method of constructing isomorphism between function sets in the same executable file but in different versions [15]. Pewny et al. observe the IO behavior of basic blocks and obtain their semantics, thereby effectively revealing the bugs in the binary code [16]. These methods all rely on accurate graphic matching technology, and have high time complexity, and are not suitable for large-scale binary vulnerability detection. DiscovRE [17] pre-filtered function pairs through digital features in order to reduce the costly calculation of graph matching. However, this method is not reliable and will produce a large number of false negatives.

In order to reduce the expensive cost of graph matching, the method of graph embedding has become a good choice. Graph embedding refers to the mapping of high-dimensional features in a graph to low-dimensional vector representations. The embedding vector can accurately represent the structural features in the graph, the attribute features of each vertex, and the interactive information between vertices and vertices [18]. For graph embedding vectors, we can use distance formulas between vectors, such as cos distance, Euclidean distance etc. to compare the similarity between graphics more easily. In 2016, Feng et al. [6] first used a codebook-based method to convert the ACFG of a binary function into a numerical vector, which makes it easier to calculate the similarity between graphs. After that, CVSSA [19] accurately extracts the features of ACFG at the binary function level through SVM. Gemini [10] proposed by Xu et al. uses a neural network to calculate the embedding, which extracts features at the basic block level, and then expresses the embedding of ACFG through an aggregate function, which further improves the accuracy of graph embedding. However, Gemini only expresses the embedding of the basic block through the statistical features of the basic block, completely ignoring the semantic features in the basic block, which will have a great limitation. When two basic blocks with completely different semantics have similar statistical features, Gemini will consider the two basic blocks to be similar. FIT [20] extracts the semantic features of instructions through the Word2vec, but instructions of different architectures are embedded in different spaces. FIT ignores the relevance of semantically equivalent instructions under different architectures, which leads to inaccurate comparisons of semantic features of functions under different architectures.

3 Embedded Network

This section will introduce how to convert the ACFG of the binary function into a graph embedding. For the embedded vector, the distance of the vector is calculated by the *cos* distance formula, and then the similarity between the binary functions is obtained. Here we introduce the theoretical model of the Siamese Network, which can better explain how the graph embedding network works.

3.1 Siamese Network

Siamese Network is a new type of neural network architecture. Siamese Network can learn a similarity metric from training data, which is often used to evaluate the similarity of input sample pairs. It has shown better capabilities in certain fields, such as face recognition and signature verification etc. As shown in Fig. 2, the Siamese Network architecture contains two identical sub-networks (the sub-networks have the same configuration and parameters). In this paper, these two networks are designed as ACFG graph embedded networks. These two sub-networks can convert the input ACFG sample pair into a vector, and then judge the similarity of the sample pair through the distance formula of the vector.

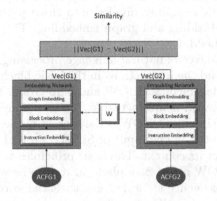

Fig. 2. Siamese network.

The training goal of Siamese Network is to maximize similarity when a given pair of ACFG samples belong to the same category. The similarity should be minimized when the sample pairs belong to different categories. Whether the sample pairs belong to the same category depends on whether they are compiled from the same source function. As shown in Fig. 2, the input sample pair ACFG1 and ACFG2 are converted into vectors Vec_1 and Vec_2 through the graph embedding network. The similarity is measured by the *cos* distance of the vector, the measurement formula is as follows:

$$cos(Vec_1, Vec_2) = \frac{Vec_1 \cdot Vec_2}{||Vec_1||||Vec_2||} \tag{1}$$

For the input sample pair, we will mark it, if the input is the same category, mark it as +1, otherwise mark it as −1. Therefore, when training the Siamese Network, the input is in the form of triples $\langle ACFG_1, ACFG_2, Label \rangle$. In this paper, the loss function is only considered related to the parameters and input, so the loss function is defined as follows:

$$L = (Label - cos(Vec_1, Vec_2))^2 \tag{2}$$

When the sample pair belongs to the same category, the closer the *cos* similarity value is to 1, the smaller the loss value L. When the sample pairs belong to different categories, the closer the *cos* similarity value is to 0, the smaller the loss value L. Therefore, reducing the loss value L in the iterative process can meet the training goal of Siamese Network.

3.2 Embedding of Instruction Semantic Features

In Sect. 3.1, the overall architecture of Siamese Network is introduced. The most important part is the graph embedding sub-network. How to convert ACFG into vector representation is also the core work of this paper. As shown in Fig. 2, the embedded network is mainly divided into three parts, namely instruction embedding, block embedding and graph embedding. This section mainly introduces instruction embedding.

Analogous to Word2vec of natural language processing, we regard each basic block as a sentence, and the instructions in the basic block as words. The classic word embedding models include CBOW and Skip-Gram. Both are composed of three layers of feedforward neural networks, which are input layer, hidden layer and output layer. The input of CBOW is the context of the word, and the context is used to predict the word. The input of Skip-Gram is the word itself, and the word is used to predict its context. The basic principles of the two are the same. This paper takes CBOW as an example to introduce its working principle.

For a given word sequence $w_1, w_2, ..., w_n$, w_k is the word to be predicted, and the sliding window size is c. The input layer is the context of w_k in the sliding window, and these words are represented by One-hot encoding. The weight matrix from the input layer to the hidden layer is W_1, and the word vector of the input layer is multiplied by the weight matrix and averaged to obtain the vector of the hidden layer. The weight matrix from the hidden layer to the output layer is W_2, and the vector of the hidden layer is multiplied by W_2 to get the vector of the output layer. The vector of the output layer is normalized by the softmax function and the value with the largest corresponding position in the vector is the predicted word. The objective function is to maximize the maximum likelihood estimation:

$$\frac{1}{n}\sum_{t=1}^{n}\sum_{-c<j<c} logp(w_k|w_{k+j}) \tag{3}$$

Whether using the CBOW model or the Skip-Gram model will cause a problem, the instruction embedding of the MIPS architecture and the instruction embedding of the ARM architecture are not in the same space. This ignores the semantic association of equivalent instructions between the two architectures, resulting in inaccurate comparisons of cross-architecture similarity. Inspired by [21] cross-language embedding, this paper uses CCA to embed MIPS and ARM instructions into the same space. First, the MIPS and ARM instructions are embedded in different spaces using the Word2vec model, and let $\Sigma \in \mathbb{R}^{n_1 \times d_1}$ and $\Omega \in \mathbb{R}^{n_2 \times d_2}$ respectively denote the vector spaces of the instructions of the two architectures. Instructions with equal semantics under the two architectures are mapped to the same space, which is not as easy as multilingual embedding in natural language. Because in natural language, the semantically equivalent words in different languages can be obtained through the dictionary. The instructions are different, and there is no dictionary-like translation between instructions of different architectures. At the same time, instructions are not atomically structured like words. Instructions are composed of mnemonics and operands, and different operands generate a large number of different instructions. In order to solve this problem, we artificially regard instructions with the same mnemonic as the same type of instructions, because most of the operations performed by instructions with the same mnemonic are similar. Based on prior knowledge, this paper uses mnemonics to map MIPS and ARM instructions. For example, 'move' in MIPS and 'MOV' in ARM are considered equivalent. Through the instruction dictionary, let the instructions in the two subsets of $\Sigma' \subseteq \Sigma$ and $\Omega' \subseteq \Omega$ map one by one. x and y denote a pair of equivalent instructions from Σ' and Ω' respectively. a and b represent the projection direction, then the vector of x and y after the projection is expressed as:

$$x' = a^\mathrm{T} x, y' = b^\mathrm{T} y \tag{4}$$

The correlation between the projection vectors x' and y' is expressed as:

$$\rho(x', y') = \frac{E\left[x'y'\right]}{\sqrt{E\left[x'^2\right] E\left[y'^2\right]}} \tag{5}$$

The goal of our optimization is to maximize the correlation $\rho(x', y')$ and output two projection vectors a and b. Using these two projection vectors, all instructions of MIPS and ARM can be projected, which can be summarized as:

$$A, B = CCA(\Sigma', \Omega') \tag{6}$$

$$\Sigma^* = A^\mathrm{T} \Sigma, \Omega^* = B^\mathrm{T} \Omega \tag{7}$$

3.3   Embedding of Structural Features of ACFG

After the instruction embedding is generated, the instruction sequence in the basic block needs to be aggregated to generate the embedding of the basic block. Considering that in natural language processing, word embedding is used to represent sentence embedding. For an ordered sequence of instructions, the RNN model can effectively mine its semantic information and timing information. However, the instruction sequence in some basic blocks is too long. If the RNN model is used in training, the problem of gradient disappearance and gradient explosion will occur. Therefore, this paper chooses the LSTM model that performs better in long sequences. The LSTM model can summarize the instruction sequence in the basic block, and finally express all the instruction sequences with internal correlation through a vector. At the same time, the statistical features of the combined basic block are shown in Table 1. The combined vector represents the embedding of the basic block. The basic block embedding formula is as follows:

$$B_{fea} = W_{b1} B_{emb} + W_{b2} B_{sta} \tag{8}$$

W_{b1} and W_{b2} represent the weight matrix of instruction semantic feature and statistical feature, respectively.

After the feature of each basic block is generated, the features of all basic blocks need to be aggregated as the feature of ACFG. A simple method is to add the features of all basic blocks to represent the features of ACFG. However, this method cannot extract the structure of the graph, resulting in insufficient accuracy of feature extraction. Inspired by Structure2vec, Gemini recursively aggregates the features of basic blocks through the topological structure of graph. After a few steps of recursion, the graph embedding network will calculate a new vector representation for each basic block. This vector includes the features of the basic block and the structural features of the graph. Gemini trains the interaction between nodes through a fully connected neural network. The formula is as follows:

$$\mu_v^{(t)} = tanh(W_1 x_v + \sigma(\sum_{u \in N_{(v)}} \mu_u^{(t-1)})) \tag{9}$$

x_v represents the feature vector of the basic block; W_1 is the matrix coefficient of the basic block feature; μ_v represents the new vector representation calculated by the graph embedding network for node v; $N_{(v)}$ represents the adjacent node of the basic block v; σ represents the fully connected neural network. The above formula can be understood as for any basic block v, the graph embedding network calculates a new feature vector for it. This feature vector is obtained by summing the features of all adjacent nodes of the basic block v and then undergoing nonlinear changes, and finally adding to the feature vector of the basic block v. This formula does consider the features of the basic block itself and the topological features of the graph. But let all adjacent nodes of the basic block have the same influence factor for summation. Although σ has a very strong nonlinear transformation, it is still not accurate enough to represent the structural features of the graph.

This paper has made improvements to this. Using GCN to extract the structural features of the topological graph has become one of the most effective methods. GCN uses the Laplacian matrix of the graph to implement the convolution operation of the topological graph, and its propagation rules are as follows:

$$Z_F = H^{(l+1)} = \sigma(\widetilde{D}^{-\frac{1}{2}} \widetilde{A} \widetilde{D}^{-\frac{1}{2}} H^{(l)} W) \tag{10}$$

Where $\widetilde{A} = A + I_N$; A are the adjacency matrix of the graph; I_N is the identity matrix; $\widetilde{D}$ is the degree matrix of $\widetilde{A}$; H is the feature of each layer, for the input layer H is the feature of the basic block; σ is the nonlinear activation function; and W is the training parameter. This propagation formula can extract the features of undirected graphs better. Unfortunately, ACFG is a directed graph. If the propagation formula of GCN is used, the direction information of the directed graph will inevitably be lost, which will have a great impact on ACFG. In order to be able to use the powerful ability of GCN to extract graphic features, we are inspired by the DGCN proposed by [11], and retain the direction information of the graphic when using the GCN propagation formula.

As shown in Fig. 3, we add two matrices to ACFG, the in-degree matrix A_{Sin} and the out-degree matrix A_{Sout}. In-degree matrix means that there is a node k, and two nodes i and j point to node k at the same time $\{i \Rightarrow k \Leftarrow j\}$, let $A_{Sin}+ = 1$. On the contrary, if there is node k pointing to node i and j at the same time $\{i \Leftarrow k \Rightarrow j\}$, let $A_{Sout}+ = 1$. These two matrices are symmetric because $A_{Sin}(i,j) = A_{Sin}(j,i)$ and $A_{Sout}(i,j) = A_{Sout}(j,i)$. Therefore, these two matrices can be constructed similar to undirected graph convolution, the formula is as follows:

$$Z_{Sin} = H^{(l+1)} = \sigma(\widetilde{D}_{Sin}^{-\frac{1}{2}} \widetilde{A}_{Sin} \widetilde{D}_{Sin}^{\frac{1}{2}} H^{(l)} W) \tag{11}$$

$$Z_{Sout} = H^{(l+1)} = \sigma(\widetilde{D}_{Sout}^{-\frac{1}{2}} \widetilde{A}_{Sout} \widetilde{D}_{Sout}^{-\frac{1}{2}} H^{(l)} W) \tag{12}$$

Through these two auxiliary formulas, the directionality of the graph can be effectively expressed, and then the convolution formula of the undirected graph is merged. The fusion method used in this paper is splicing, and the fusion formula is as follows:

$$Z = Concat(Z_F, \alpha Z_{Sin}, \beta Z_{Sout}) \tag{13}$$

α and β represent the different weights of in-degree convolution and out-degree convolution, and this weight is obtained through learning. In this way, the structure of the directed graph ACFG can be extracted through the fused convolution formula.

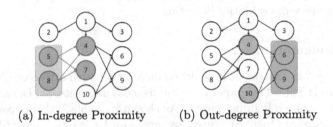

(a) In-degree Proximity   (b) Out-degree Proximity

Fig. 3. DGCN second-order proximity.

Similar to the representation of basic block features, we combine graph embedding and graph statistical features, as shown in the Function-level of Table 1. The features of the final ACFG are expressed as follows:

$$F_{fea} = W_{f1} Z + W_{f2} F_{sta} \tag{14}$$

W_{f1} and W_{f2} are the matrix coefficients of the graph embedding feature and the graph statistical feature, and F_{sta} is the graph statistical feature.

Table 1. Statistical features

Type	Attribute name	Type	Attribute name
Block-Level	No.of String Constants	Function- level	No.of Arithmetic Instructions
	No.of Numeric Constants		No.of Logic Instructions
	No.of Arithmetic Instructions		No.of Transfer Instructions
	No.of Logic Instructions		No.of Transmit Instructions
	No.of Transfer Instructions		No.of Basic Blocks
	No.of Transmit Instructions		No.of Edges
	No.of Instructions		No.of Function Calls
	No.of Calls		No.of Incoming Calls
	No.of Offspring		No.of Instructions
	Betweeness		No.of Variables

4 Evaluation

This section mainly introduces the details of the experiment, as well as evaluating the effectiveness of instruction embedding for spatial projection and evaluating the effectiveness of using DGCN to extract ACFG graph structures. This paper compares the most advanced methods such as Gemini and FIT to prove the effectiveness of the improved method. Finally, this paper detects real firmware vulnerabilities and proves that the method proposed in this paper can be applied to real firmware vulnerabilities detection.

4.1 Implementation

The experiment in this paper is deployed on a server with a 16-core CPU, 128GB RAM, and 1TB SSD. This paper has established 3 data sets: (1) Data set I is used to train the graph embedding model. As shown in Table 2, this papaer compiles different versions of OpenSSL, BusyBox, and FindUtils into binary files of MIPS and ARM architectures, and opens four different optimization levels: O0, O1, O2, and O3. The data in the table represents the number of functions under different architectures of different programs, each function represents an ACFG, a total of 59410 ACFGs. The extraction of ACFG uses IDA pro script written by Gemini, which can effectively extract the features of ACFG. (2) Data set II is used to verify the effectiveness of the graph embedding model. As shown in Table 3, we compile multiple Unix Shell programs such as cat, shown, and cp into binary programs under the two architectures of ARM and MIPS, and open O0 to O3 four optimization levels. There are 13587 ACFGs in total. (3) Data set III is the firmware image obtained from real manufacturers, including manufacturers such as D-Link, TP-Link, Netgear and Buffalo. This paper mainly obtains firmware with corresponding vulnerabilities from various manufacturers, and is mainly used for the detection of three vulnerabilities: CVE-2020-1967, CVE-2020-1971 and CVE-2017-15873. For each of these three vulnerabilities, 50 firmware images are selected for detection.

This paper uses data set I to train Siamese Network, the Batch Size is 10, and 5 sets of similar sample pairs and 5 sets of dissimilar sample pairs are selected each time. Similarity means that ACFG sample pairs are derived from the same original function. Similar sample pairs are marked as <ACFG1,ACFG2,+1>, and dissimilar sample pairs are marked as <ACFG1,ACFG2,-1>. The iterative principle of the model training process can refer to the third section of this paper. The learning rate during training is 0.001, the embedding depth of the model is 128, and the maximum number of iterations is 100. The trained model is tested on data set II. The Batch Size is also set to 10 during the test, and 5 groups of similar sample pairs and 5 groups of dissimilar sample pairs are selected each time. Finally, the TPR (true positive) and FPR (false positive) under different test sets are obtained, and the ROC curve is obtained.

Table 2. Data set I

	OpenSSL	BusyBox	FindUtils
MIPS	21085	6700	2360
ARM	20513	6512	2240
Total	41598	13212	4600

Table 3. Data set II

	cat	chown	cp	dd	ls	rm
MIPS	528	1062	1466	788	2092	1048
ARM	480	980	1411	716	2039	977
Total	1008	2042	2877	1504	4131	2025

4.2 Effectiveness of Instruction Embedding Projection

As shown in Fig. 4(a), this paper takes the 'MOV R0, R8' instruction in ARM as an example. It can be seen that due to the heterogeneity of the two architectures, only the instruction with the mnemonic 'MOV' is close to the embedding space of 'MOV R0, R8'. Although Skip-Gram does embed instructions with similar semantics in the same architecture into similar spaces. But for instructions with similar semantics under different architectures, they are not in a similar embedding space. In this regard, this paper constructs equivalent translations of MIPS and ARM instructions, and uses CCA to project instructions in different spaces into the same space. This allows instructions with similar semantics under different architectures to have similar spatial embeddings. As shown in Fig. 4(b), the similar embedding of the 'MOV R0, R8' instruction is no longer only the instruction with 'MOV' as the mnemonic in ARM, but includes the instruction with 'move' as the mnemonic in MIPS. This is in line with the expectation that similar instructions in the same architecture have similar embeddings, and instructions with similar semantics in different architectures also have similar embeddings.

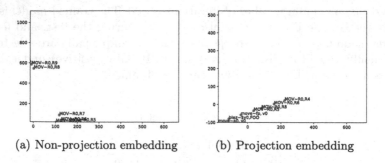

(a) Non-projection embedding   (b) Projection embedding

Fig. 4. Instruction embedding space.

In order to prove that the effect of instruction embedding after projection is better than that of instruction embedding without projection, this paper makes a comparison. The embedded instruction after projection is represented by Skipgram2, and the embedded instruction without projection is represented by Skipgram1. The block embedding of the two methods adopts the LSTM model, and the graph embedding adopts the aggregation algorithm of Gemini. The result is shown in Fig. 5. In the three different test sets, the model using Skipgram2 has a higher AUC value. It can be proved that the effect of instruction embedding after projection is better.

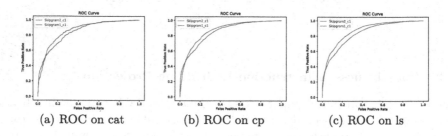

(a) ROC on cat   (b) ROC on cp   (c) ROC on ls

Fig. 5. Comparison of the effectiveness of instruction projection

4.3   Evaluation of Graph Embedding

The above has proved that the projected instructions have better performance. But instruction projection is only optimized at the level of instruction embedding. As described in Sect. 3.4, the graph embedding aggregation algorithm proposed by Gemini is not accurate enough to extract the graph features of ACFG. Therefore, we have improved the algorithm. We use c2 to represent the improved aggregation algorithm, and c1 to represent the original algorithm of Gemini. At the same time, because FIT uses SkipGram and Gemini's aggregation algorithm, we use Skipgram1_c1 to represent FIT. As shown in Fig. 6, the ROC curves of CBOW2_c2 and Skipgram2_c2 are basically similar, where CBOW2 indicates that the original instruction is embedded using CBOW, and then the instruction is embedded in the re-projection. The effect of instruction embedding using CBOW and Skipgram is similar, which is also easy to understand, because the two models are the same in principle. In addition, we can see that the improved effect of the aggregation algorithm is stronger than Skipgram2_c1, which further proves that the aggregation algorithm we proposed can extract the features of the graph more effectively.

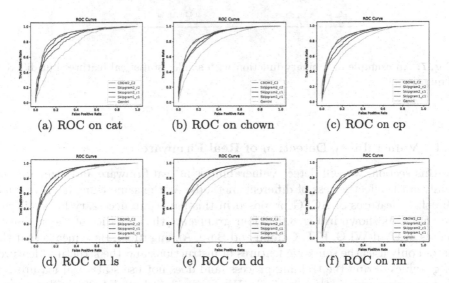

(a) ROC on cat   (b) ROC on chown   (c) ROC on cp

(d) ROC on ls   (e) ROC on dd   (f) ROC on rm

Fig. 6. Comparison of the effectiveness of instruction projection

It can be seen from the ROC curve that Gemini's performance is not good. We found that the data set used by Gemini, although the same source code has been optimized by different compilers, has different optimization levels. But most functions of the same origin have the same statistical features, which cause the statistical features to occupy a large proportion in the learning process of the graph embedding network. This will lead to a defect that the graph embedding network ignores the semantic features of instructions in the learning process. As shown in Fig. 7, Gemini will mistakenly regard basic blocks with similar statistical features but completely different semantic information as similar, resulting in a high number of false positives. In response to this problem, this paper modified the data set. We also compiled the same source code into binary codes with different optimization levels and different architectures. But we will try to select similar functions with large differences in statistical features. The similar functions defined here are the same as Gemini. Different binary functions compiled from the same source function are similar functions.

Func1	Func2
PUSH R7,LR	PUSH {R7,LR}
SUB SP,SP,#8	SUB SP,SP,#8
ADD R7,SP,#0	ADD R7,SP,#0
STR R0,[R7,#8+var_4]	STR R0,[R7,#8+var_4]
STR R1,[R7,#8+var_8]	STR R1,[R7,#8+var_8]
MOVS R1,#0 ; oflag	BLX getpid
MOV R0,#Aarm ; file	MOVS R3,#0
BLX open	MOV R0,R3
MOVS R3,#0	ADDS R7,#8
MOV R0,R3	MOV SP,R7
ADDS R7,#8	POP {R7,PC}
MOV SP,R7	
POP R7,PC	
(0,5,1,0,13,3,0)	(0,4,1,0,11,3,0)

Fig. 7. An example of a binary function with similar statistical features but different semantics.

4.4 Vulnerability Detection of Real Firmware

In this section, we will detect vulnerabilities in real firmware and compare and analyze the effectiveness of different methods. At the same time, it proves that the three features of ACFG proposed in this paper are necessary for similarity detection. As shown in Fig. 8, the four graphs are the statistics of the similarity scores of DVul-WLG, FIT, Gemini and Base. Among them, Base means that the model only uses the semantic features of instructions and the structural features of graphics during the training process, and does not use statistical features, so as to compare with other methods. We randomly selected 4000 similar sample pairs from the data set (compiled by the same original function), among which the top 80% with the highest DVul-WLG similarity score were in the interval of [0.797, 1.0]. Therefore, the threshold of DVul-WLG is selected as 0.797. For firmware functions that use DVul-WLG for similarity detection, if the similarity score is higher than 0.797, it is considered that there are vulnerabilities in the firmware function. Similarly, the threshold selection for FIT, Gemini and Base is 0.741, 0.628 and 0.584 respectively. This also reflects that the model proposed in this paper has a higher similarity score for similar function pairs.

As shown in Table 4, there are three types of vulnerabilities to detecte: (1) CVE-2020-1967 is a high-risk vulnerability in OpenSSL. This vulnerability is caused by the incorrect use of TLS and will lead to a null pointer reference. Cause the server or client to crash when calling the SSL_check_chain() function. This vulnerability mainly affect OpenSSL 1.1.1d, 1.1.1e and 1.1.1f versions. This

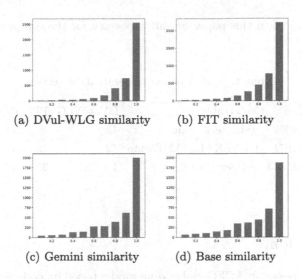

(a) DVul-WLG similarity   (b) FIT similarity

(c) Gemini similarity   (d) Base similarity

Fig. 8. Similarity scores of similar samples.

paper selects 50 firmwares with these three versions for testing. DVul-WLG successfully identified 47 (94%), FIT successfully identified 40 (80%), Gemini successfully identified 33 (66%) and Base successfully identified 25 (50%). (2) CVE-2020-1971 is a denial of service vulnerability in OpenSSL. The failure to properly handle the GENERAL_NAME_cmp function results in a null pointer reference, which may lead to a denial of service. The main affected versions are OpenSSL 1.1.1~1.1.1 h and OpenSSL 1.0.2~1.0.2w. Among 50 selected firmwares, DVul-WLG successfully identified 42 (84%), FIT successfully identified 38 (76%), Gemini successfully identified 35 (70%), and Base successfully identified 23 (46%). (3) CVE-2017-15873 is an integer overflow vulnerability in BusyBox, which can cause write access violations. The mainly affects the version of BusyBox 1.27.2. Among 50 selected firmwares, DVul-WLG successfully identified 45 (90%), FIT successfully identified 39 (78%), Gemini successfully identified 42 (84%), and Base successfully identified 30 (60%).

The above results can prove that the model DVul-WLG proposed in this paper has higher accuracy than FIT. This is because this paper improves the accuracy of extracting the structural features of ACFG graphics through the improved GCN method, which proves that the structural features of graphics are necessary when comparing the similarity of ACFG. The accuracy of DVul-WLG and FIT is higher than that of Gemini. This is because Gemini did not consider the semantic features of instructions, which can prove that the semantic features of instructions are necessary when comparing ACFG similarities. Finally, the accuracy of Base is the lowest. This is because Base does not use the statistical features of ACFG. Therefore, statistical features are also necessary when comparing the similarity of ACFG. In summary, the three features of ACFG proposed in this paper are all necessary for the comparison of ACFG similarity.

Table 4. Real firmware vulnerability detection

CVE Number	Vulnerability	DVul-WLG	FIT	Gemini	Base
CVE-2020-1967	SSL_check_chain	47	40	33	25
CVE-2020-1971	GENERAL_NAME_cmp	42	38	35	23
CVE-2017-15873	get_next_block	45	39	42	30

5 Conclusion

This paper proposes an ACFG embedding model based on code similarity detection, which can be used for firmware vulnerability detection. This paper uses the method of instruction embedding to improve the accuracy of extracting semantic information of instructions in ACFG. At the same time, in order to better compare the similarity of instructions across architectures, this paper uses the canonical correlation analysis (CCA) method to project instructions in different spaces to the same space. Regarding the extraction of structural features of ACFG graphics, because ACFG is a directed graph, the traditional GCN method cannot be used to extract structural features. Therefore, this paper uses the improved GCN method DGCN to extract the structural features of ACFG. The model proposed in this paper can be used for actual firmware vulnerability detection and has practical significance.

References

1. Davis, D.B.: ISTR,: Internet of things cyber attacks grow more diverse. Symatec. Blogs/Exp. Perspect. **2019**, 9 (2019)
2. Chen, D., et al.: Towards automated dynamic analysis for Linux-based embedded firmware. In: NDSS, vol. 1 (2016)
3. Shoshitaishvili, Y., et al.: Firmalice-automatic detection of authentication bypass vulnerabilities in binary firmware. In: NDSS, vol. 1 (2015)
4. Gauthier, F., Lavoie, T., Merlo, E.: Uncovering access control weaknesses and flaws with security-discordant software clones. In: Proceedings of the 29th Annual Computer Security Applications Conference. (2013)
5. Jang, J., Agrawal, A., Brumley, D.: ReDeBug: finding unpatched code clones in entire OS distributions. In: 2012 IEEE Symposium on Security and Privacy. IEEE (2012)
6. Feng, Q., et al.: Scalable graph-based bug search for firmware images. In: Proceedings of the 2016 ACM SIGSAC Conference on Computer and Communications Security (2016)
7. Hex Rays.https://hex-rays.com/

8. Kenter, T., Borisov, A., De Rijke, M.: Siamese cbow: optimizing word embeddings for sentence representations. arXiv preprint arXiv:1606.04640 (2016)

9. Song, Y., et al.: Directional skip-gram: explicitly distinguishing left and right context for word embeddings. In: Proceedings of the 2018 Conference of the North American Chapter of the Association for Computational Linguistics: Human Language Technologies, vol. 2 (Short Papers). (2018)

10. Xu, X., et al.: Neural network-based graph embedding for cross-platform binary code similarity detection. In: Proceedings of the 2017 ACM SIGSAC Conference on Computer and Communications Security (2017)

11. Tong, Z., et al.: Directed graph convolutional network. arXiv preprint arXiv:2004.13970 (2020)

12. Gao, D., Reiter, M.K., Song, D.: BinHunt: automatically finding semantic differences in binary programs. In: Chen, L., Ryan, M.D., Wang, G. (eds.) ICICS 2008. LNCS, vol. 5308, pp. 238–255. Springer, Heidelberg (2008). https://doi.org/10.1007/978-3-540-88625-9_16

13. Ming, J., Pan, M., Gao, D.: iBinHunt: binary hunting with inter-procedural control flow. In: Kwon, T., Lee, M.-K., Kwon, D. (eds.) ICISC 2012. LNCS, vol. 7839, pp. 92–109. Springer, Heidelberg (2013). https://doi.org/10.1007/978-3-642-37682-5_8

14. Bourquin, M., King, A., Robbins, E.: Binslayer: accurate comparison of binary executables. In: Proceedings of the 2nd ACM SIGPLAN Program Protection and Reverse Engineering Workshop (2013)

15. Flake, H.: Structural comparison of executable objects. Detection of intrusions and malware & vulnerability assessment. In: GI SIG SIDAR Workshop, DIMVA 2004. Gesellschaft für Informatik eV (2004)

16. Pewny, J., et al.: Cross-architecture bug search in binary executables. In: 2015 IEEE Symposium on Security and Privacy. IEEE (2015)

17. Eschweiler, S., Yakdan, K., Gerhards-Padilla, E.: discovRE: efficient cross-architecture identification of bugs in binary code. In: NDSS, vol. 52 (2016)

18. Goyal, P., Ferrara, E.: Graph embedding techniques, applications, and performance: a survey. Knowl.-Based Syst. **151**, 78–94 (2018)

19. Lin, H., et al.: Cvssa: cross-architecture vulnerability search in firmware based on support vector machine and attributed control flow graph. In: 2017 International Conference on Dependable Systems and Their Applications (DSA). IEEE (2017)

20. Liang, H., et al.: FIT: inspect vulnerabilities in cross-architecture firmware by deep learning and bipartite matching. Comput. Secur. **99**, 102032. (2020)

21. Faruqui, M., Dyer, C,: Improving vector space word representations using multilingual correlation. In: Proceedings of the 14th Conference of the European Chapter of the Association for Computational Linguistics (2014)

Machine Learning for Security

Detect and Remove Watermark in Deep Neural Networks via Generative Adversarial Networks

Shichang Sun[1], Haoqi Wang[1], Mingfu Xue[1(✉)], Yushu Zhang[1], Jian Wang[1], and Weiqiang Liu[2]

[1] College of Computer Science and Technology, Nanjing University of Aeronautics and Astronautics, Nanjing 211106, China
{sunshichang,haoqi.wang,mingfu.xue,yushu,wangjian}@nuaa.edu.cn
[2] College of Electronic and Information Engineering, Nanjing University of Aeronautics and Astronautics, Nanjing 211106, China
liuweiqiang@nuaa.edu.cn

Abstract. Deep neural networks (DNN) have achieved remarkable performance in various fields. However, training a DNN model from scratch requires expensive computing resources and a lot of training data, which are difficult to obtain for most individual users. To this end, intellectual property (IP) infringement of deep learning models is an emerging problem in recent years. Pre-trained models may be stolen or abused by illegal users without the permission of the model owner. Recently, many works have been proposed to protect the intellectual property of DNN models. Among these works, embedding watermarks into DNN based on backdoor is one of the widely used methods. However, the backdoor-based watermark faces the risk of being detected or removed by an adversary. In this paper, we propose a scheme to detect and remove backdoor-based watermark in deep neural networks via generative adversarial networks (GAN). The proposed attack method consists of two phases. In the first phase, we use the GAN and few clean images to detect the watermarked class and reverse the watermark trigger in a DNN model. In the second phase, we fine-tune the watermarked DNN with the reversed backdoor images to remove the backdoor watermark. Experimental results on the MNIST and CIFAR-10 datasets demonstrate that, the proposed method can effectively remove watermarks in DNN models, as the watermark retention rates of the watermarked LeNet-5 and ResNet-18 models reduce from 99.99% to 1.2% and from 99.99% to 1.4%, respectively. Meanwhile, the proposed attack only introduces a very slight influence on the performance of the DNN model. The test accuracy of the watermarked DNN on the MNIST and CIFAR-10 datasets drops by only 0.77% and 2.67%, respectively. Compared with existing watermark removal works, the proposed attack can successfully remove the backdoor-based DNN watermarking with fewer data, and can reverse the watermark trigger and the watermark class from the DNN model.

Keywords: Deep neural networks · Intellectual property protection · Watermark removal · Generative adversarial networks · Fine-tuning

© Springer Nature Switzerland AG 2021
J. K. Liu et al. (Eds.): ISC 2021, LNCS 13118, pp. 341–357, 2021.
https://doi.org/10.1007/978-3-030-91356-4_18

1 Introduction

In recent years, deep neural networks (DNN) have achieved remarkable performance in many tasks [25,27], such as face recognition and natural language processing. However, training a DNN model is expensive because it requires a lot of training data and expensive computing resources. It is extremely difficult for individual users to train high-performance DNN models. To this end, machine learning as a service (MLaaS) [16] has become an emerging business paradigm [25]. However, the copyright of DNN models may be infringed by malicious users. For instance, unauthorized users may steal, illegally copy, abuse the DNN models, or use the pirated models to provide illegal services without permission [25,29]. The copyright of the DNN model has a high commercial value thus needs to be protected [25], which has aroused serious concerns.

A variety of methods [1,14,20,26,29] have been proposed to protect the intellectual property (IP) of deep neural networks. Among them, the backdoor-based watermarking method [1,29] is one of the most popular methods. In backdoor based watermarking method, the model owner first injects a specific watermark trigger pattern, such as logo pattern or noise pattern [29], into clean images to generate backdoor instances. Then, with these backdoor instances and the incorrect label, the model owner embeds the watermark into the DNN model through training. During copyright verification, the model owner can send watermark trigger samples (backdoor instances) to the suspicious DNN model to verify whether the model is a pirated model.

However, recent works [2,6,13,17,28] have shown that the backdoor-based watermarking method is vulnerable to watermark removal attacks. Shafieinejad et al. [17] designed two attacks, the black-box attack and the white-box attack, to remove the backdoor-based DNN watermark. The black-box attack is based on the model extraction attack [19], and the white-box attack is achieved by regularization and fine-tuning. Yang et al. [28] demonstrated that the DNN watermark can be removed by distillation. Chen et al. [6] proposed a fined-tuning based method to remove the watermark in deep neural networks. Liu et al. [13] incorporated data augmentation and fine-tuning to remove DNN watermark when a small amount of training data is available. Aiken et al. [2] proposed a neural network laundering method based on *Neural Cleanse* [21] to remove the backdoor-based watermarking. The works [17,28] do not actually remove the watermark in the DNN model. Instead, they replace the original model with a surrogate model. The works [6,13] require a lot of training data, thus are difficult to be deployed in real-world scenarios. In this paper, we attempt to attack the backdoor-based watermarking method from the following two aspects: reversing the DNN watermark (more stronger capability) and removing the watermark by using few training data (more feasible).

In this paper, we propose a novel two-phase watermark removal method via generative adversarial networks (GAN) [8]. In the first phase, we use GAN to detect and reverse the watermark from the watermarked DNN. Specifically, we iteratively train GAN to generate perturbation patterns to simulate the watermark trigger pattern. During the training process, GAN will gradually modify the generated perturbation pattern based on the output of the watermarked DNN. After training, GAN can generate a perturbation pattern that is similar to the real watermark trigger pattern. Additionally, we define a metric named *class normality* to determine whether a class is a watermarked class. During the training process, all classes will be detected. If the *class normality* of a certain class is less than the threshold, this class is considered as a watermarked class. In the second phase, we fine-tune the watermarked DNN model with the reversed backdoor images to remove the watermark. The proposed method can obtain an excellent watermark removal effect by using only a small number of training images (i.e., 5% of training data). As a comparison, existing watermark removal methods, REFIT [6] and WILD [13], require at least 10% of training data to remove the watermark. Besides, compared with REFIT [6] and WILD [13], another significant advantage of our method is that, the proposed method can not only remove the watermark, but can also reverse the watermarked class and the watermark trigger from the watermarked model.

The contributions of this paper are summarized as follows:

- We propose a novel method to remove the backdoor-based DNN watermark using GAN. First, the AdvGAN [23] is used to generate perturbations in clean training images. Based on the feedback of the watermarked model, the GAN is able to reverse an approximate watermark trigger with the generated perturbations. Second, we utilize the reversed watermark trigger images and corresponding ground truth labels to fine-tune the watermarked DNN to remove the watermark.
- The proposed GAN-based attack can not only detect the watermark, but can reverse the watermark trigger. The attacker can obtain the precise target class of the backdoor-based watermark, and the approximate position and rough shape of the watermark trigger pattern.
- We have performed experiments on the MNIST [7] and CIFAR-10 [11] datasets to evaluate the proposed method. Experimental results show that, the test accuracy of the watermarked model trained on the MNIST [7] dataset only drops by 0.77%, while the watermark retention rate of the model drops from 99.99% to 1.2%. For the watermarked model trained on the CIFAR-10 [11] dataset, the watermark retention rate after the proposed attack is only 1.4%, and the test accuracy of the model only drops by 2.67%. Overall, the proposed method can effectively remove the watermark in the DNN model, while only have a very small influence on the performance of the DNN model.

The organization of this paper is as follows. The related work is reviewed in Sect. 2. The proposed GAN-based watermark removal attack is elaborated in Sect. 3. Experimental results are presented in Sect. 4. Finally, this paper is concluded in Sect. 5.

2   Related Work

In this section, we review the DNN watermarking methods, DNN watermark removal attacks, and GAN-based backdoor defense method.

2.1   DNN Watermarking Works

Many DNN watermarking [1,14,20,29] methods have been proposed to protect the IP of DNN. Uchida *et al.* [20] proposed to use a binary string as the watermark. They embedded the watermark into a selected layer of the host DNN model through a parameter regularizer. Merrer *et al.* [14] leveraged a set of adversarial examples as the watermark key set to query the suspected remote model.

Backdoor used to be an attack method on DNN [5,24]. In the field of DNN copyright protection, there are also many works [1,29] use backdoor to protect the copyright of DNN. Adi *et al.* [1] proposed a backdoor-based DNN watermarking method, in which the abstract images and randomly selected classes are treated as the trigger set. The backdoor watermark is embedded into the DNN model via the trigger set during training [1]. Zhang *et al.* [29] proposed three backdoor-based watermark generation methods, which are the content-based method, the unrelated data based method, and the noise-based method.

2.2   DNN Watermark Removal Works

At present, a few works have been proposed to attack the DNN watermarking methods. Yang *et al.* [28] proposed to utilize a distillation method to remove the DNN watermark. They demonstrated that parameters responsible for memorizing the watermark are irrelevant to DNN model's main functionality, thus the distillation method can remove these redundant parameters (i.e., the watermark) [28]. However, since the distillation method aims at training a surrogate model, the real watermark in the original DNN model has not been removed. Wang *et al.* [22] attacked the watermarking scheme proposed in work [20] by analyzing the statistical distribution of watermarked model's parameters. The attack method is a white-box attack, which is inapplicable to scenarios where an attacker cannot obtain the model's parameters.

There are also many works [2,6,13,17] aimed at attacking backdoor-based watermarking methods [1,29]. Shafieinejad *et al.* [17] proposed two attacks to remove the backdoor-based watermarking, which are the black-box attack and the white-box attack. The black-box attack is achieved via the model extraction attack [19], while the white-box attack is achieved based on regularization and fine-tuning. It also aims at training a surrogate model rather than removing the real watermark in the DNN model. Aiken *et al.* [2] proposed a neural network laundering method based on Neural Cleanse [21]. Specifically, first, the Neural Cleanse method [21] is performed to reverse the watermark pattern. Then a neuron pruning approach is conducted to reset the backdoored neuron. Finally, a model retraining method is used to remove the backdoor-based DNN watermarks [2]. The main difference between the work [2] and this paper is as follows: (i) The work [2] uses Neural Cleanse [21] to reverse the watermark, while our method use AdvGAN [23] to reverse the watermark; (ii) The work [2] combines neuron resetting and model retraining to remove the backdoor-based watermark in DNN, while our method uses fine-tuning [18] to remove the backdoor-based

DNN watermark. Chen *et al.* [6] proposed a fine-tuning based method, named REFIT, to remove the backdoor-based watermarks in DNN models. REFIT utilizes unlabeled data and a learning rate schedule to fine-tune the model to remove the watermark. Liu *et al.* [13] proposed a watermark removal attack, named WILD, where a data augmentation approach along with a distribution alignment approach are used to fine-tune the watermarked model. Compared with the works [6,13], our proposed method has the following advantages: (i) Our proposed attack can not only detect the watermarked class, but can also reverse the watermark trigger. By using the perturbations generated by GAN, our attack can detect which class is the watermarked class. In addition, the proposed attack can reverse the approximate watermark trigger, including the rough shape and the rough location of the watermark trigger pattern. However, REFIT [6] and WILD [13] can neither detect the watermarked class nor reverse the watermark trigger. (ii) Our proposed attack method requires less training data, which ensures that the proposed method is easier to be deployed in real-world scenarios.

2.3 Backdoor Defense Based on GAN

In the context of deep learning, two works based on GAN have been proposed to defend against the DNN backdoor attack. Zhu *et al.* [30] proposed a method (GangSweep) based on GAN to detect backdoors. Specifically, GangSweep first generates some perturbation masks [30] as possible triggers for each class. Then, it performs an outlier detection on these triggers to determine whether the model has been attacked. After detecting the backdoor, GangSweep attempts to remove the backdoor by using the generated trigger [30]. Chen *et al.* [4] proposed DeepInspect to detect neural backdoors in black-box settings. Using a conditional generative model (cGAN) [15], DeepInspect reconstructed the backdoor trigger from the black-box backdoored model. Our work is different from GangSweep [30] and DeepInspect [4] in the following aspects: (i) Different usages in different fields. Our method is an attack method used to remove the backdoor-based DNN watermarking, while GangSweep [30] and DeepInspect [4] are defense methods that are used to detect whether a model is implanted with a backdoor. (ii) The structure of the used GAN is different. In our method, the AdvGAN [23] that consists of a generator, a discriminator and the target model is used to reverse the watermark trigger, while in GangSweep [30] and DeepInspect [4], the GAN is composed of a generator and a discriminator. (iii) Implementation details are different. Compared with GangSweep [30] and DeepInspect [4], we use a different loss function to train the GAN.

3 The Proposed Method

3.1 Overview

The overview of the proposed attack is shown in Fig. 1. It can be divided into two phases, i.e., watermark reversing and watermark removal. We will discuss these two phases in Sect. 3.2 and Sect. 3.3, respectively.

1) **Watermark Reversing**: We attempt to reverse the watermark trigger pattern with perturbations generated by GAN [8]. Given a small amount of training data and a target DNN model, we construct a GAN to output special perturbation patterns. During the training process of GAN, all classes of the target DNN model will be enumerated to find the possible watermark class. Additionally, a metric named *class normality* is calculated to determine whether a class is watermarked. The *class normality* measures the L_2 distance of the generated perturbation. If the *class normality* of a certain class is less than the threshold, the class is considered to be watermarked. Furthermore, the perturbations generated by GAN are considered as the reversed watermark trigger pattern.

2) **Watermark Removal**: We remove the watermark in the DNN by leveraging fine-tuning [18]. Specifically, we use reversed watermark images with corresponding ground truth labels to fine-tune the watermarked model so as to remove the watermark.

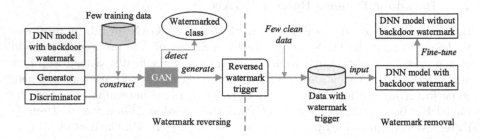

Fig. 1. Overview of the proposed watermark removal attack.

3.2   Watermark Reversing

In the watermark reversing phase, we adopt the AdvGAN [23] to infer whether there is a watermark in the target DNN model. The AdvGAN [23] consists of a generator G, a discriminator D, and the target DNN model f, which is shown in Fig. 2. The process of watermark reversing through AdvGAN is as follows [23]. First, a clean image x is fed into the generator G, which will output a specific perturbation $G(x)$. Second, the perturbation $G(x)$ is added to the clean image to craft an adversarial example $G(x) + x$. Third, $G(x) + x$ will be input to the discriminator and the target DNN model simultaneously. Discriminator D is used to distinguish sample $G(x) + x$ from the clean image x. The output of D will be fed back to the generator G to encourage G to generate a more indistinguishable sample in the next iteration. The generator and the discriminator are optimized via the loss L_{GAN} [23]:

$$L_{GAN} = MSE(D(x), 1) + MSE(D(G(x) + x), 0) \qquad (1)$$

where MSE represents the mean square error [3]. L_{GAN} ensures that the generated adversarial example is close to the original image x.

The target DNN model f takes the sample $G(x) + x$ as input and outputs the loss L_{wm}. In the proposed attack, L_{wm} is calculated as follows [23]:

$$L_{wm} = \max(\max\{f(G(x) + x)_i : i \neq t\} - f(G(x) + x)_t, 0) \tag{2}$$

where t is the ground truth class of the image x, and i represents any other class except for t. L_{wm} ensures that the generated adversarial example $G(x) + x$ is classified as an incorrect class by the target model f.

In order to constrain the magnitude of the generated perturbation $G(x)$, the loss L_{pert} is calculated as follows:

$$L_{pert} = ||G(x)||_2 \tag{3}$$

Then, the overall objective function for attacking the target DNN model is as follows:

$$L = \lambda_1 L_{wm} + \lambda_2 L_{pert} \tag{4}$$

where λ_1 and λ_2 are two hyperparameters that are used to balance the above two loss terms.

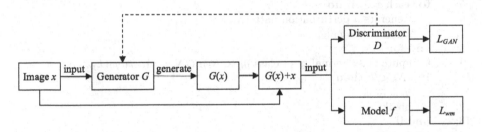

Fig. 2. The structure and workflow of AdvGAN [23], where G denotes the generator and D denotes the discriminator.

In order to detect whether there is a watermark in the DNN model and which class is the watermarked class, we define a metric named *class normality*. For each class, the *class normality* is defined as the average value of L_{pert}. Generally, the *class normality* of the watermarked class is much smaller than the *class normality* of other normal classes. Given a DNN model f with a small number of training images X, the process of detecting whether there is a watermark in the target model f is summarized in Algorithm 1. First, we enumerate all N classes and calculate the *class normality* for each class, as shown in lines 1–9 of Algorithm 1. We denote the i-th class in the DNN model as y_i ($i = 1, 2, ..., N$). The steps of calculating the *class normality* are as follows.

1) Select a set of images A_i' from training data X, where the ground-truth label of the image is not y_i.
2) Train the generator G with these selected images A_i' and model f.
3) For each image x in A_i', generate a perturbation pattern $G(x)$ and calculate the loss L_{pert}.
4) Based on 3), calculate the *class normality* of class y_i.

Then, the *class normality* of each class is sequentially compared with the threshold T, as shown in lines 10–13 of Algorithm 1. If the *class normality* of a class y_i is smaller than T, y_i is considered as a watermarked class y_{wm}, where $i = 1, 2, \ldots, N$. Note that, based on experimental results, we empirically set the threshold T to be 10.

Algorithm 1. Watermark reversing algorithm

Input: A small amount of training data X, target DNN model f, number of data classes N, threshold T
Output: Watermarked class label y_{wm}
1: **for** $i = 1$ to N **do**
2:     Select some data A_i with the label y_i from X;
3:     Obtain train data $A_i' = X - A_i$;
4:     Train the generator G with A_i' and f;
5:     **for** each $x \in A_i'$ **do**
6:         Generate a perturbation pattern $G(x)$;
7:         $L_{pert} \leftarrow ||G(x)||_2$;
8:     **end for**
9:     Compute class normality of class y_i (CN_i): $CN_i = Average(L_{pert})$;
10:    **if** $CN_i < T$ **then**
11:        $y_{wm} = y_i$;
12:        break;
13:    **end if**
14: **end for**
15: **return** y_{wm}

After detecting the watermarked class y_{wm}, the perturbation $G(x)$ generated by GAN is considered as the reversed watermark trigger. Generally, GAN can generate a perturbation pattern for each image, which means that for different images, different perturbation patterns will be generated. We empirically find that, the perturbation pattern with the minimal L_2 distance is more like the real watermark trigger than other perturbation patterns, thus we consider the perturbation pattern with minimal L_2 distance as the watermark trigger.

In the proposed attack, we attempt to reverse the watermark trigger based on perturbations. The generative adversarial networks is able to generate perturbations without destroying the image content, thus we leverage the GAN [23] architecture to generate perturbations and reverse watermark triggers. The target DNN model f makes the GAN generate perturbation pattern towards the real watermark trigger. Based on the feedback of loss L_{wm}, the generator

G tends to craft perturbations in the opposite direction of the ground truth label. If there exists a watermark in the model f, the generated perturbations tend to trigger the watermark. More specifically, GAN will generate a rough perturbation pattern at the position of the watermark trigger.

Figure 3 presents several example images of the reversed watermark trigger, including clean images, watermarked images, and reversed watermark images. As shown in Fig. 3(b) and Fig. 3(c), on the MNIST [7] dataset, the white square trigger reversed by GAN is very similar to the real white square trigger. On the CIFAR-10 [11] dataset, the position and the shape of the watermark trigger in the reversed image are roughly correct. Similarly, as shown in Fig. 3(d) and Fig. 3(e), the position and shape of the reversed "TEST" trigger roughly match the real "TEST" trigger.

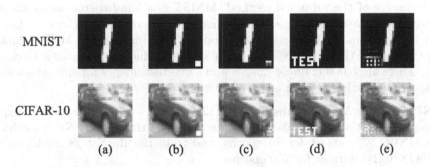

Fig. 3. Example images on the MNIST and CIFAR-10 datasets. (a) Clean images; (b) watermarked images with a white square; (c) reversed watermark images (white square); (d) watermarked images with a "TEST" pattern; (e) reversed watermark images ("TEST" pattern).

3.3 Watermark Removal

In the watermark removal phase, we attempt to remove the DNN watermark with the reversed watermark trigger. A fine-tuning [18] approach is performed with the following steps.

1) Superimpose the reversed watermark trigger on few clean images. These images with the watermark trigger are treated as training samples.
2) Assign the correct labels (i.e., the ground truth labels) to these training samples.
3) Fine-tune the watermarked DNN model with the above training samples.

The above fine-tuning process can effectively remove the watermark by using a small amount of training data (i.e., only 5% training data of the dataset). In addition, our watermark removal attack only has a slight impact on the performance of the DNN model.

4 Experimental Results

In this section, we evaluate the proposed watermark removal attack. First, we introduce the experimental setup, including the dataset, DNN models, watermark triggers, and evaluation metrics. Then, we evaluate the performance of the proposed attack. Next, we discuss three parameters that may affect the performance of the proposed method, i.e., the watermarked class, the amount of training data during fine-tuning, and the number of fine-tuning epochs. Finally, we compare the proposed attack with two existing watermark removal works [6,13].

4.1 Experimental Setup

Datasets. We use the MNIST [7] and CIFAR-10 [11] datasets to evaluate the performance of the proposed method. MNIST is a handwritten image dataset consisting of grayscale images with 10 classes [7]. There are 6,000 training images and 1,000 test images for each class. The size of each image in the MNIST dataset is 28×28. CIFAR-10 is a colored image dataset, which also contains 10 classes [11]. There are 5,000 training images and 1,000 test images for each class. Each image is a color image with a size of 32×32.

DNN Models. We adopt the LeNet-5 [12] and ResNet-18 [10] models for experimental evaluations. To embed the watermark, we train the LeNet-5 model on the MNIST [7] dataset for 80 epochs, and train the ResNet-18 model on the CIFAR-10 [11] dataset for 100 epochs.

Watermark Triggers. We adopt two widely used patterns, the white square [13] and the "TEST" logo [29] as watermark triggers. The white square is added in the lower right corner of each image, and the "TEST" logo is added in the lower left corner of each image. To embed the watermark, we sample 5% of the data from the training set of the MNIST [7] and CIFAR-10 [11] datasets to craft backdoor instances, and assign the label "7" as the target label. Note that, in the CIFAR-10 [11] dataset, the label "7" corresponds to the "horse" class.

Evaluation Metrics. We use the following three metrics to evaluate the performance of the proposed method.

1) **Test Accuracy** [9]: We evaluate the performance of DNN models by calculating the test accuracy before and after the proposed attack.
2) **Watermark Retention Rate** [13]: We adopt the watermark retention rate to measure the watermark removal effect after applying the proposed attack. Assuming that the number of watermark samples that are classified as the target class is S_y, and the total number of watermark samples is S, then the watermark retention rate is calculated by S_y/S [13]. The smaller the watermark retention rate, the better the watermark removal effect.
3) **Class Normality:** We define a metric, named *class normality*, to determine whether or not the DNN model has a watermark. As mentioned in Sect. 3.2, for K training images, *class normality* of a class y_i $(i = 1, 2, \ldots, N)$ is defined as the average of all K losses (L_{pert}). If the *class normality* of y_i is greater

than the predefined threshold T, the class y_i is a watermark-free class. If the *class normality* of y_i is less than T, y_i is a watermarked class. In our experiment, T is empirically set to be 10.

4.2 Experimental Results

In this section, we evaluate the proposed attack on the MNIST [7] and CIFAR-10 [11] datasets, respectively. Two types of watermarks (i.e., white square [13] and "TEST" pattern [29]) are embedded in LeNet-5 [12] and ResNet-18 [10] models, respectively.

The performance of the proposed attack is shown in Table 1. It can be seen that, for the DNN model with a "TEST" watermark, the test accuracy before the attack is 99.34% (watermarked LeNet-5) and 86.11% (watermarked ResNet-18), and the watermark retention rate before the attack is 99.99% (watermarked LeNet-5) and 99.99% (watermarked ResNet-18). After applying the proposed attack, the watermark retention rate of the watermarked LeNet-5 drops from 99.99% to 1.2%, while the test accuracy of the watermarked LeNet-5 is only reduced by 0.77%. Similarly, on the CIFAR-10 dataset, the watermark retention rate of the watermarked ResNet-18 drops from 99.99% to 1.4%, while the test accuracy of the watermarked ResNet-18 only drops by 2.67%. As shown in Table 1, the proposed attack performs well on removing both the white square watermark and the "TEST" pattern watermark. In a word, our proposed attack can effectively remove watermarks in DNN models, while only having a slight impact on the test accuracy of the DNN.

The reason why the proposed method is effective in removing watermarks in DNN models is summarized as follows. First, we perform a GAN-based watermark reversing process, where the perturbation generated by GAN is considered as a watermark trigger pattern. Then, we label the reversed watermark trigger images with the correct class labels. Through fine-tuning [18], the watermarked model can discard the previously learned watermark. In addition, the fine-tuning process can enable the DNN model to maintain its test accuracy. The reason is that the DNN model has many local minima, and through the fine-tuning, another sub-optimal test accuracy can be found [6,20].

4.3 Parameter Discussion

In this section, we discuss the influence of different parameters on the performance of the proposed attack. First, the impact of different watermarked classes on the performance of the proposed attack is evaluated. Second, the impact of the amount of training data and the number of epochs on the proposed attack is discussed.

Table 1. Test accuracy and watermark retention rate of the DNN model before and after the watermark removal attack.

Dataset	Model	Watermark types	Before the proposed attack		After the proposed attack	
			Test accuracy	Watermark retention rate	Test accuracy	Watermark retention rate
MNIST [7]	Watermarked LeNet-5 [12]	White square	99.59%	99.93%	98.67%	1%
		TEST pattern	99.34%	99.99%	98.57%	1.2%
CIFAR-10 [11]	Watermarked ResNet-18 [10]	White square	86.53%	99.96%	84.08%	1.42%
		TEST pattern	86.11%	99.99%	83.44%	1.4%

We first discuss the impact of different watermarked classes on the watermark detection capability of the proposed attack. To this end, we perform experiments on two benchmark datasets (i.e., MNIST [7] and CIFAR-10 [11]) for 4 times respectively, and each time a target class is used as the watermarked class. In addition, the threshold T used to identify the watermarked class is set to be 10. On the MNIST [7] dataset, the selected target classes for embedding watermarks are 1, 4, 7, and 9, respectively. The *class normality* of all ten classes are shown in Table 2. It can be seen that the proposed method can accurately detect the watermarked class. Specifically, among all the ten classes, only the *class normality* of the watermarked class is lower than threshold T and significantly lower than the *class normality* of other normal classes. For instance, when the watermarked class is 1, the *class normality* of class 1 is 7.565 (lower than 10), while *class normality* of other classes are all in the range of 14–17 (higher than 10). On the CIFAR-10 [11] dataset, the watermarked classes are set to be 0, 2, 5, and 7, respectively. The *class normality* of all the ten classes are presented in Table 3. It is shown that, after the proposed attack, the *class normality* of the watermarked class (in a range of 7–8) is significantly smaller than the *class normality* of other normal classes (in a range of 11–16). Therefore, the attacker can easily determine whether the DNN model has a watermark from the *class normality*. In conclusion, the proposed attack can accurately detect the watermarked class from the watermarked model regardless of which class is the watermarked class.

In addition, we discuss the impact of different amounts of training data and different numbers of fine-tuning epochs on the effect of watermark removal. We set the training data used for fine-tuning to be 2%, 5%, and 10% of the training set, respectively. Specifically, on the MNIST dataset [7], 1,200, 3,000, 6,000 images are used to fine-tune the watermarked DNN, respectively. On the CIFAR-10 dataset [11], 1,000, 2,500, 5,000 images are used to fine-tune the watermarked DNN, respectively. Moreover, we use 10 epochs, 40 epochs, and 80 epochs to

Table 2. *Class normality* of ten different classes on the MNIST dataset. Four experiments are performed, and the target classes (i.e., watermarked classes) are 1, 4, 7, and 9, respectively. The data in bold is the *class normality* below threshold T.

Target class \ Class	0	1	2	3	4	5	6	7	8	9
1	14.865	**7.565**	16.214	15.012	16.11	15.421	15.742	14.365	15.458	15.897
4	15.14	14.623	15.562	15.354	**7.569**	14.424	15.286	16.656	14.195	16.433
7	15.403	16.436	15.487	15.15	16.175	14.975	15.468	**7.077**	15.743	16.124
9	15.101	16.109	15.981	15.008	15.754	15.343	15.788	14.412	15.98	**7.961**

Table 3. *Class normality* of ten different classes on the CIFAR-10 dataset. Four experiments are performed, and the target classes (i.e., watermarked classes) are 0, 2, 5, and 7, respectively. The data in bold is the *class normality* below threshold T.

Target class \ Class	0	1	2	3	4	5	6	7	8	9
0	**7.112**	14.589	13.124	14.124	12.441	13.745	12.118	13.547	12.778	12.745
2	12.578	12.734	**7.11**	13.254	12.52	14.112	12.584	14.257	13.122	11.245
5	13.589	12.968	12.475	13.785	12.714	**7.569**	12.325	12.956	13.678	11.989
7	12.449	12.495	11.973	13.252	11.955	15.456	11.545	**7.692**	12.214	12.488

fine-tune the watermarked DNN to remove the watermark, respectively. The experimental results are presented in Table 4 and Table 5, respectively. It is shown that, first, the amount of fine-tuning data will only slightly affect the performance of the proposed method. The more the amount of fine-tuning data, the better the watermark removal effect (i.e., the greater the difference between the watermark retention rate before and after the attack) of the proposed method. When using only 5% training data to fine-tuning the watermarked model, the proposed method is sufficient to achieve a good watermark removal effect. Second, as shown in Table 4 and Table 5, the number of fine-tuning epochs has a certain impact on the proposed attack. The more the number of fine-tuning epochs, the better the watermark removal effect of the proposed method. In conclusion, the proposed method is able to effectively remove the backdoor-based watermark with a small amount of fine-tuning data and a number of fine-tuning epochs.

Table 4. Test accuracy and watermark retention rate after watermark removal on the MNIST [7] dataset.

Watermark	Percentage of training data	Test accuracy after watermark removal			Watermark retention rate after watermark removal		
		10 epochs	40 epochs	80 epochs	10 epochs	40 epochs	80 epochs
White square	2%	87.92%	95.69%	96.63%	10.1%	8.42%	4.3%
	5%	94.33%	97.7%	98.37%	3.2%	2.13%	1.8%
	10%	96.79%	98.07%	98.67%	1.65%	1.57%	1%
TEST pattern	2%	87.71%	95.1%	96.68%	10.12%	8.79%	4.3%
	5%	94.13%	97.33%	98.04%	3.12%	2.33%	1.2%
	10%	96.32%	98.27%	98.57%	2.14%	1.99%	1.2%

Table 5. Test accuracy and watermark retention rate after watermark removal on the CIFAR-10 [11] dataset.

Watermark	Percentage of training data	Test accuracy after watermark removal			Watermark retention rate after watermark removal		
		10 epochs	40 epochs	80 epochs	10 epochs	40 epochs	80 epochs
White square	2%	38.93%	62.17%	65.93%	11.03%	10.22%	8.86%
	5%	53.31%	77.1%	81.6%	10.1%	5.52%	1.5%
	10%	73.13%	82.18%	84.08%	12.33%	5.48%	1.42%
TEST pattern	2%	42.93%	61.86%	67.95%	11.42%	10.86%	8.32%
	5%	51.97%	75.32%	81.08%	10.4%	5.81%	1.2%
	10%	74.67%	83.6%	83.44%	12.17%	6.12%	1.4%

4.4 Comparison with Existing Works

We compare the proposed watermark removal method with two existing watermark removal methods, REFIT [6] and WILD [13], both of which are aimed at removing the backdoor-based DNN watermark. Since the two works [6,13] do not provide the source codes, it is difficult for us to reproduce these two works. Besides, the work [6] does not provide relevant experimental results on watermark retention rate, so we cannot directly compare our attack method with REFIT. Since Liu *et al.* [13] performs relevant experiments for both REFIT and WILD, in this paper, we directly compare our work with the experimental results presented in [13]. Specifically, we compare the proposed method with REFIT [6] and WILD [13] on watermark removal, watermark detection, and watermark reversing. Table 6 presents the compared results of the proposed watermark removal method with REFIT [6] and WILD [13].

As shown in Table 6, on the MNIST [7] dataset, the watermark retention rates of watermarked models before attacks are all close to 100%. After attacked by REFIT [6], WILD [13] and our method, the watermark retention rates of watermarked models are 3.27% (REFIT), 0.92% (WILD), 1.2% (ours), respectively. Similarly, on the CIFAR-10 [11] dataset, the watermark retention rates of watermarked models before attacks are close to 100%. After attacks, the watermark retention rates are 1.71% (REFIT), 2.78% (WILD), 1.4% (ours), respectively. It is shown that the proposed attack has a similar watermark removal capability as

REFIT [6] and WILD [13]. However, in addition to removing the watermark, the proposed method can detect the watermarked class (watermark detection capability) and reverse the watermark trigger (watermark reversing capability). By using the proposed method, an attacker can obtain knowledge about the target class of the backdoor-based watermarks, and the approximate position and shape of the backdoor trigger in images. The attacker can exploit the above information for further attacks, such as illegally tampering with the watermarked model and fraudulently claiming ownership of the model. For REFIT [6] and WILD [13], they can neither detect the watermark nor reverse the watermark trigger. The proposed method leverages the reversed watermark trigger to fine-tune the watermarked model, which enables the proposed method can remove the backdoor-based DNN watermark with only 5% of the training data. As a comparison, both REFIT [6] and WILD [13] require at least 10% of training data to remove the backdoor-based watermark.

Table 6. Comparison of the proposed method with existing work on watermark removal. The experimental results of REFIT [6] and WILD [13] are from [13], and the watermark is based on "TEST" pattern. The percentage of training data refers to the proportion of the amount of training data used in the fine-tuning process in the entire dataset. Watermark detection capability means whether a method can detect the watermarked class from the watermarked DNN. Watermark reversing capability means whether a method can reverse the backdoor-based watermark trigger from the watermarked DNN.

Dataset	Method	Watermark retention rate before attack	Percentage of training data	Watermark retention rate after attack	Watermark detection capability	Watermark reversing capability
MNIST [7]	REFIT [6]	99.86%	10%	3.27%	No	No
	WILD [13]	99.86%	10%	0.92%	No	No
	Ours	99.99%	10%	1.2%	Yes	Yes
		99.99%	5%	1.2%		
CIFAR -10 [11]	REFIT [6]	99.38%	10%	1.71%	No	No
	WILD [13]	99.38%	10%	2.78%	No	No
	Ours	99.99%	10%	1.4%	Yes	Yes
		99.99%	5%	1.2%		

5   Conclusion

Existing backdoor-based DNN watermarking methods are vulnerable to watermark removal attacks. This paper presents a GAN-based watermark removal method. The proposed attack consists of two stages. In the first stage, an attacker utilizes GAN [23] to detect the watermarked class and reverse the potential watermark trigger in the DNN model. In the second stage, the attacker uses the reverse watermark trigger pattern to fine-tune the watermarked model to remove the watermark. The proposed attack can effectively remove the backdoor-based DNN watermarking by using only 5% training data. Experimental results show that, under the proposed attack, the watermark retention rate of watermarked LeNet-5 [12] reduces from 99.99% to 1.2%, and the watermark retention rate of watermarked ResNet-18 [10] reduces from 99.99% to 1.4%. In the meantime, the test accuracy of the DNN model is only slightly affected. Compared with the existing watermark removal methods REFIT [6] and WILD [13], another advantage of the proposed attack is that, this attack can reverse the watermark class and trigger from the watermarked DNN model. This work reveals the vulnerability of the current backdoor-based DNN watermarking methods. In future works, we will explore effective countermeasures against the proposed attack.

Acknowledgement. This work is supported by the National Natural Science Foundation of China (No. 61602241).

References

1. Adi, Y., Baum, C., Cissé, M., Pinkas, B., Keshet, J.: Turning your weakness into a strength: watermarking deep neural networks by backdooring. In: 27th USENIX Security Symposium, pp. 1615–1631 (2018)
2. Aiken, W., Kim, H., Woo, S.S., Ryoo, J.: Neural network laundering: removing black-box backdoor watermarks from deep neural networks. Comput. Secur. **106**, 1–14 (2021)
3. Allen, D.M.: Mean square error prediction as a criterion for selecting regression variables. Technometrics **13**(3), 469–475 (1971)
4. Chen, H., Fu, C., Zhao, J., Koushanfar, F.: DeepInspect: a black-box trojan detection and mitigation framework for deep neural networks. In: Proceedings of the 28th International Joint Conference on Artificial Intelligence, pp. 4658–4664 (2019)
5. Chen, X., Liu, C., Li, B., Lu, K., Song, D.: Targeted backdoor attacks on deep learning systems using data poisoning. arXiv:1712.05526 (2017)
6. Chen, X., et al.: REFIT: a unified watermark removal framework for deep learning systems with limited data. In: ACM Asia Conference on Computer and Communications Security, pp. 321–335 (2021)
7. Deng, L.: The MNIST database of handwritten digit images for machine learning research [best of the web]. IEEE Sig. Process. Mag. **29**(6), 141–142 (2012)
8. Goodfellow, I.J., et al.: Generative adversarial nets. In: Advances in Neural Information Processing Systems, pp. 2672–2680 (2014)
9. Harrington, P.: Machine Learning in Action, 1st edn, Manning Publications, Shelter Island, April 2012
10. He, K., Zhang, X., Ren, S., Sun, J.: Deep residual learning for image recognition. In: IEEE Conference on Computer Vision and Pattern Recognition, pp. 770–778 (2016)
11. Krizhevsky, A.: Learning multiple layers of features from tiny images. Technical Report (2009)
12. LeCun, Y., Bottou, L., Bengio, Y., Haffner, P.: Gradient-based learning applied to document recognition. Proc. IEEE **86**(11), 2278–2324 (1998)
13. Liu, X., Li, F., Wen, B., Li, Q.: Removing backdoor-based watermarks in neural networks with limited data. In: 25th International Conference on Pattern Recognition, pp. 10149–10156 (2020)

14. Merrer, E.L., Pérez, P., Trédan, G.: Adversarial frontier stitching for remote neural network watermarking. Neural Comput. Appl. **32**(13), 9233–9244 (2020)
15. Mirza, M., Osindero, S.: Conditional generative adversarial nets. arXiv:1411.1784 (2014)
16. Ribeiro, M., Grolinger, K., Capretz, M.A.M.: MLaaS: machine learning as a service. In: 14th IEEE International Conference on Machine Learning and Applications, pp. 896–902 (2015)
17. Shafieinejad, M., Lukas, N., Wang, J., Li, X., Kerschbaum, F.: On the robustness of backdoor-based watermarking in deep neural networks. In: Proceedings of the ACM Workshop on Information Hiding and Multimedia Security, pp. 177–188 (2021)
18. Simonyan, K., Zisserman, A.: Very deep convolutional networks for large-scale image recognition. In: Proceedings of the 3rd International Conference on Learning Representations, pp. 1–14 (2015)
19. Tramèr, F., Zhang, F., Juels, A., Reiter, M.K., Ristenpart, T.: Stealing machine learning models via prediction APIs. In: 25th USENIX Security Symposium, pp. 601–618 (2016)
20. Uchida, Y., Nagai, Y., Sakazawa, S., Satoh, S.: Embedding watermarks into deep neural networks. In: Proceedings of the ACM on International Conference on Multimedia Retrieval, pp. 269–277 (2017)
21. Wang, B., et al.: Neural cleanse: identifying and mitigating backdoor attacks in neural networks. In: IEEE Symposium on Security and Privacy, pp. 707–723 (2019)
22. Wang, T., Kerschbaum, F.: Attacks on digital watermarks for deep neural networks. In: IEEE International Conference on Acoustics, Speech and Signal Processing, pp. 2622–2626 (2019)
23. Xiao, C., Li, B., Zhu, J., He, W., Liu, M., Song, D.: Generating adversarial examples with adversarial networks. In: Proceedings of the 27th International Joint Conference on Artificial Intelligence, pp. 3905–3911 (2018)
24. Xue, M., He, C., Wang, J., Liu, W.: One-to-N & N-to-one: Two advanced backdoor attacks against deep learning models. IEEE Transactions on Dependable and Secure Computing, pp. 1–17, early access (2020)
25. Xue, M., Wang, J., Liu, W.: DNN intellectual property protection: taxonomy, attacks and evaluations (Invited paper). In: Great Lakes Symposium on VLSI, pp. 455–460 (2021)
26. Xue, M., Wu, Z., He, C., Wang, J., Liu, W.: Active DNN IP protection: a novel user fingerprint management and DNN authorization control technique. In: 19th IEEE International Conference on Trust, Security and Privacy in Computing and Communications, pp. 975–982 (2020)
27. Xue, M., Yuan, C., Wu, H., Zhang, Y., Liu, W.: Machine learning security: threats, countermeasures, and evaluations. IEEE Access **8**, 74720–74742 (2020)
28. Yang, Z., Dang, H., Chang, E.: Effectiveness of distillation attack and countermeasure on neural network watermarking. arXiv:1906.06046 (2019)
29. Zhang, J., et al.: Protecting intellectual property of deep neural networks with watermarking. In: Proceedings of the Asia Conference on Computer and Communications Security, pp. 159–172 (2018)
30. Zhu, L., Ning, R., Wang, C., Xin, C., Wu, H.: GangSweep: sweep out neural backdoors by GAN. In: The 28th ACM International Conference on Multimedia, pp. 3173–3181 (2020)

Targeted Universal Adversarial Perturbations for Automatic Speech Recognition

Wei Zong[1]([✉]), Yang-Wai Chow[1][iD], Willy Susilo[1][iD], Santu Rana[2][iD], and Svetha Venkatesh[2][iD]

[1] Institute of Cybersecurity and Cryptology (iC2), School of Computing and Information Technology, University of Wollongong, Wollongong, NSW, Australia
{wzong,caseyc,wsusilo}@uow.edu.au
[2] Applied Artificial Intelligence Institute (A2I2), Deakin University, Geelong, VIC, Australia
{santu.rana,svetha.venkatesh}@deakin.edu.au

Abstract. Automatic speech recognition (ASR) is an essential technology used in commercial products nowadays. However, the underlying deep learning models used in ASR systems are vulnerable to adversarial examples (AEs), which are generated by applying small or imperceptible perturbations to audio to fool these models. Recently, universal adversarial perturbations (UAPs) have attracted much research interest. UAPs used to generate audio AEs are not limited to a specific input audio signal. Instead, given a generic audio signal, audio AEs can be generated by directly applying UAPs. This paper presents a method of generating UAPs based on a targeted phrase. To the best of our knowledge, our proposed method of generating UAPs is the first to successfully attack ASR models with connectionist temporal classification (CTC) loss. In addition to generating UAPs, we empirically show that the UAPs can be considered as signals that are transcribed as the target phrase. We also show that the UAPs themselves preserve temporal dependency, such that the audio AEs generated using these UAPs also preserved temporal dependency.

Keywords: Audio adversarial example · Universal adversarial perturbations · Automatic speech recognition · Deep learning · Machine learning

1 Introduction

To date, automatic speech recognition (ASR) [2,6,9,19] systems have been deployed ubiquitously in popular commercial products, such as Google Assistant, Amazon Alexa, and so on. An ASR system converts speech from audio into text before further processing. Deep learning techniques play an important role in modern ASR systems. Specifically, end-to-end ASR, which relies on recurrent neural network (RNN), was able to achieve human level performance when tested on several benchmark datasets [2].

© Springer Nature Switzerland AG 2021
J. K. Liu et al. (Eds.): ISC 2021, LNCS 13118, pp. 358–373, 2021.
https://doi.org/10.1007/978-3-030-91356-4_19

However, deep learning models suffer from the threat of adversarial examples (AEs), which were first found in the image recognition domain [23]. An image AE is generated by applying imperceptible perturbations to a benign (normal) image, such that the resulting modified image will fool a deep learning model. There are targeted and untargeted image AEs. Targeted AEs force a target model to output predefined labels, while untargeted image AEs merely aim to make the target model output an incorrect result [16]. In addition, adversaries can assume a white-box or black-box threat model to generate AEs [4,10,30]. Under a white-box threat model, adversaries can access the internal workings of the target model, including model weights, training data, etc. In contrast, under a black-box threat model only input and output pairs can be obtained.

Besides image recognition, researchers also found that ASR models are vulnerable to audio AEs. In seminal work conducted by Carlini and Wagner [5], they generated audio AEs by solving an optimization problem by constraining the maximum norm of perturbations. Their work was improved in Qin et al. [20] via incorporating psychoacoustics to hide perturbations below the hearing threshold. However, such adversarial perturbations can only produce an AE for a specific audio signal, and must be recalculated to produce AEs for different audio signals. To overcome this shortcoming, researchers have investigated the generation of AEs using universal adversarial perturbations (UAPs) that can be applied directly to generic audio [1]. UAPs can be used to generate both untargeted and targeted audio AEs [17,26]. It should be mentioned that the concept of UAPs was first introduced for image AEs [15].

Although a great amount of effort has been spent on attacking speaker verification models, sound classification models, etc., there is limited research focused on generating UAPs to attack ASR systems. For a given audio, ASR models deal with an excessively large number of potential transcripts. This task is typically more difficult compared to other classification models, which only output a fixed set of labels. Early work was conducted by Neekhara et al. [17], in which they generated UAPs for untargeted audio AEs. Compared to targeted audio AEs, untargeted audio AEs are less interesting as they only make ASR models output incorrect or even meaningless transcripts. Lu et al. [14] recently performed a preliminary study on targeted UAPs to attack ASR models. However, their UAPs cannot generate UAPs against models with connectionist temporal classification (CTC) loss [8]. This severely limits their method since CTC loss is widely deployed in modern ASR models that achieve state-of-the-art performance [2,9].

In this paper, we fill the research gap by proposing UAPs that can be applied directly to audio to generate targeted audio AEs. Our main contributions are summarized as follows:

- To the best of our knowledge, our UAP method is the first to successfully attack CTC loss based ASR models. Most existing work focus on speaker verification models, sound classification models, etc., instead of ASR models.
- Unlike previous work by Lu et al. [14], we improve the quality of audio AEs by constraining the maximum norm of UAPs. Furthermore, we conducted

a feasibility study to hide UAPs below the hearing threshold in a piece of music.

- In addition to generating UAPs, we empirically show that UAPs can be considered to be signals that will be transcribed into the target phrase. The generation of UAPs can then be viewed as training (modifying) UAPs to be robust against modification using audio containing speech.
- We show that the UAPs themselves preserve temporal dependency, such that the audio AEs generated by applying these UAPs also preserve temporal dependency.

2   Related Work

Early work in this field by Neekhara et al. [17], studied the generation of untargeted UAPs by maximizing CTC loss for each input audio. Compared to random noise, their UAPs can more effectively cause DeepSpeech [9] to output incorrect transcripts. However, untargeted attack cannot predetermine the output of a target model, and this makes untargeted attack less interesting than targeted attack. In contrast, our work focuses on targeted UAPs which pose severe threats because an adversary is able to control the output from a target model. Abdoli et al. [1] proposed UAPs that can generate targeted audio AEs. Instead of attacking ASR models, they attacked environmental sound classification and speech command recognition models.

In other work, Xie et al. [26] proposed to incorporate transformations by simulated room impulse response (RIR), so that audio AEs generated by their UAPs were robust against such transformations. The purpose is to make audio AEs still adversarial when played through speakers and received by microphones. They focused on fooling speaker verification models. Compared to ASR models which transcribe voice input, speak verification models aim to identify whether input voice comes from a valid user. Li et al. [13] demonstrated that it is unnecessary to perturb all samples in an audio signal. They generated UAPs that were much shorter than the input audio and the UAPs can be applied to an arbitrary position within the input audio. To make audio AEs physically adversarial, they used datasets of physically recorded RIRs instead of simulated RIRs.

As opposed to generating input-agnostic UAPs, another line of work focused on training a generative model, so that perturbations can be efficiently generated for previously unknown audio. Broadly speaking, the generative model represents UAPs that are input-dependent. Wang et al. [24] trained a generative adversarial network (GAN) to produce specific perturbations for an input audio. The output of GAN can fool the prediction of command classification and music classification models into outputing predetermined labels. Recent work by Li et al. [12] trained a generator that can map random noise to targeted UAPs given an input audio.

In contrast with existing work, this research investigates targeted UAPs against ASR models.

3 Problem Definition and Assumptions

Our goal is to generate UAPs δ that will result in targeted audio AEs when applied to input audio. Note that δ is specific to a target phrase, such that a different target phrase will require a different δ. We assume a white-box threat model, under which the internal workings of the target model are accessible and gradients with respect to the input can explicitly be calculated. Formally, let $\delta \in \mathbb{R}^m$ be perturbations of length m. $\delta_{i:j} = (\delta_i, \ldots, \delta_j)$ denotes a slice of δ from the ith to j^{th} elements. Let $f(\cdot)$ represent the ASR model. Let $\mathcal{D}$ be a set of audio with audio sample values ranging from $[-1, 1]$, i.e. if $x \in \mathcal{D}$ then $||x||_\infty \leq 1$. It should be noted that the length $x \in \mathcal{D}$ varies. Without loss of generality, let n represent the length of x: $x \in \mathbb{R}^n$. It is required that $n \leq m$, as given an input audio, δ will first be truncated to the same length as the input. Then, an audio AE is generated by applying δ to the input audio.

Specifically, we want to generate δ that satisfies:

$$\underset{x \in \mathcal{D}}{P}\left(f(x') = t\right) \geq \eta$$

$$\text{such that } ||\delta||_\infty \leq \tau \tag{1}$$

where t is a predefined target phrase, x' is the modified audio with elements clipped into $[-1, 1]$: $x' = \max(\min(x + \delta_{1:n}, 1), -1)$, η denotes the minimal success rate of attack, and τ constrains the maximum norm of δ.

3.1 Evaluation

Given an input audio $x \in \mathbb{R}^n$, we measure the distortion caused by δ in decibels (dB):

$$dB_x(\delta) = 20 \cdot \log_{10} \frac{\max_i \delta_i}{\max_i x_i}$$

$$\text{for } i \in \{1, 2, \ldots, n\} \tag{2}$$

This metric was initially defined by Carlini and Wagner [5] and is also used in other work [1,14,17,26]. This metric is analogous to the maximum norm measurement in the image AE domain.

4 Proposed Method

4.1 Universal Adversarial Perturbations

To generate UAPs that satisfy the requirements defined in Eq. 1, we solve the following optimization problem:

$$\min_{\delta} \frac{1}{|\mathcal{D}|} \sum_{x \in \mathcal{D}} \ell_{adv}(f(x'), t) + \lambda \cdot \ell_{reg}(\delta, \tau)$$

$$\text{such that } \underset{x \in \mathcal{D}}{P}\left(f(x') = t\right) \geq \eta \tag{3}$$

where $\mathcal{D}$ is a set of input audio, x' is the modified audio clipped into the range $[-1, 1]$: $x' = \max(\min(x + \delta^\tau_{1:n}, 1), -1)$. δ^τ is the perturbations applied to x and equals to δ clipped into a specific range: $\delta^\tau = \max(\min(\delta, \tau), -\tau)$, with τ constraining the maximum norm. $\ell_{adv}(\cdot)$ calculates the loss of the ASR model and minimizing $\ell_{adv}(\cdot)$ encourages the modified input x' be to transcribed as t. If a solution is found, δ^τ is returned as a UAP. To make δ^τ less suspicious, it is preferred that τ be as small as possible. Thus, τ should be initialized to a large value, then gradually decreased until a valid solution can no longer be found.

Instead of viewing x as the input audio and δ^τ as noise, we consider δ^τ as a signal which is transcribed as t. From this perspective, x is considered as "noise" applied to δ^τ, and δ^τ is robust against modification by adding $x \in \mathcal{D}$. We will validate this point of view later in Sect. 5. A recent study by Zhang et al. [29] presented a similar idea in the image AE domain. They showed that UAPs were highly correlated with the output logits of image classifiers so that the classification was actually dominated by UAPs.

$\ell_{reg}(\cdot)$ is the regularization term with λ for weighting. $\ell_{reg}(\cdot)$ is defined as follows:

$$\ell_{reg}(\delta, \tau) = \sum_{i=1}^{m} \max(|\delta_i| - \tau, 0) \tag{4}$$

Minimizing $\ell_{reg}(\cdot)$ encourages the maximum norm of δ to be within τ. This prevents $\frac{\partial \ell_{adv}(f(x + \delta'_{1:n}), t)}{\partial \delta_i}$ from always being 0 when $|\delta_i| > \tau$.

In practice, we split the generation process into two stages. During stage 1, we set $\tau = 1$ and gradually let δ^τ be effective for more and more audio in $\mathcal{D}$. Stage 1 finishes when δ^τ can attack all audio in $\mathcal{D}$, i.e. an audio AE is generated by applying δ^τ to any audio in $\mathcal{D}$. The purpose of this stage is to quickly find a valid δ^τ, even though δ^τ may be too noisy. In stage 2, we focus on making δ^τ less noisy by gradually decreasing τ until no valid solution can be found. This two stage generation process is provided in Algorithm 1.

4.2 Robustness Against Room Impulse Response

In the audio AE domain, expectation over transformation (EOT) has been widely used to make audio AEs robust against RIRs [20,22,25]. The purpose of being robust against RIRs is to let audio AEs still be adversarial when played through speakers and received by microphones. EOT [3] was initially proposed to make image AEs robust against camera transformations.

In this research, we also deploy EOT to make our UAPs robust against RIR. It should be mentioned that computation will be prohibitively expensive if too many RIRs are considered [7]. To incorporate EOT, the optimization problem define in Eq. 3 is modified as follows:

$$\min_{\delta} \underset{h \in \mathcal{H}}{\mathbb{E}} \left[\frac{1}{|\mathcal{D}|} \sum_{x \in \mathcal{D}} \ell_{adv}(f(x' * h), t) \right] + \lambda \cdot \ell_{reg}(\delta, \tau)$$

$$\text{such that } \underset{h \in \mathcal{H}}{\mathbb{E}} [\underset{x \in \mathcal{D}}{P} (f(x' * h) = t)] \geq \eta \tag{5}$$

Algorithm 1. Two stage process for generating universal perturbations.

Input: target model, f; a set of audio, $\mathcal{D}$; target phrase, t; the minimum success rate η;
Output: universal perturbations, δ^τ

initialize $\delta = 0$
$\delta^\tau =$ Stage1(δ) // generate valid UAPs
return Stage2(δ^τ, η) // make UAPs less noisy

function Stage1(δ)
    initialize a subset $\mathcal{G} \subset \mathcal{D}$
    while iterations < max iterations **do**
        set success number $s = 0$
        for each audio $x \in \mathcal{G}$ // $\mathcal{G}$ is shuffled for each iteration
            increase s by 1 if $f(x') = t$ // x' is the modified audio from Equation 3
            modify δ via gradient decent
        end for
        if s is equal to $|\mathcal{G}|$ **then**
            return δ^τ if $|\mathcal{G}| = |\mathcal{D}|$
            add more audios into $\mathcal{G}$ from $\mathcal{D}$
        end if
    end while
end function

function Stage2(δ^τ, η)
    while failed iterations < max iterations **do**
        set success number $s = 0$
        for each audio $x \in \mathcal{D}$ // $\mathcal{D}$ is shuffled for each iteration
            increase s by 1 if $f(x') = t$ // x' is the modified audio from Equation 3
            modify δ via gradient decent
        end for
        if $\frac{s}{|\mathcal{D}|} \geq \eta$ **then**
            set failed iterations $= 0$
            decrease τ
        else
            increase failed iterations by 1
        end if
    end while
    return δ^τ
end function

where $\mathcal{H}$ is the distribution of RIRs considered, and $*$ denotes convolution operation.

Algorithm 2 provides the process used to solve the optimization problem shown in Eq. 5. Specifically, δ is initialized as the solution found in Stage 1 of Algorithm 1. For each audio, we randomly select an RIR to transform the audio.

Algorithm 2. Process for generating robust universal perturbations.

Input: target model, f; a set of audio, $\mathcal{D}$; target phrase, t; a set of RIR, $\mathcal{H}$; minimum success rate η; initial values for δ, δ_{init};

Output: robust universal perturbations, δ^τ

initialize $\delta = \delta_{init}$, $\tau = 1$
while failed iterations < max iterations **do**
    set success number $s = 0$
    for each audio $x \in \mathcal{D}$ // $\mathcal{D}$ is shuffled each time
        select a random RIR $h \sim \mathcal{H}$
        increase s by 1 if $f(x' * h) = t$ // x' is the audio from Equation 5
        modify δ via gradient decent
    end for
    if $\frac{s}{|\mathcal{D}|} \geq \eta$ **then**
        set failed iterations = 0
        decrease τ
    else
        increase failed iterations by 1
    end if
end while
return δ^τ

τ constrains the maximum norm of δ^τ, and it gradually decreases until no valid solution can be found.

5   Results and Discussion

5.1   Setup

In this study, we used DeepSpeech2 as the target model, which is an end-to-end RNN based ASR model with CTC loss [2]. We used the open source implementation of DeepSpeech2 V2[1] with Librispeech [18] as the dataset since a pre-trained model on this dataset was released. Specifically, we randomly extracted 150 audio with durations from 2 to 4 seconds from the "dev-clean" dataset to generate UAPs. We also extracted all audio with duration 2 to 4 seconds from the "test-clean" dataset for evaluation. We used the following 5 target phrases to generate UAPs: "power off", "open the door", "turn off lights", "use airplane mode", "visit malicious dot com". It should be noted that target phrases cannot be too long. This is because it is overly challenging to force a target model to output transcripts that are too long for short input audio.

Throughout the experiments, if not otherwise indicated, we used the following settings. The Adam method [11] was used for optimization with a learning rate of 0.001. τ, which controls the maximum norm of UAPs as shown in Eq. 3 and

---

[1] https://github.com/SeanNaren/deepspeech.pytorch.

Eq. 5, was initially set to 1.0 then decreased by being multiplied with 0.8. The minimum success rate η was fixed at 0.8 for both Eq. 3 and Eq. 5. Without incorporating EOT, the maximum iterations to lower the maximum norm of UAPs was set to 30. If EOT was incorporated, the maximum iterations was set to 60, because it is more computationally expensive to converge in this case.

5.2   Generating Universal Adversarial Perturbations

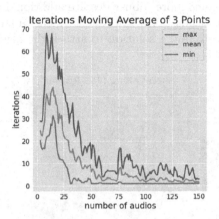

Fig. 1. Iteration trend when generating UAPs.

We first used the Stage1 function in Algorithm 1 to generate UAPs for the 5 target phrases. As previously mentioned, the aim of this stage is to generate valid UAPs, even though they may be noisy. The time taken to generate UAPs for the target phrases: "power off", "open the door", "turn off lights", "use airplane mode", "visit malicious dot com", it took 5.0, 2.8, 7.8, 4.2 and 7.9 hours respectively. Obviously, the generation time for different target phrases is different. This may be because target phrases that are seen less frequently during training of the target model will require more iterations. At the start of the generation process, the audio set only contained 1 audio. When the generated UAPs were able to attack all audio in the current set, we added a new audio to the set, i.e. the size of the set increased by 1. This strategy is beneficial for convergence since the UAPs for a specific set only needs to handle one new audio. The set at the end of the process contained 150 audio.

Figure 1 shows the iteration trend to generate UAPs capable of attacking all audio as we gradually increase the size of the audio set. To clearly show the iteration trend, we present a moving average based on 3 data points. The horizontal axis represents the number of audio used to train UAPs, while the vertical axis indicates the number of iterations needed for the UAPs to attack all audio in the set. Early on when the size of the set was small, the number of iterations increased as more audio were added to the set. This is reasonable since the UAPs had to attack a greater number of audio, so more computation was required to find a solution. However, interestingly the iterations started to decrease when the size of the audio set reached around 20. This can be explained from the point of view that the generated UAPs are considered as signals that are transcribed into the target phrase, while audio containing speech are considered as noise being applied to UAPs. From that perspective, it is intuitive that after a while, the UAPs become more robust despite additional audio being added to the set. In other words, when UAPs are robust against a large set of audio, fewer iterations are required to find a solution to attack the newly added audio.

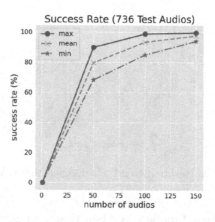

Fig. 2. Increase in success rate as the UAPs attacked an increasing number of audio.

To test the performance of the generated UAPs, we applied the UAPs to all audio with a duration between 2 to 4 s from the "test-clean" set. As shown in Fig. 2, the success rate of UAPs increased as more audio was used for training. In the Figure, the horizontal axis represents the number of audio used to train UAPs, while the success rate was calculated by applying UAPs to all 736 audio with a duration between 2 to 4 seconds from "test-clean" set. The increase in success rate is complementary to the above discussion that UAPs become more robust against new audio as the size of training set increases.

UAPs generated using Stage1 alone were too noisy to be used in practice as they easily cause suspicion. Stage2 was used to constrain the maximum norm of UAPs. To effectively decrease the maximum norm, UAPs were only required to attack 80% of audio in the audio set by setting $\eta = 0.8$. Intuitively, lowering η will lead to smaller maximum norm of UAPs.

Table 1. Minimized maximum norm of universal perturbations

Target phrase	Success rate (S1)*	Max norm (S1)+	Median dB
"Power off"	66.71% (97.42%)	0.107 (0.991)	−12.47
"Open the door"	51.63% (99.59%)	0.044 (0.673)	−19.37
"Turn off lights"	46.88% (97.55%)	0.086 (0.997)	−13.54
"Use airplane mode"	46.33% (99.32%)	0.069 (0.902)	−15.44
"Visit malicious dot com"	59.51% (94.02%)	0.107 (0.994)	−12.03

*:The success rate of UAPs by Stage2 compared to Stage1 (S1).
+:Maximum norm of UAPs by Stage2 compared to Stage1 (S1).

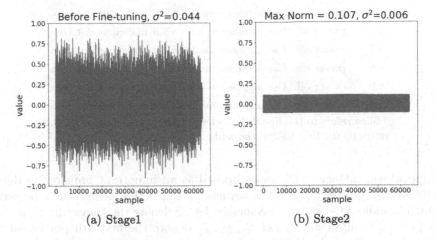

(a) Stage1   (b) Stage2

Fig. 3. Comparing UAPs generated using Stage1 and Stage2 with the target phrase "power off". (a) UAPs generated using Stage1 alone were very noisy; (b) Stage2 constrained the maximum norm of UAPs to a small value.

Table 1 presents the results of the 5 UAPs. It took around 1 hour to finish Stage2 for each UAPs. We can see that the maximum norm of UAPs was greatly reduced after Stage2. UAPs generated using Stage1 and Stage2 with "power off" as the target phrase is compared in Fig. 3. Although the success rate on the test audio decreased because we set $\eta = 0.8$ instead of 1.0, the UAPs were still effective to attack over 45% of audio from the test set.

To give a sense of the distortion cause by our UAPs, Carlini and Wagner [5] reported that the 95% interval for distortion using their approach was between −15 dB to −45 dB. While our UAPs introduce more distortion compared with their approach, the key thing to note is that their perturbations are only effective for a specific audio input and must be recalculated for different audio, as opposed to UAPs which are universal and able to attack generic audio.

5.3   Preserving Temporal Dependency

Table 2. An example depicting preserved temporal dependency for UAPs

Slice*	Power off	Use airplane mode	Visit malicious dot com
0.1	p	Use	
0.2	pon	Use	Visit
0.3	po	Use air	Visit mali
0.4	po	Use airplane	Visit malicious
0.5	power	Use airplane mode	Visit malicious dotd co
0.6	power off	Use airplane mode	Visit malicious dot com
0.7	power off	Use airplane mode	Visit malicious dot com
0.8	power off	Use airplane mode	Visit malicious dot com
0.9	power off	Use airplane mode	Visit malicious dot com
1.0	power off	Use airplane mode	Visit malicious dot com

*:Slice refers to the first kth portion of the input audio, e.g., 0.5 refers to the first half of the audio.

Temporal dependency (TD) was proposed as an important property to detect audio AEs by Yang et al. [27]. The key assumption is that benign audio preserves TD while audio AEs do not. Specifically, let S_k denote the transcript of the first kth portion of input audio. Let $S_{\{whole,k\}}$ denote the first kth portion of the entire transcript, such that the length of $S_{\{whole,k\}}$ is equal to the length of S_k. If $S_{\{whole,k\}}$ is not consistent with S_k, this means the audio is potentially adversarial.

In our experiments, we found that UAPs generated by Stage2 can be transcribed as the target phrase and preserved TD. This finding is complementary to our point view that UAPs can be considered as signals that are transcribed as the target phrase. The results for the target phrases: "power off", "use airplane mode" and "visit malicious dot com", are shown in Table 2. The experimental results show that the transcripts of differently sliced UAPs were consistent with the corresponding portions of the target phrase. An interesting observation is that when $k \geq 0.6$, all the partial UAPs were accurately transcribed as the target phrase. This is intuitive because the duration of the UAPs was 4 seconds, and were required to attack 80% of audio with duration between 2 to 4 seconds by design. Thus, the first portion of the UAPs were transcribed as the target phrase and robust against modification. The remaining parts of UAPs then aimed to suppress output from DeepSpeech2, i.e. forcing DeepSpeech2 to output nothing for those parts.

Table 3. AUC of temporal dependency detection*

| | k = 1/2 | | | k = 2/3 | | | k = 3/4 | | |
	WER	CER	LCP	WER	CER	LCP	WER	CER	LCP
Power off	**0.91**	0.37	**0.91**	0.70	0.45	0.73	0.56	**0.47**	0.60
Open the door	**0.43**	**0.43**	**0.31**	0.35	0.36	0.19	0.28	0.35	0.18
Turn off lights	**0.61**	**0.45**	0.32	0.48	0.41	0.31	0.49	0.45	**0.36**
Use airplane mode	**0.84**	**0.51**	**0.55**	0.60	0.43	0.41	0.45	0.40	0.34
Visit malicious dot com	**0.72**	**0.54**	**0.65**	0.53	0.49	0.51	0.43	0.43	0.40

*:The maximum value for WER, CER and LCP for each target phrase is highlighted.

As the UAPs preserved TD, this suggests that audio AEs generated by applying UAPs would also preserve TD. Therefore, we calculated the same metrics proposed by Yang et al. [27] to validate if our audio AEs generated using the UAPs were able to avoid TD detection[2]. These metrics were area under curve (AUC) score of word error rate (WER), AUC of character error rate (CER), and AUC of longest common prefix (LCP).

The audio AEs used in the experiment were those successfully generated by applying our Stage 2 UAPs to the test audio. Table 3 shows the experimental results for $k = \frac{1}{2}, \frac{2}{3}, \frac{3}{4}$. We can see that TD detection only achieved good performance with WER and LCP on detecting audio AEs with the target phrase "power off" when $k = \frac{1}{2}$. This implies that the first half of the UAPs for "power off" was not robust enough. To improve the robustness against TD detection for "power off" when $k = \frac{1}{2}$, a potential solution is to increase the value of η in Stage 2. If $\eta = 1.0$, the first half of the UAPs for "power off" will be forced to be robust, although this will result in a larger maximum norm for UAPs. Other than the "power off" target phrase, we can see from Table 3 that most AUC scores were below 0.75. This indicates that audio AEs generated by our UAPs were overall robust against TD detection.

5.4 Robustness Against Gaussian Noise

Table 4. Success rates of audio AEs generated using UAPs against Gaussian noise

	std = (0.001)	std = (0.01)	std = (0.1)
"Power off"	98.57%	85.95%	0.00%
"Open the door"	98.42%	69.21%	0.00%
"Turn off lights"	98.84%	81.16%	0.00%
"Use airplane mode"	97.36%	72.14%	0.00%
"Visit malicious dot com"	98.63%	87.90%	0.00%

As discussed above, UAPs were trained to be robust against modification using audio containing speech. Table 4 further shows that audio AEs generated by

---

[2] We used the open source implementation from https://github.com/AI-secure/Characterizing-Audio-Adversarial-Examples-using-Temporal-Dependency.

applying UAPs to test audios were also robust against Gaussian noise until $std = 0.01$.

5.5 Robustness Against Room Impulse Response

Table 5. Robustness of UAPs their corresponding audio AEs against RIRs

	Stage2			Robustness		
	UAPs	AEs	Max Norm	UAPs	AEs	Max Norm
"Power off"	0.00%	0.00%	0.107	85.00%	55.57%	0.210
"Open the door"	70.00%	1.90%	0.044	100.00%	61.41%	0.086
"Turn off lights"	0.00%	0.00%	0.086	55.00%	33.83%	0.210
"Use airplane mode"	0.00%	0.00%	0.069	70.00%	40.49%	0.210
"Visit malicious dot com"	0.00%	0.00%	0.107	60.00%	41.71%	0.328

We generated 100 RIRs from virtual rooms with dimension ($width, length, height$) using pyroomacoustics 0.4.2[3]. 80 RIRs were used for training while 20 RIRs used were for testing. $height$ was set to 3.5 while $width = length$ and we randomly sampled their values from $\mathcal{U}(4, 6)$. The time it takes for the RIR to decay by 60 dB was randomly sampled from $\mathcal{U}(0.15, 0.20)$. Locations of microphones and audio sources were randomly sampled inside the virtual rooms.

To test the robustness against RIR, each audio AE was transformed by a random RIR from the 20 RIRs. We also transformed the UAPs by all the 20 RIRs and to check whether UAPs themselves are robust against RIRs. When using Algorithm 2 to generate robust UAPs, we set the maximum iterations to 60.

Table 5 shows the results of comparing robust UAPs generated using Algorithm 2 with UAPs generated by Stage2. Table 5 also compares the robustness of audio AEs, which were generated by applying the corresponding UAPs to test audio. Although there was an exception for UAPs of "open the door", UAPs generated by Stage2 and corresponding audio AEs were obviously not robust against RIRs. In contrast, UAPs generated using Algorithm 2 and their corresponding audio AEs were robust against RIRs. It should be noted that robustness against RIRs was obtained at the cost of significantly larger maximum norm.

5.6 Limitation

Our experiments showed that the quality of audio AEs generated by applying UAPs was poor. The distortion caused by UAPs will be worse if we make them robust against RIRs. While it will be difficult to lower the maximum norm of UAPs further while keeping them adversarial, we can potentially hide UAPs below the hearing threshold of unsuspicious sound. This may be a promising

---

[3] https://pypi.org/project/pyroomacoustics/.

future direction. A potential scenario is where an adversary plays unsuspicious adversarial audio in the background, while the victim speaks to a voice interface, thereby causing the underlying ASR model to be fooled. A similar idea was proposed by Commandersong [28], in which they hid perturbations within a song. However, their method may not be robust for speech, which is common for voice interfaces.

In this section, we present a feasibility study on hiding UAPs below the hearing threshold in a piece of piano music. We incorporated the masking loss proposed by Qin et al. [20], which hid perturbations below the hearing threshold of speech. Specifically, we replaced the $l_{reg}(\cdot)$ in Eq. 3 with the masking loss. Instead of generating UAPs from scratch, we used UAPs generated by Stage2 of Algorithm 1 as initial values. It should be mentioned that audio AEs were generated by applying UAPs together with the music.

Measuring the maximum norm of UAPs is meaningless in this case because large values in UAPs would be masked by the music. Therefore, we measured the Perceptual Evaluation of Speech Quality (PESQ), which was proposed to automatically measure degradation in the context of telephony [21]. The values range from 1.0 to 4.5 with larger values indicating better quality.

After running 30 iterations, we successfully generated UAPs by setting $\eta = 0.5$. The PESQ between the original music and music distorted by UAPs was 2.97, which means moderate quality. The success rate of generating audio AEs from test audios was 30.71%. This shows UAPs hidden in music are still able to attack generic audio.

6 Conclusion and Future Work

In the audio AE domain, there is limited work focusing on generating UAPs against ASR models. In this research, we filled this research gap by proposing the first successful targeted UAPs against ASR models with CTC loss. We analyzed UAPs from the point of view that UAPs can be considered as signals that were transcribed as the target phrase. To decrease the distortion caused by UAPS, we tried to minimize the maximum norm of UAPs. In addition, we showed that UAPs themselves preserved temporal dependency, such that the audio AEs generated by applying UAPs also preserved temporal dependency. UAPs and the corresponding audio AEs were also robust against Gaussian noise. We demonstrated the possibiliy of hiding UAPs below the hearing threshold of unsuspicious sound, such as music. Future work will focus on generating UAPs with reduced distortion.

References

1. Abdoli, S., Hafemann, L.G., Rony, J., Ayed, I.B., Cardinal, P., Koerich. A.L.: Universal adversarial audio perturbations. arXiv preprint arXiv:1908.03173 (2019)
2. Amodei, D., et al.: Deep speech 2: end-to-end speech recognition in English and mandarin. In: International Conference on Machine Learning, pp. 173–182 (2016)

3. Athalye, A., Engstrom, L., Ilyas, A., Kwok, K.: Synthesizing robust adversarial examples. In: International Conference on Machine Learning, pp. 284–293. PMLR (2018)
4. Carlini, N., Wagner, D.: Towards evaluating the robustness of neural networks. In: 2017 IEEE Symposium on Security and Privacy (SP), pp. 39–57. IEEE (2017)
5. Carlini, N., Wagner, D.: Audio adversarial examples: targeted attacks on speech-to-text. In: 2018 IEEE Security and Privacy Workshops (SPW), pp. 1–7. IEEE (2018)
6. Chan, W., Jaitly, N., Le, Q.V., Vinyals, O.: Listen, attend and spell: a neural network for large vocabulary conversational speech recognition. In: 2016 IEEE International Conference on Acoustics, Speech and Signal Processing, ICASSP 2016, Shanghai, China, 20–25 March 2016, pp. 4960–4964. IEEE (2016)
7. Du, X., Pun, C., Zhang, Z.: A unified framework for detecting audio adversarial examples. In: Chen, C.W., et al. (eds.), MM 2020: The 28th ACM International Conference on Multimedia, Virtual Event/Seattle, WA, USA, 12–16 October 2020, pp. 3986–3994. ACM (2020)
8. Graves, A., Fernández, S., Gomez, F., Schmidhuber, J.: Connectionist temporal classification: labelling unsegmented sequence data with recurrent neural networks. In Proceedings of the 23rd International Conference on Machine Learning, pp. 369–376 (2006)
9. Hannun, A., et al.: Deep speech: scaling up end-to-end speech recognition. arXiv preprint arXiv:1412.5567 (2014)
10. Ilyas, A., Engstrom, L., Athalye, A., Lin, J.: Black-box adversarial attacks with limited queries and information. In: Dy, J.G., Krause, A. (eds.), Proceedings of the 35th International Conference on Machine Learning, ICML 2018, Stockholmsmässan, Stockholm, Sweden, 10–15 July 2018, volume 80 of Proceedings of Machine Learning Research, pp. 2142–2151. PMLR (2018)
11. Kingma, D.P., Ba. J.: Adam: a method for stochastic optimization. In: Bengio, Y., LeCun, Y. (eds.) 3rd International Conference on Learning Representations, ICLR 2015, San Diego, CA, USA, 7–9 May 2015, Conference Track Proceedings (2015)
12. Li, J., et al.: Universal adversarial perturbations generative network for speaker recognition. In: IEEE International Conference on Multimedia and Expo, ICME 2020, London, UK, 6–10 July 2020, pp. 1–6. IEEE (2020)
13. Li, Z., Wu, Y., Liu, J., Chen, Y., Yuan. B.: Advpulse: universal, synchronization-free, and targeted audio adversarial attacks via subsecond perturbations. In: Ligatti, J., Ou, X., Katz, J., Vigna, G. (eds.), CCS 2020: 2020 ACM SIGSAC Conference on Computer and Communications Security, Virtual Event, USA, 9–13 November 2020, pp. 1121–1134. ACM (2020)
14. Lu, Z., Han, W., Zhang, Y., Cao. I.: Exploring targeted universal adversarial perturbations to end-to-end ASR models. arXiv preprint arXiv:2104.02757 (2021)
15. Moosavi-Dezfooli, S.-M., Fawzi, A., Fawzi, O., Frossard., P.: Universal adversarial perturbations. In: Proceedings of the IEEE Conference on Computer Vision and Pattern Recognition, pp. 1765–1773 (2017)
16. Moosavi-Dezfooli, S.-M., Fawzi, A., Frossard, P.: Deepfool: a simple and accurate method to fool deep neural networks. In: Proceedings of the IEEE Conference on Computer Vision and Pattern Recognition, pp. 2574–2582 (2016)
17. Neekhara, P., Hussain, S., Pandey, P., Dubnov, S., McAuley, J.J., Koushanfar, F.: Universal adversarial perturbations for speech recognition systems. In: Kubin, G., Kacic, Z. (eds.) Interspeech 2019, 20th Annual Conference of the International Speech Communication Association, Graz, Austria, 15–19 September 2019, pp. 481–485. ISCA (2019)

18. Panayotov, V., Chen, G., Povey, D., Khudanpur, S.: Librispeech: an ASR corpus based on public domain audio books. In: 2015 IEEE International Conference on Acoustics, Speech and Signal Processing (ICASSP), pp. 5206–5210. IEEE (2015)
19. Park, D.S., Chan, W., Zhang, Y., Chiu, C., Zoph, D.S., Cubuk, E.D., Le, Q.V.: Specaugment: A simple data augmentation method for automatic speech recognition. In: Kubin, G., Kacic, Z. (eds.) Interspeech 2019, 20th Annual Conference of the International Speech Communication Association, Graz, Austria, 15–19 September 2019, pp. 2613–2617. ISCA (2019)
20. Qin, Y., Carlini, N., Cottrell, G.W., Goodfellow, I.J., Raffel, C.: Imperceptible, robust, and targeted adversarial examples for automatic speech recognition. In: Proceedings of the 36th International Conference on Machine Learning, ICML 2019, 9–15 June 2019, Long Beach, CA, USA, pp. 5231–5240 (2019)
21. Rix, A.W., Beerends, J.G., Hollier, M.P., Hekstra, A.P.: Perceptual evaluation of speech quality (PESQ)-a new method for speech quality assessment of telephone networks and codecs. In: IEEE International Conference on Acoustics, Speech, and Signal Processing, ICASSP 2001, 7–11 May, 2001, Salt Palace Convention Center, Salt Lake City, Utah, USA, Proceedings, pp. 749–752. IEEE (2001)
22. Schönherr, L., Eisenhofer, T., Zeiler, S., Holz, T., Kolossa, D.: Imperio: Robust over-the-air adversarial examples for automatic speech recognition systems. In: ACSAC 2020: Annual Computer Security Applications Conference, Virtual Event/Austin, TX, USA, 7–11 December, 2020, pp. 843–855. ACM (2020)
23. Szegedy, C., et al.: Intriguing properties of neural networks. In: Bengio, Y., LeCun, Y. (eds.) 2nd International Conference on Learning Representations, ICLR 2014, Banff, AB, Canada, April 14–16, 2014, Conference Track Proceedings (2014)
24. Wang, D., Dong, L., Wang, R., Yan, D., Wang, J.: Targeted speech adversarial example generation with generative adversarial network. IEEE Access **8**, 124503–124513 (2020)
25. Xie, Y., Li, Z., Shi, C., Liu, J., Chen, Y., Yuan, B.: Enabling fast and universal audio adversarial attack using generative model. arXiv preprint arXiv:2004.12261 (2020)
26. Xie, Y., Shi, C., Li, Z., Liu, J., Chen, Y., Yuan, B.: Real-time, universal, and robust adversarial attacks against speaker recognition systems. In: 2020 IEEE International Conference on Acoustics, Speech and Signal Processing, ICASSP 2020, Barcelona, Spain, 4–8 May 2020, pp. 1738–1742. IEEE (2020)
27. Yang, Z., Li, B., Chen, P., Song, D.: Characterizing audio adversarial examples using temporal dependency. In: 7th International Conference on Learning Representations, ICLR 2019, New Orleans, LA, USA, 6–9 May 2019. OpenReview.net (2019)
28. Yuan, X., et al.: Commandersong: A systematic approach for practical adversarial voice recognition. In 27th {USENIX} Security Symposium ({USENIX} Security 18), pages 49–64, 2018
29. Zhang, C., Benz, P., Imtiaz, T., Kweon, I.S.: Understanding adversarial examples from the mutual influence of images and perturbations. In: Proceedings of the IEEE/CVF Conference on Computer Vision and Pattern Recognition, pp. 14521–14530 (2020)
30. Zhao, P., et al.: On the design of black-box adversarial examples by leveraging gradient-free optimization and operator splitting method. In: Proceedings of the IEEE International Conference on Computer Vision, pp. 121–130 (2019)

Voxstructor: Voice Reconstruction from Voiceprint

Panpan Lu[1], Qi Li[2], Hui Zhu[1], Giuliano Sovernigo[2], and Xiaodong Lin[2(✉)]

[1] Xidian University, Xi'an, China
lupanpan@stu.xidian.edu.cn, zhuhui@xidian.edu.cn
[2] University of Guelph, Guelph, Canada
{qli15,gsovernigo,xlin08}@uoguelph.ca

Abstract. With the rapid development of machine learning technologies, voiceprint has become widely used as a personal identifier in daily life. Because of that, it is essential to determine to what extent a voiceprint derived from machine learning can be inverted to obtain the original speaker characteristic. However, the reconstruction of voiceprint templates is still a challenging issue. It has also not been proven whether the widespread use of voiceprint poses a privacy leakage risk. In this paper, we implement the first comprehensive, holistic, and systematic reconstruction study targeting voiceprint templates. We present Voxstructor, a voiceprint-based voice constructor that can be used for bulk template reconstruction attacks. An attacker can reconstruct a new voice based only on the victim's voiceprint data instead of the voice itself. Specifically, we formalize the voice reconstruction work as an objective optimization problem and merge voice cloning with voiceprint template conversion work. We have conducted extensive experiments on multiple mapping models, loss functions, voiceprint template extraction models, scoring methods, and two types of speaker verification attacks. Thorough experiments show that our attacks are effective, achieving a fairly high success rate which is similar to the results generated by voice cloning methods. The time overhead of Voxstructor is far less than other attacks. Our study not only demonstrates the need for protection of voiceprint templates in speaker recognition systems, but also shows that Voxstructor can be used as a privacy measure tool for voiceprint privacy-preserving schemes.

Keywords: Privacy · Reconstruction · Speaker verification · Voiceprint

1 Introduction

The application of speaker recognition systems is on the rise, such as in banking, voice assistants, online authentication among numerous others. At the same time, the attacks against speaker recognition systems become correspondingly more

---

P. Lu and Q. Li—Contributed equally.

J. K. Liu et al. (Eds.): ISC 2021, LNCS 13118, pp. 374–397, 2021.
https://doi.org/10.1007/978-3-030-91356-4_20

common. Several representative attack methods have been proposed separately, such as adversarial noise [1–3], replay attack [4], speech synthesis [5], and others. All these attacks point out the vulnerability of some modules in the speaker recognition system.

It is well known that a speaker recognition system operates by extracting the voiceprint vector from the speaker's speech, and then comparing it with the stored voiceprint to calculate the similarity. This process can be used to determine the identity of the speaker. Voiceprints are typically compact binary or real-valued feature representations that are extracted from voice samples or voice features to increase the efficiency and accuracy of similarity computation. Over the past couple of decades, a large number of approaches have been proposed for voiceprint [6–8].

In this paper, we focus on template reversibility and reconstruction attacks in speaker recognition systems. In a voiceprint reconstruction attack, if voice can be reconstructed from the target's voiceprint, it can be used to gain access to the target through the target or other user-registered systems, thus threatening the target's interests and safety. Template reconstruction attacks generally assume that templates of target subjects and the corresponding black-box template extractor can be accessed [9]. First, templates of target users can be exposed in hacked databases. Second, the corresponding black-box template extractor can potentially be obtained by purchasing the speaker recognition SDK. To our knowledge, almost all of the speaker recognition vendors store voiceprints without template protection.

There are existing works on face template reconstruction [9], but these cannot be applied to voiceprint reconstruction. Faces are static features and do not change dynamically. Human voice however, changes dynamically with content, emotion, and other factors. Voiceprints are text-independent for increasing recognition accuracy, which makes it more difficult to reconstruct the target's speech. Similar work has been done such as voice synthesis [5,10], and adversarial voice attack [1–3]. However, such work requires the original speech of the target as input, which is difficult to obtain these speeches in reality.

To address the issues of voiceprint reconstruction, inspired by voice cloning [5,10], we propose a voice constructor from voiceprint, called Voxstructor ("vox", as derived from the etymology of "voice"). First, we use a common voiceprint extractor such as i-vector as a black box to extract voiceprint. Second, we use multiple neural networks to construct a mapping transformation model from voiceprint to speaker embedding in voice clones. Third, the speaker embedding is used to generate speech from existing voice cloning technology. In our study of voiceprint reconstruction attacks, we made no assumptions about subjects used to train the target speaker recognition system. Therefore, we use Kaldi's pre-trained voiceprint extractors in our research, and use public datasets to train our attack model. We experiment and analyze our mapping transformation model from multiple loss functions and multiple model structures. We also abstract several attack scenarios, conduct experiments and analysis for these scenarios. In summary, we make the following contributions:

- We conduct a comprehensive study on the reversibility of voiceprint. To our best knowledge, this is the first study on voiceprint reconstruction and voiceprint privacy.
- Voxstructor is developed for reconstructing voice samples from voiceprint. We implement and analyze voiceprint reconstruction under three mapping network structures, three loss functions, three voiceprint extractors and three discrimination thresholds while achieving a very high attack success rate.
- We discuss the multiple implications of our scheme. It not only exposes the reversibility and sensitivity of the voiceprint, but also demonstrates the need for privacy protection. Moreover, it can be used in several aspects such as computer forensics, and privacy-preserving effect metrics.

The remainder of this paper is organized as follows. We review the relevant background information in Sect. 2. The proposed scheme and the performance evaluation are followed in Sect. 3 and Sect. 4 respectively. In Sect. 5, we review some related works. Finally, we draw our conclusion in Sect. 6.

2   Background

In this section, we introduce the basic knowledge of the speaker verification system and threat model.

2.1   Speaker Verification System

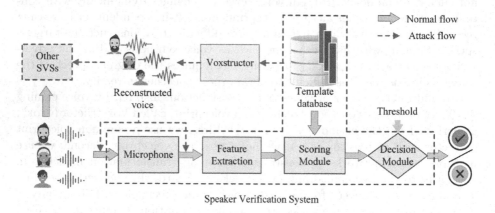

Fig. 1. Overview of the proposed system for reconstructing voices from the corresponding templates.

Speaker recognition is an automatic technology which can recognize the speaker's identity according to the sound characteristics extracted from their speech. The flow of a speaker verification system (SVS) is shown with the dashed box in the normal flow in Fig. 1, which mainly includes five modules. **Microphone** is used to collect user's registered voice and verification voice. **Extractor** is used to extract speaker characteristics in voice. **Database** is used to store user's registered voiceprint template. **Scoring module** is used to match speaker feature vector extracted from verification voice with registered voiceprint template stored in database and outputs a similarity score. **Decision module** is used to compare the result of scoring module with threshold and gives the decision result of pass or fail.

At present, there are several popular technologies used in speaker recognition system as follows.

I-Vector. The method based on the i-vector involves modeling the global difference, and modeling the speaker and channel as a whole [6]. In this way, the restrictions on the training corpus are relaxed, the calculation is simple, and the performance is better. The i-vector contains both the speaker differential information and the channel differential information, so it is necessary to remove the channel interference in the i-vector and use channel compensation technology to eliminate the channel interference. An i-vector can be written as 400 or 600 dimensional vector.

X-Vector. Snyder et al. [7] defined the x-vector and proposed an extraction model based on a multi-layer delayed neural network, which can transform the input features at the frame level into the feature expression at the sentence level. The embedded vector extracted from the model is called the x-vector, which can be used similarly to the i-vector. The dimension of this vector is 512, and it also contains the channel information. Channel compensation technology is needed to eliminate the interference (PLDA classifier is used in the training process).

Resnet34 Model. Heo et al. [8] proposed the Resnet34 voiceprint extraction model based on residual networks. In this paper, different loss functions are used to train the model. Comparing the accuracies of the models, GE2E and the original network (AP + softmax) have the highest accuracy.

Scoring Methods. It consists of three main scoring methods in SVS systems: PLDA, cosine distance, and Euclidean distance. As a channel compensation algorithm of i-vector and x-vector, PLDA is widely used in SVS because its compensation effect is better than other channel compensation algorithms (such as LDA) and the scoring methods are based on calculating log likelihood. Research shows that channel information will cause the size of feature vector to change, while speaker information mainly affects the direction of i-vector feature vector [6], so cosine distance weakens the influence of channel information to a certain extent. Finally, Euclidean distance is widely used as a way to measure the distance between two points (vectors). Here we combine it with the Resnet34 model as an SVS to show the effect of Euclidean distance in the field of voiceprint feature recognition.

2.2 Threat Model

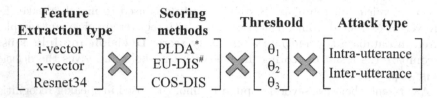

Fig. 2. Attack scenarios, where * means that PLDA is not used for SVS with Resnet34 as the voiceprint extractor, and # means that EU-DIS is only used for SVS with Resnet34 as the voiceprint extractor. $\theta_1, \theta_2, \theta_3$ are based on EER, high user experience degree, and high security degree respectively.

We assume that the adversary has the voiceprint template of the registered speaker and hopes to design a voice sample to defeat the SVS.

The scenario of the template reconstruction attack is shown in Fig. 1. The adversary obtains the target's voiceprint template through some means, such as purchasing it illegally or obtaining it through unauthorized access, for example, caused by software vulnerabilities in the SVS such as buffer overflow privilege escalation. Then the adversary uses it to reconstruct the target's voice through voxstructor, and uses the voice to attack the target's speaker verification system. According to whether the voiceprint template obtained by the adversary is from the target SVS, there are two types of attacks in voiceprint reconstruction attack: (1) intra-utterance, the reconstructed voiceprint template comes from the victim registration voiceprint template stored in the target SVS; (2) inter-utterance, the reconstructed voiceprint template comes from the victim's unregistered voiceprint template.

Our proposed voiceprint reconstruction attack is a black-box attack. In other words, the attacker can attack the system without knowing the neural network model in the SVS (such as structure, parameters, and training data set, etc.). The reason is that the proposed voiceprint reconstructor does not need to understand the neural model, and only needs to input the voiceprint template to reconstruct the victim's voice.

In our attack model, in order to fully demonstrate the effect of voiceprint reconstruction attack, we design six SVSs based on three mainstream voiceprint extraction models (i-vector, x-vector, Resnet34) and three popular scoring methods (PLDA, Euclidean distance, cosine distance). According to the system's availability and security requirements, we set three different thresholds based on the system accuracy evaluation target equal error rate (EER), high user experience degree, and high security degree for each SVS. Including two types of attacks, as shown in Fig. 2, there are a total of 36 attack scenarios.

3   Voxstructor

Voxstructor is mainly realized by voice cloning technology [5] and voiceprint mapping model. Figure 3 shows the structure diagram of voxstructor. Voiceprint templates are transformed into the speaker embedding vectors by mapping model, and the vector and text content are synthesized into mel spectrograms by the synthesizer, and the reconstructed speech is generated by the vocoder. In this section, we will introduce the details and technologies in the process of voiceprint reconstruction.

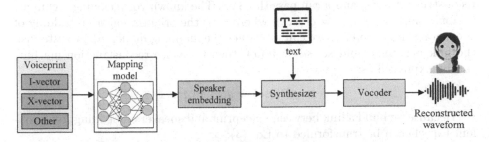

Fig. 3. Voxstructor structure diagram.

3.1   Voice Cloning

Google proposes real-time voice cloning (RTVC) technology, which is based on a text-to-speech (TTS) synthesis system that can generate speech audio in different speaker's voices [5]. The technology consists of three main components: (1) Speaker encoder network: a multilayer LTSM network, trained as a speaker verification task, that generates a fixed dimensional embedding vector speaker embedding from only a few seconds of reference speech of the target speaker, which has the characteristics of the speaker; (2) Synthesizer: a Tacotron 2-based [11] inter-sequence synthesis network that generates mel spectrograms from text conditional on the speaker embedding vector generated in the speaker encoder; (3) Vocoder: an autoregressive WaveNet-based [12] vocoder network that converts the generated in the synthesizer mel spectrograms into time domain waveform samples, thus generating the speech audio of the target person. While voice cloning provides our research with a strong base, our voiceprint reconstruction converts different forms of voiceprint templates into speaker embedding vectors, synthesizes mel spectrograms with text through Synthesizer, and finally generates speech files through the vocoder.

3.2   Problem Formation

Given a target person's voiceprint template x, the target person's voice v is reconstructed from x, and v must be similar enough to the target person's voice in order to pass the SVS. In other words, the voiceprint x' extracted from v by the voiceprint extractor in the SVS and the registered template x can be scored against the threshold after passing the scoring method. Therefore, we wish the difference between x and x' to be as small as possible. Then the problem is formalized as:

$$\min d(x, x'), \tag{1}$$

where d represents the distance between the two vectors.

Our ultimate goal is to reconstruct the voice from the voiceprint, i.e., we wish to construct a voiceprint reconstructor $v = R(x, t)$, where t is the text of the reconstructed voice, and v can pass the SVS. The known voice cloning technique [5] for cloning voice is: $v = g(se, t)$, where se is the origin speaker embedding of speaker's voice. Therefore we can introduce the mapping model $m(.)$ to establish the link between x and se: $se' = m(x)$, then the voice reconstruction machine can be expressed as:

$$v = R(x, t) = g(m(x), t). \tag{2}$$

Because we build a link between voiceprint and speaker embedding, the problem Eq. (1) can be transformed to Eq. (3):

$$\min d(se, se'). \tag{3}$$

In summary, our goal is to find mapping model $m(.)$, which can achieve min $d(se, se')$.

3.3   Mapping Model

The mapping models are three-layer fully connected structures and convolutional neural network, which have simple structures, easy implementation, and few parameters. The normalization of the voiceprint is needed before the input model. According to three different types of voiceprint characteristics, we design three different mapping models. (1) I2E: this model maps i-vector to speaker embedding; (2) X2E: this model maps x-vector to speaker embedding; (3) R2E: this model maps the voice eigenvector extracted by Resnet34 to speaker embedding. The mapping model we proposed is not limited to these three types.

Let $D(\cdot, \cdot)$ denote the reconstruction loss function between different speaker embedding, v denote a training voice sample from the public datasets, $f(\cdot)$ denote voiceprint extractor function, $g(\cdot)$ denote voice cloning function, t denote the text in the reconstructed voice, θ denote the parameters of mapping model, e denote the speaker embedding extractor function. According to Eq. (1) and Eq. (3), the objective function for training mapping models can be formulated as

$$\arg\min_{\theta} \mathcal{L}(v, \theta) = \arg\min_{\theta} \frac{1}{N} \sum_{i}^{N} \mathcal{D}(f(v_i), f(g(m_{\theta}(f(v_i)), t))) \tag{4}$$

$$\approx \arg\min_{\theta} \frac{1}{N} \sum_{i}^{N} \mathcal{D}(m_{\theta}(f(v_i)), e(v_i)), \tag{5}$$

where N denotes the number of voice samples. After training, we can get the reconstructed voice sample v' using the target's voiceprint x: $v' = g(m_\theta(f(v_i)), t)$.

We use three different loss functions (MSELoss, L1Loss and SmoothL1Loss) as $D(\cdot, \cdot)$ in Eq. (4) to train our model, so as to show the influence of different distance measurement methods on the voiceprint mapping model. For each mapping model, we use the above loss functions to train the mapping models, which contains nine models.

4   Experiment Evaluation

We evaluate the reconstruction attack capability of Voxstructor[1] in a SVS from the following four aspects: effectiveness, efficiency, human perceived similarity and privacy-reserving methods effect metric. Then, we introduce the datasets, experimental design and the above four aspects. For convenience and clarity, we list the abbreviations used in the experiment in Table 1.

Table 1. The list of notations used in the experiments.

Notations	Descriptions
Average-utterance	Voxstructor based on the mean voiceprint
CONV	MSE & convolutional network
Inter-utterance	Voxstructor based on the Unregistered voiceprint
Intra-utterance	Voxstructor based on the registered voiceprint
IV-COS	i-vector & cosine distance as score
IV-PLDA	i-vector as voiceprint & PLDA as score
L1L	L1 loss & fully connected network
L1L-text2	L1L & use second text to generate
L1LNO	L1L & without normalization
MSE	MSE loss & fully connected network
Rand-vector	Randomly generated voiceprint vectors
Rand-wav	4874 randomly generated voices
RN-EU	Resnet & euclidean distance as score
RN-COS	Resnet & cosine distance as score
Smooth	Smooth loss & fully connected network
RTVC	Voice generated by voice cloning tool
RTVC-text2	RTVC & use second text to generate
XV-PLDA	x-vector as voiceprint & PLDA as score
XV-COS	x-vector & cosine distance as score

---

[1] https://github.com/voxstructor/voxstructor.

4.1 Dataset and Design

Dataset. The databases we used are voxceleb1 [13] and librispeech [14]. Voxceleb1 contains about 100000 voice samples of 1251 celebrities from YouTube Videos. The data is reasonably gender balanced (55% male). For the speaker verification system, the data set can be divided into a development set and a test set, and there is no overlap between them.

Librispeech is the most authoritative mainstream open-source dataset to measure speech recognition technology. It is an audiobook data set containing text and voice. The data comes from the audio recordings of reading materials from the Librivox project, and is carefully subdivided and consistent. Each recording is split into segments of 10 s and linked to its corresponding section of the accompanying text.

Design. In order to better and more comprehensively evaluate the voice reconstruction attack capability of Voxstructor, we target three speaker verification systems: i-vector, x-vector and deep residual network ResNset34 model. These are test in the most popular open-source platform-kaldi [15]. In addition, we use the more popular PLDA, cosine distance, and Euclidean distance as the scoring methods for speaker verification systems. The i-vector extractor and the corresponding PLDA use the pre-trained model from the open source tool Kaldi[2]. The x-vector model and its PLDA also use the pre-trained Kaldi model[3]. The Resnet34 model uses the pre-trained model from Joon et al. [16]. The performance of these six systems can be seen in Table 2.

To be able to fully represent the Voxstrutor voice reconstruction capability, we use all the voices in the test set (40 users, 4874 voices) to register the speaker verification system and reconstruct the voices according to the corresponding voiceprint. We also consider the case that some current speaker verification systems register users with a voiceprint template that averages the vectors extracted from multiple voices of the user. Therefore, we also use the average voiceprint of the four voices of each user in the test set to register the system and reconstruct the voice based on this voiceprint template. In addition, we selected 100 speakers from the tran-clean-100 in LibriSpeech with clear and noiseless speech to test the reconstruction ability of Voxstructor.

Evaluation Criteria. We use false rejection rate (FRR), false acceptance rate (FAR), and equal error rate (EER) to express the performance of the SVS. We use the attack pass rate to evaluate the ability of the voice-reconstruction attack, i.e., the percentage of voices reconstructed from the voiceprint that pass the speaker verification system. To evaluate the efficiency of the voice reconstruction attack, the execution time of the reconstructed voice is used as a metric.

---

[2] https://github.com/kaldi-asr/kaldi/tree/master/egs/voxceleb/v1.
[3] https://github.com/kaldi-asr/kaldi/tree/master/egs/voxceleb/v2.

Table 2. Performance of the six baseline SVSs (%).

SVS	Threshold	EER	FRR	FAR
IV-PLDA	−1.000	5.342	5.371	5.313
	−6.000	—	1.193	17.487
	3.000	—	14.846	1.278
IV-COS	0.060	13.831	13.807	13.855
	−0.020	—	1.283	67.869
	0.128	—	41.559	1.012
XV-PLDA	−3.000	3.134	3.303	2.964
	−8.000	—	1.288	7.635
	1.000	—	7.269	1.103
XV-COS	0.670	9.722	9.369	10.074
	0.530	—	1.082	32.847
	0.770	—	33.330	1.145
RN-EU	80.000	5.199	5.795	4.602
	87.000	—	1.129	18.722
	75.000	—	13.971	1.145
RN-COS	0.350	1.880	1.023	2.736
	0.390	—	2.322	1.198

4.2 Effectiveness

Target Model. In order to evaluate the effectiveness of the voiceprint reconstruction attack, we designed six speaker verification systems (IV-PLDA, IV-COS, XV-PLDA, XV-COS, RN-EU, RN-COS) using a combination of the three most popular voiceprint extraction methods and three scoring methods, PLDA, Euclidean distance, and cosine distance. For simplicity, IV is used to denote i-vector, XV to denote x-vector, RN to denote Resnet34, and PLDA, EU, COS to denote the three scoring methods of PLDA, Euclidean distance, and cosine distance, respectively.

Here, we set three thresholds for each system. The first threshold is determined based on the EER, which is a relatively good compromise between availability and security of the verification system. The second will be determined based on the FRR value of 1.0% , i.e., the verification system focuses on availability. The third will be determined based on the FAR value of 1.0% , i.e., the verification system focuses on security. It is worth noting that similar to other biometric verification techniques, the input voice (or extracted voiceprint from the user input) and the stored voiceprint usually do not match perfectly. As a result, a matching score threshold must be set for SVS to verify the identity of user. In the RN-COS system, the FRR can be taken as 1.023% when the EER is 1.88%, so the second threshold is not set.

Table 3. The pass rates of Voxstructor, RTVC and rand guessing under intra-utterance type (%).

Model	SVS	Threshold	Voxstructor	RTVC	Rand_vector	Rand-wav
I2E	IV-PLDA	−1.000	77.754	84.773	1.950	0.636
		−6.000	97.106	98.071	10.979	6.731
		3.000	41.822	54.853	0.082	0.041
	IV-COS	0.060	41.137	52.626	11.264	15.224
		−0.020	88.162	91.711	66.886	66.639
		0.128	7.817	13.993	0.431	1.847
X2E	XV-PLDA	−3.000	72.522	79.889	3.099	2.586
		−8.000	90.971	93.803	16.745	16.068
		1.000	48.964	60.456	0.349	0.369
	XV-COS	0.670	89.208	86.869	0.000	0.041
		0.530	99.713	99.036	0.000	0.759
		0.770	45.466	46.492	0.000	0.000
R2E	RN-EU	80.000	64.854	67.357	0.533	12.946
		87.000	88.531	90.008	5.929	52.216
		75.000	40.870	44.276	0.021	1.785
	RN-COS	0.350	63.192	70.086	0.000	1.149
		0.390	45.568	53.037	0.000	0.041

Voiceprint Reconstruction Results. To evaluate the voice reconstructed based on different voiceprint forms, we test the pass rate of the voice reconstructed with different types of voiceprints in the corresponding SVS. In addition, we designed two sets of comparison experiments, one is to test the pass rate of the original voice of registered users directly synthesized by the real-time voice cloning tool (RTVC) [5] in six speaker verification systems. The other is to verify the pass rate of random guesses, we generated two forms of data sets randomly based on the test set of voxceleb1, one randomly generated voice vector set (rand_vector) and the other randomly generated voice set (rand_wav). The pass rates of Voxstructor, RTVC and rand guessing under intra-utterance case are shown in Table 3, where the loss function of the Voxstructor is the L1Loss function. We verify the impact caused by the voiceprint after reconstruction on the SVS based on 4874 voices in the voxceleb test set. The results show that our attack scheme is fully effective and can achieve similar results to RTVC, far exceeding the two random guesses.

As shown in Table 4, the pass rates of voice reconstructed based on average voiceprint are higher than common intra-uttenance case. This result indicates that the mean voiceprint-based reconstruction attack is much more effective against the SVS based on their models than the single speech-based voiceprint reconstruction attack. That is, the mean voiceprint of multiple voices of a user is better at characterizing the user's voice than the voiceprint of a single voice.

Table 4. The pass rates of different datasets, average-utterance, intra-utterance and inter-utterance (%).

Model	SVS	Threshold	librispeech	voxceleb	Average	Intra	Inter
I2E	IV-PLDA	−1.000	96.000	77.754	85.000	77.754	48.133
		−6.000	100.000	97.106	97.500	97.106	83.772
		3.000	84.000	41.822	47.500	41.822	18.366
	IV-COS	0.060	81.000	41.137	52.500	41.137	28.706
		−0.020	95.000	88.162	90.000	88.162	80.764
		0.128	43.000	7.817	20.000	7.817	4.369
X2E	XV-PLDA	−3.000	94.000	72.522	72.500	72.522	44.944
		−8.000	100.000	90.971	95.000	90.971	71.989
		1.000	84.000	48.964	42.500	48.964	23.544
	XV-COS	0.670	100.000	89.208	100.000	89.208	71.729
		0.530	100.000	99.713	100.000	99.713	95.758
		0.770	66.000	45.466	85.000	45.466	23.293
R2E	RN-EU	80.000	82.000	64.854	87.500	64.854	49.968
		87.000	92.000	88.531	100.000	88.531	80.064
		75.000	66.000	40.870	80.000	40.870	28.112
	RN-COS	0.350	93.000	63.192	92.500	63.192	40.027
		0.390	82.000	45.568	80.000	45.568	24.624

In the inter-utterance case, the pass rate of the reconstructed speech from our voiceprint reconstruction scheme is about 20% lower in SVSs than in the intra-utterance case. This shows that even for different voices of the same person, there are still relatively large differences and it is still not a good way to model a person's speech characteristics. The result is a good illustration of the limitations and drawbacks of short speech registration in speaker verification systems. However, this pass rate is still fatal to SVSs, and once the voiceprint of a registered user of all SVSs is leaked, then SVS using the same model as that SVS will also be threatened.

The pass rates of two datasets in the intra-utterance case are shown in Table 4, where the loss function of the model is the L1Loss function. As can be seen from the table, among these six SVSs, the pass rate of the speech reconstructed by Voxstructor based on the voiceprint in librispeech speech can reach more than 90% in the SVS with the threshold value of voxceleb, which is about 20% higher than the pass rate tested with voxceleb data. This is mainly due to the fact that the voxceleb speech is mainly from YouTube videos, which contains additional background noise, while the librispeech speech is clean speech from audiobook readings.

Effect of Loss Functions. In order to test the effect of different loss functions on the mapping models, we designed three loss functions, L1Loss, MSELoss, and SmoothL1Loss, to train our proposed three models, I2E, X2E, R2E, and test their pass rates. The pass rates of the mapping models trained with different loss functions are shown in Table 5. The results show that SmoothL1Loss has the highest accuracy for i-vector voiceprints and MSELoss has the highest accuracy for x-vector and Resnet voiceprints.

Table 5. The pass rates of different loss function under intra-utterance type (%).

Model	SVS	Threshold	L1L	MSE	Smooth
I2E	IV-PLDA	−1.000	77.754	76.790	80.176
		−6.000	97.106	96.696	97.496
		3.000	41.822	41.740	43.854
	IV-COS	0.060	41.137	43.906	45.507
		−0.020	88.162	89.516	89.577
		0.128	7.817	9.643	10.423
X2E	XV-PLDA	−3.000	72.522	72.604	71.681
		−8.000	90.971	91.525	90.806
		1.000	48.964	49.292	48.245
	XV-COS	0.670	89.208	88.346	89.229
		0.530	99.713	99.815	99.733
		0.770	45.466	43.188	44.337
R2E	RN-EU	80.000	64.854	67.111	64.198
		87.000	88.531	91.075	88.941
		75.000	40.870	42.388	39.352
	RN-COS	0.350	63.192	65.429	64.362
		0.390	45.568	47.476	46.984

Model Structure. For the mapping models in the proposed scheme, we also design a set of comparison experiments using three different structures of mapping models for the acoustic vectors. These are namely the fully connected, convolutional, and unnormalized.

The pass rates of the fully connected mapping model, the fully connected mapping model without normalization of the voiceprint, and the convolution-based mapping model in the speaker verification system are shown in Table 6. As we can see, the pass rate for the unnormalized fully-connected mapping model of the voiceprint is very low, about 70% lower than that of the normalized fully-connected model. It was observed that in the reconstruction for i-vector and Resnet voiceprint, the pass rates of the fully connected structure is almost the same as that of the convolutional structure. And the fully connected structure outperforms the convolutional structure in the reconstruction for the x-vector. This indicates that the correlation between the components of the voiceprint template is small and there is no local receptive field.

Table 6. The pass rates of different mapping models under intra-utterance type (%).

Model	SVS	Threshold	L1L	L1LNO	CONV
I2E	IV-PLDA	−1.000	77.754	8.537	77.940
		−6.000	97.106	21.547	97.189
		3.000	41.822	1.642	42.110
	IV-COS	0.060	41.137	13.500	44.112
		−0.020	88.162	66.229	89.516
		0.128	7.817	0.985	10.176
X2E	XV-PLDA	−3.000	72.522	1.847	52.473
		−8.000	90.971	6.587	79.356
		1.000	48.964	0.451	29.079
	XV-COS	0.670	89.208	21.892	78.539
		0.530	99.713	29.237	99.056
		0.770	45.466	7.571	28.272
R2E	RN-EU	80.000	64.854	2.400	61.202
		87.000	88.531	11.899	86.725
		75.000	40.870	0.472	36.048
	RN-COS	0.350	63.192	1.805	57.858
		0.390	45.568	0.677	41.157

Due to the limited space, we only show the pass rates in the intra-utterance attack type here, and the pass rate for the inter-utterance type can be found in the Appendix.

Text Independence. Finally, to characterize the text-independent speaker verification system, two different texts were used to synthesize two sets of speech. Text 1 is: "This is being said in my own voice. The computer has learned to do an impression of me." Text 2 is: "The prince loves his roses, but felt disappointed by something the rose said. As doubt grows, he decides to explore other planet." We synthesize two sets of speech based on the two texts after mapping the voiceprints using a mapping model trained with the L1Loss loss function. In addition, to compare and demonstrate the effect of our reconstruction scheme to reconstruct two different contents of speech in a text-independent system, we take the speech from the voxceleb1 test set directly through the RTVC tool to synthesize two sets of speech with different texts.

The pass rates of the voice reconstructed using two different English texts with the mapped vectors through the speaker verification system is shown in Table 7 and Table 16 (see Appendix). The results indicate that our attack can still achieve a high pass rate even when generating a voice with different text content than the original registered voice. The pass rate for both texts is essentially the same. This shows that Voxstructor is fully applicable to diverse attacks and can generate commands with sensitive semantics to further threaten the security of smart voice assistants, smart homes, and other environments.

Table 7. Pass rate of text-independent under Intra-utterance type (%).

Model	SVS	Threshold	L1L	L1L-TEXT2	RTVC	RTVC-TEXT2
I2E	IV-PLDA	−1.000	77.754	74.635	84.773	82.865
		−6.000	97.106	95.834	98.071	97.353
		3.000	41.822	39.113	54.853	52.719
	IV-COS	0.060	41.137	39.598	52.626	51.252
		−0.020	88.162	88.059	91.711	92.983
		0.128	7.817	6.483	13.993	12.659
X2E	XV-PLDA	−3.000	72.522	67.063	79.889	76.093
		−8.000	90.971	86.723	93.803	91.340
		1.000	48.964	45.392	60.456	56.105
	XV-COS	0.670	37.669	36.808	52.626	51.252
		0.530	86.972	86.233	91.711	92.983
		0.770	7.448	6.011	13.993	12.659
R2E	RN-EU	80.000	64.854	88.141	67.357	86.438
		87.000	88.531	98.420	90.008	97.435
		75.000	40.870	69.696	44.276	67.152
	RN-COS	0.350	63.192	67.009	70.086	69.655
		0.390	45.568	49.097	53.037	53.775

4.3 Efficiency

We test the time of synthesizing sound in our voiceprint reconstruction scheme on a Windows PC with NVIDIA p5000 GPU. The test time is shown in Table 8. Our voiceprint reconstruction attack can reconstruct the user's voice from the voiceprint vector without accessing the verification system. However, the FAKE-BOB proposed in the paper [1] not only needs a segment of speech as the original speech of the target speech, but also needs to visit the verification system many times to make the speech conversion successful. Therefore, the time consumed by our proposed voiceprint reconstruction attack is much less than that of FAKE-BOB attack, which is 80 times faster than that of FAKEBOB attack.

Table 8. The time consumed by voiceprint reconstruction attack and FAKEBOB attack (seconds).

	I2E	X2E	R2E	FAKEBOB
Time (seconds)	23.781	27.254	25.340	2014

4.4 Manual Listening Experiment

We randomly select 10 people from librispeech and pick 2 sentences each at random. We extract three voiceprints for each sentence and reconstruct them using Voxstructor to get $3*2*10 = 60$ new voices. At the same time, we use RTVC to generate the same $2*10 = 20$ strips. These are combined, and we invite 10 volunteers to perform a manual listening test to evaluate the similarity with the original speech. We ask the testers to score the speech on a scale of 0–5, where a score of 0 indicates that it is completely unlike the original speech and a score of 5 indicates that it is identical. The results of the manual scoring are shown in Table 9.

Table 9. The manual listening scores of voxstructor and voice cloning [5].

	I2E	X2E	R2E	Average of three	RTVC
Scores	4.12	3.86	3.94	3.97	4.25

From Table 9, we can see that the average score of Voxstructor reconstructed out is 3.97, and the average score of RTVC is 4.25. The results show that the effect of our reconstructed speech using voiceprints is very close to the effect of RTVC using voice directly. Furthermore, both resemble the original voice so much that humans cannot distinguish whether it is the generated voice or not.

4.5 Privacy-Preserving Methods Metric

Due to the sensitive nature of voiceprint biometrics, many privacy-preserving speaker recognition schemes have been developed in recent years. Thus, it is important to evaluate the effectiveness of these privacy protection mechanisms. In order to show the effectiveness of Voxstructor on the metric of voiceprint-based privacy-preserving schemes, we designed the following experiments.

Setup: This experiment is also conducted mainly under the intra-utterance case. The test data are obtained from 20 different speakers' voices in librispeech's tran-clean-100. We test the pass rates of reconstructed voice from the three kinds of protected voiceprints by Voxstructor in their SVSs. In order to exclude the influence of the voice text in the metric of the privacy protection scheme of the voiceprint, we reconstruct the voice content as well as the content of the original voice text. We metric for four current privacy-preserving methods for voiceprint.

- MR: multiplying the voiceprint value by a random number for protection purpose.
- ARV: Adding the voiceprint by a random vector for protection purpose.
- MOM: multiplying the voiceprint by an orthogonal matrix for protection purpose.
- MMV: multiplying the voiceprint by an orthogonal matrix followed by a random vector for protection purposes, where the elements in the random vector and the random orthogonal matrix are generated by normal distribution, and we designed the mean value to be 0 and the scalar vertebral difference to be 0, 0.5, 1, 2, 3, 4, 5, to verify its pass rate in the SVS, respectively.

Results: For the MR approach, the protection method of multiplying the voiceprint by a random number does not achieve the effect of protecting the voiceprint because the voiceprint will be normalized when the voiceprint mapping model of Voxstructor is passed.

Table 10. Pass rate of Voxstructor for ARV privacy-preserving schemes (%).

SVS	Threshold	std-0	std-0.5	std-1	std-2	std-3	std-4	std-5
IV-PLDA	−3.000	95.000	95.000	95.000	60.000	25.000	40.000	25.000
	−8.000	100.000	100.000	100.000	75.000	60.000	50.000	45.000
	1.000	95.000	80.000	70.000	40.000	20.000	20.000	10.000
IV-COS	0.060	100.000	95.000	100.000	80.000	75.000	65.000	60.000
	−0.020	100.000	100.000	100.000	100.000	100.000	95.000	95.000
	0.128	80.000	75.000	65.000	35.000	30.000	30.000	20.000
XV-PLDA	−3.000	100.000	100.000	100.000	100.000	95.000	95.000	85.000
	−8.000	100.000	100.000	100.000	100.000	100.000	100.000	100.000
	1.000	95.000	95.000	100.000	100.000	85.000	85.000	70.000
XV-COS	0.670	100.000	100.000	100.000	100.000	100.000	90.000	90.000
	0.530	100.000	100.000	100.000	100.000	100.000	100.000	100.000
	0.770	65.000	75.000	80.000	65.000	55.000	50.000	35.000
RN-EU	80.000	95.000	100.000	100.000	100.000	100.000	95.000	90.000
	87.000	100.000	100.000	100.000	100.000	100.000	100.000	100.000
	75.000	95.000	95.000	95.000	95.000	90.000	85.000	80.000
RN-COS	0.350	95.000	100.000	95.000	90.000	90.000	75.000	55.000
	0.390	80.000	90.000	90.000	80.000	80.000	65.000	45.000

For the ARV, MOM, and MMV approaches, our test data are shown in Table 10, Table 11, and Table 12 respectively. When the variance is small, the Voxstructor pass rate is very high. When the variance is large, the pass rate of the reconstructed speech is low. The privacy of the voice template is fully protected at this time. Therefore, we can conclude that the pass rate of Voxstructor is inversely correlated with the degree of privacy protection. In conclusion, Voxstructor can be used as a tool for evaluating privacy-preserving approaches for speaker verification systems.

Table 11. Pass rate of Voxstructor for MOM privacy-preserving schemes (%).

SVS	Threshold	std-0	std-0.5	std-1	std-2	std-3	std-4	std-5
IV-PLDA	−3.000	95.000	10.000	25.000	20.000	10.000	30.000	10.000
	−8.000	100.000	45.000	40.000	45.000	45.000	45.000	40.000
	1.000	95.000	0.000	10.000	10.000	5.000	20.000	0.000
IV-COS	0.060	100.000	60.000	75.000	85.000	70.000	70.000	55.000
	−0.020	100.000	85.000	90.000	95.000	95.000	95.000	90.000
	0.128	80.000	20.000	30.000	20.000	25.000	25.000	5.000
XV-PLDA	−3.000	100.000	20.000	15.000	0.000	15.000	15.000	5.000
	−8.000	100.000	25.000	35.000	20.000	25.000	20.000	20.000
	1.000	95.000	15.000	0.000	0.000	10.000	10.000	0.000
XV-COS	0.670	100.000	10.000	10.000	10.000	10.000	10.000	20.000
	0.530	100.000	40.000	50.000	40.000	45.000	40.000	35.000
	0.770	65.000	5.000	5.000	0.000	0.000	0.000	0.000
RN-EU	80.000	95.000	60.000	40.000	50.000	35.000	45.000	60.000
	87.000	100.000	90.000	85.000	85.000	80.000	95.000	95.000
	75.000	95.000	45.000	15.000	25.000	10.000	35.000	45.000
RN-COS	0.350	95.000	25.000	5.000	10.000	10.000	15.000	5.000
	0.390	80.000	10.000	5.000	5.000	5.000	10.000	5.000

5 Related Work

At present, there are many studies on the security of intelligent voice system. In this part, we discuss the attacks on an intelligent voice system and compare them with Voxstructor.

Li et al. [2] introduce an imperceptible disturbance into the original speech signal to defeat the SVS. From the perspective of voiceprint template, they generate the sample voice for spoofing SVSs by leveraging the Genetic algorithm, the fitness function in which is mainly designed according to the similarity score between the target's voiceprint and the voiceprint extracted from the sample speech. Comparatively, Voxstructor does not need multiple iterations to reconstruct voice, so its efficiency is high. Additionally, Voxstructor can realize the black-box attack without knowing the voiceprint extraction model. The

Table 12. Pass rate of Voxstructor for MMV privacy-preserving schemes (%).

SVS	Threshold	std-0	std-0.5	std-1	std-2	std-3	std-4	std-5
IV-PLDA	−3.000	95.000	15.000	40.000	20.000	20.000	52.000	20.000
	−8.000	100.000	35.000	65.000	45.000	30.000	30.000	35.000
	1.000	95.000	0.000	20.000	10.000	10.000	5.000	0.000
IV-COS	0.060	100.000	55.000	60.000	55.000	50.000	70.000	70.000
	−0.020	100.000	100.000	95.000	85.000	95.000	90.000	90.000
	0.128	80.000	30.000	25.000	30.000	15.000	30.000	30.000
XV-PLDA	−3.000	100.000	10.000	20.000	10.000	15.000	20.000	20.000
	−8.000	100.000	35.000	40.000	40.000	25.000	45.000	35.000
	1.000	95.000	5.000	10.000	0.000	5.000	5.000	15.000
XV-COS	0.670	100.000	5.000	15.000	20.000	15.000	15.000	30.000
	0.530	100.000	30.000	55.000	50.000	50.000	40.000	55.000
	0.770	65.000	5.000	0.000	5.000	0.000	0.000	0.000
RN-EU	80.000	95.000	60.000	45.000	65.000	70.000	50.000	55.000
	87.000	100.000	95.000	85.000	90.000	85.000	85.000	85.000
	75.000	95.000	20.000	30.000	40.000	35.000	20.000	25.000
RN-COS	0.350	95.000	10.000	5.000	35.000	25.000	15.000	5.000
	0.390	80.000	10.000	0.000	10.000	15.000	5.000	0.000

voiceprint mimicry attack [3], realized the gray box or black box attack, but it is in essence an adversarial voice attack. That is to say, only through most iterations can the sample speech contain the target's voiceprint template. The FAKEBOB proposed by Chen et al. [1] attacks speaker recognition systems (e.g. SV, OSI, CSI). However, FAKEBOB also needs to access the system several times, while Voxstructor does not need access to one. In summary, compared with adversarial voice attacks, our voiceprint reconstruction attack can quickly reconstruct the target's voice from the voiceprint template without additional voice samples.

The spoofing attack is to mimic the target's voice to trick the SVS. There are four main kinds of attacks. The first and second attacks are mimicking and replaying. The attacker creates a speech sample by mimicking or pre-recording the speech sample of a given target speaker, which are the simplest ways to cheat the speaker verification system. However, playback technology can not meet the requirements of text-dependent SVS when producing specific utterances, and mimic is quite hard to find in reality. Our voiceprint reconstruction attack can meet this kind of attack scenario. The third one is voice synthesis [17]. The attacker uses text to speech (TTS) synthesis system to synthesize the target's audio. However, the training of this synthesis model requires the target's speech set of at least tens of minutes. Voxstructor does not need to obtain any speech set of the target, it only needs the target's voiceprint. The fourth attack is voice conversion [18]. It is to modify the voice of one speaker (source) to make it sound like the voice of another speaker (target) without changing the language content. However, this kind of attack also needs the target's voice to train the transfer function. In addition, our attack can reconstruct the voice of most targets in a short time, which other spoofing attacks cannot achieve.

6 Conclusion

In this paper, we conducted the first comprehensive and systematic research on voiceprint reconstruction, by proposing a novel, efficient voiceprint reconstructor, called Voxstructor. At the same time, our voiceprint reconstruction attack was verified under 36 attack scenarios. This paper not only reveals the high sensitivity of voiceprint template through a large number of experiments, but also has the following significance:

- Voxstructor can carry out high simulation and batch spoofing attack on speaker recognition system. And it automatically completes the attack end-to-end without human participation.
- Voxstructor can be used to measure the effect of voiceprint privacy protection method; it can also be used to measure privacy in voiceprint. For noise-added privacy-preserving schemes, Voxstructor can also reconstruct the voice sample very well and achieve a high pass rate.
- Voxstructor can be used in computer forensics. This technology can also restore the voice of the suspect from the voiceprint of the suspect to provide evidence or clues for the police.

Acknowledgments. This work was supported by National Natural Science Foundation of China (61972304 and 61932015), National Natural Science Foundation of Shaanxi Province (2019ZDLGY12-02), and Natural Sciences and Engineering Research Council of Canada (NSERC).

Appendix

Experimental Results About Inter-utterance Case

The pass rates of Voxstructor, RTVC and rand guessing under inter-utterance case are shown in Table 13. The pass rate of Voxstructor is close to that of RTVC with speech as direct input and significantly higher than that of the two random guessing schemes. These results illustrate that Voxstructor is still valid under inter-utterance case.

Table 13. Pass rate of Voxstructor, RTVC and rand guessing under inter-utterance case.

Model	SVS	Threshold	L1L	RTVC	Rand_vector	Rand-wav
I2E	IV-PLDA	−1.000	48.133	57.194	1.782	0.743
		−6.000	83.772	88.186	11.039	7.480
		3.000	18.366	26.122	0.228	0.058
	IV-COS	0.060	28.706	33.622	11.659	15.747
		−0.020	80.764	83.648	65.292	66.840
		0.128	4.369	6.389	0.562	1.644
X2E	XV-PLDA	−3.000	44.944	49.326	3.188	2.822
		−8.000	71.989	74.143	16.625	15.501
		1.000	23.544	28.997	0.403	0.292
	XV-COS	0.670	71.729	69.077	0.000	0.037
		0.530	95.758	94.677	0.000	0.732
		0.770	23.293	23.844	0.000	0.000
R2E	RN-EU	80.000	49.968	51.723	0.514	12.349
		87.000	80.064	80.938	5.790	51.909
		75.000	28.112	28.818	0.016	1.713
	RN-COS	0.350	40.027	46.288	0.000	1.002
		0.390	24.624	29.915	0.000	0.095

The pass rates of three loss functions under inter-utterance case are shown in Table 14. The pass rates of three mapping models under inter-utterance case are shown in Table 15. The pass rates of text-independent reconstructed voice under inter-utterance case are shown in Table 16. These results show that the discussion we made in the main text for the intra-utterance case is also applicable in the inter-utterance case.

By comparing the results in both cases, the pass rate in the intra-utterance case is higher than that in the inter-utterance case. This once again shows that there are still relatively large differences even for different voices of the same person, and short voice sample is still not a good source to model a person's speech characteristics in SVSs.

Table 14. Pass rates of three loss function under inter-utterance case (%)

Model	SVS	Threshold	L1L	MSE	Smooth
I2E	IV-PLDA	−1.000	48.133	46.456	48.027
		−6.000	83.772	81.459	83.756
		3.000	18.366	17.528	17.294
	IV-COS	0.060	28.706	28.955	29.194
		−0.020	80.764	81.437	80.488
		0.128	4.369	4.343	4.894
X2E	XV-PLDA	−3.000	44.944	44.462	43.464
		−8.000	71.989	71.162	71.013
		1.000	23.544	23.698	22.446
	XV-COS	0.670	71.729	69.852	70.053
		0.530	95.758	95.970	96.124
		0.770	23.293	20.827	21.193
R2E	RN-EU	80.000	49.968	50.917	48.059
		87.000	80.064	81.400	79.539
		75.000	28.112	27.736	25.361
	RN-COS	0.350	40.027	40.308	40.758
		0.390	24.624	25.027	25.180

Table 15. Pass rates of three mapping models under inter-utterance case (%)

Model	SVS	Threshold	L1L	L1LNO	CONV
I2E	IV-PLDA	−1.000	48.133	8.313	46.822
		−6.000	83.772	21.332	84.371
		3.000	18.366	1.650	16.218
	IV-COS	0.060	28.706	13.547	29.517
		−0.020	80.764	64.862	80.323
		0.128	4.369	1.071	4.592
X2E	XV-PLDA	−3.000	44.944	1.873	32.446
		−8.000	71.989	6.626	61.347
		1.000	23.544	0.408	14.292
	XV-COS	0.670	71.729	21.797	62.306
		0.530	95.758	28.823	95.180
		0.770	23.293	8.187	14.825
R2E	RN-EU	80.000	49.968	2.126	47.879
		87.000	80.064	11.893	78.298
		75.000	28.112	0.477	25.764
	RN-COS	0.350	40.027	1.803	38.234
		0.390	24.624	0.530	23.712

Table 16. Pass rates of text-independent reconstructed voice under inter-utterance case

Model	SVS	Threshold	L1L	L1L-TEXT2	TRVC	TRVC-TEXT2
I2E	IV-PLDA	−1.000	48.133	45.332	57.194	54.578
		−6.000	83.772	80.085	88.186	86.462
		3.000	18.366	16.881	26.122	23.947
	IV-COS	0.060	28.706	26.808	33.622	33.473
		−0.020	80.764	80.398	83.648	84.093
		0.128	4.369	3.197	6.389	5.483
X2E	XV-PLDA	−3.000	44.944	40.801	49.326	45.003
		−8.000	71.989	65.767	74.143	69.220
		1.000	23.544	21.814	28.997	25.973
	XV-COS	0.670	71.729	77.200	69.077	71.898
		0.530	95.758	96.739	94.677	95.599
		0.770	23.293	28.181	23.844	24.173
R2E	RN-EU	80.000	49.968	78.287	51.723	76.485
		87.000	80.064	95.594	80.938	94.639
		75.000	28.112	53.218	28.818	52.195
	RN-COS	0.350	40.027	42.815	46.288	46.760
		0.390	24.624	26.007	29.915	30.636

References

1. Chen, G., et al.: Who is real bob? adversarial attacks on speaker recognition systems. In: 2021 2021 IEEE Symposium on Security and Privacy (SP), pp. 55–72, Los Alamitos, CA, USA, IEEE Computer Society, May 2021
2. Li, Q., Zhu, H., Zhang, Z., Lu, H., Wang, F., Li., L.: Spoofing attacks on speaker verification systems based generated voice using genetic algorithm. In: ICC 2019–2019 IEEE International Conference on Communications (ICC), pp. 1–6. IEEE (2019)
3. Zhang, L., Meng, Y., Yu, J., Xiang, C., Falk, B., Zhu, H.: Voiceprint mimicry attack towards speaker verification system in smart home. In: IEEE INFOCOM 2020-IEEE Conference on Computer Communications, pp. 377–386. IEEE (2020)
4. Huang, L., Pun, C.-M.: Audio replay spoof attack detection by joint segment-based linear filter bank feature extraction and attention-enhanced Densenet-Bilstm network. IEEE ACM Trans. Audio Speech Lang. Process. **28**, 1813–1825 (2020)
5. Jia, Y., et al.: Transfer learning from speaker verification to multispeaker text-to-speech synthesis. arXiv preprint arXiv:1806.04558 (2018)
6. Dehak, N., Kenny, P., Dehak, R., Dumouchel, P., Ouellet, P.: Front-end factor analysis for speaker verification. IEEE Trans. Speech Audio Process. **19**(4), 788–798 (2011)

7. Snyder, D., Garcia-Romero, D., Sell, G., Povey, D., Khudanpur, S.: X-vectors: robust DNN embeddings for speaker recognition. In: 2018 IEEE International Conference on Acoustics, Speech and Signal Processing (ICASSP), pp. 5329–5333. IEEE (2018)
8. Soo Heo, F., Lee, B.-J., Huh, J., Chung. J.S.: Clova baseline system for the voxceleb speaker recognition challenge 2020. arXiv preprint arXiv:2009.14153 (2020)
9. Mai, G., Cao, K., Yuen, P.C., Jain, A.K.: On the reconstruction of face images from deep face templates. IEEE Trans. Pattern Anal. Mach. Intell. **41**(5), 1188–1202 (2019)
10. Seong, J.-W., Lee, W., Lee, S.: Multilingual speech synthesis for voice cloning. In: Unger, H., et al. (eds.) IEEE International Conference on Big Data and Smart Computing, BigComp 2021, Jeju Island, South Korea, 17–20 January 2021, pp. 313–316. IEEE (2021)
11. Shen, J., et al.: Natural TTS synthesis by conditioning Wavenet on Mel spectrogram predictions. In: 2018 IEEE International Conference on Acoustics, Speech and Signal Processing (ICASSP), pp. 4779–4783. IEEE (2018)
12. van den Oord, A., et al.: Wavenet: a generative model for raw audio. arXiv preprint arXiv:1609.03499 (2016)
13. Nagrani, A., Chung, J.S., Zisserman, A.: Voxceleb: a large-scale speaker identification dataset. arXiv preprint arXiv:1706.08612 (2017)
14. Panayotov, V., Chen, G., Povey, D., Khudanpur, S.: Librispeech: an ASR corpus based on public domain audio books. In: 2015 IEEE International Conference on Acoustics, Speech and Signal Processing (ICASSP), pp. 5206–5210. IEEE (2015)
15. Povey, D., et al.: The Kaldi speech recognition toolkit. In: IEEE 2011 Workshop on Automatic Speech Recognition and Understanding. IEEE Signal Processing Society, IEEE Catalog No.: CFP11SRW-USB,December 2011
16. Chung, J.S., et al.: In defence of metric learning for speaker recognition, In: Interspeech (2020)
17. De Leon, P.L., Pucher, M., Yamagishi, J., Hernaez, J., Saratxaga, I.: Evaluation of speaker verification security and detection of HMM-based synthetic speech. IEEE Trans. Audio Speech Lang. Process. **20**(8), 2280–2290 (2012)
18. Mukhopadhyay, D., Shirvanian, M., Saxena, N.: All your voices are belong to us: stealing voices to fool humans and machines. In: Pernul, G., Ryan, P.Y.A., Weippl, E. (eds.) ESORICS 2015. LNCS, vol. 9327, pp. 599–621. Springer, Cham (2015). https://doi.org/10.1007/978-3-319-24177-7_30

Word-Map: Using Community Detection Algorithm to Detect AGDs

Futai Zou[✉], Qianying Shen, and Yuzong Hu

School of Cyber Science and Engineering, Shanghai Jiao Tong University,
Shanghai 200240, China
{zoufutai,sjtusqy,huyz97}@sjtu.edu.cn

Abstract. Domain generation algorithms (DGA) are widely used by malware families to realize remote control. Researchers have tried to adopt deep learning methods to detect algorithmically generated domains (AGD) automatically. Some detection methods based on only domain strings alone are proposed. Usually, such methods analyze the structure and semantic features of domain strings. Among various types of AGDs, dictionary-based AGDs are unique for their semantic similarity to normal domains, which makes such detection based on only domain strings difficult. In this paper, we observe that the relationship between domains generated based on a same dictionary shows graphical features. We focus on the detection of dictionary-based AGDs and propose Word-Map which is based on community detection algorithm to detect dictionary-based AGDs. Word-map achieved great accuracy, recall rate, false positive rate, and missing rate on testing sets.

Keywords: Algorithmically generated domains · Community detection · Machine learning

1 Introduction

In cyberattacks such as botnets and APT attacks, when attackers successfully invade a computer, the next step is to establish a communication channel between the server and the infected machine to facilitate further manipulation and information theft. Domain generation algorithm (DGA) plays a key role in the communication between and C&C servers [1]. In order to avoid detection, usually, attackers will not hard-code the server's IP address or set a fixed domain in the malicious code but apply DGA to dynamically generate a batch of algorithmically generated domains (AGDs) [2].

Algorithmically generated domains (AGDs) refer to a group of domains generated in batches based on a string of random seeds [3]. The random seeds are shared between the malicious code inserted in the infected machines and attackers. Since the cost of registering a domain is relatively high nowadays, attackers often choose several domains to register from a set of AGD generated based on a certain seed. The malicious codes inserted in the infected machines generate

© Springer Nature Switzerland AG 2021
J. K. Liu et al. (Eds.): ISC 2021, LNCS 13118, pp. 398–414, 2021.
https://doi.org/10.1007/978-3-030-91356-4_21

all the alternate domains through the seed, and then tries these domains one by one until successfully connect to the malicious server. Since it is impossible to know in advance which domain names the attacker will register every day, all of these AGDs must be detected in order to achieve an effective defense effect. Random seeds are often hidden and may change with time, which makes them more difficult to detect. According to different generation algorithms, AGDs can be roughly divided into four categories: arithmetic based, hashing based, permutation based, and word dictionary based [4]. The first three types of AGDS are often in the forms of a random combination of letters and numbers, which is obviously different from the normal domain names in aspects of lexical and semantic characteristics. There are many methods that use only the domain strings for detection based on this distinction. Dictionary based AGDs discussed in this paper are generated from a random combination of commonly used English words, the lexical and semantic characteristics of which show little difference with normal domains. As a result, detection methods based on the lexical and semantic characteristics are not effective anymore. Information beside the domain strings themselves are needed to achieve a good detection rate.

In this paper, a new method named Word-Map is proposed to solve the problem that dictionary-based AGDs are difficult to detect using lexical and semantic characteristics. Word-Map is designed to achieve two effects: actively mine DGA dictionaries and accurately detect dictionary-based AGDs. The key idea of Word-Map is to convert the problem of dictionary-based AGDs detection into a community detection problem on a word map which is constructed based on the co-occurrence of words in a certain set of domains. Data used as a training set and testing set in this paper are composed of Suppobox domains from DGArchive dataset and Alexa Top 1M domains. Suppobox domains come from three different dictionaries. Word-Map has achieved good results on testing sets. The accuracy and recall rate of Word-map on domains from same DGA dictionaries, domains from different DGA dictionaries and imbalanced dataset is respectively above 98.0% and 93.0%.

This paper has 3 main contributions:

1) We are the first to apply community detection algorithm to solve the problem of detecting dictionary based AGDs. We prove that community detection algorithm performs well in extracting DGA dictionaries from a mix of DGA dictionary words and normal words.

2) We provide a light, efficient and accurate method called Word-Map to detect dictionary based AGDs. By detecting DGA words community on word graphs obtained from a domain string set first, we extract structure features of these communities to train a decision tree to classify word communities as a DGA dictionary word or a normal word.

3) We optimize the domain splitting and AGD dictionary distraction methods, thus improving the word splitting effect and minimize the size of AGD dictionaries.

2   Related Work

The low cost and flexibility of DGA technology makes it widely used in malicious code, which seriously threatens network security. Therefore, researches on the detection methods of AGDs have always been a hot issue. The earliest AGDs detection methods focused on the reverse of the domain generation algorithms. Theoretically, such methods are able to completely capture all the AGDs, however, they consume too many resources, and are challenged by the rapid change of domain generation algorithms and random seeds. Subsequent research methods began to utilize characteristics of AGDs, such as the statistical characteristics of DNS traffic [5,6] and the characteristics of the domain strings themselves [7,8]. To lower cost, it is best to detect AGDs using domain strings only without relying on any other information such as context information of DNS traffic. This section focuses on the researches that use domain strings only for detection. Word-Map proposed in this paper also belongs to this type of detection method.

AGD strings are often a random combination of letters and numbers, which are obviously different from normal domain strings in aspects of lexical and semantic characteristics. At present, AGD detection methods are generally based on this difference. Detection methods develop from the extraction of statistical features to the use of machine learning, and then the application of deep learning and generative adversarial networks. In 2014, Miranda et al. [7] proposed a detection method based on the length distribution of domains, which extracts the n-gram distance of single characters, number of layers, number of digits, number of upper and lower case letters, number of hyphens and other features of second-level domain strings, and then use these features to train a regression model to detect AGDs. This method can detect 12 DGA families, and its accuracy on testing set is higher than 95%. Tommy Chin et al. [9] proposed a two-layer machine learning model to detect and cluster AGDs.

With the development of deep learning, there are also many researchers attempt to apply natural language processing experience to the detection of AGDs. Jonathan Woodbridge et al. [10] proposed a detection method based on LSTM. This method does not need to extract features in advance, but get the embeddings of domain strings in advance and then trains a LSTM network to classify domains into AGDs or benign domains. Koh J Jet al. [11] proposed a context-sensitive domain string embedding method, and apply a simple fully-connected classifier to achieve domain detection. This method performs well on small data sets. Some researchers also try to address the problem that dictionary-based AGDs are not easy to detect. Hyrum S et al. [12] found in the research that the letter distribution of Suppobox AGDs (a typical kind of dictionary based AGDs) are consistent with the Alexa Top 1,000,000 domains, which means there exists no significant difference statistically between Suppobox AGDs and Alexa domains. The research group further proposed using the idea of adversarial learning to realize the detection of AGDs. Through the confrontation between the generator and the detector, the detector is strengthened, and thus its ability to detect dictionary based domains is improved. Mayana Pereira et al. [13] tried to start from the perspective of graph structure to realize the detection of dictionary AGDs names. This method uses the longest substring method to extract the AGDs name dictionary, and judges whether a group of words is a DGA dictionary based on the graph's node degree, path length, ring number, and other characteristics. Kate Highnam et al. [14] proposed a hybrid neural network Bilbo, using CNN and LSTM networks in parallel to score the possibility of domain strings being generated based on dictionaries.

Many previous AGD detection methods are based on the statistical,lexical and semantic characteristics of the domain strings, and therefore were limited in the face of dictionary based AGDs. The introduction of deep learning and adversarial learning can solve this problem to a certain extent but perform not that well in the face of domains generated from unknown dictionaries. In response to this problem, this paper proposes a new method named Word-Map which analyzes the co-occurrence relationship of words in a certain set of domains and applies community detection algorithm to actively mine DGA dictionaries and detect the dictionary based AGDs. It is flexible and light, as well as performs well on testing data.

3   Methodology

Overview. This section will introduce Word-Map. Word-Map can realize the extraction of unknown DGA dictionary and the detection of dictionary based AGDs. In order to better understand this method, this section will introduce the graph structure, community detection algorithm, and the final dictionary based AGDs classification method in detail.

The key idea of Word-Map is to convert the detection of dictionary-based AGDs into a community detection problem. An obvious phenomenon is that the co-occurrence probability of words from the same DGA dictionary in the dictionary based AGDs is much higher than the co-occurrence probability common words in benign domains. First, we cut domain based AGDs into words, and then use the co-occurrence relationship in original domains to associate these words. It can be intuitively understood that the connections between the words from DGA domains composed of a same DGA dictionary will be very tight, which means these words are more likely to form a community. However, the words obtained from benign domain strings often do not show such characteristics. Since this method can actively detect DGA dictionaries, it is able to effectively detect dictionary based AGDs without knowing DGA dictionaries in advance.

The main workflow of Word-Map is as follows: After obtaining the domain string, firstly pre-process the domain string by removing the top-level domain name and only retaining the second-level domain strings. For AGDs, group them according to the top-level domain strings. Then, cut the second-level domain strings into words, and construct these words into a word graph according to their co-occurrence in original domain strings. As to the word graphs, use the infomap algorithm to detect communities. At last, extract the features of these independent word communities to train a decision tree. Use the decision tree to determine whether a certain word community is a DGA dictionary or not. For a domain, if the components of its second-level domain all belong to a single DGA dictionary, it is determined as a dictionary based AGD.

Word Graph

Word Graph Construction. For a domain string set D = d1, d2, ..., di, ..., dn, we process each domain name by removing the top-level domain string, and only retaining the second-level domain string. Then we get a second-level domain string set S = s1, s2,... ..., si,..., sn. Then we cut each element in S into single English words.

The splitting of second-level domain strings is actually a word splitting problem of English words without spaces. A mature tool named Wordninja [15] can be used to solve this problem efficiently. This paper uses Wordninjia to cut the domain strings into words. Inspired by Pereira M et al. [13], we also tried to use the longest substring method for word splitting. However, it's proved to have several limitations which would be explained later.

For a domain name set D, after domain string splitting, a word set W can be obtained, and each word in the word set is a vertex. These word vertexes will then be connected by edges according to their co-occurrence relationship in D. If two vertexes have appeared together in any domain string in D, then they will be connected with 2 directed edges. In this way, for a domain name set D, a word graph G = (V, E) can be obtained, where V represents the vertex set, of which the elements are words; and E represents the edge set, indicating the co-occurrence relationship between word vertexes. An example of the composition process is shown below:

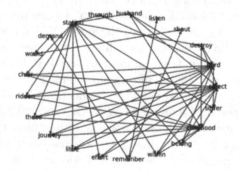

Fig. 1. Word graph of dictionary based AGDs

Fifty domain strings are randomly chosen from the dictionary based AGDs dataset which are from the same dictionary. After cutting domain strings into words, a word graph is constructed according to the co-occurrence relationship between words. As shown in Fig. 1, there are 21 word nodes and 100 directed edges.

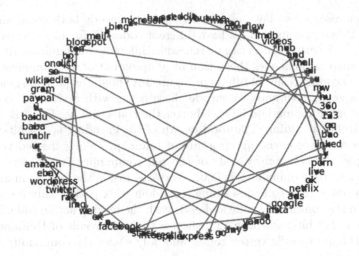

Fig. 2. Word graph of Alexa Domains

Fifty domain strings are randomly chosen from the Alexa domains dataset. After cutting domain strings into words, a word graph is constructed according to the co-occurrence relationship between words. As shown in Fig. 2, there are 72 word nodes and 60 directed edges. We can see that the average degree of vertexes in this graph is less than 1. It's because some domains are too short to be cut, therefore becoming isolated vertex in the word graph.

Through 2 word graphs above, it can be intuitively observed that for an equivalent amount of dictionary based AGDs and Alexa domains, dictionary based AGDs will be cut into fewer word vertexes, however dictionary based AGDs word vertexes of are more closely connected, and the average degree of vertexes is higher. This shows that the word vertexes obtained from dictionary based AGDs are more closely related, which makes them easier to be classified into a community.

Community Detection on Word Graph

Introduction of Infomap. The key idea of Word-Map is to convert the detection of dictionary-based AGDs into a community detection problem on word graphs. The key step is to use the Infomap [16,17] algorithm to perform community detection on word graphs.

Infomap is a community detection algorithm based on information theory. Infomap uses the principle of minimum entropy to address the problem of community detection as an optimal encoding and compression problem. Probability flows between vertexes are used to represent the information flow between nodes. The random walk method is used to simulate the flow of information between vertexes. The core premise assumption of the Infomap algorithm is that a reasonable community division can lead to shorter codes.

Infomap uses a two-layer coding structure to encode both communities and vertexes. Different communities have different codes. Different vertexes have different codes. A vertex code s can be reused in different communities. At the same time, Infomap also encodes the action of jumping out of a community. Figure 3 shows the encoding result of Infomap. Figure 3-A shows the path of some random walks in a graph. We hope to encode these paths with a string of codes. The better the encoding method is, the shorter the codes will be; Fig. 3-B shows the result of Huffman coding. The total length of the encoding is 314 bits; Fig. 3-C shows the two-layer encoding structure of Infomap. Taking the red vertexes as an example, the community code of the red community is 111, and the code of leaving the red community is 0001. Vertexes inside the red community have their own codes. The code describing a random walk path within a community starts with the community code and ends with the leaving action code. This coding result is 243 bits, which is 32% shorter than the result of Huffman coding. Figure 3-D blurs specific vertex codes, and only shows the community codes.

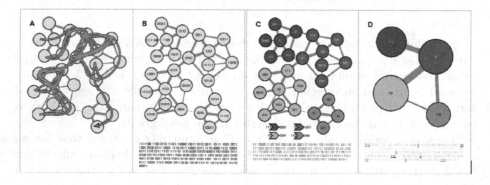

Fig. 3. Workflow of Infomap [16]

The Infomap algorithm can be simply summarized as the following three steps:

1) Initialization, each vertex is regarded as an independent community;
2) Randomly sample a sequence of vertexes in the graph, try to assign each vertex to the community where its neighbor vertex is located in order, and then compute the average length of codes. Assign the vertex into the current community if the average code length is shorter and do nothing if not;
3) Repeat step 2 until L(M) can no longer be optimized.

Words Community. The following figures are examples of community detection results of word graphs obtained from dictionary based AGDs, Alexa domains, and mixed domains.

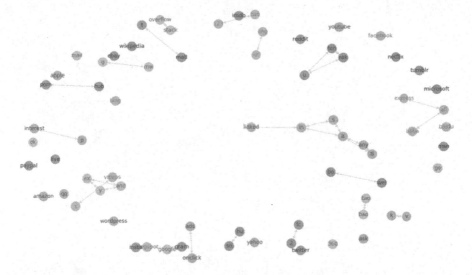

Fig. 4. Communities detected from the word graph of Alexa domains

As shown in Fig. 4, 46 communities were detected on the word graph obtained from 50 Alexa domains as shown in Fig. 2. The largest community is composed of 6 blue-colored vertexes in the center of Fig. 4, of which the total degree is 14 and the average degree is 2.33. For other communities, The number of vertexes is 1 (isolated vertex), 2 (word vertexes obtained from a same domain string) or 3. It can be seen that words obtained by splitting Alexa domains have no obvious clustering characteristics.

As shown in Fig. 5, 2 communities were detected on the word graph obtained from 50 dictionary based AGDs as shown in Fig. 1. The two communities are composed of 40 and 24 vertexes respectively, of which the total degrees is 739 and 261 respectively and the average degree is 18.48 and 10.88 respectively. Compared to Fig. 4, it can be seen that words obtained by splitting dictionary based AGDs have obvious clustering characteristics. Also, there are obvious differences in aspects of the number of vertexes, the total degrees of vertexes, and the average degree of vertexes between AGD communities and Alexa communities.

Mix the 50 Alexa domains and 50 dictionary based AGDs mentioned before and get the word graph of the mixed domains. 48 communities were detected on the word graph. The biggest two communities (blue and green colored vertexes in the center of Fig. 6) have 40 and 24 vertexes respectively. Their total degrees are 739 and 261, and their average degrees are 18.48 and 10.88. The number of vertexes of the remaining communities is all no bigger than 6, and their total degrees are no bigger than 14, while average degrees no bigger than 2.5. Comparing Fig. 6 with Fig. 4 and Fig. 5, it can be seen that dictionary based AGDs and Alexa domains have been effectively distinguished from each other.

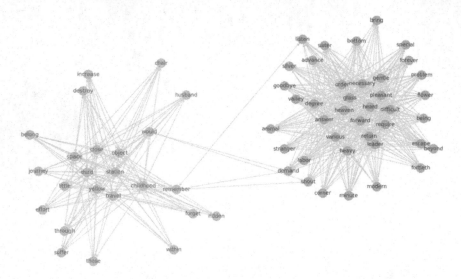

Fig. 5. Communities detected from the word graph of Dictionary based AGDs

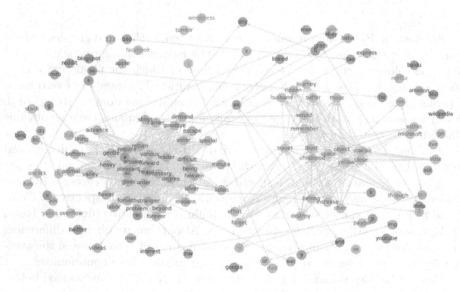

Fig. 6. Communities detected from the word graph of mixed domains

It can be seen intuitively that there are several differences between dictionary based AGD community and Alexa community: 1) The number of vertexes in dictionary based AGD communities is much bigger than that of Alexa communities. 2) The total and average degrees of the vertexes of dictionary based AGD are much bigger than those Alexa communities. Therefore, after community detection, these two features can be collected to train a decision tree to classify whether a community is dictionary based AGD community or not.

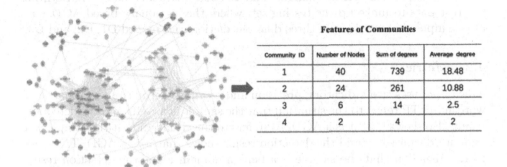

Features of Communities

Community ID	Number of Nodes	Sum of degrees	Average degree
1	40	739	18.48
2	24	261	10.88
3	6	14	2.5
4	2	4	2

Fig. 7. Extract features of word communities

After extracting AGD dictionaries from the domain sets, we use a simple method to determine whether a domain string is a dictionary based AGD.

Dictionary-Based AGDs Detection. After extracting AGD dictionaries from the domain sets, we use a simple method to determine whether a domain string is a dictionary based AGD or not. For a domain string, if all the words obtained from this string belonging to a same AGD dictionary, the domain string is judged as a dictionary based AGD.

4   Experiments and Results

4.1   Dataset

Dataset used in the experiments contains a total of 1,313,571 dictionary based AGDs domains and 1,000,000 benign domains. Dictionary based AGDs come from the Suppobox domains in the DGArchive dataset [18], and benign domains are chosen from Alexa Top 1M domains. Ground Truth Data As shown in Table 1,

Table 1. Ground truth data

Type	Count	Dictionary
Alexa Domain	100,000	/
	100,000	Dictionary 1
Dictionary-based AGD	100,000	Dictionary 2
	100,000	Dictionary 3

we randomly select 1,000,000 Alexa domains and 1, 200, 000 dictionary based AGDs to make up the training set, where the dictionary based AGDs are composed of words from three different dictionaries named D1, D2, and D3. We randomly select 100,000 Alexa domains and 100,000 dictionary based AGDs from the rest data to make up the testing set, where the dictionary based AGDs are also composed of words from three different dictionaries named D1, D2, and D3.

4.2 Metrics

This paper uses two indicators, precision and recall, to verify the performance of word-map. TP refers to the situation that the sample is a AGD and the detection result also shows that it is a AGD; FP refers to the situation that the sample is a benign domain while and the detection result shows that it is a AGD; TN refers to the situation that the sample is a benign domain name the detection result also shows that it is a benign domain; FN refers to the situation that the sample is a AGD, while and the detection result shows that it is a benign domain.

Accuracy = (TP+TN)/(TP+FN+FP+TN) refers to the proportion of all correctly classified domains to all domains. Recall rate = (TP)/(TP+FN)) refers to the proportion of all dictionary based AGDs that are found. False positive rate = FN/(TP+FN). Missing rate = 1 − recall rate.

4.3 Performance on Testing Data

We designed three different experiments to verify the performance of Word-map on domains from the same DGA dictionary, domains from different DGA dictionaries and imbalanced data sets. The first group of experiments verifies the performance of Word-map on domains from the same DGA dictionary. A total of 3 rounds of independent experiments were conducted. The specific composition of the training set and testing set is shown in Table 2.

The results of three independent experiments are shown in Table 3.

The second group of experiments verifies the performance of Word-map on domains from different DGA dictionaries. A total of 3 rounds of independent experiments were conducted. The specific composition of the training set and testing set is shown in Table 4.

The results of three independent experiments are shown in Table 5.

Table 2. Experiments on domains from same DGA dictionaries

Dataset	Training set				Testing set			
	Alexa	D1	D2	D3	Alexa	D1	D2	D3
Round1	50,000	50,000	0	0	50,000	50,000	0	0
Round2	50,000	0	50,000	0	50,000	0	50,000	0
Round3	50,000	0	0	50,000	50,000	0	0	50,000

Table 3. Performance on domains in same DGA dictionaries

	Round1	Round2	Round3	Average
Accuracy	99.72%	99.53%	99.84%	99.67%
Recall rate	100.0%	99.94%	99.97%	99.97%
Missing rate	0.00%	0.06%	0.03%	0.03%
False positive rate	0.56%	0.88%	0.29%	0.58%

Table 4. Experiments on domains from different DGA dictionaries

Dataset	Training set				Testing set			
	Alexa	D1	D2	D3	Alexa	D1	D2	D3
Round1	50,000	50,000	0	0	50,000	0	25,000	25,000
Round2	50,000	0	50,000	0	50,000	25,000	0	25,000
Round3	50,000	0	0	50,000	50,000	25,000	25,000	0

Table 5. Performance on domains from different DGA dictionaries

	Round1	Round2	Round3	Average
Accuracy	99.29%	99.43%	99.14%	99.29%
Recall rate	99.72%	99.91%	99.57%	99.73%
Missing rate	0.28%	0.09%	0.43%	0.27%
False positive rate	1.14%	1.04%	1.29%	1.16%

The third group of experiments verifies the performance of Word-map on the imbalanced dataset. A total of 3 rounds of independent experiments were conducted. The specific composition of the training set and testing set is shown in Table 6.

Table 6. Experiments on imbalanced datasets

Dataset	Training set				Testing set			
	Alexa	D1	D2	D3	Alexa	D1	D2	D3
Round1	50,000	500	500	500	50,000	500	500	500
Round2	50,000	500	500	0	50,000	0	0	500
Round3	50,000	500	0	0	50,000	500	0	0

The results of three independent experiments are shown in Table 7.

Table 7. Performance on imbalanced dataset

	Round1	Round2	Round3	Average
Accuracy	98.76%	98.63%	98.85%	98.80%
Recall rate	93.07%	92.87%	93.26%	93.07%
Missing rate	6.93%	7.13%	7.74%	7.27%
False positive rate	0.57%	0.80%	0.59%	0.68%

Based on the results of three rounds of experiments, it can be seen that Word-map performs best on a single dictionary to generate DGA domain name data sets, with the highest accuracy rate, and both the accuracy rate and the recall rate are about 99%. This shows that when the generation dictionary has been mastered, Word-map can accurately detect the dictionary based AGDs. The performance of Word-map on domains from different DGA dictionaries is slightly inferior to the performance on domains from same DGA dictionaries, but it also remains above 99%, which shows that Word-map has good enough ability to mine new dictionaries. On the imbalanced data set, the accuracy rate of Word-map is maintained above 98%, and the recall rate is maintained at about 93%, which fully shows that Word-map can adapt to the situation in the real world where the AGDs is far less than the normal domains.

4.4 Improvement in Word Splitting and Dictionary Extraction

For word splitting and dictionary extraction, Pereira M et al. [14] applied the longest substring method. The longest substring method refers to finding the longest substring of each pair of strings in the domain string set. If the length of a longest substring is greater than the threshold (in[14], set to 3) and does not overlap with any previous substring, this substring is added to the AGD dictionary. To avoid adding benign words into the dictionary, they filter out words with degrees less than 3.There are two main limitations of the longest substring method. One is that the algorithm has a high complexity; the second is that the threshold of the longest substring is difficult to determine. If the threshold is too low, common letter combinations like "ere" will be added into the dictionary, making the dictionary too large and introduce a lot of noise; if the threshold is too high (for example, 5), many short words will be filtered out, affecting the extraction effect of the final DGA dictionary.

To improve the word splitting efficiency and minimize the size of AGD dictionary, we adopt Wordninja to split domain strings and Infomap to detect AGD words. We respectively select 1, 000 domains from W1, W2, W3, and Alexa domains randomly. As shown in Table 8, the size of word dictionaries extracted by Word-Map is far smaller than that extracted by Longest Substring Method.

Table 8. Dictionary size

	Word-Map	LSM
W1	106	1094
W2	194	2194
W3	158	1543
Alexa	1236	17892

*LSM: Longest Substring Method

Table 9. False positive rate

	Word-Map	LSM
W1	0.62%	6.11%
W2	0.58%	5.79%
W3	0.59%	6.09%

As shown in Table 9, it's proved that optimizing the word splitting and dictionary extraction can help to get a lower false positive rate. Compared to longest substring method, Word-Map extracted a smaller AGD dictionary and achieve a lower false positive rate.

4.5   Comparison with Other Methods

This section will compare the pros and cons of the algorithm proposed in this article with machine learning detection methods based on artificial feature extraction and deep learning detection methods based on automatic feature extraction in detecting dictionary based AGDs.

For artificial features, We extract two aspects of domains: formation feature and network features, including Domain Name Length, Maximum Count of Consecutive Characters, Count of Uppercase Letters in Domain Name, Numbers in Domain Name, Count of Special Characters in Domain Name, Ratio of Vowels and Consonants, Entropy Calue of Domain Name, Probability of Character Conversion, Count of IP Addresses, Count of NS Records, Geographical Distribution of IP Addresses, Average TTL, Standard Seviation of TTL, Survival Time of Domain Name, and Domain Name Active Time.

As shown in Table 10, the detection effect of machine learning methods based on manual feature extraction is generally not rational. The accuracy of the logistic regression algorithm and naive Bayes algorithm is less than 80%, and the

Table 10. Comparison with feature based machine learning methods

Algorithms	Same dictionary		Different dictionaries		Imbalanced dataset	
	Accuracy	Recall rate	Accuracy	Recall rate	Accuracy	Recall rate
LR	78.92%	48.28%	72.36%	40.17%	68.52%	38.09%
SVM	**85.75%**	**84.31%**	**80.54%**	**81.21%**	**79.15%**	**74.10%**
Decision Tree	82.95%	70.37%	80.06%	69.07%	76.94%	63.25%
Random forest	80.57%	68.73%	74.42%	63.98%	72.94%	60.52%
Naive Bayesian	79.25%	49.88%	74.66%	42.74%	70.13%	39.79%
Word-map	**99.67%**	**99.97%**	**99.29%**	**99.73%**	**98.80%**	**93.07%**

Table 11. Comparison with deep learning methods

Algorithms	Same dictionary		Different dictionaries		Imbalanced dataset		Embedding method
	Accuracy	Recall rate	Accuracy	Recall rate	Accuracy	Recall rate	
RNN	89.29%	88.98%	87.03%	86.73%	86.29%	85.81%	Character level
LSTM	**90.89%**	**90.91%**	**88.93%**	**88.29%**	**87.12%**	**87.03%**	
GRU	89.12%	89.04%	87.86%	87.58%	87.15%	86.99%	
CNN	87.63%	87.12%	85.98%	85.17%	84.09%	83.70%	
BPTT	89.32%	89.07%	88.05%	87.74%	86.92%	86.63%	
RNN	90.58%	90.34%	89.21%	89.05%	87.91%	87.39%	Word level
LSTM	**92.09%**	**91.13%**	**91.21%**	**90.92%**	**89.93%**	**89.42%**	
GRU	90.67%	90.32%	89.16%	88.87%	88.05%	87.76%	
CNN	88.24%	87.83%	87.11%	86.39%	86.28%	85.83%	
BPTT	91.13%	90.98%	90.06%	89.27%	89.25%	88.77%	
Word-map	**99.67%**	**99.97%**	**99.29%**	**99.73%**	**98.80%**	**93.07%**	—

recall rate is less than 50%. Decision tree algorithm and random forest algorithm perform slightly better, but the accuracy rate is just over 80%, and the recall rate is basically less than 70%. In contrast, the accuracy rates of the best performing SVM algorithm on the three data sets are only 85.75%, 80.54% and 79.15%, and the recall rates are only 84.31%, 81.21% and 74.10%. The accuracy of this algorithm on the three data sets is 99.67%, 99.29% and 98.80%, and the recall rate is 99.97%, 99.73% and 93.07%. Through comparison, it can be found that the accuracy and recall rate of the machine learning algorithm is far lower than the algorithm in this paper, especially in the recall rate, the gap is very large. This fully shows that for dictionary-type DGA domain names, the detection rate of the machine learning algorithm based on artificial features is very unsatisfactory, and the algorithm in this paper has a good performance.

As shown in Table 11, the detection effect of the deep learning method based on automatic feature extraction is slightly better when using word-level embedding than using character-level embedding. Compared with the two, word-level embedding can learn the characteristics of dictionary DGA domain names. For different deep learning models, LSTM performs best in comparison. With single-level embedding, the accuracy rates on the three data sets are only 92.09%, 91.21% and 90.92%, which are still significantly lower than 99.67%, 99.29% and 98.80% of the algorithm in this paper.

At the same time, it can be seen from the experimental results that the detection effect of the deep learning method based on automatic feature extraction on multi-dictionary domain names and unbalanced data sets is far lower than that on a single dictionary domain name. Compared with this article In terms of algorithm, the stability of the detection effect is slightly inferior.

Experiments show that the Word-map algorithm proposed in this article has obvious advantages on accuracy, recall, or pan-China capabilities of different datasets and negative samples compared with the deep learning detection algorithm based on automatic feature extraction.

5   Conclusion

This paper proposes a new method named Word-map to the problem that dictionary based AGDs are difficult to detect, which converts the problems of DGA dictionary extraction and AGD detection into a problem of community discovery on word graphs. Word-map applies decision tree to classify DGA dictionary word Communities and normal domain word communities so that to discover DGA dictionaries actively and detect dictionary based AGDs accurately. This paper uses Suppobox domains and Alexa Top 1M domains from the DGArchive dataset as the training set and testing set. Suppobox domains comes from three different dictionaries. The accuracy and recall rate of Word-map on domains from same DGA dictionaries, domains from different DGA dictionaries and imbalanced dataset is respectively above 98% and 93.0%. Compared with state-of-art machine learning methods, Word-map also performs better.

The main contribution of Word-map is that it apply community detection algorithm to dictionary based AGDs name detection for the first time. Word-map uses the community detection algorithm to mine DGA dictionaries, extract features of the DGA dictionary word communities from the perspective of the graph structure. In general, Word-map is low cost and flexible, as well as has a high detection rate of dictionary based AGDs.

Acknowledgements. This work is supported by National Key Research and Development Program of China under Grant No.2020YFB1807500.

References

1. Zeidanloo, H.R., Manaf, A.A.: Botnet command and control mechanisms. In: 2009 Second International Conference on Computer and Electrical Engineering. vol. 1, pp. 564–568. IEEE (2009)
2. Feily, M., Shahrestani, A., Ramadass, S.A.: Survey of botnet and botnet detection. In:2009 Third International Conference on Emerging Security Information, Systems and Technologies, pp. 268–273. IEEE (2009)
3. Plohmann, D., Yakdan, K., Klatt, M., et al.: A comprehensive measurement study of domain generating malware. In: 25th USENIX Security Symposium (USENIX Security 2016). pp. 263–278 (2016)
4. Sood, A.K., Zeadally, S.: A taxonomy of domain-generation algorithms. IEEE Secur. Privacy **14**(4), 46–53 (2016)
5. Tu, T.D., Guang, C., Xin, LY.: Detecting bot-infected machines based on analyzing the similar periodic DNS queries. In: 2015 International Conference on Communications, Management and Telecommunications (ComManTel), pp. 35–40. IEEE (2015)
6. Luo, X., Wang, L., Xu, Z., An, W.: LagProber: detecting DGA-based malware by using query time lag of non-existent domains. In: Naccache, D., et al. (ed.) ICICS 2018. LNCS, vol. 11149, pp. 41–56. Springer, LagProber: detecting DGA-based malware by using query time lag of non-existent domains (2018). https://doi.org/10.1007/978-3-030-01950-1_3

7. Mowbray, M., Hagen, J.: Finding domain-generation algorithms by looking at length distribution. In: 2014 IEEE International Symposium on Software Reliability Engineering Workshops, 395–400. IEEE (2014)

8. Yu, B., Pan, J., Hu, J., et al.: Character level based detection of AGDs names. In: 2018 International Joint Conference on Neural Networks (IJCNN), pp. 1–8 IEEE (2018)

9. Chin, T., Xiong, K., Hu, C., et al.: A machine learning framework for studying domain generation algorithm (DGA)-based malware. In: International Conference on Security and Privacy in Communication Systems, pp. 433–448. Springer, Cham (2018)

10. Woodbridge, J., Anderson, H.S., Ahuja, A., et al.: Predicting domain generation algorithms with long short-term memory networks. arXiv preprint arXiv:1611.00791 (2016)

11. Koh, J.J., Rhodes, B.: Inline detection of domain generation algorithms with context-sensitive word embeddings. In: 2018 IEEE International Conference on Big Data (Big Data). pp. 2966–2971. IEEE (2018)

12. Anderson, H.S., Woodbridge, J., Filar, B.: DeepDGA: adversarially-tuned domain generation and detection. In: Proceedings of the. ACM Workshop on Artificial Intelligence and Security, vol. 2016, pp. 13–21 (2016)

13. Pereira, M., Coleman, S., Yu, B., et al.: Dictionary extraction and detection of algorithmically generated domain names in passive DNS traffic. In: International Symposium on Research in Attacks, Intrusions, and Defenses, pp. 295–314. Springer, Cham (2018)

14. Highnam, K., Puzio, D., Luo, S., et al.: Real-time detection of dictionary dga network traffic using deep learning. arXiv preprint arXiv:2003.12805 (2020)

15. Wordninja. https://github.com/keredson/wordninja. Accessed July 2021

16. Rosvall, M., Bergstrom, C.T.: Maps of information flow reveal community structure in complex networks. arXiv preprint physics.soc-ph/0707.0609 (2007)

17. Rosvall, M., Axelsson, D., Bergstrom, C.T.: The map equation. The Eur. Phys. J. Special Topics **178**(1), 13–23 (2009)

18. Plohmann, D., Yakdan, K., Klatt, M., Bader, J., Gerhards-Padilla, E.: A comprehensive measurement study of domain generating malware. In: 25th USENIX Security Symposium, pp. 263–278 (2016)

Author Index

Printed in the United States
by Baker & Taylor Publisher Services

Printed in the United States
by Baker & Taylor Publisher Services